READER FOR RACE AND ETHNICITY

Third Edition

Materials Selected By

Chuck O'Connell

University of California, Irvine

Pearson
Custom
Publishing

ISBN 0–536–70699–9

BA 996188

 PEARSON CUSTOM PUBLISHING
75 Arlington Street, Suite 300, Boston, MA 02116
A Pearson Education Company

CONTENTS

INTRODUCTION

This course reader was created to address characteristic shortcomings in many textbooks and popular discussions of race, ethnicity, and nationalism. These shortcomings consist of a number of intellectual "blind spots" or failures to address certain issues. These issues involve the failure to see the following:

- race, ethnicity, and nationalism as fluid phenomena created and manipulated by people themselves
- racism as a political project enforced by the State and society's upper class mainly for economic reasons
- racism as involving not only the "stick" of repression but also the "carrot" of co-optation and opportunism
- racism as a facilitator of imperialism
- antiracism as a powerful evolving force which has changed the world for the better

The course reader is organized around each of these five points.

Part 1

THE SOCIAL CONSTRUCTION OF RACE, ETHNICITY, AND NATIONALISM

Race is a way of differentiating people by physical characteristics which themselves are said to signify something about a person's intellectual and moral qualities. With this physical or biological basis, race is generally treated as definite and immutable. You should be able to tell a person's race just by looking. But can you? If you can't, then you have to know other things such as family ancestry or "bloodlines" to "see" race. If, however, you need to know family history to know race, just how "obvious" is race? Furthermore, who gets to define the meaning of biological characteristics? Clearly, we do not have an instinctual comprehension of the meanings of various physical characteristics; therefore, we must *learn* these meanings. But if we must be taught the significance of biological markers, *who* writes the curriculum of racial interpretation? Does the canon of racial definition remain the same year after year, place after place, or does it change? If it changes, why? Who makes the changes? If racial definitions change, can they be real in an essentialist sense or are they simply socially constructed fictions? If they have no basis in biological fact, then why do we believe them and keep them? The first two selections in this section, "Race: Can You Tell By Looking?" and "Transforming White into Black," touch on these questions.

Ethnicity is a way of differentiating people by cultural characteristics such as language and social customs. Nationality is the ethnicity of the nation-state. Both are social constructions and, as such, raise questions about *what* precisely constitutes *authentic* ethnic and national identity and *who* gets to define such identities. Included here are essays dealing with the fictive and fluid nature of ethnic and national identity. First is "Peeling the Ethnic Onion"—Avi Katzman's interview with Professor Anthony Smith on the distinctions between

1

ethnicity and nationality and the artificial quality of each. Next is "Buscando América," a reflection by UCI history professor Mike Davis on the current transformations of Latino and Anglo identity. Third, in "Latino/Hispanics . . . What Next!" sociology professor, Martha Gimenez, offers, "some reflections on the politics of identity in the U.S." Finally, Bob Blauner offers comments on the confusion over race and ethnicity and the meaning of racism in his essay "Talking Past Each Other."

RACE: CAN YOU TELL BY LOOKING?

Look at the photograph below and identify the people by race.

Who is black and who is white?

I'll see you at lecture to compare answers.

2

The Social Construction of Race: Transforming "White" into "Black"

Today the Irish are considered "white" but 150 years ago they were considered by many to be "black" or, more precisely, "white Africans." Consider the following drawings from the mid to late 1800s in *Harper's Weekly* (subtitled: "Journal of Civilization"):

In the first drawing from the mid–1800s the modern Irish are depicted as a mix of an African race (the Iberians) and Irish "savages" of the Stone age—a mix producing an inferior race.

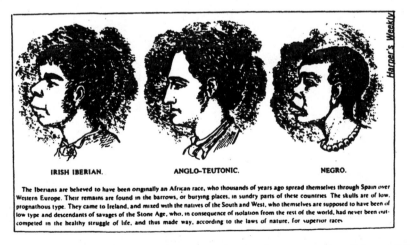

IRISH IBERIAN.   ANGLO-TEUTONIC.   NEGRO.

The Iberians are believed to have been originally an African race, who thousands of years ago spread themselves through Spain over Western Europe. Their remains are found in the barrows, or burying places, in sundry parts of these countries. The skulls are of low, prognathous type. They came to Ireland, and mixed with the natives of the South and West, who themselves are supposed to have been of low type and descendants of savages of the Stone Age, who, in consequence of isolation from the rest of the world, had never been out-competed in the healthy struggle of life, and thus made way, according to the laws of nature, for superior races.

The second drawing is the cover of the December 9, 1876 edition of *Harper's Weekly*. Although the Irishman sits on a scale labeled "white," he is clearly depicted as ape-like and thus white only in color but not in essence. It takes many years before the light skinned Irish enter the "white race" in America. The process also works in reverse apparently. According to a *Washington Post* article in 2002, some Ethiopian immigrants to the U.S. have found themselves described as "black Europeans."

HARPER'S WEEKLY.

JOURNAL OF CIVILIZATION

Vol. XX.—No. 1041.]   NEW YORK, SATURDAY, DECEMBER 9, 1876.   [WITH A SUPPLEMENT. PRICE TEN CENTS.

Entered according to Act of Congress, in the Year 1876, by Harper & Brothers, in the Office of the Librarian of Congress, at Washington.

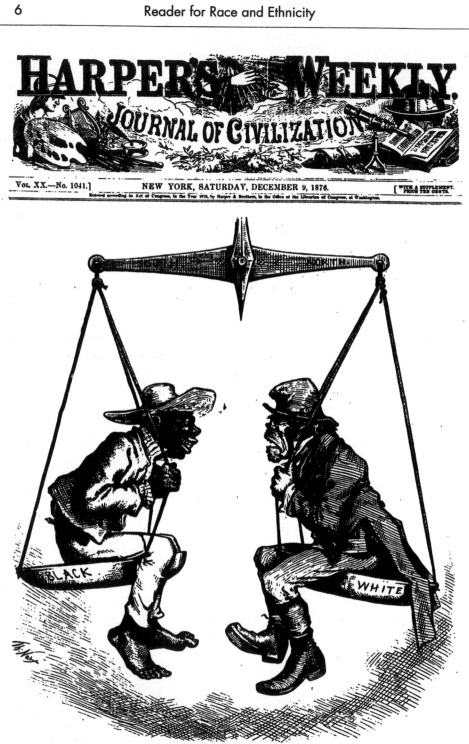

THE IGNORANT VOTE—HONORS ARE EASY.

3

PEELING THE ETHNIC ONION

Avi Katzman

Ethnicity can become a nationality. Nationality can become an ethnicity. Both are fictive—resting on myths of common origins and sacrifice.

An increasing number of Professor Anthony Smith's colleagues at universities around Great Britain have been receiving hate mail and death threats signed by the Armenian underground, the IRA and other radical organizations. Just a few weeks ago, the nationalist Serbian underground announced that it was responsible for the killing of Jill Dando, a leading BBC broadcaster. Prof. Smith, one of the world's leading experts on nationality, is extremely cautious. Under no circumstances will he allow a photograph of himself to appear in the paper. The study of nationality, it seems, is one of the most sensitive topics in academia today. Theories are not the problem, says Smith. The trouble starts when one brings examples. There will always be hot-headed nationalists who take umbrage. Smith, 63, a professor at the London School of Economics, is in Israel this week as a guest of the Israel Historical Society and the Zalman Shazar Center, the organizers of an annual lecture series in Jerusalem in memory of Prof. Menachem Stern. Like many of the experts in his field, Anthony Smith is Jewish. His Polish grandfather and quite a few family members died in the Holocaust. "I am British," he says, responding to a question about his nationality, "but also Jewish." It was the tension between his "Englishness" and his "Jewishness" that diverted him from the classics and piqued his interest in identity. Smith's research sharpens the potential clash between ethnicity and nationality. Ethnicity, he says, is "belonging to a group of people with a myth of common origins, which may or may not be true, shared historical memories, at least one common element of culture, usually language but often religion or customs, a link with some sort of homeland, but not necessarily residing in it or occupying it, and if you are a community, some measure of solidarity."

Unlike nationality, ethnicity is a very ancient concept. Within ethnic groups, there are also sub-ethnicities and even sub-sub-ethnicities. "Ethnicity is like an onion," Smith explains. "It ends, ultimately, in kinship. This is not to say that ethnicity is biological. It includes marriage, first of all. Secondly, ethnic groups might have originally started as kin groups but they grew and grew, so the sense of relatedness is often fictive. The Khazars

joined the Jews by conversion. They are not related by blood by any stretch of the imagination. But they became Jews over time, and lots of people in the Roman Empire converted to Judaism. We will never know if any of us are descended from Abraham or
some Roman nobleman who converted. But the myth of common origins is powerful."

People began to talk about nationality only 300 years ago, in Europe. Nationality is
"belonging to a state which has jurisdiction over a territory, and which confers on the
members of that state the rights and duties of citizenship. There is also a common code
of laws under which those citizens dwell, and—very important—a common public culture: a common language, a sense of shared history, institutions and customs that overlap but on occasion even conflict." In contrast to nationality, which is a fluid concept (as
in the case of the Welsh and the Bretons), ethnicity is generally fixed and immutable. A
person can change his nationality, but not his ethnicity. "I don't think that you as an
individual can," says Smith, "but through intermarriage, through migration, certainly
your grandchildren can. For your children, it is still a difficulty. There are limits to what
we can do. But over time, and in a totally new environment, if you intermarry and consciously bring up your children in a different set of customs, with different memories
and give them a different sense of myth and common origin, then gradually you can.
But it is a debatable point."

Education, says Smith, serves as the battlefield for ethnicity and nationality. In the
public domain, nationality is encouraged. An attempt is made to subsume ethnicity, to
assimilate different groups and fuse them into a new shared mythology. Ethnic leaders
seek to repel these pressures and to foster ethnic belonging and continuity. There are
very few countries where a policy of ethnic pluralism and multi-culturalism is cultivated, although one does find this in Canada, as opposed to France, for instance. Even
then, however, there are areas which the state will reserve to itself, such as the military
and the police. Ethnicity will always be off limits in these spheres.

An ethnicity can become nationality, of course, but can nationality become an ethnicity? "Certainly that is what the African state-nations would like to do. Kenya consists
of a number of ethic communities—Kikuyu, Luo and others," says Smith. "It is a state
forged along a railway line which linked the sea to mines at Kampala, completely artificial territory. The peoples were pre-existent to colonial rule, and the state that was
formed sought to unify these peoples and create a common Kenyan nationality. The
question now is, can a Kenyan nation survive without the myths, memories, symbols and
so forth, that we find in ethnicity. Can it be manufactured in some way? My view is that
manufacturing has serious limits. Besides the conscious volition of elites, what is required
is an ethnic basis upon which the nation can be created. Kenya, of course, has a dominant ethnic group, the Kikuyu. Although the battle continues very strongly, there is no
doubt that if the Kenyan nation were to be forged, it would have a lot of the symbol-
ism, myths, etc. of this dominant group . . . If the state is to succeed, it will have to make
itself into an ethnic community, but it cannot do that out of nothing. It has to have
already—it's a chicken and egg question—some sort of ethnic base.

"The one exception to this rule that makes sense to me is not Eritrea, which people have pointed out, which is at a far too early stage of development, but Tanzania, which is composed of a lot of small ethnic communities, no one of which is dominant. . . . It is possible that here we have a nation-in-the-making, that does not have a specific ethnic group upon which it is grounded.

"There isn't really an ideology of ethnism. Nobody proclaims ethnism as the panacea for the world's ills. There is my ethnicity and your ethnicity, but there is no theory of ethnicity which has a legitimacy, whereas there is a theory of nations, namely nationalism, which large numbers of people believe in as a general view of the world: That the world is divided into nations, that each of them has a particular character and destiny, and that political power belongs to the nation and to be free, you must be a member of the nation."

Smith feels that the lure of nationality lies "in the sense that we are ancestrally related, that this widely believed tale about the past, which may or may not be true, has a powerful effect on the present. It is a tale that powerfully involves us. A special tale. This is what is crucially important, together with shared memories. Mythology is the way in which intellectuals, or perhaps their predecessors—chroniclers, bards and so on, explained this sense. It is not ornamentation but elaboration." Also important is the element of sacrifice, "being called upon to die," which does not normally come into play in the family, the workplace or the political party.

Often, nationality is associated with the sense of being a "chosen people," which the Jews have always embraced, but which also exists among the Chinese, Japanese, the Armenians, the Scots, [the Americans], and many other peoples. On the whole, says Smith, a small nation's claim of making a great contribution to the world is a defense mechanism. Moral superiority becomes a refuge or compensation for powerlessness, political subjection or economic hardship.

Prof. Smith does not foresee the end of nationalism or nationalistic world views any time soon. Ethnic conflicts, from Kosovo to the island of Timor, are flourishing today precisely because of the threat posed by a "global village." "Identity," says Smith, "is often fluid. The Bavarians fought in the French revolution and later became part of Germany. So who are they? These things are not absolutely clear cut. One watches certain processes build up."

Smith feels that Israeli nationality emerged with the Balfour Declaration in 1917. He regrets that fact that the secular liberal nationality created in this country is succumbing more and more to the restrictive and misleading definition of the Orthodox rabbinate which is not, in fact, related to Jewish nationality. The principles of Jewish law, acceptable to a small religious community, cannot replace the great mythology of shared origins that go back to ancient times, the sense of belonging, or the pressures of the outside world which produce a recognized ethnicity.

4

BUSCANDO AMÉRICA

Mike Davis

The Latino Metropolis is, in the first place, the crucible of far-reaching transformations in urban culture and ethnic identity. For half a century the designers of the US Census have struggled to create a category that would successfully capture all the individuals, regardless of race or household language, who share distinctive Latin American cultural roots. After early vacillations over whether Mexicans were a "race" (yes in 1930; no in 1940), several alternate statistical universes, including the category of "Persons of Spanish Mother Tongue" (1950) and "Spanish Surname" (1960), were tried and abandoned because of heavy numerical leakage. In population sampling for the 1990 Census, census workers simply asked people if they identified with any of twelve national identities: Mexican, Puerto Rican, Cuban and so on. Households with positive replies, independent of answers to other identity questions, were enumerated as "Hispanic"—a category adopted in the 1970s by the Nixon administration and first deployed in the 1980 Census.[32]

This is at best a bureaucratic expediency. In California and Texas, for example, "Latino" is generally preferred to "Hispanic," while in South Florida it is considered bad etiquette; on the East Coast both labels are common currency.[33] Scholars, meanwhile, have tried to draw battlelines between what they discern as different politics of usage. Juan Flores, for example, condemns "the superficiality and invidiousness of the term 'Hispanic' in its current bureaucratic usage." Agreeing with him, Suzane Oboler (who devotes an entire book to the subject) and Rodolfo Acuña both claim that "Hispanic" is principally favored by eurocentric Spanish-surname elites in opposition to grassroots identification with "Latino." In the same vein, "to identify oneself today as a 'Hispanic,'" Neil Foley writes, "is partially to acknowledge one's ethnic heritage without surrendering one's 'whiteness.' Hispanic identity thus implies a kind of 'separate but equal' whiteness with a twist of salsa, enough to make one ethnically flavorful and culturally exotic without, however, compromising one's racial privilege as a White person."[34] Geoffrey Fox, on the other hand, argues that "'Hispanic,' with its emphasis on Spanish-language heritage as the foundation of meta-ethnicity, has no implied racial or class agendas and is simply preferred by most immigrants from Latin America."[35]

The debate is unlikely to be resolved. Indeed, there is broad critical awareness that both labels fail to acknowledge the decisive quotient of indigenous genetic and cultural heritage in the populations they describe. Both meta-categories, in fact, were originally nineteenth-century ideological impositions from Europe: "Hispanicity" from Liberal Spain and "Latinity" from the France of Napoleon III.[36] Consanguinity (expunged, as Paul Edison has emphasized, or any indigenous component) was invoked to legitimize the reconquests attempted by both powers in the 1860s: France in Mexico and Spain in Santo Domingo.[37] Bolívar's and Martí's encompassing *Americanismo* meanwhile, has been stolen and parochialized by *los gringos*. It goes to the very heart of the history of the New World that there is no current, consensual term that adequately reflects the fusion of Iberian, African and "Indian" origins shared by so many tens of millions.

Moreover "Hispanic" and "Latino" can no longer by decoded as synonyms for "Catholic." Certainly syncretic New World Catholicism, with a thousand-and-one Aztec and African gods masquerading as *santos*, remains, together with the mother tongue, the most important common heritage of Latino immigrant communities. And few cross-cultural trends are as impressive as the recent flocking of other Latin American Catholics and even Anglo New-Agers to the cult of Mexico's Virgin of Guadalupe (who also reincarnates the powers of the goddess Tonantzin) as she has made her way *al otro lado*. (A digital laser replica of her image recently completed a triumphal procession of the Los Angeles archdiocese. "The 3-by-5-foot copy, blessed by the pope, toured some 50 local parishes before a farewell appearance in front of 50,000 worshippers at the L.A. Coliseum.")[38] Yet if murals of La Morena, radiant in her blue, star-studded shawl, sanctify the sides of *tiendas* from San Diego to Atlanta, the adjoining storefront will most likely be a Pentecostal church. Even in the city that the *pobladores* named "Nuestra Señora" (La Reina de Los Angeles), Spanish-language Protestant denominations (especially Pentecostals) are running neck-to-neck with the Pope. Latinos equally reinvigorate US Catholicism (supplying 71 percent of its growth since 1960) *and* energize its evangelical competitors.[39] In this new dispensation, the traditional antinomy of Latino/Hispanic versus Protestant collapses, and, as Carlos Monsiváis wryly suggests, the immigrant may now pray to the Virgin of Guadalupe: "*Jefecita*. I am still faithful to you, who represents the Nation, even though I now may be Pentecostal, Jehovah's Witness, Adventist, Baptist, or Mormon."[40]

Yet, if there is no reducible essence to *latinidad*—even in language or religion—it does not necessarily follow that there is no substance. In playing with the Rubik's Cube of ethnicity, it is important to resist the temptation of prematurely resolving its contradictions. "Hispanic/Latino" is not merely an artificial, racialized box like "Asian-American," invented by the majority society to uncomfortably contain individuals of the most emphatically disparate national origins who may subsequently develop some loosely shared identity as a reaction-formation to this labeling. Nor is it simply a marketing ploy—like right-wing Coors brewery's opportunist promotion of the 1980s as the "Decade of the Hispanic"—that exploits superficial national similarities in language, cuisine and fashion.[41] To be Latino in the United States is rather to participate in a unique process of

Table 3
US Latinos as a Latin American Nation
(Millions)

2000		2050	
1. Brazil	170.7	1. Brazil	241.0
2. Mexico	98.9	2. Mexico	144.9
3. Colombia	42.3	3. US Latinos	96.5
4. Argentina	37.0	4. Colombia	71.6
5. US Latinos	35.3	5. Argentina	54.5

Source: CEPAL (UN), "America Latina: Proyecciones de población, 1970-2050," *Boletín Demográfico* 62 (July 1998). Other estimates put the US Latino population as high as 100 million by 2040.

cultural syncretism that may become a transformative template for the whole society. *Latinidad*, Flores emphasizes, has nothing to do with "post-modern aesthetic indeterminacy. . . . It is *practice* rather than *representation* of Latino identity. And it is on this terrain that Latinos wage their cultural politics as a social movement."[42] As in Octavio Paz's famous definition of *mexicanidad*, to be Latino is "not an essence but a history."[43]

It is a history that will largely be made over the next generation. It has geopolitical significance because US Latinos are already the fifth largest "nation" in Latin America, and in a half-century they will be third only to Brazil and Mexico. Alternately, they will become the world's second largest Spanish-language-origin nation. Because contemporary US big cities contain the most diverse blendings of Latin American cultures in the entire hemisphere, they seem destined to play central roles in the reshaping of hemispheric as well as national US identities. There is a parallel here, of course, with the role of postwar London as a melting pot of anglophone Caribbean diasporas that has simultaneously transformed the meanings of "Englishness" and "Caribbeaness." The dialectics

Table 4
National Composition of Latino Populations in the US, 1990

1. Los Angeles	Mexican (80%)	Salvadorean (6%)	Guatemalan (3%)
2. Miami	Cuban (66%)	Nicaraguan (11%)	Puerto Rican (6%)
3. New York	Puerto Rican (46%)	Dominican (15%)	Colombian (5%)
	Mexican (4%)	Ecuadorean (4%)	

Source: US Census 1990. What is hidden in these figures as well as ignored in most discussions of Latin identity is the rapidly growing population that identifies as multiple nationalities or heritages, ranging from, say, Mexican-Salvadorean to Cuban-Korean and Ecuadorean-Jewish. "Other" is the spanner in the works of the US ethnic-racial hierarchy.

of identity in the US case, however, are more complex because in each of the three cities that have made claims to be the "capital of Latin America"—Los Angeles, New York and Miami—the recipes for *latinidad* involve strikingly different national ingredients.

Moreover, these national components of identity are themselves not pregiven or unchanging essences. As immigration researchers have been reminding us since the days of Thomas and Znaniecki's monumental *The Polish Peasant in Europe and America* (1919), identities brought to the United States are reassembled into "ethnicities" within the contemporary force-field of the majority culture and its "others."[44] The complex and often conflicting elements of immigrants' previous identities, including fierce subnational allegiances to region and locality, as well as deep ideological divisions between religious and secular-radical subcultures, are strategically edited (and usually simplified) into usable ethnicities in the face of competing claims and pressures of other similarly constructed groups. Diasporic "Mexicanness" in El Paso, for example, does not mean the same thing as being Mexican *en la patria* just across the river in the twin city of Ciudad Juárez, just as being "Dominicanyork" or "Nuyorican" is significantly different from being Dominican in Santo Domingo or Boriquen in San Juan. (These, of course, are not necessarily exclusive identities, but situational identities between which individuals move back and forth in daily or annual itineraries.)[45]

Nor are ethnic identities necessarily stable over time. In Los Angeles, for example, each major generation of Mexican-origin youth has elaborated a different self-conception vis-à-vis Anglo society. Caught in a no-man's-land between ascriptive systems of race and ethnicity, "Mexican-Americans" in the 1930s through the 1950s expressed the pragmatic preference to be recognized as a hyphenated-ethnic minority along the lines of Polish- or Italian-Americans rather than to become a racialized caste like Blacks or Chinese.[46] Mexican-Americans during the 1940s and 1950s, Foley argues, signed a "Faustian pact with whiteness . . . in order to overcome the worst features of Jim Crow segregation."[47]

Failed mobility and reinforced barrioization, together with the charismatic influence of militant Black nationalism, led "Chicanos" in the 1960s and 1970s to discard Mexican-American assimilationism in favor of separatist claims to an indigenous origin in a south-western Aztlan.[48] (In privileging the myth of the Mexica, however, the Chicano movement unfortunately simplified a cultural heritage of magnificent diversity: Olmec, Tarascan, Zapotec, Mayan . . . even Morisco and Converso.) The striking reemergence of *mexicanidad* in the 1980s and 1990s, on the other hand, is rooted in massive immigration and the expansion of the Spanish-language public sphere. (It is also, as we shall see later, an expression of the new structural synchronicity and intensification of ties between most immigrants' old and new homes.)[49] Recently, it has become popular in Southern California for younger people to hyphenate their identities as either "Mexicana-Chicana" or "Chicana-Mexicana," depending on whether their families are first-generation immigrants or not.

Some Chicana/o intellectuals and writers, moreover, have tried to shift the debate about ethnicity beyond rhetorics of hyphenation. Much like their counterparts in the "Irish Studies" movement, they are exploring the terrain that lies beyond the antinomies shaped by Anglo-Saxon colonization or the cultural reifications that ground traditional nationalism. Indeed, some of the most influential avantegardists, like Rubén Martínez and Guillermo Gómez-Peña, have embraced the "Border"—everything that represents the interpenetration of social formations and stands between simple choices of national identity—as a distinctively Latino and dialectical epistemology. ("We de-Mexicanized ourselves to Mexi-understand ourselves, some without wanting to, others on purpose. And one day, the border became our house, laboratory, and ministry of culture.")[50] Aptly titled *Frontera Magazine*—editorially committed to "poking around at the fringes, in the dustpiles and under the heaps of what's left over after all the definitions have been established"—provides a regular stage for the delirious subversion of reified ethnicity, as well as reaching that larger audience of young, hip Chicanos tuned into Culture Clash, Tijuana NO, and Rage Against the Machine.[51] Yet "post-nationalism" may have acquired its current purchase among border literati precisely because of the massive reassertion, over the last generation, of the physical and cultural continuity of Mexico in the US Southwest. Complex experiments in identity politics—unthinkable in the white-majority 1960s—are anchored in the confidence that Aztlan is no longer nationalist myth but historical fact.

For Puerto Ricans, by contrast, the national question is agonizingly unresolved and in some sense untranscendable, with a majority of the island's voters in a recent plebiscite endorsing "none of the above" rather than the Hobson's choice between culturally self-liquidating statehood and economically inviable independence.[52] The largest remaining nineteenth-century colony has by narrow but persistent electoral pluralities preferred the limbo of "commonwealth" to any definitive resolution of its status. As in the nearby French Antilles, *independistas* contribute decisive leadership to every social, labor and environmental struggle but, in the face of debilitating economic dependency, cannot find a fulcrum to enlarge their stable but tiny 5 percent of the vote.[53] This structural stalemate, together with the declining fortunes of the mainland diaspora, gives Puerto Rican identity politics a traumatic urgency, sometimes bordering on revolutionary desperation (for example, the Macheteros), that is only reinforced by the US media's virtual blackout of island life. Indeed, as one *boriqueña* wryly suggests, the only thing visibly Puerto Rican in mainstream culture is Jennifer Lopez's voluptuous *culo*.[54]

Furthermore, these split-level processes of identity formation—the forging of ethnicity and meta-ethnicity—take place in regional contexts of unequal ethnic control over media and symbol systems. The programming of the 500 Spanish-language radio stations and two Spanish-language television networks in the United States often fails to reflect the true heterogeneity of Latino cultural and experiential worlds.[55] In Los Angeles, for example, Salvadoreans, Guatemalans and Ecuadoreans—as well as indigenous immigrants like Zapotecs, Yaquís, Kanjobals and Mixtecs—struggle to defend their distinctive identities within a hegemonically Mexican/Chicano popular culture.[56] In Chicago, on the other hand, comparably sized Mexican and Puerto Rican communities gingerly explore their cultural and political common ground, using *latinismo*, as Felix Padilla has shown, to leverage their clout within Cook County machine politics. (He usefully contrasts two modes of constructing *latinidad*: the fundamentally "weak" mode of passive, symbolic identification with a common language community; and the "strong" mode of active mobilization as an ethnic political bloc.)[57]

In Miami's Little Havana, meanwhile, the poorer Nicaraguan community (estimated South Florida population: 200,000) chafes under the cultural and economic dominance of Cuban elites. (With 5 percent of the national Latino population, Miami has nearly half of all Spanish-surname businesses.)[58] Although the Cuban percentage of Dade County's Spanish-surname population fell from 83 percent in 1970 to 66 percent in 1990, the counter-revolutionary agenda of aging exile leaders still exercises authoritarian censorship over Miami's major Latino cultural and media institutions, as well as influencing national Spanish-language television programming, which is skewed toward "white" Cuban-American talk shows and Venezuelan *telenovelas*.[59] There has been considerable local resentment, sometimes expressed in public protest, against Miami's "exploitation" of the huge captive Spanish-language media markets in Los Angeles and New York.

In New York, by contrast, the Puerto Rican community, which in 1960 comprised four-fifths of the Latino population, now accounts less than two-fifths in the wake of the great Dominican migration of the 1980s and the new Mexican influx of the 1990s. (The Dominican population is now projected to surpass the Puerto Rican by 2010.)[60] The disappearance of a single dominant group has spurred intercultural exchange as well as competition between all the Spanish-speaking and Caribbean-origin communities. Latinization, moreover, has been intertwined warp and woof with New York's Caribbeanization. The racial diversity of New York Latinos, including so many black Puerto Ricans, Cubans and Dominicans, promotes, as Flores points out, a "more reciprocal and fluid relationship" to African-American culture.[61] Younger writers and artists in *La Gran Manzana*, like the stellar Dominicanyorker Junot Diaz (*Drown*), openly advocate a radical politics of color. And, again in contrast to Los Angeles (where only 14 percent of married people of Mexican origin were married to someone from another ethnicity)[62] or Miami, fully half of the Spanish-surname marriages in New York are intermarriages between different Latino nationalities.[63] The cosmopolitan result is a rich, constantly evolving *sabor tropical* in food, music, fashion and language—always freshly spiced by the latest arrivals from Latin America.

Some prominent Latino intellectuals, embracing a messianic neo-Bolívarism, see in this New York-style cultural syncretism the seeds of new creolized identities on national, even hemispheric scales. "Ironically," writes Silvio Torres-Saillant, "Simon Bolívar's desideratum of a unified Latin American nation and the ideal upheld by Eugenio María de Hostos of an Antillean federation find in us a strange kind of fulfillment. We have

Table 5
Largest Latino Markets, 1996

Market	Annual Retail Sales
1. Los Angeles	$28.9 billion
2. New York	$17.6 billion
3. Miami	$9.0 billion
4. San Francisco	$6.0 billion
5. Chicago	$6.0 billion

Source: Website www.hispanic.market (1999).

come to articulate a collective identity, not in our native homelands, as Bolívar and Hostos had dreamed, but within the insecure space of the diaspora."[64] Likewise for Flores, Latinos are the new American counter-culture. "As each group and regional culture manifest itself in the new setting, and as they increasingly coalesce and interact in everyday life, New York is visibly becoming the source of a forceful, variegated alternative to mainstream North American culture."[65] Ilan Stavans, on the other hand, believes that the mainstream culture itself is being inexorably Latinized within a complex dialectic of transcultural exchange between old and new Americas. The rise of "Latinos agringados" addicted to hamburgers and Friday night football, he asserts, is tendentially balanced by the emergence of "gringo hispanizados" infatuated with chiles and merengue.[66] (He was writing before the current "cross-over" celebrity-boom of Selena, Ricky Martin, Christina Aguilera, Sammy Sosa and Jennifer Lopez.)[67] Similarly, the Brazilian futurist Alfredo Valladão, fascinated by the store signs in Miami and Los Angeles that say "Se habla inglés," sees the new Spanish-language "beachheads" in US cities as research laboratories for the cross-fertilization of North and South American cultures. The result, he confidently predicts, will be a new hegemonic global culture: "a Pan-American twenty-first century."[68]

5

LATINOS/HISPANICS . . . WHAT NEXT! SOME REFLECTIONS ON THE POLITICS OF IDENTITY IN THE U.S.

Martha E. Gimenez

1. It is fitting that, in an issue of *Cultural Logic* dedicated to the examination of "Post–Marxist Aporias," this critical assessment of identity politics be included. Among those aporias, the contradiction between the universal and the particular is perhaps one of the most striking. One of its manifestations is the contradiction between the rejection of metanarratives for the sake of enshrining localized "voices"/"identities," and the submission to the universalizing effects of the dominant "voice" inherent in the very process of attempting to escape it through the construction of difference.

2. I became interested in identity politics and its contradictions when I found out, some years ago, that I was included among the "minority faculty" in the university where I work. As I am a foreigner (I was born and grew up in Argentina and came to this country as an adult), I thought, naively, that the affirmative action office might have made a mistake. They informed me, orally as well as in writing, that I was a "Hispanic" and, therefore, they had the right to count me as a "minority." This was indeed a surreal and upsetting experience first because of the racism entailed in the denial of my identity and the imposition of a spurious "hispanicity" loaded with negative connotations, and also because of the administrative uses to which I was subject by becoming part of the statistics used to show compliance with the law. It was also absurd and even funny in a weird sort of way because, for anyone like myself, aware of the heterogeneity of the populations thrown together under the label, the idea is nonsensical, to say the least.

3. But this is no laughing matter, for labels have consequences and these became increasingly clear to me as I began to search for critiques of the "Hispanic" label. I thought I would find plenty, for I mistakenly considered that the problems inherent in the label were obvious, but I was wrong: I found only a handful of articles which, critical of the "Hispanic" label, suggested that "Latino" was more historically and politically

adequate. Upon reflection, I concluded that neither label was acceptable for reasons I will outline as follows:

4. These labels are intended to identify a "minority group"—i.e., a population which the "majority" considers inferior, which has been historically oppressed for generations, and which, objectively, is socially rejected, economically excluded, and lacks political power. The invention of the "Hispanic" label erases the difference between the historically oppressed populations of Mexican and Puerto Rican origin and newly arrived immigrants from Central and South America. Moreover, it does not differentiate between those populations and people from Spain. Altogether this blurring of distinctions has many negative implications for members of local minorities, for arriving immigrants, and for the average American, whose relative ignorance about the world beyond U.S. boundaries is strengthened by labels that stereotype practically the entire world. The bombardment of the population with statistics that constantly stress the differences among whites, Asians, Blacks, and "Hispanics," together with ethnic/racial politics and practices that minoritize everyone who is not from Europe must contribute to the strengthening of racial stereotypes and an oversimplified view of the world, especially among the very young, the uneducated and the prejudiced, for whom the world might easily now appear to be populated primarily by minorities.

5. Both "Hispanic" and "Latino" carry contradictory meanings: positive when linked to culture (understood in terms of ways of life or as concrete cultural/artistic productions) by, for example, minority leaders, educators, and politicians; and negative when placed in the context of what the mass media and the average person associate with them: drug abuse, low income, high incidence of AIDS, high fertility, school dropouts, criminal behavior, high rate of poverty, high proportion of families headed by women, large numbers of welfare recipients, and so on.

6. Let's examine the positive side first. In the context of the present politics of identity and public concern with multiculturalism, the labels are viewed by many, especially those in the intellectual and artistic elites, as sources of cultural pride. But, exactly what are the major components of that all-encompassing culture they seem to have in mind? Which components of the culture should people be proud of? And whose culture? Mexican? Mexican American? Puerto Rican? Colombian? The culture of Spain? When travelling in Central and South America, I was struck with the differences between Argentina and the other countries; when I visited Spain and Italy, I was amazed at how much more at home I felt in Italy than in Spain. Divisions in terms of national origin, social class, ethnicity, race, length of stay in the U.S., and so on make it exceedingly problematic to find common cultural denominators in this population beyond the language. And even the language itself divides, for each Latin American country has its own version of Spanish which is itself divided by region, class, ethnicity, race, etc. Just as heterogeneous are the populations of Mexican, Puerto Rican and Spanish descent living in this country, in which the younger generations have at best a superficial knowledge of Spanish. Here one runs into a concept of culture as a thing that somehow should be pre-

served and passed on from one generation to the next. But culture is not a thing; it is the outcome of the lived experience of people, and it changes as that experience changes, subject to the processes that are constantly changing the society as a whole. To gloss over the living nature of culture, to posit instead some objective "Hispanicity" common to everyone remotely connected to Spain or born in a Spanish-speaking country, while glossing over the historical cultural differences that divide this population is a state-imposed hegemonic project that culturalizes economic exploitation and political oppression.

7. These populations and a large proportion of immigrants from Central and South America are where they are, politically and economically, not because of their "Hispanic" or "Latin" culture but because of their class location in the economic system. I would argue that, culturally, the labels distort reality and create false perceptions which deepen the ignorance of the average person about the "real" culture of these populations. For example: to throw together the cultural productions of Spain; Central and South America; the immigrants of those countries who live in the U.S.; and the many different populations of Mexican and Puerto Rican descent who live in this country under the "Latino" or "Hispanic" label can yield only mystifications. It is as enlightening to say that Borges and Cervantes are "Hispanic" writers as to say that Shakespeare and Faulkner are "Anglo" writers.

8. When examining the negative side of labeling, the first thing to catch one's attention is that the labels hide more than they reveal. For example, they hide the fact that a large proportion of these populations are of Native American and of European descent. The labels perform neat tricks; they "minoritize" foreigners from Spanish speaking countries (many of whom are of European descent), make Native Americans disappear under the pseudo-European veneer of "Hispanic," or transform all "Latinos" into Native Americans because, as a Chicano scholar noted, the real reason why populations of Mexican, Puerto Rican, and Spanish descent have been historically subject to racist practices had nothing to do with their "Spanish" culture but with the fact that a large proportion had Native American blood. The minoritization of foreigners—especially of middle class, professional and technical workers—creates misleading evidence of progress in affirmative action recruiting. The minoritization of the "brain drain" of the Third World is legal because all the labels used to identify "minority" populations make no distinctions in class or national origin. While that might seem good, the implications for populations who have been excluded and oppressed for generations are far from desirable.

9. I cannot end without restating some of my personal views on these matters. What I have written would seem to indicate my rejection of the "Hispanic" and the "Latina" labels. That would be a correct inference. It makes sense to me to consider myself, besides Argentine, Latin American. These are descriptions of myself, partial aspects of my historically developed identity. They give me a partial understanding of who I am and were I to adopt them as alternatives or negations of the racial/ethnic labels

currently in use I would be falling in the trap set by their "ideological interpellations." As Althusser (1972) argued, the main function of ideology is the constitution of individual subjects and these, in turn, are who they are in dialectical relationship to the interpellating Subject (God, the State, the Nation, the Race, etc.). Acquiescing to this interpellation means agreeing to the support of the status quo even as we believe we are challenging it or changing it. The labels "Hispanic," Latina/Latino are, from my standpoint, adaptations to U.S.-imposed conditions of political discourse which disable rather than enable the populations so labelled. Why? Because, in the last instance, these ethnic/cultural labels are euphemisms for referring to important sectors of the U.S. working-class. The kinds of political issues which concern the men and women who self-identify as Latino/Latina tend to be working-class issues, common to all working-class people regardless of cultural heritage and skin color: jobs, good wages, housing, schools, safety in the streets, health care, etc. But the politics of class has been silenced while the politics of identity flourish. It has become legitimate to state political claims only as members of ethnic/racial minorities or majorities, not in terms of class locations. As long as this situation is not challenged, these labels will continue to shape our perceptions, strengthening the racial/ethnic divisions among people and, therefore, strengthening racism itself. On the other hand, even though the "Latina" label does not resonate with me, personally I consider it more acceptable than "Hispanic" for it grapples with the historical links between people who, while living both north and south of the U.S. border between the U.S. and Latin America, do have a common history. The "Hispanic" label, on the other hand, seeks to obscure that history while stressing the links to the former colonizer, in fact granting the former colonizer cultural hegemony over its former subjects.

10. Ultimately, how we call ourselves is our own business, although whatever we do as individuals, we are powerless to change the way others label us. As a sociologist, I am aware that insofar as the politics of identity remain "in command," critiques cannot change the status quo. Labels can be abolished only through political practices aimed at rejecting the "victim" status the system imposes upon people as the indispensable precondition for listening to their grievances. People, men and women, cannot at this time voice their grievances as workers but only as victims of their gender or their race or their ethnicity. In a process of reaction formation, people may embrace these victimized identities as banners of struggle, thus, for example, positing "Latino" against the state-created "Hispanic." But while there might be short-term gains in embracing these general identities that cut across class differences, class divisions have a way of reasserting themselves, as those individuals able to experience upward social mobility are then denounced, accused of having renounced their race, while they themselves do not understand why they are put down for their success. These contradictions should alert us to the need to be aware of the many meanings of culture, so that we can differentiate culture as the expression of free creativity and self-expression, from the culture which is the expression of state-imposed ethnicity or from the use of "Hispanic" as a code word to replace

the "culture of poverty" standby explanation of the effects of social exclusion and economic exploitation.

11. In the end, clarity about the sources of common grievances, needs, and aspirations matters more than labels. When that clarity is achieved, a clarity that necessitates a return to the discredited "metanarrative" that illuminates the crucial commonalities underlying the multiplicity of "identities" that today divide us, we are likely to realize that unity and strength can emerge more quickly from the frank recognition of differences despite our underlying class-based commonalities than from the often instrumental adoption of panethnic identities.

BIBLIOGRAPHY

Althusser, Louis. *Lenin and Philosophy.* New York: Monthly Review Press, 1972.

Gimenez, Martha E. "Minorities and the World System—The Theoretical and Political Implications of the Internationalization of Minorities," in Joan Smith et al, eds., *Racism, Sexism, and the World System.* Westport, CT: Greenwood Press, 1988.

————."Latino/'Hispanic": Who Needs a Name? The Case Against a Standardized Terminology," in *International Journal of Health Services,* Vol. 19, No. 3 (1989): 557–571.

————."The Political Construction of the Hispanic," pp. 66–85 in M. Romero and Cordelia Candelaria, eds., *Estudios Chicanos and the Politics of Community.* Selected Proceedings, National Association for Chicano Studies, 1989.

————."U.S. Ethnic Politics: Implications for Latin Americans," in *Latin American Perspectives,* Vol. 19, No. 4 (1992): 7–17.

6

TALKING PAST EACH OTHER: BLACK AND WHITE LANGUAGES OF RACE

Bob Blauner

For many African-Americans who came of age in the 1960s, the assassination of Martin Luther King, Jr. in 1968 was a defining moment in the development of their personal racial consciousness. For a slightly older group, the 1955 lynching of the fourteen-year-old Chicagoan Emmett Till in Mississippi had been a similar awakening. Now we have the protest and violence in Los Angeles and other cities in late April and early May of 1992, spurred by the jury acquittal of four policemen who beat motorist Rodney King.

The aftermath of the Rodney King verdict, unlike any other recent racial violence, will be seared into the memories of Americans of *all* colors, changing the way they see each other and their society. Spring 1992 marked the first time since the 1960s that incidents of racial injustice against an African-American—and by extension the black community—have seized the entire nation's imagination. Even highly publicized racial murders, such as those of African-American men in two New York City neighborhoods—Howard Beach (1986) and Bensonhurst (1989)—stirred the consciences of only a minority of whites. The response to the Rodney King verdict is thus a long-overdue reminder that whites still have the capacity to feel deeply about white racism—when they can see it in unambiguous terms.

The videotaped beating by four Los Angeles police officers provided this concreteness. To be sure, many whites focused their response on the subsequent black [sic] rioting, while the anger of blacks tended to remain fixed on the verdict itself. However, whites initially were almost as upset as blacks: An early poll reported that 86 percent of European-Americans disagreed with the jury's decision. The absence of any black from the jury and the trial's venue, Simi Valley, a lily-white suburban community, enabled mainstream whites to see the parallels with the Jim Crow justice of the old South. When we add to this mixture the widespread disaffection, especially of young people, with the nation's political and economic conditions, it is easier to explain the scale of white emotional involvement, unprecedented in a matter of racial protest since the 1960s.

In thirty years of teaching, I have never seen my students so overwrought, needing to talk, eager to do something. This response at the University of California at Berkeley cut across the usual fault lines of intergroup tension, as it did at high schools in North-ern California. Assemblies, marches, and class discussions took place all over the nation in predominantly white as well as nonwhite and integrated high schools. Considering that there were also incidents where blacks assaulted white people, the scale of white involvement is even more impressive.

While many whites saw the precipitating events as expressions of racist conduct, they were much less likely than blacks to see them as part of some larger pattern of racism. Thus two separate polls found that only half as many whites as blacks believe that the legal system treats whites better than blacks. (In each poll, 43 percent of whites saw such a generalized double standard, in contrast to 84 percent of blacks in one survey, 89 percent in the other.)

This gap is not surprising. For twenty years European-Americans have tended to feel that systematic racial inequities marked an earlier era, not our own. Psychological denial and a kind of post-1960s exhaustion may both be factors in producing the sense among mainstream whites that civil rights laws and other changes resolved blacks' racial grievances, if not the economic basis of urban problems. But the gap in perceptions of racism also reflects a deeper difference. Whites and blacks see racial issues through dif-ferent lenses and use different scales to weigh and assess injustice.

I am not saying that blacks and whites have totally disparate value systems and world-views. I think we were more polarized in the late 1960s. It was then that I began a twenty-year interview study of racial consciousness published in 1989 as *Black Lives, White Lives*. By 1979 blacks and whites had come closer together on many issues than they had been in 1968. In the late 1970s and again in the mid-to-late 1980s, both groups were feel-ing quite pessimistic about the nation's direction. They agreed that America had become a more violent nation and that people were more individualistic and less bound by such traditional values as hard work, personal responsibility, and respect for age and authority. But with this and other convergences, there remained a striking gap in the way Euro-pean-Americans and African-Americans evaluated racial change. Whites were impressed by the scale of integration, the size of the black middle class, and the extent of demon-strable progress. Blacks were disillusioned with integration, concerned about the people who had been left behind, and much more negative in their overall assessment of change.

In the 1990s this difference in general outlook led to different reactions to specific racial issues. That is what makes the shared revulsion over the Rodney King verdict a significant turning point, perhaps even an opportunity to begin bridging the gap between black and white definitions of the racial situation.

I want to advance the proposition that there are two languages of race in America. I am not talking about black English and standard English, which refer to different structures of grammar and dialect. "Language" here signifies a system of implicit under-standings about social reality, and a racial language encompasses a worldview.

Blacks and whites differ on their interpretations of social change from the 1960s through the 1990s because their racial languages define the central terms, especially "racism," differently. Their racial languages incorporate different views of American society itself, especially the question of how central race and racism are to America's very existence, past and present. Blacks believe in this centrality, while most whites, except for the more race-conscious extremists, see race as a peripheral reality. Even successful, middle-class black professionals experience slights and humiliations—incidents when they are stopped by police, regarded suspiciously by clerks while shopping, or mistaken for messengers, drivers, or aides at work—that remind them they have not escaped racism's reach. For whites, race becomes central on exceptional occasions: collective public moments such as the recent events, when the veil is lifted, and private ones, such as a family's decision to escape urban problems with a move to the suburbs. But most of the time European-Americans are able to view racial issues as aberrations in American life, much as Los Angeles Police Chief Daryl Gates used the term "aberration" to explain his officers' beating of Rodney King in March 1991.

Because of these differences in language and worldview, blacks and whites often talk past one another, just as men and women sometimes do. I first noticed this in my classes, particularly during discussions of racism. Whites locate racism in color consciousness and its absence in color blindness. They regard it as a kind of racism when students of color insistently underscore their sense of difference, their affirmation of ethnic and racial membership, which minority students have increasingly asserted. Many black, and increasingly also Latino and Asian, students cannot understand this reaction. It seems to them misinformed, even ignorant. They in turn sense a kind of racism in the whites' assumption that minorities must assimilate to mainstream values and styles. Then African-Americans will post an idea that many whites find preposterous: Black people they argue cannot be racist, because racism is a system of power, and black people as a group do not have power.

In this and many other arenas, a contest rages over the meaning of racism. Racism has become the central term in the language of race. From the 1940s through the 1980s new and multiple meanings of racism have been added to the social science lexicon and public discourse. The 1960s were especially critical for what the English sociologist Robert Miles has called the "inflation" of the term "racism." Blacks tended to embrace the enlarged definitions, whites to resist them. This conflict, in my view, has been at the very center of the racial struggle during the past decade.

THE WIDENING CONCEPTION OF RACISM

The term "racism" was not commonly used in social science or American public life until the 1960s. "Racism" does not appear, for example, in the Swedish economist Gunnar Myrdal's classic 1944 study of American race relations, *An American Dilemma*. But even when the term was not directly used, it is still possible to determine the prevailing understandings of racial oppression.

In the 1940s racism referred to an ideology, an explicit system of beliefs postulating the superiority of whites based on the inherent, biological inferiority of the colored races. Ideological racism was particularly associated with the belief systems of the Deep South and was originally devised as a rationale for slavery. Theories of white supremacy, particularly in their biological versions, lost much of their legitimacy after the Second World War due to their association with Nazism. In recent years cultural explanations of "inferiority" are heard more commonly than biological ones, which today are associated with such extremist "hate groups" such as the Ku Klux Klan and the White Aryan Brotherhood.

By the 1950s and early 1960s, with ideological racism discredited, the focus shifted to a more discrete approach to racially invidious attitudes and behavior, expressed in the model of prejudice and discrimination. "Prejudice" referred (and still does) to hostile feelings and beliefs about racial minorities and the web of stereotypes justifying such negative attitudes. "Discrimination" referred to actions meant to harm the members of a racial minority group. The logic of this model was that racism implied a double standard, that is, treating a person of color differently—in mind or action—than one would a member of the majority group.

By the mid-1960s the terms "prejudice" and "discrimination" and the implicit model of racial causation implied by them were seen as too weak to explain the sweep of racial conflict and change, too limited in their analytical power, and for some critics too individualistic in their assumptions. Their original meanings tended to be absorbed by a new, more encompassing idea of racism. During the 1960s the referents of racial oppression moved from individual actions and beliefs to group and institutional processes, from subjective ideas to "objective" structures or results. Instead of intent, there was now an emphasis on process: those more objective social processes of exclusion, exploitation, and discrimination that led to a racially stratified society.

The most notable of these new definitions was "institutional racism." In their 1967 book *Black Power*, Stokely Carmichael and Charles Hamilton stressed how institutional racism was different and more fundamental than individual racism. Racism, in this view, was built into society and scarcely required prejudicial attitudes to maintain racial oppression.

This understanding of racism as pervasive and institutionalized spread from relatively narrow "movement" and academic circles to the larger public with the appearance in 1968 of the report of the commission on the urban riots appointed by President Lyndon Johnson and chaired by Illinois Governor Otto Kerner. The Kerner Commission identified "white racism" as a prime reality of American society and the major underlying cause of ghetto unrest. America, in this view, was moving toward two societies, one white and one black (it is not clear where other racial minorities fit in). Although its recommendations were never acted upon politically, the report legitimated the term "white racism" among politicians and opinion leaders as a key to analyzing racial inequality in America.

Another definition of racism, which I would call "racism as atmosphere," also emerged in the 1960s and 1970s. This is the idea that an organization or an environment might be racist because its implicit, unconscious structures were devised for the use and comfort of white people, with the result that people of other races will not feel at home in such settings. Acting on this understanding of racism, many schools and universities, corporations, and other institutions have changed their teaching practices or work environments to encourage a greater diversity in their clientele, students, or work force.

Perhaps the most radical definition of all was the concept of "racism as result." In this sense, an institution or an occupation is racist simply because racial minorities are underrepresented in numbers or in positions of prestige and authority.

Seizing on different conceptions of racism, the blacks and whites I talked to in the late 1970s had come to different conclusions about how far America had moved toward racial justice. Whites tended to adhere to earlier, more limited notions of racism. Blacks for the most part saw the newer meanings as more basic. Thus African-Americans did not think racism had been put to rest by civil rights laws, even by the dramatic changes in the South. They felt that it still pervaded American life, indeed, had become more insidious because the subtle forms were harder to combat than old-fashioned exclusion and persecution.

Whites saw racism largely as a thing of the past. They defined it in terms of segregation and lynching, explicit white supremacist beliefs, or double standards in hiring, promotion, and admissions to colleges or other institutions. Except for affirmative action, which seemed the most blatant expression of such double standards, they were positively impressed by racial chance. Many saw the relaxed and comfortable relations between whites and blacks as the heart of the matter. More crucial to blacks, on the other hand, were the underlying structures of power and position that continued to provide them with unequal portions of economic opportunity and other possibilities for the good life.

The newer, expanded definitions of racism just do not make much sense to most whites. I have experienced their frustrations directly when I try to explain the concept of institutional racism to white students and popular audiences. The idea of racism as an "impersonal force" loses all but the most theoretically inclined. Whites are more likely than blacks to view racism as a personal issue. Both sensitive to their own possible culpability (if only unconsciously) and angry at the use of the concept of racism by angry minorities, they do not differentiate well between the racism of social structures and the accusation that they, as participants in that structure, are personally racist.

The new meanings make sense to blacks, who live such experiences in their bones. But by 1979 many of the African-Americans in my study, particularly the older activists, were critical of the use of racism as a blanket explanation for all manifestations of racial inequality. Long before similar ideas were voiced by the black conservatives, many blacks sensed that too heavy an emphasis on racism led to the false conclusion that blacks could only progress through a conventional civil rights strategy of fighting prejudice and discrimination. (This strategy, while necessary, had proved very limited.) Overemphasizing racism, they feared, was interfering with the black community's ability to achieve greater self-determination through the politics of self-help. In addition, they told me that the prevailing rhetoric of the 1960s had affected many young blacks. Rather than taking responsibility for their own difficulties, they were now using racism as a "cop-out."

In public life today this analysis is seen as part of the conservative discourse on race. Yet I believe that this position originally was a progressive one, developed out of self-critical reflections on the relative failure of 1960s movements. But perhaps because it did not seem to be "politically correct," the left-liberal community, black as well as white, academic as well as political, has been afraid of embracing such a critique. As a result, the neoconservatives had a clear field to pick up this grass-roots sentiment and to use it to further their view that racism is no longer significant in American life. This is the last thing that my informants and other savvy African-Americans close to the pulse of their communities believe.

By the late 1970s the main usage of racism in the mind of the white public had undoubtedly become that of "reverse racism." The primacy of "reverse racism" as "the really important racism" suggests that the conservatives and the liberal-center have, in effect, won the battle over the meaning of racism.

Perhaps this was inevitable because of the long period of backlash against all the progressive movements of the 1960s. But part of the problem may have been the inflation of the idea of racism. While institutional racism exists, such a concept loses practical utility if every thing and every place is racist. In that case, there is effectively nothing to be done about it. And without conceptual tools to distinguish what is important from what is not, we are lost in the confusion of multiple meanings.

BACK TO BASICS

While public discourse was discounting white racism as exaggerated or a thing of the past, the more traditional forms of bigotry, harassment, and violence were unfortunately making a comeback. (This upsurge actually began in the early 1980s but was not well noticed, due to some combination of media inattention and national mood.) What was striking about the Bernhard Goetz subway shootings in New York, the white-on-black racial violence in Howard Beach, the rise of organized hate groups, campus racism, and skinhead violence is that these are all examples of old-fashioned racism. They illustrate the power and persistence of racial prejudices and hate crimes in the tradition of classical lynching. They are precisely the kind of phenomena that many social analysts expected to diminish, as I did.

If there was one positive effect of this upsurge, it was to alert many whites to the destructive power of racial hatred and division in American life. At the same time, these events also repolarized racial attitudes in America. They have contributed to the anger and alienation of the black middle class and the rapid rise of Afrocentrism, particularly among college students.

As the gap in understanding has widened, several social scientists have proposed restricting the concept of racism to its original, more narrow meaning. However, the efforts of African-Americans to enlarge the meaning of racism is part of that group's project to make its view of the world and of American society competitive with the dominant white perspective. In addition, the "inflated" meanings of racism are already too rooted in common speech to be overturned by the advice of experts. And certainly some way is needed to convey the pervasive and systematic character of racial oppression. No other term does this as well as racism.

The question then becomes what to do about these multiple and confusing meanings of racism and their extraordinary personal and political charge. I would begin by honoring both the black and white readings of the term. Such an attitude might help facilitate the interracial dialogue so badly needed and yet so rare today.

Communication can only start from the understandings that people have. While the black understanding of racism is, in some sense, the deeper one, the white views of racism (ideology, double standard) refer to more specific and recognizable beliefs and practices. Since there is also a cross-racial consensus on the immorality of racist ideology and racial discrimination, it makes sense whenever possible to use such a concrete referent as discrimination, rather than the more global concept of racism. And reemphasizing discrimination may help remind the public that racial discrimination is not just a legacy of the past.

The intellectual power of the African-American understanding lies in its critical and encompassing perspective. In the Rodney King events, we have an unparalleled opportunity to bridge the racial gap by pointing out that racism and racial division remain essential features of American life and that incidents such as police beatings of minority people and stacked juries are not aberrations but part of a larger pattern of racial abuse and harassment. Without resorting to the overheated rhetoric that proved counterproductive in the 1960s, it now may be possible to persuade white Americans that the most important patterns of discrimination and disadvantage are not to be found in the "reverse racism" of affirmative action but sadly still in the white racism of the dominant social system.

And, when feasible, we need to try to bridge the gap by shifting from the language of race to that of ethnicity and class.

RACE OR ETHNICITY?

In the American consciousness the imagery of race—especially along the black-white dimension—tends to be more powerful than that of class or ethnicity. As a result, legitimate ethnic affiliations are often misunderstood to be racial and illegitimate.

Race itself is a confusing concept because of the variance between scientific and common sense definitions of the term. Physical anthropologists who study the distribution of those characteristics we use to classify "races" teach us that race is a fiction because all peoples are mixed to various degrees. Sociologists counter that this biological fiction unfortunately remains a sociologist's reality. People define one another racially, and thus divide society into racial groups. The "fiction" of race affects every aspect of peoples' lives, from living standards to landing in jail.

The consciousness of color differences, and the invidious distinctions based on them, have existed since antiquity and are not limited to any one corner of the world. And yet the peculiarly modern division of the world into a discrete number of hierarchically ranked races is a historic product of Western colonialism. In precolonial Africa the relevant group identities were national, tribal, or linguistic. There was no concept of an African or black people until this category was created by the combined effects of slavery, imperialism, and anticolonial and Pan-African movements. The legal definitions of blackness and whiteness, which varied from one society to another in the Western hemisphere, were also crucial for the construction of modern-day races. Thus race is an essentially political construct, one that translates our tendency to see people in terms of their color or other physical attributes into structures that make it likely that people will act for or against them on such a basis.

The dynamic of ethnicity is different, even though the results at times may be similar. An ethnic group is a group that shares a belief in its common past. Members of an ethnic group hold a set of common memories that make them feel that their customs, culture, and outlook are distinctive. In short, they have a sense of peoplehood. Sharing critical experiences and sometimes a belief in their common fate, they feel an affinity for one another, a "comfort zone" that leads to congregating together, even when this is not forced by exclusionary barriers. Thus if race is associated with biology and nature, ethnicity is associated with culture. Like races, ethnic groups arise historically, transform themselves, and sometimes die out.

Much of the popular discourse about race in America today goes awry because ethnic realities get lost under the racial umbrella. The positive meanings and potential of ethnicity are overlooked, even overrun, by the more inflammatory meanings of race. Thus white students, disturbed when blacks associate with each other, justify their objections through their commitment to *racial* integration. They do not appreciate the ethnic affinities that bring this about or see the parallels to Jewish students meeting at the campus Hillel Foundation or Italian-Americans eating lunch at the Italian house on the Berkeley campus.

When blacks are "being ethnic," whites see them as being "racial." Thus they view the identity politics of students who want to celebrate their blackness, their *chicano-ismo*, their Asian heritages, and their American Indian roots as racially offensive. Part of this reaction comes from a sincere desire, almost a yearning, of white students for a color-blind society. But because the ethnicity of darker people so often gets lost in our over-racialized perceptions, the white students misread the situation. When I point out to my class that whites are talking about race and its dynamics and the students of color are talking about ethnicity and its differing meaning, they can begin to appreciate each other's agendas.

Confounding race and ethnicity is not just limited to the young. The general public, including journalists and other opinion makers, does this regularly, with serious consequences for the clarity of public dialogue and sociological analysis. A clear example comes from the Chicago mayoral election of 1983. The establishment press, including leading liberal columnists, regularly chastised the black electorate for giving virtually all its votes to Harold Washington. Such racial voting was as "racist" as whites voting for the other candidate because they did not want a black mayor. Yet African-Americans were voting for ethnic representation just as Irish-Americans, Jews, and Italians have always done. Such ethnic politics is considered the American way. What is discriminatory is the double standard that does not confer the same rights on blacks, who were not voting primarily out of fear or hatred as were many whites.

Such confusions between race and ethnicity are exacerbated by the ambiguous sociological status of African-Americans. Black Americans are *both* a race and an ethnic group. Unfortunately, part of our heritage of racism has been to deny the ethnicity, the cultural heritage of black Americans. Liberal-minded whites have wanted to see blacks as essentially white people with black skins. Until the 1960s few believed that black culture was a real ethnic culture.

Because our racial language is so deep-seated, the terminology of black and white just seems more "natural" and commonsensical than more ethnic labels like African-American or European-American. But the shift to the term African-American has been a conscious attempt to move the discourse from a language of race to a language of ethnicity. "African-American," as Jesse Jackson and others have pointed out, connects the group to its history and culture in a way that the racial designation, black, does not. The new usage parallels terms for other ethnic groups. Many whites tend to dismiss this concern about language as mere sloganeering. But "African-American" fits better into the emerging multicultural view of American ethnic and racial arrangements, one more appropriate to our growing diversity. The old race relations model was essentially a view that generalized (often inappropriately) from black-white relations. It can no longer capture—if it ever could—the complexity of a multiracial and multicultural society

The issue is further complicated by the fact that African-Americans are not a homogeneous group. They comprise a variety of distinct ethnicities. There are the West Indians with their long histories in the U.S., the darker Puerto Ricans (some of whom identify themselves as black), the more recently arrived Dominicans, Haitians, and immigrants from various African countries, as well as the native-born African-Americans, among whom regional distinctions can also take on a quasi-ethnic flavor.

Blacks from the Caribbean are especially likely to identify with their homeland rather than taking on a generic black or even African-American identity. While they may resist the dynamic of "racialization" and even feel superior to native blacks, the dynamic is relentless. Their children are likely to see themselves as part of the larger African-American population. And yet many native-born Americans of African descent also resist the term "African-American," feeling very little connection to the original homeland. Given the diversity in origin and outlook of America's largest minority, it is inevitable that no single concept can capture its full complexity or satisfy all who fall within its bounds.

For white Americans, race does not overwhelm ethnicity. Whites see the ethnicity of other whites; it is their own whiteness they tend to overlook. But even when race is recognized, it is not conflated with ethnicity. Jews, for example, clearly distinguish their Jewishness from their whiteness. Yet the long-term dynamic still favors the development of a dominant white racial identity. Except for recent immigrants, the various European ethnic identities have been rapidly weakening. Vital ethnic communities persist in some cities, particularly on the East Coast. But many whites, especially the young, have such diverse ethnic heritages that they have no meaningful ethnic affiliation. In my classes only the Jews among European-Americans retain a strong sense of communal origin.

Instead of dampening the ethnic enthusiasms of the racial minorities, perhaps it would be better to encourage the revitalization of whites' European heritages. But a problem with this approach is that the relationship between race and ethnicity is more ambiguous for whites than for people of color. Although for many white groups ethnicity has been a stigma, it also has been used to gain advantages that have marginalized blacks and other racial minorities. Particularly for working-class whites today, ethnic community loyalties are often the prism through which they view their whiteness, their superiority.

Thus the line between ethnocentrism and racism is a thin one, easily crossed—as it was by Irish-Americans who resisted the integration of South Boston's schools in the 1970s and by many of the Jews and Italians that sociologist Jonathan Rieder describes in his 1985 book *Canarsie*.

White students today complain of a double standard. Many feel that their college administrations sanction organization and identification for people of color, but not for them. If there can be an Asian business organization and a black student union why can't there be a white business club or a white student alliance? I'd like to explain to them that students of color are organized ethnically, not racially, that whites have Hillel and the Italian theme house. But this makes little practical sense when such loyalties are just not that salient for the vast majority.

Out of this vacuum the emerging identity of "European-American" has come into vogue. I interpret the European-American idea as part of a yearning for a usable past. Europe is associated with history and culture. "America" and "American" can no longer be used to connote white people. "White" itself is a racial term and thereby inevitably associated with our nation's legacy of social injustice.

At various California colleges and high schools, European-American clubs have begun to form, provoking debate about whether it is inherently racist for whites to organize as whites—or as European-Americans. Opponents invoke the racial analogy and see such organizations as akin to exclusive white supremacist groups. Their defenders argue from an ethnic model, saying that they are simply looking for a place where they can feel at home and discuss their distinctive personal and career problems. The jury is still out on this new and, I suspect, burgeoning phenomenon. It will take time to discover its actual social impact.

If the European-Americans forming their clubs are truly organizing on an ethnic or panethnic rather than a racial model, I would have to support these efforts. Despite all the ambiguities, it seems to me a gain in social awareness when a specific group comes to be seen in ethnic rather than racial terms. During the period of the mass immigration of the late nineteenth century and continuing through the 1920s, Jews, Italians, and other white ethnics were viewed racially. We no longer hear of the "Hebrew race," and it is rare for Jewish distinctiveness to be attributed to biological rather than cultural roots. Of course, the shift from racial to ethnic thinking did not put an end to anti-Semitism in the United States—or to genocide in Germany; where racial imagery was obviously intensified.

It is unrealistic to expect that the racial groupings of American society can be totally "deconstructed," as a number of scholars are now advocating. After all, African-Americans and native Americans, who were not immigrants, can never be exactly like other ethnic groups. Yet a shift in this direction would begin to move our society from a divisive biracialism to a more inclusive multiculturalism.

To return to the events of spring 1992, I ask what was different about these civil disturbances. Considering the malign neglect of twelve Reagan-Bush years, the almost two decades of economic stagnation, and the retreat of the public from issues of race and poverty, the violent intensity should hardly be astonishing.

More striking was the multiracial character of the response. In the San Francisco Bay area, rioters were as likely to be white as nonwhite. In Los Angeles, Latinos were prominent among both the protesters and the victims. South Central Los Angeles is now more Hispanic than black, and this group suffered perhaps 60 percent of the property damage. The media have focused on the specific grievances of African-Americans toward Koreans. But I would guess that those who trashed Korean stores were protesting something larger than even the murder of a fifteen-year-old black girl. Koreans, along with other immigrants, continue to enter the country and in a relatively short time surpass the economic and social position of the black poor. The immigrant advantage is real and deeply resented by African-Americans, who see that the two most downtrodden minorities are those that did not enter the country voluntarily.

During the 1960s the police were able to contain riots within the African-American community. This time Los Angeles police were unable to do so. Even though the South Central district suffered most, there was also much destruction in other areas including Hollywood, downtown, and the San Fernando Valley. In the San Francisco Bay area the violence occurred primarily in the white business sections, not the black neighborhoods of Oakland, San Francisco, or Berkeley. The violence that has spilled out of the inner city is a distillation of all the human misery that a white middle-class society has been trying to contain—albeit unsuccessfully (consider the homeless). As in the case of an untreated infection, the toxic substances finally break out, threatening to contaminate the entire organism.

Will this widened conflict finally lead Americans toward a recognition of our common stake in the health of the inner cities and their citizens, or toward increased fear and division? The Emmett Till lynching in 1955 set the stage for the first mass mobilization of the civil rights movement, the Montgomery bus boycott later that year. Martin Luther King's assassination provided the impetus for the institution of affirmative action and other social programs. The Rodney King verdict and its aftermath must also become not just a psychologically defining moment but an impetus to a new mobilization of political resolve.

Part II

THE ECONOMIC CLASS BASIS OF THE POLICIES OF THE RACIAL STATE

Among the points I emphasize in lecture are these: Racism is more about profit than prejudice, power than privilege, policies of the State than actions of individuals. Many scholars and students focus on prejudice, cultural racism, and hate crimes. While these are important topics, the almost exclusive focus on them takes attention away from provocative questions about the possible benefits of racial and ethnic exploitation for an economic upper class and about the role of the State in implementing and institutionalizing race-based policies which have far wider and more tragic ramifications than episodes of interpersonal violence. In this section of the reader you will find essays relevant to these questions.

The selection by Stephen Steinberg, " 'Race Relations': The Problem with the Wrong Name," offers a critique of social science for its failure to see oppression and exploitation as the essential features of racism. The essay by Kushnick gives a historical overview of the "political economy" of white supremacy. He offers a plausible argument for the economic rationale underlying this incipient racism and for the use of the State apparatus to *institutionalize* racism. The word "institutionalize" is important—it means that, because the racist social order was based on law, refusal to comply with racism was punishable by the State authorities. Racism was not left to chance or individual prejudice—it was *policy* enforced by the State. The subsequent uses of the State as enforcer of racial oppression are covered in the following selections.

Stephen Steinberg's article examines the class forces and interests instrumental in resubjugating African-Americans after the Civil War. Jill Quadagno points out how the New Deal of the 1930s created welfare measures benefiting whites but excluding blacks. The role and interest of the Anglo upper class in exploiting Chicano labor is discussed by Tomás Almaguer. During World War Two, more than 100,000 Japanese-Americans living in the West Coast were imprisoned in concentration camps. Many people to this day attribute this imprisonment to a prevalent racist hysteria. Ronald Takaki uncovers the class forces behind the roundup and detention of Japanese-Americans and points out how upper class interests and power prevented the imprisonment of Japanese on Oahu (the Hawaiian Island with the Pearl Harbor naval base). Former FBI agent, M. Wesley Swearingen, discusses the role of the State in attacking anti-racist activists. This particular excerpt deals with the FBI's COINTEL-PRO operations against the Black Panther Party. The introduction to Swearingen's book was written by Ward Churchill and is included because of its valuable background information.

In an article for *The Nation* reviewing Diane McWhorter's book, *Carry Me Home: Birmingham, Alabama—The Climatic Battle of the Civil Rights Revolution,* UCI history professor Jon Wiener notes that power in Birmingham rested with the owners of US Steel who used the Ku Klux Klan as an anti-union, anti-black death squad and protected it with friends in local government and in the FBI (which itself was tied to beatings and murders of civil rights activists). This is further evidence that white supremacy has its basis in the political economy of capitalism.

A final article, "The Banality of 'Ethnic War,'" by John Mueller debunks the popular notion that ethnic conflict is "ethnic conflict." Focusing on conflicts of the 1990s in Croatia, Bosnia, and Rwanda, he shows that while particular ethnicities were targeted in violent, murderous attacks, these assaults were not the result of longstanding and allegedly "natural" ethnic hatreds. They were, instead, the work of "small bands of opportunistic marauders recruited by political leaders and operating under their general guidance." Ethnicity was a factor but worked as an "ordering device" more than an "impelling force." Because the killings were ordered and directed by political elites, they were *not* the inevitable result of ethnic differences. They had more to do with economics and politics than with ethnicity and prejudice.

7

"RACE RELATIONS": THE PROBLEM WITH THE WRONG NAME

Stephen Steinberg

> Which deception is most dangerous? Whose recovery is more doubtful, that of him who does not see or of him who sees and still does not see? Which is more difficult, to awaken one who sleeps or to awaken one who, awake, dreams that he is awake?
>
> Søren Kierkegaard

In *The Feminine Mystique,* published in 1963, Betty Friedan came up with an ingenious formulation for the malaise she detected among middle-class suburban housewives. She called it "the problem that has no name." Implicit here is a critique of sociological practice. Except for a few pieces by those rare women in American sociology—for example, Helen Hacker's 1951 article on "Women as a Minority Group"—the categorical subordination of women was not even on the radar screen of the sociological establishment. "Sexism" had not yet entered the sociological lexicon. The idea that women were consigned to uphold the patriarchal family and the suburban dream was beyond the sociological imagination. The relegation of women to traditional roles was accepted by the male professoriat as an unquestioned fact of life.

Thanks to Daniel Horowitz's biography *(Betty Friedan and the Making of* The Feminine Mystique), we now know that Friedan was no ordinary housewife who arrived at her epiphany through experience and introspection. She was a seasoned political activist who had been schooled in radical thought at Smith College in the 1940s, worked as a labor journalist for two decades, and was steeped in the feminist thought and politics of the 1950s. By the 1960s Friedan was also a suburban housewife, but she brought a conceptual and ideological lens to this experience that allowed her to see clearly what was opaque to most others. Friedan knew better, but as a skillful rhetorician, she refracted social reality through the lens of the average suburban housewife that this was a "problem that has no name."

Race in America presents quite another situation: a problem that has been *mis*diagnosed and *mis*labelled—a problem with the *wrong* name. The term that has dominated sociological discourse on race for seven decades is "race relations." Ponder for a moment the implications of applying this designation to the subject at hand. In the 1930s, when Robert Park introduced "race relations" into the sociological lexicon, blacks were a totally downtrodden people. All but 13 percent fell below the poverty line. Three-quarters lived in the South where they were denied elementary rights of citizenship, were subjected to an all-encompassing system of racial segregation, and were threatened with violence and death for even minor deviations from a debasing system of racial etiquette. During the 1930s there were 119 lynchings. Yes, Robert Park had a point: "race relations" were a problem. Small wonder that mainstream sociology still celebrates his perspicacity!

How is it that we apply such benign language to such a malignant problem? It is rather like diagnosing a melanoma as a skin rash, and prescribing a topical salve. Putting the wrong name on a problem is worse than having no name at all. In the latter instance, one is at least open to filling the conceptual void. In the first instance, however, words lead us down a blind alley. They divert us from the facets of the problem that should command our attention, and as the analogy to melanoma suggests, they lead to remedies that are ineffectual or worse.

Sociology can hardly be accused of turning a blind eye to the problem of race. As Franklin Frazier pointed out in 1947, the first two treatises on sociology in America concerned race (actually, they were pro-slavery tracts), and sociology has since produced an enormous body of research and writing on race and racism. But is this a case of seeing and still not seeing? What is the conceptual lens that the sociologist brings to the study of race? Does it illuminate or does it obscure? And what are we to say of a field whose very name—"race relations"—is already an artful obfuscation?

What terminology would more accurately capture the essence of race in America? The right name, I submit, is "racial oppression." This in fact was the term used by Marxist writers in the 1930s, and it entered sociological parlance in the 1970s with the publication of Bob Blauner's *Racial Oppression in America*. Unlike "race relations," "racial oppression" conveys a clear sense of the nature, magnitude, and sources of the problem. Whereas the race relations model assumes that racial prejudice arises out of a natural antipathy between groups on the basis of difference, "racial oppression" locates the source of the problem within the structure of society. Whereas "race relations" elides the issue of power, reducing racism down to the level of attitudes, "racial oppression" makes clear from the outset that we are dealing here with a system of domination, one that entails major political and economic institutions, including the state itself. Whereas "race relations" implies mutuality, "racial oppression" clearly distinguishes between the oppressor and the oppressed. Whereas "race relations" rivets attention on superficial aspects of the racial dyad, "racial oppression" explores the underlying factors that engender racial division and discord. Whereas the sociologist of "race relations" is reduced to the social equivalent of a marriage counselor, exploring ways to repair these fractured relationships, the sociologist of "racial oppression" is potentially an agent of social transformation.

As Thomas Pettigrew suggested in 1964, the ultimate fallacy of the race relations model was that it placed more importance on reducing prejudice among whites than on improving conditions among blacks. Think about it: here was a praxis that ministered to the oppressor rather than the oppressed! In effect, black aspirations for deliverance from poverty and racism were put on hold while whites underwent a therapeutic transformation. What clearer evidence that sociologists, despite their best intentions, have practiced white social science?

I hope it is clear that I am raising issue not just with the term "race relations" but with the entire paradigm that the term represents. Other terms of discourse are equally problematic. In 1984 Barton Meyers, a psychologist at Brooklyn College, wrote an incisive paper entitled "Minority Group: An Ideological Formulation." Meyers argued, much as I do here, that the term "minority group," coined by Louis Wirth in 1945, presents "a distorted understanding of reality," whose effect is "to make obscure, especially to subordinate groups, the prevailing system of power and the intentions of the powerful." Needless to say, his proposal to expunge "minority group" from the sociological lexicon, and to substitute "oppressed groups," has fallen on deaf ears. Is it that we hear, but we still do not hear?

The terms "prejudice" and "discrimination" are also ideologically laden. Marxists have long argued that prejudice and discrimination are the mere epiphenomena of *systems* of racial domination. Oliver Cox wrote sardonically: "If beliefs per se could subjugate a people, the beliefs which Negroes hold about whites should be as effective as those which whites hold about Negroes." The tendency in social science has been to reify prejudice, to treat it as a problem unto itself, and to pretend that racism could be ameliorated by disabusing whites of the distorted beliefs that they harbor about blacks. This set of assumptions has given rise to a stream of redundant studies, conducted over five decades, that chart the prevalence and distribution of prejudiced beliefs. We measure—with meticulous care—but we measure the "wrong" things, or more exactly, the epiphenomena of racism. Or we measure the right things—glaring inequalities between blacks and whites in wealth, status, and power—but we attribute them to the wrong causes: to deficits in human capital or to aberrant or dysfunctional cultures that are said to perpetuate poverty from one generation to the next.

"Discrimination" suffers from the same problem. Instead of focusing on the historical and structural processes that reproduce racial inequalities from one generation to the next, discrimination is reduced to the level of discrete acts by discrete individuals. However, far more is involved here than individual acts of discrimination, even as they constitute larger aggregates. We are dealing here with the systematic exclusion of an entire people from whole job sectors through all of American history. To describe this as "discrimination" is to trivialize the issue, to elide its institutional character, and again, to obscure its magnitude and sources. I prefer the term "occupational apartheid," which captures the *systemic* character of the problem, and provides a logic for affirmative action—which is aimed, not at atomized individuals, but at large-scale organizations, such as corporations, unions, and universities.

As I argued in *Turning Back*, the racial crisis of the 1960s provided stark proof of the failure of the race relations paradigm to explain, much less do anything about, the forces that were tearing American society apart. This opened up the canon to radical and minority voices that had long been cast to the periphery. In *Racial Oppression in America* Blauner explicitly rejected the race relations model and, picking up on the rhetoric and politics of Third World movements, he used the term "internal colonialism" to describe the encapsulation and plight of blacks and other Third World groups in America. Another key conceptual innovation was proposed in a book that was a collaboration between a political activist and a political scientist. In *Black Power* Stokely Carmichael and Charles Hamilton drew a distinction between "individual racism" and "institutional racism." The latter, they said, did not depend on intentional acts of racial animus, but was embedded in established and respected institutions of society. Here was a truly revelatory way of looking at racism, one that avoided the reductionist tendencies within sociology, and that treated racism as a systemic problem that required systemic change. Despite these theoretical advances, the insurgent sociology of the 60s never developed a full-fledged alternative paradigm. Reflecting the racial backlash in the society at large, mainstream sociology has reverted to the language and logic of "race relations."

Like the Confederate flag, the race relations paradigm has endured the challenges of history. A recent study published in *Race and Society* examined the 34 course syllabi included in the 1997 edition of the ASA's publication on *Teaching Race and Ethnic Relations*. All but one course had prosaic titles such as "Minority Groups," "Minority Relations," "Race and Minority Relations," "Race and Ethnic Relations," and for a new but equally obfuscating twist, "Race and Ethnic Diversity." The exception was a course entitled "White Racism," which aroused fierce controversy when introduced at the University of Connecticut.

One might argue that the Chicago sociologists who pioneered the study of race were "products of their times." But why is it that sociologists are still wedded to these same obfuscating categories seven decades later, as though the Civil Rights Revolution never happened? Why is a course entitled "White Racism" seen as a provocation? Why has sociology failed to develop a discourse that illuminates, instead of obscures, the systemic character of racism?

Like Cox and Du Bois in an earlier time, the proponents of a critical sociology on race are reduced to carping from the sidelines. It is fundamentally a question of hegemony: of which perspectives prevail; which command resources; which are central to intellectual discourse, both inside and outside the academy; which are influential when it comes to the formation of public policy. To pursue the question of hegemony, one would have to examine the web of relationships among elite universities, professional associations, government, the media, book publishers and book review editors, "dream teams," and those all-important foundations—which together constitute a power elite that has a decisive influence on discourse, intellectual production, and social policy.

Nowhere is the hegemonic status of the race relations paradigm more evident than in the recent report issued by the advisory board for President Clinton's Initiative on Race. The initiative itself illustrates the schizophrenic split between social reality and the construction of that reality that is endemic to the race relations model. Here is a President who helped to instigate and enact the repeal of welfare, removing billions of dollars of subsidies to poor minority families; who signed a crime bill that has increased the prison population to over two million people, two-thirds of them black and Latino; who promised to "mend, not end" affirmative action, and yet did little or nothing to oppose Proposition 209 in California, and presided over the quiet dismantling of affirmative action policy.

Instead of public policies to attack structural racism, Clinton provided us with the spectacle of a national conversation on race predicated on the assumption that dialogue "helps to dispel stereotypes," and is "a tool for finding common ground." However, these bland assumptions are not politically innocent, as Adolph Reed argued in his column in *The Progressive* (December 1997):

> The problem isn't racial division or a need for healing. It is racial inequality and injustice. And the remedy isn't an elaborately choreographed pageantry of essentializing yackety-yak about group experience, cultural difference, pain, and the inevitable platitudes about understanding. Rather, we need a clear commitment by the federal government to preserve, buttress, and extend civil rights *and* to use the office of the Presidency to indicate that commitment forcefully and unambiguously. As the lesson of the past three decades in the South makes clear, this is the only effective way to change racist attitudes and beliefs.

The report finally issued by the Commission represents at once the nullification of the 1968 Kerner Commission Report, and the reinstatement of the race relations model as the intellectual framework for race policy in America. Whereas the Kerner Report confronted the nation with the harsh reality that it was "moving toward two societies, one black, one white—separate and unequal," the Franklin Report provides a reassuring illusion of "One America in the 21st Century." Whereas the Kerner Report presented the grisly facts about racial inequality and racial conflict, designed to galvanize the nation to action, the Franklin Report is replete with platitudes about "accomplishments, challenges, and opportunities."

The most glaring point of difference pertains to social policy. The Kerner Report concluded with 73 pages of policy recommendations that envisioned a comprehensive program of economic development and social reconstruction targeted at poverty areas and racial ghettos. Not only does the Franklin Report lack any major policy initiatives, but there is no sense of crisis that the three pillars of anti-racist public policy—affirmative action, school desegregation, and racial districting—have all been gutted, effectively bringing the Second Reconstruction to an unceremonious end.

It is true that the Franklin Report includes an endorsement of affirmative action, albeit a tepid one, along with a litany of proposals for reforming housing, health care, education, and criminal justice. Its main emphasis, however, is on bridging the racial divide through dialogue. Nero has been subjected to the judgment of history for fiddling while Rome burned. In this case we are asked to dialogue—and the Commission's report provides us with a dazzling array of alternatives: One America Conversations, Campus Weeks of Dialogue, Statewide Days of Dialogue, meetings, forums, conferences, public service announcements, and visits to the One America Web Site. Finally, the Franklin Report concludes with a section entitled "Ten Things Every American Should Do To Promote Racial Reconciliation."

It is as though Durkheim concluded his masterpiece with "Ten Things That Everybody Should Do to Avoid Suicide." Or Weber offered ten tips for succeeding in business. Or Marx advocated a WPA-style jobs program for the lumpen proletariat. If the President's Advisory Board on Race has displayed an abysmal failure of sociological imagination, who are we to blame but the sociologist of "race relations" who has betrayed the promise of sociology's intellectual tradition by reducing social facts down to the level of individual predispositions? What can we hope of a Presidential commission or the public at large if sociologists, despite their assiduous labors, still do not see that good race relations are unattainable—indeed, inconceivable—unless there is a basic parity of condition between the black and white citizens of this nation?

8

THE POLITICAL ECONOMY OF WHITE RACISM IN THE UNITED STATES

Louis Kushnick

> The plight of the white working class throughout the world today is directly traceable to Negro slavery in America, on which modern commerce and industry was founded, and which persisted to threaten free labor until it was partially overthrown in 1863. The resulting color caste founded and retained by capitalism was adopted, forwarded and approved by white labor, and resulted in subordination of colored labor to white profits the world over. Thus the majority of the world's laborers, by the insistence of white labor, became the basis of a system of industry which ruined democracy and showed its perfect fruit in World War and Depression.
>
> Du Bois, *Black Reconstruction in America* (1966, p. 30)

In the 14 years since the first edition of *Impacts of Racism on White Americans,* there has been a massive increase in racial polarization in the United States, Britain, and the rest of Europe, both East and West. There has been an increase in racial violence in these areas and increasing scholarly recognition of the centrality of racism in the organization of modern Western societies (Cornacchia & Nelson, 1992; Horton, 1991; Stanfield, 1991). The successful playing of the race card in election after election has been accompanied by a rightward shift of mainstream political parties and a narrowing of the parameters of legitimate political discourse in the United States and Western Europe (Kushnick, 1995; Marable, 1993). This rightward shift in political and governmental action led to an increase in popular racism—the racism of common sense. Politicians then used this increase as a justification for further racist state actions, which in turn exacerbated popular racism. . . . This growth of racism has accompanied, and made politically possible, greater class inequality and a restructuring of the political economies of the advanced capitalist countries at the expense of the working classes. All these events were anticipated in the first edition chapter (Kushnick, 1981), and developments in the decade and a half that have passed since 1981 have validated that analysis.

Another tendency that has appeared in the intervening years is an intellectual/ideological distancing of mainstream policy commentators from the analysis that sees the class implications and functions of racism in a global capitalist system. It is the argument of this chapter that the events of the 1980s and 1990s in the United States, Britain, and Europe have validated the analysis of the first edition and made it more necessary than ever for the relationship between racism and capitalism to be put on the political agenda. The dynamic, described by Du Bois in the introductory quotation, is as central and valid today as it was when he first wrote it.

The fundamental argument is not only that racism has blighted the lives of tens and hundreds of millions of people of color all over the world. It has also functioned worldwide to maintain class-stratified societies (Du Bois, 1966, p. 30). However, this racist system has been contested terrain for its entire history. Whites and people of color as both individuals and groups have resisted the imposition of the racist ideology and the racialized organization of society (Aptheker, 1992). It is important to study that resistance and to understand the conditions within which Whites opted for a more inclusive definition of "us" as opposed to the racially exclusive basis of identification that has been the dominant mode for most of the period under review.

In this chapter I will look at the development of racism during the development of capitalism, paying particular attention to the roles of slavery and imperialism. I will outline the institutionalization of racism in the early 20th century and its implications for different races in the metropole, and I will develop this theme in the context of the growth of working-class consciousness and organization. Finally, I will look at the contemporary position of the working class, the crisis in the capitalist system and its impact on workers in the metropole, and the resistance to that racism and the construction of alternative visions and practices.

SLAVERY, EARLY CAPITALISM, AND THE ORIGINS OF RACISM

Plantation economies based on slavery in the New World provided for the development of manufacturing in the center of the world system, particularly in Britain. The triangular trade was a stimulus for British manufacturers and for economic development in the British settler colonies in North America. Africans were bought with British manufactured goods. Those who survived the middle passage in British ships had to be clothed and fed by British firms, and the crops they produced on the plantations provided both the raw materials for industry and the capital for investment in new plant and equipment in the South and New England (Bailey, 1990; Williams, 1967). The importance of the slave trade can be gauged by the following quote from a Liverpudlian authority writing in 1797:

> This great annual return of wealth may be said to pervade the whole town,
> increasing the fortunes of the principal adventurers, and contributing to the

support of the majority of the inhabitants; almost every man in Liverpool is a merchant, and he who cannot send a bale will send a bandbox. It will therefore create little astonishment that the attractive African meteor has from time to time so dazzled their ideas that almost every order of people is interested in a Guinea cargo (Pope-Hennessy, 1970, p. 155).

Leo Huberman (1968) quotes a Professor H. Merrivale, who delivered a series of lectures in 1840 at Oxford on the theme "Colonisation and Colonies" in which he asked two important questions and gave an equally important answer:

> What raised Liverpool and Manchester from provincial towns to gigantic cities? What maintains now their ever active industry and their rapid accumulation of wealth? . . . Their present opulence is as really owing to the toil and suffering of the Negro as if his hands had excavated their docks and fabricated their steam engines (p. 167).

The importance of slavery and the plantation system for the United States as a whole, not merely the Southern slave states, is equally obvious (Bailey, 1990). The political structure created by the Constitutional Convention of 1787 reflected that importance. Slavery was incorporated into the basic structure of the new political system in a number of ways: The slave trade was protected until 1807, slaves were counted as three fifths of a human being for both taxation and representation, and a fugitive slave provision was incorporated.

These material acts were reflected in the ideological sphere and produced the ideological contradictions inherent in an economic system based on human slavery. In the first instance, this dependence on slavery posed a moral question. Equiano, an ex-slave and one of the leaders of the antislavery movement in 18th-century Britain, posed the problem: "Can any man be a Christian who asserts that one part of the human race were ordained to be in perpetual bondage to another?" (Fryer, 1984, p. 109). Interestingly enough, on the other side of the English Channel the French philosopher Montesquieu articulated the problem in similar terms when he wrote, "It is impossible for us to suppose these creatures to be men, because, allowing them to be men, a suspicion would follow that we ourselves are not Christians" (Drinnon, 1980, p. 138).

At the same time, capitalism in its struggle against the remnants of feudalism and mercantilism had evolved as an ideology alongside a political liberalism based on the individual as the key actor. Individual transactions in the free market were seen as the basis of economic activity and social progress; each individual was "free" to sell her or his labor to any would-be purchaser. People were to be "freed" from feudal ties to the land, and, of course, landowners would be "free" to displace labor no longer required to maximize profitable use of the land as a commodity. How, then, was it possible to create a new economic, political, and philosophical system dedicated to individualism, freedom, and profit on the backs of slaves?

The resolution of these problems was not the ending of slavery and of the slave trade until economic change and the resistance of the slaves made the alternative of free labor of the ex-slaves a satisfactory alternative. In a development very similar to that adopted earlier *vis-à-vis* the Irish Catholics whose land and freedom had been stolen by England, all of the victims of these processes, whether they were Irish or Africans, were defined as apelike, less than human, savage (see Hechter [1975], Rai [1993], and Rolston [1993] for discussion of the Irish dimension; see Rawick [1972] and Fryer [1984] for the African dimension). This "solution"—slavery—has had fundamental and continuing consequences. It facilitated a justification of barbaric practices in terms of the superior civilization of the British and other Europeans that was to be used subsequently to justify imperial conquest of Africa at the end of the 19th century.

At the time that slavery and the plantation economies were underwriting the development of capitalism in Britain and the United States, conditions of absolute misery were created for the mass of the population that was displaced from the land and was then exploited in the mills, mines, and factories. There was an ideological congruity between stereotypes of the white poor and the slaves. The poor were poor because they were lazy, they lived from hand to mouth, they seldom thought of the future; poverty was the necessary goad to their activity and to their children's activity in the labor market. Increasing their pay and removing the threat of hunger would only make things worse for them and for society as a whole. But, of course, the rich and the powerful were motivated by other considerations such as ambition and initiative, which required material incentives and rewards. These ideas of Thomas Malthus were by no means deviant at the time, nor, as we shall see, are they deviant in our own time. So, objectively and in terms of stereotypes, the poor in Britain were paying a high price for a production surplus that, alongside the surplus generated by the superexploitation of people of color, fueled the triumph of capitalism as a world system. The fact that there was this congruity in the ideology was, however, not the whole story. There was also the racist ideology that posited the particular inferiority of the Irish and of the peoples of the conquered periphery. The white and English poor were encouraged to adopt racism in order to have a feeling of superiority over someone else in a hierarchical society. But this construction of a racialized identity was not a reflection of a "natural" racism of the white, English working class.

Indeed, the history of class struggle is the history of attempts by major sections of the working class to develop their own consciousness and agenda. It is significant that at crucial points in this struggle they overthrew during brief periods of activism and creativity the exclusive definitions of "us" as the ignorance, the prejudices, the disunion and distrust that had kept them powerless. For example, John Foster (1974), in his study of the development of class consciousness among 19th-century workers, found militants in Oldham, Lancashire, very conscious of the need for solidarity, for an inclusive definition, as an alternative.

In 1834 a mass meeting demanded the elimination of wage differentials and the levelling up of labourers' pay. The year before there had been a call for an end to coercion in Ireland. And throughout the period a predominantly English population was willing to accept Irishmen among its leaders, The very fact of class formation meant that the controlling spell of the ruling-class had been broken, and with it, the subgroup system by which people accommodated "unfairness" (p. 185).

But within a decade of the defeat of these attempts to change society in the interests of a united working class, it became clear that state policy underpinned and reinforced the racist ideology that was being constructed to limit the consequences of the dislocations, tensions, and conflicts that accompanied the rise of the new order. State policy played a crucial part in the elimination of competition from Africans, Asians, and the other indigenous peoples encountered by white expansionism. The British government destroyed the textile industry in India and opened that enormous market to the domination of Lancashire textiles (Mukherjee, 1973). The slave trade, the plantation economies, and their ideological justifications were paralleled by conscious policies to separate physically in Britain the Irish and the English working class, and ideologically the white working class from the people of color on the periphery.

Within Britain's North American colonies, using both indentured white labor and black labor, either indentured or semi-enslaved, the need for separation and antagonism was made apparent by Bacon's Rebellion in Virginia in the mid-17th century. Bacon's Rebellion fundamentally threatened the status quo because it was a joint action by both racial groups. A way had to be found to maintain stability and order, to increase the supply of cheap, controllable plantation labor, and to avoid adding to the future numbers of yeoman farmers contesting for political power with the planter elite. The solution involved the enslavement of black labor and the nonenslavement of white labor. This strategy was bolstered by a series of concessions to white labor, which worked to divide the two groups further. Clearly, if no White could be a slave, and if all slaves were black, the objective conditions for racial separation were well established. Furthermore, laws were passed further providing for white supremacy. Thus, we see yet again the crucial role of state racism constructing and underpinning popular racism by providing material and psychic rewards for accepting a white identity, that is, a racialized identity in opposition to a more inclusive identity.

The ideology of racism was incredibly effective, even given the costs to the vast majority of the Southern population. So important was this separation of Whites from Blacks that George Fitzhugh, the slaveholding sociologist, could declare,

> The poor (whites) constitute our militia and our police. They protect men in the possession of property, as in other countries; and they do much more, they

secure men in the possession of a kind of property which they could not hold a day but for the supervision and protection of the poor (Allen, 1975).

Thus, in the United States white supremacy was constructed and reinforced by race-based chattel slavery and a racialized definition of *us* as opposed to *them*, which was an integral part of racist ideology (Drinnon, 1980; Ringer, 1983; Roediger, 1991; Saxton, 1991; Takaki, 1980). This was underscored by the Naturalization Act of 1790, which established the requirements for citizenship, one of which was the necessity of being white. It was not merely that one had to be white to be an American, but obviously to be white was to be superior. The construction of a white identity provided the basis for incorporation of European immigrants into the society. So the Irish driven out of their own country by the consequences of Anglo-Saxon imperialism arrive in another country largely controlled by Anglo-Saxon elites but are able to avoid permanent suppression and inferiority by virtue of being able to become white rather than remaining Irish and Celtic. Thus, angry Irish miners in Pennsylvania denounced Daniel O'Connell, the Irish Republican leader, for his call for Irish American opposition to slavery. Despite their own exploitation and the attacks on them from nativist forces, they declared that they would never accept Blacks as "brethren," for it was only as Whites that they could gain acceptance and opportunity in the United States.

Furthermore, acceptance and opportunity are of crucial importance in the construction of "whiteness." Although the Irish suffered discrimination at the hands of the "white, Anglo-Saxon Protestant" (WASP) elites, they had the basis of gaining acceptance in U.S. society as Whites rather than as Catholic Celts (Roediger, 1991). It is also conceptually important in challenging the "ethno-racial umbrella" thesis advanced by scholars such as Glazer (1971), with the argument that ethnicity was "an umbrella term subsuming all racial, religious and nationality groupings" to form a part of a single family of social identities (Cornacchia & Nelson, 1992, p. 103). Cornacchia and Nelson test the validity of this ethno-racial umbrella thesis in contrast with the "black exceptionalism" thesis and conclude that it is the latter that has greater validity: "The findings on the Black political experience demonstrate that it would be inappropriate to treat racial minorities as merely ethnic groups competing in the interest group arena for entitlements and preferments. The political system was nearly sealed shut to Blacks" (Cornacchia & Nelson, 1992, p. 120).

The extension of democracy in the United States, particularly during the Jacksonian era, was an extension of democracy—or at least of formal incorporation into the Republic as citizens—to white males. The outcome was the creation of a "Herrnvolk democracy" or, in Roediger's terms, "Herrnvolk Republicanism." This incorporation of Whites regardless of class played a crucial role in ensuring the triumph of racism throughout the United States, in the free states and in the slave states. Before the Civil War, poor Whites and the non-slaveholding yeomanry in the South, free soil farmers in the West, and artisans and the emerging working class—immigrant and native—in the

North were all made citizens in the great white Republic and given an identity that was oppositional to people of color, slave or free.

Because "Herrnvolk Democracy" was not and could not be a reality in terms of "Democracy" despite its state constructed and supported "Herrnvolk" character, there remained a class tension within American society. This class tension became central at various points and remained more marginal at others in societal terms; for some working people it was more central to their identity than for others. The point is that it was part of an ongoing set of struggles and that the racially defined identity as Whites was not always hegemonic. As Herbert Aptheker has argued, the rank and file of the antislavery and abolitionist movements among Whites were made up largely of poor people:

> The hundreds of thousands of people who signed anti-slavery petitions were common people, the poor and the working class. The subscribers to the abolitionist newspapers had to struggle to assemble their pennies. . . . It was also common white people who took risks during this period. Those who saved Garrison from lynching were plain and ordinary people (Aptheker, 1987).

There were, therefore, white people who acted on the basis of values that were alternative to those based on an identity as Whites. The triumph of the white identity, therefore, was not an inevitable consequence of natural or genetic forces but the outcome of unequal struggles.

In fact we find that opposition to racism could and did go hand in hand in antislavery movements in Britain and the United States with attitudes and politics that opposed slavery without rejecting racism. Thus, the outcomes of the struggle against slavery, including the Civil War in the United States, did not lead to systems of racial justice or of class equality. For example, the ending of slavery in the British West Indies followed the rise of alternative centers of political/economic power. Fears of successful slave uprisings such as Haiti's, the increasing cost of suppressing such uprisings, and diminishing levels of profit overshadowed the moral crusade that had been waged against the evils of the slave trade and of slavery.

Emancipation, however, did not mean the dismantling of the plantation system and the transfer of land to the Afro-Caribbean peoples. Instead, barriers were placed in their way when they tried to obtain land. Indentured Asian labor was brought in until the 1920s, political control remained in London, and new forms of superexploitation were devised. As a consequence of these actions, future class and racial relations in the Caribbean were shaped by imperialism for the benefit of the countries of the metropole. Similarly in the United States, the Civil War was fought by the leaders of the Union less to free the slaves than to extend the sway of the emergent industrial capitalists and serve the interests of their free soil allies. Emancipation in neither the Caribbean nor the United States required the overthrow of racialist attitudes or of racist structures, despite the commitment of antiracist Whites and free people of color and slaves struggling for freedom. Thus, in both cases, slavery died so that capitalism could continue to flourish, and with it, racism.

RACISM IN THE POSTSLAVERY PERIOD

Prejudices, disunion, and distrust were all characteristics of the response of the major part of the working class in both Britain and the United States to the triumph of capitalism. This response involved the acceptance of hierarchy itself and the situating of oneself and one's group into hierarchies based on skill, job status, ethnicity, gender, and race. One owed and was owed respect in relation to one's position along these scales. These divisions were reinforced by the distribution of material resources. State action directly and indirectly maintained this invidious social order and made possible the continued functioning of the system to control the production and distribution of the material resources. Politics based on an inclusive class consciousness had to confront and overcome these ideological and material reinforcements, including state repression, and it was not entirely surprising that such politics had an up-hill battle and were successful less frequently than they failed.

THE UNITED STATES

The development of class consciousness among the rapidly growing working class in the post-Civil War United States, was, as in Britain, fundamentally shaped and distorted by racism (Sexton, 1991). There was the presence of freed slaves and of other racially distinct colonized peoples within the metropole itself in large numbers. There was a massive immigration of European workers into the United States. Racism provided the ideological and material framework within which the millions of European immigrants who joined the labor force in the half century between 1865 and 1914 became "American." Then they and the indigenous white working class were given a racialized identity (or a racialized working-class identity) as an alternative to a working-class identity and this shaped their responses to being made wage-laborers.

The choice that presented itself throughout this period in U.S. history was between a politics based on an inclusive definition of "us" and one based on an exclusive racial definition. An inclusive definition and political strategy would have necessitated challenging the racialist ideology that had become a dominant characteristic of American identity in the antebellum period (Roediger, 1991). It would have required that workers recognize a common interest and need to cooperate to achieve common objectives. Although this was not the path chosen by most of the white working class and its organizations, there is evidence that there was consideration of such an option and evidence of attempts to develop such a politics. The Address of the National Labor Congress to the Workingmen of the United States in 1867, for example, declared that "unpalatable as the truth may be to many," Negroes were now in a new position in the United States, and the actions of white working men could "determine whether the freedman becomes an element of strength or an element of weakness" in the labor movement.

The solidarity option was not chosen. The exclusive racial definition of "us" was the dominant response. This divisive definition was based both on possession of craft skills and on racial prejudice. As Du Bois put it,

> [the National Labor Union] began to fight for capital and interest and the right of the upper class of labor to share in the exploitation of common labor. The Negro as a common laborer belonged, therefore, not in but beneath the white American labor movement. Craft and race unions spread. The bettered skilled and intelligent American labor formed itself into closed guilds and, in combination with capitalist guild-masters, extorted fair wages which could be raised by negotiation (Du Bois, 1966, pp. 569–571).

The craft- and race-based unionization operated to retard the development of mass unionism until the Great Depression. It culminated in the formation of the CIO (Congress of Industrial Organizations) industrial unions of the late 1930s. Exclusiveness ensured the availability of large pools of workers willing to, or having no choice but to strike-break and thus weaken the effectiveness of the craft unions. These factors were reinforced by racial and ethnic divisions in the workplace and in housing, education, and social and political activities. This situation goes a long way toward explaining the present political weakness and lack of class consciousness of the American working class (Davis, 1986).

Matters were further complicated by white labor being encouraged to feel superior to non-Whites and thus become "White." Central Pacific Superintendent Charles Crocker, for example, pointed out the benefits to white labor from Chinese immigration:

> I believe that the effect of Chinese labor upon white labor has an elevating instead of degrading tendency. I think that every white man who is intelligent and able to work, who is more than a digger in a ditch . . . who has the capacity of being something else, can get to be something else by the presence of Chinese labor more than he could without it. . . . There is proof of that in the fact that after we got Chinamen to work, we took the more intelligent of the white laborers and made foremen of them. I know of several of them now who never expected, never had a dream that they were going to be anything but shovelers of dirt, hewers of wood and drawers of water, and they are now respectable farmers, owning farms. They got a start by controlling Chinese labor on our railroad (Takaki, 1980, p. 238).

Not only could white male workers be elevated by the use of Chinese labor, and become "White" men, so could white women become "White" women. Takaki quotes an article by Abby Richardson in *Scribner's Monthly* titled "A Plea for Chinese Labor," in which she argued: "This is the age when much is expected of woman. She must be the ornament of society as well as the mistress of a well-ordered household." Thus, "Chinese labor could become a feature of both the factory and the home." Tensions of class conflict in white society could be resolved if Chinese migrant laborers became the "mudsills" of society, white men became "capitalists," and their wives "ornaments of society" (Takaki, 1980, p. 239).

These privileges, or more correctly for many white working-class men and women, these promises of privileges were only part of the process through which racism remained a dominant characteristic of the American ideology. Repression of those who challenged that response of the working class to their designated position in society also existed. There is a long history in the United States of legal and extralegal repression, ranging from the terrorism directed against Blacks and their white allies during reconstruction in the post-Civil War South, to the suppression of the Molly McGuires, the Industrial Workers of the World (IWW), to the judicial murders of Sacco and Vanzetti and then the Rosenbergs in this century.

Clearly, the threat posed by class-conscious interracial cooperation was perceived by the ruling class and its agents in control of the state. Repression was accompanied by propaganda campaigns against Populists efforts in the last two decades of the 19th century. There was a massive campaign appealing to white supremacist attitudes. The specter of black equality was used to divert the poor Whites away from any incipient class consciousness, toward a renewed racial consciousness. For example, the power of racial identity was tested in Lawrence County, Alabama, which represented Alabama's "strongest and most persistent opposition to the Democratic party" and in which "Free labor ideology and biracial class politics survived . . . because of the efforts of local black and white radical Republicans, who during Congressional Reconstruction refused to be intimidated by Ku Klux Klan terror" (Horton, 1991, p. 65).

Horton (1991) identifies the campaign waged by the local, Democrat newspaper, the *Advertiser:*

> Because the Democratic party was threatened by the possible emergence of a bi-racial brotherhood of working men . . . the *Advertiser* resorted to a campaign of racial hatred that resembled its earlier pronouncements in support of the Klan. . . . To stir up racial discontent, the *Advertiser* on election day fell back on its tried and tested formula—race-baiting. The front page of the *Advertiser* was filled with reports of assaults by blacks on white women. "The Negroes . . . were getting very troublesome" in Mississippi. "Several Negro women of Tuscumbia" were reported to "have addressed a very insulting letter to several respectable white ladies." Jourd White (the editor) stated that they would "hug a barrel or look up a rope," as a just reward for the insult. The "white men of

Lawrence County," were urged by White to "do" their "duty" to "protect the white race from this animalism" (pp. 76, 77).

Horton concludes that, "A strong tradition of free labor-oriented biracial politics coupled with worsening agricultural depression during the post-Reconstruction period could not overcome the dominance of racial politics even in a county where a legitimate space had been created for class politics" (p. 83).

The Southern state governments legitimated the process by establishing the Jim Crow system of de jure segregation, that is, of apartheid. The federal government accepted and legitimated the process through a number of Supreme Court decisions culminating in the 1896 *Plessy v. Ferguson* decision, which established the "separate but equal" principle. This decision justified segregation in all aspects of life in the South. The federal government's acceptance of the disenfranchisement of the Southern black population, of the lynch terror that took hundreds of black lives a year, and of the total denial of Black's citizenship rights were crucial developments. So was Northern capitalist support. This took the form of not recruiting Southern black labor into the growing industrial proletariat and by largely excluding the Northern black population as well. Capitalist reinforcement of racial hatred also meant recruiting Blacks solely as strikebreakers. This ensured the maintenance of the controlled labor force necessary for the Southern sharecrop system that produced the cotton that was still so crucial to the economy of the United States. This also ensured the exclusion of black labor from the national industrial proletariat just like it had been excluded from the previous fundamental determinant of American life, the frontier. Now when Blacks entered the labor force, they would be entering turf considered by Whites as White.

In addition to the psychological privileges that poor Whites obtained from the Jim Crow system (being told that they were superior to all African Americans regardless of their own class position), they received some material privileges. These privileges were unequally distributed within the white working class and were tenuously held. There was the ever-present threat of cheap substitute black labor if Whites stepped out of line. The price white labor paid in the South for its superior position included wages significantly lower than those in other regions, lower levels of public services than in other regions, and the contempt of their ruling class "white allies" who looked upon them in much the same way as they did the Blacks. A politics characterized by the absence of issues and the absence of opportunities for poor Whites to obtain benefits, even by the standards of the rest of the country, became normal. Poor Whites, in effect, gave up their own suffrage through the denial of suffrage to African Americans as part of the price paid to become "White."

Faced with the political culture of racism, the white working class failed to create its own culture to challenge the class-based ethos or to defend and maintain the attempts to do so that were made during this period. Thus, the white working class was unable to meet the growing attacks on its interests that the rise of monopoly capital represented. The growing concentration of capital and centralization of control brought with it increased exploitation of the population by suppressing wages and benefits. It made possible the process of "de-skilling" and the degradation of labor associated with "Scientific Management" (Braverman, 1974). The skilled/unskilled hierarchy was reinforced in ethnic and racial terms, and the craft-based unions were unable to defeat the power of the monopoly capitalists and their political allies. Rather than reconsider its basic assumptions, the American Federation of Labor (AFL) became more and more exclusionist as it faced the competition of cheaper labor. This pattern was similar to that which characterized British trade unions in the same period. In 1898 an article in the AFL's official organ, the *American Federationist,* declared that Blacks were unfit for union membership because they were "of abandoned and reckless disposition," lacking "those peculiarities of temperament such as patriotism, sympathy, sacrifice, etc., which are peculiar to most of the Caucasian race." The AFL therefore recommended deportation of Blacks to Liberia or Cuba. Samuel Gompers went further in a speech in 1905 when he declared that "the Caucasians are not going to let their standard of living be destroyed by negroes, Chinamen, Japs, or any others" (quoted in Saxton, 1970, p. 115).

White opposition to such attitudes came from movements that posited a class, rather than a sectional or racial, analysis of society. The IWW, for example, took a principled inclusive position and was consequently the target of repressive action by state and capital. The threat that such a position would challenge the commonsense popular racism that was being pushed by capital and the state and would offer an alternative identity for the new immigrants to that of "White American" was a serious one. This elicited a mixture of propaganda and repression, with the additional weight of science thrown in for good measure. As science and technology became more central to the economy, scientists and engineers became more important as authority figures (Noble, 1977).

For example, the expanding field of psychology became an especially important ally of the capitalists, who in their role as philanthropists provided the resources for the scientists. Edward Thorndike received $325,000 from the Carnegie Foundation from 1918 to 1934 and was the author of one of the basic textbooks used until the 1950s in major American universities. He and his colleagues, Terman and Goddard, adapted Binet's intelligence test for American use, propagandized the theories of genetically inherited intelligence, and offered scientific "proof" of the superiority of some races (the Nordic and Teutonic) and the inferiority of others. Coincidentally, the "inferiors" were not only the victims of the "white man's burden" overseas, and were the nonwhite super-exploited races within the United States itself; they were also the recent immigrant employees of the philanthropists, such as the Italians, the Poles, the Slavs, and others. Science simply documented that the class hierarchy was as it should be. If the United States was the land of opportunity, those at the top got there because of their intelligence and hard work. Those at the bottom deserved to be there.

The scientifically objective data produced by such experts as Thorndike were used to justify the racist 1921 and 1924 Immigration Acts that kept out further immigrants from Southern and Eastern Europe. The demands for such control on immigration from the AFL and from nativist groups such as the Immigration Restriction League had all failed until after World War I. Why? Although sections of the working class supported such restriction, it was not in response to their wishes that restriction was adopted. World War I had stopped the flow of immigrant workers from Europe. There was a continuing, and indeed increasing, need for workers in the United States, first to supply the British and French war efforts and then its own. This need was met by recruiting black workers from the South. Racialist attitudes and—crucially—the construction of institutional racism by the local state, ensured that there would be antagonism between white workers and their new African American colleagues. Racist practices ensured that the latter would be concentrated in particular low-level jobs and in particular ghetto residential areas that were then systematically denied the level of public services to which they were entitled. Thus, the labor force would continue to be divided and controllable (Tuttle, 1977; Vittoz, 1978).

After the war, fear of the spread of Bolshevism made the prospect of recruiting labor from areas contaminated by its virus particularly unsatisfactory. Segregated reserves of black labor in the South made it unnecessary for capitalists and the state to take that risk. The racist culture provided the guarantee that lower levels of white immigrants and the new black industrial proletariat would be divided. The consequences for the white working class of adherence of most of its members to a system in which they were exploited as workers and were recipients of privileges, or the promise of privileges, as Whites can be seen in their political weakness, low level of unionization, high level of economic insecurity, and low level of state benefits. This situation was challenged by large sections of the working class during the Great Depression. How successful that challenge was to be and to what extent white workers would develop a class, rather than a racial, consciousness is the subject of the next section.

RACISM, WELFARE CAPITALISM, AND THE AUTHORITARIAN STATE

The development of welfare capitalism in the aftermath of the Great Depression and World War II has been one of the major developments of the contemporary period. It has been argued that capitalism has thus changed its nature. The state was now the protector of the weak and defenseless, the provider of a safety net to catch those who fell, for whatever reason, and the provider of services on the basis of need rather than the ability to pay. The corporations themselves were seen to have become "soulful," in Carl Kaysen's felicitous phrase. Power was seen to have become dispersed because of widespread stock ownership, the separation of ownership and control, and the responsiveness of the new managers in the postindustrial society to interests wider than the hitherto exclusive concern for profit maximization. There were no longer to be struggles over the distribution of scarce resources in an age of plenty and affluence. Class had become an irrelevant concept and, consequently, there was an end to ideology.

During this same period, there had been major changes in race relations. Civil Rights legislation, executive action, judicial decisions, and political leadership had all been responsive to liberal ideology and political pressure from the civil rights movement. The state no longer endorsed racism, *de jure* segregation was overturned, and racial minorities could now compete and rise on the basis of their own worth. Although prejudice might still remain as a residual problem, racism was not—and could not be seen as—a structural characteristic of society in the United States.

Given the reality of capital's most recent counterattacks and revocations of most of these concessions over the past decades, it is, perhaps, hard to remember how taken-for-granted such fairy tales were in the dominant ideologies of American society from the end of the Great Depression to the present. The soulful corporation has turned out to be a transnational corporation moving production and jobs around the globe in search of ever-greater profits and using its ability to do so to force its remaining workforce in the metropole to accept an escalating series of "take-backs" as a condition of being allowed to continue to work. The state has turned out to be more committed to capitalism than to welfare, which is being eroded as a condition of keeping and attracting jobs. The ending of *de jure* segregation did not mean the end of racial polarization. But these challenges to the dominant ideology have not led to a reconsideration of the ideological assumptions of mainstream commentators. Far from it: It is either the genetic or cultural inferiority of the victims that accounts for continuing and increasing inequality Indeed, it is the very welfare system itself that created a dependency culture in unemployment, homelessness, drug abuse, and so on (Gilder, 1982; Murray, 1986; for critique of these ideas see Boston, 1988; Reed, 1992). Racism, in both its material and ideological forms, continues to be a central characteristic of American society and has played a crucial role in capital's ability, along with the state's, to overturn what were supposed to have been fundamental changes in the nature of capitalism and in the nature and operations of the liberal democratic state.

THE MODERN PERIOD

The Great Depression, the New Deal, World War II, and the working-class response to these events played a major role in extracting concessions from capital and in shaping the forms of the state. The federal government came to play the central role in subsidizing capital, in ensuring that a favorable investment climate existed within the United States and abroad, and in ensuring order and stability within the United States. Performing these tasks often brought the federal government into conflict with the states and with local authorities and into conflict with the belief in free enterprise, minimal government, and the inferiority of Blacks. For example, in order to ensure that black struggles in the postwar period did not continue the link with the Communist

Party and with issues of class, it was necessary to combine repression of those wishing to continue that link, Du Bois and Robeson, for example, with sufficient concessions to ensure the triumph of Americanism, despite racism.

Such concessions required changes in the Jim Crow system of the South. De jure segregation was no longer necessary to maintain the Southern system of agriculture, which was being rapidly mechanized, in part supported by the policies of the New Deal. These policies served as a lightning rod for black demands and were a force of instability that the newer power centers in the South associated with industry and commerce wished to defuse. Racial segregation was a contradiction for the United States in its efforts to shape the world order after World War II, a world in which two thirds of the people were not white and in which U.S. apartheid was available for the Soviets and other nationalist critics to challenge U.S. claims to moral leadership. Plus, incorporation of African Americans into the formal democracy would channel the African American middle class into the system rather than run the danger of it becoming a counter-elite. This reasoning did not mean that the white leaders of the old order in the South would give up their power and privileges without a struggle. Also, poor Whites in the South were not going to give up power either, especially after being assured by word and deed by those with power in the South and in the nation as a whole that they too were superior to Blacks because they were white.

The federal government was, therefore, going to be in conflict with rural Southern elites as it attempted to overturn *de jure* segregation, with African Americans taking the lead and being beaten and killed as a necessary part of the campaign. The national administration had, at the same time, to deal with overt racial discrimination in the rest of the country where racial segregation was not legally required. Here, the federal government came into conflict with the principles of private property, which held that individuals could do whatever they wished to with their property and could hire whom they wished, and rent to whom they wished. The level of struggle by African Americans and the imperatives of running the world required that overt racial discrimination be outlawed (see Kushnick, 1991; Marable, 1991).

The desegregation efforts of the federal government did not mean the end of institutional racism or the end of the role of the state in legitimating popular racism. Racism continued to be part of the normal operations of the state at every level. For example, one of the key engines of state intervention in support of the economy in the postwar years was support for suburbanization, which by 1965 had led to the construction of more than $120 billion worth of owner-occupied housing—98 percent of which was owned and occupied by Whites. This was the result of official government policies administered through the lending decisions of the Veterans Administration and the Federal Housing Agency. State and local governments made similar decisions that led to the construction of what Arnold Hirsch has called Chicago's Second Ghetto (Hirsch, 1983). The racialized economic consequences of encouraging and financially subsidizing white flight to the suburbs included the loss of jobs, tax revenues, and affordable housing in the inner cities—which were becoming more black as African Americans were displaced from Southern sharecropping and came North looking for work. The decisions of the state at every level constructed the increasingly racialized ghettos with their underresourced education and health systems, appalling housing, and high levels of un- and underemployment. The construction of racialized criminal justice systems ensured the lack of police protection and a massively racialized disparity in imprisonment. These realities of state policy have to be set against statements in favor of tolerance and brotherhood and even against assertions of the decline of racism and the presumption that past civil rights legislation have fundamentally eliminated systematic racism in the United States.

Just as there is this contradiction between the ostensible purposes of the state in the field of race, so there is a similar contradiction in the state's relations with the white working class. An essential part of the construction of Pax Americana was the great or Keynesian accommodation that augmented the new era of welfare capitalism discussed above. Workers in the primary sector of the economy were allowed to enjoy high pay, job security, and a social wage. But the price they had to pay actually undermined their ability to protect these gains. The purge of the Left from the unions associated with the anti-Communist purges and the requirements of the Taft-Hartley Act was accompanied by the acceptance of the ideology and practice of the Cold War, of anti-Communism, of Military Keynesianism, and by the cessation of serious attempts to unionize the non-union majority of the working class (see Bowles, Gordon, & Gintis, 1984; Davis & Huttenback, 1986).

The consequences of these concessions have proven devastating over the medium term for those workers who were to be the beneficiaries of this accommodation and devastating for those excluded. The purges of the unions had driven out those militants and activists who had wanted to challenge the structural racism within the workplace and within the unions themselves. It was these workers who wanted to create objective conditions of racial equality The failure to continue unionizing drives, particularly in the South, created a potential region where capital could locate future investment and employ labor with a lower social wage. The lack of unionization created the basis upon which capital, the state, and the media could scapegoat organized labor as the cause of inflation and other ills of the society. The ensuing weakness of the working class made it even more difficult for members of that class to resist the transmission of the dominant racist ideology of white supremacy. The acceptance of Pax Americana helped capital and the state to define the national interest in terms most favorable to themselves.

This defining of interest included seeing any foreign government on the periphery that attempts to improve the living conditions of its people by taking control of its economy as an enemy of the United States and as part of the International Communist Conspiracy of the Evil Empire. The consequence of such a hegemonic definition of the national interest has been political, military, covert, and economic interventions to overthrow such governments and to put and keep in power regimes that would allow transnational capital a free run in their countries, that would sell their people more cheaply than their neighbors and thus provide opportunities for the export of jobs from the metropole to the periphery (Sivanandan, 1990). The limitation of private sector unionization primarily to the major industrial sectors had another consequence—the expanding sectors of the economy (service, sales, and clerical) were not unionized and consequently were based on cheap labor. The weakening influence of organized labor, a political system that was coming to be more and more under the control of capital, and no meaningful alternatives offered by the Democratic Party has left large parts of the white working class alienated from the system and from the Democratic Party.

The essence of the Republican strategy since 1964 has been an appeal to the white South and to Whites in the rest of the country on the basis that the Democratic Party had been captured by Blacks and was no longer the White Man's Party. Race has become the best single predictor of voting behavior: For example, two thirds of all white voters voted for Reagan in 1984 and 60 percent voted for Bush in 1988. Manning Marable has calculated that overall white support in the South for Republican presidential candidates has been 70 percent and among white evangelical Christians, 80 percent. "Since the election of Ronald Reagan in 1980, in presidential contests the Republican Party operates almost like a white united front, dominated by the most racist, reactionary sectors of corporate and finance capital, and the most backward cultural and religious movements" (Marable, 1993, p. 76).

Racialized politics has made it possible for capital to use the electoral system to restructure the political economy, as done in Britain under Thatcher and Major, with large portions of those who will pay, and have paid, the highest price. For example, the median family income in the United States in 1993 in real terms was lower than it was in 1973, and it takes more family members working to earn that lower income. Deskilling, deindustrialization, decertification of trade unions, take-backs by capital from unionized workers, and cuts in the social wage have all been imposed during the decade since the first edition of this volume was published. During this period there has been an ideological assault on state and collective provision; on the supposed "dependency culture"; and on large sections of the reserve labor force, now called the "underclass." The level of state attacks on African American and Latino communities has increased massively during this period, and the level of imprisonment has escalated exponentially with the United States now the most imprisoned nation in the world. The United States is racialized to the extent that an African American male is more likely to be imprisoned than to be in higher education and is five times more likely to be imprisoned than is an African in South Africa (Mauer, 1990; Shine & Mauer, 1993).

The racial and gender divisions of the working class have weakened its ability to resist the dominant racialized and gendered ideology. This lack of working-class consciousness and autonomous culture severely weakens its ability to respond to these attacks on its living standards and hopes for the future. The increasing level of scapegoating of African Americans and women is an indication of the determination of those in power to stay in power and to use the system to their maximum advantage. Their ability to buy acquiescence through material concessions to white working-class men is becoming more and more limited and therefore they are relying more and more on scapegoating and division.

Until the working class creates its own identity and a racially inclusive consciousness and culture, it will continue to be unable to advance its own interests. The European American working class will have to reject the white part of that identity and the illusory privileges based on racism and sexism. The damage done is not only to people of color: European Americans are damaged as well. The dominant ideology of white racial supremacy has served, and continues to serve, the interests of capital and its political allies. Opposition has come from individuals and groups of whites, African Americans, Latinos, and others. This opposition to a racialized identity illustrates that it is possible to choose an alternative identity to that constructed and transmitted by agents of capital. Thus, it is possible for the individual effort and talent used in everyday struggles to survive and to resist class oppression, to be used to create a just and truly democratic society

9

THE RECONSTRUCTION OF BLACK SERVITUDE AFTER THE CIVIL WAR

Stephen Steinberg

> They could call it some other name—it is fertile in names; it has been called
> "the peculiar institution," the "impediment," etc., and it will again turn up under
> some new and hateful guise to curse and destroy this nation.
>
> Frederick Douglass, *New York Times*, May 11, 1865

The end of the Civil War was a critical juncture in American race history Slavery had been abolished at a time when the North was on the verge of an economic breakthrough that would transform the United States into the world's most industrialized nation within a single generation. The labor shortages associated with this rapid growth presented the nation with a unique opportunity to integrate black workers into the industrial mainstream. As the British economist Brinley Thomas has written: "After the Civil War the best thing that could have happened to the black workers of the United States would have been a fair opportunity to contribute to satisfying the great demand for labour in the rapidly growing cities of the North and West."[1] However, blacks were almost totally excluded from these burgeoning industries, and instead the nation looked to European immigrants to fill its manpower needs. In the half century between the end of the Civil War and the beginning of the First World War, over 24 million immigrants entered the United States; at the end of this period 89 percent of the nation's 10 million blacks remained in the South.

The reasons for this categorical exclusion of blacks from northern industry are far from clear, as Gunnar Myrdal noted in *An American Dilemma:* "There was enough industrial activity . . . in many of the smaller centers of the North to permit a significant immigration of Negroes. That Negroes have not migrated to these places is . . . a mystery. . . ."[2] It is often implied that, as a rural people, blacks were tied to the soil and reluctant to migrate to northern cities. Any such interpretation, however, is belied by a considerable body of evidence showing that emancipated slaves explored every conceivable channel of escape from southern oppression.

Both as individuals and as groups, blacks experimented with migration to under-populated and developing areas of the South and West (especially Florida and Texas), to Kansas and other homesteading areas of the Midwest, to the urban North, to Canada, to Haiti and other Caribbean islands, and even to Africa. If none of these "colonization schemes" developed into significant movements, it is because none offered a realistic solution to the plight of the black masses. It was for this reason, and not out of any lack of knowledge or motivation, that more blacks did not flee the South after the Civil War.

Whenever promising alternatives to the South were found, information spread like wildfire through the Black Belt. In the case of the "exoduster movement" to Kansas in the late 1870s, itinerant black leaders met with prospective migrants in churches through-out the South, and blacks working on steamboats and railroads circulated leaflets and passed on word of cheap land and black settlement in Kansas. No amount of propa-ganda, appeasement, or intimidation on the part of white Southerners succeeded in stemming the exodus.[3]

It is tempting to dismiss the preference given immigrants over blacks in northern industry simply as a case of racism, as Robert Allen does in his book *Black Awakening in Capitalist America:*

> It would have made sense at the close of the Civil War to plan for the assimila-tion of black people as a group into the American mainstream. Racism made this impossible. . . . Hence racism, the stepchild of slavery, prevented black people from following in the footsteps of other ethnic groups.[4]

To be sure, there was a color line in northern industry that barred blacks from employment in any but the most menial positions. However, racism per se cannot explain the existence of this color line. In the South where racism was carried to its most malevolent extremes, there was a general preference for black laborers over foreigners, despite public rhetoric to the contrary. Indeed, from the end of the Civil War until the Great Depression, the South frequently resorted to violence to obstruct the movement of blacks to labor markets in the North. On the other hand, whenever black labor was needed in northern industry—for example, when immigration was cut off by the First World War—employers were all too willing to put aside their racist attitudes and to inte-grate blacks into the labor force.

Thus, what needs to be explained is why black labor was indispensable in the South and, until the First World War, superfluous in the North. Simple "racism" cannot explain why black laborers were excluded from northern industry in the first decade of the twen-tieth century and employed by the hundreds of thousands in the second decade.

The key to solving the "mystery" of why blacks were excluded from the early stages of industrialization has to do with the critical role that cotton played, not just in the South but in the national economy as a whole. The South was unable, despite considerable effort, to attract immigrants to the cotton fields, and came to realize that it was utterly dependent on black labor. On the other hand, as long as the North had access to cheap foreign labor, there was no reason to raid the labor supply of the South, especially when its own economic well-being depended on an abundant supply of cheap cotton.

In short, major economic interests were served by the deployment of blacks to southern agriculture and immigrants to northern industry. Yet there was no conspiratorial design to regulate the racial composition of the labor force on a regional basis. What needs to be explained, therefore, is how emancipated slaves were forced to remain in a region of the country and a sector of the economy that was so inimical to their collective interests.

THE "NEGRO QUESTION" AFTER THE CIVIL WAR: THE NORTH

The end of the Civil War and the abolition of slavery raised a great question that was debated by journalists and politicians in both the North and the South. The question, in Lincoln's own words, was: "What shall we do with the Negroes after they are free?"[5] The nation's quandary over the future of four million emancipated slaves stemmed from the fact that the status of blacks in America had always been defined in terms of slavery. Had their emancipation made them expendable? In 1867 one vitriolic Southerner actually proposed the mass expulsion of blacks:

> No permanent lodgment, no enduring part nor lot, must the black and baneful negroes be permitted to acquire in our country. Already have they outlived their usefulness—if, indeed, they were ever useful at all. . . .[6]

Expulsion was not altogether a new concept. Since 1816 the American Colonization Society had been active, with the help of a congressional subsidy, in the "repatriation" of freed blacks to Africa. Lincoln himself became a champion of colonization, and in 1862 he prevailed upon Congress to pass legislation subsidizing the voluntary emigration of ex-slaves to various destinations in the Caribbean. The naked truth is that white America valued blacks only as property. Notwithstanding the sectional conflict, few Northerners—indeed, few abolitionists—could conceive of living with blacks as equals.

Even before the war was over, the North was practically obsessed with a fear that emancipation would unleash an "invasion" of southern blacks to the northern states. These fears were especially pronounced among ordinary laborers, many of them immigrants, who found themselves in competition for jobs with the small black population living in northern cities. This was particularly true of Irish immigrants, who rapidly became as racist as any segment of northern society simply because they competed with blacks for jobs at or near the bottom of the occupational ladder. The antagonisms that built up prior to the Civil War finally exploded into the bloody Draft Riots, when Irish mobs ravaged New York City for four days, randomly lynching blacks, razing a black orphanage, and driving blacks out of the city.[7]

By 1862 blacks who had escaped from the South or been liberated by the Union Army were already drifting into northern cities, and in Cincinnati there was a riot following the employment of blacks on the wharves. In August the *Boston Pilot,* an Irish-Catholic newspaper, reported that "we have already upon us bloody contention between white and black labor. . . . The North is becoming black with refugee Negroes from the South. These *wretches* crowd our cities, and by overstocking the market of labor, do incalculable injury to white hands."[8]

Even before the Civil War, northern politicians frequently exploited fears of labor competition to rally popular opposition to the extension of slavery to the territories. William Seward, the governor of New York who was later to become Lincoln's influential secretary of state, explicitly defined immigration and slavery as two competing sources of labor, and in 1856 he delivered a speech entitled "Immigrant White Free Labor or Imported Black African Slave Labor" to an audience in Oswego, New York, made up largely of immigrants. After extolling the contributions immigrants had made to the prosperity of Oswego and the entire nation, Seward issued the following admonition:

> Only grant now that this great end of the slaveholders can be attained, and you
> will need no argument to prove that African slaves will be found in the ports,
> not merely of New York, New Orleans, and Philadelphia, and in the fields
> of Kansas and Nebraska, but even in the ports of Oswego, Rochester, and Buf-
> falo, and in the fields of Western New York, forcing the free white labor, equally
> of native Americans, and of Englishmen, Irishmen, and Germans, no matter
> whether they be Protestants or Roman Catholics, into Canada, Russian Amer-
> ica, Australia, and wherever else throughout the whole earth, free white indus-
> try can find refuge.[9]

As reflected in Seward's speech, much of the North's opposition to the extension of slavery had all along been predicated on racist assumptions. Prevailing sentiment favored not the abolition of slavery but rather its containment to the South where blacks posed no economic threat. As an English observer of the American working class wrote in 1865: "At present the working-men in the Northern States, though they have neither sympathy nor fellow feeling for the coloured race, make no objection to their emancipation providing they remain south of Dixie's line."[10]

Given their working-class constituency, Democratic politicians actively played on fears of labor competition, and according to one historian, "opposition to negro immigration [to the North] and citizenship was one of the cardinal principles of the Democratic party."[11] For example, in 1862 the Democratic Party of Pennsylvania denounced Republicans as:

> . . . the party of fanaticism, or crime, whichever it may be called, that seeks to turn the slaves of the Southern states loose to overrun the North and enter into competition with the white laboring masses, thus degrading and insulting their manhood by placing them on an equality with Negroes in their occupations is insulting to our race, and merits our most emphatic and unqualified condemnation.

On the same day, the Democratic State Convention of Ohio passed a similar resolution:

> Because . . . emancipation would throw upon the border free states, and especially upon Ohio, an immense number of negroes . . . to compete with . . . the white laborers of the State . . . we would deem it most unjust to our gallant soldiers to see them compelled to free the negroes of the South and thereby fill Ohio with a degraded population, to compete with these same upon their return to peaceable avocation of life.[12]

Republican leaders and abolitionists countered that, once freed, blacks would have little reason to leave their "natural home" in the South. However, the principal tactic for allaying fears of a black invasion of the North was to link emancipation with colonization. As a writer in the abolitionist newspaper *The Liberator* observed in 1863:

> Everywhere . . . denunciations of slavery and advocacy of the emancipation policy are coupled with the proposition that the two races cannot occupy the same territory in peace, and that we must choose between slavery with all its countless brood of evils, and the deportation of the black race.[13]

In his annual address to Congress in 1862, Lincoln proposed his plan to colonize ex-slaves to islands in the Caribbean, and explicitly justified it as a way of reducing labor competition between the races. As he said: "Reduce the supply of black labor by colonizing the black laborer out of the country and precisely by so much you increase the demand for and wages of white labor."[14]

It was not for lack of popular support that colonization was never implemented on a major scale. Black labor was simply too valuable to be discarded so recklessly, as was recognized by Representative Thomas Eliot of Massachusetts:

> You ought not to do it, because besides its intrinsic and fatal injustice, you will deprive the country of what it most needs, which is labor. Those freedmen on

the spot are better than mineral wealth. Each is a mine out of which riches can
be drawn. . . .[15]

The real function of the colonization proposals was to make the war and abolition more
palatable to public opinion in the North, and to win the support of groups such as the
Tammany Club in New York, which in 1862 went on record as "opposed to emanci-
pating negro slaves, unless on some plan of colonization, in order that they may not
come in contact with the white man's labor."[16]

Several other schemes were proposed which would "mine the riches" of black
labor without posing a threat to white workers in the North. The most far-reaching
proposal, advanced by a small group of Radical Republicans, would have broken up the
large plantations and redistributed confiscated land to ex-slaves. That more than considerations of justice went into this proposal is reflected by an 1863 editorial in the New
York Daily Tribune that favored a land distribution program because it would allay fears
among workers that "they are to be swamped by a vast importation of blacks."[17]

Another plan, proposed by Senator James Lane of Kansas in 1864, would have set
aside large tracts of land in Texas for Negro colonization.[18] Still another proposal,
advanced by Carl Schurz and John Palmer Usher, the secretary of the interior, would
have employed blacks in railroad construction and other public works projects.[19] The
common feature in all these plans is that blacks would have been safely removed from
the industrial labor markets. Even Charles Sumner, who in 1863 weighed the possibility of using freedmen to build the transcontinental railroad, later reversed himself on the
ground that "their services can be more effectively bestowed at home, as laborers and
soldiers."[20]

Thus, even these benevolent schemes for dealing with the "Negro question" never
contemplated an integration of black workers into the nation's industrial labor force. On
the contrary, policy in the North was expressly designed to preclude this possibility, and
even before emancipation, Pennsylvania, Ohio, and Illinois passed laws restricting black
migration into their states.[21] Surveying this situation in 1863, Montgomery Blair, the
postmaster general, was moved to ask: "When the Northern free States have framed
laws prohibiting the colored freedman from obtaining a foothold on their soil, upon
what terms can it be supposed the master race, in the slave states, would consent to associate with negroes made free by the hand of war?"[22]

THE "NEGRO QUESTION" IN THE SOUTH

If the North was apprehensive about black encroachment on "white" labor markets, the problem was quite different in the South, where blacks constituted the chief
source of agricultural labor. Here the "Negro question" assumed the form: "Will the
Negro work now that he is free?"[23] To some extent southern thought was trapped in its
own myths, in that slavery had always been justified as having rescued blacks from a

slothful existence in the bush, and it was argued that blacks would never work unless forced to do so. As the author of an 1866 letter in the *Southern Cultivator,* a planters' journal, put it: "With some two hundred years experience, it has been found that the only way to make the negro work is to keep the fear of corporeal punishment continually before him; rewards for diligence uniformly ruin him."[24] Now that Negroes had been freed from the salubrious constraints that slavery placed on their nature, the author speculated, they would inevitably die off.

Like the northern schemes to colonize blacks out of the country, however, such rhetoric should not be taken at face value. It reflected the South's difficulty in reconciling itself ideologically to dealing with blacks in a state of freedom, but behind the rhetorical excesses were more rational concerns. Would ex-slaves be willing to return to their previous station as farm laborers? What wages would they exact, and given the dearth of capital after the war—complicated by the fact that cotton has a two-hundred-day growing season—how were they to be paid? Finally, now that the economic advantages of slavery had been eliminated, why employ blacks at all? Why not tap the vast pool of immigrant labor that had proved so valuable to the North?

When *DeBow's Review,* the South's leading economic journal, resumed publication after the war, labor problems were in the forefront of the journal's concerns. The first edition contained no fewer than three articles—one written by DeBow himself—proclaiming the advantages that white immigration would have for the South, as well as a fourth article assessing the sundry plans for colonizing blacks out of the country. For the next half century, the South would try, often through official agencies established by state governments, to promote European immigration, but with almost no success. Immigrants who were destined for farming generally moved to the developing areas west of the Mississippi where land was cheap and where no established social hierarchy denied them status and opportunity. Those who did not have the requisite experience and capital to become independent farmers typically opted for jobs in northern industry. Given these alternatives, there was no reason why immigrants should voluntarily enter the South's feudalistic system of agriculture as ordinary laborers.[25]

Nor given the South's access to cheap black labor was there any incentive for developing a reward system that might have attracted immigrants to the region. Indeed, the South rapidly became disenchanted with those few immigrants who settled there, for reasons that were foreshadowed in DeBow's 1866 article. DeBow quoted a southern planter as saying: "Germans do not aim to become merely day laborers, but landowners."[26] The same observation was made by a traveller to the South in 1866 who reported that "Germans of a better class . . . wouldn't contract with you, unless they saw a chance to become, after a time, the owners of the soil they cultivated."[27] Another traveler in 1867 described the European immigrant as "simply an unbloated aristocrat without the slightest intention of working for anybody except himself," an accusation that would later be made of Italians in particular.[28] The crux of the matter was that unlike blacks, immigrants could not be forced into a quasi-serfdom. If their conditions as agricultural laborers became intolerable, there were always alternatives. As a result the South's experiment with immigration ended in dismal failure.[29]

A proposal to import Chinese to do the work previously done by slaves aroused particular enthusiasm. "We can drive the niggers out and import coolies that will work better at less expense, and relieve us from the cursed nigger impudence," exclaimed one planter in 1866."[30] A year later *DeBow's Review* proposed importing half a million Chinese laborers, whom the journal extolled as "docile and obedient" workers.[31] Just as the North used the reservoir of black labor to subdue white workers, the South now turned to Chinese for much the same purpose. With the coming of the Chinese, a Kentucky editor wrote gleefully, "the tune . . . will not be 'forty acres and a mule,' but . . . 'work nigger or starve.'"[32]

However, the experiment with Chinese labor also yielded meager results. Few Chinese went South, opting instead for more lucrative and less degrading employment on the railroads or in the mines of the West. And those who did migrate to the cotton or cane fields of the South rapidly made their way into more rewarding niches in the regional economy—often as storekeepers, and in the case of Louisiana's Chinese, as independent fishermen and truck farmers.[33] If Chinese laborers proved to be less "docile and obedient" than their employers hoped, it was because there were channels of escape open to them.

In the end the South had to reconcile itself to the fact that it was as dependent as ever on black labor. On a note of resignation, *DeBow's Review* wrote in 1867: "Our sole reliance hereafter, as heretofore, for farm hands must be on the negroes."[34] The one difficulty, however, was that blacks had never worked in the cotton fields by choice. Now that they were ostensibly free, how could they be forced to take employment that no other segment of the labor force would accept on more than a temporary basis? This was the dilemma facing the postbellum South. Vanquished in war, the South could not achieve this fateful objective of getting blacks to work for their former masters without the active support and collaboration of the North.

THE POLITICS OF COTTON

With characteristic acumen, Alexis de Tocqueville wrote in *Democracy in America:* "It is not for the good of Negroes but for that of the whites that measures are taken to abolish slavery in the United States."[35] This applies with equal force to the granting of full citizenship to ex-slaves, which was motivated less by altruism than by a self-serving desire on the part of the victorious North to curtail the political power of the southern oligarchy and, in effect, to drive a thirteenth nail in the Confederate coffin. For example, the Fifteenth Amendment enfranchising black men was viewed by the reigning Republicans as a device for securing a permanent Republican foothold in the South.[36] In short, nothing in the race history of the North—not even its advocacy of black civil rights—augured well for the future of blacks once the sectional conflict was settled.

Rather, there were powerful economic and political pressures in the North to restore the southern economy, and cotton production in particular, to prewar levels, even if this meant compromising the freedom that had been reluctantly granted to ex-slaves.

As already indicated, cotton was the most expansive force in the American economy during the early nineteenth century. It provided the raw material for the nascent textile industry which functioned as a base for industrial development; it alone accounted for over half of American exports, which served as a critical source of foreign capital; and it unleashed a chain of economic forces that led to sustained growth. By 1860, however, the North had emerged as a full-fledged industrial and commercial center with its own self-sustaining economic base, and as Douglass North points out, "the dependence of both the Northeast and the West on the South waned."[37] Nevertheless, cotton still accounted for 58 percent of the dollar value of all American exports, and the domestic textile industry's demand for raw cotton was never greater.[38] Southern apologists for slavery had long contended that the North profited from slavery as much as the South, and complained that southern profits were siphoned off to build up the northern economy—a claim that was not without justification. In the first place, much of the capital for the plantation economy came from northern banks and financial institutions. Secondly, northern traders and ports reaped most of the benefit from the profitable commerce in raw cotton, and cotton manufacturing was concentrated almost exclusively in northern cities. Finally, most of the profits made by southern planters were eventually spent purchasing farm machinery, supplies, and consumer goods produced in the North. Despite its best efforts, the South lacked the capital resources and the home market to develop its own industrial base and to diversify economically, and was reduced to being little more than a supplier of cotton and a few other raw materials to the North.[39] This prompted one southern senator to comment that "the South is nothing else now but the very best colony to the North any people ever possessed."[40]

This helps to explain why, in the aftermath of the Civil War, there was such an urgent need to normalize economic relations between North and South. Northern businessmen were in the forefront of those calling for political conciliation and a rebuilding of the shattered southern economy. The drift of business sentiment can be gleaned from the pages of the *Commercial and Financial Chronicle,* a new publication that, according to one historian, functioned as "a business propaganda offensive for Jacksonianism."[41] The first issue appeared in July 1865, and began on this sanguine note: "The end of the war, through which the country has just passed, inaugurates an era of peace and prosperity which only needs wise legislation to find encouragement." The *Chronicle* did not leave it to the imagination of its readers to decipher what was meant by "wise legislation":

> It is to our advantage as much as theirs that their lands shall be tilled, their channels of trade reopened, their villages, towns and cities redeemed from the ravages of war, their railroads, canals and highways repaired and put in working

order, and their minds relieved from vague apprehensions of impending chas-
tisement for past misconduct. They have sinned much, they have suffered
much. . . . Help them to retrieve their fallen fortunes, and in doing so we make
them more efficient helpmates in achieving the general prosperity.[42]

Further, the task of rehabilitating the crippled southern economy took precedence
over social reform and social justice:

> The question, therefore, which, as practical men, the administrators of our
> public affairs have to settle, at this moment, as it seems to us, is not the ideally
> desirable in the way of reconstructing Southern society, but the really practica-
> ble in the way of remitting the Southern communities at the earliest possible
> day to their normal relations of production and consumption with the rest of
> the republic.[43]

An immediate restoration of the southern state governments, the *Chronicle* believed,
would redound to the benefit of all concerned. But what about the Negro? The *Chronicle's* answer was vague in expression but clear in its import: "Social questions must be
left, in great degree, to adjust themselves."[44]

Implicit in the *Chronicle's* endorsement of "benign neglect" was a repudiation of the
idea that the federal government should intervene on behalf of ex-slaves, either to guarantee their rights or to redistribute land seized from slave owners. No doubt, the *Chronicle's*
editors recognized that a land redistribution might establish an ideologically dangerous
precedent, as was pointed out, on a note of sarcasm, in an 1867 issue of *DeBow's Review:*
"We are inclined to think that if the agrarian ball should be set in full motion in ten states
of the Union," then laborers in the North "would be very apt to consider their claim
upon the wealth of the North quite as good as that of the negro upon the wealth of
the South."[45] When it came to protecting wealth and property, there was no dispute
between northern businessmen and southern planters, and it was this harmony of interest between the ruling elites of the two regions that ultimately defeated the hopes of
freedmen for their own land.

Northern businessmen had all along assumed that a system of free labor would be
not only more effective, but more profitable as well. From the vantage point of northern industrialists, slavery was a wasteful and inefficient labor system that needlessly tied
up large amounts of capital in "fictitious property," and instead of providing incentives
for hard work, did the exact opposite. Industrialists boasted that for modest wages, their
employees reported to work promptly, labored long hours, and did not have to be
supervised after the workday ended, or supported during their unproductive years. They
were convinced that a system of free labor would eliminate the inefficiencies inherent
in slavery and, not incidentally, make cotton production more competitive by breaking
the monopolistic control of large southern planters.

This was the logic that allowed Edward Atkinson, a leading business critic of slavery, to say to himself, "I am a cotton manufacturer, at the same time an anti-slavery man."[46] In 1861 Atkinson published a pamphlet under the revealing title: *Cheap Cotton by Free Labor*. Atkinson argued that the experience of the West Indies proved that slaves would work after emancipation, just as the experience of Texas proved that, contrary to the claims of slave owners, whites could work in the cotton fields. Not only could cotton be grown by free labor, according to Atkinson, but it would actually be cheaper. Finally, Atkinson issued a statement that might well be called "the cotton manifesto":

> Have not the cotton spinners of the world the right to say to the slaveholder: "You have proved by the experience of the last few years that with your slave labor you cannot give us cotton enough."[47]

The Civil War presented Atkinson with an opportunity to prove that cotton could be produced by emancipated slaves. In 1863 he organized the Free Labor Cotton Company which followed on the heels of the Union Army as it conquered the lower Mississippi Valley. Under a program administered by the federal government's Commission on Plantations, Atkinson leased confiscated land and employed ex-slaves at prescribed wages. Due to the unstable economic conditions as well as Confederate raids, the scheme was not very successful. Northern investors had better luck on the Sea Islands off the Georgia coast, which were insulated from the hostilities on the mainland and produced a large and profitable harvest on land worked by ex-slaves.[48]

No sooner were the Confederate armies defeated on the battlefield than northern businessmen rushed in to take advantage of the opportunities afforded by the collapse of the plantation system. The war had left southern planters on the verge of bankruptcy, and more dependent than ever on credit from outside sources. The situation was ripe for northern capital, especially since land values had plummeted at a time when cotton was selling at a premium due to wartime shortages. Some investors bought huge parcels of land at depressed prices, others provided credit to southern middlemen who in turn extended credit to planters and tenant farmers.[49] Though it is not precisely known to what extent cotton production in the postbellum South was owned and financed by northern interests, it was enough to prompt one southern politician to remark in 1868 that "it is the Northern capitalist as well as the Southern planter that the poor freedman has to contend against now."[50]

In other ways, too, the freedmen had to cope with the northern capitalist as well as the southern planter. The South, after all, had been prostrated by the war, and at least during the Reconstruction period, it was the North that wielded the political power that would determine the ultimate fate of the freedmen. This was the historical moment when the North's legacy of racism and its own stake in the exploitation of black labor would deal a devastating blow to the hopes of the ex-slaves for economic and social redemption.

The two possible outcomes that would have been most advantageous to blacks—a massive redistribution of land in the South, or integration into the industrial labor force in the North—were never given more than fleeting consideration. Excluded from the industrial labor markets, blacks were pushed back onto the South; denied an opportunity to become independent farmers, they were forced to work as farm laborers, or as sharecroppers or tenant farmers under a system that in some respects was almost as bad as slavery itself. The South's historic role in oppressing blacks after slavery is well understood. What is not generally recognized is the role that the North played in creating the larger framework in which southern racism operated.

Aside from fateful acts of omission in failing to institute constructive policies that might have redistributed land to ex-slaves or integrated blacks into the industrial labor force, the North was an active agent in the development of the sharecropping system that functioned as an economic surrogate for slavery. And the chief instrument for the North's reorganization of southern agriculture into a sharecropping system was the agency that was established ostensibly to promote the welfare of emancipated slaves—the Freedmen's Bureau.

WHOSE FREEDMEN'S BUREAU?

The initial step toward the development of the Freedmen's Bureau came from a committee representing several freedmen's aid societies, voluntary groups dedicated to the "elevation" of ex-slaves, who petitioned President Lincoln in 1863 to establish an official bureau that would put the machinery of government behind their lofty mission. The petitioners included prominent clergy and abolitionist leaders—such as Henry Ward Beecher, the brilliant antislavery preacher, and Levi Coffin, a Quaker leader in the Underground Railroad. But along with these selfless individuals whose repudiation of slavery rested on high moral principle appears the name of Edward Atkinson, the Boston cotton manufacturer who that same year had organized the Free Labor Cotton Company.[51] Here was the first sign that more than altruism went into the creation of the Freedmen's Bureau.

From its inception the bureau was designed to facilitate the transition from slavery to freedom in a manner that would not disrupt the Southern economy or jeopardize the North's supply of cheap and abundant cotton. To be more precise, the abolitionist voice which had been so reviled prior to the Civil War was now used to provide an ideological facade for an agency whose covert function was to ease the emancipated Negro into a new form of subjugation.

That the Freedmen's Bureau would serve narrow business interests was forewarned by some of its opponents in Congress. A New York congressman denounced it as a "money-making scheme" which was "for the use of the black race by northern masters," while a Kentucky congressman criticized it for putting "the control of three or four million men seated in southern and western states in the hands of the commercial and manufacturing parts of the country . . ."[52] Indeed, beneath the philanthropic pretensions of the bureau and the sanctimony of its most ardent supporters were raw economic interests that had a stake in prodding ex-slaves back to the cotton fields. As a congressional proponent of the Bureau argued: "The welfare of the people of the North demands it. They need the commodities yielded by this territory. Their industry is paralyzed by want of cotton which will be produced on these fields and by the labor of these people."[53]

In theory, distribution of land to ex-slaves could have restored cotton production, and the promise of "forty acres and a mule" in fact attained a prominent place in the political discourse of the postbellum period. Indeed, the legislation establishing the Freedmen's Bureau specifically provided that "abandoned or confiscated land"—that is, land of Confederate soldiers and supporters that had been seized by the government—should be distributed to freedmen in 40-acre tracts. However, the government possessed only 800,000 acres of such land, which, at best, could have provided 20,000 homesteads for the four million ex-slaves. Besides, this provision of the bill never received more than token implementation. No sooner did Otis Howard, the embattled commissioner of the Freedmen's Bureau, initiate a land distribution to freedmen than President Johnson forced him to rescind the order. By 1866 half the land in government possession had been returned to the original owners, and in a number of cases, blacks were forced—sometimes at the point of a bayonet—to relinquish land that they had been previously granted.

Instead of effecting a land redistribution program, the Freedmen's Bureau became the chief instrument for organizing a system of contract labor that reduced the black population of the South to a state of virtual peonage. The bureau's strategy was to draw up model contracts, and to prevail upon planters and laborers alike to sign them. On the surface, the contract provided benefits to both parties. Freedmen were guaranteed specific wages, or in lieu of wages, a share of the crop raised. In addition, their employers were enjoined to provide shelter, food, and medical care for their employees. In return, employers received a binding obligation from their laborers to work for the duration of the contract. The bureau arrogated to itself the right to supervise the contracts and to adjudicate any disputes.

Here was the North's answer to the Negro question—a system of contract labor that had all the earmarks of a voluntary agreement that conferred benefits on both parties, that would restore agricultural production and revitalize commerce in the South's precious commodity.

The one stumbling block was that ex-slaves were less than eager to sign the contracts. Above all else, they were repelled by the idea of returning to work for their former masters. Furthermore, by signing the contracts, they were essentially surrendering their freedom to quit their jobs or to strike for higher wages, and would be bonded to their employers and subject to a regimentation, including the possibility of harsh punishment, that was not very different from slavery itself. Thus it is hardly surprising that freedmen balked at signing contracts, and jealously guarded their newly acquired freedom to choose the conditions of their own employment.[54]

Nevertheless, the Freedmen's Bureau zealously promoted its system of contract labor. Its first task was to disabuse ex-slaves of their expectations of "forty acres and a mule," which was accomplished "by constant exertions on the part of officers of the bureau."[55] In addition, agents exhorted ex-slaves to prove by their labor that they were deserving of the freedoms that had been bestowed upon them. For example, the very first communication issued to freedmen by the Freedmen's Bureau of South Carolina began with these unctuous words of advice:

> Freedmen, let not a day pass ere you find some work for your hands to do, and do it with all your might. Plough and plant, dig and hoe, cut and gather in the harvest. Let it be seen that where in slavery there was raised a blade of corn or a pound of cotton, in freedom there will be two.[56]

This evangelical tone, characteristic of the bureau's dealings with ex-slaves, was typically invoked for the purpose of sanctifying labor contracts and compliance with authority. "This thing you must learn above all else," sermonized an assistant commissioner of the bureau, "a contract must be sacredly observed."[57]

Where moral suasion failed, the bureau resorted to more coercive methods. Even before the bureau was established, the government had begun systematically to cut back on the rations provided to ex-slaves crowded into refugee camps, and this policy was continued by the Freedmen's Bureau. The bureau's stated policy was to issue rations "so as to include none that are not absolutely necessitous and destitute."[58] According to official records, in August 1865 there were about 148,000 freedmen receiving relief. But by September, when the bureau had become fully operational, the number had been reduced to 75,000. A year later the figure was 30,000; a year later, 12,000.[59] Though the bureau routinely doled out money to transport refugees back to their former homes, it refused to pay transportation expenses for refugees who wished to go to other parts of the country, including the areas of the West and South that had recently been opened for homesteading.[60]

In effect, then, relief provided to ex-slaves was used as a lever to force them to resume their previous roles as farm laborers in southern agriculture. In June 1865, the *New York Times* took obvious satisfaction in reporting that "the throngs of colored people that were visible in our midst some time ago have scattered and settled down on the plantations. The short supply of rice in the government's storehouses doubtless had much to do with their departure."[61] Blacks who had sought refuge in government camps had been pushed to the brink of starvation by the very people to whom they had turned for protection. In a sense, it was the Freedmen's Bureau that carried out the southern planters' dictate, "Work, nigger, or starve."

An equally oppressive device, specifically designed to force blacks to sign labor contracts, was the use of vagrancy laws and the threat of vagrancy arrest. According to Daniel Novak, in his recent history of black forced labor after slavery, this practice was pioneered by the Freedmen's Bureau in Mississippi, which threatened black laborers with arrest if they did not sign labor contracts.[62] Between 1865 and 1867 most southern states passed Black Codes which included vagrancy laws that not only provided for the arrest of "idle" blacks, but also provided that "vagrants" could be hired out at public auction for as long as a year. Novak presents this synopsis of Mississippi's vagrancy laws:

> Mississippi's opening effort, ironically titled "An Act to Confer Civil Rights on Freedmen," barred the freedman from renting land outside city limits, thus ensuring that blacks could not begin farming on their own. Further, by the following January, and annually thereafter, each freedman had to hold written proof of lawful employment (*i.e.,* a labor contract). The absence of such evidence was prima facie proof of vagrancy. Should a freedman breach his contract "without good cause," he was subject to arrest by the police or other civil officer. The arresting officer was entitled to a reward of five dollars (plus ten cents per mile traveled), to be paid out of the laborer's wages. As a further insurance against flight, the old Fugitive Slave Laws were reborn: any person attempting to "entice" a laborer from his master, employ him, or otherwise aid or harbor him was subject to criminal as well as civil penalties.[63]

In Florida the definition of a "vagrant" was broadened to include laborers found guilty of "a willful disobedience of orders," "impudence," "disrespect to his employer," or "idleness." Still other laws empowered courts to remove children from parents declared unwilling or unable to provide for them, and bind them out to employers, preferably their former owners, under an apprenticeship system.[64]

In some states the Freedmen's Bureau nullified the Black Codes, but in other states it either acquiesced or actively encouraged their enforcement. Novak concluded that "the Black Codes regulating labor were little more than local validations of the regulations initiated and enforced by the federal authorities."[65]

Finally, if these indirect methods failed to produce the desired results, the bureau could intervene militarily. In South Carolina, for example, agents visited each plantation, presented laborers with contracts drawn up by planters, mediated any differences, and evicted any laborers unwilling to sign.[66] By the summer of 1866, agents had approved about 8,000 contracts involving 130,000 black farm laborers.[67] Indeed, after the initial period of providing relief to refugees, implementation and enforcement of the contract system received the agency's highest priority. By its own account, as stated in the bureau's annual report for 1868, "every bureau officer became an employment agent for the purpose of securing homes and employment for all who were without work."[68]

Despite the various forms of coercion that were applied to ex-slaves, the bureau's agents could pretend, perhaps even to themselves, that they were engaged in a noble experiment to prove the viability of a free labor system, and hence the obsolescence of slavery. As William McFeeley, Otis Howard's biographer, has noted, "the Freedmen's Bureau always tried to veil its enforcement of the contract system with talk of mutually beneficial arrangements freely entered. . . ."[69] In actual practice, however, blacks were hardly acting out of free choice, and the system was far from equitable. As long as they were prevented from withholding their labor, black workers were not in a position to negotiate their wages or the conditions of their employment. Furthermore, planters' organizations generally conspired to impose a ceiling on wages, and laws were passed prohibiting planters from "enticing" laborers already under contract. Consequently, black laborers never received a fair wage for their labor, nor benefited from the high price of cotton or the great demand for their labor in the aftermath of the Civil War. Finally, blacks had little protection from outright fraud, and the Freedmen's Bureau was far from even-handed in enforcing the contracts. In 1866 a northern teacher wrote of the Bureau:

> They are more proslavery than the rebels themselves, and only care to make the blacks work—being quite unconcerned about making the employers pay. Doing justice seems to mean . . . seeing that the blacks don't break contract and compelling them to submit cheerfully if the whites do.[70]

Sharecropping arrangements were also subject to abuse. Problems arose over the distribution of shares, and it was not uncommon for planters to renege altogether after the cotton was harvested. Of even greater consequence was the routine exploitation inherent in the sharecropping system itself. Lacking any resources of their own, ex-slaves were dependent upon their employer, or upon local merchants extending credit on their employer's account, for food, clothing, seed, and other provisions to carry them through the growing season. More often than not, the costs of goods advanced, typically at usurious rates of interest, exceeded the value of the laborer's share at the end of the season. Thus sharecroppers had little or nothing to show for a year's labor, and as they borrowed again for the next season, they were kept permanently in debt. Except for the fact that sharecropping usually freed blacks from working in closely supervised field gangs, it amounted to a form of economic bondage that made a chimera of their emancipation.

Given the role that the Freedmen's Bureau played in the evolution of these new forms of servitude, it is not surprising that southern planters overcame their initial antipathy toward the bureau and came to see it as an ally in resolving the "Negro question." The annual reports of the Freedmen's Bureau are peppered with statements of appreciation on the part of planters for the bureau's work. For example, the 1866 report indicated that "many of the planters in the wealthy districts, where a large number of freedmen are employed, acknowledge the aid rendered to the planting interests by the bureau."[71] This was reiterated in the 1868 report: "Many planters have expressed their approbation of the conduct of the freedmen, and given officers of the bureau credit for aiding in settling labor upon just principles."[72] Indeed, southern planters had good reason to exonerate the Freedmen's Bureau from the charge that it was an instrument of Yankee domination of the South. Not only were their landholdings secure, but through the contract system, the bureau had helped to resolve their most serious problem—a stable supply of cheap labor. One planter in 1866 calculated that labor was as cheap as it was during slavery:

> Before the war able-bodied negroes were commanding from fifteen hundred to three thousand dollars in the New Orleans market. Counting only ten percent interest on the investment, we find it nearly as cheap to hire the negroes as it was in the old days to own them and get their labor for nothing.[73]

Not only was labor cheap, but cotton production was increasing. In its 1868 annual report, the Freedmen's Bureau could trumpet the success of the newly installed labor system:

> .... the great mass of freedmen are now self-supporting. And in spite of the misfortunes that have fallen upon the south during the last two planting seasons—the floods, the caterpillar, and the army worm—the voluntary labor of the freedmen has produced nearly all the food which has supported the whole people, besides nearly two millions of bales of cotton in 1866, and above two millions of bales in 1867, which have paid a tax of more than forty millions of dollars into the United States treasury, and furnished exports amounting in value to more than 300 millions of dollars.[74]

In effect, the Freedmen's Bureau had vindicated northern businessmen who had argued that a free labor system would work in the South and that cotton would be as plentiful as ever. Never mind that in proving its point the bureau had mutilated the concept of free labor. Never mind that the nation had again made a sham of its equalitarian principles, and reneged on its promises to the emancipated slaves. Never mind that in the aftermath of the Civil War blacks had been reduced to a state of virtual peonage. These compromising details were easily brushed aside as the North bathed in self-congratulation for having freed the slaves.

CONCLUSION

Thus, the most notable and enduring achievement of Reconstruction was the reconstruction of black servitude. Though the Civil War had ended slavery, the underlying economic functions that slavery had served were unchanged, and a surrogate system of compulsory paid labor developed in its place.

While the Freedmen's Bureau was a powerful instrument in the development of this surrogate system of exploitation, it is doubtful that the coercive tactics used to get ex-slaves back onto the cotton fields would have succeeded had other avenues of escape been open. Four million emancipated slaves were, in effect, trapped in the South, and unlike Alex Haley's family at the end of *Roots,* they had no teams of horses to carry them to less oppressive homes, and no capital to buy land or develop homesteads. As it was, a large number of ex-slaves made their way to Texas and other developing areas of the South and West where their labor was in demand, but as in the Old South, they worked primarily as agricultural laborers. Though the federal government possessed over one billion acres of public lands which it generously doled out to European settlers, railroads, and other special interests, almost none was made available for black settlement.[75] Though northern industry absorbed tens of millions of immigrants in the decades following the Civil War, a color line barred the employment of black labor until the supply of white labor had been exhausted. In short, ex-slaves were encircled by discriminatory barriers in other parts of the country, and, pushed to the brink of starvation, were forced to struggle for survival as wage laborers, sharecroppers, and tenant farmers in southern agriculture.

Once again, blacks paid the price and carried the burden of the nation's need for cheap and abundant cotton.

ENDNOTES

1. Brinley Thomas, *Migration and Economic Growth* (London: Cambridge; University Press, 1973), p. 330.
2. Gunnar Myrdal, *An American Dilemma* (New York: McGraw-Hill, 1974), pp. 189–90. Commenting on the paucity of research on black migration prior to the First World War, one demographer attributed this to a failure to study nonmigration. Peter Uhlenberg, "Noneconomic Determinants of Nonmigration: Sociological Considerations for Migration Theory," *Rural Sociology,* 38 (Fall 1973), p. 290.
3. Nell Painter, *The Exodusters* (New York: Knopf, 1977), chap. 15.
4. Robert L. Allen, *Black Awakening in Capitalist America* (Garden City NY.: Doubleday, 1970), p. 51.
5. Quoted in Charles W. Wesley, "Lincoln's Plan to Colonize the Emancipated Negroes," *Journal of Negro History,* January 1919, p. 20. Also see *DeBow's Review,* IV (AWS), 1867, p. 363; Congressional Globe, 38th Congress, 1st Session (February 17, 1864), p. 43; *New York Tribune,* May 25, 1865, p. 4.
6. Hinton Helper, *Nojoque* (New York: G.W. Carleton, 1867), p. 251.
7. Albion P. Mann, "Labor Competition and the New York Draft Riots of 1863," *Journal of Negro History* 36 (October 1951). For a graphic description of the "black pogrom," see Adrian Cook, *The Armies of the Streets* (Lexington: University Press of Kentucky, 1974),

chap. 4. In her *History of Chicago* (New York: Knopf, 1937), Bessie Louise Pierce writes that in 1864 a mob of Irish assaulted a dozen blacks working in a lumber dock. The *Annual Cyclopedia* for 1862 (p. 754) reports disturbances in Chicago, Brooklyn, Cincinnati, Toledo, and New Albany, Indiana, all provoked by the hiring of blacks.

8. Article reprinted in *The Liberator,* August 22, 1862, p. 1.

9. Speech of William Seward, "Immigrant White Free Labor or Imported Black African Slave Labor," at Oswego, New York, November 3, 1856, p. 4. Schomburg center for Research and Black Culture, New York City Public Library.

10. James D. Burns, *Three Years among the Working Classes in the United States During the War* (London, 1865), p. xii.

11. Norman Dwight Harris, *The History of Negro Servitude in Illinois, 1719–1864* (Chicago Lakeside Press, 1904), p. 241.

12. Quoted in Williston Lofton, "Northern Labor and the Negro During the Civil War," *Journal of Negro History* 34 (July 1949), pp. 254–55.

13. *The Liberator,* November 27, 1863, p. 2.

14. Quoted in Wesley, op. cit., pp. 14–15.

15. Quoted in Wesley, op. cit., pp. 11–12. Much the same point of view was expressed in *The Liberator:* " 'Expatriate him,' say the haters of the Negro. Expatriate him for what? He has cleared the swamps of the South, and has put the soil under cultivation; he has built up the towns and cities and villages, he has enriched the North and Europe, and for this you would drive him out of the country?" May 16, 1863.

16. Quoted in James McPherson, "Abolitionist and Negro Opposition to Colonization During the Civil War," *Phylon,* 4th quarter, 1965, p. 391.

17. February 12, 1863, p. 4.

18. Congressional Globe, 38th Congress, 1st Session, pp. 672–75.

19. "Schurz Report," *Senate Executive Documents,* 39th Congress, 1st Session, No. 2, pp. 2–105; "Report of the Secretary of the Interior," *House Executive Documents,* vol. 3, no. 1, 38th Congress, 1st Session, 1863–64, p. 414.

20. Charles Sumner, *Complete Works,* vol. IX (New York: Negro Universities Press, 1969), p. 319.

21. Edward Raymond Turner, *The Negro in Pennsylvania* (Washington: American Historical Association, 1911), pp. 153–67; Frank U. Quillin, *The Color in Ohio: A History of Race Prejudice in a Typical Northern State* (Ann Arbor: Univ. of Michigan, 1913), published thesis, p. 45; Pierce, op. cit., p. 12; Harris, op. cit., pp. 234–43.

22. *The Liberator,* June 26, 1863, p. 1.

23. *DeBow's Review,* vol. I, no. I, AWS (January 1866), p. 7; vol. IV (1867), p. 363.

24. *Southern Cultivator* 24 (January 1866), p. 5.

25. This was well recognized by contemporary observers: "The immigrant laborer does not strive long to rival him [the black worker] because no such laborer is content to live on the same humble plane of existence; in this, the latter resembles the native white laborer, only

that he is far more irritable and complaining."—Philip A Bruce, *The Plantation Negro as a Freedman* (New York: Knickerbocker Press, 1889), p. 188. "The farm laborer of the North would be foolish indeed to go to the South to compete with the negro in the cultivation of cotton or any other staple at the prices which labor receives in that region. Not only can he earn the equivelent thereof in half the time upon a Northern farm, but with his labor there he receives also bed and board of a character that would seem ruinously extravagant to the Southern landlord."—Albion Winegar Tourgee, *An Appeal to Caesar* (New York: Fords, Howard, & Hulbert, 1884), p. 161.

26. *DeBow's Review*, vol. I, no. I, AWS (January 1866), p. 11.

27. Whitelaw Reid, *A Southern Town, May 1, 1865 to May 1, 1866* (New York: Moore, Wilstack, and Baldwin, 1866), p. 564.

28. Henry Latham, *Black and White* (New York University Press, 1869; orig. 1867), p. 141. For similar statements concerning the Italians, see Robert L. Brandfon, "The End of Immigration to the Cotton Fields," *Mississippi Valley Historical Review* 50 (March 1964), p. 606.

29. Ibid., pp. 591–611; Bert James Loewenberg "Efforts of the South to Encourage Immigration," *The South Atlantic Quarterly* 33 (October 1934), pp. 363–85

30. Quoted in Oscar Zeichner, "The Transition from Slave to Free Labor in the Southern States," *Agricultural History* XIII (1939), p. 26.

31. *DeBow's Review*, vol. IV, AWS (1867), p. 364.

32. Quoted in Gunther Barth, *Bitter Strength: A History of the Chinese in the United States, 1850–1870* (Cambridge Harvard University Press, 1964) pp. 188–89. A similar refrain is found in a message to the freedmen printed in *DeBow's Review*, in 1867 (vol. IV, p. 421).

33. James W. Loewen, *Mississippi Chinese* (Cambridge Harvard University Press, 1971).

34. Zeichner, op. cit., p. 494.

35. Alexis de Tocqueville, *Democracy in America*, vol. 1 (New York: Vintage, 1954), p. 360.

36. William Gillette, *The Right to Vote* (Baltimore: Johns Hopkins Press, 1965), chaps. 2–3.

37. Douglass North, *The Economic Growth of the United States, 1790–1860* (New York: W. W. Norton, 1966), p. 70.

38. Ibid., p. 233.

39. See Eugene Genovese, "The Significance of the Slave Plantation for Southern Economic Development," *Journal of Southern History* 28 (1962) p. 424.

40. Senator Robert Rhett of South Carolina, quoted in John W. Stormont, *The Economics of Secession and Coercion* (Victoria, Tex.: Victoria Advocate Publishing Co., 1957), p. 11. Also, Robert Albion, *The Rise of the New York Port 1815–1860* (New York: Scribner, 1939).

41. George Ruble Woolfolk, *The Cotton Regency* (New York: Bookman Associates, 1958).

42. *Commercial and Financial Quarterly*, July 1, 1865, pp. 1, 5.

43. Ibid., April 26, 1866, p. 260.

44. Ibid., September 23, 1865, p. 388.

45. *DeBow's Review*, vol. IV (1867), p. 587.

46. Harold Francis Williamson, *Edward Atkinson* (New York: Arno Press, 1972), p. 4.

47. Edward Atkinson, *Cheap Cotton by Free Labor* (Boston: A. Williams and Co., 1861), p. 25.

48. See Willie Lee Rose, *Rehearsal for Reconstruction: The Port Royal Experiment* (Indianapolis University of Indiana Press, 1965).

49. Fred Shannon, *The Farmer's Last Frontier, 1860–1897* (New York: Farrar & Rinehart, 1945), p. 100.

50. Quoted in James Allen, *Reconstruction* (New York: International Publishers, 1937), p. 71.

51. George R. Bentley, *A History of the Freedmen's Bureau* (New York: Octagon Press, 1970), p. 31.

52. Ibid., pp. 38–39.

53. Ibid., p. 39

54. Joel Williamson, *After Slavery* (Chapel Hill: University of North Carolina Press, 1965), p. 69; Martin Abbott, *The Freedmen's Bureau in South Carolina, 1865–1872* (Chapel Hill: University of North Carolina Press, 1967), pp. 70–72; Zeichner, op. cit., pp. 25–26.

55. "Report of the Commissioner of the Bureau of Refugees, Freedmen, and Abandoned Lands," House Executive Documents, vol. 3, 39th Congress, 2nd Session, 1866–67, p. 3; Charles William Ramsdell, *Reconstruction in Texas* (New York, 1910), pp. 48, 73.

56. Quoted in Laura Josephine Webster, "The Operation of the Freedmen's Bureau in South Carolina," *Smith College Studies in History* (January 1966), p. 107.

57. Quoted in William McFeeley, *Yankee Grandfather* (New Haven: Yale University Press, 1968), p. 180.

58. "Report of the Commissioner of the Bureau of Refugees, Freedmen and Abandoned Lands," r868, 40th Congress, 3rd Session, p. 9.

59. Ibid.

60. The 1866 Report of the Freedman's Bureau indicated that "no transportation has yet been given in the work of transferring freedmen to the public lands. . . ." "Report of the Commissioner of the Bureau of Refugees, Freedmen, and Abandoned Lands," 1866, op. cit., p. 7.

61. Quoted in Williamson, op. cit., p. 67.

62. Daniel A. Novak, *The Wheel of Servitude* (Lexington: University Press of Kentucky, 1978), p. 11.

63. Ibid., pp. 2–3. Also see W. Kloosterboer, *Involuntary Labour Since the Abolition of Slavery* (Leiden: E. J. Brill, 1960), chap. 5.

64. Novak, op. cit., pp. 3–6.

65. Novak, op. cit., p. 9.

66. Williamson, op. cit., p. 69.

67. Abbott, op. cit., p. 91.

68. "Report of the Commissioner of the Bureau of Refugees, Freedmen, and Abandoned Lands," 1868, op. cit., p. 8.

69. McFeeley, op. cit., p. 180.

70. Ibid., p. 157; see also Zeichner, op. cit., pp. 495–96.

71. "Report of the Commissioner of the Bureau of Refugees, Freedmen, and Abandoned Lands," 1867, 40th congress, and session, op. cit., p. 41.

72. "Report of the Commissioner of the Bureau of Refugees, Freedmen and Abandoned Lands," 1868, p. 8.

73. Reid, op. cit., p. 278.

74. "Report of the Commissioner of the Bureau of Refugees, Freedmen, and Abandoned Lands," 1868, op. cit., p. 9.

75. Kloosterboer, op. cit., p. 59.

10

CREATING THE RACIAL WELFARE STATE REGIME

Jill Quadagno

Franklin Delano Roosevelt took office in 1932 with a mandate to inaugurate a new era in government intervention. The cornerstone of his New Deal was the Social Security Act of 1935, which provided old-age insurance and unemployment compensation for the industrial labor force. Under the old-age insurance program, workers paid payroll taxes of 1 percent on the first $3,000 earned, matched by their employers, in exchange for a $15 pension upon retirement. Under the unemployment insurance program, states levied a payroll tax on employers to protect workers against downturns in the business cycle. Although the unemployment program was technically voluntary, generous tax credits that offset most of the payroll tax provided incentives to employers to participate.

The Social Security Act also included two means-tested social assistance programs, Aid to Dependent Children and Old Age Assistance, in which state expenditures were matched by federal funds. These programs provided minimal support to those outside the wage labor pool. Old-age assistance paid eligible elderly men and women a maximum grant of $30 a month, though most states, especially those in the South, paid less. Aid to Dependent Children was restricted to single-parent families and paid benefits only to children.

The Social Security Act laid the groundwork for a national welfare state and established some benefits as an earned right. Through such measures, the New Deal liberalism of the Democratic party came to mean active, positive intervention for the public good. Public support was high for programs that protected the many against the abuses of the few and taxed the few for the benefit of the many.

Government intervention did not extend to support for civil rights, however, as Roosevelt sought to stabilize his unwieldy coalition of northern workers and white southerners by refusing to back legislation abolishing lynching or poll taxes and by weaving racial inequality into this new welfare state. This was accomplished by excluding agricultural workers and domestic servants from both old-age insurance and unemployment compensation and by failing to provide national standards for unemployment compensation. These omissions were not random. Rather, they reflected a compromise reached with southern Democrats over the structure of the welfare state.

THE REPRESSION OF RIGHTS

By 1935 the North was industrialized and democratic. It had two active political parties, and its citizenry had full civil and political rights. The South was neither industrialized nor democratic. Its economy was driven by cotton production, which flourished through a sharecropping system that locked tenants—both black and white—to the land. Sharecropping was a system of servitude that denied to African Americans the first civil right, "the right to follow the occupation of one's choice in the place of one's choice." Sharecropping operated without cash. Planters loaned money to croppers for seeds, equipment, food, and rent. Often at year's end a cropper family owed more than it had earned in the entire year. Debt kept the sharecroppers nearly enslaved.

Politically, the South was an oligarchy. Such measures as poll taxes and literacy tests introduced at the end of the nineteenth century had not only disfranchised African Americans but most poor whites as well. Disfranchisement reduced opposition to the Democratic party majority and allowed one-party politics to reign. With no competition for elective office, southern Democrats earned seniority in Congress and thus were able to control key committees in the House and Senate. This power allowed them to exert a negative, controlling influence on national politics.

Although Roosevelt's electoral victory did not hinge on southern support, he needed southern Congressmen to move his programs past the key House and Senate committees. They opposed any program that would grant cash directly to black workers, because direct cash could undermine the entire foundation of the plantation economy. In 1935 more than three-quarters of African Americans still lived in the South. Most sharecropped. Those not sharecropping worked as day laborers when planters needed extra hands at picking time. The going rate for day laborers was two dollars per one hundred pounds of cotton, a day's labor for a strong worker. Outside the cotton fields black women worked as maids, earning perhaps $2.50 a week. Federal old-age insurance paid directly to retired black men and women, even at the meager sum of $15 a month, would provide more cash than a cropper family might see in a year.

Because of southern opposition, agricultural workers and domestic servants—most black men and women—were left out of the core programs of the Social Security Act. Instead they were relegated to the social-assistance programs, where local welfare authorities could determine benefit levels and set eligibility rules. Even in these programs, southern Congressmen vigilantly defended "states' rights." They demanded that two clauses be removed from the old-age assistance legislation, one compelling the states to furnish assistance at "a reasonable subsistence compatible with decency and health" and another requiring states to designate a single state authority to administer the plan. Southerners simply would not allow the federal government to dictate standards or set benefit levels. They sought control over any social program that might threaten white domination, so precariously balanced on cotton production.

The unemployment insurance program also perpetuated racial inequality by charging Employment Service offices with implementing the legislation. Established in 1933, the U.S. Employment Service was a federal–state organization that provided job placement for the unemployed. In administering unemployment insurance, however, Employment Service offices devoted little attention to job placement. Instead, they spent most of their time figuring benefits. When they did connect workers to jobs, they did so in a highly prejudiced manner, either excluding minority clients entirely or offering them the most menial, low-paying jobs.

Racial inequality was not confined to the South, however. By legitimating discrimination in work and housing, New Deal legislation reinforced racial barriers in other parts of the nation. Skilled craft workers had been organized into unions since the nineteenth century. Most became members of the American Federation of Labor (AFL) and its affiliates. But unskilled workers in the expanding mass-production industries—iron and steel, autos, rubber, and meat packing—had fought a losing battle against employers over the right to organize. When the National Labor Relations Act, or Wagner Act, of 1935 granted workers the right to organize unions and bargain collectively with employers, unskilled workers clamored to join unions. The issue of race contributed to the already fractious relationship between them and their skilled comrades.

Throughout its history, the AFL had discriminated against black workers. Some affiliates, like the Brotherhood of Railway Carmen, banned black workers by ritual or constitutional provision. Others granted black unions separate charters or established segregated locals as second-class members under the supervision of white workers. Only the United Mine Workers, an AFL affiliate comprised mainly of unskilled workers, had integrated unions.

On November 9, 1935, unskilled workers walked out of the AFL convention and founded the Committee for Industrial Organization (CIO). Among their grievances was the refusal of the AFL to address union discrimination. They knew that industrial unionism required inter-racial cooperation. After all, African Americans comprised more than 18 percent of iron and steel workers, 68 percent of tobacco workers, 40 percent of meat packers, and 9 percent of coal miners. Without their participation, any union of the unskilled would fail. From its inception the CIO opened its doors to black workers on an equal basis. Following a massive organizing campaign, by 1940 the CIO had more than 500,000 black members.

Black leaders had little enthusiasm for the Wagner Act, because it legalized closed shops. Since black workers were excluded from most skilled trade unions, they feared that the closed shop provision would permanently lock them out of these jobs. The National Association for the Advancement of Colored People (NAACP) tried to have a clause barring discrimination by labor unions written into the Wagner Act, but the AFL refused to support the legislation if the clause was included. The final legislation permitted labor organizations to exclude African Americans, denied the status of "employee" to black workers engaged in strike breaking, and permitted the establishment of separate, racially segregated unions. From 1936 to 1955, when the AFL merged with the CIO, the skilled trade unions maintained policies of racial exclusion and segregation with the tacit approval of the federal government.

The New Deal also preserved and reinforced patterns of racial segregation through housing policy. The government first intervened in the housing market to restore the confidence of lenders in average homebuyers, thousands of whom had defaulted on loans. The National Housing Act of 1934 sought both to stimulate a depressed economy and to calm the fears of bankers. It authorized low down payments, set up extended loan maturities (as long as 40 years), and regulated interest rates so that working-class families could afford mortgage payments. The Act also established the Federal Housing Admin- istration (FHA) to insure lending institutions against loan defaults. The FHA was to behave like a conservative bank, only insuring mortgages that were "economically sound." In practice, economic soundness was translated into "red-lining": a red line was literally drawn around areas of cities considered risky for economic *or* racial reasons. Redlining meant that most black families were ineligible for federally insured loans. Until 1949 the FHA also encouraged the use of restrictive covenants banning African Americans from given neighborhoods and refused to insure mortgages in integrated neighborhoods. Thanks to the FHA, no bank would insure loans in the ghetto, and few African Americans could live outside it.

What housing the federal government did provide to African Americans was racially segregated. The Housing Act of 1937 allowed local housing authorities to use proceeds from tax-free bonds to build public housing projects. Federal subsidies would pay the difference between the housing costs and what tenants could afford to pay in rent. From the start, public housing authorities located new projects in racially segre- gated neighborhoods and selected tenants by race. Thus, federal housing provided secure loans for the middle class and subsidized rentals in public housing for the poor. The working poor, much of black America but also white families outside the industrial labor force, were left out in the cold.

The New Deal thus united the industrial working class around a party that pro- vided income security against job loss, injury, and old age to working men and their families. At the same time it left intact—indeed reinforced—the rigid color line. The extension of social rights thus had paradoxical consequences for racial equality. In the words of T. H. Marshall, it granted a modicum of economic welfare and security to whites while denying to others the full perquisites of democracy.

11

THE BASES OF CHICANO OPPRESSION

Tomás Almaguer

Controversies over U.S. immigration policy have highlighted the recently growing role of Latinos in the United States. The U.S. Latino population has a long history dating back to the annexation of Florida from Spain in 1819 and the usurpation of Texas from Mexico in the 1830s. The histories of Latinos and blacks in this country differ considerably; yet, as in the case of blacks, Latinos experience lower incomes and higher rates of unemployment. In the following reading Tomás Almaguer discusses the specific historical and contemporary bases of this oppression for one major part of the Latino population: Chicanos.

Excerpted from Tomás Almaguer, "The Historical Roots of Chicano Oppression," *Socialist Revolution,* 25 (July–September 1975).

Racial and class domination form the principal basis of Chicano oppression. I will attempt to trace historically the development of both racial and class oppression in North America as it has affected Chicanos and our historical forefathers in Mexico. I will show that in the history of the colonization that has affected the Chicano people, class exploitation has taken on a very definite racial form. The racism and racial oppression faced by colonized people has been more than just part of an "ideological superstructure," for it has a very real structural basis in the organization of production.

In the colonial situation in Mexico, and in capitalist societies like the United States that have a history of colonial expansion within the continent, the class system has taken a marked racial form, and racial oppression has been mediated through the organization of class relations. In these societies class relations have given substance to and concretized racial domination.

In the United States, this class domination of racial minorities has shaped and conditioned their history of social oppression. In order to maintain the subordinate position of racial minorities within the class structure, an entire system of social control and political and cultural domination, as well as racial ideology, was developed. The effect of this "ideological superstructure" was not only to justify racial domination but also to maintain this subordination of racial minorities within the lowest strata of the working class.

The colonization of the Indio-mestizo [largely the blood line of the Chicano] in the Southwest originated in a classic colonial conquest, but it did not follow the "classic" colonial form, in which the exploitative relationship is generally carried out between the metropolis and a spatially separated colony. Having soon become a numerical minority on their own land, and having had that land "annexed" to the American metropolis, Mexicanos found themselves members of an "internal colony."[1] The colonization of the Mexicano unfolded *within* the political boundaries of the metropolitan nation.

What is crucial in defining the colonial situation of Mexicanos within the United States was their use as a super-exploitable labor force. Unlike white wage-labor and like colonized laborers elsewhere, Chicanos were confined largely to employment sectors like agriculture and mining, and were often hired out by owners on a seasonal basis or were bound to contractors and used as gang laborers. Unlike white immigrants who worked within sectors of the economy based on free labor, Chicanos formed a sub-proletariat within the labor force of the United States.[2] This peonage-like status as contracted or gang laborers was justified by a view of Chicanos as an inferior mongrel race. Historically, this sub-proletarianization of Mexican labor played an important part in the development and stabilization of American capitalism.

First of all, the use of Mexican labor greatly helped transform the Southwest from a relatively underdeveloped area into an agricultural oasis. This development of agriculture in the West would not have been possible nor profitable without the super-exploitation of Mexican labor. Agriculture in the West, like cotton in the slave South, greatly contributed to the capital accumulation that made the transformation of these areas possible.

> Testifying before congressional committees in the twenties, the principal employers of Mexican labor in the Southwest presented facts and figures showing that Mexicans had been a vital factor in the development of agricultural and industrial enterprises valued at $5,000,000,000. Starting with a scant production in 1900, the Southwest was by 1929 producing between 300,000 and 500,000 carloads of vegetables, fruits, and truck crops—forty percent of the nation's supply of these products. Most of this development took place in less than two decades and was directly based on the use of Mexican labor which constituted from sixty-five to eighty-five percent of the common labor used in the production of these crops.[3]

Second, the use of Chicano labor and technical skills provided for the development of the mining and railroad industry. Both of these sectors were crucial components of the "mineral-transport-communications" infrastructural base needed for future industrialization and modernization of the area. Chicano labor was used extensively both in the maintenance of the railroads at the turn of the century and in the development of mining in the Southwest. "From 1900 to 1940 Mexican workers constituted sixty percent of the common labor in the mines and from sixty to ninety percent of the section and extra gangs employed on eighteen western railroads."[4] By helping lay the foundation upon which the later industrial development of this region was built, Chicano labor played a central role in the development and spread of capitalism in the Southwest.

Third, as a largely mobile and seasonal work force, Chicano labor was used as an integral part of the "reserve army of labor." In times of intense labor needs Mexicanos have been actively recruited into the Southwest to work in agriculture, mining, the livestock industry, or the railroads (*circa* 1900–1940). Displaced by the Mexican Revolution at the turn of the century and by the intense United States foreign investment that hastened the break-up of traditional social and economic life in Mexico, thousands of Mexicanos became a highly exploitable work force that the American economy was able to draw upon. In times of economic and social crisis, the United States has been able to deport, repatriate, or simply disemploy this surplus labor with relative ease. In the depression years, for example, it is estimated by both Mexican and United States government officials that well over 415,000 Mexicanos were "repatriated" back to Mexico.[5] These wholesale deportations had no criminal offenses as a basis for cause; rather they were justified on the basis of "illegal entry." Similarly, during the economic downturn of the 1950s we witnessed the second major deportation of unwanted Mexican labor under the auspices of "Operation Wetback" (sic). From as far away as Chicago, St. Louis, and Kansas City, hundreds of thousands of Mexican workers were sent back to Mexico. This rising tide of deportations began to swell from 69,111 in 1945 to a high point of 1,108,000 in 1954.[6] From the mid-forties to the mid-fifties, the mass deportation of Mexican workers expelled no fewer than *four million*.

Today, we see a continuation of these same exploitative relationships and a reaffirmation of the use of the policy of widespread deportation of undocumented workers. As a result, the Chicano people have the dubious distinction of far outnumbering any other racial or ethnic minority in the number of forced repatriations or deportations from the territorial United States. Chicano labor has served as a "reserve army of labor" *par excellence*.

Finally, we have acted as "shock absorbers" for the class contradictions of society, *i.e.,* any social or economic crisis that this society produces is generally felt most strongly and "absorbed" by third-world people within the United States.[7] As part of this community, the Chicano feels the force of the contradictions produced within this society. The class contradictions that Marx described as being endemic to this capitalist mode of production have largely manifested themselves as racial contradictions. The weight of social oppression and class contradictions of monopoly capitalism has fallen on the backs of people of color.

As the United States has developed industrially and as labor needs have increased and diversified, the American labor force has become increasingly segmented. Historically, as well as today, the racial form that the class structure in the United States has taken has been largely brought about through the occupational placement of racial and ethnic groups within the working class. Commenting on the role that race and colonized racial minorities have played in the organization of production in the United States, Robert Blauner has observed:

> *What has not been understood is the fact that racial realities have a material basis.* They are built into the economic structure as well as the culture of all colonial societies, including those capitalist nations which developed out of conquest and imported African slaves to meet labor needs. . . . From the very beginning race has been central to the social relations of production in America. The right to own property, the right not to become property, and the distribution of labor were all essentially matters of color. Southern slavery was a system of production based on race. But not only in the ante-bellum South, elsewhere and after, the racial principle continued to organize the structure of the labor force and the distribution of property. The free laborers, the factory proletariat, was largely recruited from white ethnic groups, whereas people of color (Mexicans, Asians, to a lesser degree Indians, and of course, Blacks) were employed in various unfree labor situations. The ethnic labor principle appears to be a universal element of the colonial situation and this is why race and racism are not simply aspects of cultural "superstructure," but cut through the entire social structure of colonial societies.[8]

By *"concentrating people of color in the most unskilled jobs, the least advanced Sectors of the economy, and the most industrially backward regions of the nation,"*[9] the material basis of racism and racial oppression has become structurally incorporated into the organization of labor-systems in this society, and more concretely into the relation that workers (white and nonwhite) have to the means of production. In this society, the social relations of production have been largely cast in racial and ethnic terms. The racism and racial oppression that developed in the United States have been much more than a ploy on the part of the bourgeoisie to "divide the working class," for the real basis of racial contradictions is grounded in the different positions that white and nonwhite workers have held in the production process in the United States.

CHICANO LABOR AFTER 1940

Until 1940, Chicanos and other racial minorities were largely used in precapitalist employment sectors outside of urban, industrial centers. We were principally used as a super-exploitable semifree labor force. After 1940, Chicanos and other racial minorities came increasingly to occupy the lowest parts of the working class. During and after

World War II, the needs of the defense industry combined with the introduction of technological innovations in agriculture caused the large-scale migration of Chicanos from the rural areas of the Southwest. For Chicanos, this movement into areas of urban industrial production did not bring with it the opportunity for social mobility that had been open to immigrant ethnic minorities in an earlier period. As the new colored migrant began to take over blue-collar jobs in the working class proper, the white sector of the working class increasingly moved into higher-paid white-collar and "new working class" jobs. The upgrading of racial minorities within the working class was to a great extent made possible through the automation of their old jobs and by entry into areas of production left open by the occupational upgrading of white workers. One social scientist has described this process in the following way:

> During and after the Second World War blacks and browns from the rural backwaters of the South and Mexico came by the millions to northern and western industrial cities. But the era of increasing absorption of unskilled and semi-skilled labor into the industrial system, and thereby into the mainstream of class society, was rapidly drawing to a close. Blacks and browns were relegated to employment in the most technologically backward or labor-intensive sectors (menial services, construction labor, corporate agriculture) and to unemployment, the squalor of ghetto life, and welfare handouts. Today, the black, Chicano, and Puerto Rican colonies remain indispensable sources of cheap labor for the technologically backward and labor-intensive sectors. They also provide a servant class to relieve the affluent of the chores of ordinary living and to enhance their status and feeling of superiority. For the highly technological corporate and the rapidly expanding public sectors which require high skill levels, however, the minorities have become superfluous labor.[10]

These observations are confirmed when one examines the changes that have occurred in the placement of Chicanos in the occupational hierarchy. An examination of U.S. Census materials on Chicano occupational distribution shows that in the thirty-year period from 1930 to 1960, male Chicano workers moved from unskilled labor classifications (laborer and farm labor) into the operative and crafts area of production. Nearly 65 percent of male Chicano workers in 1930 were employed in unskilled, manual laboring jobs. By 1960, this proportion had declined to 32 percent while Chicano employment in the operative and crafts group rose from 16 percent to 41 percent (see Table 1). The decline in the use of Chicano labor as a largely unskilled cheap labor force was accompanied by the steady rise in our being used as semi-skilled and low-skilled urban workers. Table 1 indicates a steady rise in the relative concentration of male Chicano worker in the crafts and operative occupations. While there has been a proportional increase of the Chicano labor force in these areas, many Chicano workers remain as farm and urban-based manual laborers.

Table 1: Occupational Distribution and Relative Concentration of
Mexican-American Men in the Southwest, 1930–60

Occupation	Percent Distribution			Relative Concentration*		
	1930	1950†	1960†	1930	1950	1960
Professional and technical	0.9	2.2	4.1	0.18	0.25	0.33
Managers and proprietors	2.8	4.4	4.6	0.28	0.35	0.36
Sales	2.4	††6.5	3.6	0.29	††0.48	0.47
Clerical	1.0		4.8	0.18		0.69
Craft	6.8	13.1	16.7	0.47	0.67	0.81
Operative	9.1	19.0	24.1	0.92	1.16	1.35
Service	4.0	6.3	7.5	0.68	0.98	1.15
Laborer	28.2	18.7	15.2	2.22	2.22	2.12
Farm managers	9.8	5.1	2.4	0.59	0.65	0.61
Farm labor	35.1	24.7	16.8	2.62	3.87	4.16

*The figures for these columns were obtained by dividing the proportion of Mexican-American men employed in each occupation for the years given by the corresponding proportion of all men in that occupation. Thus, the figure of 0.33 for the professional group in 1960 indicates that the fraction of Mexican-American employment which was in this category in 1960 war just one-third as large as the fraction for the total population.

†Computed on a base which omitted employed persons who did not report an occupation.

††The 1950 Census of Population combined the sales and clerical occupations into one category for the purpose of reporting occupations of persons with Spanish surname.

Source: Census of Population: 1930, 1950, 1960 (US. Bureau of the Census), as compiled by Walter Fogel, *Mexican-Americans in Southwest Labor Markets* (Los Angeles: University of California, Mexican-American Study Project, 1967).

More recent figures from March 1973 show a continued increase in Chicano workers in the crafts and operatives area, from 16.7 percent and 24.1 percent of the total male Chicano work force in 1960 to 20.0 percent and 28.4 percent respectively in 1973 (see Table 2). There has also been a recent increase in Chicanos as employed as service workers (from 7.5 percent in 1960 to 12.0 percent in 1973). The other side of this increase is the dramatic decline in the proportion of Chicanos employed as farm workers (from 16.8 percent in 1960 to 8.4 percent in 1973). This trend is largely the result of the rapid automation of agriculture.

By 1973 over 83 percent of Chicano males were in the non–white-collar areas of production (*i.e.*, blue-collar, farm workers, and service workers occupations). This is to be contrasted with the 59.7 percent figure for the total United States male employment in these areas for the same year. This of course means that over 40 percent of the male labor force in the United States was employed in white-collar jobs compared to only 16.7 percent of Chicano males (see Table 2).

To make matters worse, one writer has recently noted that while Chicano employment in the crafts and operatives occupations has risen, these are two areas in which aggregate employment significance has actually *declined*.[11] "Far from being able to take advantage of the changing structure of employment opportunities, Chicanos seem to have increased their labor market handicaps by moving into occupations which face declining demand. By 1970, as a result of these adjustments [in the location of changing employment opportunities] fully 57.5 percent of all Anglos were employed in expanding occupational groups but for Chicanos this figure was only 20.8 percent."[12]

Table 2: Total Employed Men 16 Years and Over by Major Occupation and Total Mexican Origin for the United States: March 1973

	(numbers in thousands)	
Occupation	Total Men, 16 Years Old and Over	Total Mexican Origin
Total employed	50,890	1,303
percent	100	100
White-collar workers:		
Professional and technical	13.6	4.8
Managers and administrators, except farm	13.6	5.3
Sales	6.2	2.5
Clerical	6.8	4.1
Blue-collar workers:		
Craftmen and kindred workers	20.9	20.0
Operatives, including transportation	18.9	28.4
Laborers, except farm	7.1	14.0
Farm workers:		
Farm and farm managers	3.0	0.4
Farm laborers and foremen	1.6	8.4
Service workers:		
Service workers, except private	8.2	12.0
Household workers		
Private household workers	—	0.1

Source: U.S. Bureau of the Census, Current Population Reports, P–20, No. 26: *Persons of Spanish Origin in the United States: March 1973*. Adapted from Table H.

Thus, this shift in the composition of Chicano labor from a rural, unskilled labor force to the urban, blue-collar working class has not brought with it true social mobility nor a meaningful improvement in the condition of the Chicano people. Despite these changes in our areas of employment, Chicanos remain at the bottom of the working class, and in occupations that provide no real opportunity for group advancement. Moreover, the median income of Chicanos in the Southwest remains three-quarters that of their Anglo counterparts.[13] Even within the same occupations, Chicago workers earn less than Anglos.[14]

The position that Chicano workers occupy in the working class is clearly reflected in the income received by Chicano men and women. Table 3 shows that in 1972 over 75 percent of Chicana wage earners had an income of less than $4,000. In fact, nearly 50 percent earned less than $2,000 for the entire year. Chicano workers on the other hand were largely concentrated in the $3,000 to $7,000 income bracket. Nearly 40 percent of all Chicano workers were in this income range with our median individual income amounting to $5,489.

White workers, on the other hand, remained predominantly located in areas of production that enable them to benefit from changes in the occupational hierarchy. The

Table 3: Income in 1972, Chicago Men and Women
    16 Years and Over for the United States

Income	Male	Female
Total persons, 16 years old and over (thousands)	1,741	1,812
Persons with income (thousands)	1,604	1,029
Percent	100.0	100.0
$1 to $999 or loss	9.2	26.7
$1,000 to $1,999	7.6	21.8
$2,000 to $2,999	8.2	14.7
$3,000 to $3,999	10.5	12.1
$4,000 to $4,999	10.2	9.3
$5,000 to $6,999	17.1	9.3
$7,000 to $7,999	7.5	2.8
$8,000 to $9,999	12.2	1.7
$10,000 to $14,999	13.7	1.0
$15,000 to $24,999	2.7	0.1
$25,000 and over	0.3	—
Median income of persons with income	$5,489	$2,105

—Represents zero or rounds to zero.

Source: U.S. Bureau of the Census, Current Population Reports, P-20, No. 264, *Persons of Spanish Origin in the United States: March 1973. Adapted from Table 11.*

implication here, of course, is that racism has in fact helped to maintain the subordination of Chicanos within the lowest level of the working class. Racism in the United States has not only provided benefits to the capitalist class but it has also provided real material advantages for the white working class. Along with providing important social and psychological benefits for Anglos, racism in the labor market has provided a modicum of security and advantages in employment for white workers. Racism is in this sense more than just a trick used to "divide the working class" or a form of "false consciousness" imposed on white workers. Racism in the United States does in fact reflect the privileged position that some white workers have held over racial minorities within the working class.

Historically, changes in the form of this super-exploitation of racial minorities have caused shifts in the type of racial ideology that is used to justify and maintain their subordinate position.[15] Using Frantz Fanon's classic insight into the nature of racism we see how racial ideology has coincided and changed with shifts in this racial exploitation.

> The complexity of the means of production, the evolution of economic relations inevitably involving the evolution of ideologies, unbalance the system. Vulgar racism in its biological form corresponds to the period of crude exploitation of man's arms and legs. The perfecting of the means of production inevitably brings about the camouflage of techniques by which man is exploited, hence of the forms of racism.[16]

While as a group we toiled primarily with our hands, the type of racial oppression and exploitation we faced was physical in nature and forms of racism we confronted were based on biological premises. This is the period in which Chicanos labored primarily as captives of agricultural production and as exploited laborers in all facets of mining, the railroads, and the livestock industry.

In the period when the economy caused a large shift in the Chicano population from the fields into the cities, racial ideologies shifted from a biological to a cultural basis. As social contact between Anglos and Chicanos increased with this movement into the urban setting, Chicano "biological abnormalities" were increasingly replaced with "cultural" explanations for our backwardness. The reasons used to justify racist practices and poor living conditions were no longer merely that Chicanos had inherited "low-grade" biological traits but that our culture was "backward" or "traditional" and we were "culturally deprived."

Today, as the state has come to play an increasing role in dealing with racial minorities, racism is increasingly mediated by the state institutions—the educational system, the legal system, and the welfare system. Racism and racial exploitation are steadily being transformed from a biological racial ideology used to justify the widespread exploitation of colonial labor to an institutionally-mediated cultural ideology used to justify the subordination of Chicanos within the blue-collar working class.

From this it becomes clear that Chicano oppression in the United States has not been simply the outgrowth of a "culture conflict" between Anglos and Chicanos, nor merely the result of a vicious racist ideology. Rather, the many forms of social, political, and cultural oppression Chicanos have faced have ultimately been shaped by the material conditions of our labor. The racial oppression of the Chicano, and of other racial minorities, has largely stemmed from the place we occupy within the working class and from the fact that class exploitation in the United States has taken on a racial form. To do away with the class basis of this racial oppression, however, will not automatically ensure that racism will altogether disappear. For racial minorities, the end to class exploitation is not a panacea but merely an essential precondition for our true liberation and self-determination.

If meaningful political alliances between oppressed peoples are to take place then the left must face the fact that large sectors of the white working class do receive very real short-term benefits from racism. The question of how to convince these workers that they share overriding long-term interests with all sectors of the working class cannot be squarely faced if racism continues to be seen as merely a form of "false consciousness."

What is needed now is an honest appraisal of the many ways in which the working class has become segmented and divided. An assessment of racial minorities within the working class is but one step in this direction. It is only when oppressed peoples begin to seek out the commonalities—as well as differences—in their oppression that we can hope to build those political alliances that will be both meaningful and ultimately effective.

ENDNOTES

1. For discussion of the view that the Chicano is a colonized people see Tomás Almaguer, "Towards the Study of Chicano Colonialism," *Aztlan,* vol. 2, no. I (Spring 1971); Mario Barrera, Carlos Muñoz, and Charles Ornelas, "The Barrio as Internal Colony," in Harlan Hahn, ed., *Urban Politics and People: Urban Affairs Annual Reviews,* vol. 6, 1972; and Guillermo Flores, "Internal Colonialism and Racial Minorities in the U.S.: An Overview," in Frank Bonilla and Robert Girling, eds., *Structures of Dependency* (Palo Alto, Calif.: Stanford University Press, 1973).
2. See Robert Blauner, *Racial Oppression in America* (New York: Harper & Row, 1972). The discussion here relies heavily on Blauner's chapter on "Colonized and Immigrant Minorities."
3. Carey McWilliams, *North from Mexico* (New York: Greenwood Press, 1966), pp. 18–86.
4. Ibid.
5. Abraham Hoffman, *Unwanted Mexican Americans in the Great Depression* (Tucson University of Arizona Press, 1974), p. 126.
6. Ernesto Galarza, *Merchants of Labor* (Charlotte, N.C.: McNally & Lofton, 1964), p. 59.

7. This discussion is primarily based on a lecture given by Robert Allen, "The Illusions of Progress," University of California, Berkeley, 30 November 1973.

8. Robert Blauner, "Marxist Theory, Nationalism, and Colonialism," unpublished manuscript (emphasis in original).

9. Robert Blauner, *Racial Oppression,* p. 62.

10. Dale Johnson, "On Oppressed Classes," in Cockcroft, Frank, and Johnson, eds., *Dependence and Underdevelopment,* p. 286.

11. Tim D. Kane, "Structural Change and Chicano Employment in the Southwest, 1950–70: Some Preliminary Observations," *Aztlan: Chicano Journal of the Social Sciences and Arts,* vol. 4, no. 2 (Fall 1973), p. 391.

12. Ibid.

13. Paul M. Ryscavage and Earl F. Mellor, "The Economic Situation of Spanish Americans," *Monthly Labor Review,* vol. 96, no. 4 (April 1973), p. 6.

14. Ibid.

15. This point is made by both Guillermo Flores, "Race and Culture in the Internal Colony," and by Jeffrey Prager, "White Racial Privilege and Social Change: An Examination of Theories of Kacism," *Berkeley Journal of Sociology,* vol. 17, 1972–73.

16. Frantz Fanon, *Towards the African Revolution* (New York: Grove Press, 1967), p. 35.

12

THE MYTH OF "MILITARY NECESSITY" FOR JAPANESE-AMERICAN INTERNMENT

Ronald Takaki

"**O**ne morning—I think it was a Sunday—while I was working at Palama Shoe Factory I heard, '*Pon! pon! Pon! pon!*'" recalled Seichin Nagayama. He was only a few miles away from the navy base at Pearl Harbor. "I was drinking coffee and I thought, 'Strange. Are they having military practice?' At the corner of Liliha and Kuakini streets, a bomb fell in the back of a cement plant. We felt like going to see what happened, the noise was so loud. We found out that the war had started." The reverberations of the bombs falling near the Palama Shoe Factory and on Pearl Harbor were heard across the ocean; in a small Japanese farming community in California, Mary Tsukamoto was in church when she also suddenly felt the shocks of the explosions. "I do remember Pearl Harbor," she said years later as if it had happened that morning. "It was a December Sunday, so we were getting ready for our Christmas program. We were rehearsing and having Sunday school class, and I always played the piano for the adult Issei service. . . . After the service started, my husband ran in. He had been home that day and heard [the announcement] on the radio. We just couldn't believe it, but he told us that Japan attacked Pearl Harbor. I remember how stunned we were. And suddenly the whole world turned dark."

As it turned out, Nagayama and Tsukamoto faced very different futures during World War II. Nagayama quit his job at the Palama Shoe Factory because the pay was too low and started work at Primo Beer. His life, like the lives of most of the 158,000 Japanese in the islands representing 37 percent of Hawaii's population, was not dramatically interrupted by the war. But Tsukamoto and 94,000 fellow Japanese in California, representing only one percent of the state's population, had their lives severely disrupted: along with some 25,000 Japanese from Washington and Oregon, they were forcefully placed in internment camps by the U.S. government. Everyone was given short notice for removal. "Signs had been nailed to the telephone poles saying that we had to report to various spots," Tsukamoto recalled. "They told us to register as families.

We had to report to the Elk Grove Masonic Building where we were given our family number. No. 2076." While the Japanese in the islands had become "locals," members of the community in Hawaii, their brethren on the mainland had been forced to remain "strangers." Different histories were coming home to roost in Hawaii and in California.

Shortly after inspecting the still-smoking ruins at Pearl Harbor, Navy Secretary Frank Knox issued a statement to the press: "I think the most effective fifth column work of the entire war was done in Hawaii, with the possible exception of Norway." Knox's assessment turned out to be inaccurate, for investigations by naval intelligence and the Federal Bureau of Investigation agreed that in fact no sabotage had occurred. But Knox's alarming announcement fueled rumors of sabotage committed by Japanese Americans in the islands—Japanese plantation laborers on Oahu had cut swaths in the sugar cane and pineapple fields to guide the Japanese bombers to the military installations, Japanese had parked cars across highways to block the traffic, and Japanese had given signals to enemy planes. At a cabinet meeting on December 19, Knox recommended the internment of all Japanese aliens on an outer island.

But in a radio address aired two days later, General Delos Emmons, as military governor of Hawaii declared: "There is no intention or desire on the part of the federal authorities to operate mass concentration camps. No person, be he citizen or alien, need worry, provided he is not connected with subversive elements. . . . While we have been subjected to a serious attack by a ruthless and treacherous enemy, we must remember that this is America and we must do things the American Way. We must distinguish between loyalty and disloyalty among our people."

A schism in policy was developing between Washington and Honolulu. Pursuant to Secretary Knox's recommendation, the War Department sent General Emmons a letter on January 10, 1942, asking for his view on the question of evacuating the Japanese from Oahu. Emmons replied that the proposed program would be dangerous and impractical. Such evacuation would require badly needed construction materials and shipping space, and would also tie up troop resources needed to guard the islands. Moreover, the mass evacuation of Japanese would severely disrupt both the economy and defense operations of Oahu, for the Japanese represented over 90 percent of the carpenters, nearly all of the transportation workers, and a significant proportion of the agricultural laborers. Japanese labor was "absolutely essential" for the rebuilding of the defenses destroyed at Pearl Harbor. A shrewd bureaucrat, General Emmons probably realized his analysis would fall on deaf ears in Washington and concluded his report by offering an alternative policy: if the War Department should decide to evacuate the Japanese from Oahu, it should remove them to the mainland.

In early February, Emmons informed Washington that he did not want to evacuate more than a few hundred Japanese until some 20,000 white-civilian women and children had first been transported to the mainland. He also estimated that 100,000 Japanese would have to be evacuated in order to remove all potentially disloyal Japanese, implying such a program would be impractical. On February 9, the War Department ordered

General Emmons to suspend all Japanese workers employed by the army. But the order was rescinded after Emmons argued that the Japanese workers were indispensable and that the "Japanese question" should be handled "by those in direct contact with the situation."

General Emmons was hoping his bureaucratic foot-dragging and his resistance against orders from Washington would wear down the War Department. His strategy seemed to be paying off: Washington agreed to scale down the number to be evacuated. On March 13, President Franklin Roosevelt, acting on the advice of his Joint Chiefs of Staff, approved a recommendation for the evacuation of 20,000 "dangerous" Japanese from Hawaii to the mainland. Two weeks later, General Emmons reduced the number drastically to only 1,550 Japanese who constituted a potential threat. But, on April 20, Secretary Knox again insisted that "all of the Japs" should be taken out of Oahu. The War Department then circulated a report received from the Justice Department warning of dangerous conditions in Hawaii. In a letter to Assistant Secretary of War John J. McCloy, Emmons angrily dismissed the report as "so fantastic it hardly needs refuting" and then directly attacked the credibility of the War Department and the Justice Department: "The feeling that an invasion is imminent is not the belief of most of the responsible people. . . . There have been no known acts of sabotage committed in Hawaii."

The bureaucratic pushing and shoving between the War Department in Washington and the Hawaiian Department under the command of General Emmons continued. On October 29, Secretary of War Henry L. Stimson informed President Roosevelt that General Emmons intended to remove approximately 5,000 Japanese from Hawaii during the next six months as shipping facilities became available. "This, General Emmons believes, will greatly simplify his problem, and considering the labor needs in the islands, is about all that he has indicated any desire to move although he has been given authority to move up to fifteen thousand." Irritated by Emmons, President Roosevelt wrote to Stimson four days later: "I think that General Emmons should be told that the only consideration is that of the safety of the Islands and that the labor situation is not only a secondary matter but should not be given any consideration whatsoever."

In the end, General Emmons had his way. He had seen no military necessity for mass evacuation and ordered the internment of only 1,444 Japanese (979 aliens and 525 citizens). Emmons saw that martial law had given the military government the authority to control Hawaii's Japanese population. But Emmons's success in resisting pressures from Washington depended not only on his administrative savvy and his ability to wage a waiting war of bureaucracy but also on widespread local opposition to mass internment.

In an article on "Hawaii's 150,000 Japanese" published in *The Nation* in July 1942, journalist Albert Horlings questioned whether the military authorities in Hawaii made their decision against mass internment based on their trust for the Japanese. He suspected "pressure" had been brought on the military, warning that the economic life of the islands would collapse without the Japanese. Horlings argued that businessmen appeared to favor "a liberal policy" toward the Japanese simply because they favored "business as usual."

Indeed, economic pressure groups in Hawaii were advising General Emmons to resist relocation. A few isolated local businessmen favored mass internment. "At least 100,000 Japanese should be moved to inland mainland farming states," John A. Balch of the Hawaiian Telephone Company wrote to Admiral Chester Nimitz in August 1942. "If such a step as this was taken . . . not only the danger of internal trouble could be avoided, but the future of Hawaii would be secured against the sure political and economic domination by the Japanese within the next decade." But most of Hawaii's leading businessmen and *kamaaina haoles* (old-timer whites) opposed the proposal for mass internment. The president of the Honolulu Chamber of Commerce called for just treatment of the Japanese in Hawaii: "There are 160,000 of these people who want to live here because they like the country and like the American way of life. . . . The citizens of Japanese blood would fight as loyally for America as any other citizen. I have read or heard nothing in statements given out by the military, local police or FBI since December 7 to change my opinion. And I have gone out of my way to ask for the facts." The kamaaina elite, possessing a sense of genteel paternalism and a long history of interaction with the Japanese in the islands, were unwilling to permit their mass uprooting. They also knew the evacuation of over one third of Hawaii's population would decimate their labor force and destroy the economy of the islands.

Politicians and public officials also urged restraint and reason. Hawaii's congressional delegate, Sam King, advised the military that nothing should be done beyond apprehending known spies. Honolulu Police Captain John A. Burns refuted rumors of Japanese snipers firing on American soldiers during the attack on Pearl Harbor. "In spite of what . . . anyone . . . may have said about the fifth column activity in Hawaii," stated Robert L. Shivers, head of the FBI in Hawaii, "I want to emphasize that there was no such activity in Hawaii before, during or after the attack on Pearl Harbor. . . . I was in a position to know this fact. . . . Nowhere under the sun could there have been a more intelligent response to the needs of the hour than was given by the entire population of these islands." When schools were reopened in January 1942, the Superintendent of Public Instruction sent a directive to all teachers:

> Let us be perfectly frank in recognizing the fact that the most helpless victims, emotionally and psychologically, of the present situation in Hawaii will be children of Japanese ancestry and their parents. The position of loyal American citizens of Japanese ancestry and of aliens who are unable to become naturalized, but who are nonetheless loyal to the land of their adoption, is certainly not enviable. Teachers must do everything to help the morale of these people. Let us keep constantly in mind that America is not making war on citizens of the United States or on law-abiding aliens within America.

The press in Hawaii behaved responsibly. Newspaper editors like Riley Allen of the Honolulu *Star Bulletin* and Mrs. Clarence Taylor of the Kauai *Garden Island* expressed confidence in the loyalty of the local Japanese and criticized the federal government's treatment of the Japanese on the mainland. "It was an invasion of the rights of the Japanese citizens on the Pacific coast to be picked up and shipped to the interior," editorialized the *Garden Island*. Newspapers also cautioned their readers not to spread or be influenced by rumors generated by the war situation. Within days after the attack on Pearl Harbor, the Honolulu *Star Bulletin* dismissed reports of Japanese subversion in the islands as "weird, amazing, and damaging untruths." "Beware of rumors always," urged the *Paradise of the Pacific* magazine in February 1942, "avoid them like a plague and, when possible, kill them as you would a reptile. Don't repeat for a fact anything you do not know is a fact."

The reasons behind Hawaii's refusal to intern the Japanese were complex and did include the self-serving economic concern of the business community for the uninterrupted maintenance of its labor force. Still, in this moment of crisis an image of what Hawaii represented began to take a more definite form and content, drawing from the particular history of the islands and defining more sharply Hawaii's identity as a multiethnic community. Political and economic circumstances had provided an occasion for cultural development. In his radio message broadcast two weeks after the attack on Pearl Harbor, General Emmons declared: "Hawaii has always been an American outpost of friendliness and good will and now has calmly accepted its responsibility as an American outpost of war. In accepting these responsibilities, it is important that Hawaii prove that her traditional confidence in her cosmopolitan population has not been misplaced." While what Emmons described was a myth, it nonetheless also contained within it the possibility of an ideological counterpoint to the reality of racial hierarchy in the islands.

The actions of the Japanese gave concreteness to the idea of Hawaii as a cosmopolitan community. During the morning of the attack, two thousand Nisei serving in the U.S. Army stationed in Hawaii fought to defend Pearl Harbor against enemy planes. Everywhere Japanese civilians participated in the island's defense. They rushed to their posts as volunteer truck drivers for Oahu's Citizens' Defense Committee. They stood in long lines in front of Queen's Hospital, waiting to give their blood to the wounded. Many of these civilians were Issei. "Most of us have lived longer in Hawaii than in Japan. We have an obligation to this country," they declared. "We are *yoshi* [adopted sons] of America. We want to do our part for America."

Then that night, as the people of the islands tensely waited in the darkness for the expected invasion, thousands of Nisei members of the Hawaii Territorial Guard—youngsters from the high schools and the University of Hawaii ROTC program—guarded the power plants, reservoirs, and important waterfronts. For them, there was simply no doubt how they viewed the event: Japan had attacked their country. "As much as we would hate to see a war between the United States and Japan," Nisei Shigeo Yoshida had explained in 1937 during the hearings on statehood for Hawaii, "and as much as we would hate to see the day come when we would have to participate in such a conflict, it would be much easier, for us I think, if such an emergency should come, to face the enemy than to stand some of the suspicion and criticism, unjust in most cases, leveled against us. It is extremely difficult to bear up under the gaff of suspicion and expressions of doubt which have been leveled at us. It would be easier for me to pack a gun and face the enemy." Four years later, on December 7, that day did come and thousands of Nisei stood tall in defense of their country.

"Japan's dastardly attack leaves us grim and resolute," declared Shunzo Sakamaki of the Oahu Citizens Committee for Home Defense on December 11. "There is no turning back now, no compromise with the enemy. Japan has chosen to fight us and we'll fight." The Japanese of Hawaii fought wholeheartedly. On June 5, 1942, more than seventeen hundred Japanese presented a check to the federal government for "bombs on Tokyo." In January 1943 General Emmons issued a call for fifteen hundred Nisei volunteers for the U.S. Army. "OK Tojo—you asked for it," announced a newspaper advertisement published in the Honolulu *Star Bulletin* on January 23 and signed by Akagi, Fukushima, Hiyama, Isoshima, Kanda, Kataoka, Kawashima, Komenaka, Musashiya, Ogata, Nagao, and Yamamoto. "You dished it out with a head start by treachery—now we're going to see how you can take it." In response to Emmons's call, 9,507 Nisei men volunteered for service. Many of them were sent to Camp Shelby, Mississippi, where they became members of the 442nd Regimental Combat Team and gave their unit the slogan, "Go for Broke," a pidgin-English phrase from the plantation gambling experience. "I wanted to show something, to contribute to America," explained Minoru Hinahara, who served as a Japanese-language interpreter in the U.S. 27th Army Division and participated in the invasion of Okinawa. "My parents could not become citizens but they told me, 'You fight for your country.'"

If the Japanese in Hawaii were not interned, why were their brethren on the mainland evacuated and imprisoned in internment camps? Why did the mainland do "things the American Way" differently?

On the day after the attack on Pearl Harbor, Representative John M. Coffee declared in Congress: "It is my fervent hope and prayer that residents of the United States of Japanese extraction will not be made the victim of pogroms directed by self-proclaimed patriots and by hysterical self-anointed heroes. . . . Let us not make a mockery of our Bill of Rights by mistreating these folks. Let us rather regard them with understanding, remembering they are the victims of a Japanese war machine, with the making of the international policies of which they had nothing to do."

Perhaps Coffee was overly hopeful and naive, but there were reasons to think Japanese Americans would not become victims of hysteria unleashed by the war. A confidential report on the question of Japanese-American loyalty had already been submitted to President Franklin Roosevelt. The president had secretly arranged to have Chicago businessman Curtis Munson gather intelligence on the Japanese in the United States and assess whether they constituted an internal military threat. After Roosevelt received the Munson report on November 7, 1941, he asked the War Department to review it. In his discussion on sabotage and espionage, Munson informed the President that there was no need to fear or worry about America's Japanese population: "There will be no armed uprising of Japanese [in this country]. . . . Japan will commit some sabotage largely depending on imported Japanese as they are afraid of and do not trust the Nisei. There will be no wholehearted response from Japanese in the United States. . . . For the most part the local Japanese are loyal to the United States or, at worst, hope that by remaining quiet they can avoid concentration camps or irresponsible mobs. We do not believe that they would be at least any more disloyal than any other racial group in the United States with whom we went to war."

A month later the assessment of the Munson report was tested at Pearl Harbor. In his investigation of the Japanese in Hawaii and on the mainland, Lieutenant Commander K. D. Ringle of the Office of Naval Intelligence found that the large majority of them were at least passively loyal to the United States. In late January 1942, Ringle estimated that only about 3,500 Japanese could potentially be military threats and stated there was no need for mass action against the Japanese. Meanwhile, the FBI had also conducted its own investigation of the Japanese. On December 10, Director J. Edgar Hoover informed Washington that "practically all" suspected individuals whom he had initially planned to arrest were in custody: 1,291 Japanese (367 in Hawaii, 924 on the mainland), 857 Germans, and 147 Italians. In a report to the Attorney General submitted in early February, Hoover concluded that the proposed mass evacuation of the Japanese could not be justified for security reasons.

Despite these intelligence findings. Lieutenant General John L. DeWitt, head of the Western Defense Command, behaved very differently from his counterpart General Emmons in Hawaii. Within two weeks after the attack on Pearl Harbor, General DeWitt requested approval to conduct search-and-seizure operations in order to prevent alien Japanese from making radio transmissions to Japanese ships. The Justice Department refused to issue search warrants without probable cause, and the FBI determined the problem was only a perceived one. In January, the Federal Communications Commission, which had been monitoring all broadcasts, reported that the army's fears were groundless. But the army continued pursuing plans based on the assumption of Japanese disloyalty. General DeWitt also wanted to be granted the power to exclude Japanese aliens as well as Americans of Japanese ancestry from restricted areas. On January 4, 1942, at a meeting of federal and state officials in his San Francisco headquarters, DeWitt argued that military necessity justified exclusion: "We are at war and this area—eight states—has been designated as a theater of operations. . . . [There are] approximately 288,000 enemy aliens . . . which we have to watch. . . . I have little confidence that the enemy aliens are law-abiding or loyal in any sense of the word. Some of them yes; many, no. Particularly the Japanese. I have no confidence in their loyalty whatsoever. I am speaking now of the native born Japanese—117,000—and 42,000 in California alone."

The Western Defense Command ignored the Munson report as well as the information from the FCC and shunned Lieutenant Commander Ringle. Serving under DeWitt, Major General Joseph W. Stilwell had an insider's view of the situation at the

Command's headquarters in San Francisco. In his diary, Stilwell described how DeWitt was responding irrationally to rumors: "Common sense is thrown to the winds and any absurdity is believed." But Stilwell did not understand the reasons for DeWitt's conduct. FBI director Hoover was more perceptive: while he also saw that the WDC's intelligence information reflected "hysteria and lack of judgment," he noticed that the claim of military necessity for mass evacuation was based "primarily upon public and political pressure rather than on factual data."

Immediately after the press had been told by Navy Secretary Knox about Japanese subversive activity at Pearl Harbor, West Coast newspapers gave his claim headline attention: "Fifth Column Treachery Told" and "Secretary of Navy Blames 5th Column for Raid." Nonetheless, newspapers were initially restrained, advising readers to remain calm and considerate toward the Japanese. But in early January, press sentiments began shifting suddenly. On January 5, John B. Hughes of the Mutual Broadcasting Company began firing a month-long salvo against the Japanese in California. The Japanese were engaged in espionage, he charged, and their dominance in produce production and control of the food supply were part of a master war plan. On January 19, *Time* reported Japanese fifth-column activities in Hawaii in an article entitled: "The Stranger within Our Gates." The next day, the *San Diego Union* stirred anti-Japanese hysteria: "In Hawaii . . . treachery by residents, who although of Japanese ancestry had been regarded as loyal, has played an important part in the success of Japanese attacks. . . . Every Japanese . . . should be moved out of the coastal area and to a point of safety far enough inland to nullify any inclination they may have to tamper with our safety here." Meanwhile the *Los Angeles Times* editorialized: "A viper is nonetheless a viper wherever the egg is hatched—so a Japanese American, born of Japanese parents—grows up to be a Japanese, not an American." On January 29, Henry McLemore blasted the Japanese in his syndicated column for the Hearst newspapers: "I am for immediate removal of every Japanese on the West Coast to a point deep in the interior. I don't mean a nice part of the interior either. Herd 'em up, pack 'em off and give 'em the inside room in the badlands." Two weeks later, in a *Washington Post* article entitled "The Fifth Column on the Coast," prominent columnist Walter Lippmann called for the mass removal of Japanese Americans: "The Pacific Coast is in imminent danger of a combined attack from within and without. . . . The Pacific Coast is officially a combat zone. . . . And nobody ought to be on a battlefield who has no good reason for being there. There is plenty of room elsewhere for him to exercise his rights."

As the press mounted its campaign for Japanese removal, it was joined by patriotic organizations. In January the California Department of the American Legion began to demand that all Japanese known to possess dual citizenship be placed in "concentration camps." Shortly afterward American Legion posts in Washington and Oregon passed resolutions urging the evacuation of all Japanese. In the January issue of their publication, *The Grizzly Bear*, the Native Sons and Daughters of the Golden West told their fellow Californians: "We told you so. Had the warnings been heeded—had the federal and state authorities been 'on the alert,' and rigidly enforced the Exclusion Law and the Alien Land Law . . . had the legislation been enacted denying citizenship to offspring of all aliens ineligible to citizenship . . . had Japan been denied the privilege of using California as a breeding ground for dual-citizens (Nisei);—the treacherous Japs probably would not have attacked Pearl Harbor on December 7, 1941, and this country would not today be at war with Japan."

Beginning in January and early February, the anti-Japanese chorus included voices from farming interests such as the Grower-Shipper Vegetable Association, the Western Growers Protective Association, and the California Farm Bureau Federation. "We've been charged with wanting to get rid of the Japs for selfish reasons," the Grower Shipper Vegetable Association stated in the *Saturday Evening Post* in May. "We might as well be honest. We do. It's a question of whether the white man lives on the Pacific Coast or brown man. They came into this valley to work, and they stayed to take over. . . . If all the Japs were removed tomorrow, we'd never miss them in two weeks, because the white farmers can take over and produce everything the Jap grows."

Meanwhile, local and state politicians were already leading the movement for Japanese removal. The boards of supervisors of sixteen California counties, including Los Angeles County, passed resolutions urging removal. California Attorney General Earl Warren pressed federal authorities to remove Japanese from sensitive areas on the West Coast. The Japanese in California, he warned, "may well be the Achilles heel of the entire civilian defense effort. Unless something is done it may bring about a repetition of Pearl Harbor." On January 16, Congressman Leland Ford of Los Angeles wrote to the secretaries of the departments of War and the Navy and the FBI Director, insisting that "all Japanese, whether citizens or not, be placed in concentration camps." Two weeks later, several House members from the Pacific Coast states asked President Roosevelt to grant the War Department "immediate and complete control over all alien enemies, as well as United States citizens holding dual citizenship in any enemy country, with full power and authority" to evacuate and intern them.

The Western Defense Command operated within the context of this clamor for Japanese removal. The situation was very different from Hawaii's. Economic interests in California did not need Japanese labor, and many white farmers viewed Japanese farmers as competitors. Representing a small, rather than numerically significant racial minority, the Japanese were more vulnerable to xenophobic attacks. Furthermore a mythology of California as a "cosmopolitan" society did not exist to protect its Japanese residents. In fact, the state's image as protected by politicians in the 1920 vote on the alien land law was "Keep California White." On February 1, in a telephone conversation with Provost Marshal General Allen Gullion, General DeWitt said he had "travelled up and down the West Coast," talked to "all the Governors and other local civil authorities," and decided to press for mass evacuation. Protection against sabotage, he said, "only can be made positive by removing those people who are aliens and who are Japs of American citizenship." On February 5, after he had received DeWitt's views in writing, Gullion drafted a War Department proposal for the exclusion of "all persons, whether aliens or citizens . . . deemed dangerous as potential saboteurs" from designated "military areas."[75]

But a decision on evacuation still had not been made in Washington. During lunch with President Roosevelt on February 7, Attorney General Francis Biddle said "there were no reasons for mass evacuation." In his diary on February 10, Secretary of War Henry L. Stimson wrote: "The second generation Japanese can only be evacuated either as part of a total evacuation . . . or by frankly trying to put them out on the ground that their racial characteristics are such that we cannot understand or trust even the citizen Japanese. This latter is the fact but I am afraid it will make a tremendous hole in our constitutional system to apply it."

President Roosevelt was willing to make such a tremendous hole in the Constitution. In fact, he had been considering the internment of Japanese Americans for a long time. On August 10, 1936, President Roosevelt had written a memorandum to the Chief Naval Operation; "One obvious thought occurs to me—that every Japanese citizen or non-citizen on the island of Oahu who meets these Japanese ships or has any connection with their officers or men should be secretly but definitely identified and his or her name placed on a special list of those who would be the first to be placed in a concentration camp in the event of trouble." Thus, five years before the attack on Pearl Harbor, Roosevelt was already devising the imprisonment of Japanese aliens and citizens in a "concentration camp" without due process of law.

On February 11, 1942, Roosevelt met with Stimson, and shortly after the meeting, Assistant Secretary of War John J. McCloy telephoned the Provost Marshal General's office in San Francisco. "We talked to the President," McCloy said to Karl Bendetsen, chief of the Aliens Division, "and the President, in substance, says go ahead and do anything you think necessary. He says there will probably be some repercussions, but it has got to be dictated by military necessity. . . ." Three days after he had received his signal from Washington, General DeWitt sent Stimson his formal recommendation for removal, buttressing it with a racial justification: "In the war in which we are now engaged racial affinities are not severed by migration. The Japanese race is an enemy race and while many second and third generation Japanese born on United States soil, possessed of United States citizenship, have become 'Americanized,' the racial strains are undiluted. . . . It, therefore, follows that along the vital Pacific Coast over 112,000 potential enemies, of Japanese extraction, are at large today."

Three days later, Attorney General Biddle wrote a memorandum to President Roosevelt, opposing DeWitt's recommendation for evacuation: "My last advice from the War Department is that there is no evidence of imminent attack and from the FBI that there is no evidence of planned sabotage." Biddle tried to exercise reason and restraint, and his efforts to derail DeWitt's recommendation angered Congressman John Ford. "I phoned the Attorney General's office," said Ford, "and told them to stop fucking around. I gave them twenty-four hours notice that unless they would issue a mass evacuation notice I would drag the whole matter on the floor of the House and of the Senate and give the bastards everything we could with both barrels."

The next day, February 18, Secretary of War Stimson met with Attorney General Biddle and several others from the Department of Justice and the War Department. In his autobiography, Biddle described the meeting: "The decision [for evacuation] had been made by the President. It was, he said, a matter of military judgment. I did not think I should oppose it any further." The following morning, President Roosevelt signed Executive Order 9066, which directed the Secretary of War to prescribe military areas "with respect to which, the right of any person to enter, remain in, or leave shall be subject to whatever restrictions the Secretary of War or the appropriate Military Commander may impose in his discretion." The order did not specify the Japanese as the group to be excluded. But they were the target: a few months later, when President Roosevelt learned about discussions in the War Department to apply the order to Germans and Italians on the East Coast, he wrote to inform Stimson that he considered enemy alien control to be "primarily a civilian matter except in the case of the Japanese mass evacuation on the Pacific Coast." Unlike the Germans and Italians, the Japanese were "strangers from a different shore."

President Roosevelt had signed a blank check, giving full authority to General DeWitt to evacuate the Japanese and place them in assembly centers and eventually in internment camps. And so it happened, tragically for the Japanese and for the U.S. Constitution, for there was actually no "military necessity."

Under General DeWitt's command, the military ordered a curfew for all enemy aliens and all persons of Japanese ancestry and posted orders for evacuation: "Pursuant to the provisions of Civilian Exclusion Order No. 27, this Headquarters, dated April 30, 1942, all persons of Japanese ancestry, both alien and non-alien, will be evacuated from the above area by 12 o'clock noon, P. W. T., Thursday May 7, 1942." The evacuees were instructed to bring their bedding, toilet articles, extra clothing, and utensils. "No pets of any kind will be permitted." Japanese stood in silent numbness before the notices. Years later, Congressman Robert Matsui, who was a baby in 1942, asked: "How could I as a 6-month-old child born in this country be declared by my own Government to be an enemy alien?" But the order applied to everyone, including children. An American birthright made absolutely no difference. "Doesn't my citizenship mean a single blessed thing to anyone?" asked Monica Sone's brother in distress. "Several weeks before May, soldiers came around and posted notices on telephone poles," said Takae Washizu. "It was sad for me to leave the place where I had been living for such a long time. Staring at the ceiling in bed at night, I wondered who would take care of my cherry tree and my house after we moved out."

Notice of evacuation
One spring night
The image of my wife
Holding the hands of my mother.[81]

Believing the military orders were unconstitutional, Minoru Yasui of Portland refused to obey the curfew order: "It was my belief that no military authority has the right to subject any United States citizen to any requirement that does not equally apply to all other U.S. citizens. If we believe in America, if we believe in equality and democracy, if we believe in law and justice, then each of us, when we see or believe errors are being made, has an obligation to make every effort to correct them." Meanwhile Fred Korematsu in California and Gordon Hirabayashi in Washington refused to report to the evacuation center. "As an American citizen," Hirabayashi explained, "I wanted to uphold the principles of the Constitution, and the curfew and evacuation orders which singled out a group on the basis of ethnicity violated them. It was not acceptable to me to be less than a full citizen in a white man's country." The three men were arrested and convicted; sent to prison, they took their cases to the Supreme Court, which upheld their convictions, saying the government's policies were based on military necessity. Most Japanese however, felt they had no choice but to comply with the evacuation orders.[82]

Instructed they would be allowed to take only what they could carry, evacuees had to sell most of their possessions—their refrigerators, cars, furniture, radios, pianos, and houses. "I remember how agonizing was my despair," recounted Tom Hayase, "to be given only about six days in which to dispose of our property." "It is difficult to describe the feeling of despair and humiliation experienced by all of us," said another evacuee, "as we watched the Caucasians coming to look over our possessions and offering such nominal amounts knowing we had no recourse but to accept whatever they were offering because we did not know what the future held for us."

At the control centers, the evacuees were registered and each family was given a number. "Henry went to the Control Station to register the family," remembered Monica Sone. "He came home with twenty tags, all numbered '10710,' tags to be attached to each piece of baggage, and one to hang from our coat lapels. From then on, we were known as Family #10710." When they reported at the train stations, they found themselves surrounded by soldiers with rifles and bayonets.

> *Like a dog*
> *I am commanded*
> *At a bayonet point.*
> *My heart is inflamed*
> *With burning anguish.*

From there they were taken to the assembly centers. "I looked at Santa Clara's streets from the train over the subway," wrote Norman Mineta's father in a letter to friends in San Jose. "I thought this might be the last look at my loved home city. My heart almost broke, and suddenly hot tears just came pouring out. . . ." They knew that more than their homes and possessions had been taken from them. "On May 16, 1942, my mother, two sisters, niece, nephew, and I left . . . by train," said Teru Watanabe. "Father joined us later. Brother left earlier by bus. We took whatever we could carry. So much we left behind, but the most valuable thing I lost was my freedom."

When they arrived, the evacuees were shocked to discover that they were to be housed at stockyards, fairgrounds, and race tracks. "The assembly center was filthy, smelly, and dirty. There were roughly two thousand people packed in one large building. No beds were provided, so they gave us gunny sacks to fill with straw, that was our bed." Stables served as housing. "Where a horse or cow had been kept, a Japanese American family was moved in." "Suddenly you realized that human beings were being put behind fences just like on the farm where we had horses and pigs in corrals."

> *If you live in a*
> *Horse stable*
> *The winds of cities*
> *Blow through.*

Conditions were crowded and noisy. "There was a constant buzzing—conversations, talk. Then, as the evening wore on, during the still of the night, things would get quiet, except for the occasional coughing, snoring, giggles. Then someone would get up to go to the bathroom. It was like a family of three thousand people camped out in a barn." Everywhere there were lines. "We lined up for mail, for checks, for meals, for showers, for washrooms, for laundry tubs, for toilets, for clinic service, for movies." There were curfews and roll calls, and "day and night camp police walked their beats within the center."

After a brief stay in the assembly centers, the evacuees were herded into 171 special trains, five hundred in each train.

> *Snow in mountain pass*
> *Unable to sleep*
> *The prison train.*

They had no idea where they were going. In their pockets, some carried photographs of themselves and the homes they had left behind, and they occasionally turned their gaze away from the landscape whizzing by them and pulled out their pictures.

13

FBI COINTELPRO TARGET: THE BLACK PANTHER PARTY

M. Wesley Swearingen

> During the ten years that I was on the U.S. Intelligence Board . . . never once did I hear anybody, including myself, raise the questions: "Is this course of action which we have agreed upon lawful, is it legal, is it moral and ethical?" We never gave any thought to that realm of reasoning, because we were just naturally pragmatists. The one thing we were concerned with was this: Will this course of action work, will it get us what we want, will it reach the objective we desire to reach?
>
> William C. Sullivan, former FBI Assistant Director,
> Domestic Intelligence Division

INTRODUCTION

Beginning with the 1971 citizens' break-in at the Media, Pennsylvania Resident Agency FBI office, in which a large number of Top Secret documents were stolen and subsequently made public, the past quarter-century has been replete with revelations concerning pervasive criminal activities engaged in by the Federal Bureau of Investigation. Over the years, it has become increasingly apparent that such conduct on the part of the "nation's police force" has, overwhelmingly, been directed against politically dissident individuals and organizations. This is how the bureau has functioned from its inception in 1908 to today. In effect, the FBI exists, as much as anything else, as a national political police.

Much of the operational history of the bureau's many campaigns against political diversity in the United States has been detailed in the voluminous reports of a Senate Select Committee (Church Committee) during the mid-70s, and in such books as Robert Justin Goldstein's *Political Repression in Modern America*, Cathy Perkus' *COINTELPRO*, Athan Theoharis' *Spying on Americans*, David Wise's *The American Police State*, Peter Matthiessen's *In the Spirit of Crazy Horse*, Brian Glick's *War at Home*, David Garrow's

The FBI and Martin Luther King, Jr., Ross Gelbspan's *Break-ins, Death Threats and the FBI,* and my own collaborations with Jim VanderWall, *Agents of Repression* and *The COIN-TELPRO Papers.*

From this array of sources, both primary and secondary, emerges a portrait of a massive, deeply entrenched and increasingly ubiquitous institutional entity devoted to the curtailment of domestic political action and expression. The individual objects of the bureau's attentions in this respect have been people as different in their lives and outlooks as Ernest Hemingway and Dr. Martin Luther King, Jr., the Berrigan brothers and Russell Means, Bernardine Dohrn and Malcolm X, Janis Joplin and Kathy Boudin, Huey P. Newton and Joan Baez, George Jackson and Walter Reuther. The organizations subject to FBI counterintelligence operations have been equally wide-ranging, extending from the Black Panther Party, American Indian Movement, Puerto Rican *independentistas* and the Weathermen faction of the Students for a Democratic Society, to the entirety of the labor movement and the Communist and Socialist Workers parties, and onward still, to the Student Nonviolent Coordinating Committee, Committee in Solidarity with the People of El Salvador (CISPES), Every Mother for Peace, Clergy and Laity Concerned, Silo Plowshares, even Duke University.[4]

On record, the methods employed against such "deviants" have included every sort of tactic from discrediting targeted persons or groups by circulating defamatory rumors about them in their communities and/or planting false reports about them in the media, to causing "politically objectionable individuals" to be evicted from their homes and fired from their jobs by contacting their landlords and employers, to orchestrating the repeated arrests on spurious charges of those targeted, to obtaining the conviction and consequent imprisonment of "key activists" by introducing fabricated evidence against them at trial, to provoking inter- and intra-group violence, to outright assassination of selected leaders. Although the profile of the FBI's lexicon of illicitly repressive modes and methods is in some ways substantially complete, there has always been an important missing ingredient: namely, detailed tales of the bureau's adventures and wrongdoings. In contrast, much has been written about the activities of the Central Intelligence Agency (CIA), the FBI's figurative counterpart in U.S. external affairs. Several former CIA agents and officials have offered up details that corroborate and amplify the information about CIA techniques available from official and unofficial sources. The dramatic stories of Philip Agee, John Stockwell, Victor Marchetti, Frank Snepp, and Ralph McGehee have clarified and confirmed our knowledge of "The Company."

Unfortunately, it seems the bureau has produced virtually nobody—until now—with the requisite conscience, courage, and personal integrity to match their CIA counterparts in disclosing their insider's direct knowledge of what the FBI has done. Indeed, the major example of an agent who "quit and told" has until now been Joseph Schott, whose 1975 book, *No Left Turns,* was designed to embarrass the memory of FBI Director J. Edgar Hoover. An earlier effort by former agent William Turner, *Hoover's FBI,* was so limited as to be nearly useless in today's research on the FBI.

Given the veritable vacuum into which it injects itself, then, the present book is not only unique but vitally important. Here at last is a career veteran of the bureau's clandestine wars against political freedom in America—a participant in literally hundreds of burglaries, disinformation campaigns, and worse—who has, however belatedly, demonstrated the fortitude and character necessary to admit, first to himself and then to the rest of us, not just the illegality but the intrinsic *wrongness* of what he did "in service to the bureau." Thus, the author, M. Wesley Swearingen, has finally positioned himself to reveal what he learned in the course of his decades as an active-duty FBI agent.

This, to be sure, is a lot. The chapters which follow are laced with privileged information. Exposed, for example, are the mechanics of how Los Angeles Black Panther leader Geronimo ji Jaga Pratt was railroaded into an ongoing life term in prison by agents with whom the author worked during the early 1970s. Similarly, Swearingen recounts a drinking scene in which another agent, a friend with whom he had long worked in Chicago, confessed the bureau's involvement in the December 1969 assassinations of Illinois Panther leaders Fred Hampton and Mark Clark.[10] Light is also shed on the victimization of others, Jean Seberg and Leonard Peltier among them.[11] Additional vignettes highlight the FBI's more-or-less continuous subversion of "objectionable" electoral candidates, the hyper-reactionary racial and sexual attitudes of the average agent, and much more.

Altogether, *FBI Secrets* serves much the same purpose as Agee's *Inside the Company* or Stockwell's *In Search of Enemies,* providing an indispensable validation of certain conclusions already drawn by independent analysts and researchers.[12]

Swearingen's Los Angeles counterintelligence colleagues also played a role in bringing about the murders of other Panthers—Fred Bennett, for instance, and Frank Diggs, Sandra Lane Pratt, Jimmie Carr, Bunchy Carter, and Jon Huggins—and were probably involved in setting up the 1970 Marin County Courthouse disaster that resulted in the deaths of Jonathan Jackson and several others, while very nearly ending the career of activist/intellectual Angela Davis. Scholars and activists are still debating the question of the bureau's possible participation in orchestrating the assassination of George Jackson in 1971.

The FBI also used street gangs during the late-60s and early '70s as surrogates with which to destroy the Panthers. The Party, of course, is known to have fielded a strong and tentatively viable anti-drug program in many inner cities during that period. The gangs with which the bureau aligned itself, and to which it appears to have extended some sort of criminal immunity as a *quid pro quo*—the Black P. Stone Nation *cum* El Rukn group in Chicago is a salient example—largely went on to become primary drug distributors in their respective localities once the Panthers had been obliterated. The FBI's activities on such matters illuminate the meaning of the Reagan/Bush "War on Drugs" and the present Clinton "Get Tough on Crime" initiative.

FBI Secrets represents a giant step toward lifting the shroud of secrecy under which the bureau has sought to conceal its true malignancy. It stands as a singular testimony, a precedent, one which may quite possibly lay the groundwork for other agents or former agents, with other knowledge and other anecdotes, to step forward to share their own insights and experiences. This is certainly an outcome to be hoped for. But, whether or not such a potential is ever borne out, the material herein cries out to be read in its own right, and its author is deserving of genuine respect for having proven himself courageous enough to have written it.

Ward Churchill
Boulder, Colorado
October 1994

THE BLACK PANTHER PARTY

The racial squad investigated the Black Panther Party, the Black Liberation Army, the United Slaves, and other black organizations that were unacceptable to J. Edgar Hoover. The S-2 also investigated various white hate groups such as the American Nazi Party and the Sheriff's Posse Comitatus. It also investigated a very small group of young Hispanic political activists known as the Brown Berets.

The Black Panther Party was established as the Black Panther Party for Self-Defense in the San Francisco Bay area by two Merrit College students, Huey Newton and Bobby Seale, in October 1966. The Black Panthers had a ten-point program that resembled a political platform for a member of Congress or a presidential candidate. Its demands included freedom, power to determine the destiny of their community, full employment, the end to robbery by the white man of their community, decent housing, education that taught black history, exemption of black men from military service, an immediate end to police brutality and the murder of black people, freedom for black men in jail, fair trials in court by a jury of their peers as defined by the U.S. Constitution, and peace. The Black Panthers' platform was legal, but their ten-point program was unacceptable to Hoover and his all-white FBI.

By 1967, the Black Panther Party had organized a free breakfast program for black children and offered free health care to ghetto residents. They also had a community education project and an anti-heroin campaign.

In February 1968, Bobby Seale and Eldridge Cleaver planned the merger of the Black Panther Party with the Student Nonviolent Coordinating Committee (SNCC). Stokely Carmichael was designated as honorary prime minister of the Panthers, H. Rap Brown as minister of justice, and James Forman as minister of foreign affairs.

FBI officials saw a strengthening coalition within the black community that they felt had to be stopped immediately. The FBI framed Stokely Carmichael as an informer for the CIA by planting an informant report in his car where other members could find it, with the help of another FBI informer. The report was discovered and the Panthers sent a "hit team" after Carmichael, who as a result departed immediately for an extended period in Africa.

The FBI's COINTELPRO had successfully neutralized the coalition between the Panthers and the Student Nonviolent Coordinating Committee, instigated by Hoover's paranoia of African Americans, but the Panthers were gaining respect in the black community across the country. Hoover wanted the Black Panther Party neutralized immediately, one way or the other.

In November 1968, Hoover wrote to the various FBI field offices in cities with growing Panther organizations that a serious struggle was developing between the Panthers and the United Slaves organization. Hoover wrote that the struggle had reached such proportions that it was taking on the aura of gang warfare with threats of murder.

Then, in December 1968, Hoover ordered these offices to submit letters every two weeks outlining the counterintelligence measures that were being taken to neutralize the Black Panther Party. These bi-weekly letters were to list the accomplishments achieved in attacking the Panthers.

Soon after I had been assigned to the Los Angeles racial squad, I was told by a fellow agent, *Joel Ash,* that another agent on the squad, *Nick Galt,* had arranged for Galt's informers in the United Slaves to assassinate Alprentice Carter, the Panther's Los Angeles minister of defense, and John Huggins, the deputy minister of information. Following Galt's instructions, informants George Stiner and Larry Stiner shot them to death on the UCLA campus on January 17, 1969.

I had thought Joel Ash had been kidding me because this was beyond any corruption or wrongdoing that I had witnessed or heard of by FBI agents.

I later reviewed the Los Angeles files and verified that the Stiner brothers were FBI informants. I knew they must be real informants, even though the informant programs that I knew about in Chicago and Los Angeles were approximately 75 percent phony, because Hoover wanted the Panthers in jail or dead. That was why he had ordered bi-weekly reports from the field about the campaign against the Black Panther Party.

Darthard Perry, a self-admitted and publicly acclaimed informer for the FBI, filed an affidavit in a Black Panther Party lawsuit against the government charging that he knew that the United Slaves members who were responsible for the murders of the Panthers were FBI informers. Perry claims that the murders committed by the Stiner brothers, who were convicted and sent to jail in 1969, and their subsequent escape in the 1974 prison break from San Quentin, were engineered by the FBI. I then discovered the unthinkable, that FBI informants had actually been instructed by FBI agents to assassinate several other Black Panther members.

As of 1992, the Stiner brothers were still listed as fugitives. Either the FBI has disposed of the Stiners or they are in the FBI's Witness Protection Program. I know that Darthard Perry was an FBI informant and that he is telling the truth about the FBI.[1]

United Slaves member *Bill Stark,* an FBI informer, shot and killed Panther member *Al Holt,* another FBI informer, on March 14, 1969.[2]

The Los Angeles files revealed that a Panther member was shot by a United Slaves member on March 17, 1969. Julius Carl Butler, an informer for the Los Angeles Police

Department and the FBI for several years, retaliated by shooting up the home of James Doss. United Slaves member Jerry Horne shot and killed Panther member John Savage on May 23, 1969. On August 14, 1969, United Slaves members wounded two Black Panthers. Sylvester Bell, another Panther member, was killed by FBI informers in the United Slaves on August 15, 1969.

The FBI eagerly took credit for this high degree of unrest in a communication to Hoover that stated, "It is felt that a substantial amount of the unrest is directly attributable to this program," referring to the FBI's counterintelligence program, code named COINTELPRO. The FBI has denied any wrongdoing, but agents have told me what happened and I have read the files of the Los Angeles FBI office.

Panther Leader Elmer Pratt was framed by the FBI and the Los Angeles Police Department in 1972, and he is now serving life in prison. [Pratt was released in 1997. —Editor's note.]

After four months on the racial squad, our supervisor, Dred Scott, held a squad conference to brief the new members, including me, on the forthcoming May 1972 trial of Elmer "Geronimo" Pratt for murder.

Elmer Pratt had become the leader of the Panthers in Los Angeles after the assassination of Alprentice Carter and John Huggins. Pratt had served two tours of duty in Vietnam as a decorated paratrooper and he had received an honorable discharge in 1968. He then had attended UCLA on the GI Bill. Soon after Pratt had joined the Panthers, the FBI had arranged to have his veterans benefits cut off in November 1968.

At the squad conference in April 1972, Dred Scott said that Kenneth Olsen and Caroline Olsen had been attacked on a tennis court in Santa Monica on December 18, 1968, by two black men. Caroline was shot and killed. Kenneth had tentatively identified several persons from photographs shown to him by the Santa Monica Police Department and positively identified one person from a photograph.

Scott told us how the Los Angeles Police Department (LAPD) had explained to Mr. Olsen that Pratt was the leader of the Panthers in Los Angeles and that a car like Pratt's had been seen in the area of the tennis court on the night of the shooting. Scott said that Olsen positively identified Geronimo Pratt as Caroline's killer after being pressured by the LAPD.

I recognized the old cop ploy immediately. I have used it myself. You show a confused witness a photograph of the person you want in jail and, nine times out of ten, if you press hard enough, the witness will say what you want to hear. After more than three years, Mr. Olsen had suddenly become clairvoyant enough to tell the LAPD that Geronimo Pratt was the one who had shot Caroline Olsen.

Then Dred Scott dropped the clincher. Scott said, "The LAPD won't tell the jury that Olsen positively identified at least three other suspects before he identified Pratt."

Scott continued. He told how the Los Angeles Police Department had recovered a weapon from John Huggins' house after the UCLA murders. He said that the LAPD ballistics expert would testify that the weapon found in Huggins' house belonged to

Pratt and that it was the gun that was used to kill Caroline Olsen, even though the barrel was missing.

I knew enough about ballistics to know that you had to compare rifling marks on a round of ammunition as it slammed out of the barrel of a gun with the rifling in the gun barrel to prove that the round that killed a certain person had come from the gun in question. The Los Angeles Police Department did not follow that procedure and they did not tell the jury so.

Scott gave us a rundown on Julius Carl Butler, the prime witness against Pratt, who had been an informer for the Los Angeles Police Department and the FBI for several years. Scott said Pratt had expelled Butler from the Black Panther Party because Butler was a violent person. Julius Butler was no longer effective as an informer, so Butler decided to get even with Pratt by claiming that Pratt had confessed to Butler to having killed Caroline Olsen.

Dred Scott said, "We will close our informant file on Butler during the trial so that Butler can say he is not an FBI informant."

I looked around the room. Scott and some of the agents were smiling. Two other agents winked at each other.

Scott said, "It took some doing, but it looks as though we have Pratt cold this time."

I thought to myself that Pratt would not be convicted if the Black Panther attorney in San Francisco, Charles R. Garry, represented Pratt. The trial started and I did not give it a second thought because I believed in our system of justice. I thought that an innocent person could not be convicted in a court of law in these United States. I had lost cases against guilty persons. How could an innocent person go to jail? I learned later that I still had been naive. Elmer "Geronimo" Pratt was convicted in Los Angeles Superior Court and sentenced to life in prison.

My supervisor and several agents on the racial squad knew that Pratt was innocent because the FBI had wiretap logs proving that Pratt was in the San Francisco area several hours before the shooting of Caroline Olsen and that he was there the day after the murder.

The Los Angeles office had had a wiretap on Panther headquarters in Los Angeles for a two-week period covering the date of December 18, 1968. These wiretap logs could prove that Elmer Pratt was in the San Francisco area on the day Caroline Olsen was shot to death.

I reviewed the Black Panther Party file that showed that the Los Angeles FBI office had had a wiretap on the Panther office at 4115 South Central Avenue from November 15, 1968 through 2:00 P.M., December 20, 1968. In other cases for which I had reviewed wiretaps, such as on radical attorneys such as Charles R. Garry and William Kunstler, I simply asked the clerk who handled the "JUNE" files—the records pertaining to wiretaps and other electronic surveillances—for the records and telephone logs. I had worked with wiretap information since 1952, and this was the first time in my twenty-five-year career that I could not find the Panther wiretap logs for the period

November 15 through December 20, 1968. Someone had destroyed these logs so there would be no proof that Elmer Pratt had been in the San Francisco area on December 18, 1968.

A wiretap by the San Francisco FBI office on Panther headquarters placed Pratt in the Bay area just hours before the shooting. An illegal wiretap in Oakland, which was paid for by the FBI from a bogus informant file under the name of Ozzie Penz, possibly a code name for the Oakland Police, placed Pratt in Oakland the day after the murder.

This is a total of three wiretaps known to the FBI with information that placed Pratt in the San Francisco area before, during, and after the murder of Caroline Olsen, and yet the FBI withheld this information from the court and the jury.

When Julius Carl Butler testified under oath in the Pratt trial, he said he had not been an informer for the police or the FBI. I reviewed Butler's FBI informant file, number 170–1259. The file shows that FBI agents, including Richard Wallace Held, who retired as Special Agent in Charge of the San Francisco FBI office in 1993, had been in contact with Butler for more than two years before the Pratt trial and that an FD–209 Informant Contact form had been filled out more than two dozen times. The Butler informant file was opened on a memo from agent Richard Wallace Held dated July 9, 1970. Butler was contacted by the FBI at least once a month for a two-year period. The Butler informant file was closed before the trial started and it was re-opened after Elmer Pratt was convicted. Both Butler and the FBI deny that Butler was an informant, but the informant file has now been made available to Pratt's attorneys, and it is there for anyone to review. The information on Butler's status as an informer for the LAPD and the FBI is now a matter of public record in the courts, but Pratt is still serving time. The FBI did not tell the court or the jury that Elmer Pratt also had been a target of COINTEL-PRO to be neutralized.

Pratt was not the only case of FBI-orchestrated miscarriages of justice that I learned about.

Sometime later, I attended a special seminar at the FBI's National Academy at Quantico, Virginia. Friends from other offices were there, as was *Gregg York,* a long-time friend from Chicago. York and I had conducted nearly 100 bag jobs together in Chicago and we came to trust each other with our jobs and our lives. We shared some of the FBI's darkest secrets.

There is a lounge at the FBI National Academy which sells low-alcohol beer in the evening after classes, but no hard liquor. Gregg York and I had finished a few pitchers of beer one night as we discussed old times. I don't recall just how the subject of the Black Panther Party came up. I may have started the conversation by comparing the work on the Los Angeles racial squad to the bag jobs Gregg and I had done in Chicago.

I told York that some agents in Los Angeles had informants who had assassinated Black Panther members and I told him how Geronimo Pratt had been framed for murder and had been sentenced to life in prison.

York grinned and said he had a better story than that.

York told me about the December 1969 raid on the Chicago Panther headquarters in which Fred Hampton and Mark Clark had been killed by the Chicago police. He said the FBI had arranged for the raid by telling the police that the Panthers had numerous guns and explosives, and that they would shoot any police officer who entered the building.

As York outlined the details of what had happened during the pre-dawn raid on December 4, 1969, directed by the state attorney general's office, his smile went away. His mouth tightened. York looked as though he was about to confess to a horrible sin. We had been through some tough times together and I admired him as a friend and fellow agent. York had always been there when we needed him on a difficult bag job. He was one of the best agents with whom I had ever worked. From his expression I felt he was about to tell me something I did not want to hear and something he should not tell me. York looked over his shoulder in both directions, to be sure no one was listening. We were alone at a corner table. I poured another glass of beer and sipped it while York told his story.

York explained that agent Roy Mitchell had an informant in the Chicago Black Panther Party and that the informant had given Mitchell a detailed floor plan of Panther headquarters along with a description of their weapons cache. He explained that the Chicago FBI office had held a conference with the Chicago police and had detailed the violent background of the Panthers and their collection of firearms. He said, "We gave them a copy of the detailed floor plan from Mitchell's informant so that they could raid the place and kill the whole lot."

I was speechless. Gregg York had just confessed to me his part, as a supervisor in the Chicago office, in the FBI's plot to assassinate the Panthers in a style similar to the Chicago gangland murders of the 1950s. York had confessed to being an accessory to murder. The judge later ruled that indeed there had been a conspiracy between the FBI and the police in this case.

We did not speak for what seemed a long time. I kept thinking of how my old friend thought I was on his side when it came to killing African Americans. I felt sorry for Gregg York because he was still fighting Hoover's imaginary enemies: the communists, the Native Americans and the African Americans.

We began to talk again, and York said, "We expected about twenty Panthers to be in the apartment when the police raided the place. Only two of those black nigger fuckers were killed, Fred Hampton and Mark Clark."

I could not take anymore of York's depraved attitude. I changed the subject to our upcoming retirements.

On the last day of the seminar I said good-bye to York and wished him well in his retirement. I never spoke to him again. During my career I had done many things that I was not proud of, but I never had been involved in a plot to murder or assassinate anyone. I knew it would be hard for me to live down the transgressions I had committed against the Constitution in what I thought were honorable acts in the defense of our country, but I had no idea how Gregg York and the other agents involved in plots to assassinate and murder innocent citizens could ever have a peaceful night's sleep.

ENDNOTES

1. From my work with false identification on the Weathermen in 1971, I learned that the FBI had arranged for Perry to give Elmer Geronimo Pratt phony identification in 1972 from the Weatherman files. Perry was to assist Pratt in a jail break so that the FBI could track Pratt's contacts in the black nationalist underground, via the National Crime Information Center (NCIC). If Pratt were arrested after the jail break while using the phony identification, the FBI would have short-circuited a police inquiry through NCIC. Later, the FBI would do an innocuous follow-up interview with the arresting officer to determine Pratt's city of operation and then would have developed, through informers, the black nationalist underground contacts in that city.

2. According to a May 26, 1970 memo from the Los Angeles Special Agent in Charge to the Director, the racial squad "is aware of the mutually hostile feelings harbored between the organizations and the first opportunity to capitalize on the situation will be maximized. It is intended that U.S. Inc. will be appropriately and discreetly advised of the time and location of BPP activities in order that the two organizations might be brought together and thus grant nature the opportunity to take her due course."

14

SOUTHERN EXPLOSURE

Jon Wiener

Thirty-eight years after the bombing of Birmingham's 16th Street Baptist Church, two of the four principals are dead, but the issues are still full of life. Thomas Blanton Jr. is one of two surviving Klan bombers, and after a jury convicted him in early May of murdering the four black girls that Sunday morning, former Alabama Attorney General Bill Baxley wrote a blistering Op-Ed for the *New York Times* accusing the FBI of concealing evidence and aiding the Klan for decades after the event. The FBI's denial made page one the next day: "There's no reason we would have done that," a bureau spokesperson declared. The *Times* also published a letter from the special agent in charge of the FBI's Birmingham office, calling Baxley's Op-Ed "a disservice to all the agents who tirelessly investigated the 1963 bombing."

Diane McWhorter's *Carry Me Home* is a history of that bombing, of the FBI "investigation," of the people responsible for it—high and low—and of the civil rights movement in Birmingham. She grew up there—she was 10 years old at the time of the bombing—and later she worried, because her father, who had fallen from an elite family, had spent many evenings attending what her mother called "civil rights meetings." But Diane knew he had Klan literature around. Eventually she realized that her father could have been attending Klan meetings, and might even have been one of the bombers. Many years later she set out to find out the truth about him—and ended up writing this magnificent book.

Although the 16th Street Baptist Church served as a rallying point for demonstrators in the 1963 campaign, it was not a Movement church. McWhorter calls it "the snootiest black congregation in the city," and its founding minister worked with the local industrialists to persuade blacks not to join the union. At services they didn't sing gospel songs but rather "the sedate hymns of white Christianity." And 16th Street Baptist was the only church in the city that charged the Movement for using its facilities.

The bomb was a huge one—perhaps a dozen sticks of dynamite. When the blast was heard across town, Klansman Ross Keith, almost certainly one of the bombers, told a friend, "I guess it's somebody discriminating against them niggers again." The four girls who were killed were in the women's lounge, freshening up for their roles as ushers in the main service. Denise McNair was 11; the three others were 14: Carole Robert-son, Addie May Collins and Cynthia Wesley—Wesley was wearing high heels for the first time, "shiny black ones bought the day before."

There is a survivor who was in the women's lounge with the other four: 12-year-old Sarah Collins, sister of Addie May. When they found Sarah in the rubble, her face was spurting blood. She was loaded into an ambulance—a "colored" one. On the way to the hospital she sang "Jesus Loves Me" and occasionally said, "What happened? I can't see." Today she is 50 and still blind in one eye.

Immediately after the four girls were identified, the authorities began "furious background checks on them, the search for some flaw deserving punishment." But their records were clean: None, that is, had participated in the recent civil rights demonstrations. Thus, even the city fathers and the local press had to agree they were "innocent."

The big question was never who the bombers were—they were identified by the FBI and the police almost immediately. The big question, McWhorter shows, is what permitted them to get away with it—"the state's malevolence or the FBI's negligence." Dozens of bombings had been carried out by the Klan in the preceding few years, vir-tually none of which were prosecuted. The FBI's informant in the local Klan, Gary Thomas Rowe, participated in some of them. McWhorter's index has ninety entries for "bombings," starting in the late 1940s. Most Klan bombings in the fifties targeted upwardly mobile blacks moving into middle-class white neighborhoods.

After the 16th Street church bombing, local authorities kept suggesting that blacks were the bombers. The police took the church custodian in for questioning. The FBI's pursuit of witnesses was unhurried, which gave the Klansmen more time to coordinate alibis. FBI informant Rowe told a Birmingham policeman that the man who put up the money to have the church bombed was Harry Belafonte.

The man convicted just weeks ago, Thomas Blanton Jr., was part of an extremist subgroup of the Klan. Initially he focused his violent hatred on Catholics, like the Klan of the 1920s. He had a neighbor, a widow, who was Catholic; she received regular "anonymous calls" from a voice she recognized as his—she had known him for eigh-teen years—telling her "Niggers and Catholics have to die." Once he threw red paint on her new white Ford and slashed her tires. Earlier in 1963 Blanton had been talking about organizing a church bombing, but he wanted to bomb a Catholic church, not a Negro one. "His associates pronounced him not intelligent enough to make a bomb but dumb enough to place it."

The other man recently charged with the bombing has been judged mentally inca-pable of standing trial. But in 1962–63, Bobby Frank Cherry was 32 years old, had "no upper front teeth, a 'Bobby' tattoo on his arm, seven kids, and a wife he beat and cheated on." He had been a police suspect in the 1958 attempted bombing of Birm-ingham's Temple Beth El, and McWhorter has evidence strongly suggesting that he also participated in bombing churches in January 1962, almost two years before the four girls were killed. If the FBI had investigated him after the 1962 explosions, that might have prevented the 16th Street Baptist Church bombings, but as McWhorter points out, "instead the FBI was investigating Martin Luther King," proposing to, as the bureau put it, "expose, disrupt, discredit, or otherwise neutralize" the leader of the civil rights movement. (In the middle of the Birmingham battle, Bobby Kennedy agreed to let J. Edgar Hoover wiretap King.)

The killing of the four black girls finally spurred the Kennedy Administration to propose, Congress to pass and new President Lyndon Johnson to sign the Civil Rights Act of 1964, outlawing racial discrimination in public facilities—the first significant civil rights legislation in a century. The bombing followed the biggest and most successful mass civil rights demonstrations in US history—police met the thousands of marchers with fire hoses and dogs. Today the history of the civil rights movement seems like one of steady progress: first the Montgomery bus boycott in 1955, which propelled King to national prominence and established nonviolent direct action as the new tactic, supplanting the legal gradualism of the NAACP; then, in 1960–61, the sit-in movement, in which small groups of courageous students across the South took the lead in a direct personal challenge to segregation; then the Freedom Rides, where a few brave people provoked racist violence that compelled the Kennedy Administration to enter the civil rights arena; and finally Birmingham, where mass protests filled the jails and finally won national legislation outlawing segregation in public accommodations.

What's been forgotten is the grim situation that faced King and the Movement at the outset of the Birmingham campaign in 1962. It had been seven long years since the Montgomery bus boycott—seven years with intermittent acts of immense heroism but without concrete victories. The Southern states were defiant, and the Kennedys, as Victor Navasky argued in *Kennedy Justice,* considered activists like Martin Luther King to be a problem that endangered their real initiatives, like a tax cut and fighting communism. By 1963 King and the Movement desperately needed a nationally significant victory, somewhere.

King himself had not, up to 1963, initiated any civil rights protest himself—starting with Montgomery in 1955, he was brought in as a spokesman after the action had already begun. Birmingham was no different. Here the real hero and moving force was Fred Shuttlesworth, in many ways the opposite of King—a man of the people, not of the elite; a man who courted danger and pushed the envelope, who stayed till the end, unlike King, who was criticized for leaving town early and leaving "a community stranded with false hope and huge legal fees." Much of the story of Birmingham is the story of Shuttlesworth's brilliant strategic initiatives and awesome physical courage—and King's more cautious efforts to negotiate a settlement by enlisting the White House, in exchange for calling off the demonstrations. It was Shuttlesworth who set out to launch mass demonstrations, fill the jails and compel the city leaders to desegregate downtown businesses and public facilities. McWhorter's book also shows just how close the Birmingham campaign came to failure. A month into the campaign, few people had signed up to go to jail—barely 300 in total, even though King himself had gone to jail. "There are more Negroes going to jail for getting drunk," one Movement leader commented.

What turned this around was an idea of James Bevel's—he had been a Student Nonviolent Coordinating Committee (SNCC) leader, who later became field secretary for King's organization, the Southern Christian Leadership Conference. His idea for Birmingham: Fill the jails with children. The adults were full of doubt and fear, but the kids were eager. Hundreds boycotted school on May 2, 1963, instead gathering at the 16th Street Baptist Church, then marching into the streets—more than a thousand of them. The children confronted the cops, singing in high voices "Ain't Gonna Let Nobody Turn Me Around" and "Which Side Are You On?" and then were ushered into buses to go to jail. For the first time, King and his lieutenants had achieved Gandhi's goal— fill the jails.

The next day thousands more showed up to march. That was the day of the fire hoses. The city's fire chief initially resisted officials' attempts to enlist the fire department in attacking demonstrators, on the grounds that the national union of firefighters officially opposed using fire equipment to "control" crowds. But when the orders came, they turned on high-pressure hoses powerful enough to knock a big man off his feet, blast the shirts off people's backs and flush individuals down the gutters.

The success of the civil rights movement on the national political landscape required not just heroic action by large numbers of ordinary black people; it also required that the viciousness of the opponents of civil rights be presented vividly and dramatically to ordinary American newspaper readers and TV watchers. In this, the Birmingham movement turned out to be supremely fortunate to have the grotesque Eugene "Bull" Connor as police commissioner. Photos of young demonstrators linking arms and standing up to the high-pressure hoses made page one around the world. *Life* magazine ran a two-page spread of the most dramatic photo of firemen blasting demonstrators, headlined "They Fight a Fire That Won't Go Out." The photos of police dogs attacking demonstrators had the same effect. The *New York Times* ran a photo of a dog biting a demonstrator on page one, three columns wide and above the fold, headlined "Dogs and Hoses Repulse Negroes at Birmingham."

Key reporters had already found the civil rights drama a compelling story. In 1960, the *New York Times* published a blazing Harrison Salisbury story on page one before the Birmingham campaign got going: "Every reasoned approach, every inch of middle ground has been fragmented by the emotional dynamite of racism, reinforced by the ship, the razor, the gun, the bomb, the torch, the club, the knife, the mob, the police and many branches of the state's apparatus." State authorities responded by charging Salisbury with forty-two counts of criminal libel. The *Times*'s response was to order its reporters to stay out of Alabama—not exactly a fighting stance—which meant that other news organizations would henceforth get the story while the *Times* relied on wire copy for the climactic battles. The *Times* didn't return until a year later, when Claude Sitton persuaded executives to let him cover the aftermath of the Freedom Rides.

While the *Times* proved gun-shy on Alabama, CBS-TV didn't; network president Frank Stanton sent reporter Howard K. Smith to Birmingham to make a documentary. (Even though Stanton was not exactly a civil rights advocate; he also "blacked out all Negro speakers at the Democratic and Republican presidential conventions.") Smith's crew set out to interview leading whites; the head of the elite Women's Committee told him on camera that "one of the contributing factors to our creativeness in the South is sort of a joyousness of the Negro." But she was worried because it had been four or five years since she had "heard Negroes just spontaneously break into song." Smith also turned out to be the only national reporter on the scene when the Freedom Riders arrived and were savagely beaten by a white mob while the police stood by.

Who Speaks for Birmingham? aired on CBS in 1961 and featured Smith's account of the mob attack on the Freedom Riders. Network executives complained that the program "presented Birmingham's Negroes in a better light than its whites," but executive producer Fred Friendly fought to keep the whole thing, and in the end gave up only Smith's closing line, a quote from Edmund Burke: "The only thing necessary for the triumph of evil is for good men to do nothing." But when the same Howard K. Smith criticized Kennedy in his regular Sunday radio commentary, asking whether "we really deserve to win the cold war" in view of the racist violence in Birmingham, CBS News suspended him from his job as Washington bureau chief.

The media coverage was crucial, but one of the secrets of the demonstrations was that neither the police nor the media distinguished between marchers and spectators. Only a couple of hundred people joined the early official demonstrations, but a thousand or more turned out to watch and see what happened. The police attacked everybody, and the press reported thousands of demonstrators.

Carry Me Home includes the most detailed account ever of the Birmingham Movement's strategy and tactics, day by day and hour by hour, but what makes it unique is its account of the local opposition to civil rights, and particularly the links between the "Big Mules," who ran Birmingham's industrial economy, and the Klan bombers. The book's most important contribution is its decisive evidence that the bombing of the 16th Street Baptist Church "was the endgame in the city fathers' long and profitable tradition of maintaining their industrial supremacy through vigilantism."

Birmingham had never been what you would call a happy place—the New South's one center of heavy industry, it was a city where the ruling elite fought working-class militancy with the most blatant racism. Power in Birmingham centered on US Steel, which ran the town along fascist lines—one Communist organizer in the 1930s was sentenced to a shackled road crew for possessing "seditious" literature, which included *The Nation* magazine. The dirty work of the Big Mules was carried out by the Alabama Klan, which was reorganized in the 1930s, as an antiunion shock force.

Charles DeBardeleben headed the Big Mules—he ran the biggest coal company in the state, and his father had pretty much founded Birmingham as a coal and iron center. By the mid-1930s DeBardeleben was also a secret corporate benefactor of the Constitutional Educational League, part of a global network of pro-Nazi propagandists. The league's 1938 banquet featured George Van Horn Moseley, who "advocated sterilizing all Jewish immigrants to the US." McWhorter names the names of the other key Big Mules and shows their connections to the bombers of the 1950s and 1960s.

History also loomed large for the Jewish businessmen who owned the downtown department stores that were the target of the demonstrators' demands for integration and jobs. Birmingham's Jews had been traumatized a generation earlier during the Scottsboro trial, when the nine "Boys" were defended during their rape trial by a Jewish attorney from New York named Samuel Liebowitz. The state's closing statement challenged the jury to "show them that Alabama justice cannot be bought and sold with Jew money from New York." The jury obliged.

That was 1933. Thirty years later, Birmingham's Jews were still feeling defensive. One liked to tell his gentile friends, "It wasn't the Birmingham Jews who killed Jesus. It was the Miami Jews." Now they declared that they were as opposed to "outside agitators" as Bull Connor—indeed, one Birmingham Jewish organization issued a public statement demanding not only that Martin Luther King stay away but that the Anti-Defamation League stay out of Birmingham.

Birmingham is also famous as the place where Martin Luther King composed his best-known written work, "Letter From a Birmingham Jail." It wasn't King's idea. Harvey Shapiro, an editor at *The New York Times Magazine*, suggested that King write a "letter from prison" for the magazine. The missive that King wrote turned out to be a classic, "the most eloquent treatment of the nexus between law and injustice since Thoreau's essay 'Civil Disobedience.'" But when King submitted his piece, the *Times* editors rejected it. It wasn't printed for another two months, and then in *The Atlantic Monthly*.

The Martin Luther King who appears in McWhorter's account is not very heroic. His claim that "unearned suffering is redemptive," made at the March on Washington earlier that year, seemed irresponsible to more and more blacks, ranging from SNCC militants to ordinary Birmingham blacks. In King's first statement after the bombing, he asked, "Who murdered those four girls?" and answered, "The apathy and complacency of many Negroes who will sit down on their stools and do nothing and not engage in creative protest to get rid of this evil." Carole Robertson's mother had not participated in the demonstrations; she was so outraged at King blaming her for her daughter's murder that she refused to join the three other families in a mass funeral for the girls.

At the other end of the spectrum in black Birmingham were the men who saw the events as providing "a chance to kill us a cracker." The Movement's insistence that marchers take a pledge of nonviolence was based on leaders' knowledge of the deep rage that black men in particular bore for whites. "At mass meetings, King began passing around a box for people to deposit razors, knives, ice picks, and pistols, and salted his inspirational calls to dignity with reminders that being black did not in itself constitute a virtue." People need courage and hope before they could take the pledge of nonviolence.

McWhorter's panoramic cast includes blacks on the wrong side of the Movement. "Rat Killer" ran the 17th Street Shine Parlor, a popular after-hours spot where visiting stars like Jackie Wilson, Sam Cooke and the Temptations hung out, and where Movement preachers got their shoes shined. But Rat Killer was "Bull Connor's right-hand man" in the black community—he traded information for informal permission to sell bootleg liquor and do some pimping.

McWhorter weaves her personal story throughout the book, and these sections provide uniquely rich and revealing evidence of the blindness of middle-class whites in this era. The book opens at Birmingham's elite white country club on a Sunday, when McWhorter was having brunch as usual with her family. It turns out to have been the morning the church was bombed. McWhorter was a year younger than the youngest of the four girls killed. Although the bombing marked a turning point in the nation's history, her family took little note of it. She doesn't remember it at all, and her mother's diary entry for that day says only that Diane's rehearsal for the community theater production of *The Music Man* was cancelled—not in mourning over the deaths but because whites feared that black people would riot.

The police dogs that horrified the world were well-known to McWhorter. Before the historic day they attacked the demonstrators, the police brought one of the dogs to an assembly at her school to demonstrate its crime-fighting abilities. McWhorter was so excited by the event that she changed her career goal to police-dog handler (she had planned to become an Olympic equestrian).

At the end of the book, McWhorter finally confronts her father on tape. He says he's told friends his daughter is writing a book about "the nigger movement," but says he wasn't in the Klan and was never involved in murdering anyone. She concludes he was a camp follower but not much of an activist.

The rest of the key figures in the story are mostly dead now: Bull Connor died in 1973; Robert Chambliss, until Blanton the only man convicted in the bombing (in a 1977 trial brought by then–Alabama Attorney General Baxley), died in 1985 while serving his prison term. (Baxley ran for governor in 1978 and lost.) The FBI's Klan informant, Gary Thomas Rowe, admitted that he and three Klan members shot and killed Viola Liuzzo on the 1965 Selma-to-Montgomery march; the killers were acquitted of murder (but not of violating her civil rights), and Rowe went into the witness protection program after the trial and died in 1998. The other Klan bombers died too, until the only ones left seemed to be Bobby Frank Cherry and Tommy Blanton.

Chambliss's 1977 trial exploded back to life early this May with Baxley's *New York Times* Op-Ed. He wrote that he had "requested, demanded and begged the FBI for evidence" from 1971 through 1977; that his office was "repeatedly stonewalled"; that the bureau practiced "deception," the result of which was that Blanton went "free for 24 years" while the FBI had "smoking gun evidence hidden in its files." He concluded by describing "the disgust" he felt over the FBI's conduct. No state attorney general has ever spoken so forcefully in criticizing the bureau.

Now Blanton has been convicted, but virtually all the other Southern white men who killed blacks during the heyday of the civil rights movement have gone unpunished. In the end the Klan bombers may not be the biggest villains in this story. It's the city and state officials, including the police and the FBI, who tolerated and sometimes encouraged racist violence, and the Kennedy brothers, who didn't want to do anything about it until they were forced to. Diane McWhorter started writing about "growing up on the wrong side of the civil rights revolution"; she ended up with the most important book on the movement since Taylor Branch's *Parting the Waters*. It should become a classic.

15

THE BANALITY OF "ETHNIC WAR"

John Mueller

On December 7, 1941, as it is commonly put, "the Japanese" attacked Pearl Harbor. No one of course takes this expression literally to suggest that the entire population of Japan, or even a major portion of it, directly participated in the assault. Rather it is understood to mean that some of Japan's military forces, ordered into action by Japan's government and perhaps supported to varying degrees by the Japanese population, launched the attack. In discussions of ethnic war, by contrast, such distinctions are often missing. When we say "the Serbs" and "the Croats" are engaged in ethnic war, the implication frequently is that those two groups have descended into a sort of Hobbesian war of all against all and neighbor against neighbor.

In this article I assess the violence that took place in the former Yugoslavia and in Rwanda in the 1990s and argue that the whole concept of "ethnic warfare" may be severely misguided. Specifically, insofar as it is taken to imply a war of all against all and neighbor against neighbor—a condition in which pretty much everyone in one ethnic group becomes the ardent, dedicated, and murderous enemy of everyone in another group—ethnic war essentially does not exist. I argue instead that ethnic warfare more closely resembles nonethnic warfare, because it is waged by small groups of combatants, groups that purport to fight and kill in the name of some larger entity. Often, in fact, "ethnic war" is substantially a condition in which a mass of essentially mild, ordinary people can unwillingly and in considerable bewilderment come under the vicious and arbitrary control of small groups of armed thugs.

I consider first the violent conflicts in Croatia and Bosnia. These were spawned not so much by the convulsive surging of ancient hatreds or by frenzies whipped up by dem-agogic politicians and the media as by the ministrations of small—sometimes very small—bands of opportunistic marauders recruited by political leaders and operating under their general guidance. Many of these participants were drawn from street gangs or from bands of soccer hooligans. Others were criminals specifically released from prison for the purpose. Their participation was required because the Yugolsav army, despite years of supposedly influential nationalist propaganda and centuries of supposedly pent-up ethnic hatreds, substantially disintegrated early in the war and refused to fight.

133

A group of well-armed thugs and bullies encouraged by, and working under rough constraints set out by, official security services would arrive or band together in a community. Sometimes operating with local authorities, they would then take control and persecute members of other ethnic groups, who would usually flee to areas protected by their own ethnic ruffians, sometimes to join them in seeking revenge. Carnivals of often-drunken looting, destruction, and violence would take place, and others—guiltily or not so guiltily—might join in. Gradually, however, many of the people under the thugs' arbitrary and chaotic "protection," especially the more moderate ones and young men unwilling to be pressed into military service, would emigrate to safer places. In all this, nationalism was not so much the impelling force as simply the characteristic around which the marauders happened to have arrayed themselves.

To explore the possibilities for generalizing from the Yugoslav experience, I assess very briefly the extreme case of Rwanda in 1994, when ethnic Hutus engaged in genocidal massacres of ethnic Tutsis. In recent history this is probably the instance in which the Hobbesian all-against-all and neighbor-against-neighbor idea of ethnic warfare is most likely to hold. Nevertheless, even in this case, it seems clear that the main momentum of the killings was carried by a relatively small number of specially trained Hutus who, allying themselves with often-drunken criminal and hooligan opportunists, went on a murderous rampage coordinated by local officials acting on orders from above. By contrast, the vast majority of Hutus seem to have stood by in considerable confusion and, often, indifference.

The mechanism of violence in the former Yugoslavia and in Rwanda, then, is remarkably banal. Rather than reflecting deep, historic passions and hatreds, the violence seems to have been the result of a situation in which common, opportunistic, sadistic, and often distinctly nonideological marauders were recruited and permitted free rein by political authorities. Because such people are found in all societies, the events in Yugoslavia and Rwanda are not peculiar to those locales, but could happen almost anywhere under the appropriate conditions. On the other hand, there was nothing particularly inevitable about the violence: with different people in charge and with different policing and accommodation procedures, the savagery could have been avoided.

Because the violence in Yugoslavia and Rwanda was carried out chiefly by small, ill-disciplined, and essentially cowardly bands of thugs and bullies, policing the situation would probably have been fairly easy for almost any organized, disciplined, and sizable army. An extreme aversion to casualties and a misguided assumption that the conflicts stemmed from immutable ethnic hatreds, however, made international military intervention essentially impossible until the violence appeared to have run its course.[1]

ETHNIC WARFARE IN CROATIA AND BOSNIA

Two explanation are commonly given for the wars in the former Yugoslavia. One is that elemental and ancient ethnic hatreds had only temporarily and superficially been kept in check by communism and that with its demise, murderous nationalism erupted. This perspective has been developed most famously and influentially by Robert Kaplan, who described the Balkans as "a region of pure memory" where "each individual sensation and memory affects the grand movement of clashing peoples," and where the processes of history and memory were "kept on hold" by communism for forty-five years, "thereby creating a kind of multiplier effect for violence."[2] The other explanation holds that the violence was a reaction to continuous nationalist propaganda spewed out by politicians and the media, particularly on Serbian television, that played on old fears and hatreds. As a Belgrade journalist put it to an American audience, "You must imagine a United States with every little television station everywhere taking exactly the same editorial line—a line dictated by David Duke. You too would have war in five years."[3]

THE SHALLOWNESS OF MILITANT NATIONALISM IN YUGOSLAVIA

Actually, support for militant nationalism in Yugoslavia was not all that deep even at the time of its maximum notice and effect in the early 1990s. The rise of some militant nationalists in elections during that period stemmed less from their wide appeal and more from their ability to manipulate the system and from the disarray of their opposition. In their key victories in 1990, Franjo Tudjman's nationalists in Croatia massively outspent the poorly organized opposition, using funds contributed by well-heeled militants in the Croatian diaspora—particularly in North America. And their success was vastly exaggerated by an electoral system, foolishly designed by the outgoing communists, that handed Tudjman's party 69 percent of the seats with only 42 percent of the vote. In the same election, less than a quarter of Serbs in Croatia voted for their nationalist party. The same sort of distortions, though to a lesser degree, took place in the elections in Bosnia. In early elections in Serbia, Slobodan Milošević controlled the media and essentially bought the vote by illegally using public funds—hardly a sign of enormous public appeal, and an act that was foolhardy as well because it greatly accelerated the breakup of the country. Moreover, like Tudjman's party, Milošević's party was comparatively well organized and widely based and had an enormous advantage under the election rules. Although it garnered less than half the vote, it gained 78 percent of the seats. Milošević's fortunes were further enhanced because Kosovo Albanians boycotted the election, allowing his party to win that area.[4]

A poll conducted throughout Yugoslavia in the summer and autumn of 1990, even as nationalists were apparently triumphing in elections, more accurately indicates the state of opinion after centuries of supposed ethnic hatreds and after years of nationalist propaganda. The question, "Do you agree that every (Yugoslav) nation should have a national state of its own?" elicited the following responses: completely agree, 16 percent; agree to some extent, 7 percent; undecided, 10 percent; do not agree in part, 6 percent; and do not agree at all, 61 percent.[5]

At times, particularly in Serbia during the rise of Milošević, militant nationalists were able to orchestrate huge public demonstrations, which have often been taken to suggest their popular appeal. But in general it is unwise to take large, noisy crowds, which clearly are heavily self-selected, as representing public opinion more generally.[6] Moreover, much of the crowd behavior in Yugoslavia in the early 1990s was manipulated—Milošević's party often paid mobs with free food, transportation, and liquor.[7] And if crowd behavior is to be taken as indicative of wider attitudes, it should be pointed out that even the poorly organized opposition was able to mount massive demonstrations in 1991 and 1992 in Zagreb, Belgrade, and Sarajevo.[8]

Finally, the casual notion that each ethnic or national group in Yugoslavia (or indeed anywhere) is united by deep bonds of affection is substantially flawed. Serbs in Serbia have expressed little affection for the desperate and often rough rural Serbs who have fled to their country from war-torn Croatia and Bosnia.[9] Indeed, as Christopher Bennett argues, in profound contrast with Kaplan, after World War II the "great divide" within Yugoslav society was increasingly that between rural and urban communities, not that between peoples."[10]

ARMED THUGS AND THE BANALITY OF "ETHNIC WARFARE" IN YUGOSLAVIA

The violence that erupted in Yugoslavia principally derived not from a frenzy of nationalism—whether ancient or newly inspired—but rather from the actions of recently empowered and unpoliced thugs. Politicians may have started the wars, and they may have whipped up a fair amount of hatred. But the effective murderous core of the wars were not hordes composed of ordinary citizens ripped loose from their repression or incited into violence against their neighbors. Rather the politicians found it necessary to recruit thugs and hooligans for the job.

Significantly, the Serbian (or Yugoslav) army substantially disintegrated early in the hostilities. There may well have been hatreds, and there surely was propaganda. But when ordinary Serb soldiers were given an opportunity to express these presumed proclivities or to act in response to the ingenious televised imprecations in government-sanctioned violence, they professed they did not know why they were fighting and often mutinied or deserted en masse.[11] Meanwhile, back in Serbia young men reacted mainly by determined draft-dodging. Some 150,000 or more quickly emigrated or went underground. In one city, only two of the 2,000–3,000 "volunteers" expected in a call-up showed up, and in several towns there were virtual mutinies against conscription. Overall, only 50 percent of Serbian reservists and only 15 percent in Belgrade obeyed orders to report for duty.[12]

Because Serbs from Serbia proper were unwilling to fight outside their own republic, Belgrade had to reshape its approach to the wars in Croatia and Bosnia in major ways. As a Serbian general put it, modification of Belgrade's military plans was made necessary by "the lack of success in mobilisation and the desertion rate."[13] Part of the solution involved arming the locals, particularly in Serb areas of Croatia and Bosnia.[14] But in general the fighting quality of the militaries, especially initially, was very poor:

There was a lack of discipline, ineffective command and control, and, especially in the case of the Serbs, a reluctance to take casualties. Such deficiencies, as Steven Burg and Paul Shoup observe, "led all sides to reply on irregulars and special units."[15]

The appearance in the wars of the paramilitaries was caused in part by the collapse of the army morale, but their presence may also have helped to aggravate that collapse. An internal Yugoslav army memo from early in the conflict found them to be dangerous to "military morale" because their "primary motive was not fighting against the enemy but robbery of private property and inhuman treatment of Croatian civilians."[16]

The most dynamic (and murderous) Serbian units were notably composed not of committed nationalists or ideologues, nor of locals out to get their neighbors, nor of ordinary people whipped into a frenzy by demagogues and the media, but rather of common criminals recruited for the task. Specifically, the politicians urged underworld and hooligan groups to get into the action, and it appears that thousands of prison inmates, promised shortened sentences and enticed by the prospect that they could "take whatever booty you can," were released for the war effort.[17] Thus, to a substantial degree the collapse of the army led to a privatization of the war, and loot comprised the chief form of payment. The releasees, together with other criminals and like-minded recruits, generally worked independently, improvising their tactics as they went along. However, there does seem to have been a fair amount of coordination in Serb areas mainly by Milošević's secret police. The army, such as it was, enforced an overall framework of order and sometimes directly participated in the deprivations as well.[18]

Some of the thugs and hooligans joined and bolstered what remained of the Yugoslav army. According to Miloš Vasib, a leading Serb journalist, however, "they behaved in a wholly unsoldierly way, wearing all sorts of Serb chauvinist insignia, beards, and knives, were often drunk (like many of the regular soldiers, too), looted, and killed or harassed civilians. Officers rarely dared discipline them."[19]

Others joined semicoherent paramilitary groups like Vojislav Šešelj's Chetniks[20] and Arkan's Tigers, organizations already heavily composed of criminals, adventurers, mercenary opportunists, and, in the case of the Tigers, soccer hooligans. Arkan (Zeljko Raznjatovib) had been the leader of Delije, the official fan club of Belgrade's Red Star soccer team, which, not unlike other soccer clubs, had become a magnet for hoodlums and unemployable young men; the Tigers seem to have been built from that membership.[21] Arkan's forces seem to have functioned essentially as mercenaries: As one Bosnian Serb government official put it, "He is very expensive, but also very efficient."[22]

Still others seem to have gone off on their own, serving as warlords in the areas they came to dominate. These independent or semi-independent para-military and warlord units, estimates Vasib, "consisted on average of 80 per cent common criminals and 20 per cent fanatical nationalists. The latter did not usually last long (fanaticism is bad for business)."[23] There were also many "weekend warriors," men who joined the war from Serbia and elsewhere only intermittently and then mainly to rob and pillage, enriching themselves in the process.[24] Similarly, the initial fighting forces of Bosnia and of Croatia were also substantially made up of small bands of criminals and violent opportunists recruited or self-recruited from street gangs and organized mobs.[25]

Arkan began as a juvenile delinquent and later developed into a skilled bank robber, plying his trade mostly in northern Europe (dashingly, he often left the tellers bouquets of roses). He also became a prison breakout artist, escaping from jails in Belgium, the Netherlands, and Germany. Returning to Belgrade, the fugitive became a respected member of the criminal underground, enjoyed a special relationship with the police and with the internal affairs ministry, and ran a successful ice cream and pastry shop.[26] Another Serb paramilitary leader, who called himself "Captain Dragan," had reportedly been a pimp in the Sydney underworld (working in the Knin area, his men were known as "Knindjas" after the cartoon characters).[27] For their part, the Muslims were protected by Celo, a convicted rapist, and by Juka, a former mob boss, racketeer, and underworld thug.[28] And the Croats had Tuta, a former protection racketeer, the mere mention of whose name could "cause an entire village to panic."[29]

As Warren Zimmermann observes, "the dregs of society—embezzlers, thugs, even professional killers—rose from the slime to become freedom fighters and national heroes." Robert Block notes that "gangsters, outlaws, and criminals have had a special place in the war in the former Yugoslavia. Their skills in organizing people and their ruthlessness made them natural choices for Balkan rabble-rousers looking for men to defend cities or serve as nationalist shock troops." And David Rieff points out that "one of the earliest, deepest, and most pervasive effects of the fighting" was "to turn the social pyramid on its head. . . . Simple boys from the countryside and tough kids from the towns found that their guns made them the ones who could start amassing the Deutschemarks and the privileges, sexual and otherwise."[30]

There was also Rambo-like affectation: Each fighter dressed as if "he had been cast as a thug by a movie director," observes Block. Indeed, one Serbian paramilitary unit called itself "the Rambos" and went around in webbed masks and black gloves with black ribbons fetchingly tied around their foreheads.[31] Naser Orib, a muscular and charismatic former bodyguard who became the Muslim warlord of Srebrenica, and, until 1995, its protector, liked to wear leather jackets, designer sunglasses, and thick gold chains. Members of the Muslim paramilitary group the "Black Swans," which sometimes served as the bodyguard for Bosnia's president when he ventured outside Sarajevo, wore a round patch depicting a black swan having intercourse with a supine woman.[32]

Thus, as Susan Woodward notes, "paramilitary gangs, foreign mercenaries, and convicted criminals roamed the territory under ever less civil control." And "war crimes," observes Norman Cigar, were their "primary military mission."[33] Vladan Vasilijevib, an expert on organized crime, says that most of the well-documented atrocities in Bosnia were committed by men with long criminal records. And a United Nations (UN) commission notes a "strong correlation" between paramilitary activity and preports of killing of civilians, rape, torture, destruction of property, looting, detention facilities, and mass graves.[34]

THE STAGES OF WAR AND ETHNIC CLEANSING

What passed for "ethnic warfare" in Bosnia and Croatia thus seems to have been something far more banal: the creation of communities of criminal violence and pillage.[35] In the end, the wars rather resembled the movie images of the American Wild West or of gangland Chicago, and often had far less to do with nationalism than with criminal opportunism and sadistic cruelty, often enhanced with liquor—liquid courage. There seem to have been four stages to the process: takeover, carnival, revenge, and occupation and desertion.

TAKEOVER. Recruited and encouraged by leading politicians, and operating under a general framework of order provided by the army, a group of well-armed thugs—or skinhead or redneck or soccer hooligan or Hell's Angels types—would emerge in an area where the former civil order had ceased to exist or where the police actually or effectively were in alliance with them. As the only group willing—indeed, sometimes eager—to use force, they would quickly take control. Members of other ethnic groups would be subject to violent intimidation at best, atrocities at worst, and they would leave the area in despair. Because there was no coherent or unbiased police force to protect these victims, their best recourse was to flee, and it would not take much persuasion to get them to do so—indeed, rumors or implied threats could often be sufficient. Once the forces of Arkan and Šešelj had established their murderous reputations, for example, the mere warning that they were on their way was often enough to empty a village of its non-Serb residents.[36]

Any co-ethnics who might oppose the thugs' behavior would be subject to even more focused violence and would either be forced out, killed, or cowed into submission. One unusually candid Croatian ex-militiaman recalled that his unit had killed mostly Serb civilians but also unsympathetic Croats.[37] And a UN report notes, "In places where the local Serb population was initially fairly friendly, once Arkan's thugs arrived the situation changed, and they were intimidated into ostracizing the Muslims and behaving toward them with hostility."[38]

In many cases, the dominating forces could be remarkably small. The Bosnian town of Višegrad on the Drina River, for example, was substantially controlled for years by a returned hometown boy, Milan Lukib, and some fifteen well-armed companions including his brother, a cousin, and a local waiter who often went barefoot. Using violent and often sadistic intimidation, this tiny band forced the 14,500 Muslims in the town to leave and suppressed any expressions of dissent from local Serbs—many of whom took advantage of the situation to profit from the Muslim exodus.[39] Then there is the town of Teslib, controlled, it is estimated, by "five or six men, well placed and willing to use violence."[40] The violence that in 1992 tore apart Srebrenica, a town of 37,000 people, was perpetrated by no more than thirty Serb and Muslim extremists. Orib, the Muslim warlord who controlled Srebrenica for several years (and who was mysteriously absent with his gang when Serb forces overran the town in 1995), led an armed band with a nucleus of only fifteen men.[41] Arkan's much-feared forces consisted of a core of 200 men and perhaps totaled no more than 500–1,000.[42]

The most common emotion among ordinary people caught up in this cyclone of violence and pillage seems to have been bewilderment rather than rage. Working with Muslim refugees early in the Bosnia war, Cheryl Benard found them "to be totally at a loss to explain how the hostility of the Serbs was possible. All of them, without exception, say they lived and worked with and were close friends with Serbs." Far from seeing the violence as the delayed eruption of ancient hatreds and as evidence of the strength of ethnic ties, Benard suggests that "one could argue that Bosnia shows how weak and how fluid political identity really is."[43]

CARNIVAL. The thugs often exercised absolute power in their small fiefdoms and lorded it over their new subjects. Carnivals of looting and destruction would take place, as would orgies of rape, arbitrary violence and murder, and roaring drunkenness; pay often came in the form of alcohol and cigarettes.[44]

Sadists may make up a small percentage in any population, but in these circumstances, they rose to the occasion and reveled in it. In a number of places, notes Tim Judah, "real psychopaths were rampaging across the countryside indulging in cruel, bizarre, and sadistic killings." Peter Maass reports "an odd enthusiasm on the part of the torturers, who laughed, sang, and got drunk while inflicting their crimes. They weren't just doing a job, they were doing something they enjoyed," and "there were plenty of Serbs who enjoyed killing civilians and eagerly sought the opportunity to do so. . . . These killers never had so much fun."[45]

In the words of a UN official, in this unrestrained new world run by "gunslingers, thugs, and essentially criminals," others might opportunistically join the carnivals and orgies. After all, if the property of a local Muslim is going to be looted and set afire (like the store of a local Korean during the Los Angeles riots of 1992), it may seem sensible to some—even rational—to join the thieves: No high-minded moral restraint about such vulture-like behavior will do the departed owner any good. Additionally, various adventurers, mercenaries, and revenge-seekers—often belonging to the police—might join in. And so might some of those (particularly teenagers) who find excitement, comradeship, clarity, and theatricality—not to mention material profit—in war and in its terrifying, awesome destructiveness.[46] In the process, many ordinary residents might become compromised, sometimes willingly. For example, one Bosnia Serb policeman used his position, Schindler-like, to save the lives of several Muslims, but under the extraordinary conditions of the time, he also probably raped two or more of them—in at least one instance after proposing marriage.[47]

REVENGE. Some among the brutalized might wish to fight—and to seek revenge against—their persecutors. In general, they found that they were best advised not to try to improvise local resistance, but rather to flee with their fellow ethnics and then to join like-minded armed bands in more hospitable parts of the country. Thus the special Muslim unit, Black Swans, was supposedly made up of volunteers aged twenty to twenty-two who had been orphaned by the war. And the Muslims' "elite" Seventeenth Krajina brigade was labeled "the angry arm of the dispossessed," though questions have been raised about how adequately it actually fought.[48]

Members of each group would quickly find, sometimes to their helpless disgust, that their thugs at least were willing to fight to protect them from the murderous thugs on the other side. Often the choice was essentially one of being dominated by vicious bigots of one's own ethnic group or by vicious bigots of another ethnic group: Given that range of alternatives, the choice was easy.

OCCUPATION AND DESERTION. Life in areas controlled by the thugs could be miserable, as the masters argued among themselves and looked for further prey among those remaining, whatever their ethnic background.[49] As Rieff observes, the involvement of gangsters on all sides meant that the "political aims of the war became hopelessly intertwined on a day-to-day level with profiteering and black market activities."[50]

Corruption and nepotism in the Serb areas of Croatia and Bosnia, including the Bosnian Serb capital of Pale, were so endemic that the war effort was substantially harmed.[51] Meanwhile, in the Muslim enclave of Srebreanica, men loyal to Orib controlled the few jobs in town, lived in the larger houses, and had more food than others. They prospered by exaggerating the population size in order to get excess humanitarian aid, and then hoarding it to drive up prices before selling it on the black market at a killing. When three opponents to this feudal arrangement come forward, they were ambushed and, in one case, killed. Because the refugees were essentially being used as human shields to protect the property and income of Orib and his men, Muslims were not allowed to leave, yet little effort was made to improve the lives of the people, especially the refugees, unless it brought personal profit to the ruling gang.[52]

In war-torn Sarajevo, Juka's men, who had defended the city from the Serbs in 1992, soon began plaguing the defended without regard to ethnicity. They stole automobiles; extorted money and valuables; abducted, abused, and raped civilians; and looted the city's warehouses and shops, making off with 20,000 pairs of shoes in one venture. In addition, they monopolized the black market that made up the city's only trade, earning fortunes in a city where many people spent their days scavenging for water and bread.[53]

Gradually, many of the people under the thugs' arbitrary and chaotic "protection," especially the more moderate ones and young men unwilling to be impressed, would manage to emigrate to a safer place. And in time the size of the "protected" group would be substantially reduced—by half or more.[54] The remnants ever more disproportionately consisted of fanatics, economic marauders, militant radicals, common criminals, opportunistic sycophants, embittered revenge-seekers, and murderous drunks.[55]

Those in the right positions quickly discovered a lucrative opportunity to trade with the enemy, and hundreds of millions of Deutschemarks' worth of weaponry, ammunition, fuel, and goods were exchanged across the front lines. The Serbs in Bosnia, after all, enjoyed a major military advantage in that, because of the deft manipulations of Milošević and crew early in the war, they inherited masses of weaponry from the Yugoslav national army. Once the war settled down a bit, many of the Serb leaders in Bosnia went looking for buyers and found them nearby: the Croats and the Muslims were eager for weapons with which to attack the Serbs in Croatia and Bosnia (and, for a time, each other). There were opportunities in the other direction as well; the speaker of the Bosnian Serb assembly, for example, made millions buying fuel from Croatia and then selling it to Croatia's Serb enemies in Bosnia. One senior Serbian commander in Bosnia sold a Muslim village some heavy artillery and then retired with his family to Serbia. Croats could sometimes rent tanks from the Serbs at a going rate of DM 1,000 per day.[56] Whether they had to pay extra for insurance is not recorded.

The relationship of such banal behavior to "nationalism" and "ethnic hatred," ancient or otherwise, is less than clear as is its bearing on the notion of "clashing civilizations." Its relation to common criminality, however, is evident.[57]

A COMPARISON: RWANDA

I have stressed the importance of vicious and opportunistic, but often substantial nonideological, criminals and criminal-like elements in the development of the wars in Croatia and Bosnia. This approach seems much sounder than ones that seek to explain the wars as conflicts in which murderous communal rage, exploding from pent-up ancient hatreds or the cynical manipulation of malevolent, shortsighted politicians, induces a Hobbesian conflict of all against all and neighbor against neighbor. There are doubtless instances, however, in which the Hobbesian vision comes closer to being realized. The 1994 genocide inflicted by ethnic Hutus against Tutsis in Rwanda may be a case in point. Closer examination, however, suggests a number of similarities with the wars in Croatia and Bosnia.

Much of the writing about the genocide, in which some 500,000 to 800,000 perished in a matter of weeks—mostly by being hacked to death with machetes or hoes—gives the impression that the conflict was one of all against all, friends against friends, neighbors against neighbors, even Cain against Abel. Friends and neighbors (and even brothers perhaps) did kill each other, but it seems that by far the greatest damage, as in Croatia and Bosnia, resulted from the rampages of murderous thugs.

Far from a spontaneous eruption, the basic elements of the genocidal process had been planned for years by Hutu extremists who were substantially in charge of the ruling party, the government bureaucracy, and the police.[58] Throughout the country Hutus and Hutu police were urged—or ordered—to engage in killing, and many do seem to have responded enthusiastically. Joining was the Presidential Guard, numbering 700–1,500 men, and the Hutu army, which consisted of some 50,000 men, most of them hastily recruited in the previous few years from landless peasants, the urban unemployed, and foreign drifters who had chiefly signed up not for ideological reasons, but rather for the guaranteed food and drink (each man was entitled to two bottles of beer a day, a luxury by Rwandan standards) and for the opportunity to loot, because pay was low and irregular.[59]

Finally, there was the Interahamwe, militia bands that had been created and trained by Hutu extremists. As Philip Gourevitch points out, the Interahamwe had its genesis in soccer fan clubs, and it recruited jobless young men who were "wasting in idleness and its attendant resentments," and who tended to see the genocide as a "carnival romp."[60] Moreover, their ranks were expanded by hordes of opportunists once the genocide began. Gérard Prunier notes that a "social aspect of the killings has often been overlooked": As soon as the killing groups "went into action, they drew around them a cloud of even poorer people, a *lumpenproletariat* of street boys, rag-pickers, car-washers, and homeless unemployed. For these people the genocide was the best thing that could ever happen to them. They had the blessings of a form of authority to take revenge on socially powerful people as long as these were on the wrong side of the political fence. They could steal, they could kill with minimum justification, they could rape, and they could get drunk for free. This was wonderful. The political aims pursued by the masters of this dark carnival were quite beyond their scope. They just went along."[61] "Drunken militia bands," notes Gourevitch, "fortified with assorted drugs from ransacked pharmacies, were bused from massacre to massacre."[62] There were about 1,700 "professional Interahamwe" who received training and uniforms, and thousands or tens of thousands joined up (sometimes under coercion) after the genocide began.[63]

As in Yugoslavia, criminals were released from jail to participate in the destruction,[64] and the prospect for enrichment by looting was vastly escalated during the genocide and was used as a specific incentive by the leaders—many of whom were happy to take booty as well.[65] The killers were fully willing to murder fellow Hutus suspected of not being loyal to the cause, and they often forced other Hutus, on pain of instant death, to join the killings.[66] Others participated by manning roadblocks or by pointing out local Tutsis to the marauding *génocidaires*. "I didn't have a choice," one cooperating priest pointed out. "It was necessary to appear pro-militia. If I had had a different attitude, we would all have disappeared."[67]

Many Hutus, however, did hide and protect Tutsi neighbors and sometimes strangers despite the pressure, and despite the fact that the punishment for such behavior could be instant, brutal death.[68] The number of Hutus who did so probably was as high as the number who, under pressure from the often-drunken and always-murderous *génocidaires,* indicated where some Tutsis might reside or be hiding.[69] Most of the others, it appears, simply withdrew whether in approval or disapproval of the cataclysm surrounding them: "We closed the door and tried not to hear," said one.[70]

Although an extensive study by Human Rights Watch ventures no direct estimates, it does suggest at various points that the killers numbered in the "tens of thousands."[71] A study by African Rights in London amasses a detailed listing of those in the Hutu elite who directed the genocide and comes up with 600 or 700 names.[72] As indicated earlier, the Presidential Guard comprised some 700–1,500, the army perhaps 50,000, and the Interahamwe militias another 50,000. A year after defeating the genocidal regime, Tutsi forces had 33,000 people incarcerated under suspicion of participating in the genocide—a figure that later rose to at least 125,000.[73]

It may be reasonable to suggest from all this that there some 50,000 hard-core killers. This would easily be enough to have accomplished the genocide: If each of these people killed one person a week for the course of the 100 day holocaust, more than 700,000 would have perished. This number would represent some 2 percent of the male Hutu population over the age of thirteen. That is, 98 percent of the male Hutu population older than thirteen was not in this group.

It is possible that 200,000 participated in the massacres, though this is likely to be a rather high figure that would include people who, under pressure from the hard-core *génocidaires,* did nothing more than point out where local Tutsi lived or simply manned roadblocks under orders. This would still represent less than 9 percent of the Hutu male population over the age of thirteen. (Though by all accounts very much outnumbered by men and boys, women and girls did join in the genocide. In addition, boys younger than thirteen also often participated.[74] If these groups are added to the base, the percentages would be much lower.)

In some sense, of course, these are astoundingly high figures. In a normal year, by comparison, the proportion of males older than thirteen who committed murder in Rwanda was probably something like 1 in 2,000. Nonetheless, a situation in which more than 90 percent of the over-thirteen male Hutu population did not participate in killings hardly seems to justify the notion that the situation was one of all against all or neighbor against neighbor. As in Croatia and Bosnia, the chief dynamic of the depredations seems to have been furnished by marauding bands of violent, opportunistic, and often drunken thugs.

CONCLUSIONS

That analysis of the experiences in the former Yugoslavia and Rwanda suggests that ethnicity is important in "ethnic wars" more as an ordering device than as an impelling force; that the violence would probably have been fairly easy to police; that the wars did not necessarily derive from the ethnic peculiarities of those regions; and that the wars were by no means inevitable. In addition, some of the wars' key dynamics may have considerable applicability to other violent conflicts.

ETHNICITY IS IMPORTANT ONLY AS AN ORDERING DEVICE

Michael Ignatieff compares the conditions that prevailed in the former Yugoslavia to a Hobbesian state of nature.[75] But the experience in Yugoslavia and in Rwanda calls this image into question. People did not descend into the war of "every man against every man" that Hobbes so vividly depicted and so ardently abhorred. What happened in Croatia, Bosnia, and Rwanda did resemble a Hobbesian state of nature, but it came about not because people generally gave into murderous enmity, but because they came under the arbitrary control of armed thugs. Ethnicity proved essentially to be simply the characteristic around which the perpetrators and the politicians who recruited and encouraged them happened to array themselves. It was important as an ordering device or principle, not as a crucial motivating force.

The same sort of dynamic could hold if the thugs' organizational principle were class or ideological allegiance or even handedness or loyalty to a specific soccer team. If they took control in a town determined to cleanse it violently of, say, left-handers or of supporters of an opposing team, those in that group would quickly find it in their interest to leave. Meanwhile right-handers or fans of the thug-favored team would, often reluctantly, come to recognize that the thugs had become their only protection against revenge-seeking thugs of another group. And as they hunkered down behind their protecting thugs, or as they sought gradually to flee the war zone, members of each group would probably reflect in bewilderment from time to time that before the thugs came, they often did not even know the handedness or the soccer loyalties of their friends, neighbors, and schoolmates. Under such conditions, identity, as Chaim Kaufmann notes, "is often imposed by the opposing group, specifically by its most murderous members."[76]

None of this is to argue that no neighbor ever persecuted a neighbor in these conflicts. Some locals did join in the process, sometimes out of ethnic loyalty, sometimes to settle old scores, most often, it seems, opportunistically to pursue profit in the chaos. In many cases, the war conditions did bring out the worst in some people, and victims did sometimes know their victimizers—though this is something that happens in most civil wars, not just ethnic ones. And, of course, once the thugs took over, former cross-ethnic relationships were often warily broken off because the thugs were likely to punish such sympathies. The crucial dynamic of the wars, however, was not in the risings of neighbor against neighbor, but in the marauding of comparatively small groups of thugs recruited and semicoordinated by politicians.

INTERNATIONAL POLICING COULD PROBABLY HAVE BEEN EFFECTIVE

Hobbes's greatest mischief comes from his solution to the problem he invents. He assumes that *every* person is, at base, "radically insecure, mistrustful of other men, and afraid for his life." Therefore the only way out of the mess is for everyone permanently to surrender to an authoritarian ruler, one who primarily values glory and stability over doctrinal orthodoxy or ideological purity, and one who will maintain the necessary force to keep all people from once again giving in to their natural proclivities for isolation, hostility, and insensitivity to the rights of others.[77]

But the experience in the former Yugoslav and Rwanda suggests that this monumental—perhaps even impossible—task is hardly required. Most people most of the time do not have much difficulty getting along and creating useful rules and patterns of conduct that allow them to coexist peacefully.[78] Police may be needed, even necessary, to maintain order, but they need not normally be numerous. Nor does their control need to be Leviathan-like, because they mainly need simply to protect the many from the few, rather than everyone from everyone else as Hobbes would have it.

It follows that policing the situation in Yugoslavia and in Rwanda would not have been the major challenge often anticipated. Essentially, the intimidating, opportunistic thugs were successful mainly because they were the biggest bullies on the block. But, like most bullies (and sadists and torturers), they substantially lacked organization, discipline, coherent tactics or strategy, deep motivation, broad popular support, ideological commitment, and essentially, courage.[79] Consequently, if confronted by a military force with these qualities, their most likely reaction would be to flee. And, to a considerable degree, this seems to be what happened both in Yugoslavia and in Rwanda.

While Serbe forces remained criminal-dominated, their opponents began to develop real armies. Unprepared and badly outgunned at the beginning, independent Croatia, despite an international arms embargo, gradually built up and trained a conventional military force using Western advisers.[80] And an important step in buildings *its* army was the Bosnian government's risky but successful military operation in October 1993 to destroy the criminal gangs in Sarajevo that had helped defend the capital in the 1992 but that had then taken control in various areas of the city, terrorizing non-Muslims and Muslims alike.[81]

As early as January 1993, only a year after Serbs had effectively partitioned the country, the new Croatian army launched an attack on several important targets in Serb-held territory in Croatia and encountered little resistance.[82] In May 1995, it achieved the same success in another Croatian area, taking control in thirty-two hours. Then, over three or four days in August, using plans partly devised by retired American generals, the army pushed from most of the rest of Croatia the remaining Serb opposition, which for the most part followed the example of its erstwhile "protectors" and simply ran. As Marcus Tanner puts it, "As soon as the bombardment started the Serb troops fled the frontlines, provoking a panicked flight into Bosnia by thousands of civilians, who left their houses with washing on the lines and meals half eaten on kitchen tables." Similar results were soon achieved in neighboring Bosnia by organized Croat and Bosnian forces.[83]

As in Yugoslavia, the marauders in Rwanda were put down fairly easily when confronted with a reasonably coherent military force. Several thousand refugees were saved in a Kigali stadium because the United Nations Assistance Mission to Rwanda, which Prunier characterizes as "the powerless UN 'military' force," simply forbade the murder squads entry. And when the Tutsis eventually were able to get their comparatively capable army into the country, they had to battle for the capital city, but took over the rest of the country with a minimum of fighting. For the most part, Hutu authorities, like their counterparts in the former Yugoslavia, simply ordered their forces to flee when confronted with military force.[84]

Thus it seems likely that a large, impressively armed, and well-disciplined international policing force could have been effective in pacifying the thug-dominated conflicts in Yugoslavia and Rwanda. The approach could have resembled the technique used to suppress riots in U.S. cities or those successfully applied by the U.S. military in Haiti in the mid-1990s or by Australian and other international policing troops in East Timor in 1999. Well-armed and disciplined troops would occupy an area; the thugs would either flee or blend back into the population; and the troops would then gradually be reduced in number. The thugs would still exist of course, and many might remain in the area, as they do in U.S. cities. But, insofar as they remained unpacified, the thugs would be reduced to sporadic and improvised crime and violence, not town mastery.

There seem to be two reasons why such a force was never put together by concerned members of the international community. First, they assumed that the wars were essentially inexplicable Kaplanesque all-against-all conflicts, rooted in old hatreds that could hardly be ameliorated by well-meaning, but innocent and naïve, outsiders.[85] As the discussion above suggests, this explanation, so convenient to those favoring passivity, was substantially flawed. But, as Brian Hall observes, "Literary clichés do not die easily, especially when informed by superficialities."[86]

Second, the international community had, and has, an extremely low tolerance for casualties in peacekeeping ventures in which clear national interests do not appear to be at stake. The international mission to Somalia in 1993 saved many lives, but U.S. policy there is held to be a "failure" in large part because eighteen Americans were killed in the process. In essence, when Americans asked themselves how many American lives peace in Somalia was worth, the answer came out close to zero.[87] The general reluctance to become involved in the fighting in Bosnia (despite, incidentally, years of the supposedly action-impelling "CNN effect") suggests that Americans and others reached a similar conclusion for that trouble spot. By 1997, after Spain had suffered seventeen deaths policing the Bosnian conflict, it withdrew from further confrontation. Similarly, when ten of its policing troops were massacred and mutilated early in the Rwandan genocide, Belgium abruptly withdrew—and, to save face, urged others to do the same. It seems clear that policing efforts will be politically tolerable only as long as the cost in lives for the policing forces remain extremely low—and perhaps not even then.[88]

WHAT HAPPENED IN YUGOSLAVIA AND RWANDA COULD HAPPEN ANYWHERE

If my assessment is essentially correct, it suggests that what happened in Yugoslavia and Rwanda is not unique, but could happen just about anywhere. The Serbian writer Aleksandar Tisma has gloomily concluded from his country's tragedy that "there are civilized people and less civilized people. Here in the Balkans, people don't belong to the civilized but to the less civilized."[89] But the wars in Yugoslavia did not break out because the peoples there are "less civilized." When criminals and sadists are given free rein, they can easily debase the conditions of life.

And thugs are everywhere—at least in small numbers—and only small numbers are necessary if the conditions are ripe. England may seem rather tranquil and well ordered in many respects, but it is also the home of some of the world's most notorious soccer hooligans. Canada often seems to be a nation of eminently reasonable people, but that is not the conclusion one would draw from watching a hockey game. Denmark may today remind people mainly of Hans Christian Andersen and little mermaids, but it once was the home of world-class marauders, and it seems unlikely that that propensity has been fully bred out of the race in the intervening centuries.[90] Moreover, as various studies have suggested, it is often possible to get ordinary people to participate in acts of considerable cruelty when they are placed, voluntarily or involuntarily, in a supportive environment—ideological or ethnic hatred is by no means necessary for this capacity to emerge.[91] Under the right conditions, thugs can rise to a dominant role, others can lend a hand or withdraw into terrified isolation or studied indifference, and any place can degenerate into a Bosnia or a Rwanda.

WHAT HAPPENED IN YUGOSLAVIA AND RWANDA WAS NOT INEVITABLE

That catastrophes that engulfed Bosnia, Croatia, and Rwanda did not have to happen. They emerged not out of inevitable historic necessities, but were instigated and orchestrated by designing politicians and local extremists who, however, often did not know how to control the violent processes they had set into motion.

Yahya Sadowski finds that cultural strife is found about as much in developed countries as in poorer ones, but that such strife is less likely to turn violent in prosperous societies. From this he concludes that economic advancement tends to reduce cultural violence.[92] But it seems, rather, that the actions of leading politicians and police organizations are most important in keeping ethnic and cultural conflict from leading to major violence. Prosperous societies do seem to do better in this regard than poorer ones (which in fact is probably one of the reasons for their comparative prosperity). Prosperity may therefore be beneficial if it helps to develop competent governments and police forces, but wealth itself is not the key operative factor. Thus it is entirely possible to imagine Bosnian-like chaos in prosperous Quebec or Northern Ireland if the Canadian or British authorities had attempted to deal with cultural conflicts by encouraging murderous rampage rather than through patient policing and political accommodation.

On the other hand, because of sound political policies, ethnic violence has been avoided in Bulgaria and Romania even though those countries are hardly more developed than Serbia or Bosnia. And the experience in Macedonia, where political leaders have sought calm accommodation, suggest that the disasters in the more prosperous areas of the former Yugoslavia, far from being inevitable, could almost certainly have been avoided if politicians and police had behaved more sensibly.[93]

EXTRAPOLATIONS

The degree to which this analysis can be transferred to the dozens of "ethnic wars" taking place in any given year remains to be seen. But ideas developed in an analysis of the wars in the former Yugoslavia do have at least some bearing on the extreme, genocidal war in Rwanda. This suggests that an approach that applies as a crucial mechanism the elite-encouraged rampages of opportunistic and often drunken thugs may, in many cases, more adequately explain what passes for "ethnic war' than one that envisions such conflicts as Hobbesian all-against-all upheavals stemming from previously suppressed ancient ethnic hatreds or from media- or politician-induced mass frenzies.

Michael Ignatieff finds the "new architects" of "postmodern war" in "the paramilitaries, guerrillas, militias, and warlords who are tearing up the failed states of the 1990s." Similarly, Martin van Creveld has proclaimed that we have entered a "new era," in which "war will not be waged by armies but by groups whom we today call terrorists, guerrillas, bandits, and robbers."[94] Banditry and depredations by roving militias are hardly new of course, but Ignatieff and van Creveld may be correct in suggesting that regular soldiers are no longer engaging in combat nearly as much as they used to. It is not, as van Creveld would have it, that low-intensity conflict has risen to "dominance." Rather it is that, increasingly, warfare at that sort is the only kind still going on—war by thugs is the residual, not the emerging, form.[95]

Moreover, if some states (like Serbia, Croatia, Bosnia, and Rwanda) came to depend on irregulars, it is not because they find this approach preferable, but because they are unable to muster an adequate number of recruits to field a real army. And if, again like Serbia and Rwanda, but unlike Croatia and Bosnia, they continue to rely on such corrupt, opportunistic, inept, and often cowardly forces, they are likely eventually to go down in pathetic defeat.

In the end, the basic operation—and the fundamental banality—of much ethnic violence is neatly summed up in a Bosnian expression: "Teško narodu kad pametni ubute, budale progovore, a fukare se obogate." That is, "It is difficult for the people when the smart keep quiet, fools speak out, and thugs get rich."[96] The mistaken—even racist—notion that an entire ethnic group is devotedly out to destroy another ethnic group can in such cases shatter any ability to perceive nuance and variety, and it can be taken to suggest that efforts to foster elite accommodation are essentially irrelevant and therefore bound to prove futile. Further, the all-against-all image can discourage policing because it implies that the entire ethnic group—rather than just a small, opportunistic, and often cowardly subgroup—must be brought under control.

ENDNOTES

1. I am concerned here with ethnic violence and warfare—a condition in which combatants arrayed along ethnic lines seek to kill each other—not particularly with ethnic hatreds. It is important to distinguish common, knee-jerk, and sometimes hateful ethnic slurs—no matter how unpleasant and politically incorrect their expression may often be—from prejudice that is expressed in violence. As James D. Fearon and David D. Laitin have pointed out, ethnic violence is actually exceedingly rare when one considers how many Archie Bunkers there are in the world and how many opportunities there are for it to occur. Fearon and

Laitin, "Explaining Interethnic Cooperation," *American Political Science Review,* Vol. 90, No. 4 (December 1996), pp. 716–717. Some analysts argue that "conflicts among nations and ethnic groups are escalating." Samuel P. Huntington, "Why International Primacy Matters," *International Security,* Vol. 17, No. 4 (Spring 1993), p. 71. Others believe "there is a virtual epidemic of armed civil or international conflict." See David A. Haumburg, *Preventing Contemporary Intergroup Violence* (New York: Carnegie Corporaton of New York, 1993). But such wars and conflicts did not increase in number or intensity in the 1990s. See Yahya Sadowski, *The Myth of Global Chaos* (Washington, D.C.: Brookings, 1998); Ernest J. Wilson and Ted Robert Gurr, "Fewer Nations Are Making War," *Los Angeles Times,* August 22, 1999, p. M2; Steven R. David, "Internal War: Causes and Cures," *World Politics,* Vol. 49, No. 4 (July 1997), pp. 552–576; and James D. Fearon and David D. Laitin, "Weak Sates, Rough Terrain, and Large-Scale Ethnic Violence since 1945," paper presented at the annual meeting of the American Political Science Association, Atlanta, Georgia, September 25, 1999. Rather, what is new is that some of these wars and conflicts have taken place in Europe, an area that had previously been free from substantial civil warfare for nearly half a century. However, militant nationalism—whether violent or not—may well already have had its day in Central and Eastern Europe. Hypernationalists (and even some that are not so hyper), who sometimes appeared threateningly formidable at the polls in the early 1990s, have been reduced in elections in many places to the point of extinguishment.

2. Robert D. Kaplan, "A Reader's Guide to the Balkans," *New York Times Book Review,* April 28, 1993, pp. 1, 30–32. See also Robert D. Kaplan, "History's Cauldron," *Atlantic Monthly,* June 1991, pp. 93–104; and Kaplan, *Balkan Ghosts: A Journey through History* (New York: St. Martin's, 1993). For Kaplan's more recent doomsaying, now focused also on Africa, see his "The Coming Anarchy," *Atlantic,* February 1994, pp. 44–76. For a devastating critique of the argument, see Noel Malcolm, "Seeing Ghosts," *National Interest,* Summer 1993, pp. 83–88. See also V.P. Gagnon, Jr., "Ethnic Nationalism and International Conflict: The Case of Serbia," *International Security,* Vol. 19, No. 3 (winter 1994/95), pp. 133–134; Russell Hardin, *One for All: The Logic of Group Conflict* (Princeton, N.J.: Princeton University Press, 1995), chap. 6; Sadowski, *Myth of Global Chaos;* and Brian Hall, "Rebecca West's War," *New Yorker,* April 15, 1996, p. 83. For Kaplan's more recent reflections, see his "Reading Too Much into a Book," *New York Times,* June 13, 1999, p. 4–17.

3. Quoted in Noel Malcolm, *Bosnia: A Short History* (New York: New York University Press, 1994), p. 252. On this argument, see, for example, Christopher Bennett, *Yugoslavia's Bloody Collapse* (New York: New York University Press, 1995), pp. viii, 10, 242; Warren Zimmermann, *Origins of a Catastrophe: Yugoslavia and Its Destroyers* (New York: Times Books, 1996), pp. 120–122; Christopher Cviib, "A Culture of Humiliation," *National Interest,* Summer 1993, p. 82; Jack Snyder and Karen Ballentine, "Nationalism and the Marketplace of Ideas," *International Security,* Vol. 21, No. 2 (Fall 1996), pp. 25–30; Michael Ignatieff, "The Balkan Tragedy," *New York Review of Books,* May 13, 1993, p. 3; Noel Malcolm, "The Roots of Bosnian Horror Lie Not So Deep," *New York Times,* October 19, 1998; Tim Judah, *The Serbs: History, Myth, and the Destruction of Yugoslavia* (New Haven, Conn.: Yale University

Press, 1997), pp. 285, 309; and Peter Maass, *Love Thy Neighbor: A Story of War* (New York: Vintage, 1996), p. 227.

4. On Tudjman's spending, see Susan L. Woodward, *Balkan Tragedy: Chaos and Dissolution after the Cold War* (Washington, D.C.: Brookings, 1995), pp. 119, 229; Bennett, *Yugoslavia's Bloody Collapse*, p. 199; Lenard J. Cohen, *Broken Bonds: Yugoslavia's Disintegration and Balkan Politics in Transition*, 2d ed. (Boulder, Colo: Westview, 1995), p. 95; Marcus Tanner, *Croatia: A Nation Forged in War* (New Haven, Conn: Yale University Press, 1977), p. 222; and David Binder, "Gojko Susak, "Defense Minister of Croatia Is Dead at 53," *New York Times*, May 5, 1998, p. A25. On Tudjman's electoral success, see Bennett, *Yugoslavia's Bloody Collapse*, p. 127; Woodward, *Balkan Tragedy*, pp. 117–119; Laura Silber and Allan Little, *Yugoslavia: Death of a Nation* (New York: Penguin, 1997), p. 90; and Cohen, *Broken Bonds*, pp. 99–100. On the Serb vote in Croatia, see Gagnon, "Ethnic Nationalism and International Conflict," p. 155; and Bennett, *Yugoslavia's Bloody Collapse*, p. 127. Somewhat similarly, a large portion of those Serbs in Bosnia who lived outside areas controlled by Serb nationalists voted with the Muslims for independence from Serbia in a 1992 referendum; see Gagnon, "Ethnic Nationalism and International Conflict," p. 163. On Bosnia, see Steven L. Burg and Paul S. Shoup, *The War in Bosnia-Herzegovina: Ethnic Conflict and International Intervention* (Armonk, N.Y.: M. E. Sharpe, 1999), pp. 50–51, 57. On Serbia, see Gagnon, "Ethnic Nationalism and International Conflict," p. 154; Bennett, *Yugoslavia's Bloody Collapse*, p. 121; Brian Hall, *The Impossible Country: A Journey through the Last Days of Yugoslavia* (New York: Penguin, 1994), p. 48; Woodward, *Balkan Tragedy*, pp. 130, 448–449; Mladjan Dinkic, *The Economics of Destruction* (Belgrade: Video Nedeljnik, 1995), pp. 30, 61–66; see also Judah, *The Serbs*, p. 260. On vote percentages, see Cohen, *Broken Bonds*, p. 158. On the Albanian vote, see Woodward, *Balkan Tragedy*, p. 121.

5. Laslo Sekelj, *Yugoslavia: The Process of Disintegration* (Highland Lakes, N.J.: Atlantic Research and Publications, 1992), p. 277.

6. Thus, because anti–Vietnam War demonstrators in the 1960s in the United States were predominantly young, most commentators came to hold that young people were more opposed to the war than older people; yet poll data clearly show the opposite to have been the case. John Mueller, *War, Presidents, and Public Opinion* (New York: Wiley, 1973), pp. 136–140.

7. Bennett, *Yugoslavia's Bloody Collapse*, p. 98.

8. On Zagreb, see "Yugoslavia: Death of a Nation," Discovery Channel, 1995. On Belgrade, see Gagnon, "Ethnic Nationalism and International Conflict," pp. 157–158; Silber and Little, *Yugoslavia*, chap. 9; Judah, *The Serbs*, p. 174; and Chuck Sudetic, *Blood and Vengeance: One Family's Story of the War in Bosnia* (New York: W.W. Norton, 1998), p. 85. On Sarajevo, see Judah, *The Serbs*, p. 211; and Robert J. Donia and John V.A. Fine, Jr., *Bosnia and Hercegovina: A Tradition Betrayed* (New York: Columbia University Press, 1994), p. 1.

9. Christine Spolar, "Lesser Serbs in Greater Serbia: Refugees of Croatia Fighting Find Little Welcome from Fellow Serbs," *Washington Post*, May 15, 1995, p. A36; Woodward, *Balkan Tragedy*, p. 364; Stephen Kinzer, "Yugoslavia Deports Refugee Serbs to Fight for Rebels in

Bosnia and Croatia," *New York Times*, July 6, 1995, p. A6; and Roger Cohen, *Hearts Grown Brutal: Sagas of Sarajevo* (New York: Random House, 1998), p. 296.

10. Bennett, *Yugoslavia's Bloody Collapse*, p. 63. See also Woodward, *Balkan Tragedy*, pp. 238, 241; Ignatieff, "Balkan Tragedy," p. 4; John R. Bowen, "The Myth of Global Ethnic Conflict," *Journal of Democracy*, Vol. 7, No. 4 (October 1996), pp. 3–14; and Sadowski, *Myth of Global Chaos*, pp. 78–80. Interestingly, in his discussion of the Bosnian war, Peter Maass observes that "to a surprising extent, this was a war of poor rural Serbs against wealthier urban Muslims, a *Deliverance* scenario." Maass, *Love Thy Neighbor*, p. 159. Donia and Fine note that it was the "relatively uneducated armed hillsmen, with a hostility toward urban culture and the state institutions (including taxes) that go with it" who proved "susceptible to Serbian chauvinist propaganda," "allowed themselves to be recruited into Serb paramilitary units," and formed a significant portion of those shelling Bosnia's cities. Donia and Fine, *Bosnia and Hercegovina*, p. 28. See also Fearon and Laitin, "Weak States, Rough Terrain."

11. Norman Cigar, "The Serbo-Croatian War, 1991: Political and Military Dimensions," *Journal of Strategic Studies*, Vol. 16, No. 3 (September 1993), pp. 317–319; Woodward, *Balkan Tragedy*, p. 238; Bennett, *Yugoslavia's Bloody Collapse*, p. 167; Ed Vulliamy, *Seasons in Hell: Understanding Bosnia's War* (New York: Simon and Schuster, 1994), p. 19; Miloš Vasib, "The Yugoslav Army and the Post-Yugoslav Armies," in David A. Dyker and Ivan Vejvoda, eds., *Yugoslavia and After: A Study in Fragmentation, Despair, and Rebirth* (London: Longman, 1996), p. 128; Burg and Shoup, *War in Bosnia-Herzegovina*, p. 51; Gagnon, "Ethnic Nationalism and International Conflict," p. 162; Silber and Little, *Yugoslavia*, p. 177; Tanner, *Croatia*, p. 269; and Judah, *The Serbs*, pp. 185, 189.

12. Jasminka Udovicki and Stojan Cerovic, "The People's Mass Murderer," *Village Voice*, November 7, 1995, p. 27; Stipe Sikavica, "The Collapse of Tito's Army," in Jasminka Udovibki and James Ridgeway, eds., *Yugoslavia's Ethnic Nightmare* (New York: Lawrence Hill, 1995), p. 138; Cigar, "Serb-Croatian War," p. 315; Tanner, *Croatia*, p. 270; Judah, *The Serbs*, p. 185; and Burg and Shoup, *War in Bosnia-Herzegovina*, p. 51. See also Silber and Little, *Yugoslavia*, p. 177; and Gagnon, "Ethnic Nationalism and International Conflict," p. 162. See also Silber and Little, *Yugoslavia*, p. 177. In all communist countries, certainly including Yugoslavia, people were determinedly subject to decades of communist propaganda in the media. Yet, as history has shown, many—probably most—failed in the end to be convinced by it. If media promotion could guarantee lasting impact, all Yugoslavs would today be worshiping Tito, and all Americans would be driving Edsels. For a discussion, see John Mueller, *Policy and Opinion in the Gulf War* (Chicago: University of Chicago Press, 1994), pp. 129–136. Warren Zimmerman observes, "My most difficult task has been to convey the conviction that all Yugoslavs weren't the bloodthirsty extremists so ubiquitously visible in Western news accounts. Most of the people my wife and I met in six years of living in Yugoslavia were peaceful and decent, without a trace of the hostility on which nationalism feeds. . . . What amazed me was how many Yugoslavs resisted the incessant racist propaganda." Zimmerman, *Origins of a Catastrophe*, p. xi; see also pp. 209–210.

13. Tanner, *Croatia*, p. 269. See also United Nations commission of Experts, *Final Report of*

the United Nations Commission of Experts Established Pursuant to Security Council Resolution 780 (1992), Annex III. A Special Forces, ed. M. Cherif Bassiouni, December 28, 1994, par. 29.

14. Burg and Shoup, *War in Bosnia-Herzegovina,* p. 130; and Judah, *The Serbs,* pp. 170–172, 192–195.

15. Burg and Shoup, *War in Bosnia-Herzegovina,* p. 137. There were at least eighty-three of these groups operating in Croatia and Bosnia: fifty-six Serbs, thirteen Croat, and fourteen Muslim, with 36,000-66,000 members. See UN Experts, *Final Report,* par. 14.

16. UN Experts, *Final Report,* par. 100.

17. Julian Borger, "The President's Secret Henchmen," *Guardian Weekly,* February 16, 1997, p. 8; Cohen, *Hearts Grown Brutal,* pp. 192, 410–411; UN Experts, *Final Report,* par. 3, 30; and David Firestone, "Serb Lawmaker Is Called Vicious Killer," *St. Louis Post-Dispatch,* January 3, 1993, p. 1A. See also Woodward, *Balkan Tragedy,* pp. 238, 249, 265; Vasib, "Yugoslav Army," p. 128; Udovicki and Cerovic, "People's Mass Murderer"; and Michael Ignatieff, *The Warrior's Honor: Ethnic War and the Modern Conscience* (New York: Henry Holt, 1997), p. 132.

18. Vasib, "Yugoslav Army," p. 134; Borger, "President's Secret Henchmen"; Silber and Little, *Yugoslavia,* pp. 177–178; Tanner, *Croatia,* p. 245; Judah, *The Serbs,* chap. 9; and UN Experts, *Final Report,* par. 18, 24.

19. Vasib, "Yugoslav Army," p. 128.

20. One of the most fanatical of Serb nationalists, the political scientist Šešelj, who spent a year teaching at the University of Michigan in his younger years, later seems to have become mentally unbalanced as the result of the torture and beatings he endured while in prison in Yugoslavia for counterrevolutionary activities. One academic colleague described him as "disturbed, totally lost, and out of his mind." See UN Experts, *Final Report,* par. 107, 108; see also Judah, *The Serbs,* p. 187.

21. UN Experts, *Final Report,* par. 129; Judah, *The Serbs,* p. 186; and Sudtic, *Blood and Vengeance,* p. 98. The overlap between soccer hooligans and criminals seems to be very high. See Bill Buford, *Among the Thugs* (New York: W.W. Norton, 1991), p. 28. Also associated are racist attitudes, a proclivity for extreme right-wing politics; a capacity to imbibe huge amounts of liquor; a strident and vicious boorishness; a deep need for camaraderie and for being accepted by the "lads"; and an affinity for, even a lusting after, the thrill of violence. On the war-anticipating pitched battle between supporters of the Zagreb and Belgrade soccer clubs in 1990, see Tanner, *Croatia,* p. 228.

22. UN Experts, *Final Report,* par. 23, 26.

23. Vasib, "Yugoslavia Army," p. 134.

24. Sikavica, "Collapse of Tito's Army," p. 137. There was one paramilitary group, identified as "The Weekenders," that ventured from Bijeljina to Breko each weekend over a three-year period to plunder and vandalize. See UN Experts, *Final Report,* par. 317.

25. Particularly in the case of Croatia, as Bennett notes, many of the most extreme fighters were emigré adventurers from abroad. See, Bennett, *Yugoslavia's Bloody Collapse,* p. 165. See also Hall, *Impossible Country,* p. 11; David Rieff, *Slaughterhouse* (New York: Simon and Schuster, 1995), p. 66. Tony Horwitz met German skinheads in Zagreb who had come "for

a bit of graduate training." See Horwitz, "Balkan Death Trip: Scenes from a Futile War," *Harper's*, March 1993, p. 41.

26. UN Experts, *Final Report*, par. 125–128; see also Sudetic, *Blood and Vengeance*, pp. 97–98. He was assassinated gangland-style in Belgrade in January 2000.

27. UN Experts, *Final Report*, par. 206; and Tanner, *Croatia*, p. 245. There was also a group identified as the "Knindža Turtles," but it is not clear whether this is the same band as the one led by Captain Dragan. See UN Experts, *Final Report*, n. 493. For completeness, it should be reported that a paramilitary unit in Bosnia was led by a man calling himself "Commander Turtle." See ibid., par. 311.

28. Cohen, *Hearts Grown Brutal*, p. 280; Robert Block, "Killers," *New York Review of Books*, November 18, 1993, p. 9; UN Experts, *Final Report*, n. 74; and Maass, *Love Thy Neighbor*, p. 31.

29. Block, "Killers," p. 9. On these issues, see also Anna Husarska, "Rocky-Road Warrior," *New Republic*, December 4, 1995, pp. 16–17; Tanner, *Croatia*, p. 245; Rieff, *Slaughterhouse*, pp. 131–132; Vulliamy, *Seasons in Hell*, pp. 314–316; Ignatieff, *Warrior's Honor*, p. 131; Burg and Shoup, *War in Bosnia-Herzegovina*, pp. 137–139; and Sadowski, *Myth in Global Chaos*, p. 163.

30. Zimmermann, *Origins of a Catastrophe*, p. 152. Block, "Killers," p. 9. Rieff, *Slaughterhouse*, p. 130. Reportage by Peter Maass is peppered with such phrases as "drunken hillbillies," "death and thuggery," "they don't wear normal uniforms, they don't have many teeth," "the trigger fingers belonged to drunks," "the Bosnians might be the underdogs, but most of their frontline soldiers were crooks," "bullies," "a massive oaf," "a foul-smelling warlord," "mouthing the words, 'Bang, you're dead,' through rotten teeth," "an unshaven soldier would point his gun at a desired item and grunt," "only drunks and bandits ventured outside," "goons with guns," "Serb soldiers or thugs—and the difference is hard to tell." See Maass, *Love Thy Neighbor*, pp. 6, 7, 16, 30, 42, 48, 61, 69, 77, 79, 80, 85. Reporter Ed Vulliamy describes them as "boozy at their best, wild and sadistic at their worst" or as "toothless goons" with "inflammable breath." See Vulliamy, *Seasons in Hell*, pp. 19, 46.

31. Block, "Killers"; UN Experts, *Final Report*, par. 291; and Cohen, *Hearts Grown Brutal*, p. 126.

32. Burg and Shopu, *War in Bosnia-Herzegovina*, p. 137; and UN Experts, *Final Report*, at par. 142.

33. Woodward, *Balkan Tragedy*, pp. 254, 356, 485; and Cigar, "Serbo-Croatian War," p. 323. See also Mischa Glenny, *The Fall of Yugoslavia: The Third Balkan War* (New York: Penguin, 1993), p. 185; Chuck Sudetic, "A 'Wild East' Revival in Serbian-Held Croatia," *New York Times*, September 21, 1992, p. A6; Cheryl Benard, "Bosnia: Was It Inevitable?" in Zalmay M. Khalilzad, ed., *Lessons from Bosnia* (Santa Monica, Calif: RAND Corporation, 1993), pp. 18–25; Vulliamy, *Seasons in Hell*, pp. 307–316; and Bob Stewart, *Broken Lives: A Personal View of the Bosnian Conflict* (London: HarperCollins, 1994), pp. 318–319. See also Rieff, *Slaughterhouse*, p. 83; Ignatieff, *Warrior's Honor*, p. 131; and Sikavica, "Collapse of Tito's Army," p. 138. Vulliamy quotes Reuters reporter Andrej Gustincib: "Gangs of gun-toting Serbs rule Foca, turning the once quiet town into a nightmare landscape of burning streets

and houses. . . . Some are members of paramilitary groups from Serbia, self-proclaimed crusaders against Islam and defenders of the Serbian nation, others are wild-eyed local men, hostile towards strangers and happy to have driven out their Muslim neighbors. No one seems to be in command, and ill-disciplined and bad-tempered gunmen stop and detain people at will." See Vulliamy, *Seasons in Hell,* pp. 90–91. Many of the "wild-eyed local men," according to another report, were local criminals who "donned uniforms and took part enthusiastically in the subsequent looting." See Julian Borger, "Friends or Foes?" *Guardian Weekly,* January 19, 1997, p. 23. Similarly, the town of Bosanski Novi was ruled by five roaming Serbian armed groups, the most brutal of which was a well-known local mafia known as the "Spare Ribs" that had donned uniforms. See Judah, *The Serbs,* p. 227.

34. On Vasilijevic, see Firestone, "Serb Lawmaker Is Called Vicious Killer." UN Experts, *Final Report,* par. 21.

35. A partial exception to this pattern was the slaughter of thousands of Muslim men by Serbs after they successfully invaded the "safe area" of Srebrenica in 1995, a seemingly calculated and rather orderly massacre that was carried out by what appears to have been the regular army. On this issue, see Sadowski, *Myth of Global Chaos,* p. 133. Given that the army had become increasingly thuggish by this time, a formal distinction with less-organized bands of thugs may be somewhat strained. Nevertheless, this murderous episode does seem to show more method and less madness than the more capricious and improvisatory killings that had taken place during the main period of ethnic cleansing in 1992. As was typical in this war, however, the killing squads at Srebrenica were often shored up with generous quantities of liquor. See Judah, *The Serbs,* p. 241. Although in no way excusing the massacre, it may be relevant to point out that the Serbs were deeply bitter because, although they had allowed the city to become a UN safe area in 1993 under an agreement that it would be demilitarized, it had repeatedly been used as a base for attacks on Serb civilians. David Rhode, *Endgame: The Betrayal and Fall of Srebrenica, Europe's Worst Massacre since World War II* (New York: Farrar, Straus and Giroux, 1997), pp. xvi, 215–216, 409.

36. UN Experts, *Final Report,* par. 104.

37. Chris Hedges, "Croatian's Confession Describes Torture and Killing on Vast Scale," *New York Times,* September 5, 1997, p. A1.

38. Quoted in Husarska, "Rocky-Road Warrior," p. 16; see also Bennett, *Yugoslavia's Bloody Collapse,* p. 191; Mike O'Connor, "Nationalism Checkmates Pawns, Too, in Bosnia," *New York Times,* March 28, 1996, p. A3; Rieff, *Slaughterhouse,* p. 110; Judah, *The Serbs,* p. 195; and Peter Maass, "In Bosnia, 'Disloyal Serbs' Share Plight of Opposition," *Washington Post,* August 24, 1992, p. A1.

39. Chris Hedges, "From One Serbian Militia Chief: A Trail of Plunder and Slaughter," *New York Times,* March 25, 1996, p. A1. Ed Vulliamy, "Bloody Train of Butchery at the Bridge," *Guardian,* March 11, 1996, p. 9. Maass, *Love Thy Neighbor,* pp. 12–14, 157. UN Experts, *Final Report,* par. 246–250, 540–556. Sudetic, *Blood and Vengeance,* pp. 120–125. Lukib is reported to be spending the postwar years in Serbia, a wealthy man. Vulliamy. "Bloody Train of Butchery." Other reports, however, indicate that he has sought psychiatric

care, has become unhinged, sleeps with all the lights on, and drives around in a different car all the time. Still, he claims to be proud he killed so many Muslims in the war and says he has an almost uncontrollable urge to kill again. Sudetic, *Blood and Vengeance,* pp. 355–356, 358.

40. Mike O'Connor, "Moderate Bosnian Serbs Plot in Secrecy for Unity," *New York Times,* July 31, 1996, p. A3.

41. Rhode, *Endgame,* pp. xiv, 60, 354, 355.

42. Vasib, "Yugoslav Army," p. 134; and UN Experts, *Final Report,* par. 92, 138.

43. Benard, "Bosnia," p. 24. See also Malcolm, "Roots of Bosnian Horror." Halina Grzymala-Moszczcynska, a Polish sociologist working with Muslim refugees in Poland, reports that the refugees she has interviewed never refer to their persecutors as "Serbs," but always as "criminals." Personal conversation.

44. Woodward, *Balkan Tragedy,* p. 249.

45. Judah, *The Serbs,* p. 233; and Maass, *Love Thy Neighbor,* pp. 52, 111. See also Julian Borger, "Day of Reckoning for the Men of Death," *Guardian Weekly,* July 20, 1997, p. 7.

46. Woodward, *Balkan Tragedy,* p. 249; and Sudetic, "A 'Wild East' Revival." On the phenomenon more broadly, see John Mueller, *Quiet Cataclysm* (New York: HarperCollins, 1995), chap. 8; J. Glenn Gray, *The Warriors: Reflections on Men in Battle* (New York: Harper and Row, 1959); William Broyles, Jr., "Why Men Love War," *Esquire,* November 1984, pp. 55–65; and Dave Grossman, *On Killing: The Psychological Cost of Learning to Kill in War and Society* (Boston: Little, Brown, 1995).

47. Borger, "Friends or Foes?"

48. Burg and Shoup, *War in Bosnia-Herzegovina,* p. 137.

49. Some of this behavior surfaced early—in the fighting in Croatia in 1991. As one Serb from the area recalled, "I don't deny that I myself did some shooting, but the worst crimes were committed by the irregulars who came in from Serbia. First they looted the homes of Croats. When they came back a second time they started looting Serb houses, because the Croat houses had already been robbed clean." Another Serb from the same village reports that after defending their homes for six months (and never seeing a single regular army officer or soldier), they were ordered, together with some of their Croat neighbors who had joined them in home defense, to evacuate for resettlement in Bosnia. On the way, they were all robbed by the Serbian forces of Šešlj. Ejub Štitkovac, "Croatia: The First War," in Udovicki and Ridgeway, *Yugoslavia's Ethnic Nightmare,* p. 160.

50. Rieff, *Slaughterhouse,* p. 132.

51. Judah, *The Serbs,* pp. 221–223, 252–255.

52. Rohde, *Endgame,* pp. 107–109; and Sudetic, *Blood and Vengeance,* pp. 223, 244.

53. UN Experts, *Final Report,* par. 84, 86; John F. Burns, "2 Gang Leaders in Sarajevo Face Crackdown in Bosnia," *New York Times,* October 27, 1993, p. A6; and Maass, *Love Thy Neighbor,* p. 31.

54. Vasib, "Yugoslav Army," p. 133; Woodward, *Balkan Tragedy,* p. 246; Charles G. Boyd, "Making Peace with the Guilty: The Truth about Bosnia," *Foreign Affairs,* Vol. 74, No. 5

(September/October 1995), p. 29; Noel Malcolm, "Bosnia and the West: A Study in Failure," *National Interest*, Spring 1995, p. 9; Judah, *The Serbs*, pp. 223, 237, 296; Chuck Sudetic, "Serbs of Sarajevo Stay Loyal to Bosnia," *New York Times*, August 26, 1994, p. A6; and Maass, "In Bosnia, 'Disloyal Serbs' Share Plight of Opposition." The population of the once thoroughly integrated city of Mostar declined from 130,000 to 60,000. Chris Hedges, "A War-Bred Underworld Threatens Bosnia Peace," *New York Times*, May 1, 1996, p. 8. Sarajevo declined from 450,000 to something close to 280,000, including some 100,000 refugees from ethnically cleansed areas of the country. Chris Hedges, "War Turns Sarajevo Away from Europe," *New York Times*, July 28, 1995, p. A4. By September 1992, only nine months after their brief war for independence had ended, the number of Serbs from the Krajina section of Croatia who had moved to Serbia was reaching "disastrous proportions," according to a Belgrade daily, a situation it blamed on the endemic corruption of Krajina officials. Tanner, *Croatia*, p. 283.

55. For a portrait of the clearly deranged Branko Grujić, a Serb who reigned as the mayor of Zvornik after the Muslim majority had been driven from the city, see Cohen, *Hearts Grown Brutal*, pp. 296–298.

56. Judah, *The Serbs*, pp. 242–252; and Ed Vulliamy, "Croats Who Supped with the Devil," *Guardian*, March 18, 1996, p. 8. See also Burg and Shoup, *War in Bosnia-Herzegovina*, p. 138; and Sudetic, *Blood and Vengeance*, p. 90. Serbia itself was also substantially criminalized during the war. Judah, *The Serbs*, pp. 255–256.

57. Although there are differences, the Serb rampages in Kosovo in 1999 often resembled those seen earlier in Bosnia and Croatia. The army provided a sort of generalized support, it participated directly in some areas, and it hardly escapes blame for the results in any case. But, as one report puts its, "in hundreds of interviews," Kosovo Albanians "have said that nearly all the killings of civilians were committed by Serbian paramilitary forces and not by the regular army." Blaine Harden, "Reservists a Crucial Factor in Effort against Mikosevic," *New York Times*, July 9, 1999, p. A1. Released criminals formed an important component of Serb forces. See Michael R. Gordon, "Civilians Are Slain in Military Attack on a Kosovo Road," *New York Times*, April 15, 1999, p. A1; and Charles Ingrao, "It Will Take More Than Bombs to Bring Stability," *Los Angeles Times*, April 12, 1999, p. B11.

58. Gérard Prunier, *Rwanda Crisis: History of a Genocide* (New York: Columbia University Press, 1995), p. 169; and African Rights, *Rwanda: Death, Despair, and Defiance*, rev. ed. (London: African Rights, 1995), pp. 51–52.

59. Prunier, *Rwanda Crisis*, pp. 113, 242–243; and African Rights, *Rwanda*, pp. 49, 65.

60. Philip Gourevitch, *We Wish to Inform You That Tomorrow We Will Be Killed with Our Families: Stories from Rwanda* (New York: Farrar, Straus and Giroux, 1998), p. 93.

61. Prunier, *Rwanda Crisis*, pp. 231–232. See also Allison Des Forges, *"Leave None to Tell the Story": Genocide in Rwanda* (New York: Human Rights Watch, 1999), pp. 11, 261.

62. Gourevitch, *We Wish to Inform You*, p. 115.

63. African Rights, *Rwanda*, pp. 55, 61–62, 114.

64. Gourevitch, *We Wish to Inform You*, p. 242.

65. African Rights, *Rwanda,* pp. 55, 61–62, 114.

66. Prunier, *Rwanda Crisis,* p. 247; African Rights, *Rwanda,* chap. 14; and Gourevitch, *We Wish to Inform You,* pp. 307, 309.

67. Prunier, *Rwanda Crisis,* pp. 253–254; and Gourevitch, *We Wish to Inform You,* p. 136.

68. African Rights, *Rwanda,* pp. 1017–1022.

69. Prunier, *Rwanda Crisis,* p. 253; and Des Forges, *"Leave None to Tell the Story,"* pp. 11, 260–262.

70. Des Forges, *"Leave None to Tell the Story,"* p. 262.

71. Ibid., pp. 2, 16, 260, 262.

72. African Rights, *Rwanda.*

73. Gourevitch, *We Wish to Inform You,* p. 242.

74. Bill Keller, "In Mozambique and Other Lands, Children Fight the Wars," *New York Times,* November 9, 1994, p. A14.

75. Ignatieff, "Balkan Tragedy."

76. Chaim Kaufmann, "Possible and Impossible Solutions to Ethnic Wars," *International Security,* Vol. 20, No. 4. (Spring 1996), p. 144.

77. Robert P. Kraynak, *History and Modernity in the Thought of Thomas Hobbes* (Ithaca, N.Y.: Cornell University Press, 1990), pp. 165, 176, 179.

78. On this issue, see Bruce L. Benson, "The Spontaneous Evolution of Commercial Law," in Daniel B. Klein, ed., *Reputation Studies in the Voluntary Elicitation of Good Conduct* (Ann Arbor: University of Michigan Press, 1997), pp. 165–189; Robert C. Ellickson, *Order without Law: How Neighbors Settle Disputes* (Cambridge, Mass: Harvard University Press, 1991); and John Mueller, *Capitalism, Democracy, and Ralph's Pretty Good Grocery* (Princeton, N.J.: Princeton University Press, 1999), chap. 4.

79. Judah observes of Bosnian Serb General Ratko Mladib that "his war was a coward's war. He fought few pitched battles but managed to drive hundreds of thousands of unarmed people out of their homes," and he also questions Mladib's mental stability. Judah, *The Serbs,* pp. 230–231. On this latter issue, see also Robert Block, "The Madness of General Mladic," *New York Review of Books,* October 5, 1995, pp. 7–9; and Jane Perlez, "A Grim Turn for 2 Embattled Serb Leaders," *New York Times,* December 15, 1995, p. A1.

80. Vasib, "Yugoslav Army," pp. 134–135; Silber and Little, *Yugoslavia* p. 360; Ken Silverstein, "Privatizing War? How Affairs of State Are Outsourced to Corporation beyond Public Control," *Nation,* July 28/August 4, 1997, pp. 11–17; and Tanner, *Croatia,* p. 284.

81. Vasib, "Yugoslav Army," p. 136; Judah, *The Serbs,* pp. 217–218; Maass, *Love Thy Neighbor,* p. 33; Chris Hedges, "Postscript to Sarajevo's Anguish: Muslim Killings of Serbs Detailed," *New York Times,* November 12, 1997, p. A1; Burg and Shoup, *War in Bosnia-Herzegovina,* pp. 138–139; Burns, "2 Gang Leaders in Sarajevo Face Crackdown in Bosnia"; and John F. Burns, "Bosnian Forces Kill Reputed Gang Chief in Sarajevo Gunfight," *New York Times,* October 27, 1993, p. A6. See also Rieff, *Slaughterhouse,* p. 132.

82. Bennet, *Yugoslavia's Bloody Collapse,* pp. 228–229; and Silber and Little, *Yugoslavia,* p. 353. Tanner, *Croatia,* p. 288.

83. Tanner, *Croatia*, pp. 294–297; Silber and Little, *Yugoslavia*, pp. 353–360; see also Vasib, "Yugoslav Army," p. 135. In victory, however, the discipline of the Croat forces often broke down in arson, destruction, and looting. Tanner, *Croatia*, p. 298.

84. Prunier, *Rwanda Crisis*, pp. 254, 268, 377; Gourevitch, *We Wish to Inform You*, pp. 156–157; and Alan J. Kuperman, "Rwanda in Retrospect," *Foreign Affairs*, Vol. 79, No. 1 (January–February 2000), pp. 94–118.

85. On this issue, see also Malcolm, "Bosnia and the West," pp. 4–5; and Sadowski, *Myth of Global Chaos*, pp. 24–25, 66–68. On President Bill Clinton's seduction by Kaplan's book, see Elizabeth Drew, *On the Edge. The Clinton Presidency* (New York: Simon and Schuster, 1994), p. 157; on his belated, regretful public recantation in 1999 of the Kaplan perspective, see Katharine Q. Seelye, "Clinton Blames Milosevic, Not Fate, for Bloodshed," *New York Times*, May 14, 1999, p. A12. Talking about the Bosnia conflict on national television on June 5, 1995, Vice President Al Gore had allowed as how the tragedy had been unfolding, "some would say, for five hundred years." Clinton, not to be outdone, opined in the same interview that "their enmities go back five hundred years, some would say almost a thousand years." Cohen, *Hearts Grown Brutal*, pp. 397–398. The exact identity of the hyperbolic "some" was not specified, but one source perhaps was Henry Kissinger, who has noted authoritatively that "ethnic conflict has been endemic in the Balkans for centuries" (as opposed to gentle, trouble-free Western Europe presumably), and, patronizingly and absurdly, that "none of the populations has any experience with—essentially no belief in—Western concepts of toleration." Henry Kissinger, "No U.S. Ground Forces for Kosovo," *Washington Post*, February 22, 1999, p. A15. At the source of many of these perceptions is Rebecca West's two-volume *Black Lamb and Grey Falcon* (New York: Viking, 1941). The work was written after the author had made three visits—the longest of which lasted less than two months—to Yugoslavia between 1936 and 1938, and it often propounds views that are essentially racist. For a superb assessment, see Hall, "Rebecca West's War."

86. Hall, *Impossible Country*, p. 68. In the case of Yugoslavia, outsiders also tended vastly to overestimate the fighting tenacity of the defenders under the assumption that Serbs, in particular, were fanatically dedicated fighters. This notion derives from a World War II myth that maintains that the occupying Germans, confronted with a dedicated guerrilla opposition, were forced to divert a huge number of forces to maintain their control in Yugoslavia. Even assuming the situations are comparable, the Germans occupied the country in a matter of days and rarely found the Yugoslav occupation much of a diversion. Bennett, *Yugoslavia's Bloody Collapse*, pp. 49–50; and J. P. Mackley, "The Balkan Quagmire Myth: Taking On the Serbs Would Be More Grenada than Vietnam," *Washington Post*, March 7, 1993, p. C3. In Bosnia, suggests Mackley, no Yugoslav combat unit, regular or irregular, could successfully compete with the U.S. military "in anything but a drinking contest."

87. John Mueller, "The Common Sense," *National Interest*, Spring 1997, p. 83. On the other hand, this is not such an unusual position for humanitarian ventures. If Red Cross or other workers are killed while carrying out humanitarian missions, their organizations frequently threaten to withdraw no matter how much good they may be doing. Especially

what they are saying, then, is that the saving of lives in not worth the deaths of even a few rescuers.

88. On Spain, see Chris Hedges, "On Bosnia's Ethnic Fault Lines, It's Still Tense, but World Is Silent," *New York Times*, February 28, 1997, p. A1. On Belgium, see Des Forges, "*Leave None to Tell the Story.*" pp. 618–620; Gourevitch, *We Wish To Inform You*, pp. 114–150; and African Rights, *Rwanda*, p. 1112. Poll data demonstrate that President Clinton (in part because he confronted vocal Republican opposition on the issue) was never able to increase the numbers of Americans who saw wisdom or value in sending U.S. policing troops to Bosnia even though it was expected that there would be few casualties. In fact, six months after the venture began, support for it had *still* not risen even though it was completely successful: Bosnians had stopped killing each other (even if they had not come to love each other) and, most important, no Americans had been killed. Americans have a deep concern for U.S. casualties and very little for foreign ones, and they have never had much stomach for losing American lives in humanitarian ventures. On the other hand, it seems likely that, if they are not being killed, U.S. troops can remain on peacekeeping missions almost indefinitely. See Mueller, "Common Sense"; and John Mueller, "Public Opinion as a Constraint on U. S. Foreign Policy: Assessing the Perceived Value of American and Foreign Lives," paper presented at the annual convention of the International Studies Association, Los Angeles, California, March 14–18, 2000.

89. Quoted in Jane Perlez, "Balkan Voice of Reason and Despair," *New York Times*, August 14, 1997, p. B1.

90. On the murderous rivalries of motorcycle gangs in tranquil Denmark, see Stephen Kinzer, "Biker Wars in the Land of 'The Little Mermaid,'" *New York Times*, May 6, 1996, p. A4. In this case, however, the thugs are taken to be an aberrant "social pathology," and they are not held to be typical of the entire national spirit as so often happens in Kaplanesque discussions of the Balkans.

91. Stanley Milgram, *Obedience to Authority: An Experimental View* (New York: Harper and Row, 1975); Philip G. Zimbardo, Craig Haney, Curtis Banks, and David Jaffe, "The Mind Is a Formidable Jailer," *New York Times Magazine*, April 8, 1973, pp. 38ff; Christopher R. Browning, *Ordinary Men: Reserve Police Battalion 101 and the Final Solution in Poland* (New York: HarperCollins, 1998); and Fred E. Katz, *Ordinary People and Extraordinary Evil: A Report on the Beguilings of Evil* (Albany: State University of New York Press, 1993).

92. Sadowski, *Myth of Global Chaos*, pp. 174–176.

93. In 1991 Robert Kaplan declared that "Macedonia is once again poised to erupt. Never in half a century has there been so much anger in Macedonia, as its people wake up from a Communist-imposed sleep. . . . Unable to stand on its own, like its more populous and historically grounded neighbor Serbia, Macedonia could implode under the pressures of Albanian nationalism from the west and Bulgarian nationalism from the east. And this is to say nothing of the pressures of Greek nationalism from the south. . . . The various popular convulsions in the Balkans are inexorably converging on Macedonia. . . . It is a tragic yet fas-

cinating development. Rarely has the very process of history been so transparent and cyclical." Kaplan, "History's Cauldron," p. 104. See also his "Ground Zero: Macedonia: The Real Battleground," *New Republic*, August 2, 1993, p. 15. Inspired by such wisdom, applications of the now-popular notion of "preventative diplomacy" would have concentrated on exactly the wrong place in the early 1990s. On Bulgaria, see Venelin I. Ganev, "Bulgaria's Symphony of Hope," *Journal of Democracy*, Vol. 8, No. 4 (October 1997), pp. 125–139. On Romania (and also Slovakia), see Robert H. Linden, "Putting on Their Sunday Best: Romania, Hungary, and the Puzzle of Peace," *International Studies Quarterly*, Vol. 44, No. 1 (March 2000), pp. 121–145.

94. Ignatieff, *Warrior's Honor*, pp. 3, 5–6; and Martin L. van Creveld, *The Transformation of War* (New York: Free Press, 1991), pp. ix, 197. On banditry in Chechnya, see Anatol Lieven, "A Trap for Russia," *New York Times*, November 30, 1999, p. A31. On the connection between crime and the Irish Republican Army, see Linda Grant, "Where Hard Men Face Hard Choices," *Guardian Weekly*, April 26, 1998, p. 32; on connections in Algeria, see Stathis N. Kalyvas, "Wanton and Senseless? The Logic of Massacres in Algeria," *Rationality and Society*, Vol. 11, No. 3 (August 1999), p. 268. On the role of criminals, alcohol, drugs, and armed children in war in Mozambique, see Keller, "In Mozambique and Other Lands, Children Fight the Wars"; in Cambodia, see Stephen J. Morris, "Pol Pot's Lingering Influence," *New York Times*, April 17, 1998, p. A25; in Liberia, see Howard W. French, "Liberia's Teen-Age Soldiers Find Civil War Is Over but So Is Hope," *New York Times*, September 11, 1995, p. A1; and in Sierra Leone, see Judith Miller, "U.N. Monitors Accuse Sierra Leone Peacekeepers of Killing," *New York Times*, February 12, 1999, p. A10. See also David Keen, *The Economic Functions of Violence in Civil Wars*, Adelphi Paper No. 320 (London: International Institute for Strategic Studies, 1998); and Edward C. Banfield, *The Unheavenly City Revisited* (Boston: Little, Brown, 1970), chap. 9.

95. Van Creveld, *Transformation of War*, p. 205. On the trend, see also John Mueller, *Retreat from Doomsday: The Obsolescence of Major War* (New York: Basic Books, 1989); and Mueller, *Quiet Cataclysm*, chap. 9. Those seeking to identify a truly new form of war might better focus on the economic warfare that has become more effective because the end of the Cold War allows major countries to coordinate their efforts more fully. See John Mueller and Karl Mueller, "Sanctions of Mass Destruction," *Foreign Affairs*, Vol. 78, No. 1 (May/June 1999), pp. 43–53; and John Mueller and Karl Mueller, "The Methodology of Mass Destruction: Assessing Threats in the New World Order," *Journal of Strategic Studies*, forthcoming.

Part III

RACISM AT THE TURN OF THE CENTURY: STICKS AND CARROTS FOR CONTINUED EXPLOITATION

The use of slavery, Black Codes, legal segregation, and Ku Klux Klan death squads to control the labor struggles of racially oppressed peoples—African-Americans, Latinos, Asian-Americans—has ended. Does this mean that the hyper-exploitation of the labor of people of color has ended or is it now continued with new forms? Three things suggest the latter: First, the wealth gap between whites and people of color persists (and has done so in spite of the falling wage levels of whites since the 1970s). Second, blacks and Latinos are disproportionately warehoused in the world's largest penal system. Third, the system that spawned the earlier forms of labor control—capitalism—is still with us and still has a need to extract surplus value from workers. In this section you will find a number of selections discussing new forms of control and exploitation of the labor of people of color. Some of these forms deal with repression and forced labor; others deal with "progressive" reforms such as affirmative action and multiculturalism, which make the governing institutions of America more diverse.

THE STICK: Controlling labor with prison and workfare

In the early 1970s the US capitalist class faced a decline in profits. This was at a time in which millions of workers expected a more just (less racist and sexist) social order. In order to restore lost profit margins and destroy workers' power a number of tactics were used by the upper class during the 1970s and 1980s against workers. These tactics included the following:

(1) Fire union activists during organizing drives.
(2) Hire union—busting consultants.
(3) Place anti-worker representatives on the National Labor Relations Board.

(4) Threaten layoffs or plant closings to coerce workers into accepting less pay.

(5) Hire "permanent replacements" to replace striking workers.

(6) Use bankruptcy laws to get rid of union contracts.

These tactics were accompanied by other practices. For example, many full-time, steady high-salary jobs were redefined as part-time, temporary, low-salary jobs (e.g. college and university teaching positions). Also, capital imported millions of low-wage foreign workers from Mexico, Central America, China, and India. By using Foreign Labor Contractors to recruit Mexican workers, "snake-heads" (aka "snaketails") to ship Chinese workers, and the government's own H-2 guest worker program to procure IT-educated Indian workers for the Silicon Valley computer industries, capital has encouraged immigration. Importing low-wage labor has been facilitated by a number of factors. Privatization in China has destroyed the social safety net and led to an increase in unemployment and poverty for millions thus prompting many to look overseas for work. Low-intensity warfare by the U.S. in Central America during the 1980s and early 90s pushed many traumatized peasants on to the road to El Norte. And the export of capital to the Third World disrupted subsistence economies in a number of places, creating workers superfluous to the local economy and thus adding to the pool of potential immigrants.

In spite of these assaults on labor, three problems still faced capitalists: the welfare safety net, highly paid public sector unions, and unemployment. Workers who could survive on welfare payments are not workers willing to work for less than welfare, and better-paid public sector unions provide an example to private sector workers of the higher wages and benefits that were still possible—a bad example from the capitalists' point of view. Finally, millions of unemployed workers represented a huge pool of alienated, disaffected men and women who were not absorbed into the system in a productive way; they constituted a political threat. The solutions to these problems were simple and straightforward. Welfare was cut by the Clinton administration and much of it was replaced by "workfare." As Robin D.G. Kelley explains in the first selection, the substitution of workfare for welfare allows capital to replace unionized public sector jobs with below minimum wage workers. This further erodes the bargaining position of the working class by reducing the welfare safety net and the availability of well-paying union jobs in various cities and counties across America. Of course, the unemployed remain and are, disproportionately, young black and brown men. The solution to this "problem," as Christian Parenti points out, has been to expand the prison system to warehouse unemployed youth. As the French noted some years ago, the American unemployment rate is lower than the rates of other countries because the U.S. jails so many of its unemployed.

THE CARROTS: Producing a more inclusive class of "overseers" through multiculturalism and diversity.

Because of the tremendous anti-racist movement of the 1950s into the 1970s, the attacks on minority labor could not proceed by precisely the same methods and by those institutions and organizations which maintained the same old exclusionary membership lists. The command and control institutions of the nation had to open up for women and people of color if they were to maintain any political legitimacy. And open up they did—often through affirmative action programs and countless seminars on multiculturalism. There is now "diversity in the power elite" to borrow a phrase from Bill Domhoff. How diverse are the institutions of power and privilege? And what has been the primary effect of this new diversity? Has it led to a less racist society? Or have women and minorities found themselves co-opted or contained by the rules of class politics? Answers to these questions might be found in the following readings.

First, there is a brief selection from G. William Domhoff's book, *Diversity in the Power Elite,* looking at the actual social composition of today's power structure. There then follows a longer essay by John Pilger on working class life in post-apartheid South Africa and the relationship between the new black rulers and the old white power structure (i.e. capitalist class). Returning to an American focus, sociologist Steven Rosenthal reviews Adolph Reed, Jr.'s book on black politics after 1970, and community organizer Eric Mann offers an assessment of Tom Bradley's regime in Los Angeles. Two short pieces, one by Anthony Arnove and the other by Kevin Gray, discuss the assimilation of Jesse Jackson to the class politics of corporate America. Finally, UCI Ph.D., Anthony Dawahare, discusses the politics of diversity under capitalism in his paper "Workers of the World: Separate! 'Diversity' and the Legacy of Anticommunism in the Academic Workplace." Dawahare examines the published statements of the U.S. Army, Exxon Mobil, and the CIA to see what diversity means to the upper class. This is a very revealing and provocative essay.

16

WORKFARE REPLACES WELFARE

Robin D.G. Kelley

What three decades ago were seen as rights are now cast as a burden or drain on the state, or (in the case of affirmative action) discrimination against white guys. This free-market ideology has helped make government downsizing more palatable. In addition to the erosion of municipal and state tax bases due to capital flight and suburban tax revolts, major urban governments suffered huge cutbacks, which further resulted in the shrinking of urban labor markets. The federal government cut funds for cities and for poor people and reduced guarantees for benefits and services. Perhaps the most draconian measure of the late twentieth century is the welfare reform bill, signed not by a Republican president but by a self-proclaimed liberal Democrat: Bill Clinton. (It is more than a bit ironic that the welfare reform bill Clinton signed into law was called the "Personal Responsibility and Work Opportunity Reconciliation Act of 1996.") Among other things, the act replaces entitlements to Aid to Families with Dependent Children (AFDC) with state block grants, denies benefits to *legal* immigrants, and cuts funding for low-income programs, such as food stamps, Supplemental Security Income (SSI)—a program that targets the elderly and disabled poor—by $55 billion over the next six years.

The main purpose of the law is to force welfare recipients into an extremely low-wage labor market without concern for the needs of children. Under the new law, for example, recipients whose youngest child is more than a year old must do some form of paid or unpaid work after twenty-four months of receiving benefits, or lose their benefits altogether. By the year 2002, states are required to have 50 percent of single parents receiving cash assistance in work programs. Unfortunately, in order to meet their quota, it is easier for states to drop people from the rolls than try to employ them all. And those required to work who fail to find jobs within two months of receiving assistance must enroll in a mandatory "workfare" program. The Personal Responsibility Act does not include higher education in its definition of work or "training programs"; rather, welfare recipients will be limited to vocational programs approved by the state. To make matters worse, anyone convicted of a drug felony cannot receive direct aid or welfare *for life.* Unemployed adults between eighteen and fifty with no children will be limited to just three months of food stamps in any three-year period, which essentially means that the only safety net available to them would be unemployment insurance. Altogether, welfare reform will leave some 3.5 million children without any means of support. Moreover, we must consider the startling fact that approximately 60 percent of mothers on welfare have been battered; this means that the increased use of time limits might unintentionally force women back into abusive relationships in order to survive.

Short of a massive expansion of decent paying jobs to absorb the women and men being thrown off the welfare rolls, the end result will only be more misery and exploitation under the guise of "workfare." In New York City in 1996, about 30,000 welfare recipients employed by the Work Experience Program (WEP) earned biweekly "wages" as low as $68.50 in cash and $60 in food stamps. At twenty-six hours a week, the jobs range from street sweeping to transporting corpses in city hospitals. Most WEP workers are single, childless recipients of Home Relief, who under 1994 state law must work for their benefit checks. But with federal welfare reform an increasing number of mothers receiving funds through the Temporary Assistance to Needy Families Block Grants (TANF)—which replaces AFDC under the Personal Responsibility Act—will be added to the workfare rolls. By some estimates, under the new reforms at least 70,000 recipients will be added to the city's workfare programs.

The consequences for labor are potentially disastrous. Workfare undermines union-scale wages and creates an ultracheap, superexploited workforce without the basic protections that ordinary workers have. Indeed, in New York City the MTA has already begun to hire workfare workers to clean the subway trains at below-union wages. Furthermore, federal and state labor laws have made it difficult, if not impossible, for WEP workers to organize collectively and fight back. They are not entitled to bargain as a group under federal laws, nor do they come under the jurisdiction of the National Labor Relations Board, which essentially means that they cannot hold union elections under federal law. The conditions of work and the treatment they have received from regular employees leaves much to be desired. Street cleaners often have to work without gloves, and the chances for advancement within a job are slim to none. To add insult to injury, a sign hangs over the rest room in the New York City Sanitation Department building that reads, "No WEP Workers Allowed."

17

THE "NEW" CRIMINAL JUSTICE SYSTEM: STATE REPRESSION FROM 1968 TO 2001

Christian Parenti

Consider again the numbers: in the last twenty years the Justice Department's budget grew by 900 percent; over 60 percent of all prisoners are in for non-violent drug crimes; an estimated one-in-three black men between the ages of twenty and twenty-nine are under some type of criminal justice control or sought on a warrant; nationwide some 6.5 million people are in prison, on parole or probation. From the left it is clear that the United States is an over-policed, surveillance society that uses prison as one of its central social institutions.

But how are we to understand this? A common explanation, that spans the spectrum from the radical activists to the mainstream scriveners at the *Wall Street Journal*, portrays the prison boom as driven by direct and specific economic interests. For example we hear much about private prisons or prison labor. This economistic analysis is attractively simple, all one has to do is connect the dots: bad corporation here, human rights violations there. Unfortunately explaining prison in "anti-corporate" or other directly economic terms requires ignoring the facts. Private prisons are in crisis and losing money, prison labor is not profitable nor widespread, and most guards are not well organized or pushing their agenda on legislators. Nor do prison architects and medical providers, for the most part, mount huge lobbying operations that can be said to control policy. In short, prison is not profitable. [1]

Does this mean prison growth is simply irrational, with no coherent causal link to class exploitation and racism? Hardly. The new criminal justice system has every thing to do with the needs of capital and the ideology of white supremacy. More specifically, this repression is about two things: creating political obedience and regulating the price of labor. That is what the repression of the capitalist state has always been about, from the enclosures and the Atlantic slave trade, to the many bloody wars against organized labor, to the militarized ghetto of 2001. Capitalism was born of state violence and repression will always be part of its genetic code.

To understand the wider political effects of state violence it's worth contemplating the opposite: state assistance for poor and working people. As Frances Fox-Piven and Richard Cloward wrote in the *New Class War*, "the connection between the income-maintenance programs, the labor market and profits is indirect, but not complicated." Too much social democracy, and people stop being grateful for poorly paid, dangerous work. So too with the converse; the link between state repression and labor markets and profits is indirect but not complicated. Repression manages poverty. Poverty depresses wages. Low wages increase the rate of exploitation and that creates surplus value, which is what it is all about . . . at least at one level.

This dynamic works at a macro-scale upon the society and economy as a whole. Policing and incarceration—directly profitable or more likely not—are thus part of a larger circuitry of social control. Incarceration is the motherboard but other components include county jails, INS detention centers, the militarized border, psych wards, halfway houses, hospital emergency rooms, homeless shelters, skid row, and the ghetto. All of these locations share populations and all serve to contain and manage the social impacts of poverty. But what is the specific history of the current crackdown and how does the central question of class struggle shape the story of the new criminal justice system? Answering that question requires a trip back to the late 1960s, because the current buildup started then, plateaued briefly in the late seventies, and then began a second phase in the early 1980s, which has carried on into the present.

IN THE BEGINNING THERE WERE RIOTS . . .

During one of the mid-sixties "civil disturbances," an intrepid reporter, wanting to know why black people were looting, burning stores, and fighting cops, asked a young rioter: "What do you want?" "More ammunition," came the response. Imagine the terror of U.S. elites with riots every summer in hundreds of cities from 1964 through the early seventies. But the riots—just one part of a sustained revolt by African Americans—formed the ideological backdrop for a much larger general crisis of disobedience. Elements of this gathering storm included civil rights, Black Power, Vietnam, the anti-war mobilizations, poor people's movements, wild cat labor strikes, feminism, a sagging dollar, and, by the early seventies, slow growth and plunging profits.

In response to this panorama of mayhem, a new round of law and order politics began. The opening move was President Johnson's Omnibus Crime and Safe Streets Act of 1968, a bill that Congress debated just after the assassination of Dr. Martin Luther King. As the lawgivers toiled, smoke billowed up from D.C.'s bitterly poor Shaw district a mere two miles from the Capitol. From this crucible emerged a new super agency, the Law Enforcement Assistance Administration (LEAA), which over the next ten years spent billions of dollars rationalizing and retooling American law enforcement.

Johnson laid the initial groundwork for new criminal justice but Sunbelt Republicans, like Senator Barry Goldwater, were the first to supply the rhetorical fuel for the long crackdown. As the Senator said during his 1964 presidential campaign, "Security from domestic violence, no less than from foreign aggression is the most elementary form and fundamental purpose of any government." [2] Nixon noted the power in Goldwater's script, and in 1966 told *U.S. News and World Report*: "the deterioration [in respect for law and order] can be traced directly to the spread of the corrosive doctrine that every citizen possesses an inherent right to decide for himself which laws to obey and when to disobey them." [3] As Dan Baum pointed out in *Smoke and Mirrors* (1996), Nixon was conflating street crime with civil disobedience, the left, and the larger question of resistance. Likewise, Goldwater linked the redistributive efforts of the war on poverty to criminal violence: "If it is entirely proper for the government to take away from some to give to others, then won't some be led to believe that they can rightfully take from anyone who has more than they? No wonder law and order has broken down, mob violence has engulfed great American cities, and our wives feel unsafe in the streets." [4]

At the heart of this new politics was an old trope—white racism and the need for an internal enemy. As Nixon's Chief of Staff, H. R. Haldeman, put it: "[The President] emphasized that you have to face that the whole problem is really the blacks. The key is to devise a system that recognizes this while not appearing to." [5] At the same time police began openly discussing their work as "counterinsurgency." Law enforcement trade journals ran articles such as the September 1966 piece in *The Police Chief* entitled "Police-Military Relations in a Revolutionary Environment," authored by an instructor from the U.S. Army War College, "It is now generally agreed among counterinsurgency experts that one of the most important aspects of counter-insurgency operations is the control of population and resources. . . . Techniques to control the people include individual and family identification, curfews, travel permits, static and mobile checkpoint operations, and the prevention of assemblies or rallies." The article went on to describe rising crime rates as a precursor to revolution, and to laud the "value of an effective police organization—both civil and military—in maintaining law and order, whether in California, Pennsylvania, Mississippi, or the rice paddies and jungles of Viet-Nam."

Overseeing this techno-political revolution in U.S. policing was the federal government, particularly the LEAA. As Tony Platt and other radical criminologists of the 1970s detailed at the time, the LEAA provided local cops with money, military weaponry, communications gear, and special training and forced them into new interagency forms of co-operation. Under LEAA guidance, police first started using helicopters, SWAT teams, body armor, computers, and shoulder radios; they also instituted literacy requirements and basic competency tests.

Eventually this first phase of the build-up plateaued. By the late seventies even many mainstream, middle-class, white Americans began to tire of government repression, as a series of scandals great and small exposed the seamier side of politics and policing. As the 1975 *Congressional Quarterly Almanac* noted, "It was an ironic twist on the 'law and order' theme of the first years of the Nixon administration: the crimes which drew the most attention in the administration's last years were those committed by or charged against the men who held some of the highest offices, including Nixon himself." After Watergate came the Knapp Commission hearings exposing New York Police Department corruption, the Church Committee's findings on domestic spying, and from other quarters came more revelations about the brutality in Southern prisons. All of this caused a momentary pause in the otherwise forward momentum of the criminal justice juggernaut.

NEOLIBERAL JUSTICE: MANAGING MISERY

The lull was short lived. By the early mid-eighties President Reagan's men had started escalating domestic repression once more. But this second stage of the buildup was not about crushing rebellion; that job had been done. There were no more riots; the mighty Black Panther Party was long gone; the antiwar movement dead; and even many radical community organizations had been domesticated, their rank and file demobilized, their leaders reduced to funding addicts, living obediently from one Ford Foundation grant to the next.

Instead, this second stage of repression was about "order maintenance" in an epoch of harsh economic restructuring; it was an attempt to physically contain and politically "explain away" (via racist and often sexist victim-blaming) the seismic dislocations of the Reagan-Bush-Clinton era of neo-liberal economic restructuring. But why the economic restructuring, was it simple greed or something deeper? Ultimately, the neoliberal offensive of the eighties was a response to the end of the post-war boom and to the economic stagnation and weak profits of the seventies. It was "creative destruction" designed to end a crisis of overaccumulation. By the late sixties, it was clear the recovery of the post-war era had finally played itself out and there was just too much capital, too much stuff, and not enough profitable outlets for investment; not enough consumption to keep the colossus moving.

Reagan's response was a class war against labor. Between 1979 and 1982, the real average weekly wage fell more than 8 percent. As Bennett Harrison and Barry Bluestone put it in *The Great U-Turn*, "with wage growth arrested by unemployment, what growth occurred during the Reagan period rebounded mostly to the profits side of the capital-labor ledger" (p. 92). Between 1980 and 1985, the Department of Labor estimates that some 2.3 million manufacturing jobs disappeared for good. As industrial jobs evaporated, so too did attendant retail jobs, the local tax base, and much municipal employment.

This was accompanied by a right-wing assault on the disadvantaged and dispossessed. Labor unions, which had maintained some power in the 1970s and whose members had been extremely troublesome (wildcat strikes, absenteeism, and the like), were subjected to a vicious frontal assault. In 1982 alone the Reagan administration cut the real value of welfare by 24 percent; slashed the budget for child nutrition by 35 percent; reduced funding for school milk programs by 78 percent and urban development action grants by 35 percent; shrank educational block grants by 38 percent; and simply abolished the Comprehensive Employment and Training Act which had employed four hundred thousand.

This multifaceted society-wide class assault from above had a single unifying aim: discipline for the laboring classes. Neo-conservative "theorist" George Gilder summed it up nicely. "The poor must work hard, and they must work harder than the classes above them." [6] The policy package known as "Reaganomics" was an effort to boost profit margins by increasing the rate of exploitation. And by the mid-late eighties profitability was recovering, but with enormous social costs. Chicago saw its number of ghetto census tracts increase by 61.5 percent between 1980 and 1990; cities like Cleveland, Philadelphia, and Boston saw similar changes. Overall, the number of African Americans who found themselves living in "ghetto" census tracts, due to middle class flight, job loss, etc., grew by one third. So, too, did homelessness make a dramatic comeback.

Enlarging the industrial reserve army of labor—the unemployed—brought with it serious political problems. Simply stated, capitalism always needs poverty and creates poverty, but is simultaneously always threatened by poverty. The poor keep wages down, but they also create trouble in three ways. First, their presence calls into question capitalism's moral claims (the system can't work for "everyone" when beggars are in the street). Second, the poor threaten and menace the moneyed classes aesthetically and personally simply by being in the wrong spaces. (Gourmet dining isn't quite the same when done in the presence of mendicant paupers.) And finally, the poor threaten to rebel in organized and unorganized ways. This simple fact punctuating every moment in history is systematically expunged from official texts. Yet the past is full of poor and working peoples' rebellions, from the United Mine Workers dropping dynamite on the West Virginia state militia, to the National Welfare Rights Organization flipping desks in welfare offices across the county, to the Teamsters bringing the United Parcel Service to its knees. Thus the poor and working classes must always be physically controlled.

The mechanism of the second phase of the criminal justice escalation was, of course, Reagan's vicious and hyperbolic War on Drugs. The reengaged buildup began quietly, at first FBI funding was doubled; wiretap laws were loosened; and more money was doled out for the U.S. Bureau of Prisons. Meanwhile, Reagan's Chief of Staff, Ed Meese, and his Attorney General, William French Smith, started demanding changes in the criminal code that would "increase the power of the prosecutors."

Aiding that effort came a battery of new right-wing federal judges. And from the U.S. Supreme Court came several crucial decisions, notably Gates v. Illinois, which made it easier for police to obtain search warrants based on anonymous tips, and *United States v. Leon*, which allowed police to use defective and partially false warrants in obtaining evidence.

But the buildup really took off with the Federal Crime Bill of 1984. This created the assets forfeiture laws enabling police to keep as much as 90 percent of all the "drug tainted" property they could seize. Nationwide, the total amount of all seizures grew from about $100 million in 1981 to over $1 billion by fiscal year 1987. Thus did the feds entice local police into their plans for total war at home. The next congressional election brought another massive crime bill. Only eighteen lawmakers voted against the catch-all Anti-Drug-Abuse Act of 1986, which imposed twenty-nine new mandatory minimum sentences, among them the notoriously racist disparity in the penalties for crack and for powder cocaine. This bill also shifted official rhetoric from hunting "king pins" to rounding up "users."

The escalating repression hit people of color hardest, and black people hardest of all. In 1980, African Americans made up 12 percent of the nation's population and over 23 percent of all those arrested on drug charges. Ten years later, African Americans were still 12 percent of the total population, but made up more than 40 percent of all people busted for narcotics. Still more remarkable, over 60 percent of all narcotics convictions were (and are) for African Americans. Overall, drug arrests almost doubled in the late eighties: 1985 saw roughly eight hundred thousand people taken down on drug charges; by 1989 that number had shot up to almost 1.4 million.

By the late eighties, lawmakers and the media were locked in a symbiotic hysteria— a political perpetual motion machine—and the drug war juggernaut was steaming ahead at full throttle. The racist PR of this onslaught reached its zenith with the Hill & Knowlton produced TV ads featuring convicted rapist-murderer Willie Horton who escaped prison while Michael Dukakis was governor. (As Alexander Cockburn and Jeffrey St. Clair remind us, it was Al Gore who first deployed the Willie Horton story during the Democratic primaries.) The 1988 crime bill emerging from his most grotesque of planned panics created, among other things, the cabinet level "drug czar" and pumped millions more in federal funds to police and prison construction. The bill also created a "one strike" policy for public housing. Any tenant caught with even a tiny amount of drugs or paraphernalia is now subject to automatic eviction. One recent victim of this policy was seventy-five-year-old Herman Walker of Oakland, California. A home-care attendant was caught with drug paraphernalia in Walker's apartment so the old man was "kicked to the curb."

The Clinton presidency brought new heights of viciousness. The specter of the Los Angeles riots—which were for the ruling class a frightening psychedelic blast from the past—spurred the New Democrats on in their design and implementation of the most racist and merciless policies yet. Their magnum opus was the 1994 Violent Crime Control and Law Enforcement Act, which offered up a cop's cornucopia of $30.2 billion in federal cash from which we got Clinton's one hundred thousand new police officers, scores of new prisons, and SWAT teams in even small New England towns.

Two years later, with another election on the way, Clinton gave us the Anti-Terrorism and Effective Death Penalty Act, which massively expanded the use of the death penalty and eviscerated federal habeas corpus. If this law had been in effect years earlier, one of Clinton's favorite movies, *Hurricane,* would never have been made because Rubin "Hurricane" Carter would have been denied his exonerating retrial. And for the people "inside," that same election year delivered the Prison Litigation Reform Act. This little examined law barred many prisoners from access to the civil courts; helped eliminate prison law libraries; kept liberal judges from imposing meaningful penalties on abusive prison administrators; and stripped lawyers of their ability to receive legal fees when handling prison civil rights suits. The sad election year of 1996 also delivered the ideologically named "Illegal Immigration Reform and Immigrant Responsibility Act," which eliminated the undocumented person's right to due process and helped bring Immigration and Naturalization Service (INS) funding up to four billion annually. These were the Clinton administration's demolition devices, strategically placed to take out what little remained for prisoners in the Bill of Rights. The damage from this mid-nineties frenzy of hate is so massive that a full accounting is as yet impossible.

Coinciding with these federal laws came a tsunami of state laws. California made over a thousand changes to its criminal code during the eighties and nineties. Looking back we can see clearly the effects—intentional or otherwise—of this generalized project of repression: racialize the discussion of poverty via the code of crime and then hound the victims with police narc squads, SWAT teams, and "zero tolerance" enforcement; send the INS to raid their homes; and lock up as many as possible for as long as possible.

To recap, criminal justice regulates, absorbs, terrorizes, and disorganizes the poor. At the same time it promulgates racism; demonizing, disenfranchising, and marginalizing ever-larger numbers of brown working-class people; and in so doing it creates pseudo explanations and racialized scapegoats with which to delude downwardly mobile voters; this after all is the very lifeblood of American electoral politics! And most important, prison allows for the economically heuristic effects of mass unemployment without the political destabilization mass poverty can bring. Nor does the new model of control let loose dangerous Great Society style notions of "racial equality" and "social inclusion." These ideological side effects from controlling the poor via co-optation (welfare) were almost as bad as the economic support once offered by the insipient, inadequate, but real American welfare state to the restive working classes. As Reagan's first Attorney General, William French Smith, put it, "The justice department is not a domestic agency. . . . It is the internal arm of national defense." [7]

Today, the poor are thoroughly locked-down. Law enforcement has moved to the center of domestic politics; state violence is perhaps more than ever a constant, regular a normal feature of poor people's lives. Police, private security, and closed circuit television secure revitalized city centers; while American ghettos are in political disarray, wracked by poverty, disease, addiction, and engineered illiteracy. When the best and the brightest in the 'hood do organize, the state comes down fast and furious. Take for example, the gang truce movements in Chicago, New York, and Los Angeles. In each case the political leaders were framed, busted, and replaced by apolitical thugs. This was true for the Vice Lords and the Latin Kings, as well as for the Crips and Bloods.

Thus the new criminal justice system does an excellent job of destroying the social fabric upon which any future political rebellion would rely for coherence at the same time as it has created a system of surveillance and repression that is already being used against a new protest movement. The courts—retooled by a generation of conservative judicial appointments and crazed case law—now function as social abettors, in which the poor and the dark skinned are shunted off to a concrete hell with industrial efficiency. Left behind are broken families, more addiction, more disease, more illiteracy, and thus a more docile society. All this for the political security of capital. This is how class struggle is waged from above.

NOTES

1. For a full version of this argument see the last chapter in Christian Parenti, *Lockdown America* (Verso, 2000).
2. "Goldwater's Acceptance Speech to GOP Convention," *New York Times,* July 17 1964.
3. Richard Nixon, "If Mob Rule Takes Hold in the US: A Warning from Richard Nixon," *U.S. News and World Report,* August 15, 1966, 5.
4. Quoted in Katherine Beckett, *Making Crime Pay: Law and Order in Contemporary American Politics* (Oxford: Oxford University Press, 1997), 28.
5. H. R. Haldeman, *The Haldeman Diaries: Inside the Nixon White House* (New York: P. G. Putman's Sons, 1994), 53; quoted in Baum, op citain.
6. George Gilder, *Wealth and Poverty* (New York: Basic Books, 1981), 82.
7. Quoted in Dan Baum, *Smoke and Mirrors* (New York: Little, Brown and Company, 1996), 137–138.

> The last decade has . . . seen the highest rates and fastest increase in mass incarceration in the history of the Country. These glaring facts, in conjunction with the current trends of the increasing concentration of national minority people in the prisons and the ever increasing sensitivity of the prison system to the demands of monopoly capitalism, insure that the prison problem in America can only get worse. . . . Reactionary politicians play on the fears and worries of the people about street and other crimes. Their proposals for still more repression, however, provide no solution. Longer prison sentences and harsher treatment of prisoners clearly have no bearing on the root cause of the growth of crime: unemployment and racism. . . . Short of a major social transformation, militant struggle against racism and for a new WPA (or its equivalent) is the only meaningful approach to the reduction of crime and the prison population.
> Richard D. Vogel, "Capitalism and Incarceration,"
> *Monthly Review,* March 1983

18

HAS THE POWER ELITE GONE MULTICULTURAL?

Richard L. Zweigenhaft and G. William Domhoff

Injustices based on race, gender, ethnicity, and sexual orientation have been the most emotional and contested issues in American society since the end of the 1960s, far exceeding concerns with social class, and rivaled only by conflicts about abortion. These issues are now subsumed under the umbrella terms *diversity* and *multiculturalism,* and they have been written about extensively from the perspectives of both the aggrieved and those at the middle and lower levels of the social ladder who resist any changes.

In this book we look at multiculturalism from a new angle: we examine its impact on the small group at the top of American society that we call the power elite—those who own and manage large banks and corporations, finance the political campaigns of conservative Democrats and virtually all Republicans at the state and national levels, and serve in government as appointed officials and military leaders. We ask whether the decades of pressure from civil rights groups, feminists, and gay and lesbian rights activists has resulted in a more culturally diverse power elite. If it has, what effects has this new diversity had on the functioning of the power elite and on its relation to the rest of society?

We also compare our findings on the power elite with those from our parallel study of Congress to see whether there are differences in social background, education, and party affiliation for minorities and women in these two realms of power. We explore the possibility that elected officials come from a wider range of occupational and income backgrounds than members of the power elite. In addition, we ask whether either of the major political parties has been more active than the other in advancing the careers of women and minorities.

According to many commentators, the higher circles in the United States had indeed become multicultural by the late 1980s and early 1990s. Some went even further, saying that the old power elite had been pushed aside entirely. The demise of the "old" power elite was the theme of such books as Nelson Aldrich's *Old Money* and Robert Christopher's *Crashing the Gates,* the latter emphasizing the rise of ethnic minorities.[1] There have also been wide-eyed articles in mainstream magazines, such as one in the late 1980s in *U.S. News and World Report* entitled "The New American Establishment," which celebrated a new diversity at the top, claiming that "new kinds of men and women" have "taken control of institutions that influence important aspects of American life." School and club ties are no longer important, the article announced; the new role of women was highlighted with a picture of some of the "wise women" who had joined the "wise men" who dominated the old establishment.[2]

Then, in July 1995, *Newsweek* ran a cover story on "The Rise of the Overclass," featuring a gallery of one hundred high-tech, media, and Wall Street stars, women as well as men, minorities as well as whites, who supposedly come from all rungs of the social ladder.[3] The term *overclass* was relatively new, but the argument—that the power elite was dead, superseded by a diverse meritocratic elite—was not.

We are wary about these claims announcing the arrival of new elites because they never have been documented systematically. Moreover, they are suspect because similar claims have been made repeatedly in American history and have been proved incorrect each time. In popular books and magazines from the 1830s, 1920s, and 1950s, the leading commentators of the day assert that there used to be a tightly knit and cohesive governing group in the United States, but not any longer. A closer look at the supposedly new era several decades later has invariably shown that the new power group was primarily the old one after all, with a few additions and alterations here and there.[4]

Since the 1870s the refrain about the new diversity of the governing circles has been closely intertwined with a staple of American culture created by Horatio Alger Jr., whose name has become synonymous with upward mobility in America. Born in 1832 to a patrician family—Alger's father was a Harvard graduate, a Unitarian minister, and a Massachusetts state senator—Alger graduated from Harvard at the age of nineteen. There followed a series of unsuccessful efforts to establish himself in various careers. Finally, in 1864 Alger was hired as a Unitarian minister in Brewster, Massachusetts. Fifteen months later, he was dismissed from this position for homosexual acts with boys in the congregation.

Alger returned to New York, where he soon began to spend a great deal of time at the Newsboys' Lodging House, founded in 1853 for footloose youngsters between the ages of twelve and sixteen and home to many youths who had been mustered out of the Union Army after serving as drummer boys. At the Newsboys' Lodging House Alger found his literary niche and his subsequent claim to fame: writing books in which poor boys make good. His books sold by the hundreds of thousands in the last third of the nineteenth century, and by 1910 they were enjoying annual sales of more than one million in paperback.[5]

The deck is not stacked against the poor, according to Horatio Alger. When they simply show a bit of gumption, work hard, and thereby catch a break or two, they can become part of the American elite. The persistence of this theme, reinforced by the annual Horatio Alger Awards to such well-known personalities as Ronald Reagan, Bob

Hope, and Billy Graham (who might not have been so eager to accept them if they had known of Alger's shadowed past), suggests that we may be dealing once again with a cultural myth. In its early versions, of course, the story concerned the great opportunities available for poor white boys willing to work their way to the top. More recently, the story has featured black Horatio Algers who started in the ghetto, Latino Horatio Algers who started in the barrio, Asian-American Horatio Algers whose parents were immigrants, and female Horatio Algers who seem to have no class backgrounds—all of whom now sit on the boards of the country's largest corporations.

But is any of this true? Can anecdotes and self-serving autobiographical accounts about diversity, meritocracy, and upward social mobility survive a more systematic analysis? Have very many women and previously excluded minorities made it to the top? Has class lost its importance in shaping life chances?

In this book we address these and related questions within the framework provided by the iconoclastic sociologist C. Wright Mills in his hard-hitting classic *The Power Elite,* published in 1956 when the media were in the midst of what Mills called the Great American Celebration. In spite of the Depression of the 1930s, Americans had pulled together to win World War II, and the country was both prosperous at home and influential abroad. Most of all, according to enthusiasts, the United States had become a relatively classless and pluralistic society, where power belonged to the people through their political parties and public opinion. Some groups certainly had more power than others, but no group or class had too much. The New Deal and World War II had forever transformed the corporate-based power structure of earlier decades.

Mills challenged this celebration of pluralism by studying the social backgrounds and career paths of the people who occupied the highest positions in what he saw as the three major institutional hierarchies in postwar America—the corporations, the executive branch of the federal government, and the military. He found that almost all the members of this leadership group, which he called the power elite, were white Christian males who came from "at most, the upper third of the income and occupational pyramids," despite the many Horatio Algeresque claims to the contrary.[6] A majority came from an even narrower stratum, the 11 percent of U.S. families headed by businesspeople or highly educated professionals like physicians and lawyers. Mills concluded that power in the United States in the 1950s was just about as concentrated as it had been since the rise of the large corporations, although he stressed that the New Deal and World War II had given political appointees and military chieftains more authority than they had exercised previously.

It is our purpose, therefore, to take a detailed look at the social, educational, and occupational backgrounds of the leaders of these three institutional hierarchies to see whether they have become more diverse in terms of gender, race, ethnicity, and sexual orientation, and also in terms of socioeconomic origins. Unlike Mills, we think the power elite is more than a set of institutional leaders. It is also the leadership group for the small upper class of owners and managers of large income-producing properties, the 1 percent of Americans who in 1992 possessed 37.2% of all net worth.[7] But that theoretical difference is not of great moment here. The important commonality is the great wealth and power embodied in these institutional hierarchies and the people who lead them.

We first study the directors and chief executive officers of the largest banks and corporations, as determined by annual rankings compiled by *Fortune* magazine. The use of *Fortune* rankings is now standard practice in studies of corporate size and power. Over the years, *Fortune* has changed the number of corporations on its annual list and the way it groups them. For example, the separate listings by business sector in the past, like "life insurance companies," "diversified financial companies," and "service companies," have been combined into one overall list, primarily because many large businesses are now in more than one of the traditional sectors. Generally speaking, we use the *Fortune* list or lists available for the time period under consideration.

Second, again following Mills, we focus on the appointees to the president's cabinet when we turn to the "political directorate," his general term for top-level officials in the executive branch of the federal government. We also have included the director of the Central Intelligence Agency in one chapter because of the increased importance of that agency since Mills wrote. In chapters concerning groups that have not had anyone in presidential cabinets, we profile the highest-level appointees as of 1995. Third, and rounding out our portrait of the power elite, we examine the same top positions in the military—generals and admirals—that formed the basis for Mills's look at the military elite.

As noted at the outset of this introduction, we also study Congress. In the case of senators, we do the same kind of background studies that we do for members of the power elite. For members of the House of Representatives, we concern ourselves only with party affiliation for most groups. We include findings on women and minority senators and representatives for two reasons. First, this allows us to see whether there is more diversity in the electoral system than in the power elite. Second, we do not think—as Mills did—that Congress should be relegated to the "middle level" of power. To the contrary, we believe that Congress is an integral part of the power structure in America.

Until the 1980s, most northern Republicans and most southern Democrats supported the power elite on the labor, welfare, and business regulation issues critical to it, whereas a majority of Democrats outside of the South were sympathetic to a coalition of liberals, minorities, and labor. Due to the Voting Rights Act of 1965 and the gradual industrialization of the South since World War II, southern conservatives have moved steadily into the Republican Party. At the same time, many moderate Republicans outside the South have been defeated by Democrats, leading to a situation where the two major power coalitions are increasingly housed almost exclusively in just one of the two dominant political parties. We therefore can use party preference to gauge whether women and minorities in the power elite differ from women and minorities elected to Congress in terms of how liberal or conservative they are.

In addition to studying the extent to which women and minorities have risen in the system, we focus on whether they have followed different avenues to the top than their predecessors did, and on any special roles they may play. Are they in the innermost circles of the power elite, or are they more likely to serve as buffers and go-betweens? Do they go just so far and no farther? What obstacles does each group face?

We also examine whether or not the presence of women and minorities affects the power elite itself. Do those women and minorities who become part of the power elite influence it in a more liberal direction, or do they end up endorsing traditional conservative positions, such as opposition to trade unions, taxes, and government regulation of business? In addition, in the final chapter we consider the possibility that the diversity forced on the power elite has had the ironic effect of strengthening it, at least in the short run, by providing it with people who can reach out to the previously excluded groups and by showing that the American system can deliver on its most important promise, an equal opportunity for every individual.

These are not simple issues, and the answers to some of the questions we ask vary greatly depending on which previously disadvantaged group we are talking about. Nonetheless, in the course of our research, a few general patterns emerged that we examine throughout the text and then tie together in the final chapter. Six general points may help readers to see the patterns develop as we embark upon a narrative in the next six chapters that focuses on specific issues related to entry into the power elite by Jews, women, blacks, Latinos, Asian Americans, and, finally, gays and lesbians.

(1) The power elite now shows considerable diversity, at least as compared with its state in the 1950s, but its core group continues to be wealthy white Christian males, most of whom are still from the upper third of the social ladder. They have been filtered through a handful of elite schools in law, business, public policy, and international relations.

(2) In spite of the increased diversity of the power elite, high social origins continue to be a distinct advantage in making it to the top. There are relatively few rags-to-riches stories in the groups we studied, and those we did find tended to come through the electoral process, usually within the Democratic Party. In general, it still takes at least three generations to rise from the bottom to the top in the United States.

(3) The new diversity within the power elite is transcended by common values and a sense of hard-earned class privilege. The newcomers to the power elite have found ways to signal that they are willing to join the game as it has always been played, assuring the old guard that they will call for no more than relatively minor adjustments, if that. There are few liberals and fewer crusaders in the

power elite, despite its new multiculturalism. Class backgrounds, current roles, and future aspirations are more powerful in shaping behavior in the power elite than gender, ethnicity, or race.

(4) Not all the groups we studied have been equally successful in contributing to the new diversity in the power elite. Women, blacks, Latinos, Asian Americans, and openly homosexual men and women are all underrepresented, but to varying degrees and with different rates of increasing representation. We will explore the reasons for these differences in our final chapter.

(5) Although the corporate, political, and military elites accepted diversity only in response to pressure from minority activists and feminists, these elites have benefited from the presence of new members. Some serve either a buffer or a liaison function with such groups and institutions as consumers, angry neighborhoods, government agencies, and wealthy foreign entrepreneurs.

(6) There is a greater diversity in Congress than in the power elite, and the majority of the female and minority elected officials are Democrats.

ENDNOTES

1. Nelson W. Aldrich Jr., *Old Money: The Mythology of America's Upper Class* (New York: Knopf, 1988); Robert C. Christopher, *Crashing the Gates: The De-WASPing of America's Power Elite* (New York: Simon and Schuster, 1989).

2. "The New American Establishment," *U.S. News and World Report,* February 8, 1988, pp. 39, 45–46.

3. "The Rise of the Overclass," *Newsweek,* July 31, 1995, pp. 32–46.

4. Edward Pessen, *Riches, Class, and Power Before the Civil War* (Lexington, Mass.: D. C. Heath, 1973); Edward Pessen, ed., *Three Centuries of Social Mobility in America* (Lexington, Mass.: D. C. Heath, 1974).

5. See Richard M. Huber, *The American Idea of Success* (New York: McGraw Hill, 1971), 44–46; Gary Scharnhorst, *Horatio Alger, Jr.* (Boston: Twayne, 1980), 24, 29, 141.

6. C. Wright Mills, *The Power Elite* (New York: Oxford University Press, 1956), 279. For Mills's specific findings, see 104–105, 128–129, 180–181, 393–394, and 400–401.

7. Edward N. Wolff, *Top Heavy* (New York: New Press, 1996), 67.

THE IRONIES OF DIVERSITY

Richard L. Zweigenhaft and G. William Domhoff

As the preceding chapters have shown in detail, the power elite and Congress are more diverse than they were before the social movements that emerged in the 1960s brought pressure to bear on corporations, politicians, and government. Although the power elite is still composed primarily of Christian white men, there are now Jews, women, blacks, Latinos, and Asian Americans on the boards of the country's largest corporations; presidential cabinets are far more diverse than was the case forty years ago; and the highest ranks of the military are no longer filled solely by white men. In the case of elected officials in Congress, the trend toward diversity is even greater for women and all of the minority groups that we have studied. At the same time, we have shown that the assimilation of the different groups has been uneven. In this final chapter, we explain the successful assimilation by women and minorities into the power elite and Congress in terms of four factors: identity management; the importance of class; the importance of education; and the importance of light skin. We conclude that class origin is the most important factor for all groups except blacks and "Indian-appearing" Latinos, and we offer a general explanation for the continuing exclusion of people with darker skins.

Ultimately we suggest that the increase in diversity at the top contains several ironies, the most important of which is related to what is perhaps the major unresolved tension in American life, between liberal individualism and the class structure. The diversification of the power elite has been celebrated, but this celebration ignores the continuing importance of the class structure. The movements that led to diversity in the power elite have succeeded to some extent, especially for women and minorities from privileged social backgrounds, but there has been no effect on the way the power elite functions or on the class structure itself.

IDENTITY MANAGEMENT

We have seen that newcomers who seek to join the power elite have to find ways to demonstrate their loyalty to those who dominate American institutions—straight white Christian males. We can recall, for example, Cecily Cannan Selby's decision to reduce tension at a dinner meeting with the previously all-male Avon Products board by lighting up a cigar, or Hazel O'Leary's realization that she had to learn to play golf if she expected to advance in her corporate career. We can envision William T. Coleman demonstrating his elite educational background by reciting great poetry with his fellow law clerk Elliot Richardson. Reading between the lines of traditional stereotypes, we can imagine Jewish and black executives being properly reserved, Asian-American executives acting properly assertive, gay executives behaving in traditionally masculine ways and lesbian executives in traditionally feminine ways. Thus we have seen the importance of identity management. As Terrie Miyamoto of U.S. West put it, the challenge is to move into a "comfort zone" with those who decide who is and is not acceptable for inclusion.

At the same time, in Chapter 2 we drew on the work of sociologist Rosabeth Kanter to stress that the demand for demonstrations of outward conformity by established leaders is not primarily a matter of personal prejudice or cultural heritage. It is, instead, the need for trust and smooth working relationships within complex organizations that leads to the marked preference for women and minorities who think and act like the straight Christian males running those organizations. The social movements that arose in the 1960s were able to rock the boat enough to open up some space for nontraditional leaders, but not enough to change the way in which institutions are managed. Unless and until such changes are made in institutional governance, women and minorities will be at a disadvantage in climbing the managerial hierarchy even though they are now allowed to enter the competition.

Identity management, however, is only the final step, the icing on the cake, so to speak. Before atypical candidates for acceptance into the higher circles can even think about making adjustments in their personas, they have to meet prerequisites that are attainable by only a small percentage of the population whatever their race, ethnicity, gender, or sexual orientation. It is to these prerequisites that we now turn.

THE IMPORTANCE OF CLASS

Those who brought diversity to the power elite tended to come from business and professional backgrounds, like the white Christian males whom Mills studied more than forty years ago. Fully one-third of the women who have become corporate directors are from the upper class, and many others are from the middle and upper middle classes. Most of the Cuban Americans and Chinese Americans who have risen to the top have come from displaced ruling classes, a far cry from the conventional image of the immigrant. The Jews and Japanese Americans in high positions have mostly been the products of two- and three-generational climbs up the social ladder. The first black members of the corporate elite and the cabinet tended to come from the small black middle class that predated the civil rights movement. Although there is no systematic information on the social backgrounds of gay and lesbian leaders, who are treated in most studies as if they had no class origins, our anecdotal information suggests that many visible activists and professionals come from business and professional families as well.

A high-level social background, of course, makes it easier to acquire the values, attitudes, and styles that are necessary to hire, fire, and manage the work lives of employees with blue, white, and pink collars. This point can be extended to include even those from more modest circumstances, like Lauro Cavazos, whose father was a ranch foreman, or Katherine Ortega, Sue Ginn, and David Geffen, whose families owned small businesses, or David Mixner, whose father was in charge of minority farmhands on a farm he did not own. Most of those we studied, in other words, learned firsthand that a few people boss the majority or have independent professions based on academic credentials, and that they were expected to be part of this managerial and professional stratum.

When we compare women and minority members of the power elite with their counterparts in Congress, however, two further generalizations emerge. First, members of the power elite tend to come from more privileged social backgrounds than the elected officials. Second, the elected women and minorities are more likely to be Democrats than Republicans. These two findings suggest that there are class and political dimensions to our findings on the differences between the power elite and Congress that cut across gender and ethnic lines. If the power elite comes to be housed almost exclusively in the Republican Party as well-to-do southerners leave the Democrats and as the liberal-labor coalition becomes more important within the Democratic Party, then the country's traditional regional, racial, and ethnic politics may be replaced by a more clear-cut class-and-values politics, with both the Republicans and Democrats being able to say that they are multicultural in terms of gender and minority representation.[1]

THE IMPORTANCE OF EDUCATION

Class by no means explains all of our findings, however. Education also matters a great deal. The women and minorities who make it to the power elite are typically better educated than the white males who are already a part of it. This was seen with the European-American women and African Americans on corporate boards and in presidential cabinets, as well as the successful Asian-American immigrants. Education seems to have given them the edge needed to be accepted into the power elite.

Moreover, it is not merely academic degrees that matter but also where those degrees are from. Again and again, we saw that a significant minority were from the same few schools that educate Christian white male leaders—Harvard, Yale, Princeton, and MIT on the East Coast, the University of Chicago in the Midwest, Stanford and the University of California on the West Coast. Three of the five Asian-American appointees to the executive branch, for example, have at least one degree from Harvard (Julia Chang Bloch, Elaine Chao, and Lon Hatamiya). The other two attended the University of Chicago (Patsy Mink) and the University of California (Dennis Hayashi).

These elite schools not only confer status on their graduates but also provide contacts with white male elites that are renewed throughout life at alumni gatherings and other special occasions. School connections in turn lead to invitations to attend exclusive social events and join expensive social clubs, which extend the newcomers' social networks even further. With success in business or a profession comes invitations to serve on boards of trustees of elite foundations and universities, and the circle is completed.

The newcomers become part of the ongoing institutional framework that defines and shapes the power elite in the United States, even though they are unlikely to reach the very top. The individuals in the power elite may come and go, and they may diversify in gender, ethnicity, and sexual orientation, but there is stability and continuity within the overall power structure.

As was true of social class origins, there is a difference in educational attainment between those in the power elite and those in Congress: the men and women elected to Congress are not as likely as those in the power elite to have attended elite colleges and universities or to have earned postgraduate degrees.

THE IMPORTANCE OF COLOR

Just as class alone cannot explain all of our findings, neither can the combination of class and education: color also matters. African Americans and darker-skinned Latinos find it more difficult than others to use their educational credentials as a passport to occupational success. This can be seen poignantly in our skin-color comparisons of successful blacks and Latinos. Even among those who had achieved some level of prominence (measured by inclusion in *Ebony*'s fiftieth anniversary issue or the *Hispanic Business* listing of "Hispanic influentials"), those who had made it into the power elite were lighter skinned than those who had not. On this score, our data simply reinforce earlier work by others. As the Glass Ceiling Commission reported, "Our society has developed an extremely sophisticated, and often denied, acceptability index based on gradations in skin color."[2]

There is another side of the coin: darker-skinned blacks may have a harder time finding jobs and may, if convicted of crimes, receive stiffer jail sentences.[3] Furthermore, both blacks and Latinos in the United States understand (and sometimes indulge in) the discrimination against those who are darkest. Blacks speak openly of the advantage lighter-skinned blacks have, and surveys of Latinos reveal that those who are described as "Indian" in appearance report greater discrimination than do Latinos who are described as more Caucasian in appearance.[4]

These findings on color discrimination may be useful in explaining why the assimilation of blacks into the power elite may be slowing down. The failure of American society to accept darker-skinned citizens—especially blacks—is the single most important issue that needs to be understood by social scientists.

THE IRONIES OF DIVERSITY

The impetus for greater diversity, as we have stressed, did not come from within the power elite but was the result of external pressures. Generally speaking, members of the power elite reluctantly accepted diversification as a goal for themselves only because they had little choice. This point is best demonstrated in the case of one aspect of diversity called affirmative action, a set of programs designed to create more job opportunities for African Americans.

As John Skrentny argues, the idea of affirmative action as a policy was adopted by business and political elites very hurriedly in the face of the 290 serious urban disturbances that occurred between 1963 and 1968. These elites quickly legitimized what they saw as preferential hiring through a series of special commissions and government hearings, before the concept was widely discussed, because they feared that even greater unrest might develop. Job programs were seen not only as the quickest and surest way to restore domestic tranquility but as a means of avoiding larger government programs and expanded welfare benefits as well. Moreover, it was the Nixon administration that created the stringent guidelines later attacked as a "quota" system. Once the fear of urban unrest subsided, however, the elite origins of the plan were ignored, and conservatives began to attack affirmative action as unfair to whites and unconstitutional. In the first of many ironies, liberals and minorities ended up defending a plan endorsed by white male elites in a time of crisis.[23]

Moreover, the diversity forced upon the power elite may have helped to strengthen it, at least in the short run. Diversity has given the power elite buffers, ambassadors, tokens, and legitimacy. This is an unintended consequence that few insurgents or social scientists foresaw. One who did was the late E. Digby Baltzell, who argued in the early 1960s that the acceptance of successful Jews would strengthen what he called the establishment. Baltzell believed that the exclusion of successful newcomers, whatever their social origins, would cause the establishment to become castelike and hence vulnerable.[24] But even Baltzell missed the bigger picture. As the power elite diversified far beyond the inclusion of Jews, he joined the long parade of those who lamented the alleged death of the establishment. By the late 1980s and into the 1990s, rather than praising the establishment for taking in new members, Baltzell was bemoaning the "decline of traditional class authority."[25]

The power elite has been strengthened because diversity has been achieved primarily by the selection of women and minorities who share the prevailing perspectives and values of those already in power. The power elite is not "multicultural" in any full sense of the concept, but only in terms of ethnic or racial origins. This process has been helped along by those who have called for the inclusion of women and minorities without any consideration of criteria other than sex, race, or ethnicity. Because the demand was strictly for a woman on the Supreme Court, President Reagan could comply by choosing a conservative upper-class corporate lawyer, Sandra Day O'Connor. When pressure mounted to have more black justices, President Bush could respond by appointing Clarence Thomas, a conservative black Republican with a law degree from Yale University. It is yet another irony that appointments like these served to undercut the liberal social movements that caused them to happen.[26]

It is not surprising, therefore, that when we look at the business practices of the women and minorities who have risen to the top of the corporate world, we find that their perspectives and values do not differ markedly from those of their white male counterparts. When Linda Wachner, one of the few women to become CEO of a *Fortune*-level company, the Warnaco Group, concluded that one of Warnaco's many holdings, the Hathaway Shirt Company, was unprofitable, she decided to stop making Hathaway shirts and to sell or close down the factory. It did not matter to Wachner that Hathaway, which started making shirts in 1837, was one of the oldest companies in Maine, that almost all of the five hundred employees at the factory were working-class women, or even that the workers had given up a pay raise to hire consultants to teach them to work more effectively and, as a result, had doubled their productivity. The bottom-line issue was that the company was considered unprofitable, and the average wage of the Hathaway workers, $7.50 an hour, was thought to be too high. (In 1995 Wachner was paid $10 million in salary and stock, and Warnaco had a net income of $46.5 million.) "We did need to do the right thing for the company and the stockholders," explained Wachner.[27]

Nor did ethnic background matter to Thomas Fuentes, a senior vice president at a consulting firm in Orange County, California, a director of Fleetwood Enterprises, and chairman of the Orange County Republican Party. Fuentes targeted fellow Latinos who happened to be Democrats when he sent uniformed security guards to twenty polling places in 1988 "carrying signs in Spanish and English warning people not to vote if they were not U.S. citizens." The security firm ended up paying $60,000 in damages when it lost a lawsuit stemming from this intimidation.[28]

We also recall that the Fanjuls, the Cuban-American sugar barons, have had no problem ignoring labor laws in dealing with their migrant labor force, and that the Sakioka family illegally gave short-handled hoes to its migrant farm workers. These people were acting as employers, not as members of ethnic groups. That is, members of the power elite of both genders and all ethnicities have practiced class politics, making it possible for the power structure to weather the challenge created by the social movements that began in the 1960s.

Those who challenged Christian white male homogeneity in the power structure during the 1960s not only sought to create civil rights and new job opportunities for men and women who had previously been mistreated, important though these goals were. They also hoped that new perspectives in the boardrooms and the halls of government would bring greater openness throughout the society. The idea was both to diversify the power elite and to shift some of its power to previously excluded groups and social classes. The social movements of the 1960s were strikingly successful in increasing the individual rights and freedoms available to all Americans, especially African Americans. As we have shown, they also created pressures that led to openings at the top for individuals from groups that had previously been excluded.

But as the concerns of social movements, political leaders, and the courts came to focus more and more on individual rights, the emphasis on social class and "distributive justice" was lost. The age-old American commitment to individualism, reinforced at every turn by members of the power elite, won out over the commitment to greater equality of income and wealth that had been one strand of New Deal liberalism and a major emphasis of left-wing activists in the 1960s.

We therefore have to conclude on the basis of our findings that the diversification of the power elite did not generate any changes in an underlying class system in which the top 1 percent have 45.6 percent of all financial wealth, the next 19 percent have 46.7 percent, and the bottom 80 percent have 7.8 percent.[29] The values of liberal individualism embedded in the Declaration of Independence, the Bill of Rights, and the civic culture were renewed by vigorous and courageous activists, but despite their efforts the class structure remains a major obstacle to individual fulfillment for the overwhelming majority of Americans. This fact is more than an irony. It is a dilemma. It combines with the dilemma of race to create a nation that celebrates equal opportunity but is, in reality, a bastion of class privilege and conservatism.

ENDNOTES

1. On the continuing importance of class voting in the United States, contrary to recent claims based on weak methods, see Michael Hout, Clem Brooks, and Jeff Manza, "The Democratic Class Struggle in the United States, 1948–1992," *American Sociological Review* 60, no. 6 (1995), 805–828; Jeff Manza and Clem Brooks, "Continuity and Change in the Social Bases of U.S. Political Alignments, 1960–1992," paper presented at the American Sociological Association Meetings, New York, August 1996.

On class voting by Latinos, see Barry Kosmin and Ariela Keysar, "Party Political Preferences of U.S. Hispanics: The Varying Impact of Religion, Social Class and Demographic Factors," *Ethnic and Racial Studies* 18, no. 2 (1995), 236–347. In surveys of the CEOs of the largest Hispanic-owned businesses in 1989 and 1996, *Hispanic Business* found that 78 percent of them voted Republican in 1988 and that 67 percent said they were Republicans in 1996. See "CEOs and the Entrepreneurial 80s," *Hispanic Business*, April 1989, p. 30; "HB 500 CEOs Opt for Dole," *Hispanic Business*, June 1996, p. 34. On class voting by Chinese Americans, see Wendy Tam, "Asians—a Monolithic Voting Bloc?" *Political Behavior* 17, no. 2 (1995), 223–249.

2. *Good for Business: Making Full Use of the Nation's Human Capital, a Fact-Finding Report of the Federal Glass Ceiling Commission* (Washington, D.C.: U.S. Government Printing Office, 1995), 95.

3. James H. Johnson Jr. and Walter C. Farrell Jr., "Race Still Matters," *The Chronicle of Higher Education*, July 7, 1995, p. A48.

4. Carlos H. Arce, Edward Murguia, and W. Parker Frisbie, "Phenotype and Life Chances Among Chicanos," *Hispanic Journal of Behavioral Sciences* 9, no. 1 (1987), 19–32; E. A. Telles and Edward Murguia, "Phenotypic Discrimination and Income Differences Among Mexican Americans," *Social Science Quarterly* 71 (1990), 682–696; Aida Hurtado, "Does Similarity Breed Respect? Interviewer Evaluations of Mexican-Descent Respondents in a Bilingual Survey," *Public Opinion Quarterly* 58 (1994), 77–95.

23. John David Skrentny, *The Ironies of Affirmative Action: Politics, Culture, and Justice in America* (Chicago: University of Chicago Press, 1996), 78–91. Although he concludes that affirmative action was an "elite" response to a possible loss of societal control, Skrentny abandons any consideration of class. For a critical analysis of the return to a classless paradigm in American social science, see G. William Domhoff, *State Autonomy or Class Dominance?* (Hawthorne, N.Y.: Aldine de Gruyter, 1996).

24. E. Digby Baltzell, *The Protestant Establishment: Aristocracy and Caste in America* (New York: Vintage, 1964; New Haven: Yale University Press, 1987).

25. E. Digby Baltzell, *Sporting Gentlemen: Men's Tennis from the Age of Honor to the Cult of the Superstar* (New York: Free Press, 1995), 388. At the time of his death, in August 1996, Baltzell was in the early stages of research for a book on what he called "the end of the Protestant establishment." See Eric Pace, "E. Digby Baltzell Dies at 80; Studied WASP's," *New York Times,* August 20, 1996.

26. In addition, evidence from experimental work in social psychology suggests that tokenism has the effect of undercutting the impetus for collective action by the excluded group. See, for example, Stephen C. Wright, Donald M. Taylor, and Fathali M. Moghaddam, "Responding to Membership in a Disadvantaged Group: From Acceptance to Collective Protest," *Journal of Personality and Social Psychology* 58, no. 6 (1990), 994–1003. See also Bruce R. Hare, "On the Desegregation of the Visible Elite; or, Beware of the Emperor's New Helpers: He or She May Look Like You or Me," *Sociological Forum* 10, no. 4 (1995), 673–678.

27. Sara Rimer, "Fall of a Shirtmaking Legend Shakes its Maine Hometown," *New York Times,* May 15, 1996. See also Floyd Norris, "Market Place," *New York Times,* June 7, 1996; Stephanie Strom, "Double Trouble at Linda Wachner's Twin Companies," *New York Times,* August 4, 1996. Strom's article reveals that Hathaway Shirts "got a reprieve" when an investor group stepped in to save it.

28. Claudia Luther and Steven Churm, "GOP Official Says He OK'd Observers at Polls," *Los Angeles Times,* November 12, 1988; Jeffrey Perlman, "Firm Will Pay $60,000 in Suit Over Guards at Polls," *Los Angeles Times,* May 31, 1989.

29. Edward N. Wolff, *Top Heavy* (New York: New Press, 1996), 67.

19

THE BETRAYAL OF SOUTH AFRICA'S REVOLUTION

John Pilger

On April 21, John Pilger's documentary, *Apartheid Did Not Die*, will be shown simulta-neously on British and South African television. In this exclusive report for the *Mail & Guardian*, Pilger describes his first trip back to South Africa after his banning 30 years ago.

In the early morning sunlight a watchtower stands silhouetted against Table Moun-tain; two ostriches stroll by the gently rolling surf. Robben Island is a wildlife sanctuary now, its bleak beauty and silence part of the veneer of the new South Africa. "Appar-ently that's the quarry where they worked," said the Afrikaner helicopter pilot as he banked to land, unaware that one of them was sitting next to him. Kathy looked down and nodded, his dark glasses covering eyes permanently damaged by the glare of the limestone where he and Nelson Mandela and Walter Sisulu and other dangerous men wielded a pick year upon year, decade upon decade.

"It was a bitterly cold winter's day in 1964 when the seven of us were flown here," said Kathy, whose name is Ahmed Kathrada. "We'd all been sentenced to life in the Rivonia treason trial. I was 34 years old and the youngest and the only non-African. I stood here and was issued with the regulation shirt, jersey, canvas jacket, trousers, socks, shoes. Mandela and the others were given short trousers, no socks and as a special favour shoes instead of the rubber type sandals normally given out to Africans.

"Even in winter; the rationale of apartheid was quite simple: in South Africa, Africans were regarded as children. That's still true. You'll find in whites' homes, they talk of their garden boy and their kitchen girl." A handsome, youthful man in his 60s, Kathy led me to his cell, past the sign "We Serve With Pride," down the battleship-grey corridors silent except for the sound of the wind and the ocean. "This is it," he said, turning the key in the door of what looked like a stone closet, 1.5m by 1.5m. "I slept on that floor for the first 14 years. I had a raffia mat and eventually a bookcase. When we were caught smuggling Mandela's notes, our books were taken away and our stud-ies suspended." "For how long?" "Four years." "What did you miss most of all?" I asked. "The presence and sound of children. When the warders brought their families, we were made to turn our backs. That was hard." "How long were you in this cell?" "Almost 18 years. And you know, they never switched off the light."

The struggle of people against power, wrote Milan Kundera, "is the struggle of memory against forgetting." With the release of Mandela in 1990, the spectacle of people queuing to vote four years later and the triumph of the African National Congress, the popular memory now struggles to recall the years that those like Kathy and Mandela endured and lost. "South Africa had its own Final Solution," said Father Michael Lapsley, an Anglican priest whose hands and one eye were blown off by a security police letter bomb. "Under apartheid, [the scale of the crime] was of genocidal dimensions." The Verwoerds and the Vorsters and the Bothas "removed" up to a million people to a Gulag. They wrenched families apart and denied life to the most vulnerable. In his seminal book, *The Discarded People*, published in 1970, Cosmas Desmond disclosed that more than 100,000 "removed" children starved to death in 1967 alone.

In that year I was banned from South Africa for "embarrassing the state." I had been smuggled into one of the secret hearings of the Race Classification Board where, in Room 33 every Thursday morning, apartheid's horrific quackery was on display, its moral and intellectual mutation made to appear normal, with forms and regulations and decision-making based on "criteria." Here, suited officials, men of dour, fraudulent respectability, took evidence: scribbling, whispering and now and then leaning down from their magistrate's bench in order to study the texture of a human head of hair and peer at the whites of human eyes. After due consideration, "racially borderline" people were classified or reclassified "according to appearance and acceptance," which meant a ticket to a lifetime of privilege or humiliation. Black-skinned people needed not apply.

Stepping off the plane 30 years later, I read about the white expatriate businessman who had sent an anonymous fax to a black trade union leader, calling him a "kaffir, arsehole and trash." For this, he was fined and publicly shamed: a normal act of justice in a civilised country, yet inconceivable until recently in South Africa.

There was the sight of black and white children together in a nursery; and the bold, fluent black voices of SABC radio and television; and the brilliant and brave Afrikaner and journalist Max du Preez explaining to his white compatriots that the Nazi genocidist Adolf Eichmann was also "just ordinary" like them. Among the black majority there is a new sense of pride that gives meaning to ubuntu, the traditional spirit of humanism expressed in a distinctly African notion that people are people through other people. This is not without the usual frailties, but the evidence of its resilience is everywhere in South Africa; and those seeking optimism about the human spirit need look no further.

I have never conducted interviews that began and ended with a heart-swelling song by an impromptu choir: people who simply came and stood and listened. "How beautifully they have emerged from their nightmare," the great reporter Martha Gellhorn told me on her return from her first visit, which she spent in the townships. Few whites go into the townships. For them, beyond the multiracial images of the "rainbow nation"—now celebrated, sadly, not by the power of the people's epic story but by consumerist propaganda—is another country. Here live those whose blood, sweat and tears forced the pace of change and who, wrote Allister Sparks, South Africa's great chronicler, "could feel they were proclaiming their equality and that their strength of spirit could overwhelm the guns and armoured vehicles waiting outside." These are the people to whom Mandela said their "hopes and dreams are about to be realised." It follows that they ought not to have merely an expectation of a better life, but a right to one.

The truth is that this right is still denied and South Africa is still not theirs. What is clear is that "reconciliation," to which Mandela has devoted himself to the applause of most of the world, provides little more than a facade behind which apartheid continues by other means. For the question remains: reconciliation for whom?

In 1994, as election day approached, white South Africans hoarded food and fortified their houses against the feared "takeover" by domestic servants, the homeless, the unemployed and the black masses in general. Four years later, the servants are still serving, the squatters are still squatting (and still being evicted by white-led paramilitary police), and the majority are still waiting—while the "madams" and the "baases" experience no real change in their privileged way of life. For them, there is nothing new in the "new" South Africa, apart from the shared discomfort of paranoia and the acquisition of a new burglar alarm.

Fly into any South African city and the divisions are precise and entrenched. Johannesburg offers the most vivid example. On one side, there is Sandton municipality where, in fortified splendour, live some of the most pampered people on earth. They do not all live in "Italinate" palaces, with decorative fountains rising out of rolling lawns tended by garden "boys"; and many do not conform to the stereotypes lampooned, so often hypocritically, in Britain. (Those whites who actively opposed apartheid are among the most attractive people I have met.)

But enclaves like Sandton are apartheid's unchallenged bastions, from which the 5% of the population control 88% of the nation's wealth. This grotesque imbalance of power has not changed since democracy and is not likely to. They, not the majority, have been rewarded by democracy and "reconciliation." No longer "the polecats of the world," they can now travel and play sport and do business wherever they like, protesting that they, like good Germans, were never part of the system and suffering, as David Beresford wrote, "a collective delusion that they have done enough by 'allowing' majority rule."

"And what do you think of South Africa?" is a question I remember from 30 years ago. It is more guarded now, but just as loaded: an invitation to share a view from "the white man's windows," as Breyten Breytenbach wrote, "[which] are painted white to keep the night in."

In a Sandton restaurant, a woman said, "You must understand it's very difficult for young children here." She meant white children. The rest, the 87% of African children who are in poor health, the 38% who are stunted, the 23% who suffer chronic malnutrition, do not exist. When I suggested that the whites were fortunate, given their role in apartheid, to have experienced such a peaceful transformation to democracy, she said: "I don't know what you mean."

What they like to talk about is crime—not the great crime of apartheid's genocide, but that which is "threatening lifestyle," as one commentator wrote. Certainly, there is a lot of crime in South Africa, mostly against property. Eighty per cent of crime is confined to the black townships, where several families live under one roof, often in appalling conditions, and unemployment is as high as 70%.

The gangs in the Cape Flats are the sons and grandsons of whole communities dumped there, in the shifting sand and wind and heat, without hope. Moreover, there is now evidence that organised crime mushroomed in the 1980s as a direct result of state-sanctioned alliances with the security services.

To many white South Africans, "crime" is the euphemism for the migration of impoverished, workless blacks across the old racial dividing lines. In one sense, the issue is quite useful to the corporate elite that controlled the economy under apartheid and controls it now, for it reminds the African National Congress government that it must discipline those frustrated with the lack of change.

What is amazing to me is the degree of restraint exercised by the majority, given the flaunting of wealth by a minority. About 2.5km from Sandton, literally across a road, is Alexandra. Half-a-million people live here, squeezed into a square 2.5km. When it rains, the polluted river floods and houses collapse and the roads run like caramel.

When I was there it was stinking and dry, with a flock of aproned women frantically trying to pick up the stranded rubbish; the spick and span state of people's homes is a wonder. On the hill are two great "hostels," like prison blocks: one built for men, the other for women. Apartheid's planners designed them as a cheap labour pool; everybody else was to be "removed." But the people of Alexandra resisted, and stayed.

Mzwanele Mayekiso grew up in Alexandra and, until recently, was head of the local branch of the South African National Civics Organisation, whose boycotts and direct action during the 1980s helped to bring down the regime. "Most people over there don't know we exist," he said. "I mean, literally. Our women go over as domestics, our men as labourers and gardeners. No one asks where they return home to. Nothing has changed.

"Long before Mandela was released, the old regime had already dismantled the trappings of segregation. They left intact the most important part, which was always economic apartheid; and this has been adapted and reinforced by the ANC government. I think we are being designed like the United States: divided by class, which generally means race. We are even learning to speak the new jargon of separation, with the majority of people referred to not as the heroes of our struggle, but as an 'underclass.'"

For most of his life, Cosmas Desmond has been an independent and eloquent voice of the homeless and landless, having suffered arrest and banning by the apartheid regime; and he continues to infuriate its successor by challenging the new received wisdom. I asked him what had gone wrong. "The ANC was in exile for so long, it was willing to accept power at any price," he said. "It is considered blasphemous to say so, but Mandela seemed never to spell out a vision for South Africa, not like a Nehru or a Cabral. There is no political philosophy: it's like candyfloss, all sweet and fluffy and lovely with a spurious notion of 'reconciliation' between those with nothing and those with everything. The people who were the power behind apartheid, the great corporations like Anglo American, are still here, undiminished."

Before FW de Klerk announced the unbanning of the ANC and Mandela's release on February 2, 1990, he and the white establishment had reached a kind of gentlemen's agreement with the ANC, following secret meetings, that accommodated the fears of the old order and the demands of the "international community."

The Americans, the British and the World Bank made it clear, without spelling it out publically, that South Africa would be "welcomed into the global economy" on condition that its new government pursued orthodox, "neo-liberal" policies that favoured big business, foreign investors, deregulation, privatisation and, at best, a "trickle down" to the majority who effectively were to be shut out of the economy.

Deputy President Thabo Mkebi, Mandela's successor and one of the transition negotiators, told me that the ANC had "no choice at all" but to accept a series of "historic compromises." The surface could not be disturbed; otherwise there would have been a "bloodbath" and "great suffering across the land." Certainly, at the time, the perceived threat was from a far-right third force. But if such a threat existed, it turned out to be far less important than the more subtle machinations of De Klerk and his colleagues combined with the ANC's willingness to make the "historic compromises."

As for the "great suffering," while it is true that there was no civil war, the political decisions made by the ANC, which relegated the needs of the majority, have ensured the continuation of great suffering by exclusion—in the disastrous housing and employment policies and the absence of a minimal strategy for redistribution. The reason for this is partly historical. The ANC was always a party of compromise, seeking in the beginning "a place at the table."

People were misled; in 1990, the ANC leadership made clear it would do its utmost to honour the spirit of the 1955 Freedom Charter, which declared that the people of South Africa "shall share in the country's wealth. The minerals beneath the soil and monopoly industry shall belong to the people. The land shall be shared among those who work it. There shall be houses, security and the right to work."

The ANC, said Mandela, would take over the great monopolies, including the mines, and the financial institutions. "That is the fundamental policy of the ANC," he said. "It is inconceivable that we will ever change this policy." To his people, his words carried the moral weight of a leader who, as Anthony Sampson, Mandela's biographer, has written, has "a moral influence which no politician or newspaper dare challenge."

However, on his triumphant travels abroad Mandela spoke with a different emphasis. The ANC, he said in New York, "will reintroduce the market to South Africa." The "market" in South Africa has a long and bloody history. As Basil Davidson has written, "economic invention" lay at the root of the organised racism that distinguished the British Empire long before the Boers declared apartheid as official policy in 1948.

As prime minister of the Cape in the late 19th century, Cecil Rhodes, the great liberal benefactor, encouraged the dispossession of Africans and their "removal" to cheap labour reserves for the gold and diamond mines. The Oppenheimers, who ran the Anglo American company, also had beneficent pretensions. While declaring himself an opponent of certain aspects of apartheid, Harry Oppenheimer's tentacular empire grew rich on the brutal migrant labour system.

When it was clear, in the 1980s, that the regime of PW Botha was doomed, big business changed its allegiance to the ANC, confident that its multinational interests would not be obstructed as they "opened up" the South African economy and that foolish promises about equity and the natural resources "belonging to all the people" would be abandoned.

Since the ANC has settled into office, Margaret Thatcher's infamous Tina ("there is no alternative") has become the government's touchstone. The policy is known as Gear, for growth, employment and redistribution, but it has little connection with employment, as jobs are being "shed" by the tens of thousands, and even less with redistribution, which seems confined to changing seats on a gravy train. A government adviser told me: "We refer to cautious Thatcherism"—which sounded to me like cautious apartheid.

The Ministry of Finance remains in thrall to the orthodoxy of globalisation; the Minister of Finance, Trevor Manuel, has metamorphosed from long-haired biker and Cape Flats activist to the very model of a modern Blairite capitalist, boasting of his low deficit and devoted to the "economic growth," which Joseph Schumpeter, the doyen of Harvard economists, once described as "creative destruction."

There is something surreal about all of this. Is this a country of corporate hustlers celebrating their arcane deals in the voluminous business pages? Or is it a country of deeply impoverished men, women and children whose great human resource is being repressed and wasted, yet again?

"I think the reason behind the ANC leadership going for the International Monetary Fund approach is because they are ashamed that most of the people live in the Third World," said the Africa analyst Peter Robbins. "They don't like to think of themselves as being mostly an African-type economy. So economic apartheid has replaced legal apartheid with exactly the same consequences for exactly the same people, yet it is greeted as one of the greatest achievements in world history."

The social cost was stated plainly by Mary Metcalf, education MEC in Gauteng. "The only benefit of the discredited system we inherited," she wrote, "is the opportunities it necessitates for radical change." She described schools "built deliberately without toilets" and "with no access to running water within walking distance."

For every four teachers, there is only one classroom, and no library, no laboratory, no staffroom, no desks. "What is difficult," she wrote, "is that these historic distortions are being addressed in impossible conditions of financial austerity." In other words, ANC policy has made "the provision of acceptable conditions for teaching and learning an absolute impossibility."

So dedicated are the born-again free marketeers that South Africa's deficit is almost as low as that of some developed countries. For this, the ANC has been honoured with a "Duff & Phelps credit rating for foreign currency debt." What has this to do with a country where most of the children are, as they say here, "nutritionally compromised" and live in desperate conditions?

What the ANC called its "unbreakable promise" was the Reconstruction and Development Programme (RDP). Two years after the election, the RDP office was closed down and its funds transferred to the Ministry of Finance. When he was minister for housing, Joe Slovo had estimated that half the black population lacked a secure roof over their heads and that a million-and-a-half houses would have to be built immediately. Nothing like this has happened. The poorest get a R15,000 housing grant, which seldom pays for more than a jerry-built matchbox. In Ivory Park township near Johannesburg, "RDP houses" are known as "kennels."

The ANC's Freedom Charter says: "Reconstruction of land ownership on a racial basis should be ended and all the land divided among those who work it." Since democracy, little has changed. Wealthy white farmers continue to control more than 80% of the land, and their existing property rights are guaranteed in the new Constitution. Out of 22,000 land restitution cases, only a handful have been settled.

In the Eastern Cape, where few tourists go, silhouettes of women file across the saddle of a hill to draw water from a well where cattle drink and defecate. Most rural people have no choice but to walk up to half-a-mile to get water. Most have no sanitation, no electricity and no telephone, and no work. The shadows you pass on the road are those of stunted children and their mothers, walking, carrying, enduring.

This is the successor generation of the "discarded people" Desmond wrote about 28 years ago. At Dimbaza, 70 families were dumped on a waterless, windswept hillside. Stanley Mbalala, one of the survivors, remembers a forest, which became firewood during the first winter. They lived in tents and wooden huts with zinc roofs and earthen floors. Later arrivals had boxes made from asbestos and cement; these, too, had neither floors nor ceilings and were so hot in summer and cold and damp in winter that the very young and old perished in them. A government official explained the policy: "We are housing redundant people [in Dimbaza]. These people could not render productive service in an urban area."

Physically, Dimbaza is extraordinary. In the centre is a children's cemetery. The graves are mostly of infants aged younger than two. There are no headstones. There are plastic toys among the weeds and the broken glass of shattered flower-holders; emaciated cattle graze.

You trip over aluminium pipes embedded in pieces of broken concrete. These were meant as headstones; on one is scratched: "Dear Jack, aged 6 months, missed so bad, died 12 August 1976." At least 500 children are buried here, or were. Mbalala told me that in the 1970s heavy rains washed away many of them, and little skeletons appeared at the bottom of the hill. "There has never been the money to make something of this sacred ground," said Mbalala.

During the late 1970s, the rural concentration camp became a "showcase of investment opportunity." Cheap labour and factories were laid out like a vast grandstand overlooking the children's graveyard. Since then, most of them have closed down and unemployment is now at 70%. Mbalala, the survivor, lost his last job a year ago. One of the few working factories overlooks the children's cemetery where, in the brown grass between the graves, desperate men and women wait in the hopes of a few hours' work.

By contrast, the grass at 50 St. David's Road, Upper Houghton, is green and glistening from the spray of sprinklers. Houghton is the richest suburb of Johannesburg. Here, the walls are topped with razor wire and display signs: You have been warned; 24-hour Armed Response.

On the night I was there, chauffeur-driven Mercedes and BMWs converged on an important garden party at No. 50. The guests were white and black, mostly men in business suits who knew each other and affected an uncertain bonhomie across the old racial divide. The party was hosted by an organisation called BusinessMap, which, according to its brochure, gives "guidance on . . . black economic empowerment" and staged a "forum for the globalisation of South African business." The guest of honour was Cyril Ramaphosa, former general secretary of the miners' union and the principal negotiator of the ANC's "historic compromises."

Ramaphosa and others have spoken a great deal about "black economic empowerment" as a "philosophy" for the new South Africa. What this really means is the inclusion of a small group of blacks in South Africa's white corporate masonry, which is overseen by the power of five companies to use black faces to gain access to the ANC establishment. "I am," as one new executive told me, "the black ham in the white sandwich."

Certainly, the income gap between whites and blacks has narrowed slightly. However, inequality among blacks has increased sharply as the new black elite gets richer and the majority gets poorer. The new apartheid is one of class, not race.

The tragedy is that there are immediate, practical alternatives. If the government had kept to the spirit of the Freedom Charter and invested directly in the majority of people and their "informal economy," it would transform the lives of millions. With government loans going directly to communities, run as co-operatives, millions of houses could be built, and better health care and education provided. A small-scale credit system would ensure cheap goods and services that cut out the middle men and the banks. None of this would require the import of equipment and raw materials, and it would provide millions of jobs.

Thabo Mbeki told me the problem of poverty was an "absolute priority," but as far as I could deduce, he offered no solution beyond dreams of a "trickle down" effect. He is said to be an enigma. I found him, on the contrary, a straightforward, charming and highly intelligent free market economist.

Nelson Mandela is very different, and perhaps he is the enigma. He repudiates his sainthood with characteristic style. In response to the ignorant, fatuous, snobbish attack on him by Brian Walden, he said: "When treated as an ordinary human being one was prone to do fairly well in one's work. If treated as a saint, one was likely to disappoint." It seemed to me that his authority and reputation rested on what he represented, rather than his politics. He has served as a mighty symbol, calming and reassuring; this has been his remarkable power.

He also has the rare quality of grace; he makes people feel good. "You must understand," he said when we met, "that to have been banned from my country is a great honour." He listed for me the ANC's achievements: the supply of water to more than a million people, the building of clinics, the free health care to pregnant women and children under six. (To these, I would add the new abortion laws, which have saved the lives of tens of thousands of women, whose death at the hands of back-street abortionists was a feature of apartheid.)

Then he suddenly changed course and praised privatisation "as the fundamental policy of this government," which was the diametric opposite of what he promised in 1994. He quoted an array of statistics about inflation and the deficit, while omitting the terrible facts of unemployment. By the year 2000, it is estimated that half the population will be unemployed: a bomb ticking to its inevitable detonation.

He told me he had repeatedly warned people that substantial change "could not happen over night: that the process might take as long as five years." Five years are up next April. Moreover, it has to be said that the rise of the new elite has not been inhibited by such a time restriction, that their enrichment did, in many cases, happen "overnight."

I was surprised that the president failed to see the irony in his statement that an ANC government, brought to power partly as a result of boycotts and sanctions, was willing to "do business with any regime regardless of its internal policies." The West, he said, had no monopoly on human rights, which were also the rights to health care and education. Amazingly, he gave as a model Saudi Arabia "where students enjoy benefits I have not seen anywhere in the world."

Saudi Arabia and Algeria, both of them serious human rights violators, are current clients of the billion dollar white-run South African arms industry, the source of death and suffering in the region, and which has been reinvigorated under the ANC. On one of his visits to see the dictator of Indonesia, General Suharto, Mandela offered to sell him arms, too.

More than 150 years ago the Chartists, the investors of modern democracy, said that the vote had little meaning if people's lives did not improve. It is five years since a wise Nelson Mandela addressed this in a speech to South Africa's trade union movement, which was at the forefront of the struggle for freedom and continues to draw young, courageous and principled leaders, renaissance men and women from one of the most politicised constituencies in the world.

"How many times," he said, "has the liberation movement worked together with the people and then at the moment of victory betrayed them? There are many examples of that in the world. If people relax their vigilance, they will find their sacrifices have been in vain. If the ANC does not deliver the goods, the people must do to it what they have done to the apartheid regime . . ."

20

STIRRINGS IN THE JUG: BLACK POLITICS IN THE POST-SEGREGATION ERA

Adolph Reed, Jr.
Reviewed by: Steven J. Rosenthal, Hampton University

Stirrings in the Jug consists of six previously published essays, introduced with a long essay based on lectures Adolph Reed, Jr., gave during the 1998–1999 academic year. Because the essays originally appeared as separate articles, there is repetition from chapter to chapter. Nevertheless, these essays present a coherent and valuable analysis, and they display Reed's formidable talents as a critic of liberalism, racism and nationalism.

In these essays Reed argues that, during the "post-segregation era," white corporate leaders brought about a "reconstitution of domination" by developing a "black urban regime" that presides over "the Bantustanization of inner-city minority populations." This regime caters to corporate development interests and offers only "symbolic" rather than "redistributive" benefits for black workers whom they falsely claim to represent.

The black urban regimes govern cities that are "among the most depressed." Their ability to garner support from urban blacks makes them "well suited to implement the draconian retrenchment policies" desired by capitalist circles (p. 104). Atlanta's white business elite, for example, understood that black mayor Maynard Jackson was better able to "handle" municipal unions than a white mayor would have been. Jackson broke a strike by low-paid sanitation workers in 1977 by firing 2000 black workers (p. 95).

Reed's essays on "The 'Underclass' as Myth and Symbol" (chapter 6) is one of the best in the literature. Reed writes, "The behavioral tendencies supposedly characterizing the underclass exist generally throughout the society. Drug use, divorce, educational underattainment, laziness, and empty consumerism exist no less in upper-status suburbs than in inner city Bantustans. The difference lies not in the behavior but in the social position of those exhibiting it" (p. 190). Reed points out the sexist character of "underclass" discourse and emphasizes that liberals such as William J. Wilson played a leading role in legitimizing "underclass" ideology.

Along with his damning critique of white capitalists, their black junior partners, and liberal racist academics, Reed offers a no less scathing critique of black and white radicals who, Reed thinks, have failed to comprehend these developments or to articulate an effective strategy to combat them. He argues that both cultural nationalists and Marxists have clung to an essentialist view of a "black community" with no conflict class interests.

Reed draws upon his own experience in leftist formations in the 1970s to support his argument. Many leftists supported calls for black capitalism, for black politicians, for black police, military officers, and supervisors. As Reed's critique of the "urban black regime" shows, winning these demands actually strengthened capitalist control over black workers.

Reed's critique of racism, nationalism, liberalism, and the blurring of class interests might lead readers to expect him to issue a call for black workers to lead militant class struggle against the black elite and the corporate class whom they serve. But having argued that the entire U.S. left failed to grasp the politics of the "post-segregation era," Reed has painted himself into what he acknowledges is an "exceedingly pessimistic" political corner. He asserts that we are living in a period of Marcusan "one-dimensionality." With everyone confused or complicit, all Reed thinks is possible is a minimalist program that recognizes black diversity and cultivates democratic participation and open debate. Thus, Reed offers the reader no more than what he calls "liberal formalism."

But Reed has somewhat overstated his critique of Marxists. I know from my experience that not all Marxists in the 1960s and 1970s supported nationalism and nationalist demands. For example, in Students for a Democratic Society (SDS), a "Worker-Student Alliance" (WSA) caucus under the leadership of the multiracial communist Progressive Labor Party, concluded that the old left's distinction between "progressive" and "reactionary" nationalism was untenable and that workers should not support nationalist demands. Nationalism kept black workers subordinated to black capitalists and divided the working class. Similarly, in Vietnam nationalism transformed a revolutionary struggle for socialism into a victory for national capitalism.

PLP/WSA members were attacked as racists and imperialists by pro-nationalist forces, but their consistent leadership in campus struggles against racism and imperialism won PLP growing support. In 1969, at the SDS national convention in Chicago, the pro-nationalist leadership of SDS brought in members of the Black Panther Party to condemn opponents of nationalism. Then they declared the PLP and the WSA caucus expelled from SDS and led a walkout of approximately one-third of the 1500 delegates attending the convention. PLP outlived the split and subsequent decline of SDS in the early 1970s and continues to fight both racism and nationalism today.

PLP and its allies represented only a small percentage of those activists calling themselves Marxists during the late 1960s and early 1970s. Most Marxist organizations consisted of white radicals who uncritically supported the nationalism of various black organizations. Reed is therefore basically accurate. But when he writes that SDS proclaimed in 1969 that the Black Panther Party was the "vanguard of the black revolution," he doesn't point out that this was the position only of the rump minority that had walked out of the SDS convention. By not even suggesting that there was disagreement within SDS on the question of nationalism, and by failing to recognize the existence of any anti-nationalist Marxist organizations from the 1960s up to the present, Reed overstates his point. But the core of his anti-nationalist argument and critique is sound, and Marxists who are attempting to build a new workers' movement should embrace it.

21

BRADLEYISM AS CORPORATISM

Eric Mann

Los Angeles: The mayor aided minorities but his pro-business agenda didn't help areas most in need.

Tom Bradley was the political architect of modern Los Angeles. He brought L.A. out of its Great Racist Depression into the politics of a rainbow corporatism. His epochal campaign battles with Sam Yorty (1969, 1973) were urban civil wars, for Yorty was not a harmless old curmudgeon but a cunning reactionary who busted unions, fostered racism and allowed the LAPD to operate as a publicly funded terrorist organization.

Bradley, who died Tuesday at the age of 80, was part of the first generation of black mayors in U.S. cities—which also included Carl Stokes in Cleveland, Richard Hatcher in Gary, Ind., and Ken Gibson in Newark—that was a major component of a worldwide anti-racist, anti-colonial revolution, of which the 1965 Watts rebellion was the local incarnation. But within a few years of his rise to power, many of Bradley's most liberal and militant supporters felt shunted aside and betrayed as he constructed a centrist, corporate dominated strategy for L.A. Big business—not the poor and not South-Central L.A.—were at the center of his plan.

Bradley's achievements were structural and impressive. He transformed the ruling elite from a white boys network to a multiracial and transnational one. He positioned L.A. as the financial, manufacturing and cultural center of the Pacific Rim. He worked to curtail the worst abuses of the LAPD. He orchestrated the construction of an international city with a signature downtown skyline.

However, the lower-wage and dispossessed working class and minority communities were the victims of the Bradley agenda. In 1982, I was the coordinator of the UAW Campaign to Keep GM Van Nuys Open, trying to stop GM from closing the last major industrial plant in L.A. We worked with civil rights and labor groups to organize a preemptive boycott of GM products in the largest new car market in the U.S. We asked Bradley for help, but he preferred incentives to threats, not wanting to hurt the business climate.

The campaign succeeded in spite of Bradley, keeping 5,000 union workers employed for a full decade. The Van Nuys plant—now leveled and soon to become a haven of minimum wage jobs as a new commercial center—was the last of the major factories in L.A. that, once gone, wiped out well-paying jobs for an entire generation of blacks and Latinos.

In 1992, another urban rebellion triggered by the Rodney King verdict cried out against racism, poverty and the LAPD and extended its scope to the Latino poor as well. But Bradley could offer little sympathy and even less help. He and Gov. Pete Wilson refused to make any demands on President Clinton to help L.A. with public capital for schools, hospitals, Head Start programs or living-wage jobs. Instead, Bradley and Wilson recruited Peter Ueberroth to head Rebuild LA. He gave South Los Angeles a dose of tough love, offering private sector jobs in return for environmental deregulation, low-wage labor, more police to protect property and procorporate community politics. A year later, the Strategy Center issued "Reconstrucing Los Angeles From the Bottom Up," a blistering report on the regressive impact of Rebuild LA; meanwhile, Ueberroth left town and, again, South L.A. was left holding the bag.

Bradley had hoped to use the MTA Red Line subway as the final act in his urban development plan—transportation as public monument. But as the rail system depleted its budget, it parasitically raided public funds designated for the bus system, inflicting unbearable transportation conditions upon 350,000 bus riders—95% of all MTA passengers. Separate and unequal had once again come to Los Angeles: A boondoggle rail empire for wealthy developers and a few suburban riders and a dilapidated, overcrowded, undependable bus system for the urban poor of color. In 1994, the Strategy Center and the Bus Riders Union were forced to take the MTA to court for violating the 1964 Civil Rights Act. Besides L.A. Mayor Richard Riordan, the defendants included County Supervisor Yvonne Brathwaite Burke, who is black, and Supervisor Gloria Molina and L.A. City Councilman Richard Alatorre, who are Latino—all beneficiaries of the civil rights movement. Bradley's corporate rainbow had come full circle.

My last memory of Bradley was as a tactical ally after he left office. In 1995, MTA chief Franklin White, under pressure from the Bus Riders Union, tried to slow down the rail construction program, in particular the Pasadena Blue Line that was raiding funds from the bus system. The MTA board moved to fire him. I saw the termination of his contract as a violation of his civil rights and did not like the board using a black CEO as a sacrificial lamb for its rail obsession. State Sen. Diane Watson, Bradley and I all testified on White's behalf. White, facing the firing squad, decried the MTA board as a money train and publicly apologized to the Bus Riders Union for not taking more risks on behalf of bus riders.

As Bradley shook hands with everyone in the MTA board room and left to return to his corporate law firm, I could imagine another apology, this one from Bradley:

"I, too, want to apologize to the poor and the minorities that my ambition and strategy left behind. I broke the racial—yes, the racist—codes at the top. In a country in which the shadow of the plantation still haunts us, I exemplified a black man as an honest, intelligent leader that none could impeach. I brought coherence and prosperity to the city of L.A. but, after all was said and done, not to those at the bottom. Now is your time to formulate your own agenda, to train your own leaders, to go beyond me on the next leg of the journey. I have gone as far as I can go."

For a whole new generation of allegedly progressive elected officials in Los Angeles, I hope another round of apologies won't be necessary.

22

JESSE DOES WALL STREET

Anthony Arnove

Jesse Jackson has made some new friends in high places with his recent campaign for black capitalism. To celebrate Martin Luther King Jr.'s birthday this year, Jackson held the First Annual Rainbow/PUSH Wall Street Project Conference at Windows on the World in New York. Sharing the view with some of the nation's richest CEOs, he urged them to see Black America as "a big, overlooked emerging market."

Last year, Jackson opened a Wall Street office, announcing his intention to focus on the racial composition of Fortune 500 exeuctive boards. "This is the new Jesse Jackson. Jesse Jackson the capitalist," said David C. Wilhelm, a senior managing director of Chicago-based Everen Securities Inc.

Jackson's new focus on Wall Street has won him praise from some interesting quarters. "I believe corporate America has a vital role to play in its own self-interest in expanding opportunity for all Americans," said Treasury Secretary Robert Rubin. "Inclusion is good for the bottom line." This nicely encapsulates the Clintonite view of racism: a missed profit opportunity. Fed chair Alan Greenspan, not particularly known for his progressive views, agreed with Rubin, saying "Discrimination is patently immoral, but it is now increasingly being seen as unprofitable." Continuing that theme, President Clinton was moved to add: "I thank Reverend Jackson for his insight, that he has said for years, and years, and years—[that investment banks] are missing a market here [in African-American communities]."

It should come as no surprise that Jackson's renewed initiative to court big business's "self-interest" gained the praise of Clinton, Rubin, Greenspan, & Co. As Jackson's office explained in a press release, "Our mission is not to be confrontational. Agitation and confrontation are last resorts. Our mission is to lead through enlightened self-interest. The private sector—the ones who stand to gain from the fruits of diversity—must assume more leadership in the struggle. We want to build partnerships with business leaders." The Wall Street Project has sought to further this "partnership" with big business by investing in fifty publicly traded companies "to closely monitor their investment practices and, if need be, intervene in our role as investment advisors," another press release explains.

Stocks in the project's portfolio include:

- rapacious HMO Columbia/HCA, under federal investigation for Medicare fraud;
- GM, for which, as *Counterpunch* reports, Jackson has been "operating a cover-up campaign . . . to undercut the efforts of GM's minority dealers to get justice. . . .";
- Texaco, where executives referred to African-American employees as "black jelly-beans" and which has dumped oceans of toxic waste in Ecuador;
- Shell, implicated in the murder of Nigerian activist and writer Ken Saro-Wiwa and scores of others in Ogoniland, which it viciously abuses in the name of oil; Jackson is friendly with Nigeria's ruler, Gen. Babangida, and has praised the head of Shell as "enlightened";
- and other fine citizens such as Chevron, Raytheon, Coca-Cola, and Seagram.

This strategy is as ineffective today as when Jackson first tried it. Jackson formed Operation PUSH (People United to Serve Humanity) soon after King's assassination. PUSH used boycotts to persuade companies to hire more African-American managers and to do more business with African-American businesses and banks.

In 1984, Operation PUSH split off from an AFL-CIO boycott of Coors brewery "in exchange for the company's 'pledge to redirect $625 million in investments into banks, publications and suppliers owned by black or Hispanic business executives,'" Adolph Reed Jr. notes in *The Jesse Jackson Phenomenon.* "As black leaders' racial agendas become ever more targeted to upper income, upper status black interests," Reed argues, "the programmatic basis for unity with the labor movement's social agenda recedes."

According to Manning Marable, Operation PUSH's early efforts received much publicity but did nothing to lower unemployment among African-Americans. When thousands of African-American auto workers were forced out of work, Jackson's advice was to buy more shares in the carmakers laying them off. "Blacks need trade, not aid," Jackson said at the time, a reassuringly neoconservative phrase he used again during the Wall Street Project conference.

As Marable points out, Jackson's message serves to "reinforce the capitalist spirit among those whom the system most brutally exploited." Jackson is looking to Wall Street for solutions to problems it helped generate in the first place: a growing gap between rich and poor, growing inequality and poverty, the destruction of the welfare state, and an increase in racism for most ordinary African-Americans.

Asked to comment on Jackson's Wall Street adventure, Reed said it's "a matter of Jesse going back to his original base." It echoes PUSH's strategy of "eschewing demands on the state for broadly egalitarian public policy in favor of pursuing direct negotiation of 'covenants' with corporations to provide benefits for black business professionals and contractors. His current move seems to have a man-bites-dog quality only because his left apologists have consistently denied what his politics and agenda have always been. Jackson is the product and avatar of a narrow kind of elite racial brokerage that has always been about just the opposite of popular mobilization—cutting side-payment deals with corporate and Democratic Party elites for personal and narrowly class-based payoffs. My only curiosity about this concerns what kind of contortions leftists will go through to keep from admitting the truth."

It is particularly disturbing that Jackson portrayed the conference at Windows on the World as continuing the tradition of struggle of Martin Luther King. In light of the recent tendency of many on the right to take King's words out of context, it is important to recall what King really said. At the 1967 Southern Christian Leadership Conference convention, King declared: "The movement must address itself to the question of restructuring the whole of American society. There are 40 million poor people here. And one day we must ask the question, 'Why are there 40 million poor people in America?' When you ask that question, you begin to question the capitalistic economy. . . . You begin to ask the question, 'Who owns the oil?' You begin to ask the question, 'Who owns the iron ore?' You begin to ask the question, 'Why is it that people have to pay water bills in a world that is two-thirds water?'"

These aren't the kinds of questions Jesse Jackson asks—especially of his guests at Windows on the World.

23

BIG DADDY AND THE PLANTATION

Kevin Alexander Gray

I grew up in a National Enquirer house. My mother reads it weekly and my brother works in the plant that prints them. There is something cosmic about Reverend Jesse Jackson, for whom I used to work, being in that rag. Now, every time I think of Reverend, Diana Ross's Love Child plays in my head. And I have gotten enough email cartoons like the one with Reverend's head (with a ponytail) on a little girl's body. This was low down—as low down as the state of black and progressive politics. And the latter should be our real concern.

The problem with Reverend Jesse Jackson isn't that he fathered a child with a woman he didn't marry. The problem is that Reverend has used a movement predicated on protecting rights of the many with gaining privilege for a few. Our movement is anti-privilege. Now, Reverend's privileges are being challenged. Who's to say that's a bad thing?

The new "morality" questions as well as past financial problems at Operation Breadbasket that led to his split with Martin Luther King's Southern Christian Leadership Conference are now regular fodder for the Sunday morning talk shows. The pundits' assessment: Reverend is not now and has never been accountable to anybody. Washington Post columnist David Broder gave Reverend's refusal to run for mayor of DC as evidence of his fear of accountability. Columnist Clarence Page, the only black guy on a news show on a regular basis, said the stories and financial questions were old news. Both fretted over Reverend's troubles but neither counted him completely out. Still, maybe his days as a national leader were numbered. (Maybe?)

But the problem isn't that Reverend is a has-been. It's worse: he's become an insider. That's what makes my desire to see Reverend either change or be gone from the scene different from Broder's and Page's. To them, Reverend is becoming ineffective as the "designated Negro."

There are also those awaiting the day when vice president Dick Cheney has his final heart attack so that Colin Powell becomes vice president. Understanding racial solidarity, they believe that the African Americans will predictably rally around the first black vice president. This group doesn't want Reverend to affect the dynamic. So, they beat up on him now in hopes of getting him out of the way. Things they ignored in the past make the Enquirer's cover. They have no desire to see Al Sharpton elevated to "national Negro leader" but they know that Powell trumps Sharpton or anyone else for that matter.

Workplace sex will always be around. No doubt, on the job there is sexual harassment and conniving plotters of both sexes. The problem with Reverend isn't workplace sex (except maybe to his wife Jackie and those who believe a minister and married man should act a certain way). Jesse Jackson and the Rainbow Coalition's problems are patronage and bossism.

The Rainbow "organization" is not committed to any movement—past or future (unless we are foolish enough to believe in a "Wall Street movement"). Jessephiles have no particular political goals, agenda or ideology beyond cutting the deal and protecting their privileges as part of the black bourgeoisie. It's always been about big daddyism, a concept that covers it all: sexual harassment, nepotism, exploitation, plotting, foolishness, favoritism and all kinds of other isms, schisms and confusion. A "big daddy" is a straw boss thinking he is the boss, or putting up the front that he believes it, as part of doing the boss's business. Tupac called it thug life.

To the Jessephiles, the Rainbow Coalition's biggest accomplishment was to become Rainbow/PUSH, but that's nonsense. The Rainbow Coalition was supposed to be about politics and organizing. PUSH is about "getting the gold." The "gold" comes with being silent about the exploitation and unfair practices of the corporate givers. To know who's doing the buying one needs only to read the magazines or newsletters of any black organization. In return for silence some "big daddy" gets some stock, a seat on a board, a job or a check. Reverend isn't even the master of this game; that would be Vernon Jordan.

Much of Reverend and his crew's present food fortune comes from the lawsuits or threats of lawsuits by grassroots groups whose primary concern is that their constituents receive fair treatment. Grassroots groups sued merging banks (such as Bank of America for gobbling NationsBank, which used to be Citizens and Southern/Sovran) over adherence to the Community Reinvestment Act. The outcome was that Reverend and the Jessephiles got the gold. The price was the abandonment attempts to enforce the Community Reinvestment Act. "Big daddys" often stifle grassroots protest, threats of economic actions or boycotts because there is an existing deal with the company or a deal waiting to be made. Reverend often says "the only bad deals are the ones you are not in the room for." A watered down CRA was passed last year with little public comment. Why? Because the banks and the feds now sidestep grassroots groups and cut the deal with the big daddys, who have become their straw bosses in the matter.

The powerful have learned that it is easier and cheaper to buy black leaders than to bust them. The real money is in busting street blacks in bulk. That's what racial profiling and the "war on drugs" are all about. And Reverend isn't the only one bought and paid for. Past NAACP director Ben Chavis and ex-chair Doc Bill Gibson were part of the demise of grassroots' effectiveness in extracting even a remote semblance of accountability from predatory banks. The only thing that the late Khalid Muhammed ever got right was what he said about Ben Chavis. Condemning Chavis for stealing from the people, he called him counterrevolutionary. But, that's what all the big daddies do. It's what Ben Chavis was taught, by experts. Look at the King family's exploitation of All-Things-Martin, right down to pimping footage of his speech from the March on Washington as a product advertisement.

Today many civil rights organizations work counter to black empowerment. Promotion of individuals, symbols and organizations, all living on someone else's past glories, replace movements of the poor and disenfranchised. The NAACP and the Urban League have their fair share of economic development programs. The black churches and preachers take the money with no demand on the system except maybe a bank loan to build a bigger church. Every big daddy gets as much money as he can from wherever or whoever he can get it. COINTELPRO was never so effective at turning politics in the black community to shit.

The movement business is good to Reverend and his kids. One son is an alcohol distributor in Chicago, a second is an investment banker and Jesse Junior is a Congressman. But in spite of the fact that one son is a "legal" dealer, Reverend is hypocritical on the issue of drug legalization and on the wrong side in the war on drugs. What he should do is demand that the POWs be set free. Start protesting at the prisons. Call for active resistance against the drug war. Those are things that need saying and doing. The drug war is now spawning the next wave of black voter disenfranchisement. The background checks by the Florida Republicans were possible because of that state's disenfranchisement of ex-felons for 15 years after their term of imprisonment. That's why the Republicans were able to run criminal background checks, falsely report the results, and prevent balloting by thousands of black voters. The same tactics are going on in South Carolina and across the South. The only way to stop this is to oppose drug criminalization.

Check cashing services, cash advance lending, predatory mortgage practices, property rights, land loss and decreasing home ownership are just some of the pressing economic issues affecting blacks. In cities such as Washington, DC, Charlotte, Atlanta and many others, inner city blacks are dealing with redevelopment, gentrification and eroding voting districts. So why aren't the Rainbow, Urban League, NAACP or the SCLC dealing with these problems?

Comes a recession in the country and it's a depression in the black community. The latest unemployment statistics, officially edging towards 10 percent, bear out worsening conditions in black households. How does Reverend's Wall Street Project help black Americans forced into the secondary lending markets during hard times or at any time? The high interest charges blacks pay is what makes the investment bankers on Wall Street billionaires; it's where the funding for the Wall Street Project comes from, too, and Reverend and the other big daddies know it, which is why they don't challenge it.

Ask average people what the Rainbow stands for and if they say anything it will be "it's Jesse Jackson's organization." But what has Reverend and his organization produced? What can that person on the street see, feel and touch? No one can call the organization on the phone for help. They can't get a question answered or a problem solved. They see no action. That's because there is nothing—for them.

Reverend's legacy is that he ran for president, twice. He's been out the movement for a long, long time. He's been in the movement prevention business just as long. Any chance of movement building died when he dismantled the Rainbow to suit Clinton and Ron Brown in 1988. After that Reverend truly became "Jesse Jackson Inc." The tradeoff for scattering those troublemakers brought by Jackson's 1984 and 1988 campaigns into the political tent was the job of head overseer on the Democratic Party plantation. Now Reverend holds the franchise on black votes. If he has a fear, it's of losing the franchise.

Many of those at the center of the Jackson campaigns, like Jack O'Dell who worked with Martin Luther King, Frank Watkins who worked with Reverend for more than 20 years, Ron Daniels, Nancy Ware, Steve Cobble and a host of others including me— wanted to connect to the people, build an organization and create a movement. They were not chumps. They put the larger than life photos of Reverend at the headquarters in Chicago in historical prospective. But big daddyism got the best of them. They moved on and the Rainbow's potential to really change and challenge America went with them.

As an institution, the Rainbow will fade away completely. Then maybe we will build organizations capable of responding to the people's needs. Maybe if we stop depending on the straw boss we can take protest back to the streets and begin tearing down those institutions and ideas that need to crumble. Since the glory days of 1988, we have been poor stewards of the goals of a progressive/black movement. The success of that movement is the salvation of this country; its failure is its damnation.

The goals were set at the founding of this country. Black politics is the counter to anti-black politics. It's the demand for equal opportunity, equal treatment and protection, due process and economic justice for the descendants of enslaved Africans, which is the only way those things can be ensured for everyone else.

24

WORKERS OF THE WORLD, SEPARATE!: "DIVERSITY" AND THE LEGACY OF ANTICOMMUNISM IN THE ACADEMIC WORKPLACE

Anthony Dawahare

Historically, the push for "diversity" comes out of advanced capitalism, and more specifically, a period when American imperialism and the postcolonial, antiwar, and civil rights movements it engendered forced a decentering of Eurocentric and patriarchal ideologies for millions of people. It is clear that after the '60s, American colleges and universities are not the same as they were during the Cold War. The creation of Black Studies, Women's Studies, Chicano Studies, etc., as well as the struggles against racist and sexist hiring practices, have certainly transformed academia into a site of political struggle for progressive ideas and causes.

Yet, an interesting dialectical reversal also occurs in the post-60s period. As capitalist globalization proceeds according to plan, that is, according to the dictates of capital in its insatiable need for self-valorization, and as American imperialism attracts more wage-laborers into its "national" economy and as it penetrates more deeply into other economies, it finds that the demon of diversity it calls forth can also be pressed into its service. What we are now witnessing, especially since the mid-80s, is a retrenchment of conservative forces in academia, but with a liberal cover that makes it all the more dangerous. The institutionalization of "diversity" carries on the work of Cold War anticommunism, because it functions as a means of eradicating class consciousness, and Marxism, while it provides the institutions of U.S. imperialism a new egalitarian look that conceals the exploitation and subjugation of the working class. The ways that diversity attempts to maintain the hegemony of U.S. imperialism is the subject of this talk. Not surprisingly, statements on diversity published by the CIA, ExxonMobil, and the U.S. Army—which I will read as representative expressions of U.S. capitalist political and economic interests—are very instructive to an understanding of the politics of diversity in academia.

U.S. political and economic organizations present the value of diversity from national and international considerations. On the one hand, they maintain that by promoting diversity, they promote "American values," such as democracy and equality. They are self-congratulatory in the belief that they strengthen the democratic and egalitarian structures and ethos of their organizations and the country in general. But, as we well know, the CIA, ExxonMobil, and the U.S. Army are not simply concerned with "values": behind their Americanism is the overriding concern of American capitalism and its "productivity." Diveristy allows these organizations to work better at maintaining U.S. imperialism. As Army Chief of Staff General Shinseki told participants at the second annual Army Equal Opportunity Advisor Training Conference in December of 1999, "Equal opportunity is not a luxury, it is not a 'frill,' it is not a social program . . . it is a combat necessity." Racism and sexism in the Army compromises the effectiveness of soldiers to win wars, to ensure ExxonMobil's control of Mideast oil, for example. In an ExxonMobil document entitled "Global Diversity," the corporation's Chairman and CEO Lee Raymond plainly views the benefits of diversity in terms of dollars: "As a worldwide enterprise," he writes, "our diverse workforce is a key competitive advantage." The CEO also writes, "By being attentive to ethnic and cultural differences and by hiring local employees whenever possible, our stores build a sense of community, resulting in improved sales and stronger brand loyalty." The belief that the institutionalization of "diversity" creates greater global competitive advantage is mirrored in the CIA's statement on diversity, written by its Director, George Tenet. Fully aware of the threat that the European Union, the Chinese, Russian, and Middle East bourgeoisie presents to American imperialism, Tenet states, "To combat the threats our country will be facing in the decades ahead, we will need collectors from diverse ethnic backgrounds . . . who can think and communicate like our targets and pierce their human and technical networks." He goes on to underscore the common interests of the CIA and multinational corporations like ExxonMobil when he writes, "Corporate America was among the first to recognize that diversity pays dividends." For both the CIA and ExxonMobil, diversity allows for better reconnaissance of "diverse" peoples in order to protect and expand capital investments and markets—in other words, to better exploit and oppress the "diverse" people they claim to respect. Simply put, diversity is now good for business.

These three organizations have thus had to adapt their tactics of world domination to the reality of multiculturalism that globalization itself makes apparent and progressive academics have championed. But, clearly, "diversity" is not something that these organizations are most concerned about. On the contrary, multiculturalism as they use and promote it is a lie. What they really seek is homogeneity, a homogeneity conceived in terms of the economics and ideologies of capitalism. The bourgeoisie, as Marx noted long ago, "compels all nations, on pain of extinction, to adopt the bourgeois mode of production; it compels them to introduce what it calls civilization into their midst, i.e., to become bourgeois themselves. In a word, it creates a world after its own image"). Cheap commodities act as heavy artillery to batter down cultural barriers. With the working classes the world over subject to capital, that is, turned into wage-workers, and their stores filled with cheap commodities promising enrichment, their cities filled with slums and high rises, and millions of others under and unemployed trying to piece together a living—it means little to support cultural "diversity." Therefore, when they defend diversity, they really mean they want to find ways to penetrate with their commodities or capital into any sector of the world that hasn't yet conformed to "American values." When they promote diversity they hope to find ways to convince the "diverse" working class that it's really good to "buy American" or to work in a free zone or border factory. And since the U.S. Army and the CIA only serve to defend companies like ExxonMobil, they will bomb any "diverse" people "back to the Stone Age" should they threaten U.S. investments or strategic plans for the domination of world markets. The Gulf Oil War and the Vietnam War make this painfully clear.

Now, of course we know that there are qualitative differences between the U.S. Army and the universities and colleges where we work or attend. But how important are these differences and what are the similarities?

To answer that question I'd like to suggest that we view institutions of higher education as, in large part, ideology factories. This view is based on the assumption that colleges and universities help to shape the bourgeois "values" of students and provide them with the skills to function (perhaps) within the division of labor of advanced capitalist society. More specifically, these institutions develop professional sectors of the working class in the form of teachers, managers, engineers, lawyers, physicists, etc. The increasing number of general education diversity requirements will help to train many of these workers on how to work within corporate America, or, lacking that, to join the multicultural U.S. army. The potential value of the diversity trend in higher education is not lost on ExxonMobil, since they "rely primarily on college recruiting to hire management, professional and technical employees." Thus, it is not surprising that the corporation invests millions of dollars into higher education every year and has "long-term relationships with more than 100 universities in the U.S." The institutionalization of diversity, whether or not directly funded by corporate America, seems to be very much in tune with the needs of the global economy. From this perspective, the historical era of capitalism seems to have played another trick on those intellectuals (especially in the Humanities) who believe that the "values" they teach have nothing to do with crass commercialism. As David Rieff writes, "One can respect the multiculturalists' project from a capitalist reformist point of view, just as long as one does not confuse it with the attack on power that so many if its proponents claim it to be. Were women and blacks represented proportionately at the top of corporate America, this would not change the nature of the class distinctions one iota . . ."

And I would argue that things are more crass within the hallowed halls of academia than some would think, since institutionalizing diversity is not just about training better managers, market researchers, and military personnel. It is also about fabricating racial/ethnic/gender ideologies within and outside the universities that function to *divert* workers and the teachers of workers away from the only "diversity" that threatens the functioning of capitalism, namely *class differences*. It is a remarkable fact that virtually all research and talk about diversity elides issues of class. Rather, the rhethoric of diversity functions to racialize and to gender class issues. This is significant because the more or less smooth functioning of capitalism depends upon the working class *not* thinking in its own interests or even in constituting itself subjectivity as a class. In other words, from its inception, capitalism's greatest fear has been of the working class, and, more specifically, working-class organizations and parties that fight to limit the insatiable greed of capital, and, even more specifically, communist parties that aim to abolish capitalism. The diversion of attention away from class conflict and struggle by "celebrating" cultural differences perpetuates, knowingly or not, the goal of anticommunism which is prolonging the existence of capitalism.

The erasure of issues of class in the rhetoric of diversity is plainly seen in the way that academic institutions define diversity. Diversity for them is primarily racial, ethnic, or sexual. For the diversifiers of academia, the most important thing about students, staff, and faculty is how they identify, their parents' country of origin, their last names, or even their pigmentation. By diversifying the student body, the faculty, and the curriculum in these ways, administrators believe that, like their corporate and governmental counterparts, they foster democracy and equality in and outside of academia. For example, the Association of American Colleges and Universities, which has spearheaded the research and institutionalization of diversity in higher education, maintains that "democracy cannot fulfill its aspirations without acknowledging diversity" ("American Commitments"). This well-intentioned but misguided belief that diversity equals democracy does not grasp that it, in fact, promotes the dictatorship of the bourgeoisie by ignoring the ways in which the structural qualities of the class system are incompatible with democracy. And that, as long as they promote and then "accept" so-called racial and gender differences, they work to forestall the formation of the class consciousness necessary to create real democracy—a real rule by the working people. But, of course, we cannot expect this to happen within institutions of higher education, which are part of the ideological state apparatus of capitalism. It is useful here to note that the term diversity comes from the Latin word divertere, to divert.

When we consider academia as a workplace run by managers, beholden to a corporate body concerned with profit, then we also understand that the institutionalization of diversity works in much the same way as it does for corporations. In other words, it functions to increase productivity. A central outcome of diversity workshops, lectures, and cultural events is that they enhance working relationships within educational institutions and promote good feelings necessary to a productive workplace. A recent study conducted at Loyola Marymount University on the emotional value of institutionalizing diversity (or what they term "interculturalism") notes,

> When students, staff, and faculty participate in intercultural activities, they feel more *comfortable* discussing ethnic issues with others in the campus community, are more likely to have *positive* interactions with people from different ethnic backgrounds, *believe race relations are good on campus,* and experience *enhanced feelings of control* over campus policies . . . When there is high university commitment to interculturalism, faculty and staff indicate *higher satisfaction* with the environment for teaching and learning. . . . (my emphasis, "Creating an Intercultural Campus: A New Approach to Diversity")

Feeling good about the institution acts as a narcotic, a drug that makes you forget "uncomfortable" facts that racism is institutionalized when you have a predominantly "white" faculty and, as in the case of California, home to Loyola Marymount, a predominantly black and Latino staff in charge of maintenance. But at least after the diversity workshop you can wink knowingly to the janitor that you "recognize" "his" people. Those "enhanced feelings of control" help you to forget that, as in the case of where I work, the Chancellor has imposed a contract on the faculty two years in a row, in spite of the recommendations of the "fact finders" that supported the union's positions on key issues relating to pay. In short, feeling good about democracy makes you forget that it doesn't exist even in higher education. But, then again, at least we will be more productive if we work together as a team to produce future workers who also feel good about living under the system of class inequality. I guess they figure that class consciousness is uncomfortable, especially for the ruling class.

By criticizing how diversity has been institutionalized, I do not mean to suggest that it does not open up some possibilities for addressing issues of racism, sexism, and class oppression, or for the recuperation and study of different working-class cultures. In fact, the discourse of diversity represents a political form of the class struggle, a form that we can use to address self-reflexively our use of the term and how the perpetuation of racism and sexism serves the profit system. My main point is that, at present, *the institutionalization of diversity represents and supports bourgeois class interests.* As a political expression of class struggle, the institutionalization of diversity demonstrates just how resourceful and clever the bourgeoisie and its representatives are in co-opting critiques of racism and sexism to shore up more nationalist support for "America" and capitalism. Therefore, we have to be very careful not to mistake the needs of global capitalism for our needs, for the needs of the international working class. Simply put, our most pressing need is to get rid of capital, the economic agency that feeds on the working class and the earth for profit and has created a hell for people through perpetual war, exploitation, and poverty.

Part IV

THE RACISM OF IMPERIALISM: DEHUMANIZATION, IGNORANCE, INDIFFERENCE, AND NATIONALISM

Racism is not only used to hyperexploit workers of color; it is also used to justify imperialist policies (especially war) which have the goals of controlling the resources, markets, and production processes in other lands. While some may think that wars are fought over "values" and "concepts," Michael Klare offers an explanation for U.S. involvement in the Middle East based on the desire to control the production and marketing of oil. He furthermore charts the increased deployment of American military forces to the Persian Gulf region as the U.S. prepositions itself to retake the oil fields of Iraq and Iran. Klare's writings illustrate the economic basis underlying the media treatment of Arabs and Muslims in this country.

In order for a society (the U.S.) to seize and control the economic assets (oilfields) of other lands (Iraq and Iran), its people must be psychologically and spiritually programmed to support the imperial assault. This can be done with a combination of psychological tools: dehumanization, ignorance, indifference, and nationalism. Dehumanization of the target population reduces them to the status of dangerous and irrational creatures with whom dialogue, negotiation, and trust would be folly. They are depicted as so dangerous that they must be controlled for the protection of civilization. The process of dehumanization begins years before the military campaigns and then continues as cultural accompaniment to the wars of conquest. Much of the psychological preparation is done by the "entertainment" industry which functions as a huge propaganda industry. The work of Hollywood in dehumanizing Arabs and Muslims (they are *not* synonymous) is discussed by emeritus professor, Jack Shaheen, in the introduction to his book *Reel Bad Arabs*. Long before the soldiers, sailors, and bomber pilots were deployed to the Persian Gulf, you were mentally prepared for it by Hollywood.

War, however, is a tragic, messy thing, which comes with always question-able civilian casualties. Questions about civilian wounded and dead might lead to further questions about the methods and purposes of the are itself and the possible answers to these questions might undercut public support for imperi-alism. Better, from the rulers' point of view, not to ask the questions. No ques-tions, no answers. Ignorance is bliss, politically speaking. The role of the media in fostering imperialist ignorance about war in the Mideast is discussed by Aus-tralian journalist John Pilger in a chapter, "Unpeople," from his book, *Hidden Agendas.*

The combination of dehumanization and ignorance might produce hatred of the "enemy." It may, however, produce something just as pernicious: indif-ference—a lack of concern, a "we don't care" attitude which is considered nor-mal because we "know" that those foreign peoples are less-than-human and, therefore, we need not trouble ourselves about them. This indifference perme-ates most institutions of society including those concerned with education and ethics: the schools and the churches. If your teachers and religious leaders are unconcerned about imperialism, why should you be concerned? This massive societal indifference allows the State to undertake rather brutal policies such as the campaign of sanctions against Iraq with only a murmur of dissent. The sanctions against Iraq are a form of siege warfare for the purposes of "target degradation" which means making Iraq a weaker and thus more easily con-querable country if and when the U.S. decides to invade. That this target degra-dation would entail massive civilian casualties through the outbreak of diseases resulting from the destruction of water treatment systems was known to U.S. policymakers in 1991. In "The Secret Behind the Sanctions," Thomas Nagy discusses Defense Intelligence Agency documents analyzing the effects (disease and death) on Iraqis stemming from U.S. policy. While the Iraqis die, Ameri-cans concern themselves with more pressing matters: should we keep the phrase "under God" in the pledge of allegiance, is it OK to try ecstasy at the rave, will the Lakers repeat as world champions, and, will we find the courage to call Jenny Craig today?

When the rulers decide to go to war, indifference needs to be replaced by a "gung-ho" fighting spirit. Here again, film (since you don't read much) is used to get you "hyped" in support of slaughtering the "barbarians." Journalist Larry Chin reviews the movie, *Black Hawk Down,* as an example of such war propaganda for imperialism.

25

OIL CONFLICT IN THE PERSIAN GULF

Michael T. Klare

Of all the world's major oil-producing areas, the Persian Gulf region is the one most likely to experience conflict in the next century. Possessing nearly two-thirds of global petroleum supplies, the Gulf is certain to remain the focus of intense worldwide competition as energy demand rises in the decades ahead. In addition, the region is riven by a multitude of power rivalries, religious schisms, and territorial disputes. These divisions have often triggered violence in the past and are likely to do so again in the future. And because any such upheaval can jeopardize the global supply of oil, intervention by outside powers—especially the United States—is an ever-present possibility.

Many factors contribute to the likelihood of war in the Gulf area, not all of which are connected to oil. Political ambition, religious differences, and greed regularly provoked conflict in the years before 1908, when the first significant deposits of petroleum were found in Iran. But the presence of vast supplies of energy in the Gulf is likely to increase both the frequency of warfare and its relative destructiveness. For one thing, many important energy reserves lie in areas that are claimed by two or more states or in featureless border regions with no established boundaries. Because the possession of these disputed areas can produce billions of dollars in annual oil and gas revenues, the various claimants may choose to seize the territory through force rather than allow a rival to obtain all or part of these royalties. Conflict can also arise in situations where a large oil reservoir spans the border between two countries or when one state attempts to extract a disproportionate share of the total supply. (Iraq accused Kuwait of taking more than its rightful measure of the shared Rumaila field in the late 1980s; this provided a pretext for the Iraqi invasion of 1990.)

The presence of large reserves of oil in the Gulf has increased the likelihood and potential intensity of interstate conflict in another manner, by giving the nations of the region the means to procure vast quantities of modern weapons. Ever since the OPEC oil price rises of 1973–74 brought them added income, the Gulf countries have jointly spent hundreds of billions of dollars on imported arms—in many cases, obtaining the most sophisticated and lethal systems available. The acquisition of so much advanced weaponry has inevitably fueled the expansionist impulses of certain Gulf leaders, including the former shah of Iran (who intervened in the Omani civil war in the mid-1970s) and Saddam Hussein of Iraq. Many analysts believe that Hussein's 1990 invasion of Kuwait was triggered in part by a belief that his forces were so well armed that no outside power would contest Iraq's annexation of the emirate.[1] Whenever warfare has broken out, moreover, the presence of large numbers of modern weapons has naturally elevated the scale and intensity of the fighting. (The Iran-Iraq war of 1980–88, for example, produced an estimated one million casualties and over $100 billion in property damage.)

Increased oil income has also increased the risk of *internal* conflict in the Gulf, particularly in those countries where the bulk of such funds have gone to a small princely or business elite. Although most of these countries have attempted to avert domestic strife over the distribution of petroleum revenues by providing extraordinary benefits to their citizens (including free education and medical care and subsidized food, housing, and energy), the accumulation of so much wealth in the hands of a prominent elite has naturally aroused a certain amount of resentment on the part of those who are less privileged. When this resentment has been fused with other sources of discontent—whether of a religious, political, or ideological nature—the results have often proved explosive.

Many of these factors, of course, can be found in other regions that harbor large supplies of petroleum. What sets the Persian Gulf apart from these other areas is the fact that the great powers, including Great Britain and the United States, have chosen to intervene in local disputes when they perceived a threat to the free flow of oil. Britain played a key role in Gulf affairs from before World War I until the early 1970s; the United States has been a major regional actor since the 1950s. Acting on the belief that access to Persian Gulf energy was essential to their nations' security, leaders of both countries have regularly sanctioned the use of force to overcome what were seen as impediments to continued production and supply.

Great Britain no longer exercises a major military role in the Gulf. The United States, however, has steadily expanded its military presence in the region. Even as U.S. troop strength has been diminished in other potential theaters of war, such as Europe and the Far East, additional forces have been deployed in the Gulf. In ordering these deployments, American officials have been very clear about their intentions: the United States will not permit a hostile state to acquire the ability to obstruct the free flow of oil from the Gulf to major markets in the West. This principle—first articulated by President Carter in January 1980—was invoked on several occasions in the 1980s and '90s to justify the use of force by American troops in the Gulf; it is likely to trigger additional U.S. interventions in the decades ahead.

American officials claim that the conspicuous presence of U.S. troops in the Gulf and the demonstrated willingness of successive administrations to endorse the use of force will reduce the risk of conflict by deterring potential adversaries from obstructing the flow of oil.[2] But while America might may well have discouraged some potential challengers from playing a more assertive role in the Gulf area, the very magnitude of the American military presence—along with Washington's periodic use of force—has also *provoked* opposition to U.S. policies. This is especially evident in Saudi Arabia, where the growing deployment of American troops has aroused fierce hostility from militant Islamic leaders who resent the presence of non-Muslims on their soil and decry America's close ties with Israel. Similarly, continuing U.S. air strikes on Iraq have alienated many pro-Western Iraqis who might otherwise direct their ire toward Saddam Hussein. The recurring attacks on Iraq, coupled with continuing economic sanctions, have also angered people in neighboring countries who have come to believe that the United States is more likely to employ force against Arabs and Muslims than against other likely foes.

Taken together, these factors are a recipe for recurring violence. The question, then, is not whether there will be conflict in the Persian Gulf, but when and of what sort. This chapter will examine the critical stakes at risk in the Gulf, the trajectory of U.S. military strategy in the area, and the myriad sources of potential strife.

THE UNIQUE STATUS OF THE GULF

The signal importance of the Persian Gulf area to global conflict dynamics is entirely the product of geology: an estimated 65 percent of the world's untrapped petroleum reserves are located in this area, and many geologists believe that future discoveries will add to the region's net supply. The Gulf's oil deposits are also highly concentrated and located close to the surface, meaning that they are among the easiest to find and develop. While it is possible that new supplies of petroleum will be found in the North Atlantic or Siberia, or in other remote locations, the Gulf area alone can provide the vast amounts of hydrocarbons that will be needed to satisfy rising demand in the twenty-first century.

The Persian Gulf oil-producing region comprises five major and several secondary suppliers. Heading the list of the major producers is Saudi Arabia, with an estimated 263.5 billion barrels (bbl) in proven reserves, representing approximately 25 percent of the world total. Next in line are four other states with very large reserves: Iraq (with 112.5 bbl in reserves), the United Arab Emirates (97.8 bbl), Kuwait (96.5 bbl), and Iran (89.7 bbl). Also included are a number of secondary suppliers, notably Bahrain, Oman, Qatar, and Yemen. Together, these nine countries produced an average of 21.3 million barrels of oil per day in 1999, or 30 percent of total world production; they also possessed an estimated 673 billion barrels of untapped oil, representing 65 percent of total world reserves.[3] (See Table 1.)

The key factor here is *reserves*. With proven reserves of 673 billion barrels of oil, plus an unknown quantity of uncharted supplies, the Gulf states can continue to extract oil from the ground for several decades to come at current or even higher rates of production—without depleting their available reservoirs. Other major producers have smaller reserves to begin with and tend to exploit their available supplies at a faster rate. The

Table 1: Oil Production and Reserves in the Persian Gulf Area, 1999

Country	Production mbd	Percent of World Total	Proven Reserves, bbl	Percent of World Reserves
Iran	3.55	5.1	89.7	8.7
Iraq	2.58	3.6	112.5	10.9
Kuwait	2.03	2.9	96.5	9.3
Oman	0.91	1.3	5.3	0.5
Qatar	0.72	1.0	3.7	0.4
Saudi Arabia	8.60	·11.9	263.5	25.5
UAE	2.51	3.2	97.8	9.4
Yemen	0.40	0.6	4.0	0.4
Other	0.10	0.1	0.2	–
Total	21.40	29.7	673.2	65.1

Source: BP Amoco, *Statistical Review of World Energy 2000.*
bbl = billion barrels
mbd = million barrels per day

United States, for example, is currently producing oil at the rate of about 2.8 billion barrels per year; if that rate is maintained in the years ahead and no new deposits of oil are discovered, U.S. reserves—estimated at 28.6 billion barrels in 2000—will be fully depleted by 2010. In the Gulf, however, existing reserves are so vast that even with a projected increase in the rate of production—from 20 to 40 million barrels per day—a substantial supply of oil will remain in the ground in 2010 and beyond.

In considering the matter of reserves, special mention must be made of Saudi Arabia. This desert kingdom is not only the world's leading producer of oil—extracting 8.6 million barrels per day in 1999, or 12 percent of total worldwide production—but is also the paramount owner of untapped supplies. With proven reserves of 264 billion barrels, Saudi Arabia alone harbors more oil than North America, South America, Europe, and the former Soviet Union combined. Most geologists believe, moreover, that continued exploration will result in the discovery of additional reserves, thus enhancing Saudi Arabia's status as the world's leading supplier of petroleum.[4]

The fact that Saudi Arabia and the other major Gulf suppliers possess such vast reserves of oil also means that they alone can expand production on a large enough scale to satisfy the anticipated increase in global demands. If worldwide oil consumption increases by 55 percent between 1997 and 2020, as predicted by the U.S. Department of Energy, a significant share of the additional petroleum will have to come from the Gulf—there simply is no other pool of oil large enough to sustain an increase of this magnitude. It is for this reason alone that all projections of future supply and demand assume that the Persian Gulf will account for an ever-expanding share of the world's oil requirements: from 27 percent in 1990 to 33 percent in 2010 and 39 percent in 2020.[5]

Table 2: Global Imports of Persian Gulf Oil, 1997 and 2020
(In millions of barrels per day)

Importing Region and Country	Actual Imports, 1997	Estimated Imports, 2020	Percent Increase, 1997–2020
North America★	2.0	4.1	105
Western Europe	3.5	3.7	6
Developed Asia★★	4.8	5.5	15
China	0.5	5.3	960
Developing East and Southeast Asia	4.2	9.0	114
All others	1.3	8.8	577
Total, all countries	16.3	36.4	123

Source: U.S. Department of Energy, *International Energy Outlook 2000,* Table 13.
★The United States, Canada, and Mexico
★★Japan, Australia, and New Zealand

As the century proceeds, the oil-importing states will become ever more dependent on energy supplies from the Gulf. According to the DoE, global imports of Persian Gulf petroleum will more than double between 1997 and 2020, from 16.3 to 36.4 million barrels per day. Not every country is expected to experience a big rise in imports from the Gulf area, but for some the increase will be substantial: Chinese imports, for example, are predicted to jump by 960 percent over the next two decades, from 0.5 to 5.3 mbd; imports by developing Asia will rise by 114 percent, from 4.2 to 9.0 mbd; and imports by the North American countries will rise by 105 percent, from 2.0 to 4.1 mbd, according to projections.[6] (See Table 2.)

The industrialized world's growing dependence on Persian Gulf energy will exacerbate many of the pressures described earlier in this chapter. Oil and gas deposits located in contested areas will become increasingly valuable, and so the claimants to these reserves will face greater temptation to seize and occupy them through the use of force. Similarly, ambitious leaders could be tempted to expand their oil holdings by annexing neighboring countries, as Saddam Hussein tried to do in 1990. The further concentration of petroleum income in the hands of ruling elites could also provide an increase in revolutionary fervor among those less fortunate. Any of these developments, moreover, could jeopardize the free flow of oil, leading to military intervention by the United States.[7]

Increased international dependence on Persian Gulf energy will also generate new sources of conflict. As more and more nations come to rely on the Gulf for their essential imports of petroleum, the competition for access to the available supply will intensify. Market forces will, of course, help alleviate these pressures by allowing better-off countries to procure what they need through the payment of higher fees, and by compelling less-wealthy states to somehow dampen demand. But some importing countries may seek alternative means of satisfying their requirements, such as forming military alliances with local powers and trading weapons and other forms of assistance for oil. Such arrangements have already been tried in the Gulf—France maintained ties with Saddam Hussein before 1990, while China is said to have formed such a relationship with Iran[8]—and could become more common in the years ahead. With many states competing for access to oil in this manner, relations between rivals within the region will become more strained and the risk of combat between them will grow. In a worst-case scenario, this could lead to a clash between the external backers of rising Gulf powers.[9]

Market forces can also fail in another way: by causing oil prices to rise to such a level as to create widespread economic hardship in importing countries, and so lead to demonstrations, strikes, riots, and other forms of civic strife. In such an environment, political leaders are bound to consider extreme measures to restore public order. This could mean the imposition of gasoline rationing, price controls, or the declaration of martial law. It could also include military action abroad. Such action has, in fact, been contemplated by American strategists in the past, and could emerge as the favored response to future crises of this sort.[10]

THE EVOLUTION OF U.S. STRATEGY

In the pursuit of what are viewed as vital national interests, American leaders have persistently argued that the United States must be able to employ military power if needed to ensure the continued flow of oil from the Persian Gulf producers to markets in the West. "America's vital interests in [the Gulf] are long-standing," General Anthony C. Zinni, then commander in chief of the U.S. Central Command (CENTCOM), told Congress in 1999. "With over 65 percent of the world's oil reserves located within the Gulf states," the United States and its allies "must have free access to the region's resources."[11] But while U.S. objectives have remained consistent over a long period of time, the strategies employed to achieve this goal have changed with the trend toward an ever-increasing commitment of American military power.

American policy makers first articulated the principle of securing Gulf oil supplies in 1943, when President Franklin D. Roosevelt authorized the delivery of U.S. military assistance to Saudi Arabia. Believing that the Western powers would become highly dependent on Persian Gulf oil after the war, administration officials concluded that the United States—which until that point had paid little attention to the Gulf—would have to exercise a more conspicuous role in the area. This led to the establishment of diplomatic relations with Saudi Arabia and, in 1945, to a face-to-face meeting between President Roosevelt and King Abdel-Aziz Ibn Saud, the founder of the modern Saudi state.[12] The designation of Persian Gulf oil as a vital security interest did not, however, lead to the immediate buildup of American forces in the area; instead, U.S. strength was built up over time, reflecting changes in the orientation of national strategy.

Initially, in the early Cold War period, the United States maintained a relatively low profile in the Gulf. Rather than station large numbers of American soldiers there, Washington chose to rely on Great Britain—the traditional hegemon in the area—to maintain regional stability. This changed in 1968, however, when then Prime Minister Harold Wilson announced that London would withdraw its military forces from "East of Suez" by the end of 1971. Convinced that the withdrawal of the British would produce a dangerous vacuum in the Gulf, American strategists determined that Washington would have to assume primary responsibility for the maintenance of stability. Following an intensive review of American interests in the Gulf by the National Security Council—then headed by Henry Kissinger—President Nixon signed National Security Decision Memorandum No. 92, mandating an expanded U.S. presence in the region.[13]

Coming when it did, the decision to upgrade U.S. involvement in the Gulf posed a significant dilemma for senior policy makers. With the fighting in Vietnam then at its peak, and the American public reluctant to endorse another major military commitment in a Third World area, the administration was unable to deploy large numbers of U.S. troops in the Gulf. To resolve this dilemma, Washington adopted what came to be known as the "Surrogate Strategy"—a policy of utilizing friendly local powers to serve as the "guardians" of Western interests with substantial U.S. military assistance and strategic guidance from Washington. "What we decided," Under Secretary of State Joseph J. Sisco later explained, "is that we would try to stimulate and be helpful to the two key countries in this area—namely, Iran and Saudi Arabia—that . . . they could become the major elements of stability as the British were getting out."[14]

The surrogate policy governed American strategy in the Gulf for most of the 1970s. Between 1970 and 1978 alone, Washington sold Iran over $20 billion worth of sophisticated weaponry—producing what Representative Gerry E. Studds of Massachusetts termed "the most rapid buildup of military power under peacetime conditions of any nation in the history of the world."[15] But while American weaponry helped Iran defend itself against its foreign enemies, it proved far less useful in protecting the shah, Mohammad Reza Pahlavi, against his domestic opponents. Indeed, the shah's conspicuous ties with Washington were seen by many in the country—especially among the Muslim clergy—as evidence of his pernicious and heretical embrace of the West. By late 1978, domestic opposition to the shah had reached massive proportions, and on January 16, 1979, he fled the country; within months, Iran had fallen under the control of a radical Islamic regime by Ayatollah Ruholla Khomeini.

The fall of the shah and the rise of Khomeini forced a thorough reassessment of American strategy in the Gulf. Of the two key "pillars" of the Surrogate Strategy, Iran and Saudi Arabia, the former was by far the stronger and the latter was much too weak to protect vital Western interests on its own. Although Washington attempted to bolster

Saudi defenses through massive infusions of American weaponry, it was evident to senior policy makers that the surrogate approach was no longer viable and that, as a consequence, the United States would have to assume *direct* responsibility for stability in the Gulf. It is against this backdrop that President Carter issued his famous statement of January 1980 in which described the Gulf as a "vital interest" of the United States and warned that an attack on this area "will be repelled by any means necessary, including military force."

To invest this pronouncement with credibility, President Carter established the Rapid Deployment Force (RDF)—a group of combat units based in the United States but available for use in the Gulf when the need arose. Carter also initiated the acquisition of new U.S. military bases in the region, upgraded existing bases, and authorized an expanded navy presence in Middle Eastern waters. This included the deployment of a permanent U.S. naval force in the Gulf, with its headquarters in Bahrain. Although widely derided at the time, these moves laid the foundation for the much enhanced U.S. capability now deployed in the region.[16] (In 1983, the RDF was reconstituted as the U.S. Central Command, or CENTCOM, and assigned additional responsibilities; the naval force at Bahrain later formed the nucleus of the U.S. Fifth Fleet.)

Initially, the RDF/CENTCOM was intended to protect the Gulf area against a hypothetical Soviet invasion. By the late 1980s, however, American policy makers had begun to worry about the growing military might of Iraq. Triumphant in its eight-year war with Iran (1980–88) and well-equipped with modern French and Soviet weapons, Iraq began issuing threats to its southern Gulf neighbors, particularly Kuwait and Saudi Arabia. Fearing that domination of the area by Saddam Hussein would jeopardize Western access to vital petroleum supplies, U.S. strategists turned their attention from the Soviet Union to Iraq. In late 1989, the chairman of the Joint Chiefs of Staff, General Colin Powell, authorized the newly appointed commander in chief of CENTCOM, General H. Norman Schwarzkopf, to prepare a blueprint for all-out combat with the Iraqis.[17]

General Schwarzkopf and his staff labored throughout the first five months of 1990 to develop such a blueprint. As reported in the media, the resulting document—known officially as Operational Plans (OpPlan) 1002–90—called for the deployment of several armored and mechanized divisions to the Gulf along with a powerful array of air and naval forces. To test this blueprint, CENTCOM conducted an elaborate "command post exercise" based on a hypothetical U.S.-Iraqi engagement in mid-July 1990. The exercise was barely completed when, on August 2, Saddam Hussein commenced the invasion of Kuwait. Schwarzkopf was immediately summoned to a crisis meeting with top White House officials at Camp David, Maryland; two days later he was ordered by President Bush to begin preparations for the actual implementation of OpPlan 1002–90. The result, six months later, was Operation Desert Storm.[18]

Table 3: U.S. Naval Forces in the Persian Gulf, January 1998

Type of Warship	Vessel	Principal Armament	Crew
Aircraft carriers	USS *Nimitz*	14 F-14 fighters; 36 F/A-18 fighters; 4 EA-6B electronic warfare planes; 23 other aircraft	5,500
	USS *George Washington*	14 F-14 fighters; 36 F/A-18 fighters; 4 EA-6B electronic warfare planes; 21 other aircraft	5,500
Cruiser	USS *Normandy*	Tomahawk cruise missile, Standard missile, Harpoon missile	358
Destroyers	USS *Carney*	Tomahawk cruise missile, Standard missile, Harpoon missile	339
	USS *John Young*	Tomahawk cruise missile, Standard missile, Harpoon missile	339
	USS *Barry*	Tomahawk cruise missile, Standard missile, Harpoon missile	300
	USS *Ingersoll*	n/a	300
Guided missile frigates	USS *Reuben James*	Standard missile, Harpoon missile	200
	USS *Samuel B. Roberts*	Standard missile, Harpoon missile	200
Attack submarines	USS *Annapolis*	Tomahawk cruise missile, Mk-48 torpedo	133
	USS *L. Mendel Rivers*	n/a	107
Mine warfare ships	USS *Dextrous*	Mine Neutralization System	81
	USS *Ardent*	Mine Neutralization System	81

Source: U.S. Navy (electronic communication, January 12, 1998).

n/a = not available

AFTER DESERT STORM

The 1991 Gulf conflict set an important precedent for U.S. military involvement in the region. Up until that point, American strategy had been designed to minimize the direct involvement of U.S. troops in any regional conflict; in Operation Desert Storm, however, the United States contributed the overwhelming majority of the forces involved. Once the war was concluded, moreover, senior American officials made it clear that Washington was prepared to assume the lead role again or, if required, to act entirely on its own. "The U.S. will continue to use a variety of means to promote regional security and stability [in the Gulf], working with our friends and allies," Assistant Secretary of Defense Joseph Nye declared in 1995. But it "will remain prepared to defend vital U.S. interests in the region—*unilaterally if necessary*" (emphasis added).[19]

Operation Desert Storm also established the prevailing model for American military intervention in the Gulf: a rapid buildup of air, sea, and ground forces followed by a crushing offensive employing high-tech weaponry. Every imaginable U.S. advantage in firepower, mobility, intelligence, and communications was to be employed in an effort to shatter enemy defenses with a minimum loss of American lives. "The ability to project overwhelming and decisive military power is key to CENTCOM's theater strategy as well as our ability to shape the battlefield," General Zinni told Congress in 1999.[20] These two principles—a commitment to unilateral intervention in the Gulf and a warfighting doctrine of "decisive victory"—are the key features of prevailing U.S. military strategy in the region.

These principles have been put to the test on several other occasions. In January and February of 1998, and then again in November and December of that year, the United States deployed a substantial force in the Gulf to conduct sustained air and missile attacks on Iraq. (See Table 3). The first round of attacks was called off at the last minute, after Saddam Hussein agreed to open up suspected Iraqi weapons sites to U.N. inspection; the second round was initiated in December 1998 when he refused all further cooperation with the United Nations. In neither of these instances did the United States receive significant support from the international community.[21] Nevertheless, American officials continue to state that U.S. forces are prepared to conduct further strikes against Iraq whenever such action is deemed appropriate.[22]

Since then the United States has further bolstered its strength in the Persian Gulf area. Because it is not feasible to station large numbers of American soldiers in the region on a permanent basis—the costs would be enormous, and none of America's local allies are keen to house a sizable force of non-Muslims on their territory—the Department of Defense is relying instead on deploying troops there quickly when a crisis erupts. To accomplish this, the Pentagon has "prepositioned" vast supplies of heavy equipment at depots in the region and acquired new ships and aircraft to carry a substantial combat force from the United States to the Gulf.[23] The army has already stored sufficient weaponry for an entire brigade in Kuwait, and is constructing a second such facility in Qatar. In addition, the Marine Corps has stored the heavy equipment for an expeditionary force of 15,000 soldiers aboard prepositioning ships in the area, and the air force has stockpiled sufficient hardware to establish a "bare bones" fighter base on very short notice.[24]

American strategy also seeks to strengthen the military capabilities of friendly powers, especially Kuwait and Saudi Arabia, and to reduce (or "degrade") the capabilities of hostile states, notably Iraq and Iran.

To boost the fighting capacity of its allies, the United States has provided vast quantities of modern arms to member states of the Gulf Cooperation Council (GCC), a loose alliance of Bahrain, Kuwait, Oman, Qatar, Saudi Arabia, and the United Arab Emirates. The aim is not to make these states militarily self-sufficient but rather to improve their ability to assist American forces in the event of a major conflagration.

"The GCC states will not be able to repel external aggression from either Iraq or Iran," the Pentagon's Institute for National Security Studies noted in 1998. However, with sufficient U.S. assistance, "their forces could make a distinct contribution to a joint effort with the United States."[25]

Washington has sold the GCC countries some of its most capable and sophisticated weapons systems, including F-15 and F-16 fighter aircraft, M-1 tanks, AH-64 Apache attack helicopters, and the Patriot air-defense missile. Between 1990 and 1997 alone, the United States provided these countries with arms and ammunition worth over $42 billion—the largest and most costly transfer of military equipment to any region in the world by any single supplier in recent history.[26] (See Tables 4 and 5.) The Department of Defense has also provided training to thousands of friendly military personnel, and U.S. forces regularly engage in joint military exercises with GCC member states.

The close relationship between U.S. arms transfers and the broader goals of American strategy in the Gulf is especially evident in the March 2000 sale of eighty upgraded F-16 fighters to the United Arab Emirates. The fighter deal, worth an estimated $7 billion, is unusual in several respects. To begin with, the aircraft sold to the UAE—the so-called Block-60 variant of the F-16—are to be equipped with electronic and radar systems far more sophisticated than those installed on the F-16s supplied to the U.S. Air Force.[27] Even more significant, the sales arrangement allows the United States to operate its own aircraft from the fighter base being built by the UAE to house its F-16s and to preposition military equipment there. Pentagon documents further suggest that the F-16 transaction is intended to lead to other forms of cooperation with the UAE, including the use of its ports by American naval vessels.[28] "U.S. forces could respond to the region quicker and more effectively if bases, ports, and the infrastructure they require were available [in the UAE]," the air force told Congress on March 7, 2000.[29]

To degrade the capabilities of Iran and Iraq—an approach known as "threat reduction"—the United States has imposed economic and trade sanctions and, in the case of Iraq, has conducted air and missile strikes against military installations and arms-production facilities. These policies aim to diminish Iran and Iraq's capacity to manufacture nuclear, chemical, and biological munitions—so-called weapons of mass destruction (WMD)— and ballistic missile delivery systems.* Measures of this sort are viewed as an important part of the policy of "dual containment," under which the United States has sought to constrain the political and military influence of Iran and Iraq."[30]

While sanctions remain the preferred mechanism for eroding the military power of hostile states, the United States has also engaged in direct military action to accomplish this purpose. The goal of the December 1998 bombing campaign against Iraq, known as Operation Desert Fox, was, according to President Clinton, to cripple "Iraq's nuclear,

---

*Iraq is subject to comprehensive trade sanctions in accordance with U.N. Security Council Resolution 687 of March 1991 and other Security Council resolutions; Iran is subject to a U.S. imposed ban on foreign investment under the Iran-Libya Sanctions Act of 1996.

Table 4:
U.S. Arms Transfer Agreements with Selected Persian Gulf States, 1990–97
(in millions of current U.S. dollars)

Recipient	1990–93	1994–97	Total, 1990–97
Bahrain	300	300	600
Kuwait	3,700	500	4,200
Oman	100	0	100
Saudi Arabia	32,000	4,200	36,200
UAE	600	300	900

Source: Congressional Research Service, *Conventional Arms Transfers to Developing Nations, 1990–1997*, July 31, 1998, p. 51.

chemical, and biological weapons programs and its military capacities to threaten its neighbors."[31] Since Desert Fox, the United States has continued to strike at military installations in Iraq as part of a systematic effort to degrade Iraqi capabilities.

All of these endeavors—the expansion of U.S. basing and logistical capabilities, the strengthening of allied forces, and the degradation of adversary strength—are part of a consistent, integrated policy aimed at bolstering American military dominance in the Persian Gulf area. Indeed, securing such dominance in the Gulf has been one of the most important and persistent goals of American strategy since 1980, when the Rapid Deployment Force was first established. All signs indicate that this goal will continue to govern U.S. strategy in the opening decades of the twenty-first century.

THE THREE-WAR SCENARIO

Military commanders can never be fully certain of the types and locations of the conflicts they will have to fight, so they like to prepare for a wide range of hypothetical contingencies. The American buildup in the Gulf has been carried out with no specific scenario in mind; instead it gives U.S. policy makers the capacity to prevail in any conceivable conflict situation. But American strategists have identified three basic scenarios for combat in the Gulf: (1) a recurrence of the 1990 Iraqi drive on the oil fields of Kuwait and Saudi Arabia; (2) an effort by Iran to close the Strait of Hormuz or otherwise imperil oil shipping in the Gulf itself; and (3) an internal revolt against the Saudi royal family. Under current U.S. policy, American forces must be able to prevail in all three of these scenarios—alone, or in any combination.

In a sense, the United States has been confronting these challenges for some time already. American forces continue to clash with Iraqi military units on a regular basis, U.S. warships patrol the Gulf and adjacent waters throughout the year, and Washington is orchestrating an international campaign against Osama bin Laden and other sworn

Table 5: Major U.S. Arms Transfers to Persian Gulf States, 1990–98

Recipient	Year	Value	Quantity and Item
Bahrain	1997	$303 million	20 F-16A/B aircraft
Kuwait	1992	$2.5 billion	6 Patriot air-defense fire units with 450 Patriot missiles; 6 Hawk air-defense missile batteries with 342 Hawk missiles
	1993	$4.5 billion	256 M-1A2 Abrams tanks; 125M-113 APCs, 52 M-577 command post carriers; 130,000 rounds of 120mm tank ammunition
	1994	$692 million	16 AH-64 Apache attack helicopters with 500 Hellfire antitank missiles
	1995	$461 million	16 UH-60L Blackhawk helicopters
	1998	$609 million	48 M109A6 howitzers, 18 M88A2 recovery vehicles, and 24 M-113A3 APCs
Oman	1991	$150 million	119 V-300 Commando armored vehicles
Saudi Arabia	1990	$3.4 billion	1,117 Light Armored Vehicles, 2,000 TOW antitank missiles, and related base construction for the SANG
	1990	$206 million	150 M-60A3 tanks
	1990	$2 billion	24 F15C/D Eagle fighter aircraft
	1990	$300 million	12 AH-64 Apache attack helicopters with 150 Hellfire antitank missiles
	1990	$984 million	6 Patriot air-defense fire units with 384 Patriot missiles
	1990	$3.1 billion	150 M-1A2 Abrams tanks, 200 M-2 Bradley Infantry Fighting Vehicles, 207 M-113 APCs
	1991	$3.3 billion	12 Patriot air-defense fire units with 758 Patriot missiles and support gear
	1992	$9 billion	72 F-15XP Eagle fighter aircraft plus 900 Maverick AGM missiles, 300 Sidewinder AAM missiles, and 300 Sparrow AAM missiles
	1995	$690 million	195,000 rounds of 90mm ammunition and other items for the SANG
	1997	$1.4 billion	Maintenance and construction services for 5 E-3 AWACS aircraft and 7 KE-3A aerial refueling tankers; 130 90mm turret weapons systems for Light Armored Vehicles

Recipient	Year	Value	Quantity and Item
United Arab Emirates	1991	$682 million	20 AH-64 Apache attack helicopters with 620 Hellfire antitank missiles
	1994	$330 million	10 AH-64 Apache attack helicopters with 360 Hellfire antitank missiles
	1998	$7 billion	80 F-16C/D fighter aircraft with 491 AMRAAM missiles, 267 Sidewinder AAM missiles, 1,163 Maverick AGM missiles, and other bombs and missiles

Source: Arms Control Association (ACA), "ACA Register of U.S. Arms Transfers," ACA, Washington, D.C., May 1997; also ACA lists of pending arms transfers for 1997 and 1998.
AAM = air-to-air missile
AGM = air-to-ground missile
APC = armored personnel carrier
SANG = Saudi Arabia National Guard

enemies of the Saudi regime. These activities sometimes lead to violent incidents that are duly noted in the international press. What is missing from such accounts, however, is an understanding of how these individual episodes fit into a larger, more complex set of conflict systems.

CONTAINING IRAQ

At present, the scenario receiving the greatest attention from Washington is the threat of a new Iraqi drive against Kuwait and Saudi Arabia. Although Iraqi forces are much weaker today than they were in 1990 when Saddam Hussein ordered the original invasion of Kuwait, U.S. officials continue to worry about Iraqi designs on the southern Gulf states. "Saddam's history of aggression leaves little doubt that he would resume his drive for regional domination and his quest for weapons of mass destruction if he had the chance," Samuel R. Berger, President Clinton's national security adviser, observed in 1998. For this reason, he noted, the United States has taken a variety of steps to constrain Iraqi power and to enhance America's ability to defeat a new Iraqi onslaught with a minimum risk to allied forces.[32]

American efforts to weaken Iraqi power are aimed, in the first instance, at Baghdad's conventional forces. While these forces are much less powerful than those engaged in the 1990 invasion of Kuwait, they remain substantial. According to General J. H. Binford Peay III, the former commander of CENTCOM, "Saddam continues to field the largest army in the region. . . . It is a force that has proven it can mobilize and deploy quickly and continue to threaten Kuwait and Saudi Arabia."[33] Peay and other U.S. officials place particular emphasis on the threat posed by the Republican Guards, a highly mobile force that has spearheaded many Iraqi assaults in the past.

Persian Gulf Region

Iraq is also said to possess a residual chemical and biological weapons industry along with ballistic missile delivery systems. The exact dimensions of this capacity are not fully known, as Saddam Hussein has gone to great lengths to hide the remnants of Iraq's once-formidable WMD capabilities. The bulk of these facilities were destroyed by Operation Desert Storm or by the United Nations Special Commission (UNSCOM), the body established in 1991 to oversee the implementation of U.N. Security Council Resolution 687 (which prohibits Iraq from possessing ballistic missiles and weapons of mass destruction). Nevertheless, most Western analysts believe that the Iraqis were able to hide some plans and equipment from UNSCOM inspectors—all of whom were expelled in late 1998—and so could be capable of reconstituting a limited ability to manufacture chemical and biological weapons.[34]

To diminish the threat posed by Iraqi military capabilities, the United States has engaged in a wide range of preventive efforts. These include: economic and trade sanctions, a naval blockade to enforce the trade embargo, the enforcement of a no-fly zone and no-drive zone over southern Iraqi, a no-fly zone over northern Iraqi, periodic air and missile attacks on Iraqi military installations, the prepositioning of U.S. military equipment in Kuwait and Qatar, and the constant rotation of American combat units through the region. Together these efforts represent a substantial commitment of U.S. resources, entailing the permanent deployment of over 20,000 American soldiers in the Gulf and the expenditure of many billions of dollars per year.[35]

Except at moments of heightened tension, the most taxing aspects of this costly effort are the enforcement of trade sanctions and the no-fly and no-drive zones.* Maintenance of the southern no-fly zone, which excludes all Iraqi aircraft from the airspace extending southward from the 33rd parallel to the Kuwaiti border, is an especially demanding task. By January 2000, the aircraft assigned to Operation Southern Watch—the Pentagon's name for this effort—had flown over 240,000 individual flights over the exclusion zone.[36] Since December 1998, moreover, the aircraft participating in Southern Watch have encountered increased resistance from the Iraqis and have responded with a steady barrage of missiles.[37]

The United States has also periodically engaged in what Samuel Berger called "disarmament from the air"—the systematic destruction of Iraqi military capabilities through sustained air and missile attack. During Operation Desert Fox, he noted, "We damaged or destroyed much of the machinery that Iraq uses to develop, test, and produce the delivery systems for its WMD. . . . We [also] destroyed the headquarters of the Special Republican Guard, and a number of other Republican Guard headquarters, barracks, and training facilities."[38] Nevertheless, U.S. military planners continue to warn of Iraqi military capabilities. In 1999, General Zinni observed that "due to the destruction of key facilities and specialized equipment, Iraq's ballistic missile program has been set back *one to two years*" (emphasis added).[39] Zinni's assessment implies that a fresh round of attacks will be needed every other year or so to prevent Iraq from rebuilding its missile arsenal. Indeed, it appears that Operation Southern Watch has now taken on this preemptive function: between December 1998 and August 1999, U.S. and British aircraft fired a total of 1,100 missiles against 359 targets in Iraq—or about three times the number of targets attacked during Operation Desert Fox.[40]

To preserve the combat readiness of American forces, the military conducts frequent training exercises along the Iraq-Kuwait border. The exercises, known as "Operation Desert Spring," are held three or four times a year—providing what CENTCOM calls a "near-continuous" U.S. military presence along the southern edge of Iraq. The United States also conducts periodic air and naval exercises in the region, and through Operations Bright Star (an annual field exercise) and Ultimate Resolve (an annual command post exercise), tests the Pentagon's ability to mount another large multinational campaign on the scale of Desert Storm.[41]

---

*To sustain the naval blockade of Iraq, CENTCOM arranged in 1999 for U.S. warships to refuel in the port of Aden in Yemen; on October 12, 2000, an American destroyer, the USS *Cole,* was struck by a terrorist bomb in Aden harbor after being refueled there.

IRAN AND THE STRAIT OF HORMUZ

The strategy of "dual containment" also applies to Iran, the other major obstacle to American dominance in the Persian Gulf area. With a long coastline on the Gulf and a large and growing naval capability, Iran is viewed in Washington as the "threat after next"—the nation that is most likely to oppose American oil interests once the risk of an Iraqi invasion has been reduced to marginality. As noted by General Zinni in 1999, "Iran remains potentially the most dangerous threat long-term to peace and stability in the [Persian Gulf] region. In the 20th year of its revolution, Iran's ambitions to be the dominant regional power and leader of the Islamic world remain undiminished."[42]

Iran does not pose a direct threat to Saudi Arabia and the southern Gulf kingdoms—at least not for the time being. However, by building up its navy and deploying antiship missiles along its coasts, Iran may imperil oil shipping in the Persian Gulf and the all-important Strait of Hormuz, the Gulf's narrow opening to the Arabian Sea and the larger world beyond. Although lacking major warships, Iran has acquired three submarines, twenty missile-armed patrol boats, numerous shore-based missile batteries, and a large inventory of antishipping mines. This is enough, General Zinni testified in 1999, to jeopardize "open access to Gulf shipping lanes."[43]

Only six miles wide at its narrowest point, the Strait of Hormuz is described by the U.S. Department of Energy as "the world's most important oil chokepoint" because of the sheer volume of oil—over 15 million barrels per day—that passes through it.[44] With missile batteries deployed at both entrances to the strait, and a large inventory of antishipping mines, Iran is in an ideal position to impede shipping through this vital channel. Pentagon strategies suggest, moreover, that Iran will seek to do so in the event of a future clash with the United States.[45]

Iran also seeks to extend its control over Abu Musa and both Greater and Lesser Tunb, a small group of islands that guard the western approaches to the strait. Iran seized the Tunbs from Ras al-Khaimah (part of the United Arab Emirates) in 1971 and has occupied them since. It shared Abu Musa with Sharjah (another UAE component) until 1994, when it took control of the entire island. When pressed by the UAE to submit the dispute over the islands to international mediation, Tehran declared that they were "an inseparable part of Iran."[46] Since then, the Iranians have deployed antiship missiles on Abu Musa and fortified their positions on the Tunbs.[47]

Just as it would resist any new Iraqi assault on Kuwait, the United States would greet any Iranian move to impede Persian Gulf shipping with an immediate and crushing military response. Tomahawk cruise missiles and radar-guided bombs would most likely be used to demolish Iranian ships, missile batteries, airfields, and communications facilities. Ships and aircraft already deployed in the region would carry out most of the attacks, backed up by additional units sent in from the United States and Europe. And while the Iranians might succeed in damaging a number of tankers, their ability to imperil the oil flow would quickly be eliminated by superior American firepower.[48]

The one uncertainty in this equation involves Tehran's intentions to use its ballistic missiles and weapons of mass destruction. Iran is thought to possess several hundred Soviet-type Scud missiles, as well as a number of longer-range Scud variants based on North Korean technology; at least some of these missiles may be armed with chemical warheads. If war broke out in the Gulf, Iran might launch its missiles against the southern Gulf kingdoms in a preemptive attack, or in retaliation for American and Saudi air strikes on Iranian territory. Such a barrage would not, in the end, affect the outcome of the war—this would almost certainly entail the ultimate defeat of Iran—but could result in extensive death and destruction, especially if the missiles were equipped with chemical weapons.[49] To counter this threat, the United States has deployed Patriot antimissile systems in the Gulf and attempted to impede Iran's access to missile and WMD technology.*

Acutely conscious of America's military superiority and desperate to improve the nation's economic performance, a significant faction of the Iranian leadership has sought to reduce tensions in the Gulf and to restore Iran's ties to the West. The most conspicuous advocate for this position is Mohammed Khatami, a moderate Muslim cleric who was elected president in 1997. Although Khatami's power is limited by the Iranian constitution (which reserves ultimate power to senior religious leaders), he has spoken often of his desire to improve relations with the GCC states and the major Western powers.[51] In recognition of his efforts, U.S. Secretary of State Madeleine Albright noted in June 1998 that the United States was ready to devise "a road map leading to normal relations" if Tehran addressed American concerns regarding terrorism and the pursuit of WMD.[52] It is unclear, however, whether Khatami can overcome the influence of hard-line clerics and reverse Iran's current, hostile stance toward the West.

While it is certainly possible that Iran and the United States will mend their relations in the years ahead, it is unlikely that Washington will in any way relax its concern over Iranian military capabilities; nor, for that matter, will it reduce its capacity to defeat Iran in the event of a future clash in the Gulf. As suggested by General Peay, it is Iran's long-term military potential, not its current political orientation, that most worries American strategists. "[Iran] has a population of over 60 million people, large numbers of highly educated engineers and technicians, abundant mineral deposits, and vast oil and gas reserves," he noted. "With such resources, Iran retains the means, over the long-term, to potentially overcome its current economic malaise and endanger other Gulf states and U.S. interests."[53]

---

*An even more worrisome scenario involves the acquisition by Iran of nuclear weapons. Although Tehran currently lacks the capacity to manufacture such munitions, many Western analysts believe that it is attempting to build a clandestine nuclear program. (As a signatory to the Non-Proliferation Treaty, Iran has opened its existing nuclear facilities to international inspection.) Much uncertainty exists over the scale and tempo of Iran's nuclear efforts, but most experts believe that Tehran is still a decade or more away from producing operational weapons.[50]

PROTECTING THE SAUDI REGIME

The third scenario that dominates U.S. military planning is an internal threat to the Saudi monarchy. Protection of the Saudi regime has been a basic feature of U.S. security policy since 1945, when President Roosevelt met Ibn Saud and assured him of America's support.[54] At the core of this arrangement is a vital but unspoken quid pro quo: in return for protecting the royal family against its enemies, American companies will be allowed unrivaled access to Saudi oil fields. To defend the monarchy against its external opponents, the United States has fought a war against Iraq and conducted the military buildup described above. Increasingly, however, internal defense is becoming the greater priority.[55]

The threat posed by the antigovernment underground was first revealed in November 1995, when a massive truck bomb shattered the headquarters of the Saudi Arabia National Guard in Riyadh, killing five American servicemen and two Indians working at the facility. Seven months later, on June 25, 1996, another truck bomb killed nineteen American servicemen at the Khobar Towers housing complex in Dhahran, in what proved to be the most deadly attack on U.S. forces since the end of the 1991 Gulf conflict. Although the identity of the bombers has never been fully established, they are widely assumed to be members of militant antigovernment Islamic organizations.[56] Similar groups, linked to Saudi extremist Osama bin Laden, are also thought to be responsible for the August 1998 bombing of the American embassies in Kenya and Tanzania.

Most analysts believe that the ultimate aim of the organizations involved in these and similar attacks is to overthrow the existing Saudi regime and replace it with an even more conservative Islamic government. Such a revolution is needed, Saudi dissidents argue, because the royal family has been so corrupted by its massive oil wealth and its ties to the West that it can no longer be considered worthy to govern. As evidence of such corruption, they point to Saudi Arabia's timid and ineffectual opposition to Israel and the presence, on sacred Islamic soil, of non-Muslim oilmen and soldiers. Reversing these injustices, the dissidents argue, can be accomplished only be eliminating the existing regime through jihad, or holy war. And because the United States is the leading source of protection for the regime, it, too, must be the target of jihad.[57]

For the most part, those who hold such views in Saudi Arabia are content to express them in private, or among the faithful in private religious assemblies. (Open political debate is not permitted in the kingdom, and those suspected of espousing antigovernment views are routinely arrested and confined to prison.)[58] Nevertheless, a small but significant minority within the fundamentalist community favors more vigorous action, including violent attacks on military bases and government offices.[59] "To the extremists, to declare the government as illegitimate makes it an infidel government," explained Jamal Khashoggi, a Saudi journalist. "And the moment they declare a government an infidel government, they believe they have the right to fight against it."[60]

Although driven primarily by religious belief, these groups have also tapped into other sources of discontent. Much of this discontent is of an economic nature: when oil revenues declined in the 1990s, the government cut back on the lucrative benefits provided to all Saudi citizens. Unemployment rose, expectations declined, and many young Saudis became embittered by the loss of privileges once taken for granted. With the open expression of political dissent forbidden, it is not surprising that a certain percentage of these disaffected youths have moved to the political margins.[61]

Despite determined efforts by the Saudi government to suppress dissident organizations, they continue to thrive. This is partly due to their professed religious character, which provides a certain degree of immunity from government surveillance, and partly to the fact that they enjoy the patronage of wealthy Saudi businessmen and senior clerics in Iran, Sudan, and other Muslim countries. Also contributing to the effectiveness and prestige of these organizations is the presence in their ranks of many ex-combatants (of various nationalities) from the anti-Soviet struggle in Afghanistan. "These groups' multinational composition, financial independence, and international ties to other terrorist groups make them an elusive threat," CENTCOM noted in 1997. "Trained as *mujahideen* in the Afghan war against Soviet occupation, members of these groups . . . form small, impenetrable cells to pursue an extremist agenda."[62]

To prevent these efforts from coalescing into a more substantial threat to the Saudi regime, the United States has undertaken a wide range of measures. These include assistance in the creation of a large, efficient, and well-equipped domestic security apparatus. Primary responsibility for internal stability and the protection of the royal family falls on the Saudi Arabia National Guard (SANG), an elite force of 57,000 active-duty combatants equipped with a broad array of modern weapons. From its inception, this force has received most of its training, equipment, and technical support from the U.S. Department of Defense or from American military contractors.[63] In 1990, for instance, U.S. firms were awarded a $3.4 billion contract to supply the SANG with 1,117 Light Armored Vehicles, 2,000 TOW antitank missiles, 27 M-198 towed howitzers, and related services; follow-on contracts, worth $819 million and $690 million respectively, were signed in 1993.[64]

Although it has entrusted the SANG and other Saudi security agencies with primary responsibility for protecting the royal family against internal threats, the United States has taken active measures of its own. These include extensive intelligence-collection activities designed to identify and track the leaders of Saudi extremist organizations—especially Osama bin Laden and his associates—as well as diplomatic efforts to deny them safe haven and banking privileges in neighboring countries.[65] The United States has also made it clear that it will employ military force to punish those implicated in terrorist attacks on U.S. bases and personnel, as it did following the August 1998 bombings of the American embassies in Kenya and Tanzania.*

Ultimately, the United States is prepared to intervene with its own forces to defend the regime against internal attack. This was made abundantly clear in 1981, when President Reagan declared that the United States would not allow an insurgent movement to overthrow the Saudi monarch, as had occurred in Iran two years earlier. "I will not permit [Saudi Arabia] to be an Iran," he told reporters at the White House.[67]

Direct American involvement in a civil war is, no doubt, the last thing that Washington would like to see happen. To prevent this, great emphasis is being placed on intelligence activities and the disruption of antigovernment organizations. But President Reagan's 1981 statement provides an unambiguous indication of America's determination to protect the Saudi monarchy at all costs. Nor is there any evidence to suggest that this commitment has in any way been diluted since Reagan's time; if anything, the United States is even more closely wedded to the Saudi regime now than it was in 1981. And while it is impossible to predict the exact nature of the U.S. response to any particular threat to the regime, it is likely to be swift, muscular, and lethal.

---

*Claiming that bin Laden's organization was behind the embassy bombings, the United States fired Tomahawk cruise missiles at a guerrilla training base in Afghanistan and a suspected chemical weapons (CW) facility in Sudan. Although the effort was characterized by White House officials as a damaging blow to the terrorist underground, it was later revealed that no senior bin Laden associates were killed in the raids and that evidence for CW production at the Sudanese facility—a well-known pharmaceutical plant—was meager and inconclusive.[66]

26

REEL BAD ARABS: HOW HOLLYWOOD VILIFIES A PEOPLE

Jack G. Shaheen

FOREWORD

Hollywood is our great national entertainer and also the most effective teacher of our young. It is the authoritative creator of commonly shared attitudes and feelings and even the shared experiences of Americans. Hollywood is also, as this book documents in troubling detail, the leading source of propagandistic images that damage and isolate some citizens and can destroy the possibility of ever achieving genuine democratic relationships among us. The power to depict certain "others" as innately strange and dangerous—as foul creatures not like the rest of us—is surely as devastating as the physical force of weaponry. The malign images segregate some Americans from the whole experience of citizenship, impeding their capacity to speak and act for themselves in political life or intimidating any public leaders who dare to speak for them.

This is the cloud that shadows Arab-Americans still and induces a kind of blindness among other Americans, who have unwittingly consumed the propaganda for generations in the process of being entertained. Folk prejudice is ancient among different peoples, of course, and not likely ever to disappear entirely. But Jack G. Shaheen's inquiry is about manufactured prejudice—a product that stokes feelings of distrust and loathing. We can argue at length about how much of this process is accidental and unintentional, how much is purposeful and politically motivated. But the larger point that Shaheen documents is the perpetuation of this malignancy among us at the center of American's popular culture. Indeed, he argues that, as other groups have protested and won redress against prejudicial stereotypes, as the Cold War ended and the familiar bogeyman of Soviet Communists was retired, the stereotypical confinement of Arabs has actually grown worse in films.

This book poses important challenges to the film industry, but it also asks questions of the rest of us. Why does our desire to experience a good story induce us to swallow the defamation so passively? Do we always need some one or other as villain to dread and despise? Or are we perhaps capable—as Americans, as human beings—of rising above the ugly stereotypes, escaping from their deleterious effects and joining Arab-Americans in protest? One might start the process of escape by reading Shaheen's account as if you and your children are Arabs too. As he describes your image as it is portrayed in American film, ask yourself how it feels.

—William Greider

INTRODUCTION

The culture for which Hollywood has shown its greatest contempt has been the [Arab or] Middle East culture.

—Max Alvarez, editor of *Cinecism*

The popular caricature of the average Arab is as mythical as the old portrait of the Jew. He is robed and turbaned, sinister and dangerous, engaged mainly in hijacking airplanes and blowing up public buildings. It seems that the human race cannot discriminate between a tiny minority of persons who may be objectionable and the ethnic strain from which they spring. If the Italians have the Mafia, all Italians are suspect; if the Jews have financiers, all Jews are part of an international conspiracy; if the Arabs have fanatics, all Arabs are violent. In the world today, more than ever, barriers of this kind must be broken, for we are all more alike than we are different.

—Sydney Harris

For the great enemy of truth is very often not the lie—deliberate, continued and dishonest—but the myth—persistent, persuasive and unrealistic. Too often we hold fast to the clichés of our forebears.

—President John F. Kennedy

Al tikrar biallem il hmar. By repetition even the donkey learns.

This Arab proverb encapsulates how effective repetition can be when it comes to education: how we learn by repeating an exercise over and over again until we can respond almost reflexively. A small child uses repetition to master numbers and letters of the alphabet. Older students use repetition to memorize historical dates and algebraic formulas.

For more than a century Hollywood, too, has used repetition as a teaching tool, tutoring movie audiences by repeating over and over, in film after film, insidious images of the Arab people. I ask the reader to study in these pages the persistence of this

---

William Greider is national correspondent for *The Nation* and author of *One World, Ready or Not: The Manic Logic of Global Capitalism.*

defamation, from earlier times to the present day, and to consider how these slanderous stereotypes have affected honest discourse and public policy.

Genesis

In this first comprehensive review of Arab screen images ever published, I document and discuss virtually every feature that Hollywood has ever made—more than 900 films, the vast majority of which portray Arabs by distorting at every turn what most Arab men, women, and children are really like. In gathering the evidence for this book, I was driven by the need to expose an injustice: cinema's systematic, pervasive, and unapologetic degradation and dehumanization of a people.

When colleagues ask whether today's reel Arabs are more stereotypical than yesteryear's, I can't say the celluloid Arab has changed. That is the problem. He is what he has always been—the cultural "other." Seen through Hollywood's distorted lenses, Arabs look different and threatening. Projected along racial and religious lines, the stereotypes are deeply ingrained in American cinema. From 1896 until today, filmmakers have collectively indicted all Arabs as Public Enemy #1—brutal, heartless, uncivilized religious fanatics and money-mad cultural "others" bent on terrorizing civilized Westerners, especially Christians and Jews. Much has happened since 1896—women's suffrage, the Great Depression, the civil rights movement, two world wars, the Korean, Vietnam, and Gulf wars, and the collapse of the Soviet Union. Throughout it all, Hollywood's caricature of the Arab has prowled the silver screen. He is there to this day—repulsive and unrepresentative as ever.

What is an Arab? In countless films, Hollywood alleges the answer: Arabs are brute murderers, sleazy rapists, religious fanatics, oil-rich dimwits, and abusers of women. "They [the Arabs] all look alike to me," quips the American heroine in the movie *The Sheik Steps Out* (1937). "All Arabs look alike to me," admits the protagonist in *Commando* (1968). Decades later, nothing had changed. Quips the US Ambassador in *Hostage* (1986), "I can't tell one [Arab] from another. Wrapped in those bed sheets they all look the same to me." In Hollywood's films, they certainly do.

Pause and visualize the reel Arab. What do you see? Black beard, headdress, dark sunglasses. In the background—a limousine, harem maidens, oil wells, camels. Or perhaps he is brandishing an automatic weapon, crazy hate in his eyes and Allah on his lips. Can you see him?

Think about it. When was the last time you saw a movie depicting an Arab or an American of Arab heritage as a regular guy? Perhaps a man who works ten hours a day, comes home to a loving wife and family, plays soccer with his kids, and prays with family members at his respective mosque or church. He's the kind of guy you'd like to have as your next door neighbor, because—well, maybe because he's a bit like you.

But would you want to share your country, much less your street, with any of Hollywood's Arabs? Would you want your kids playing with him and his family, your teenagers dating them? Would you enjoy sharing your neighborhood with fabulously wealthy and vile oil sheikhs with an eye for Western blondes and arms deals and intent on world domination, or with crazed terrorists, airplane hijackers, or camel-riding bedouins?

Real Arabs

Who exactly are the Arabs of the Middle East? When I use the term "Arab," I refer to the 265 million people who reside in, and the many more millions around the world who are from, the 22 Arab states. The Arabs have made many contributions to our civilization. To name a few, Arab and Persian physicians and scientists inspired European thinkers like Leonardo da Vinci. The Arabs invented algebra and the concept of zero. Numerous English words—algebra, chemistry, coffee, and others—have Arab roots. Arab intellectuals made it feasible for Western scholars to develop and practice advanced educational systems.

In astronomy Arabs used astrolabes for navigation, star maps, celestial globes, and the concept of the center of gravity. In geography, they pioneered the use of latitude and longitude. They invented the water clock; their architecture inspired the Gothic style in Europe. In agriculture, they introduced oranges, dates, sugar, and cotton, and pioneered water works and irrigation. And, they developed a tradition of legal learning, of secular literature and scientific and philosophical thought, in which the Jews also played an important part.

There exists a mixed ethnicity in the Arab world—from 5000 B.C. to the present. The Scots, Greeks, British, French, Romans, English, and others have occupied the area. Not surprisingly, some Arabs have dark hair, dark eyes, and olive complexions. Others boast freckles, red hair, and blue eyes.

Geographically, the Arab world is one-and-a-half times as large as the United States, stretching from the Strait of Hormuz to the Rock of Gibraltar. It's the point where Asia, Europe, and Africa come together. The region gave the world three major religions, a language, and an alphabet.

In most Arab countries today, 70 percent of the population is under age 30. Most share a common language, cultural heritage, history and religion (Islam). Though the vast majority of them are Muslims, about 15 million Arab Christians (including Chaldean, Coptic, Eastern Orthodox, Episcopalian, Roman Catholic, Melkite, Maronite, and Protestant), reside there as well.

Two Fulbright-Hayes lectureship grants and numerous lecture tours sponsored by the United States Information Service (USIS) enabled me to travel extensively throughout the region. While lecturing and living in fifteen Arab countries, I came to discover that like the United States, the Arab world accommodated diverse, talented, and hospitable citizens: lawyers, bankers, doctors, engineers, bricklayers, farmers, computer programmers, homemakers, mechanics, businesspeople, store managers, waiters, construction workers, writers, musicians, chefs, architects, hairdressers, psychologists, plastic surgeons, pilots, and environmentalists.

Their dress is traditional and Western. The majority are peaceful, not violent; poor, not rich; most do not dwell in desert tents; none are surrounded by harem maidens; most have never seen an oil well or mounted a camel. Not one travels via "magic carpets." Their lifestyles defy stereotyping.

As for Americans of Arab heritage, prior to World War I, nearly all the Arabs immigrating to America were Christians: Lebanese, Palestinians, and Syrians. Today, the majority of the United States' Arab-American population is also Christian; about 40 percent are Muslim.

Through immigration, conversion, and birth, however, Muslims are America's fastest growing religious group; about 500,000 reside in the greater Los Angeles area. America's six to eight million Muslims frequent more than 2,000 mosques, Islamic centers, and schools. They include immigrants from more than 60 nations, as well as African-Americans. In fact, most of the world's 1.1 billion Muslims are Indonesian, Indian, or Malaysian. Only 12 percent of the world's Muslims are Arab. Yet, moviemakers ignore this reality, depicting Arabs and Muslims as one and the same people. Repeatedly, they falsely project all Arabs as Muslims and all Muslims as Arabs. As a result, viewers, too, tend to link the same attributes to both peoples.

In reality, of course, Mideast Arabs—and Arab-Americans—are more than a bit like you and me. Consider, for example, two typical Arab-American families—the Jacobs and the Rafeedies. Jacob Mike Jacob, my grandfather, worked in the mills outside of Pittsburgh for nearly twenty years. Albert Rafeedie, my father-in-law, served in the United States Army during World War I; following the war he ran dry goods stores in Minneapolis and Los Angeles.

Both Jacob and Albert emigrated to America in the early 1900s. Their wives and children served their country during World War II and the Korean War, working in aircraft factories in the 1940s, enlisting in the US Army, Air Force, and Navy. Yet, I have never seen their likes in a Hollywood movie—Arab immigrants and their children making good in America, just like the Irish, Italian, and Polish immigrants.

Hollywood's past omission of "everyday" African-Americans, American Indians, and Latinos unduly affected the lives of these minorities. The same holds true with the industry's near total absence of regular Arab-Americans. Regular Mideast Arabs, too, are invisible on silver screens. Asks Jay Stone, "Where are the movie Arabs and Muslims who are just ordinary people?"

Why is it important for the average American to know and care about the Arab stereotype? It is critical because dislike of "the stranger," which the Greeks knew as xenophobia, forewarns that when one ethnic, racial, or religious group is vilified, innocent people suffer. History reminds us that the cinema's hateful Arab stereotypes are reminiscent of abuses in earlier times. Not so long ago—and sometimes still—Asians, American Indians, blacks, and Jews were vilified.

Ponder the consequences. In February 1942, more than 100,000 Americans of Japanese descent were displaced from their homes and interred in camps; for decades blacks were denied basic civil rights, robbed of their property, and lynched; American Indians, too, were displaced and slaughtered; and in Europe, six million Jews perished in the Holocaust.

This is what happens when people are dehumanized.

Mythology in any society is significant. And, Hollywood's celluloid mythology dominates the culture. No doubt about it, Hollywood's renditions of Arabs frame stereotypes in viewer's minds. The problem is peculiarly American. Because of the vast American cultural reach via television and film—we are the world's leading exporter of screen images—the all-pervasive Arab stereotype has much more of a negative impact on viewers today than it did thirty or forty years ago.

Nowadays, Hollywood's motion pictures reach nearly everyone. Cinematic illusions are created, nurtured, and distributed world-wide, reaching viewers in more than 100 countries, from Iceland to Thailand. Arab images have an effect not only on international audiences, but on international movie makers as well. No sooner do contemporary features leave the movie theaters than they are available in video stores and transmitted onto TV screens. Thanks to technological advances, old silent and sound movies impugning Arabs, some of which were produced before I was born, are repeatedly broadcast on cable television and beamed directly into the home.

Check your local guides and you will see that since the mid-1980s, appearing each week on TV screens, are fifteen to twenty recycled movies projecting Arabs as dehumanized caricatures: *The Sheik* (1921), *The Mummy* (1932), *Cairo* (1942), *The Steel Lady* (1953), *Exodus* (1960), *The Black Stallion* (1979), *Protocol* (1984), *The Delta Force* (1986), *Ernest In the Army* (1997), and *Rules of Engagement* (2000). Watching yesteryear's stereotypical Arabs on TV screens is an unnerving experience, especially when pondering the influence celluloid images have on adults and our youth.

Early on, Plato recognized the power of fictional narratives, asserting in his *Republic:* "Those who tell the stories also rule society." Functioning as visual lesson plans, motion pictures, like composed stories, last forever. They help to shape our thoughts and beliefs. "It is time to recognize that the true tutors of our children are not schoolteachers or university professors but filmmakers . . . ," writes Benjamin R. Barber in *The Nation.* "Disney does more than Duke; Spielberg outweighs Stanford."

Actor Richard Dreyfuss made this comment, "There are film artists who affected me more than any textbook, civics teacher, or even a lot of what my parents taught me. And, that's big." If Barber and Dreyfuss are right—and I believe they are—what can we expect our children to know and feel about Arabs? After all, teenagers not only watch a lot of television, they are avid moviegoers and nowadays purchase "four out of ten movie tickets."

Arabs, like Jews, are Semites, so it is perhaps not too surprising that Hollywood's image of hook-nosed, robed Arabs parallels the image of Jews in Nazi-inspired movies such as *Robert and Bertram* (1939), *Die Rothschilds Aktien von Waterloo* (1940), *Der Ewige Jude* (1940), and *Jud Süss* (1940). Once upon a cinematic time, screen Jews boasted exaggerated nostrils and dressed differently—in yarmulkes and dark robes—than the films' protagonists. In the past, Jews were projected as the "other"—depraved and predatory money-grubbers who seek world domination, worship a different God, and kill innocents. Nazi propaganda also presented the lecherous Jew slinking in the shadows, scheming to snare the blonde Aryan virgin.

Yesterday's Shylocks resemble today's hook-nosed sheikhs, arousing fear of the "other." Reflects William Greider, "Jews were despised as exemplars of modernism," while today's "Arabs are depicted as carriers of primitivism—[both] threatening to upset our cozy modern world with their strange habits and desires."

Though Arabs have been lambasted on silver screens since cameras started cranking, the fact remains that it is acceptable to advance anti-Semitism in film—provided the Semites are Arabs. I call this habit of racial and cultural generalization "The New Anti-Semitism." I call it "new" not because stereotypical screen Arabs are new (they aren't) or because anti-Semitism against Jews is dead (it isn't). I use the word "new" because many of the anti-Semitic films directed against Arabs were released in the last third of the twentieth century, at a time when Hollywood was steadily and increasingly eliminating stereotypical portraits of other groups.

Few would argue that today's Jew is subjected to the type of stereotyping in film that existed in the first half of the century. I hope and believe those days are gone forever. But this earlier incarnation of anti-Semitism, where Jews were portrayed as representing everything evil and depraved in the world, has in many ways found a new life in modern film—only this time, the target is Arabs.

Flashback. In the 1930s, the star director of Hitler's cinema was Vies Harlan, whose *Jud Süss* (1940) encouraged Germans to despise Jews.

Fast forward to two producers with a political agenda: Menachem Golan and Yoram Globus. In 1982 Yoram Globus was appointed Israel's director of the Film Industry Department, a unit that monitors all movies made in Israel. Meanwhile, back in the United States, Globus and co-producer Golan formed the American film company Cannon. Under the Cannon label, the producers functioned as cinematic storm troopers, churning out upward of 26 hate-and-terminate-the-Arab movies. In Cannon's *Hell Squad* (1985), *The Delta Force* (1986), and *Killing Streets* (1991), Las Vegas showgirls, US Marines, and US special forces in turn kill off Palestinians.

Writing about Edward Zwick's *The Siege* (1998), Roger Ebert picks up on this theme: "The prejudicial attitudes embodied in the film are insidious, like the anti-Semitism that infected fiction and journalism in the 1930s—not just in Germany but in Britain and America."

Though there are several major reasons why the stereotype has endured for a century-plus—politics, profitable box offices, apathy, and the absence of Arab-Americans in the industry—the fact remains: "You can hit an Arab free; they're free enemies, free villains—where you couldn't do it to a Jew or you can't do it to a black anymore," affirms Sam Keen.

Because of Hollywood's heightened cultural awareness, producers try not to demean most racial and ethnic groups. They know it is morally irresponsible to repeatedly bombard viewers with a regular stream of lurid, unyielding, and unrepentant portraits of a people. The relation is one of cause and effect. Powerful collages of hurtful images serve to deepen suspicions and hatreds. Jerry Mander observes, screen images "can cause people to do what they might otherwise never [have] thought to do . . ."

One can certainly make the case that movie land's pernicious Arab images are sometimes reflected in the attitudes and actions of journalists and government officials. Consider the aftermath of the 19 April 1995 bombing of the federal building in Oklahoma City. Though no American of Arab descent was involved, they were instantly targeted as suspects. Speculative reporting, combined with decades of harmful stereotyping, resulted in more than 300 hate crimes against them.

Months following the tragedy, even Henry Kissinger cautioned, "In an age when far more people gain their understanding from movies . . . than from the written word, the truth is not a responsibility filmmakers can shrug off as an incidental byproduct of creative license." Frequent moviegoers may even postulate that illusionary Arabs are real Arabs.

Our young people are learning from the cinema's negative and repetitive stereotypes. Subliminally, the onslaught of the reel Arab conditions how young Arabs and Arab-Americans perceive themselves and how others perceive them, as well. Explains Magdoline Asfahani, an Arab-American college student: "The most common questions I was asked [by classmates] were if I had ever ridden a camel or if my family lived in tents." Even worse, "I learned at a very early age [that] every other movie seemed to feature Arab terrorists."

It must be trying for young Arab-Americans to openly express pride in their heritage when they realize that their peers know only Hollywood's *reel* Arabs—billionaires, bombers, and bellydancers—which is to say, they don't know *real* Arabs at all.

The stereotype impacts even well established Arab-Americans. When Academy Award winner [*Amadeus* (1984)] F. Murray Abraham was asked what the "F" in F. Murray Abraham stood for, he said: "F stands for Farid. When I first began in the business I realized I couldn't use Farid because that would typecast me as a sour Arab out to kill everyone. As Farid Murray Abraham I was doomed to minor roles."

The Stereotype's Entry

How did it all start? Obviously, filmmakers did not create the stereotype but inherited and embellished Europe's pre-existing Arab caricatures. In the eighteenth and nineteenth centuries, European artists and writers helped reduce the region to colony. They presented images of desolate deserts, corrupt palaces and slimy souks inhabited by the cultural "other"—the lazy, bearded heathen Arab Muslim. The writers' stereotypical tales were inhabited with cheating vendors and exotic concubines held hostage in slave markets. These fictional renditions of wild foreigners subjugating harem maidens were accepted as valid; they became an indelible part of European popular culture. *The Arabian*

Nights stories especially impacted Western perceptions. Until 1979, the *Arabian Nights'* 200-plus tales had been printed in more languages than any other text except the Bible.

During the early 1900s, imagemakers such as the Frenchman Georges Méliès served up dancing harem maidens and ugly Arabs. In Méliès' mythic Arabia, Arabs ride camels, brandish scimitars, kill one another, and drool over the Western heroine, ignoring their own women. In Méliès' *The Palace of Arabian Nights* (1905), submissive maidens attend a bored, greedy, black-bearded potentate; a stocky palace guard cools the ruler, fluttering a huge feather fan.

From the beginning, Méliès and other moviemakers conjured up a mythical, uniform "seen one, seen 'em all" setting, which I call "Arab-land." The illusory setting functions as a make-believe theme park complete with shadowy, topsy-turvy sites, patronized by us all. Arab-land is populated with cafes and clubs like the "Shish-Ka-Bob Cafe" and "The Pink Camel Club," located in made-up places with names such as "Lugash," "Othar," "Tarjan," "Jotse," "Bondaria," and "Hagreeb."

The desert locale consists of an oasis, oil wells, palm trees, tents, fantastically ornate palaces, sleek limousines, and, of course, camels. To complement Arab-land's desert landscapes producers provide performers with "Instant Ali Baba Kits." Property masters stock the kits with curved daggers, scimitars, magic lamps, giant feather fans, and nargelihs. Costumers provide actresses with chadors, hijabs, bellydancers' see-through pantaloons, veils, and jewels for their navels. Robed actors are presented with dark glasses, fake black beards, exaggerated noses, worry beads, and checkered burnooses. Contemporary filmmakers embellished these early stereotypical settings and characters, trashing Arabs as junk dealers who smash automobiles. As ever, both autos and Arabs are recast as refuse.

In *The Desert Song* (1929), producers display devout and daring Arabs riding across swift-swept sands, helping the French protagonists defeat evil French colonialists. Flash forward to *The Desert Song* remakes of 1943 and 1953. Both films are decidedly different from the 1929 version. Here, the producers opt to frame Arabs as an unruly, unkempt, feuding lot—one of them is even pro-Nazi.

King Solomon's Mines (1950) contains no Arabs. Yet, Cannon's *Allan Quatermain and the Lost City of Gold* (1987), a remake of *King Solomon's Mines,* presents sleazy Arabs trying to rape the blonde heroine (Sharon Stone).

Only one villain, a lumbering mummy, appears in Universal's classic film, *The Mummy* (1932). Attempting to duplicate the original's success, Universal released in 1999 an $80 million movie displaying the reawakened mummy as a superhuman terminator intent on killing Western protagonists. Assisting him are hordes of Egyptian baddies: a fat and lecherous prison warden, saber-wielding mummies, desert bandits, and zombie look-a-likes carrying torches.

(Observes film critic Anthony Lane,

> Finally there is the Arab question. The Arab people have always had the roughest and most uncomprehending deal from Hollywood, but with the death of

the Cold War the stereotype has been granted even more wretched prominence. In *The Mummy* (1999), I could scarcely believe what I was watching . . .
So, here's a party game for any producers with a Middle Eastern setting in
mind; try replacing one Semitic group with another—Jews instead of Arabs—
and THEN listen for the laugh.

Unfortunately Lane's poignant comments had no effect on Universal. They still
populate their 2001 sequel, *The Mummy Returns,* with repugnant caricatures.

Islam, particularly, comes in for unjust treatment. Today's imagemakers regularly
link the Islamic faith with male supremacy, holy war, and acts of terror, depicting Arab
Muslims as hostile alien intruders, and as lecherous, oily sheikhs intent on using nuclear
weapons. When mosques are displayed onscreen, the camera inevitably cuts to Arabs
praying, and then gunning down civilians. Such scenarios are common fare.

Film criticism is an integral part of the cultural landscape. Allegations of moviemakers' discriminatory practices are hardly new. Documentary filmmakers as well as
scholars have commented upon Hollywood's stereotypes of other groups. Especially
informative are insightful and incisive texts: *The Hollywood Indian, From Sambo to Super-
spade, The Jew in American Cinema, The Latin Image in American Film, Hollywood's Wartime
Woman,* and *The Kaleidoscopic Lens: How Hollywood Views Ethnic Groups.* What I find startling is that although sordid-looking reel Arabs regularly imperil the very heartland of
civilized societies, so little attention has been given to the plethora of Arab screen portraits in cinema texts until now.

Andrew Dowdy's text *The Films of the Fifties: The American State of Mind,* for example, offers a detailed examination of the "movie culture of the fifties." More than 100
films released during the fifties featured Arab caricatures. Yet, Dowdy does not mention
a single Arab scenario.

From 1930–34 Hollywood released more than 40 fiction films featuring Arabs.
Thomas Doherty writes about this period in his 1999 *Pre-Code Hollywood: Sex, Immoral-
ity and Insurrection in American Cinema 1930–34.* He points out that "racism [propelled]
a hefty percentage of the escapist fantasies of pre-code Hollywood." To support his the-
sis, Doherty cites stereotypical portraits of American Indians, Africans and African-
Americans, Asians and Asian-Americans, Jews and Jewish-Americans, Irish and
Irish-Americans and Italians and Italian-Americans. But Doherty does not mention
Arabs or Arab-Americans at all.

From 1929 through 1956, Hollywood produced a total of 231 movie sound serials,
averaging 8.5 serials a year.

The racial attitudes of the period [were] none too enlightened. For the most
part . . . Orientals were portrayed as sinister cultists bent upon the destruction
of the white race; blacks were merely ignorant natives who followed the leader
who most successfully played upon their primitive superstitions.

write Ken Weiss and Ed Goodgold in *To Be Continued . . .*, their book on the period. The authors make no mention, however, of the Arab caricatures that appeared in thirteen movie serials from 1930–1950.

These early serials are important because they present several firsts. *The Black Coin* (1936) was the first film to portray an Arab skyjacker threatening to blow up a plane. Another, *Radio Patrol* (1937), introduced Arab immigrants as shoddy criminals threatening America, while *Federal Agents vs. Underworld, Inc.* (1948) displayed federal agents contesting "evil" Nila, the cinema's first Arab woman terrorist. During an invasion of the United States Nila, a reel Egyptian assassin, convinces her comrades to "rise up against the [Western] infidels." After Nila sets off a bomb, she tries to gun down a federal agent.

Surprisingly, all sorts of hokey Arab caricatures pop up in movie serials, beginning with the cliffhanger *Son of Tarzan* (1920) up to and including *Adventures of Captain Africa* (1955). Negative stereotyping of the Arab thrives profusely in eighteen cliffhangers, notably in the *Captain Africa* serial. This thrill-a-minute drama presents heroic Westerners and Africans crushing Arab slavers and terrorists, as well as pro-Nazi Arabs.

Some decent Arabs appear, albeit briefly, in three serials. In *The Vigilante* (1947), an Arab arrives in time to save the American protagonist. In *Queen of the Jungle* (1935), Arabs befriend Americans. And an intelligent and attractive Egyptian heroine appears in *The Return of Chandu* (1934).

As most serials are low budget ventures, the performances suffer. At times, serial actors portraying Arabs speak gibberish; other robed characters speak with Southern drawls and thick Italian accents.

Determined to maximize profits, as soon as the serials exited movie theaters, producers rushed back to the editing tables. They selected key scenes, then spliced and edited the serial footage, transforming the most interesting frames into ten feature-length motion pictures. By successfully managing to extend the staying power of yesteryear's Arab serials, the producers' serial stereotypes reached new audiences.

A Basis for Understanding

In this book, I list and discuss, in alphabetical order, more than 900 feature films displaying Arab characters. Regrettably, in all these I uncovered only a handful of heroic Arabs; they surface in a few 1980s and 1990s scenarios. In *Lion of the Desert* (1981), righteous Arabs bring down invading fascists. Humane Palestinians surface in *Hanna K* (1983) and *The Seventh Coin* (1992). In *Robin Hood, Prince of Thieves* (1991), a devout Muslim who "fights better than twenty English knights," helps Robin Hood get the better of the evil Sheriff of Nottingham. In *The 13th Warrior* (1999), an Arab Muslim scholar befriends Nordic warriors, helping them defeat primitive cavemen. And in *Three Kings* (1999), a movie celebrating our commonalities and differences, we view Arabs as regular folks, with affections and aspirations. This anti-war movie humanizes the Iraqis, a people who for too long have been projected as evil caricatures.

Most of the time I found moviemakers saturating the marketplace with all sorts of Arab villains. Producers collectively impugned Arabs in every type of movie you can imagine, targeting adults in well-known and high-budgeted movies such as *Exodus* (1960), *Black Sunday* (1977), *Ishtar* (1987), and *The Siege* (1998); and reaching out to teenagers with financially successful schlock movies such as *Five Weeks in a Balloon* (1962), *Things Are Tough All Over* (1982), *Sahara* (1983), and *Operation Condor* (1997). One constant factor dominates all the films: Derogatory stereotypes are omnipresent, reaching youngsters, baby boomers, and older folk.

I am not saying an Arab should never be portrayed as the villain. What I am saying is that almost *all* Hollywood depictions of Arabs are *bad* ones. This is a grave injustice. Repetitious and negative images of the reel Arab literally sustain adverse portraits across generations. The fact is that for more than a century producers have tarred an entire group of people with the same sinister brush.

Hundreds of movies reveal Western protagonists spewing out unrelenting barrages of uncontested slurs, calling Arabs: "assholes," "bastards," "camel-dicks," "pigs," "devil-worshipers," "jackals," "rats," "rag-heads," "towel-heads," "scum-buckets," "sons-of-dogs," "buzzards of the jungle," "sons-of-whores," "sons-of-unnamed goats," and "sons-of-she-camels."

Producers fail to recognize that "Allah" is Arabic for God, that when they pray, Arab Christians and Muslims use the word "Allah." When producers show Jewish and Christian protagonists contesting Arab Muslims, the Western hero will say to his Arab enemy in a scornful and jeering manner, "Allah." The character's disrespectful "Allah's" mislead viewers, wrongly implying that devout Arab Muslims do not worship the "true God" of the Christians and Jews, but some tribal deity.

Still other movies contain the word "Ayrab," a vulgar Hollywood epithet for Arab that is comparable to dago, greaser, kike, nigger, and gook.

All groups contain some Attila-the-Hun types; some Israelis and Latinos are militant zealots; some Irishmen and Arabs are terrorists; some Italians and Indonesians are gangsters; some Asians and Africans are rapists; and some Americans and Englishmen are child-abusers. Every group has among its members a minority of a minority committing heinous acts. Yet, the overwhelming majority of all people are regular, peace-loving individuals who vigorously object to violent crimes.

These pages represent the foundation for making sense of Hollywood's Arab narratives. The vast majority of the 900-plus features that I scrutinize here are English-language feature films and movie serials made by Hollywood. I use "Hollywood" in the generic sense, as some movies theatrically released in the United States were produced by independent American filmmakers, as well as by producers from Australia, Canada, England, France, Sweden, Spain, Germany, Italy, and Israel. Documentaries and movies made for television are not included.

Given time constraints and the vast numbers of Arab scenarios, my discussions of some non-viewed films are brief, usually one or two paragraphs. Many silent movies were destroyed, and some sound features are not yet available on video. I was unable to see about 140 features, including silent classics with stereotypical Arabs such as *Beau Sabreur* (1928), and *A Daughter of the Gods* (1916). When I refer to these non-viewed movies, I rely solely on my only available source: film reviews.

Research and Methodology

I began the research process that forms the content of this book in 1980. For two decades I searched for, collected, and studied motion pictures related to Arab portraits and themes. Assisting me was my research partner—my wife Bernice. Initially, to identify the films, we launched extensive computer searches. We put into play dozens of keywords such as bedouin, Egypt, Algiers, desert, and sheikh. Using keywords as a guide, we examined thousands of movie reviews, searching for "Arab" story lines, settings, and character casts.

I proceeded to uncover and write about more than 900 features, released between 1896 and 2001. During the research, I sometimes came across movie titles and reviews that misdirected me. For example, critics and promotions for Universal's horror film, *The Mad Ghoul* (1943), refer to Egyptians using "ancient Egyptian gases" to stun one's victims. In fact, the movie displays generic "natives," and makes no mention of Egyptians or their gases. Fully expecting to see Egyptians and harem maidens in *The Sphinx* (1933) and *Lost in a Turkish Bath* (1952), I purchased the films. But *The Sphinx*, a murder mystery, has no Arabs; and *Lost in a Turkish Bath* is about an American canary salesman, not dancing maidens.

In the late 1980s, I began visiting various research centers to screen and study those motion pictures not available on video, television, or in movie theaters. I screened scores of feature films, about a quarter of those I discuss here, at various institutions: the Library of Congress (Motion Picture, Broadcasting, and Recorded Sound Division), Washington, DC; the Film and Television Archive, University of California, Los Angeles; the Wisconsin Center for Film and Theater Research, University of Wisconsin, Madison; and the Museum of Modern Art, New York City.

At these centers, I also examined primary reference works, and thousands of motion picture reviews dating from when cameras started cranking to the present. I relied on sources such as *Motion Picture Daily, Motion Picture Guide, Motion Picture Herald, Motion Picture News, Motion Picture World, International Motion Picture Almanac, Moving Picture World, American Film Institute Catalog, Film Daily Yearbook of Motion Pictures, Halliwell's Film Guide, The New York Times, Variety, Hollywood Reporter, Photoplay, Magill's Survey of Cinema, Landers Film Reviews,* and *Showman's Reviews.* In the mid-1990s, I began using the Internet Movie Database, an invaluable resource.

Additionally, I appraised every film listed in movie/video guidebooks and catalogs, including those published by individual collectors. I shopped at obscure video rental stores and garage sales, rummaging through videos, checking out cassette covers and plot descriptions. Weekly, I scrutinized TV/film guide magazines and texts.

For those especially hard-to-find movies-on-video, I placed advertisements in film magazines. Surprisingly, channel surfing led me to discover dozens of unknown films. Without warning ugly Arabs would suddenly surface on our TV screens. And friends, colleagues, relatives, video rental clerks, and film buffs directed me to fresh films.

From the research, I came to discover that Hollywood has projected Arabs as villains in more than 900 feature films. The vast majority of villains are notorious sheikhs, maidens, Egyptians, and Palestinians. The rest are devious dark-complexioned baddies from other Arab countries, such as Algerians, Iraqis, Jordanians, Lebanese, Libyans, Moroccans, Syrians, Tunisians, and Yemeni.

Locked into a cycle of predictable plots, these five basic Arab types—Villains, Sheikhs, Maidens, Egyptians, and Palestinians—pop up in a hodgepodge of melodrama and mayhem. Repeatedly, Arab evil-doers are seen in every sort of film imaginable: sword-and-sandal soaps, Foreign Legion and terrorist shoot 'em-ups, camel-operas, musical comedies, magic-carpet fantasies, historical tales, movie serials, and even contemporary dramas and farces that have absolutely nothing to do with Arabs.

When you come across rigid and repetitive movies brandishing stereotypical slurs and images, keep in mind not all negative images are alike; there are distinctions and nuances. Some Arab portraits are dangerous and detestable and should be taken seriously; others are less offensive. And pay special attention to those Arabs you *do not see* on movie screens. Missing from the vast majority of scenarios are images of ordinary Arab men, women and children, living ordinary lives. Movies fail to project exchanges between friends, social and family events.

Nor should you expect to encounter friendly children, those real Arab youths who participate in sporting events, or who are Boy Scouts and Girl Scouts. Absent also are frames showing gracious and devout Arab mothers and fathers, grandmothers and grandfathers, caring for each other and their neighbors. Such scenes are as sparse as geysers in the Sahara.

Do not expect to see movie characters patterned after Arab scholars, those innovative individuals who provided us with the fundamentals of science, mathematics, medicine, astronomy, and botany. Arab seamen pioneered navigational techniques, enabling them to traverse oceans. The Arabs brought to Indonesia and Spain a fresh and vigorous religion, new technology, and new knowledge that helped transform the civilizations.

To guide the reader, I present more than 900 films in alphabetical order. In each of my silent and sound entries, I highlight specific scenes and dialogue pertaining to on-screen Arabs. I also include summaries of scenarios, cast listings, and production credits. Throughout, I pay particular attention to the five Arab character types—Villains, Sheikhs, Maidens, Egyptians, and Palestinians—many of which overlap.

In addition, I offer several appendices:

(1) Best List.

(2) Recommended Films. These scenarios offer balanced and humane portraits; young people may view them without being ashamed of their heritage.

(3) Worst List.
(4) Cannon (Golan-Globus) Films.
(5) Epithets Directed at the Film Arab.

Villains

Beginning with *Imar the Servitor* (1914), up to and including *The Mummy Returns* (2001), a synergy of images equates Arabs from Syria to the Sudan with quintessential evil. In hundreds of movies "evil" Arabs stalk the screen. We see them assaulting just about every imaginable foe—Americans, Europeans, Israelis, legionnaires, Africans, fellow Arabs, even—for heaven's sake—Hercules and Samson.

Scores of comedies present Arabs as buffoons, stumbling all over themselves. Some of our best known and most popular stars mock Arabs: Will Rogers in *Business and Pleasure* (1931); Laurel and Hardy in *Beau Hunks* (1931); Bob Hope and Bing Crosby in *Road to Morocco* (1942); the Marx Brothers in *A Night in Casablanca* (1946); Abbott and Costello in *Abbott and Costello in the Foreign Legion* (1950); the Bowery Boys in *Bowery to Baghdad* (1955); Jerry Lewis in *The Sad Sack* (1957); Phil Silvers in *Follow that Camel* (1967); Marty Feldman in *The Last Remake of Beau Geste* (1977); Harvey Korman in *Americathon* (1979); Bugs Bunny in *1001 Rabbit Tales* (1982); Dustin Hoffman and Warren Beatty in *Ishtar* (1987); Pauly Shore in *In the Army Now* (1994); and Jim Varney in *Ernest In the Army* (1997).

Some protagonists even refer to Arabs as "dogs" and "monkeys." As a result, those viewers laughing at bumbling reel Arabs leave movie theaters with a sense of solidarity, united by their shared distance from these peoples of ridicule.

In dramas, especially, Hollywood's stars contest and vanquish reel Arabs. See Emory Johnson in *The Gift Girl* (1917); Gary Cooper in *Beau Sabreur* (1928); John Wayne in *I Cover the War* (1937); Burt Lancaster in *Ten Tall Men* (1951); Dean Martin in *The Ambushers* (1967); Michael Caine in *Ashanti* (1979); Sean Connery in *Never Say Never Again* (1983); Harrison Ford in *Frantic* (1988); Kurt Russell in *Executive Decision* (1996); and Brendan Frasier in *The Mummy* (1999).

Perhaps in an attempt to further legitimize the stereotype, as well as to attract more viewers, in the mid-1980s studios presented notable African-American actors facing off against, and ultimately destroying, reel Arabs. Among them, Eddie Murphy, Louis Gossett, Jr., Robert Guillaume, Samuel Jackson, Denzel Washington, and Shaquille O'Neal.

In the Disney movie *Kazaam* (1996), O'Neal pummels three Arab Muslims who covet "all the money in the world." Four years later, director William Friedkin has actor Samuel Jackson exploiting jingoistic prejudice and religious bigotry in *Rules of Engagement* (2000). The effects of ethnic exploitation are especially obvious in scenes revealing egregious, false images of Yemeni children as assassins and enemies of the United States.

To my knowledge, no Hollywood WWI, WWII, or Korean War movie has ever shown America's fighting forces slaughtering children. Yet, near the conclusion of *Rules of Engagement,* US marines open fire on the Yemenis, shooting 83 men, women, and children. During the scene, viewers rose to their feet, clapped and cheered. Boasts director Friedkin, "I've seen audiences stand up and applaud the film throughout the United States." Some viewers applaud Marines gunning down Arabs in war dramas not necessarily because of cultural insensitivity, but because for more than 100 years Hollywood has singled out the Arab as our enemy. Over a period of time, a steady stream of bigoted images does, in fact, tarnish our judgment of a people and their culture.

Rules of Engagement not only reinforces historically damaging stereotypes, but promotes a dangerously generalized portrayal of Arabs as rabidly anti-American. Equally troubling to this honorably discharged US Army veteran is that *Rules of Engagement's* credits thank for their assistance the Department of Defense (DOD) and the US Marine Corps. More than fourteen feature films, all of which show Americans killing Arabs, credit the DOD for providing needed equipment, personnel, and technical assistance. Sadly, the Pentagon seems to condone these Arab-bashing ventures, as evidenced in *True Lies* (1994), *Executive Decision* (1996), and *Freedom Strike* (1998).

On November 30, 2000, Hollywood luminaries attended a star-studded dinner hosted by Defense Secretary William Cohen in honor of Motion Picture Association President, Jack Valenti, for which the Pentagon paid the bill—$295,000. Called on to explain why the DOD personnel were fraternizing with imagemakers at an elaborate Beverly Hills gathering, spokesman Kenneth Bacon said: "If we can have television shows and movies that show the excitement and importance of military life, they can help generate a favorable atmosphere for recruiting."

The DOD has sometimes shown concern when other peoples have been tarnished on film. For example, in the late 1950s, DOD officials were reluctant to cooperate with moviemakers attempting to advance Japanese stereotypes. When *The Bridge Over the River Kwai* (1957) was being filmed, Donald Baruch, head of the DOD's Motion Picture Production Office, cautioned producers not to overemphasize Japanese terror and torture, advising:

> In our ever-increasing responsibility for maintaining a mutual friendship and respect among the people of foreign lands, the use of disparaging terms to identify ethnic, national or religious groups is inimical to our national interest, particularly in motion pictures sanctioned by Government cooperation.

Arabs are almost always easy targets in war movies. From as early as 1912, decades prior to the 1991 Gulf War, dozens of films presented allied agents and military forces—American, British, French, and more recently Israeli—obliterating Arabs. In the World War I drama *The Lost Patrol* (1934), a brave British sergeant (Victor McLaughlin) guns down "sneaky Arabs, those dirty, filthy swine." An American newsreel cameraman (John Wayne) helps wipe out a "horde of [Arab] tribesmen" in *I Cover the War* (1937).

In *Sirocco* (1951), the first Hollywood feature film projecting Arabs as terrorists, Syrian "fanatics" assail French soldiers and American arms dealer Harry Smith (Humphrey Bogart). *The Lost Command* (1966) shows French Colonel Raspeguy's (Anthony Quinn) soldiers killing Algerians. And, Israelis gun down sneaky bedouins in two made-in-Israel films, *Sinai Guerrillas* (1960) and *Sinai Commandos* (1968).

Arabs trying to rape, kill, or abduct fair-complexioned Western heroines is a common theme, dominating scenarios from *Captured by Bedouins* (1912), to *The Pelican Brief* (1993). In *Brief*, an Arab hitman tries to assassinate the protagonist, played by Julia Roberts. In *Captured*, desert bandits kidnap a fair American maiden, but she is eventually rescued by a British officer. As for her bedouin abductors, they are gunned down by rescuing US Cavalry troops.

Arabs enslave and abuse Africans in about ten films, including *A Daughter of the Congo* (1930), *Drums of Africa* (1963), and *Ashanti* (1979). Noted African-American filmmaker Oscar Micheaux, who made "race movies" from 1919 to 1948, also advanced the Arab-as-abductor theme in his *Daughter of the Congo*. Though Micheaux's movies contested Hollywood's Jim Crow stereotypes of blacks, *A Daughter of the Congo* depicts lecherous Arab slavers abducting and holding hostage a lovely Mulatto woman and her maid. The maiden is eventually rescued by the heroic African-American officers of the 10th US Cavalry.

Anti-Christian Arabs appear in dozens of films. When the US military officer in *Another Dawn* (1937) is asked why Arabs despise Westerners, he barks: "It's a good Moslem hatred of Christians." Islam is also portrayed as a violent faith in *Legion of the Doomed* (1959). Here, an Arab is told, "Kill him before he kills you." Affirms the Arab as he plunges a knife into his foe's gut, "You speak the words of Allah." And, in *The Castilian* (1963), Spanish Christians triumph over Arab Muslim zealots. How? By releasing scores of squealing pigs! Terrified of the pigs, the reel Arabs retreat.

Arabs invade the United States and terrorize innocents in *Golden Hands of Kurigal* (1949), *Terror Squad* (1988), *True Lies* (1994), and *The Siege* (1998). *The Siege* is especially alarming. In it, Arab immigrants methodically lay waste to Manhattan. Assisted by Arab-American auto mechanics, university students, and a college teacher, they blow up the city's FBI building, kill scores of government agents, blast theatergoers, and detonate a bomb in a crowded bus.

I discussed the movie's violent images with director Edward Zwick in New York on April 2, 1998. Zwick told me that because some scenes show innocent Arab-Americans being tossed indiscriminately into detention centers, the film would "provoke thought." Provoke violence, more likely, I thought.

I pointed out that his scenario may be fiction, but the terrorists' on-screen killings take place in a real city—the Arabs are rounded up in Brooklyn, where many peace-loving Arab-Americans reside. After watching reel Arab terrorists murder more than 700 New Yorkers, I said, some viewers may think that Arab-Americans belong in those camps.

Zwick argued that he had created balance in the film, pointing out that actor Tony Shalhoub plays a decent Arab-American FBI agent. Zwick's token good guy reminded me how yesteryear's producers tried to justify their hostile depictions of American Indians. In movies showing savage Indians massacring settlers, they would point to Tonto, claiming balance. *The Siege*'s virulent and prejudicial images continue to trouble me, profoundly.

Oily Arabs and robed thugs intent on acquiring nuclear weapons surface in roughly ten films. See *Fort Algiers* (1958) and *Frantic* (1988).

At least a dozen made-in-Israel and Golan-Globus movies, such as *Eagles Attack at Dawn* (1970), *Iron Eagle* (1986), and *Chain of Command* (1993), show Americans and/or Israelis crushing evil-minded Arabs, many of whom are portrayed by Israeli actors.

More than 30 French Foreign Legion movies, virtually a sub-genre of boy's-own-adventure films, show civilized legionnaires obliterating backward desert bedouin. These legion formula films cover a span of more than 80 years, from *The Unknown* (1915) to *Legionnaire* (1998). Scenarios display courageous, outnumbered legionnaires battling against, and ultimately overcoming, unruly Arabs. Even Porky Pig as a legionnaire and his camel join in the melee, beating up bedouins in the animated cartoon, *Little Beau Porky* (1936).

Movies imply savage imagery by applying indiscriminately to Arabs and Native Americans both the colonialist's expression "tribes." Prototypes of cowboy shoot-'em-ups, screen legionnaires bring down Arabs much the same way as US Cavalrymen terminate Indians. Three *Beau Geste* movies, faithful adaptations of P.C. Wren's 1926 book, portray British legionnaires as American cowboys; they shoot Arabs as if they were Indians.

Though screen Arabs and Indians share commonalities, there are some differences. Celluloid Indians are projected as war-like and cruel, but unlike reel Arabs, they are seldom depicted as venal, greedy, or hypocritical. And, some films, notably *Broken Arrow* (1950), *Dances with Wolves* (1990), and *Last of the Mohicans* (1992), portray Native Americans as "noble" savages.

I never expected to encounter movies pitting Cowboys against Arabs, but I came across eight shoot-'em-ups, released from 1922 through 1952. Galloping from the Wild West to the Arabian desert in search of adventure and romance are cowboy favorites Tom Mix, Hopalong Cassidy, and Hoot Gibson. Six-shooters drawn, the men in white hats gun down "foul" Arabs. To paraphrase General Philip Henry Sheridan, the images imply that the only good Arab is a dead Arab.

Observes William Greider of the *Washington Post*, "Much of what Westerners 'learned' about Arabs sounds similar to what nineteenth-century Americans 'discovered' about Indians on this continent . . . acceptable villains make our troubles so manageable." In the past, imagemakers punctuated "anti-human qualities in these strange people," American Indians. They projected them as savages, not thinking like us, "not sharing our aspirations." Once one has concluded that Indians thrive on violence, disorder, and stealth, it becomes easier to accept rather than challenge "irrational" portraits. Today, says Greider, "The Arab stereotypes created by British and French colonialism are still very much with us."

Film producers, broadcast journalists, and military leaders echo Greider's Arab-as-Indian analogy. Seeing marauding desert Arabs approach, the American protagonist in the war movie *The Steel Lady* (1953) quips, "This is bandit area, worse than Arizona Apache." In talking up his film *Iron Eagle* (1986), producer Ron Samuels gushed: Showing an American teen hijacking a jet and wiping out scores of Arabs "was just the kind of story I'd been looking for . . . *It reminded me of the old John Wayne westerns*" [my emphasis].

Seeing Arabs about to attack, an American soldier in *Hot Shots! Part Deux* (1993) warns his buddies: "Indians on the warpath." After Demi Moore terminates Arabs in her role as a Navy SEAL recruit in *G.I. Jane* (1996), she tells her SEAL pals: "Let's get out of Dodge."

Declares *Scholastic* magazine, American Indians are our "new energy sheikhs!" To boost this absurd declaration, the editors placed on their March 5, 1980 "Senior Weekly Reader" cover a stereotypical American Indian sitting astride a camel [not a horse] laden with containers labeled Gas, Oil, and Coal. Explains Carlos Cortés in his insightful book, *The Children Are Watching: How the Media Teach about Diversity,* the editors' disrespectful Indian-as-sheikh image reinforces "the negative image of Arabs as manipulative moguls while simultaneously using 'Arabness' to frame—better yet—taint Native Americans."

In the mid-1980s, as CNN reporter Mike Greenspan was filing a report from the Israeli-Lebanese border, the camera cut to Israelis on horseback. Greenspan tagged the Israelis "Cowboys" defending against Lebanese "Indians." And days prior to the 1991 Gulf War, a US Army Colonel appeared on CNN News to tell the viewers he was dispatching "scouts" to "Indian country."

I discuss a few scenarios that focus on Iranians/Persians, such as *The Invincible Six* (1970) and *Into the Night* (1985). Though Iranians are not Arabs, I've added the films because some filmmakers and viewers mistakenly perceive them as Arabs, and for a personal reason. The heavies in *Into the Night* are tagged "Shaheen's boys." Since I'm a Shaheen myself, it grates.

Sheikhs

The word "sheikh" means, literally, a wise elderly person, the head of the family, but you would not know that from watching any of Hollywood's "sheikh" features, more than 160 scenarios, including the Kinetoscope short *Sheik Hadj Tahar Hadj Cherif* (1894) and the Selig Company's *The Power of the Sultan* (1907)—the first movie to be filmed in Los Angeles. Throughout the Arab world, to show respect, people address Muslim religious leaders as sheikhs.

Moviemakers, however, attach a completely different meaning to the word. As Matthew Sweet points out, "The cinematic Arab has never been an attractive figure . . . in the 1920s he was a swarthy Sheik, wiggling his eyebrows and chasing the [Western] heroine around a tiled courtyard. After the 1973 oil crisis . . ." producers revitalized the image of the fabulously wealthy and slothful sheikh, only this time he was getting rich at the expense of red-blooded Americans; "he became an inscrutable bully—a Ray-Ban-ed variation of the stereotypes of the Jewish money lender."

Instead of presenting sheikhs as elderly men of wisdom, screenwriters offer romantic melodramas portraying them as stooges-in-sheets, slovenly, hook-nosed potentates intent on capturing pale-faced blondes for their harems. Imitating the stereotypical behavior of their lecherous predecessors—the "bestial" Asian, the black "buck," and the "lascivious" Latino—slovenly Arabs move to swiftly and violently deflower Western maidens. Explains Edward Said, "The perverted sheikh can often be seen snarling at the captured Western hero and blonde girl . . . [and saying] 'My men are going to kill you, but they like to amuse themselves before.'"

Early silent films, such as *The Unfaithful Odalisque* (1903), *The Arab* (1915), and *The Sheik* (1921), all present bearded, robed Arab rulers as one collective stereotypical lecherous cur. In *The Unfaithful Odalisque,* the sheikh not only admonishes his harem maiden, he directs a Nubian slave to lash her with a cat-o'-nine-tails. In *The Sheik* (1921), Sheikh Ahmed (Valentino) glares at Diana, the kidnapped British lovely and boasts: "When an Arab sees a woman he wants, he takes her!"

Flash forward 33 years. Affirms the sheikh in *The Adventures of Hajji Baba* (1954): "Give her to me or I'll take her!"

Moving to kidnap and/or seduce the Western heroine, clumsy moneyed sheikhs fall all over themselves in more than 60 silent and sound movies, ranging from *The Fire and the Sword* (1914) to *Protocol* (1984). Sheikhs disregard Arab women, preferring instead to ravish just one Western woman.

But Hollywood's silent movies did not dare show Western women bedding sheikhs. Why? Because America's movie censors objected to love scenes between Westerners and Arabs. Even producers experiencing desert mirages dared not imagine such unions.

Some viewers perceived Valentino's *The Sheik* (1921) to be an exception to the rule. Not true. Valentino's Sheikh Ahmed, who vanquishes Diana, the Western heroine in the movie, is actually a European, not an Arab. This helps explain why the European lover-boy dressed in Arab garb was viewed so positively by his essentially female audience. Note the dialogue, revealing Ahmed to be a European:

DIANA, THE HEROINE: "His [Ahmed's] hand is so large for an Arab."
AHMED'S FRENCH FRIEND: "He is not an Arab. His father was an Englishman, his mother a Spaniard."

Other desert scenarios followed suit, allowing the hero and heroine to make love, but only after revealing they were actually Western Christians!

In Europe, it was otherwise. As early as 1922, a few European movies such as *The Sheikh's Wife* (1922) countered fixed themes, showing Western heroines embracing dashing Arab sheikhs.

Both good and evil sheikhs battle each other in about 60 Arabian Nights fantasies, animated and non-animated. A plethora of unsavory characters, wicked viziers, slimy slavers, irreverent magicians, and shady merchants contest courageous princes, princesses, lamp genies, and folk heroes such as Ali Baba, Sinbad, Aladdin and, on occasion, the benevolent caliph. You can see some of them in the four *Kismet* fantasies (1920, 1930, 1944, 1955), *Prisoners of the Casbah* (1955), and *Aladdin* (1992).

Even animated cartoon characters thump Arabs. My childhood hero, Bugs Bunny, clobbers nasty Arabs in *1001 Rabbit Tales* (1982). Bugs trounces an ugly genie, a dense sheikh, and the ruler's spoiled son. My other cartoon hero, Popeye, also trounces Arabs. In the early 1930s, Fleischer Studios' lengthy Popeye cartoons presented Arab folk heroes as rogues, not as champions. Popeye clobbers, not befriends, Ali Baba and Sinbad in *Popeye the Sailor Meets Ali Baba's Forty Thieves,* and *Popeye the Sailor Meets Sinbad the Sailor.*

Beginning in the mid–1970s, fresh directors also projected Arab leaders through warped prisms. Emulating their predecessors' stereotypes they, too, displayed Western heroines fending off over-sexed desert sheikhs.

Yet, there are dramatic differences in sheikh images. Once-upon-a-time Arabian Nights movies, such as *Ali Baba Goes to Town* (1937) and *Aladdin and His Lamp* (1952), show indolent sheikhs lounging on thrones. But, contemporary films present oily, militant, ostentatious sheikhs reclining in Rolls Royces, aspiring to buy up chunks of America.

Today's films present anti-Christian, anti-Jewish Arab potentates perched atop missile bases, armed with nuclear weapons, plenty of oil, and oodles of cash. Using Islam to justify violence, today's reel mega-rich hedonists pose a much greater threat to the West, to Israel, and to fellow Arabs than did their predecessors. You can catch a few of their kind in *Rollover* (1981), *Wrong Is Right* (1982), *The Jewel of the Nile* (1985), and *American Ninja 4: The Annihilation* (1991).

Scantily clad harem maidens attend sheikhs in more than 30 scenarios. The rulers shrug off some, torture others, and enslave the rest. Enslaving international beauties in the X-rated movie, *Ilsa: Harem Keeper of the Oil Sheikhs* (1976), is a depraved Arab ruler and his cohort—Ilsa, the "She-Wolf of the S.S." Depraved sheikhs also subjugate dwarfs and Africans; see *Utz* (1992) and *Slavers* (1977).

Often, producers falsify geopolitical realities. During WWII many Arab nations actively supported the Allies. Moroccan, Tunisian, and Algerian soldiers, for example, fought alongside French troops in North Africa, Italy, and France. Also, Jordanian and Libyan troops assisted members of the British armed services. And, late in the conflict, Egypt, Saudi Arabia, and Iraq declared war on Germany.

Yet, most movies fail to show Arabs fighting alongside the *good* guys. Instead, burnoosed pro-Nazi potentates, some belonging to the "Arabian Gestapo," appear in more than ten sheikh movies; see, for example, *A Yank in Libya* (1942), *Action in Arabia* (1944), and *The Steel Lady* (1953). As early as 1943, about fifty years before the Gulf War, *Adventure in Iraq* (1943) depicts the US Air Force bombing the pro-German Iraqi ruler's "devil-worshiper" minions into oblivion.

From the start, protagonists ranging from Samson to 007 have battled burnoosed chieftains. Flashback to the 1900s. Two 1918 films, *Tarzan of the Apes* and *Bound in Morocco,* show Tarzan and Douglas Fairbanks, respectively, trouncing shifty sheikhs.

Cut to the 1940s. Abbott and Costello, Bing Crosby and Bob Hope, follow suit by belittling Arabs in *Lost in a Harem* (1944) and *Road to Morocco* (1942).

Advance to the 1950s. The Bowery Boys and Tab Hunter thrash robed rulers in *Looking for Danger* (1957) and *The Steel Lady* (1953), respectively.

Flash forward to the 1960s and the 1970s. Elvis Presley, Pat Boone, and Jerry Lewis deride Arabs in: *Harum Scarum* (1965), *The Perils of Pauline* (1967), and *Don't Raise the Bridge, Lower the River* (1968). Other stars bashing sheikhs were Ron Ely in *Slavers* (1977), Michael Douglas in *The Jewel of the Nile* (1985), Cheech and Chong in *Things Are Tough All Over* (1982), and Eddie Murphy in *Best Defense* (1984). And I almost forgot—Burt Braverman drubs two of movie land's ugliest sheikhs in *Hollywood Hot Tubs 2: Educating Crystal* (1990).

The movies of the 1980s are especially offensive. They display insolent desert sheikhs with thick accents threatening to rape and/or enslave starlets: Brooke Shields in *Sahara* (1983), Goldie Hawn in *Protocol* (1984) Bo Derek in *Bolero* (1984), and Kim Basinger in *Never Say Never Again* (1986).

Finally, five made-in-Israel films lambast sheikhs. Particularly degrading is Golan and Globus' *Paradise* (1981). A combination of Western teenagers and chimpanzees finish off the "jackal," a Christian-hating bedouin chieftain, and his cohorts.

Maidens

Arab women, meanwhile, are humiliated, demonized, and eroticized in more than 50 feature films.

Half-Arab heroines as well as mute enslaved Arab women appear in about sixteen features, ranging from foreign legion films to Arabian Nights fantasies. "The Arabian Nights never end . . . ," writes William Zinsser.

> It is a place where young slave girls lie about on soft couches, stretching their slender legs, ready to do a good turn for any handsome stranger who stumbles into the room. Amid all this décolletage sits the jolly old Caliph, miraculously cool to the wondrous sights around him, puffing his water pipe . . . This is history at its best.

Stereotypical idiosyncrasies abound, linking the Arab woman to several regularly repeated "B" images:

(1) They appear as bosomy bellydancers leering out from diaphanous veils, or as disposable "knick-knacks," scantily-clad harem maidens with bare midriffs, closeted in the palace's women's quarters.

(2) Background shots show them as Beasts of Burden, carrying jugs on their heads. Some are "so fat, no one would touch them."

(3) In films such as *The Sheltering Sky* (1990) they appear as shapeless Bundles of Black, a homogeneous sea of covered women trekking silently behind their unshaven mates.

(4) Beginning in 1917 with Fox's silent *Cleopatra,* starring Theda Bara, studios labeled Arab women "serpents" and "vampires." Subsequently, the word "vamp," a derivation of that word, was added to English dictionaries. Advancing the vampire image are movies such as *Saadia* (1953) and *Beast of Morocco* (1966). Both display Arab women as Black magic vamps, or enchantresses "possessed of devils."

(5) In *The Leopard Woman* (1920) and *Nighthawks* (1981) they are Bombers intent on killing Westerners.

When those dark-complexioned femmes fatales move to woo the American/British hero, they are often disappointed. The majority of movies, such as *Outpost in Morocco* (1949), posit that an Arab woman in love with a Western hero must die.

A few films allow Arab maidens to embrace Western males. In *A Café in Cairo* (1925) and *Arabesque* (1966), actresses Priscilla Dean and Sophia Loren appear as bright and lovely Arab women. Only after the women ridicule and reject Arab suitors, does the scenario allow them to fall into the arms of Western protagonists.

Regrettably, just a handful of movies—*Anna Ascends* (1922), *Princess Tam Tam* (1935), *Bagdad* (1949), *Flame of Araby* (1951), and *Flight from Ashiya* (1964), present brave and compassionate Arab women, genuine heroines. There are also admirable queens and princesses in several Cleopatra films and Arabian fantasy tales.

The costume is one way imagemakers make personal and political statements. By covering the reel Arab woman in black and relegating her to silence, the costumer links her with oppression. But throughout the Arab world, from Bahrain to Lebanon, women wear a wide variety of apparel. Some don the traditional black cloaks and veils; others dress in the latest Western fashions, whether it be jeans, designer dresses, or bikinis.

Taken together, her mute on-screen non-behavior and black-cloaked costume serve to alienate the Arab woman from her international sisters, and vice versa. Not only do the reel Arab women never speak, but they are never in the work place, functioning as doctors, computer specialists, school teachers, print and broadcast journalists, or as successful, well-rounded electric or domestic engineers. Movies don't show charitable Arab women such as those who belong to the Mosaic Foundation, which donates millions to American hospitals. Points out Camelia Anwar Sadat, Syria and Egypt gave women the right to vote as early as Europe did—and much earlier than Switzerland. Today, women make up nearly one-third of the Egyptian parliament. You would never guess from Hollywood's portrayal of Arab women that they are as diverse and talented as any others. Hollywood has not yet imagined a woman as interesting as Ivonne Abdel-Baki, the daughter of Lebanese immigrants and Ecuador's ambassador to Washington. Abdel-Baki, a specialist in conflict resolution, graduated from Harvard University's

Kennedy School of Government and is fluent in five languages. Or De' Al-Mohammed, the University of Missouri's blind fencing star. And many, many more.

Addressing movie land's "B" stereotypes is my friend, a Palestinian film industry lawyer with two children. She, like Ms. Al-Mohammed and other bright, highly educated Arab women, defy the stereotype. Concerned about stale screen portraits of women, she questions whether future films will present more honest images. "Many Arab women like myself work outside the home," she said. "Some wear hijabs, others do not. What we wear, what kind of clothes other women choose to wear, should not matter. What matters most is how we live our lives, especially that we manage quite well to care for our little ones. Why doesn't Hollywood make movies showing us bonding with and assisting other women, those like myself who are finding the proper balance between family and professional life?" Why not, indeed?

Egyptians

Egyptian caricatures appear in more than 100 films, from mummy tales to legends of pharaohs and queens to contemporary scenarios. Reel Egyptians routinely descend upon Westerners, Israelis, and fellow Egyptians. Interspersed throughout the movies are souk swindlers as well as begging children scratching for baksheesh. An ever-constant theme shows devious Egyptians moving to defile Western women; see Cecil B. DeMille's *Made for Love* (1926) and *Sphinx* (1981).

Stephen Spielberg's films *Raiders of the Lost Ark* (1981), *Young Sherlock Holmes* (1986), and *Indiana Jones and the Last Crusade* (1989) merit special attention, as do Golan-Globus' 1960s scenarios, made-in-Israel: *Cairo Operation* (1965) and *Trunk to Cairo* (1965). The producers paint Egyptians as nuclear-crazed and pro-Nazi. Their scenarios are particularly objectionable given the real-life heroics of the Arab Brotherhood of Freedom, a group of brave Egyptians who sided with the Allies during World War II.

Imagemakers are not so harsh with Queen Cleopatra. Beginning with Helen Gardner's *Cleopatra* (1912), Hollywood enlisted stars such as Ava Gardner, Theda Bara, Vivian Leigh, Sophia Loren, Claudette Colbert, and Elizabeth Taylor to portray Egypt's seductive queen. Approximately fifteen movies show Egypt's queen, encircled by stereotypical maidens, pining over Roman leaders. Only four movies display Egyptian queens romancing Egyptians. The majority display Egyptian royals feuding with fellow Egyptians as well as Rome's soldiers.

A few movies, such as Cecil B. DeMille's *The Ten Commandments* (1923) and DreamWorks' Jeffrey Katzenberg's *The Prince of Egypt* (1998), feature Egyptian rogues trying to crush heroic Israelites. I found the animated *Prince of Egypt* to be less offensive than DeMille's scenarios. Though Katzenberg's movie displays plenty of Egyptian villains, *Prince of Egypt* offers more humane, balanced portraits than do DeMille's 1923 and 1956 versions of *The Ten Commandments*. DeMille's 1923 film shows Egyptian guards beating "the dogs of Israel" and Pharaoh's ten-year-old son whipping Moses.

From the start, moviemakers linked Egypt with the un-dead. In Georges Méliès' film *The Monster* (1903), the camera reveals a bearded Egyptian magician removing a skeleton from its casket. Presto! He transforms the bony thing into a lovely maiden. But, not for long. The cunning magician changes the woman back into a skeleton.

Say "Egypt" and producers think "Mummies" and "Money." Beginning with Vitagraph's *The Egyptian Mummy* (1914) and *Dust of Egypt* (1915), Hollywood presented about 26 mummy films. In order to spook viewers, cinematographers placed gauze over the camera's lens, creating chilling, dreamlike, and exotic moods. Topping the list is Universal's *The Mummy* (1932). Due to a fine screenplay and Boris Karloff's performance as the mummy Imhotep, this classic stands the test of time as *the* mummy film. Other popular mummy movies are *The Mummy's Hand* (1940), *The Mummy's Tomb* (1942), and *The Mummy's Revenge* (1973).

Mummy plots are relatively simple: Revived mummies and their caretaker "priests" contest Western archaeologists. In most scenarios, the ambitious gravediggers ignore tomb curses. So of course they suffer the consequences for daring to reawaken Egypt's sleeping royals. Meanwhile, the Westerners dupe ignorant, superstitious, and two-timing Egyptians.

Once fully revived, the bandages-with-eyes mummy lusts after the archaeologist's fair-skinned daughter. And, the mummy crushes panicked Egyptian workers and all crypt violators—"infidels," "unbelievers," and "heretics." Occasionally movies like *The Awakening* (1980) pump up the action by offering decomposed horrors; also in this one, a queen's evil spirit so contaminates the Western heroine, she kills her father.

Obviously, there's more to the state of Egypt, the most heavily populated of all Arab countries, than pyramids and curses. Egypt is comprised of a people who take pride in their culture and their long and honorable history. Moving to modernize its economy and to improve the living standards of its population, Egypt now boasts more than fourteen state universities. The likes of scholarly students or noted Egyptian archeologists men like the celebrated Kamal El Malakh, are absent from movie screens.

Nor do screenwriters present scenarios patterned after Egypt's renowned journalists and authors, like Rose El-Yousef and Nobel Laureate Naguib Mahfouz. Egyptians, like most other Arabs, are deeply religious and are noted for their warm hospitality. In villages and throughout cosmopolitan cities like Cairo and Alexandria, *Ahlan Wa Sahlan* (Welcome, this is your home) is spoken as often as "good morning."

Though I do not analyze Mexican "Aztec" mummy and mayhem features, its important to point out that Aztec scenarios correspond with Egyptian curse movies. See *Curse of the Aztec Mummy* (1959), *Attack of the Mayan Mummy* (1963), and *Wrestling Women Versus The Aztec Mummy* (1964). Even *Robot Versus the Aztec Mummy* (1959) emulates Hollywood's Egyptian formula films, with a tomb inscription that warns archaeologists: "He who defiles the tomb runs the risk of death. Those disregarding the warning perish."

Palestinians

Observed Mark Twain, "We are all ignorant, just about different things." When it comes to the Middle East, many Americans are ignorant about the history and plight of the Palestinian people. One reason is that moviegoers may mistakenly believe *reel* Palestinians, those ugly make-believe film "terrorists," are *real* Palestinians. Should this be true, then what must viewers think of Palestinians after exiting movie theaters?

To assume viewers acquire some true knowledge of Palestinians after watching the 45 Palestinian fiction films that I discuss here is both dangerous and misleading. It's the same as thinking that you could acquire accurate knowledge of Africans by watching Tarzan movies, or that you would know all about Americans after watching movies about serial killers.

More than half of the Palestinian movies were released in the 1980s and 1990s; nineteen from 1983–1989; nine from 1990–1998. Absent from Hollywood's Israeli-Palestinian movies are human dramas revealing Palestinians as normal folk—computer specialists, domestic engineers, farmers, teachers, and artists. Never do movies present Palestinians as innocent victims and Israelis as brutal oppressors. No movie shows Israeli soldiers and settlers uprooting olive orchards, gunning down Palestinian civilians in Palestinian cities. No movie shows Palestinian families struggling to survive under occupation, living in refugee camps, striving to have their own country and passports stating "Palestine." Disturbingly, only two scenarios present Palestinian families.

Watching these, I questioned the defamation of Palestinians. Is there an unwritten cinematic code stating Hollywood will present all Palestinians as irrational and *bad*, all Israelis as rational and *good*?

One year after the state of Israel was born, the film, *Sword of the Desert* (1949), presented Palestine according to the popular Zionist slogan, as a land without a people—even though the vast majority of people living in Palestine at the time were, in fact, Palestinians. This myth—no-Palestinians-reside-in-Palestine—is also served up in *Cast a Giant Shadow* (1966) and *Judith* (1966).

A decade after *Sword of the Desert* Paul Newman declared war on the Palestinians in *Exodus* (1960). Hollywood's heroes followed suit. In *Prisoner in the Middle* (1974), David Janssen links up with Israeli forces; together they gun down Palestinian nuclear terrorists. Films from the 1980s such as *The Delta Force* (1986) and *Wanted: Dead or Alive* (1987) present Lee Marvin, Chuck Norris, and Rutger Hauer blasting Palestinians in the Mideast and in Los Angeles. In the 1990s, Charlie Sheen and Kurt Russell obliterate Palestinians in Lebanon and aboard a passenger jet, in *Navy SEALs* (1990) and *Executive Decision* (1996).

In *Ministry of Vengeance* (1989) filmmakers dishonor Palestinians and American military chaplains as well. In lieu of presenting the chaplain, a Vietnam veteran, as a devout, non-violent man, the minister exterminates Palestinians. The minister's parishioners approve of the killings, applauding him.

Seven films, including *True Lies* (1994) and *Wanted Dead or Alive* (1987), project the Palestinian as a nerve-gassing nuclear terrorist. In more than eleven movies, including *Half-Moon Street* (1986), *Terror in Beverly Hills* (1988), and *Appointment with Death* (1988), Palestinian evildoers injure and physically threaten Western women and children.

The reader should pay special attention to *Black Sunday* (1977), Hollywood's first major movie showing Palestinians terrorizing and killing Americans on US soil. Telecast annually the week of Super Bowl Sunday, the movie presents Dahlia, a Palestinian terrorist, and her cohort Fasil. They aim to massacre 80,000 Super Bowl spectators, including the American President, a Jimmy Carter look-alike.

Dictating numerous Palestinian-as-terrorist scenarios is the Israeli connection. More than half (28) of the Palestinian movies were filmed in Israel. Nearly all of the made-in-Israel films, especially the seven Cannon movies, display violent, sex-crazed Palestinian "bastards [and] animals" contesting Westerners, Israelis, and fellow Arabs.

I believe Cannon's poisonous scenarios are not accidental, but rather propaganda disguised as entertainment. Even in the early 1900s studio moguls knew that motion pictures could serve propagandists. Following WWI, Adolph Zukor, the head of Paramount Pictures affirmed this film-as-propaganda fact, saying fiction films should no longer be viewed as simply "entertainment and amusement." The war years, he said, "register[ed] indisputably the fact that as an avenue of propaganda, as a channel for conveying thought and opinion, the movies are unequaled by any form of communication."

Gratuitous Scenes and Slurs

Shockingly, producers insert egregious, amoral Villains, Maidens, Sheikhs, Egyptians, and Palestinians in more than 250 movies that have absolutely nothing to do with Arabs or the Middle East. I refer to these films as cameos. Appearing like unexpected jumbo potholes on paved streets, nasty Arabs clutter hundreds of non-Arab scenarios—and even noted filmmakers such as Steven Spielberg, Francis Ford Coppola, and Ridley Scott participate in this. See *The Black Stallion* (1979), *Back to the Future* (1985), *Young Sherlock Holmes* (1985), and *G.I. Jane* (1997).

Renowned writers such as Neil Simon, Tom Wolfe, and Paddy Chayefsky also tarnished Arabs. About 40 films, including *Network* (1976), *Chapter Two* (1979), and *The Bonfire of the Vanities* (1990), contain discriminatory dialogue.

Between 1980–2001, Hollywood released more than 120 of these cameo features. Apparently, studio executives looked the other way, approving the insidious anti-Arab insertions. How would reasonable moviegoers react had the villains not been Arab? What if these hundreds of cameo movies had saturated audiences not with visions of "primitive" Arabs, but rather with cruel celluloid caricatures of other groups? Would you walk away in anger, thinking Hollywood's slanderous insertions were intentional and discriminatory? Or would you leave the theater in an apathetic state, believing the corruptive insertions to be harmless and accidental?

Why the Stereotype?

Ask a film industry executive, director, or writer whether it is ethical to perpetuate ethnic or racial stereotypes and you can expect a quick negative response. How then, to explain that since 1970, these very same individuals produced, directed, and scripted more than 350 films portraying Arabs as insidious cultural "others?"

Either filmmakers are perpetuating the stereotype unknowingly, and would immediately disassociate themselves from such activities were they to realize the implications of their actions, or they are doing so knowingly and will only stop when sufficient pressure is brought to bear on them.

It is difficult to imagine that screenwriters who draft scenes of fat, lecherous sheikhs ogling Western blondes, or crazed Arab terrorists threatening to blow up America with nuclear weapons, are not precisely aware of what they are doing. But we sometimes forget that one of the elements that makes stereotyping so powerful, and so hard to eliminate, is that it is self-perpetuating. Filmmakers grew up watching Western heroes crush hundreds of reel "bad" Arabs. Some naturally repeat the stereotype without realizing that, in so doing, they are innocently joining the ranks of the stereotypes' creators.

Huge inroads have been made toward the elimination of many racial and ethnic stereotypes from the movie screen, but Hollywood's stereotype of Arabs remains unabated. Over the last three decades stereotypical portraits have actually increased in number and virulence.

The Arab stereotype's extraordinary longevity is the result, I believe, of a collection of factors. For starters, consider print and broadcast "if it bleeds it leads" news reports. Like most Americans, creators of popular culture (including novelists, cartoonists, and filmmakers), form their opinions of a people, in part, based on what they read in print, hear on the radio, and see on television. Like the rest of us, they are inundated and influenced by a continuous flow of "seen one, seen 'em all" headlines and sound bites.

New reports *selectively* and relentlessly focus on a minority of a minority of Arabs, the radical fringe. The seemingly indelible Arab-as-villain image wrongly conveys the message that the vast majority of the 265 million peace-loving Arabs are "bad guys."

The image began to intensify in the late 1940s when the state of Israel was founded on Palestinian land. From that preemptive point on—through the Arab-Israeli wars of 1948, 1967, and 1973, the hijacking of planes, the disruptive 1973 Arab oil embargo, along with the rise of Libya's Muammar Qaddafi and Iran's Ayatollah Khomeini—shot after shot delivered the relentless drum beat that all Arabs were and are Public Enemy No. 1.

Right through the 1980s, the 1990s, and into the twenty-first century, this "bad people" image prevailed, especially during the Palestinian intifada and the Israeli invasion of Lebanon. In 1980, the rabid followers of Iran's Ayatollah Khomeini held 52 Americans hostage at the US Embassy in Teheran for 444 days. Nightly, TV cameras blazoned across the planet Khomeini's supporters chanting "Death to America!" and calling our country "the Great Satan" as they burned our flag and, in effigy, Uncle Sam himself.

At the height of the Iranian hostage crisis anti-Arab feelings intensified, as 70 percent of Americans wrongly identified Iran as an Arab country. Even today, most Americans think of Iranians as Arabs. In fact, Iranians are Persians, another people altogether.

Mindlessly adopted and casually adapted, the Arab-as-enemy stereotype narrows our vision and blurs reality. Juicy and marketable news headlines are picked up and repeated by the global news services, triggering further misunderstandings.

It got worse in the 1990s. Two major events, the Iraqi invasion of Kuwait that led to the Gulf War, and the bombing of New York City's World Trade Center, combined to create misguided mindset, leading some Americans to believe all Arabs are terrorists and that Arabs do not value human life as much as we do. As a result, some of us began even perceiving our fellow Americans of Arab descent as clones of Iraq's Saddam Hussein and the terrorist Osama bin Laden. Well, I think you get the picture.

Damaging portraits, notably those presenting Arabs as America's enemy, affect all people, influencing world public opinion and policy. Given the pervasive stereotype, it comes as no surprise that some of us—and the US State Department—find it difficult to accept Egyptians, Moroccans, Palestinians, and other Arabs as friends.

Not only do these violent news images of extremists reinforce and exacerbate already prevalent stereotypes, but they serve as both a source and excuse for continued Arab-bashing by those filmmakers eager to exploit the issue. In particular, the news programs are used by some producers and directors to deny they are actually engaged in stereotyping. "We're not stereotyping," they object. "Just look at your television set. Those are real Arabs."

Such responses are disingenuous and dishonest. As we know, news reports by their very nature cover extraordinary events. We should not expect reporters to inundate the airwaves with the lives of ordinary Arabs. But filmmakers have a moral obligation not to advance the news media's sins of omission and commission, not to tar an entire group of people on the basis of the crimes and the alleged crimes of a few.

Taken together, news and movie images wrench the truth out of shape to influence billions of people. Regrettably, gross misperceptions abound and continue to plaster on movie screens, those distorted "pictures in our heads" that Walter Lippmann bemoaned some 70 years ago.

Why would anyone take part in the denigration of a people knowingly? I think one answer is the Arab-Israeli conflict. Though the majority of moviemakers are fair-minded professionals, there are some who, in the interests of pursuing their own political or personal agenda, are willing to perpetuate hate. These individuals may be expected to continue to indict Arabs on movie screens for as long as unjust images are tolerated.

New York Times columnist Maureen Dowd offers another answer: "[S]tereotypes are not only offensive [but] they are also comforting. They . . . exempt people from any further mental or emotional effort. They wrap life in the arch toastiness of fairy tale and myth. They make complicated understandings unnecessary." Convenient stereotypes make everyone's job easier. Rather than having to pen a good joke, the writer inserts a stumbling, bumbling sheikh. Looking for a villain? Toss in an Arab terrorist—We all know what they look like from watching movies and TV. No thought required. As for the audience? Well, it also makes some of us feel better to see ourselves as superior to someone else. If one is no longer allowed to feel superior to Asians, Jews, Latinos, or blacks, at least we can feel superior to those wretched Arabs.

For some producers, Arabs are convenient scapegoats. Asked to explain why his *Iron Eagle* (1996) displayed heinous Arabs, writer-director Sidney J. Furie had this to say to NBC producer Arthur Lord:

> Look, [in movies] there always has to be a bad guy. And, so you make one up . . . an acceptable bad guy. I mean, it has to be something. It has to be somebody, cause there's good and evil. Something has to represent evil. And in our picture, as an example, we didn't give the country a name and we didn't say it was Arab. I mean you have to be an idiot not to think it was [Arab]. But, so what!

And, don't forget about peer pressure. I recall asking one producer why he and his co-workers never projected in comedies and dramas Arabs and Arab-Americans as "regular" folk. To my astonishment, he confided, "Jack, some of us are reluctant to present good Arabs, even good Arab-Americans in our movies, because we'll be labeled pro-Arab."

Certainly, the Department of Defense's rubber-stamping of motion pictures that lambast Arabs plays a role. The fact is, the government has a history of playing a role in what movies do and don't get made. As early as 1917, the federal government not only acknowledged the power of film to influence political thought, it took on the wrongful role of censor. As soon as the United States declared war on Germany, the government declared that no Hollywood movie could arouse prejudice against friendly nations. The 1917 film *The Spirit of '76* reveals heroic American revolutionaries such as Patrick Henry and Paul Revere. But some frames show British soldiers committing acts of atrocities. As England was our World War I ally, the government protested; a judge declared producer Robert Goldstein's movie advanced anti-British sentiments. Calling the film "potent German propaganda," the judge sentenced Goldstein to prison.

Greed, too, is an incentive. Bash-the-Arab movies make money. Thus, some producers exploit the stereotype for profit.

Other moviemakers fail to offer a corrective because they may be indolent, inflexible, and/or indifferent. Certainly, in the past, ignorance, the handmaiden of bigotry, was a contributing factor.

The absence of vibrant film criticism is another cause. A much-needed recourse against harmful Arab images would be more vigorous criticism emanating from industry executives and movie critics. I recall, still, Bosley Crowther's *New York Times* review of *Adventure in Sahara* (1938). Instead of criticizing stereotypes, Crowther advanced them, writing: "We know the desert is no picnic and you can't trust an Arab very far."

Another factor is silence. No significant element of public opinion has yet to oppose the stereotype; even scholars and government officials are mum. New York's Andrew Cuomo, for example, is running for governor of New York, a state where many Americans of Arab heritage reside. Cuomo is "very interested in the topic of discrimination" and stereotyping; he is alert to the fact that there is "a robust hunger for vulgar stereotypes in popular culture." Imagemakers, he says, are "still stereotyping Italian-Americans, Irish-Americans, African-Americans, Indian-Americans and American Jews." Yet, Cuomo fails to mention coarse stereotypes of Arab-Americans. If we are ever to illuminate our common humanity, our nation's leaders must challenge *all* hateful stereotypes. Teachers need to move forward and incorporate, at long last, discussions of Arab caricatures in schools, colleges, military, and government classrooms.

Ethnic stereotypes do not die off on their own, but are hunted down and terminated by those whom the stereotypes victimize. Other groups, African-Americans, Asian-Americans and Jewish-Americans, have acted aggressively against discriminatory portraits. Arab-Americans as a group, however, have been slow to mobilize and, as a result, their protests are rarely heard in Hollywood and even when heard, are heard too faintly to get the offenders to back off.

Another reason is lack of presence. With the exception of a few movies, *Party Girl* (1995) and *A Perfect Murder* (1998), Arab-Americans are invisible on movie screens. One reason, simply put, is that there are not many Arab-Americans involved in the film industry; not one is a famous Hollywood celebrity.

What does their absence have to do with contesting stereotypes? Well, one answer is that movie stars have clout. Consider how Brad Pitt altered the scenario, *The Devil's Own* (1996). After reading the initial script, Pitt protested, telling the studio the screenplay made him "uneasy" because it was loaded with stereotypes—"full of leprechaun jokes and green beer." The dialogue, he argued, unfairly painted his character as a stereotypical Irish "bad" guy. Explains Pitt, "I had the responsibility to represent somewhat these [Irish] people whose lives have been shattered. It would have been an injustice to Hollywood-ize it." Unless changes were made to humanize the Irish people, especially his character, Pitt "threatened to walk." The studio acquiesced, bringing in another writer to make the necessary changes.

Also, when it comes to studio moguls, not one Arab American belongs to the media elite. The community boasts no communication giants comparable to Disney's Michael Eisner, DreamWorks' Jeffrey Katzenberg, Fox's Rupert Murdoch, or Time-Warner's Ted Turner.

The lack of an Arab-American presence impacts the stereotype in another way. The industry has a dearth of those men and women who would be the most naturally inclined to strive for accurate and balanced portrayals of Arabs. But a number of high-level Arab

Americans in the industry over the course of time would rectify the situation. It's difficult to demean people and their heritage when they're standing in front of you, especially if those persons are your bosses.

Not so long ago, women and minorities were excluded from studios' executive offices. Not anymore. Explains director Spike Lee, "Look at the number of women in the film industry now—Amy Pascal is running Sony, you have Sherry Lansing at Paramount, and Stacey Snider at Universal—and twenty years ago there were no women heads of studios . . . This is a gradual process."

Contesting cinema's defamatory images is as American as apple pie. From the beginning, America's blacks, Jews, and Irish moved to break down walls of mistrust and suspicion. What did these diverse peoples have in common? Well, they formed pressure groups, lobbying the industry for more balanced images.

In the early 1900s, "Cinema's new presence as a form of mass entertainment made ethnic groups more sensitive to the way they were portrayed on the screen," explains Charles Musser. Though "film stereotypes faded only slowly," says Musser, "egregious representations were often followed by protest."

It began with the Irish. The year, 1907. The manager of the Lyric Theater in Providence, Rhode Island, screened a comedy about Murphy, a drunken Irishman. Abruptly,

> Irish film-goers in nearby Pawtucket [became] so outraged when they saw the picture that they threatened to destroy the Lyric [unless the film] was banned. [Enter] Mayor McCarthy of Providence. [He] saw the show, and banned the film.

Declared McCarthy: This movie is "a deliberate insult to a respectable race."

Another "respectable race" was tarred in D.W. Griffith's *The Birth of a Nation* (1915), in which all blacks are portrayed as brutes. As a result, the film stirred up race hatred against blacks, prompting the Ku Klux Klan to use it for Klan recruiting. The Mayor of Boston, James Curley, refused to ban or censor the film. He shrugged off protests from the NAACP's Boston branch, arguing, "the objections to *The Birth of a Nation* as racist propaganda would be no more valid than protests against Shakespeare's *Henry VIII* for maligning the Roman Catholic church."

One year later, members of the B'nai Brith protested the portrayal of Jews as Christ-killers in D.W. Griffith's biblical epic *Intolerance* (1916). Argued the B'nai Brith, too many Jewish extras surrounded the cross where Christ was to be crucified. Griffith responded by burning the protested footage. And, he re-shot the controversial crucifixion scene, adding Roman extras, deleting some Jewish ones. A decade later, Jewish groups objected to Jewish images in Cecil B. DeMille's spectacle, *The King of Kings* (1927). DeMille, too, deleted the offending scenes. Later, Will Hayes, the chairman of the film censorship board, said that in the future, he and his committee would consult the B'nai Brith on films with subjects of Jewish interest.

Regrettably, America's Arabs do not yet have an organized and active lobby in Los Angeles. To bring about fundamental changes in how motion pictures project Arabs, a systematic lobbying effort is needed. Though the Arab-American and Muslim-American presence is steadily growing in number and visibility in the United States, only a few Arab-Americans meet with and discuss the stereotype with filmmakers. When dialogue does occur, some discriminatory portraits are altered. Declares a February 3, 2001 Council on American-Islamic Relations (CAIR) fax: "The villains in Paramount's upcoming film, *The Sum of All Fears*, were changed to "European neo-Nazis." CAIR officials acknowledged Paramount for this important change, as Tom Clancy's book, on which the movie is based, presents Arab Muslims detonating a nuclear device at the Super Bowl in Denver. In a letter to CAIR, the film's director, Phil Alden Robinson, wrote: "I hope you will be reassured that I have no intention of portraying negative images of Arabs or Muslims."

Ongoing informal and formal meetings with movie executives are essential. Such sessions enable community members to more readily explain to producers the negative effects misperceptions of Arabs have on their children as well as on American public opinion and policy. Also, Arab-Americans need to reach out and expand their concerns with well-established ethnic and minority lobbying groups—with Asians, blacks, Jews, Latinos, gays and lesbians, and others.

Positives

To see is to make possible new ways of seeing. In this book, I have tried to be uncompromisingly truthful, and to expose the Hollywood stereotype of Arabs for all to see.

While it is true that most filmmakers have vilified the Arab, others have not. Some contested harmful stereotypes, displaying positive images—that is, casting an Arab as a regular person.

In memorable well-written movies, ranging from the Arabian Nights fantasy *The Thief of Bagdad* (1924), to the World War II drama *Sahara* (1943), producers present Arabs not as a threateningly different people but as "regular" folks, even as heroes. In *Sahara,* to save his American friends, a courageous Arab soldier sacrifices his life.

Note this father and son exchange from the film *Earthbound* (1980):

SON: "Why do they [the police] hate us, so?"
FATHER: "I guess because we're different."
SON: "Just because somebody's different doesn't mean they have to hate 'em. It's stupid."
FATHER: "It's been stupid for a long time."

At first, I had difficulty uncovering "regular" and admirable Arab characters—it was like trying to find an oasis in the desert. Yet, I discovered more than 50 motion pictures sans Arab villains, five percent of the total number reviewed here. Refreshingly, the movies debunk stale images, humanizing Arabs.

As for those Arabian Nights fantasies of yesteryear, only a few viziers, magicians, or other scalawags lie in ambush. Mostly fabulous Arabs appear in *The Desert Song* (1929), *Ali Baba and the Forty Thieves* (1944), *Son of Sinbad* (1955), and *Aladdin and His Magic Lamp* (1969). The movies present viewers with brave and moral protagonists: Aladdin, Ali Baba, and Sinbad. Emulating the deeds of Robin Hood and his men of Sherwood Forest, Arabs liberate the poor from the rich, and free the oppressed from corrupt rulers.

Worth noting is the presence of glittering Arabs in non-fantasy movies. A heroic Egyptian princess appears in the movie serial, *Chandu the Magician* (1932). A courageous Egyptian innkeeper assists British troops in *Five Graves to Cairo* (1943). *Gambit* (1966) displays a compassionate Arab entrepreneur. In *King Richard and the Crusaders* (1954), Saladin surfaces as a dignified, more humane leader than his counterpart, Richard.

Some independent Israeli filmmakers, notably those whose movies were financed by the Fund for the Promotion of Israeli Quality Films, allow viewers to empathize with Palestinians, presenting three-dimensional portraits. To their credit, producers of *Beyond the Walls* (1984) and *Cup Final* (1992) contest the self-promotional history and Palestinian stereotypes spun out by most other filmmakers. Both movies show the Palestinian and the Israeli protagonist bonding; the two men are projected as soul-mates, innocent victims of the Arab-Israeli conflict.

I recommend several top-notch movies, produced in Australia, France, Germany, and Italy. Three of the films offer telling illustrations of how prejudice impacts Arabs, blacks, Jews, and Germans. See *Ali: Fear Eats the Soul* (1974), *The Camel Boy* (1984), and *Hate* (1995).

Solutions

The time is long overdue for Hollywood to end its undeclared war on Arabs, and to cease misrepresenting and maligning them.

All I ask of filmmakers is to be even-handed, to project Arabs as they do other people—no better, no worse. They should enjoy at the very least relative immunity from prejudicial portrayal.

Established professionals and young, energetic moviemakers should step forward and create movies that change the way viewers perceive reel Arabs. They should incorporate this axiom: The denigration of one people, one religion, is the denigration of all people, all religions. As Holocaust survivor and Nobel Prize winner Elie Wiesel reminds us, no human race is superior, no religious faith is inferior; every nation has its share of bad people and good people.

I challenge Hollywood's producers to acknowledge unjust portraits of the past century and embrace Wiesel's wisdom, taking the high ground and projecting Arabs as ordinary and decent world citizens.

Affirms Thoreau, "It is never too late to give up our prejudices. . . . Men [and women] hit only what they aim at." Filmmakers should remember to aim high and heed the advice of DreamWorks' chairman Jeffrey Katzenberg, who told me: "Each of us in Hollywood has the opportunity to assume individual responsibility for creating films that elevate rather than denigrate, that shed light rather than dwell in darkness, that aim for the highest common denominator rather than the lowest."

A few producers did aim high, creating fresh scenarios humanizing Arabs. *The Lion of the Desert* (1981) and *The 13th Warrior* (1999), not only explored the various facets of the human heart, but also the films made money at the box office.

Imagemakers could illuminate the human condition and enhance tolerance by revising classics such as *Crossfire* (1947) and the Academy Award-winning film *Gentleman's Agreement* (1947). The producers combined truth with cinematic sensitivity and skill, resulting in two memorable films. *Crossfire* details the tragic consequences of an ex-soldier's (Robert Ryan) anti-Semitic actions. To better understand the nature of prejudice, *Gentleman's Agreement*'s protagonist, a crusading reporter portrayed by Gregory Peck, feigns being a Jew, and writes about anti-Semitism. The journalist's son questions his father's assignment:

SON: "What's anti-Semitism?"
FATHER: "Some people don't like other people just because they're Jews."
SON: "Why? Are some bad?"
FATHER: "Some are. Some aren't. Just like everybody else."

As both Arabs and Jews are Semites, revised versions of the two excellent 1947 movies would serve to sensitize viewers as well as imagemakers. An altered *Crossfire* could show an Arab American as a victim of prejudice. A fresh *Gentleman's Agreement* could reveal a reporter feigning to be Arab, writing about the new anti-Semitism.

Another way to curtail insidious portraits is to provide imagemakers with the long-awaited evidence—as found in this book—revealing that for more than a century Hollywood has targeted the Arab as the "other." The evidence documented here is intended to fill the empty desert between Hollywood and the Arabs that until now has seemed untraversable. Writing it has convinced me that the discussion of screen Arabs is not only historically relevant, but a legitimate and important undertaking.

I am confident this book will find its place in college classrooms. When young people, especially students of the cinema, are aware how moviemakers' tainted brushes have discolored Arabs, up-and-coming filmmakers will alter stereotypical portraits.

Openness to change is an American tradition. Not so many years ago, imagemakers repeatedly projected American Indians, Asians, Italians, and Latinos as cultural "others." No longer.

Ultimately, it is a matter of conscience and morality. Filmmakers opting to shed light would join a select and distinguished group—innovative, spirited men and women who not only contested stale stereotypes, but created more honest and humane portraits.

Overlooked in nearly all the films is this telling fact: The Arabs are an exceptionally hospitable people. Most Arabs I know are warm, outgoing, and friendly, abiding by the proverb, "Even this small room is space enough for 1,000 friends." I still recall my visit to Manama, Bahrain, in the summer of 1981. Seeking to escape the noonday heat and traffic snarls, I meditated at the entrance of a cool and peaceful mosque. After some time, Mohammed, a smiling cab driver who had just finished saying his ritual prayers, approached me. It was obvious to him that I was an exhausted visitor. Mohammed offered me some bottled water, insisting he take me to my host's home, gratis. His soft-spoken words and kindness ruled the moment; all I could say was "Thank you." Throughout the region, such helpful gestures are common.

When I think about how cinema's injurious stereotypes stand in stark contrast to the warm and hospitable Arabs I know, my thoughts turn to my late friend Alex Odeh, a poet, and a champion of human rights. In his poem, Alex equates stereotypes with lies:

> *Lies are like the dead ashes;*
> *when the wind of truth blows,*
> *the lies are dispersed like dust . . .*
> *and disappear.*

As for the future, I believe my children Michael and Michele will witness the demise of reel bad Arabs, and see the stereotypes slowly fade away like the smile on the Cheshire cat, into an overdue oblivion.

This book, the result of two decades of research, has been a daunting enterprise. To be sure, there are movies I have missed. Though I am appending a list of about 120 feature films that call for analysis, there are still plenty of films out there with hostile Arabs. Thus, I invite you, good reader, to rally round the cause, to join me in wiping the shadows of unjust portraits off the silver screen. Contest slanderous portraits whenever you see them—now and in the morrow.

Assist me in identifying stereotypes, beyond those cited here. I look forward to hearing from you and reading your evaluations of undiscovered and upcoming motion pictures with negative and positive Arab themes, characters, dialogue, and settings. Your role as a non-commissioned observer is especially important because it will help you bring to the cause a continuing reminder for producers and writers that they have an obligation—but also an opportunity to live up to their humanitarian responsibilities. Your input will add to my interpretation of new films I am already researching. Cumulatively, our joint efforts may lead to another edition. When and if it does, I will gratefully acknowledge the source of every contribution I can use. My e-mail address is info@interlinebooks.com.

To paraphrase an Arab proverb, *Eed wahdeh ma fiha tza'if,* one hand alone does not clap. Believe me, by working together we will shatter the stereotype.

Best List

Ali: Fear Eats the Soul (1974)
Beyond the Walls (1984)
The Black Tent (1956)
Cup Final (1992)
Gambit (1966)
King Richard and the Crusaders (1954)
Lion of the Desert (1981)
Madame Rosa (1977)
Robin Hood: Prince of Thieves (1991)
The Thief of Bagdad (1924)
The 13th Warrior (1999)
Three Kings (1999)

Recommended Films

The Adventures of Prince Achmed
    (1925)
The Adventures of Sinbad (1962)
The Adventures of Sinbad (1979)
Aladdin and the Wonderful Lamp
    (1917)
Aladdin's Lamp (1907)
Ali Baba and the Forty Thieves (1944)
Ali and the Talking Camel (1960)
Antony and Cleopatra (1972)
Arabian Love (1922)
The Battle of Algiers (1965)
Ben Hut (1959)
Caesar and Cleopatra (1946)
The Camel Boy (1984)
Captain Sinbad (1963)
Cleopatra (1934)
Cleopatra (1963)
The Desert Hawk (1950)
The Desert Song (1929)
Escape from Zahrain (1962)
Fatima (1912)
Five Graves to Cairo (1943)

Flame of Araby (1951)
Flight from Ashiya (1964)
40,000 Horsemen (1942)
The Golden Voyage of Sinbad (1974)
Hamsin (1983)
Hanna K. (1983)
Hate (1995)
Jericho (1937)
Khartoum (1966)
King of the Wind (1989)
Kismet (1944)
Kismet (1955)
The Long Kiss Goodnight (1996)
Man of Legend (1971)
The Message (1976)
Overseas (1992)
Party Girl (1995)
A Perfect Murder (1998)
Princess Tam Tam (1935)
Private Worlds (1935)
Project Z (1987)
The Return of Chandu (1934)
Sahara (1943)
The Seventh Coin (1992)
The Sheik Steps Out (1937)
The Sheik's Wife (1922)
The Son of Cleopatra (1964)
Sudan (1945)
The Vigilante (1947)
What the Moon Saw (1990)

Worst List

Abdulla the Great (1956)
American Ninja 4: The Annihilation
    (1991)
Ashanti (1979)
Back to the Future (1985)
Beau Ideal (1931)
Best Defense (1984)

Beyond Justice (1992)
The Black Stallion (1979)
The Black Stallion Returns (1983)
Blink of an Eye (1991)
The Bonfire of the Vanities (1990)
Bulletproof (1988)
Cast a Giant Shadow (1966)
Chain of Command (1993)
Code Name Vengeance (1989)
Death Before Dishonor (1987)
The Delta Force (1986)
Double Edge (1992)
Eagles Attack at Dawn (1970)
East of Sudan (1964)
Exodus (1960)
Follow That Camel (1967)
Freedom Strike (1998)
Ground Zero (1994)
Hell Squad (1985)
Hollywood Hot Tubs 2: Educating
    Crystal (1990)
Hostage (1986)
The Human Shield (1992)
Into the Sun (1991)
Iron Eagle (1986)
Ishtar (1987)
Jewel of the Nile (1985)
Killing Streets (1991)
Legion of the Doomed (1958)
Legion of Missing Men (1937)
Ministry of Vengeance (1989)
My Chauffeur (1986)
Navy SEALs (1990)
Network (1976)
Operation Condor (1997)
Paradise (1982)
Prisoner in the Middle (1974)
Protocol (1984)
Riding the Edge (1989)
Rollover (1982)

Rosebud (1975)
Rules of Engagement (2000)
The Sad Sack (1957)
Sahara (1983)
Sands of Beersheba (1966)
The Sheltering Sky (1990)
Son of the Pink Panther (1993)
Son of Tarzan (1920)
Sphinx (1981)
Tarzan the Tiger (1929)
Tarzan's Revenge (1938)
Terminal Entry (1986)
Terror in Beverly Hills (1988)
Things are Tough All Over (1982)
Tripoli (1950)
True Lies (1994)
Wanted: Dead or Alive (1987)
War Birds (1988)
Wrong Is Right (1982)

Cannon (Golan-Globus) Films

Aladdin (1986)
Allan Quatermain and the Lost City of
    Gold (1987)
The Ambassador (1984)
American Ninja 3: Blood Hunt
    (1989)
American Ninja 4: The Annihilation
    (1991)
American Samurai (1992)
Appointment with Death (1988)
Bloodsport (1988)
Bolero (1984)
Chain of Command (1993)
The Delta Force (1986)
The Delta Force 3: The Killing Game
    (1991)
Eagles Attack at Dawn (1970)
Firewalker (1986)

The Happy Hooker Goes to Washing-
    ton (1977)
Hell Squad (1985)
The Hitman (1991)
The Human Shield (1992)
Invasion U.S.A. (1985)
King Solomon's Mines (1985)

A Man Called Sarge (1990)
Prison Heat (1993)
Sahara (1983)
Sinbad of the Seven Seas (1989)
Surrender (1987)
Trunk to Cairo (1967)

Epithets Directed at the Film Arab

Aliens
Animals
Ape
Arab wrangler
Arab ass
Arabian Gestapo
Assassins
Asshole
Atomic terrorist
Ayrab
Bad-ass terrorist
Bandit chief
Bandits
Barbarian
Bastard
Bastards
Bearded Arab
Boring oil billionaires
Brown devils
Buffoons
Butchers
Bunco artist
Buzzards of the jungle
Camel-dick
Camel-driver
Camel farts
Camel humper
Camel jockeys
Carpetbaggers
Cheap-suited camel jockey
Cheese-dick
Cockroach
Crackpots
Croaking bullfrog
Crocodile
Cutthroats
Damn camel jockey
Desert bandits
Desert outlaws

Desert rat
Devil
Devil of the desert
Devil worshipers
Dirty dog
Dirty, filthy swines
Dog
Dog monkey
Dune dumpers
Empty-headed old fool
Faggot
Fairies
Fakirs
Fanatic tribesmen
Fanatics
Fat ant-eater
Filth
Filthy animal
Filthy Arabs
Filthy Ayrabs
Filthy butcher
Filthy groveling pig
Filthy swine
Fink-face
Flea-bitten bunch of pirates
Fly-in-a-piece-of-shit
Foal of a camel
Fuckers
Fuckin' fag
Fuckin' pigs
Gangsters
Goat
Goddamn Arabs
Goons
Greedy dogs
Groveling pig
Gucci terrorist
Half-breed dog
Half-man, half-horse
Half-savage
Hashish-maddened horde

Heathen
Hippopotamus
Holy hyenas
Horrid brutal brute
Idiot
Injuns
Infidel pig
Infidels
Jackal
King of beggars
Lard bucket
Lean Arab
Little bastard
Little monster
Little pig with a moustache
Mad dog
Male chauvinist
Man-eating dark savages
Man-eating savages
Maniac
Medieval fanatics
Merciless desert cult
Mick-a-muck of Morocco
Mideast maggot
Mongol Oriental
Monkeys
Monster
Moorish whore
Motherfuckers
Musselmen
Nazis
Nirwits
Nuclear-terrorist
Old goat
Old horse-face
Old witch
Pack of dogs
Phonies
Piece of shit
Pig
Pinhead potentate

Poisonous snake
Possessed of devils
Prowling bedouins
Raghead
Raghead faggot
Rat
Rat-bastard
Riff-raff
Riffians
Roaches
Sand-diviner
Sand fleas
Sand-spider
Satan
Savages
Scavengers
Scum
Scum bucket
Scum bums
Scum of the earth
Scumbags
Serpent
Sharks in the sea
Sheiss (shit)
Shit
Slob
Snake
Sneaky Arabs
Son-of-a-bitch
Son-of-a-camel
Son-of-a-dog
Son-of-a-flea-bitten-camel
Son-of-a-flea-bitten-goat
Son-of-a-thief
Son-of-a-whore
Son-of-an-owl
Son-of-an-unnamed-goat
Sons-of-she-camels
Stateless savages (Palestinians)
Stinky fellow
Strange Arab

Stupid bastard
Stupid bitch
Swine
Swine of the alleys
Terrorists
Thoroughbred mongrel
Tiger claws
Toothless Arab
Total slime
Towel head
Towel-headed creep
Treacherous dog
Treacherous scamp
Treacherous toad
Turbaned gangster
Turbaned twit

Unbelievers
Unseeable ones
Vampire
Vulture
Walking bedsheets
Wicked wolf
Wild tribes
Witch of evil
Wog farmers
Wogs
Wolf of the desert
World's bloodiest terrorist
Yellow heathen
Yellow-livered ape
Your-disgrace-ful-ness
Your-worth-less-ness

27

UNPEOPLE

John Pilger

Few of us can easily surrender our belief that society must somehow make sense. The thought that the State has lost its mind and is punishing so many innocent people is intolerable. And so the evidence has to be internally denied.

Arthur Miller

The Gulf War was the first real major action of the new Cold War. Like a videogame all the family could play, it was fun. There was a demon to fight, hi-tech weapons to fight him with, it was all over quickly and 'we' won. The bonus was the 'miraculously small number of casualties.'

'GO GET HIM BOYS,' said the London *Daily Star* on the day war broke out. The London *Daily Mirror* juxtaposed pictures of a soldier and an airman beneath the banner headline, 'THE HEROES,' with scowling Saddam Hussein, headlined 'THE VILLAIN.' 'The time has come,' opined the *Sun,* to 'punish the guilty party . . . Iraq and Saddam Hussein must be destroyed once and for all.'[1] After all, President Bush had declared Saddam 'another Adolf Hitler'; and the Foreign Secretary, Douglas Hurd, had agreed '100 per cent.'[2]

So it followed that anything short of resolute military action was, like the Munich Agreement in 1938, the work of the 'spineless appeasers' (said the London *Sun*) and 'the give-sanctions-a-chance-brigade' (*Daily Express*).[3] A Central Intelligence Agency report disclosing that sanctions had already stopped 97 per cent of Iraqi exports was ignored by all but the *Guardian.* The fact that most of the population of Iraq were Kurds and Shi'a, ethnic peoples oppressed by and opposed to Saddam Hussein, was not news. The war was 'inevitable.' 'Iraq,' like 'Russia' during the Cold War, had ceased to be a human community and become a 'guilty party' and a target for extraordinary weapons.[4]

'The world watched in awe,' reported the *Daily Mirror,* 'as Stormin' Norman played his "home video"—revealing how allied planes are using *Star Wars* technology to destroy vital Iraqi targets. Just like Luke Skywalker manoeuvring his fighter into the heart of Darth Vader's space complex, the U.S. pilots zeroed into the very heart of Saddam Hussein's Baghdad.'[5]

The similarity between the 'coverage' in the British tabloids and on television was striking. Only the style was different. The BBC's David Dimbleby spoke urgently about the 'surgical' effect of the new bombs, which were known by the name 'smart,' as if to endow them with human intelligence. As Greg Philo and Greg McLaughlin wrote in their review of the reporting of the war, the assumption that the 'surgical' weapons ensured low civilian casualties freed journalists from their humanitarian 'dilemma.'[6]

'Like two sports commentators, David Dimbleby and the BBC defence correspondent, David Shukman, were almost rapt with enthusiasm,' they wrote. 'They called for freeze-frames and replays and they highlighted "the action" on screen with computer "light-pens." "This is the promised hi-tech war," said Shukman. "Defence contractors for some time have been trying to convince everybody that hi-tech weapons can work . . . Now, by isolating [the target], they are able to destroy [it] . . . without causing casualties among the civilian population around." '[7]

Interviewing the American Ambassador to Britain, David Dimbleby was especially excited. 'Isn't it in fact true,' he said to him, 'that America, by dint of the very accuracy of the weapons we've seen, is the only potential world policeman? You may have to operate under the United Nations, but it's beginning to look as though you're going to have to be in the Middle East just as, in the previous part of this century, we and the French were in the Middle East.'[8]

Quite so.

The first graphic result of the 'surgical precision' was the American bombing of the Al-Amiriya bunker in Baghdad, in which between 300 and 400 women and children died; most of them burned to death. The *Sun* reported this as a fabrication of Iraqi propaganda. 'Saddam Hussein tried to trick the world yesterday,' it said, 'by saying hundreds of women and children died in a bomb attack on an "air-raid shelter." He cunningly arranged TV scenes designed to shock and appal . . . The hidden "civilian" casualties may have been Iraqi military casualties.'[9]

Like most of the *Sun's* reporting of the war, this was false. What was instructive was the speed with which the respectable media promoted the same falsehoods, if less crudely, while at the same time minimizing evidence of the carnage inside the bunker and American culpability. ITN, in announcing that it was censoring its report because the material was 'too distressing,' set the tone.[10]

Six months later, the unedited CNN and WTN 'feeds' of footage of the bunker were obtained by the *Columbia Journalism Review*. They had been censored for transmission in Britain, the United States, Australia and for other Western clients. 'They showed scenes of incredible carnage,' wrote the reporter who viewed the videotape. 'Nearly all the bodies were charred into blackness; in some cases the heat had been so great that entire limbs were burned off. Among the corpses were those of at least six babies and ten children, most of them so severely burned that their gender could not be determined. Rescue workers collapsed in grief, dropping corpses; some rescuers vomited from the stench of the still-smoldering bodies.'[11]

The U.S. military briefers insisted that the bunker was a 'military facility.' People living in the vicinity told researchers it was 'unbelievable' that the Americans did not know the shelter was used mostly by women and children, who came and went twice a day.[12] Abu Kulud, who lost his wife and two daughters, said, 'It was impossible for them not to know there were only civilians in the shelter. Their air [communications] were everywhere.' A woman who lost her mother and two sisters, said, 'How could they not know? They had to know. They had the satellite over our heads twenty-four hours a day, as well as photographs the planes took before they bombed.'[13]

On the day of the attack, the BBC's *Nine O'Clock News* presenter, Peter Sissons, prefaced a report from Baghdad with the American statement that the bunker was a military installation. This exchange followed:

> *Sissons:* A few moments ago, I spoke with [the BBC's] Jeremy Bowen in Baghdad and asked him whether he could be *absolutely sure* that there was no military communications equipment in the shelter, which the allies believe was there.
>
> *Bowen:* Well, Peter, we looked very hard for it . . . I'm pretty confident, as confident as I can be, that I've seen all the main rooms . . .
>
> *Sissons:* Is it conceivable that it could have been in military use and was converted recently to civilian use?
>
> *Bowen:* Well, it would seem a strange sort of thing to . . .
>
> *Sissons:* Let me put it another way, Jeremy. Is it possible to say with *certainty* that it was never a military facility?

Sissons concluded the interview by saying that Bowen was 'subject, of course, to Iraq's reporting restrictions.'[14]

Long after the war was over, a senior American official admitted privately that the bunker bombing had been 'a military mistake.' As this was never broadcast, the 'mistake' was never challenged.[15]

The bunker atrocity was passed over quickly, and the 'coverage' returned to its main theme of a sanitized, scientific war which the Allied military command in Saudi Arabia promoted, thanks to the 'pool' system. The 'pool' is a British invention, used to considerable effect in the Second World War, Korea and the Falklands. The Americans used the Falklands model for their invasions of Grenada (1983) and Panama (1989).

Under the rules, only selected journalists can visit 'the front,' and then under military escort. Their reports are then shared with colleagues remaining behind. Thus the 'news' is the same. Those who attempt to strike out on their own are often blackballed and denied military co-operation, such as transport, which means they see no more of the 'action.' The obedient see what the military want them to see. The control of journalists and the management of news are almost total. That was how it worked in the Gulf.

Press 'conferences' became the arena for dispensing propaganda, such as the entertaining videotapes showing pinpoint bombing. Here claims could be made without journalists being able to authenticate them. The Allies' claim that they were progressively 'knocking out' Scud missile sites in Iraq with 'smart' weapons was dutifully reported. In fact, no Scud sites were destroyed. So enthralled were some journalists with the wondrous performance of the hi-tech weapons—as seen on the military videotape—that few questioned their 'surgical precision' or asked to see the unedited videotape. Unknown to reporters in Saudi Arabia, less than 7 per cent of the weapons used in the Gulf War were 'smart,' as the Pentagon admitted long after the war.[16]

Most were old-fashioned 'dump' bombs, like those dropped by B-52 aircraft, and famously inaccurate. Seventy per cent of the 88,500 tons of bombs dropped on Iraq and Kuwait—the equivalent of more than seven Hiroshimas—missed their targets completely and many fell in populated areas, causing widespread 'collateral damage': the jargon for civilian casualties.[17] This was not reported. 'War is never pleasant,' declared the *Independent on Sunday*. 'There are certain actions that a civilized society can never contemplate. This carpet-bombing is undeniably terrible. But that does not make it wrong.'[18]

Editorial writers are seldom witnesses. In another war, in paddy fields not far from Saigon, I watched three ladders curve in the sky, and as each rung reached the ground there was a plume of fire and a sound which welled and rippled rather than exploded. These were the bombs of three B-52s flying in formation, unseen above the clouds; between them they dropped about seventy tons of explosives in a 'long box' pattern. Everything inside the 'box' was destroyed.

When I reached the nearest village, the street had been replaced by a crater; people a hundred yards from the point of contact left not even their scorched shadows, which the dead had left at Hiroshima. There were pieces of heads and limbs, and the intact bodies of your children who had been thrown into the air by the blast.

And so it was in Iraq. The Clark Commission—chaired by former U.S. Attorney-General Ramsey Clark—heard evidence from Paul Roberts, a freelance journalist who had travelled with Bedouins during the bombing, that he had watched three waves of bombing every night. 'I experienced bombing in Cambodia,' he said, 'but this was nothing like that . . . After twenty minutes of this carpet-bombing there would be a silence and you would hear a screaming of children and people, and then the wounded would be dragged out. I found myself with everyone else trying to treat injuries, but the state of people generally was one of pure shock. They were walking around like zombies . . .'[19] His evidence, like that of many others before the Clark Commission, was never published in the mainstream media.

Perhaps, like the Vietnamese, Iraqi civilians were obliterated in order to save them. Certainly, George Bush, in his victory speech, said the Gulf War had 'freed America from the memory of Vietnam'—though not before the truth began to trickle out. As the ceasefire was signed, a column of Iraqis retreating from Kuwait City along the Basra road towards Iraq were attacked by American carrier-based aircraft. They used a variety of rockets, cluster bombs and Napalm B, the type that sticks to the skin while continuing to burn. Returning pilots bragged to 'pool' reporters on the carriers, describing the event as a 'duck shoot' and a 'turkey shoot.' Other likened it to 'shooting fish in a barrel.' Defence-less people had been incinerated in their vehicles or strafed as they ran for cover.[20]

Television crews travelling with the Allied forces in Kuwait came upon the aftermath by chance. As the first pictures appeared on American television, the White House justi-fied the attack by referring to the dead as 'torturers, looters and rapists.'[21] However, it was obvious that the convoy included not only military lorries, but civilian vehicles: battered Toyota vans, Volkswagens, motorbikes. Their occupants were foreign workers who had been trapped in Kuwait: Palestinians, Bangladeshis, Sudanese, Egyptians and others.

In the British press, the *Observer* published a shocking photograph of a charred corpse still at the wheel of a truck. With the lips burned away, it appeared to be grinning. Most newspapers preferred a front-page photograph of a U.S. Army medic attending a wounded Iraqi soldier. Here was the supreme image of magnanimity and tenderness, a 'lifetime' the *Daily Mirror* called it, and the exact opposite of what had happened.[22]

In a memorable report for BBC radio, Stephen Sackur who, like Jeremy Bowen, distinguished himself against the odds in the Gulf, described the carnage in such a way that he separated, for his listeners, ordinary Iraqis from Saddam Hussein. He converted the ducks, turkeys and fish to human beings. The incinerated figures, he said, were sim-ply people trying to get home; he sounded angry.[23]

Kate Adie, another BBC correspondent, was there. Her television report showed corpses in the desert and consumer goods scattered among the blackened vehicles. If this was 'loot,' it was pathetic: toys, dolls, hair-dryers. She referred to 'the evidence of the horrible confusion.' She interviewed a U.S. Marine lieutenant, who appeared distressed. He said the convoy had had 'no air cover, nothing,' and he added ambiguously, 'It was not very professional at all.' Adie did not ask him what he meant, nor did she attempt to explain *why* the massacre had taken place. But she did say that 'those who fought and died for Iraq here turned out to be from the north of the country, from minority com-munities, persecuted by Saddam Hussein—the Kurds and the Turks.'[24]

This was probably the most revealing news of the war; but without contest or the barest explanation, it was almost meaningless. The massacre on the Basra road was mainly of troops conscripted from people oppressed by Saddam Hussein and who were his bitter opponents—the very people whom George Bush, John Major and General Schwarzkopf had called on to 'take heart' and 'rise up in revolt.' While Saddam's Republican Guard escaped, Iraq's coerced and demoralised army of mostly Kurds and Shi'a was slaughtered.

Basra road was only one of many massacres. The others were not reported. Throughout the short 'war,' the slaughter was carried out beyond the scrutiny of the 'pool.' Unknown to journalists, in the last two days before the ceasefire American armoured bulldozers were ruthlessly deployed, mostly at night, burying Iraqis alive in their trenches, including the wounded. Six months later, New York *Newsday* disclosed that three brigades of the 1st Mechanised Infantry Division—'the Big Red One'—'used snow plows mounted on tanks and combat earth movers to bury thousands of Iraqi soldiers—some still alive—in more than 70 miles of trenches.' A brigade commander said, 'For all I know, we could have killed thousands.'[25] The only images of this to be shown on television were used as a backdrop to a discussion about the reporting of the war on a late-night BBC arts programme.[26]

'Not a single armoured vehicle of the U.S. [or its allies] was hit by enemy fire. Not one,' wrote Ramsey Clark.[27] American pilots became so bored with the task of killing defenceless Iraqis that they began joking about 'tank plinking,' as if the armoured vehicles were tin cans. The operations officer for 'Desert Storm,' General Richard Neal, admitted that most Iraqi vehicles were destroyed from the rear.[28]

General Schwarzkopf's policy was that Iraqi dead were not to be counted.[29] One of his senior officers boasted, 'This is the first war in modern times where every screwdriver, every nail is accounted for.' As for human beings, he added, 'I don't think anybody is going to be able to come up with an accurate count for the Iraqi dead.'[30] In fact, Schwarzkopf did provide figures to Congress, indicating that at least 100,000 Iraqi soldiers had been killed. He offered no estimate of civilian deaths.[31]

The war was not a war at all. It was an old fashioned colonial massacre. Kate Adie, like most of her colleagues, had reported the news, but not the story. Long after it was all over, the BBC's foreign editor, John Simpson, commented in a documentary, 'As for the human casualties, tens of thousands of them, or the brutal effect the war had on millions of others . . . we didn't see much of that.'[32]

In the post-war period some journalists and their editors gave the impression that they knew they had been misled. There was something of an air of atonement. Editorial writers and studio presenters became exercised about 'safe havens' for the Kurds in the north of Iraq, policed by the same military force that had slaughtered thousands of Kurds on the Basra road and elsewhere. Star Wars over, the story was suddenly humanitarian. And close to home. Speaking as one, the British media accused the government of 'covering up the truth' about the deaths of nine British servicemen in the Gulf, all of them killed by American 'friendly fire.' Having been led by the nose in the cover-up of the slaughter of 'tens of thousands' of Iraqis, their indignation gave no hint of irony.

In the United States, there was some attempt to root out the truth. However, this was confined to a few newspapers, such as New York *Newsday* and its outstanding reporter Knute Royce, and *samizdat* publications like *Z* magazine and *Covert Action Quarterly*.

The famous TV anchorman, Dan Rather, told Americans, 'There's one thing we can all agree on. It's the heroism of the 148 Americans who gave their lives so that freedom could live.' In fact, a quarter of them had been killed, like their British comrades, by other Americans. Moreover, official citations describing how Americans had died heroically in hand-to-hand combat with Iraqis were fake.[33] American forces had bombed five Iraqi military hospitals; and American newscasters seldom referred to the Iraqi dead, let alone how they had died. These were a shocking omissions, as the cost of the human tragedy in Iraq was now available.[34]

Shortly before Christmas 1991, the Medical Educational Trust in London published a comprehensive study of casualties. Up to a quarter of a million men, women and children were killed or died as a direct result of the American-led attack on Iraq.[35] This confirmed American and French intelligence estimates of 'in excess of 200,000 civilian deaths.'[36]

In evidence submitted to the Parliamentary Foreign Affairs Select Committee, the major international relief agencies reported that 1.8 million people had been made homeless, and Iraq's electricity, water, sewage, communications, health, agriculture and industrial infrastructure had been 'substantially destroyed,' producing 'conditions for famine and epidemics.'[37]

The Clark Commission concluded that the nature of the American-led attacks violated the Geneva Convention of 1949, which expressly prohibits attacks on 'objects indispensable to the survival of the civilian population, such as foodstuffs, agricultural areas . . . crops, livestock, drinking water installations and supplies and irrigation works,' as well as 'dams, dykes and electrical generating stations,' without which there will be 'consequent severe losses among the civilian population.'[38]

In 1995, the United Nations Food and Agriculture Organisation (FAO) reported that the military devastation of Iraq, combined with the effect of sanctions imposed by the Security Council—in reality, by the American and British governments—had been responsible for the deaths of more than 560,000 children in Iraq.[39] The World Health Organisation confirmed this figure.[40] Jean Lennock, a field worker, reported this as the equivalent of the unnecessary death of a child every six minutes. 'At Ibn-al-Baladi hospital in Baghdad,' she wrote, 'I witnessed the death of eight-month-old Ali Hassan from diarrhoea. His life could have been saved with simple antibiotics. I also witnessed the grief of his mother. Like many of us, she could not understand why her child had been punished for the actions of the Iraqi government.'[41]

In a letter to the Security Council, Ramsey Clark, who has carried out investigations in Iraq since 1991, wrote that most of the deaths 'are from the effects of malnutrition including marasmus and kwashiorkor, wasting or emaciation which has reached twelve per cent of all children, stunted growth which affects twenty-eight per cent, diarrhoea, dehydration from bad water or food, which is ordinarily easily controlled and cured, common communicable diseases preventable by vaccinations, and epidemics from deteriorating sanitary conditions. There are no deaths crueller than these. They are suffering slowly, helplessly, without simple remedial medication, without simple sedation to relieve pain, without mercy.'[42]

In October 1996, UNICEF, the children's relief organisation, launched an appeal for help from governments, saying that 'over 50 per cent of women and children are receiving less than half their calorific needs.' In other words, they were close to starvation. Only the Government of the Netherlands made a contribution.[43]

In the meantime, the UN has sought to negotiate an 'oil-for-food' arrangement, by which Iraq would be allowed to sell $1 billion's worth of oil every three months on the world market. Half of this would go in war reparations to Kuwait and be allocated to the Kurds in the 'safe havens'; the other half would buy food and medicines and basic spare parts for water and sewage treatment facilities.

The American representatives on the UN Sanctions Committee have used every opportunity to obstruct the plan, which now appears frozen, in spite of having the approval of the Secretary-General.[44] When the U.S. Ambassador to the United Nations, Madeleine Albright, later to be appointed Secretary of State, was asked whether the lives of half a million Iraqi children were too high a price to pay, she replied, 'I think this is a very hard choice, but the price, we think, is worth it.'[45]

Ramsey Clark replied, 'The United States has forced this decision on the Security Council. Three of the five permanent members—China, France and the Russian Federation—have sought to modify the sanctions. [The US] blames Saddam Hussein and Iraq for the effects [on the Iraqi people], most recently arguing that if Saddam stopped spending billions on his military machine and palaces for the elite, he could afford to feed his people. But only a fool would offer or believe such propaganda. If Iraq is spending billions on the military, then the sanctions are obviously not working. Malnutrition didn't exist in Iraq before the sanctions. If Saddam Hussein is building palaces, he intends to stay. Meanwhile, an entire nation is suffering. Hundreds are dying daily and millions are threatened in Iraq, because of US-compelled impoverishment.'[46]

To report the real reasons why children are dying in Iraq, even to recognize the extent of their suffering, is to bracket Western governments with dictatorships and totalitarian regimes. Thus the victims become unmentionable. They become, wrote the British historian Mark Curtis, 'unpeople: human beings who impede the pursuit of high policy and whose rights, often lives, therefore become irrelevant.'[47] As Unpeople, they are not news, and their plight, as Kate Adie said of the slaughter on the Basra road, is merely 'evidence of the horrific confusion.'

There were a number of reasons for the American-led attack on Iraq, and none of them had much to do with concern for the freedom-loving tyranny in Kuwait. Saddam Hussein said he invaded Kuwait because the Kuwaiti regime was moving in on disputed oil fields on the Iraq–Kuwait border. This was probably correct, as the U.S. Chairman of the Joint Chiefs of Staff, Colin Powell, indicated when he argued against military intervention, predicting that Saddam would withdraw and put 'his puppet in [and] everyone in the Arab world will be happy.'[48] The documented fact that Saddam Hussein tried to extricate himself from Kuwait on a number of occasions was ignored by most of the American and British media, which preferred the countdown to war.[49]

As in the American invasion of Panama in 1989, Bush wanted to demonstrate the United States' new single-superpower status, and Iraq was the perfect venue. Here was an opportunity to show off American military power, and thereby conceal the decline of its economic power, as well as to test a range of new weapons. For example, munitions made from Depleted Uranium (DU) were used for the first time in Iraq. DU has a radioactive half-life of 125,000 years, and like the effects of 'Agent Orange' in Vietnam, its effect on the population and on future generations will be insidious and devastating.

There was no burning desire to get rid of Saddam Hussein. He had been the West's man, whom Reagan and Thatcher had armed and backed against the mullahs in Iran; and the last thing the West wanted was an Iraq run by socialists and democrats. For this reason, as the 1991 slaughter got under way, the British Government imprisoned as many Iraqi opposition leaders as it could round up. In 1996, the *New York Times* reported that the administration longed for the good old days when Saddam's 'iron fist held Iraq together, much to the satisfaction of the American allies, Turkey and Saudi Arabia.'[50]

The Americans also wanted to protect Saudi oil and the faltering Saudi economy from the competition of cheaper Iraqi oil. That remains Washington's real reason for opposing the lifting of sanctions. 'If Iraq were allowed to resume oil exports,' wrote Phyllis Bennis, one of the most astute American commentators, 'analysts expect it would soon be producing three million barrels a day and within a decade, perhaps as many as six million. Oil prices would soon drop . . . And Washington is determined to defend the kingdom's economy, largely to safeguard the West's unfettered access to the Saudis' 25 per cent of known oil reserves.'[51]

An important factor in this is the arms trade. In 1993, almost two-thirds of all American arms export agreements with developing countries were with Saudi Arabia, whose dictatorship is every bit as odious as the one in Baghdad.[52] Since 1990 the Saudis have contracted more than thirty billion dollars' worth of American tanks, missiles and fighter aircraft. According to the authors, Leslie and Andrew Cockburn, 'Every day, the Pentagon . . . disburses an average of 10 million dollars—some days as much as 50 million—to contractors at work on the Saudi shopping list.' As an insight into the US-sponsored 'peace process' in the Middle East, they wrote that a Pentagon officer had told them, 'If the Saudis had cancelled their F-15 [fighter aircraft] program [as a result of the fall in oil prices], Israel probably would not have bought any. Basically, that's the only thing keeping the F-15 line open.'[53]

In 1996, President Clinton attacked Iraq with Tomahawk missiles—ostensibly to 'defend' Kurds in the north of the country, but the presidential election campaign was well under way. Once again military technology dominated the news, celebrated with Top Gun Pilots and missiles sleek against the dawn light. American and British television used Pentagon footage. The Tomahawks and B-52s were said to have struck only 'radar sites' and 'strategic control centres.' Anchormen spoke inexplicably about 'the balance of power' and 'urgent Western diplomacy.'[54] Addressing the American people, Clinton invoked the paramount rule of the Old West: 'When you abuse your own people . . . you must pay a price.'[55]

It was Unpeople who paid the price, and we saw virtually nothing of them. A shot of a demolished building in a crowded part of Baghdad was, explained Trevor McDonald, the anchorman of Britain's Independent Television News, 'allegedly hit' by a Tomahawk. 'And finally,' said McDonald with that familiar transatlantic smile that says the news must now move on to the inane, 'Lottery winners say their millions have given them security for life. Good night.'[56] There was clearly no time for Iraq's dying children.

When, in 1998, Clinton attacked Sudan and Afghanistan with his missiles, demolishing a pharmaceutical factory and killing and maiming more Unpeople, there was fleeting media interest mainly in whether he had ordered the attacks to distract attention from his troubles with Monica Lewinsky, whose starring role in the news was quickly restored.

'Have we grown more wary of instant response to disaster, more indifferent to the stream of seemingly baffling conflicts which flit past on the screen?' asked the BBC's Kate Adie in a reflective article. 'Do the pictures of the displaced, the homeless and injured mean less when they are so regularly available? Have we, in short, begun to care less . . . ?'

She did not explain the 'we.' 'What has not changed,' she wrote, 'is the need to choose news priorities, to judge the importance and relevance of a story against all else that is happening in the world. And the need endlessly to debate whether some stories should be covered for a moral or humanitarian reason, *even though the majority of the audience expresses little desire to view them*' (my italics).[57]

She offered no evidence to support this last assertion. On the contrary, the generosity of those who can least afford to give is demonstrable, vivid and unending, as I know from personal experience. It is compassion, as well as anger, that gives millions of people the energy and tenacity to lobby governments for an end to state crimes committed in their name in East Timor, Burma, Turkey, Tibet, Iraq, to name but a few. Far from not wanting to know, the 'majority of the audience' consistently make clear, as the relevant surveys show, that they want *more* current affairs and documentaries which attempt to make sense of the news and which explain the 'why' of human events.[58]

During the Reagan and Thatcher years, broadcasters and journalists invented the public affliction called 'compassion fatigue,' which represented, not the public's sentiments, but conformism long served by journalists. Following the Gulf War, researchers scrutinised more than 8,000 images of the British television coverage and found that only one per cent dealt with human suffering.

There is a self-fulfilling element in this age of saturation media. In a related survey, a sample group of children were asked, 'What sticks in your mind about the television coverage of the war?' Most referred to the hi-tech weapons and equipment; some mentioned specifically the Pentagon war 'videogames.' None mentioned people.[59]

28

THE SECRET BEHIND THE SANCTIONS

HOW THE U.S. INTENTIONALLY DESTROYED IRAQ'S WATER SUPPLY

Thomas J. Nagy

Over the last two years, I've discovered documents of the Defense Intelligence Agency proving beyond a doubt that, contrary to the Geneva Convention, the U.S. government intentionally used sanctions against Iraq to degrade the country's water supply after the Gulf War. The United States knew the cost that civilian Iraqis, mostly children, would pay, and it went ahead anyway.

The primary document, "Iraq Water Treatment Vulnerabilities," is dated January 22, 1991. It spells out how sanctions will prevent Iraq from supplying clean water to its citizens.

"Iraq depends on importing specialized equipment and some chemicals to purify its water supply, most of which is heavily mineralized and frequently brackish to saline," the document states. "With no domestic sources of both water treatment replacement parts and some essential chemicals, Iraq will continue attempts to circumvent United Nations Sanctions to import these vital commodities. Failing to secure supplies will result in a shortage of pure drinking water for much of the population. This could lead to increased incidences, if not epidemics, of disease."

The document goes into great technical detail about the sources and quality of Iraq's water supply. The quality of untreated water "generally is poor," and drinking such water "could result in diarrhea," the document says. It notes that Iraq's rivers "contain biological materials, pollutants, and are laden with bacteria. Unless the water is purified with chlorine, epidemics of such diseases as cholera, hepatitis, and typhoid could occur."

The document notes that the importation of chlorine "has been embargoed" by sanctions. "Recent reports indicate the chlorine supply is critically low."

Food and medicine will also be affected, the document states. "Food processing, electronic, and, particularly, pharmaceutical plants require extremely pure water that is free from biological contaminants," it says.

The document addresses possible Iraqi countermeasures to obtain drinkable water despite sanctions.

"Iraq conceivably could truck water from the mountain reservoirs to urban areas. But the capability to gain significant quantities is extremely limited," the document states. "The amount of pipe on hand and the lack of pumping stations would limit laying pipelines to these reservoirs. Moreover, without chlorine purification, the water still would contain biological pollutants. Some affluent Iraqis could obtain their own minimally adequate supply of good quality water for Northern Iraqi sources. If boiled, the water could be safely consumed. Poorer Iraqis and industries requiring large quantities of pure water would not be able to meet their needs."

The document also discounted the possibility of Iraqis using rainwater. "Precipitation occurs in Iraq during the winter and spring, but it falls primarily in the northern mountains," it says. "Sporadic rains, sometimes heavy, fall over the lower plains. But Iraq could not rely on rain to provide adequate pure water."

As an alternative, "Iraq could try convincing the United Nations or individual countries to exempt water treatment supplies from sanctions for humanitarian reasons," the document says. "It probably also is attempting to purchase supplies by using some sympathetic countries as fronts. If such attempts fail, Iraqi alternatives are not adequate for their national requirements."

In cold language, the document spells out what is in store: "Iraq will suffer increasing shortages of purified water because of the lack of required chemicals and desalination membranes. Incidences of disease, including possible epidemics, will become probable unless the population were careful to boil water."

The document gives a timetable for the destruction of Iraq's water supplies. "Iraq's overall water treatment capability will suffer a slow decline, rather than a precipitous halt," it says. "Although Iraq is already experiencing a loss of water treatment capability, it probably will take at least six months (to June 1991) before the system is fully degraded."

This document, which was partially declassified but unpublicized in 1995, can be found on the Pentagon's web site at www.gulflink.osd.mil. (I disclosed this document last fall. But the news media showed little interest in it. The only reporters I know of who wrote lengthy stories on it were Felicity Arbuthnot in the *Sunday Herald* of Scotland, who broke the story, and Charlie Reese of the *Orlando Sentinel,* who did a follow-up.)

Recently, I have come across other DIA documents that confirm the Pentagon's monitoring of the degradation of Iraq's water supply. These documents have not been publicized until now.

The first one in this batch is called "Disease Information," and is also dated January 22, 1991. At the top it says, "Subject: Effects of Bombing on Disease Occurrence in Baghdad." The analysis is blunt: "Increased incidence of diseases will be attributable to degradation of normal preventive medicine, waste disposal, water purification/distribution, electricity, and decreased ability to control disease outbreaks. Any urban area in Iraq that has received infrastructure damage will have similar problems."

The document proceeds to itemize the likely outbreaks. It mentions "acute diarrhea" brought on by bacteria such as E. coli, shigella, and salmonella, or by protozoa such as giardia, which will affect "particularly children," or by rotavirus, which will also affect "particularly children," a phrase it puts in parentheses. And it cites the possibilities of typhoid and cholera outbreaks.

The document warns that the Iraqi government may "blame the United States for public health problems created by the military conflict."

The second DIA document, "Disease Outbreaks in Iraq," is dated February 21, 1990, but the year is clearly a typo and should be 1991. It states: "Conditions are favorable for communicable disease outbreaks, particularly in major urban areas affected by coalition bombing." It adds: "Infectious disease prevalence in major Iraqi urban areas targeted by coalition bombing (Baghdad, Basrah) undoubtedly has increased since the beginning of Desert Storm. . . . Current public health problems are attributable to the reduction of normal preventive medicine, waste disposal, water purification and distribution, electricity, and the decreased ability to control disease outbreaks."

This document lists the "most likely diseases during next sixty-ninety days (descending order): diarrheal diseases (particularly children); acute respiratory illnesses (colds and influenza); typhoid; hepatitis A (particularly children); measles, diphtheria, and pertussis (particularly children); meningitis, including meningococcal (particularly children); cholera (possible, but less likely)."

Like the previous document, this one warns that the Iraqi government might "propagandize increases of endemic diseases."

The third document in this series, "Medical Problems in Iraq," is dated March 15, 1991. It says: "Communicable diseases in Baghdad are more widespread than usually observed during this time of the year and are linked to the poor sanitary conditions (contaminated water supplies and improper sewage disposal) resulting from the war. According to a United Nations Children's Fund (UNICEF)/World Health Organization report, the quantity of potable water is less than 5 percent of the original supply, there are no operational water and sewage treatment plants, and the reported incidence of diarrhea is four times above normal levels. Additionally, respiratory infections are on the rise. Children particularly have been affected by these diseases."

Perhaps to put a gloss on things, the document states, "There are indications that the situation is improving and that the population is coping with the degraded conditions." But it adds: "Conditions in Baghdad remain favorable for communicable disease outbreaks."

The fourth document, "Status of Disease at Refugee Camps," is dated May 1991. The summary says, "Cholera and measles have emerged at refugee camps. Further infectious diseases will spread due to inadequate water treatment and poor sanitation."

The reason for this outbreak is clearly stated again. "The main causes of infectious diseases, particularly diarrhea, dysentery, and upper respiratory problems, are poor sanitation and unclean water. These diseases primarily afflict the old and young children."

The fifth document, "Health Conditions in Iraq, June 1991," is still heavily censored. All I can make out is that the DIA sent a source "to assess health conditions and determine the most critical medical needs of Iraq. Source observed that Iraqi medical system was in considerable disarray, medical facilities had been extensively looted, and almost all medicines were in critically short supply."

In one refugee camp, the document says, "at least 80 percent of the population" has diarrhea. At this same camp, named Cukurca, "cholera, hepatitis type B, and measles have broken out."

The protein deficiency disease kwashiorkor was observed in Iraq "for the first time," the document adds. "Gastroenteritis was killing children. . . . In the south, 80 percent of the deaths were children (with the exception of Al Amarah, where 60 percent of deaths were children)."

The final document is "Iraq: Assessment of Current Health Threats and Capabilities," and it is dated November 15, 1991. This one has a distinct damage-control feel to it. Here is how it begins: "Restoration of Iraq's public health services and shortages of major medical materiel remain dominant international concerns. Both issues apparently are being exploited by Saddam Hussein in an effort to keep public opinion firmly against the U.S. and its Coalition allies and to direct blame away from the Iraqi government."

It minimizes the extent of the damage. "Although current countrywide infectious disease incidence in Iraq is higher than it was before the Gulf War, it is not at the catastrophic levels that some groups predicted. The Iraqi regime will continue to exploit disease incidence data for its own political purposes."

And it places the blame squarely on Saddam Hussein. "Iraq's medical supply shortages are the result of central government's stockpiling, selective distribution, and exploitation of domestic and international relief medical resources." It adds: "Resumption of public health programs . . . depends completely on the Iraqi government."

As these documents illustrate, the United States knew sanctions had the capacity to devastate the water treatment system of Iraq. It knew what the consequences would be: increased outbreaks of disease and high rates of child mortality. And it was more concerned about the public relations nightmare for Washington than the actual nightmare that the sanctions created for innocent Iraqis.

The Geneva Convention is absolutely clear. In a 1979 protocol relating to the "protection of victims of international armed conflicts," Article 54, it states: "It is prohibited to attack, destroy, remove, or render useless objects indispensable to the survival of the civilian population, such as foodstuffs, crops, livestock, drinking water installations and supplies, and irrigation works, for the specific purpose of denying them for their sustenance value to the civilian population or to the adverse Party, whatever the motive, whether in order to starve out civilians, to cause them to move away, or for any other motive."

But that is precisely what the U.S. government did, with malice aforethought. It "destroyed, removed, or rendered useless" Iraq's "drinking water installations and supplies." The sanctions, imposed for a decade largely at the insistence of the United States, constitute a violation of the Geneva Convention. They amount to a systematic effort to, in the DIA's own words, "fully degrade" Iraq's water sources.

At a House hearing on June 7, Representative Cynthia McKinney, Democrat of Georgia, referred to the document "Iraq Water Treatment Vulnerabilities" and said: "Attacking the Iraqi public drinking water supply flagrantly targets civilians and is a violation of the Geneva Convention and of the fundamental laws of civilized nations."

Over the last decade, Washington extended the toll by continuing to withhold approval for Iraq to import the few chemicals and items of equipment it needed in order to clean up its water supply.

Last summer, Representative Tony Hall, Democrat of Ohio, wrote to then-Secretary of State Madeleine Albright "about the profound effects of the increasing deterioration of Iraq's water supply and sanitation systems on its children's health." Hall wrote, "The prime killer of children under five years of age—diarrheal diseases—has reached epidemic proportions, and they now strike four times more often than they did in 1990. . . . Holds on contracts for the water and sanitation sector are a prime reason for the increases in sickness and death. Of the eighteen contracts, all but one hold was placed by the U.S. government. The contracts are for purification chemicals, chlorinators, chemical dosing pumps, water tankers, and other equipment. . . . I urge you to weigh your decision against the disease and death that are the unavoidable result of not having safe drinking water and minimum levels of sanitation."

For more than ten years, the United States has deliberately pursued a policy of destroying the water treatment system of Iraq, knowing full well the cost in Iraqi lives. The United Nations has estimated that more than 500,000 Iraqi children have died as a result of sanctions, and that 5,000 Iraqi children continue to die every month for this reason.

No one can say that the United States didn't know what it was doing.

29

"BLACK HAWK DOWN"

HOLLYWOOD DRAGS BLOODY CORPSE OF TRUTH ACROSS MOVIE SCREENS

Larry Chin

January 3, 2002—True to its post-9/11 government-sanctioned role as US war propaganda headquarters, Hollywood has released "Black Hawk Down," a fictionalized account of the tragic 1993 US raid in Somalia. The Pentagon assisted with the production, pleased for an opportunity to "set the record straight." The film is a lie that compounds the original lie that was the operation itself.

SOMALIA: THE FACTS

According to the myth, the Somalia operation of 1993 was a humanitarian mission, and a shining example of New World Order morality and altruism. In fact, US and UN troops waged an undeclared war against an Islamic African populace that was hostile to foreign interests.

Also contrary to the legend, the 1993 Somalia raid was not a "Clinton foreign policy bungle." In fact, the incoming Clinton administration inherited an operation that was already in full swing—planned and begun by outgoing President George Herbert Walker Bush, spearheaded by deputy national security adviser Jonathan Howe (who remained in charge of the UN operation after Clinton took office), and approved by Colin Powell, then head of the Joint Chiefs.

The operation had nothing to do with humanitarianism or Africa-love on the part of Bush or Clinton. Several US oil companies, including Conoco, Amoco, Chevron and Phillips were positioned to exploit Somalia's rich oil reserves. The companies had secured billion-dollar concessions to explore and drill large portions of the Somali countryside during the reign of pro–US President Mohamed Siad Barre. (In fact, Conoco's Mogadishu office housed the US embassy and military headquarters.) A "secure" Somalia also provided the West with strategic location on the coast of Arabian Sea.

UN military became necessary when Barre was overthrown by warlord Mohammed Farrah Aidid, suddenly rendering Somalia inhospitable to US corporate interests.

Although the pretext for the mission was to safeguard food shipments, and stop the "evil Aidid" from stealing the food, the true UN goal was to remove Aidid from the political equation, and form a pro-Western coalition government out of the nation's warring clans. The US operation was met with "surprisingly fierce resistance"—surprising to US officials who underestimated Somalian resolve, and even more surprising to US troops who were victims and pawns of UN policy makers.

The highly documented series by Mark Bowden of the Philadelphia Inquirer on which the film is based, focused on the participants, and the "untenable" situation in which troops were placed. But even Bowden's gung-ho account makes no bones about provocative American attacks that ultimately led to the decisive defeat in Mogadishu.

Bowden writes: "Task Force Ranger was not in Mogadishu to feed the hungry. Over six weeks, from late August to Oct. 3, it conducted six missions, raiding locations where either Aidid or his lieutenants were believed to be meeting. The mission that resulted in the Battle of Mogadishu came less than three months after a surprise missile attack by U.S. helicopters (acting on behalf of the UN) on a meeting of Aidid clansmen. Prompted by a Somalian ambush on June 5 that killed more than 20 Pakistani soldiers, the missile attack killed 50 to 70 clan elders and intellectuals, many of them moderates seeking to reach a peaceful settlement with the United Nations. After that July 12 helicopter attack, Aidid's clan was officially at war with America—a fact many Americans never realized."

Hundreds, perhaps thousands, of Somalis were killed in the course of US incursions that took place over three months. In his book *The New Military Humanism,* Noam Chomsky cites other under-reported facts. "In October 1993, criminal incompetence by the US military led to the slaughter of 1,000 Somalis by American firepower." Chomsky writes, "The official estimate was 6–10,000 Somali casualties in the summer of 1993 alone, two-thirds women and children. Marine Lt. Gen Anthony Zinni, who commanded the operation, informed the press that 'I'm not counting bodies . . . I'm not interested.' Specific war crimes of US forces included direct military attacks on a hospital and on civilian gatherings. Other Western armies were implicated in serious crimes as well. Some of these were revealed at an official Canadian inquiry, not duplicated by the US or other governments."

Bowden's more forgiving account does not contradict Chomsky's in this regard:

"Official U.S. estimates of Somalian casualties at the time numbered 350 dead and 500 injured." Somalian clan leaders made claims of more than 1,000 deaths. The United Nations placed the number of dead at "between 300 to 500." Doctors and intellectuals in Mogadishu not aligned with the feuding clans say that 500 dead is probably accurate.

The attack on Mogadishu was particularly vicious. Quoting Bowden: "The Task Force Ranger commander, Maj. Gen William F. Garrison, testifying before the Senate, said that if his men had put any more ammunition into the city 'we would have sunk it.' Most soldiers interviewed said that through most of the fight they fired on crowds and eventually at anyone and anything they saw."

After 18 US Special Forces soldiers were killed in the final Mogadishu firefight, which included the downing of a US helicopter, television screens filled with the scene of a dead US soldier being dragged through the streets by jubilant Somalis. Clinton immediately called off the operation. US forces left Somalia in disgrace. Some 19,000 UN troops remained for a short period, but eventually left in futility.

The Somalia defeat elicited howls of protest and rage from the military brass, congressional hawks, and right-wing provocateurs itching for an excuse to declare political war on the "liberal" Clinton administration. The "Somalia syndrome" would dog Clinton throughout his presidency, and mar every military mission during his tenure.

Today, as right-wing extremist George W. Bush occupies the White House, surrounded by his father's operatives and many of the architects of the original raid, military fanaticism is all the rage. A global war "without end" has just begun. What a perfect moment to "clean up" the past.

HOLLYWOOD TO THE RESCUE

In promoting the film, producer Jerry Bruckheimer (who rewrote another humiliating episode of US military history with "Pearl Harbor") is seeking to convince Americans that the Somalia operation was "not America's darkest hour, but America's brightest hour"; that a bungled imperialist intervention was a noble incident of grand moral magnificence.

CNN film reviewer Paul Tatara describes "Black Hawk Down" as "pound for pound, one of the most violent films ever released by a major studio," from "two of the most pandering, tactless filmmakers in Hollywood history (Jerry Bruckheimer and Ridley Scott)" who are attempting to "teach us about honor among soldiers."

More important are the film's true subtexts, and the likely emotional reaction of viewers.

What viewers see is "brave and innocent young American boys" getting shot at and killed for "no reason" by "crazy black Islamists" that the Americans are "just trying to help." (Subtext one: America is good, and it is impossible to understand why "they hate us." Subtext two: "Those damned ungrateful foreigners." Subtext three: "Those damned blacks." Subtext four: "Kill Arabs.")

What viewers will remember is a line spoken by one of the "brave soldiers" about how, in the heat of combat, "politics goes out the window." (Subtext one: there is no need for thought; shoot first, talk later. Subtext two: it is right to abandon one's sanity, morality and ethics when faced with chaos. Subtext three: when the Twin Towers went down on 9/11, America was right in embracing radical militarism and extreme violence, throwing all else "out the window.")

In the currently lethal political climate, in which testosterone rage, mob mentality, and love of war pass for normal behavior (while reason, critical thinking, and tolerance are considered treasonous), "Black Hawk Down" will appeal to the most violent elements of American society. Many who have seen the film report leaving the theater feeling angry, itching to "kick some ass." In short, the film is dangerous. And those who "love" it are dangerous.

Considering the fact that Somalia is one of the targets in the next phase of the Bush administration's "war on terrorism," the timing of the film is no coincidence.

As Herbert London of the Hudson Institute said of "Black Hawk Down," "I would never deny the importance of heroism in battle, but just as we should recognize and honor heroes, we should also respect the truthfulness of the events surrounding their heroic acts. In the case of 'Black Hawk Down,' we get a lot of the former and almost nothing of the latter."

Part V

ANTI-RACISM

Running parallel to the history of racial oppression is the history of anti-racist activism. The period of slavery witnessed slave revolts, the creation of independent maroon societies, the abolitionist movement, and the underground railroad. The post-Civil War period of Jim Crow segregation and Klan terror saw the emergence of the anti-lynching campaign, the formation of biracial unions and strikes among sharecroppers, miners, steelworkers, and dockworkers, armed responses to the Klan, and the Civil Rights movement. In the 1960s, racism was challenged first by the Black Power movement, which itself influenced the subsequent development of movements for Brown Power, Yellow Power, Student Power, Women's Liberation, and anti-Vietnam War efforts (including GI Power).

Each of these movements contained divisions into liberal (nationalist) and revolutionary (socialist) factions. The nationalists espoused identity politics viewing racism as a phenomenon *sui generis* (existing of itself) unconnected to the capitalist social order. With this view, it was the task of each oppressed group *as a racial group* to organize itself for more power within the existing society. The question of class was not a salient issue. The revolutionaries tied racism to capitalism and generally advocated a postcapitalist (socialist) social order. Between these two extremes there was some confusion and overlap as nationalists appropriated some revolutionary rhetoric to hide their opportunism and appear more radical than they actually were while some revolutionaries lacked faith in the ability of workers to transcend identity politics. My general impression of the history of anti-racism from the 1960s onward is that the stick of repression was used more frequently against the revolutionary groups while the carrot of co-optation was extended more often to the nationalist groups. But this is only an impression which needs further investigation.

The first reading in this section is by Noel Ignatiev and John Garvey who recently edited a book entitled *Race Traitor*. In this volume they raise questions about the role of white racial identity as a critical factor in perpetuating the system of race-based power, privileges, and preferences. This position leads them to call for the abolition of the racial club called white. How could that happen and what would be its effects? The next article is a long excerpt from Aldon Morris' essay, "Centuries of Black Protest: Its Significance for America and the World," which focuses on the widespread beneficial effects of African-American movements against racism. The study of Black Protest movements has served as both an inspiration and a practical guide for people seeking justice the world over. In "The Rise of the Chicano Student Movement and Chicano Power," Carlos Muñoz, Jr. examines the role of Chicano university students in attacking Anglo hegemony in the curriculum, debating different definitions of Chicano identity and different analyses of the nature of the oppression of Chicanos, and working to increase Chicano admissions and support services at the university. The next reading consists of two chapters from Christian Smith's book, *Resisting Reagan: The U.S. Central America Peace Movement*. These chapters look at the actions of the movement against U.S. policies in Central America and toward Central American refugees and evaluate the movement's achievements. Although described as a "peace movement," this was a widespread anti-racist effort organized by many churches to oppose the I.N.S. persecution of Latino refugees in the U.S. and the killing of Latino peasants abroad. The next reading is a study of thirty years of Asian-American activism. In "The 'Four Prisons' and the Movements of Liberation," Glenn Omatsu traces the development of Asian-American activism against exploitation, the emergence of neo-conservative forces and their class basis in the 1980s, and the growth of new grass-roots organizations in the 1990s. It is a detailed, thought-provoking essay which should be seriously studied.

The next reading deals with the issue of liberal versus revolutionary approaches by looking at the Israel–Palestine conflict from the perspective of class analysis. In a brief essay, "What's 'Left' in the Israeli–Palestinian conflict?", Dick Platkin and Chuck O'Connell describe and analyze some movements regarded as "progressive" in the regional conflict and point out some of the problems remaining when anti-racist movements limit themselves to human rights or national liberation without facing questions of capitalism and imperialism.

The final selection is Edna Bonacich's summary of the problems of racism and capitalism under the heading, "Thoughts on Urban Unrest." She argues that only revolutionary change can possibly eliminate racism from our world.

30

ABOLISH THE WHITE RACE BY ANY MEANS NECESSARY

Noel Ignatiev and Andrew Garvey

The white race is a historically constructed social formation—historically constructed because (like royalty) it is a product of some people's responses to historical circumstances; a social formation because it is a fact of society corresponding to no classification recognized by natural science.

The white race cuts across ethnic and class lines. It is not coextensive with that portion of the population of European descent, since many of those classified as "colored" can trace some of their ancestry to Europe, while African, Asian, or American Indian blood flows through the veins of many considered white. Nor does membership in the white race imply wealth, since there are plenty of poor whites, as well as some people of wealth and comfort who are not white.

The white race consists of those who partake of the privileges of the white skin in this society. Its most wretched members share a status higher, in certain respects, than that of the most exalted persons excluded from it, in return for which they give their support to the system that degrades them.

The key to solving the social problems of our age is to abolish the white race. Until that task is accomplished, even partial reform will prove elusive, because white influence permeates every issue in U.S. society, whether domestic or foreign.

Advocating the abolition of the white race is distinct from what is called "anti-racism." The term "racism" has come to be applied to a variety of attitudes, some of which are mutually incompatible, and has been devalued to mean little more than a tendency to dislike some people for the color of their skin. Moreover, anti-racism admits the natural existence of "races" even while opposing social distinctions among them. The abolitionists maintain, on the contrary, that people were not favored socially because they were white; rather they were defined as "white" because they were favored. Race itself is a product of social discrimination; so long as the white race exists, all movements against racism are doomed to fail.

The existence of the white race depends on the willingness of those assigned to it to place their racial interests above class, gender, or any other interests they hold. The defection of enough of its members to make it unreliable as a determinant of behavior will set off tremors that will lead to its collapse.

Race Traitor aims to serve as an intellectual center for those seeking to abolish the white race. It will encourage dissent from the conformity that maintains it and popularize examples of defection from its ranks, analyze the forces that hold it together and those that promise to tear it apart. Part of its task will be to promote debate among abolitionists. When possible, it will support practical measures, guided by the principle, *treason to whiteness is loyalty to humanity.*

DISSOLVE THE CLUB

The white race is a club that enrolls certain people at birth, without their consent, and brings them up according to its rules. For the most part the members go through life accepting the benefits of membership, without thinking about the costs. When individuals question the rules, the officers are quick to remind them of all they owe to the club, and warn them of the dangers they will face if they leave it.

Race Traitor aims to dissolve the club, to break it apart, to explode it. Some people who sympathize with our aim have asked us how we intend to win over the majority of so-called whites to anti-racism. Others, usually less friendly, have asked if we plan to exterminate physically millions, perhaps hundreds of millions, of people. Neither of these plans is what we have in mind. The weak point of the club is its need for unanimity. Just as the South, on launching the Civil War, declared that it needed its entire territory and would have it, the white race must have the support of all those it has designated as its constituency, or it ceases to exist.

Before the Civil War, the leading spokesmen for the slaveholders acknowledged that the majority of white northerners, swayed above all by the presence of the fugitive slave, considered slavery unjust. The Southerners also understood that the opposition was ineffective; however much the white people of the north disapproved of the slave system, the majority went along with it rather than risk the ordinary comforts of their lives, meager as they were in many cases.

When John Brown attacked Harpers Ferry, Southern pro-slavery leaders reacted with fury: they imposed a boycott on northern manufacturers, demanded new concessions from the government in Washington, and began to prepare for war. When they sought to portray John Brown as a representative of northern opinion, Southern leaders were wrong; he represented only a small and isolated minority. But they were also right, for he expressed the hopes that still persisted in the northern population despite decades of cringing before the slaveholders. Virginia did not fear John Brown and his small band of followers, but rather his soul that would go marching on, though his body lay a-mould'rin in the grave.

When the South, in retaliation for Harpers Ferry, sought to further bully northern opinion, it did so not out of paranoia but out of the realistic assessment that only a renewal of the national pro-slavery vows could save a system whose proud facade concealed a fragile foundation. By the arrogance of their demands, the Southern leaders compelled the people of the north to resist. Not ideas but events were in command. Each step led inexorably to the next: Southern land-greed, Lincoln's victory, secession, war, blacks as laborers, soldiers, citizens, voters. And so the war that began with not one person in a hundred foreseeing the end of slavery was transformed within two years into an anti-slavery war.

It is our faith—and with those who do not share it we shall not argue—that the majority of so-called whites in this country are neither deeply nor consciously committed to white supremacy; like most human beings in most times and places, they would do the right thing if it were convenient. As did their counterparts before the Civil War, most go along with a system that disturbs them, because the consequences of challenging it are terrifying. They close their eyes to what is happening around them, because it is easier not to know.

At rare moments their nervous peace is shattered, their certainty is shaken, and they are compelled to question the common sense by which they normally live. One such moment was in the days immediately following the Rodney King verdict, when the majority of white Americans were willing to admit to polltakers that black people had good reasons to rebel, and some joined them. Ordinarily the moments are brief, as the guns and reform programs are moved up to restore order and the confidence that matters are in good hands and they can go back to sleep. Both the guns and the reform programs are aimed at whites as well as blacks—the guns as a warning and the reform programs as a salve to their consciences.

Recently, one of our editors, unfamiliar with New York City traffic laws, made an illegal right turn there on a red light. He was stopped by two cops in a patrol car. After examining his license, they released him with a courteous admonition. Had he been black, they probably would have ticketed him, and might even have taken him down to the station. A lot of history was embodied in that small change: the cops treated the miscreant leniently at least in part because they assumed, looking at him, that he was white and therefore loyal. Their courtesy was habit meant both to reward good conduct and induce future cooperation.

Had the driver cursed them, or displayed a bumper sticker that said, "Avenge Rodney King," the cops might have reacted differently. We admit that neither gesture on the part of a single individual would in all likelihood be of much consequence. But if enough of those who looked white broke the rules of the club to make the cops doubt their ability to recognize a white person merely by looking at him or her, how would it affect the cops' behavior? And if the police, the courts, and the authorities in general were to start spreading around indiscriminately the treatment they normally reserve for people of color, how would the rest of the so-called whites react?

How many dissident so-called whites would it take to unsettle the nerves of the white executive board? It is impossible to know. One John Brown—against a background of slave resistance—was enough for Virginia. Yet it was not the abolitionists, not even the transcendent John Brown, who brought about the mass shifts in consciousness of the Civil War period. At most, their heroic deeds were part of a chain of events that involved mutual actions and reactions on a scale beyond anything they could have anticipated—until a war that began with both sides fighting for slavery (the South to take it out of the Union, the North to keep it in) ended with a great army marching through the land singing. "As He died to make men holy, let us fight to make men free."

The moments when the routine assumptions of race break down are the seismic promise that somewhere in the tectonic flow a new fault is building up pressure, a new Harpers Ferry is being prepared. Its nature and timing cannot be predicted, but of its coming we have no doubt. When it comes, it will set off a series of tremors that will lead to the disintegration of the white race. We want to be ready, walking in Jerusalem just like John.

What Kind of Journal Is This?

Race Traitor exists not to make converts, but to reach out to those who are dissatisfied with the terms of membership in the white club. Its primary intended audience will be those people commonly called whites who, in one way or another, understand whiteness to be a problem that perpetuates injustice and prevents even the well-disposed among them from joining unequivocally in the struggle for human freedom. By engaging these dissidents in a journey of discovery into whiteness and its discontents, we hope to take part, together with others, in the process of defining a new human community. We wish neither to minimize the complicity of even the most downtrodden of whites with the system of white supremacy nor to exaggerate the significance of momentary departures from white rules.

We should say that there are some articles we are not interested in publishing. Since we are not seeking converts, we probably will not publish articles that lecture various organizations about their racial opportunism. Also we probably will not publish articles promoting interracial harmony, because that approach too often leaves intact differential treatment of whites and blacks and provides subtle confirmation of the idea that different races exist independently of social distinctions.

In the original film version of *Robin Hood* (starring Errol Flynn), the Sheriff of Nottingham says to Robin, "You speak treason." Robin replies, "Fluently." We hope to do the same.

31

CENTURIES OF BLACK PROTEST: ITS SIGNIFICANCE FOR AMERICA AND THE WORLD

Aldon Morris

THE MODERN CIVIL RIGHTS MOVEMENT

The modern civil rights movement fulfilled one of the unfinished tasks of the Civil War. It increased the freedom of the descendants of former slaves by overthrowing legalized Jim Crow and a significant amount of the inequity associated with it. My purpose here is not to describe or even analyze the many demonstrations and campaigns that constituted the modern civil rights movement. Such accounts and analyses have been done elsewhere (Carson 1981; Sitkoff 1981; McAdam 1982; Blumberg 1984; Morris 1984; Garrow 1986; Branch 1988). Rather, I shall examine how the modern civil rights movement affected the infrastructure of black protest, advanced a distinctive critical consciousness, and promoted the democratization process both nationally and abroad. Here I am interested in the overall meaning of the movement, what it produced, and what it said to the world.

The most distinctive aspect of the modern civil rights movement was its demonstration that, through the widespread use of social protest, power could be generated by an oppressed group at the bottom of a modern industrialized society. The civil rights movement produced what has come to be known around the world as "people power." This power from the bottom required extensive mobilization and organization, and it also required the utilization of an overall strategy.

The modern civil rights movement drew both inspiration and tactical insights from the many historic struggles against Jim Crow. Yet, thanks to modern communication technology and the growing internal and external strength of the African American community as a result of black urbanization following the two world wars, the modern civil rights movement was able to launch social protest on a scale unattainable in previous eras. The Montgomery bus boycott of 1955–1956 ushered in a new movement that was deeply rooted in African American culture and its tradition of social protest. What was distinctive about the Montgomery movement is that the entire black community became mobilized into a superbly organized protest movement that was able to sustain itself for over a year, utilizing the strategy of a mass boycott against Jim Crow buses.

At the time, Montgomery's black community was poor, consisting largely of low-paid manual workers. White supremacy reigned in Montgomery, where black people found themselves excluded from the formal political process and denied the franchise. White violence and overall oppression and exploitation were the mechanisms that kept blacks the victims of Montgomery's Jim Crow system of human domination. It is in this context that the real significance of the Montgomery protest movement is to be understood and appreciated. But how could this people-power movement flourish and flower in the heart of the land of white supremacy?

In Montgomery, the black protest machinery that originated in the hush harbor meetings of slaves and took shape in the first independent black churches during slavery was reactivated. Once again, black churches and black religion became the mobilization and organizational sinews of the movement. In this instance, the black church—as in the days of slavery, but with a greater capacity—provided the communication channels and organizational resources needed to mobilize the movement. In Montgomery during the second half of the twentieth century, the oppositional consciousness that had been soaked up in the very roots of the slaves' religious music, their prayers, and the sermons of their preachers sprang to life, animating the protest activities of ordinary African Americans. It was Martin Luther King, Jr., who seized on the tradition of protest oratory and charisma previously exemplified by Frederick Douglass. At the same time, black ministers throughout Montgomery preached protest and helped organize the activity. Following in the footsteps of Harriet Tubman and Sojourner Truth, it was a woman, Rosa Parks, who sparked the movement by refusing to give up her seat to a white man on the local Jim Crow bus. Her dignified act of courage raised the question whether the Rosa Parkses of Montgomery were not women who deserved first-class citizenship. Montgomery's black women responded by playing leading roles in organizing the mass protest. Many of them became organizers who raised money, drove bus boycotters to work, and performed the numerous invisible tasks essential to the success of mass movements.

A very important social movement organization was formed to guide the protest. The purpose of the Montgomery Improvement Association (MIA), like that of A. Philip Randolph's March on Washington Movement, was to coordinate and direct mass protest. Indeed, the MIA met Randolph's dictum that mass organization with a bold program capable of producing huge demonstrations was necessary if black people were to overthrow Jim Crow.

In Montgomery, black people developed a tactical weapon to conduct warfare with Jim Crow. That weapon was nonviolent direct action. It was a method accessible to masses of previously powerless people. The Reverend James Lawson, a key strategist of the modern civil rights movement, explained the significance of nonviolent direct action:

> The point . . . is that when people are suffering they don't want rhetoric and processes which seem to go slowly . . . many people want direct participation . . . they want to be able to say, what I'm doing here gives me power and is going to generate change. So nonviolence puts into the hands of all kind of ordinary people a positive alternative to powerlessness and frustration (quoted in Morris 1984:124).

Nonviolent direct action enabled masses of dominated people to enter into the history-making process of changing their own status as victims. Thus, mass direct action generated power from the bottom, making it no longer necessary for black people to rely primarily on the courts, outside elites, or even individual acts of protest to challenge racial inequity. In short, mass direct action was a form of warfare pursued nonviolently to accomplish social and political objectives. Its real leverage stemmed from its ability to generate profound social disruption which forced elites—federal and local governments, dominant social classes, and the dominant race—to yield to the demands of oppressed African Americans.

The year-long Montgomery bus boycott ended in victory when the Supreme Court ruled that racial segregation on buses in Montgomery was unconstitutional. But the victory was much larger than getting desegregated buses in Montgomery. This victory showed how Jim Crow itself could be overthrown. Within a short period, the African American community throughout the South, supported by the national African American community, developed mass movements based on the Montgomery model to overthrow Jim Crow. These local movements gave rise to numerous social movement organizations, including the Southern Christian Leadership Conference (SCLC), Student Nonviolent Coordinating Committee (SNCC), and hundreds of local movement organizations; and dormant social movement organizations like the Congress of Racial Equality (CORE) were rejuvenated. It is important to point out here that the rise of the SNCC was very important because it was comprised of and led by black students. What this development signaled was that students and young people were capable of helping to shape history and their destiny by engaging in widespread disciplined social protest geared toward dismantling systems of domination.

The modern civil rights movement produced thousands of organizers—both black and white—who learned the art of constructing grass-roots social movements. By building on the historic legacy of black social protest, the modern civil rights movement developed a sophisticated protest culture of oratory, poetry, and music. The music was especially crucial to the mobilization and organizing processes of the movement because it readily lent itself to mass participation, inasmuch as it was a shared product which came out of African American culture. Indeed, much of the music consisted of slave spirituals recast to match contemporary circumstances. This is why such songs as "We Shall Overcome" and "Before I'd Be a Slave I'd Be Buried in My Grave" had such power. Rooted in slave culture, they were energized by social oppression and the oppositional consciousness which they embodied.

The hallmark of the modern civil rights movement was its production of mass protest. This protest was the power that paralyzed the Jim Crow way of conducting social and political business. The tactics of social protest perfected during the movement included mass boycotts, mass marches, mass sit-ins, mass arrests, freedom rides, voter registration drives in hostile environments, wade-ins, pray-ins, phone-ins, and many other forms of nonviolent social disruption. Often these demonstrations met intense resistance and violence precisely because they threatened the Jim Crow order. Nevertheless, these widespread demonstrations continued in the face of violence, and under the glare of television cameras they revealed to the nation and the world that American democracy did not apply to African Americans. These demonstrations disrupted social and economic activities in local areas while forcing the federal government to take a public stance as to whether it was going to support white supremacy or the democratic principles enshrined in the United States Constitution.

By the early 1960s widespread intense social protest was making Jim Crow too difficult to maintain locally and nationally. That is what King referred to when he declared, "Segregation is on its deathbed and the only question is how expensive will the segregationists make the funeral." People power from the bottom led to the official overthrow of Jim Crow. The 1964 Civil Rights Act, which prohibited all forms of racial segregation and discrimination, and the 1965 Voting Rights Act, which enfranchised southern African Americans, constituted the national legislation that dismantled the legal underpinning of Jim Crow. It had taken a powerful nonviolent mass movement generated and sustained by local movement centers to complete the mission of the Civil War. Jim Crow as a social order was overthrown by the people power released through a strong grass-roots movement.

By the mid 1960s America's political landscape had been transformed in some fundamental respects. The "social movement" way of conducting political business and the "people power" it produced had become a reality. The nation now contained thousands of movement organizers, numerous SMO's, an extensive repertoire of direct action tactics, a vibrant social movement culture, a powerful oppositional consciousness stressing democracy and criticizing the dominant hegemonic consciousness, and important victories—foremost among them being the legal overthrow of Jim Crow. This new development engendered hope among millions that a true democracy could be established, where the people themselves made the decisions that governed their lives.

Outside the South during this period the oppression of African Americans emanated from a post-Jim Crow system of domination. Under this arrangement black oppression, especially in northern cities, was not mandated by law, and it received no official support from the state or local governments. Nevertheless, the masses of black people found themselves at the bottom of the economic order, on the edge of the political life usually governed by white ethnic political machines, shut out of decent housing and schools, constant victims of both police brutality and a veiled white hegemonic consciousness originating in the same ideology of white supremacy that legitimized southern Jim Crow. The nonviolent civil rights movement generated a new level of political consciousness among northern blacks, and it angered them to see their southern counterparts tear-gassed, jailed, beaten, and killed by racist whites. But most of all, the brutality and open, raw racism of southern whites made it easier for northern blacks to more clearly assess their own situation and to attribute it directly to white oppression.

Northern blacks, trapped in ghettos where internal and external violence was a daily reality, confronted a profound question: Was it correct or even wise for black people to fight nonviolently for their freedom while whites delighted in beating, jailing, cursing, and even killing them? Was not the right to self-defense basic to dignity and self-respect? Another provocative question emerged at the same time: Would real black empowerment and self-determination emerge from the strategy of racial integration so nobly pursued by the civil rights movement?

Malcolm X, more than anyone else, raised these issues with such clarity and eloquence that they could not be ignored. Malcolm X wanted economic, political, and social independence for blacks—not racial integration. And he wanted it by any means necessary. Malcolm X and his disciples rejected racial integration as the main goal for African Americans. They believed that American society was too corrupt, racist, and imperialistic for black people to become integrated into, even if such integration became possible. Thus Malcolm X and his political heirs advocated self-defense, human rights, and black self-determination, which meant that black people had a right to control their own communities. Moreover, they argued that blacks in America and blacks in Africa were intimately connected by blood, cultural, historical, and political ties. In fact, Malcolm X taught black people to think and act internationally, because in his view all Third World people shared a common history of oppression and a common fate.

Malcolm X made distinctive contributions to the black oppositional consciousness. He counseled black people to be proud of their heritage, culture, and blackness. He went to considerable lengths to demonstrate the major cultural and political achievements of historic African regimes and to show how American blacks were part of this noble legacy. Malcolm X challenged black people to recognize that "you cannot love the branches of a tree yet hate its roots." Racial pride, black solidarity, and an appreciation for the black experience globally were key components of the oppositional consciousness advocated by Malcolm X (Brisbane 1974; Bloom 1987). In this sense Malcolm X became the contemporary father of the black consciousness movement, following in the tradition of leaders like Martin Delaney of the slave period, Marcus Garvey of the 1920s, and cultural movements like the Harlem Renaissance.

The trenchant analysis of Malcolm X and the visible protest movement of southern blacks did not fail to make an impression on the African American community of the

North. Young black people trapped in northern ghettos were especially responsive. Many of them had participated in civil rights demonstrations in support of the southern movement (National Advisory Commission on Civil Disorders 1968), yet such participation did not affect the oppression and exploitation they encountered in the North. Armed with black pride, a belief in self-defense, and Malcolm X's exhortation to achieve their freedom by any means necessary, these young people initiated their own movement.

Their form of protest was the urban rebellion frequently referred to by the agents of social control and the larger white society as riots. Beginning in Harlem, in New York City, in 1964 and Watts, in Los Angeles, California, in 1965, these urban rebellions multiplied in the late 1960s, resulting in thousands of arrests, hundreds of deaths, and millions of dollars worth of property damage. In cities across the nation young black people were engaged in a physical war with the police who had brutalized and tyrannized them. They were striking out against exploitative businesses and landlords by burning and looting their property. This was the radical wing of the black protest movement coming alive in the tradition of the violent slave revolt.

The urban rebellions had a profound influence on the nonviolent civil rights movement. It pushed it leftward and markedly affected its goal of racial integration. It forced Martin Luther King, Jr., and other leaders to take a hard look at the structure of inequality in American society and to grapple with the problem of the widespread poverty and oppression that gripped the black ghettos. Indeed, by the late 1960s, King concluded that the entire economic and social system of America needed fundamental restructuring. In the midst of the urban rebellion, King concluded that inequality between blacks and whites and the haves and have-nots could be eliminated only if all Americans were guaranteed a decent income even if they could not find employment. Thus King redirected his efforts toward integrating the economy and advocating the use of radical nonviolent protest to accomplish the revolutionary goal of economic empowerment for not only blacks but also all poor people. Such a position logically led King to oppose the Vietnam War on both moral and economic grounds. For him violence, even if committed by the state, was morally wrong, and the war itself was draining away the funds needed to assuage domestic poverty.

As King and SCLC moved toward the left, other wings of the civil rights movement became even more radicalized. In particular, by 1966 SNCC and CORE developed and advocated the political and cultural goal of black power. The black power position transformed the black movement and many of its organizational engines. Stokely Carmichael, one of the architects of black power, and Charles Hamilton defined black power as a "call for black people in this country to unite, to recognize their heritage, to build a sense of community. It is a call for black people to begin to define their own goals, to lead their own organizations and to support those organizations. It is a call to reject the racist institutions and values of this society" (Carmichael and Hamilton 1967:45). With the call for black power Malcolm X's ideas had clearly reached into the heart of the black movement even though he himself had been felled by assassins' bullets in 1965. Black power was a call for black self-determination on every level of the African American community. Such a strategy demanded that black people run all their institutions—from schools to protest organizations. In fact, whites were expelled from SNCC and CORE so that these SMO's would be completely in the hands of African Americans.

Black power rejected the goal of integration, advocated self-defense, pressed for the acquisition of political and economic power for the African American community, and scrupulously reserved the right for black people to define themselves and their goals. Thus black power totally rejected the validity of the white hegemonic consciousness and replaced it with a diametrically opposed black oppositional consciousness. It also declared that American institutions and American values were not worth preserving and in fact had to be dismantled in order for the society to become nonracist and demo-cratic. Black power advocates denounced American imperialism around the globe, and they opposed the Vietnam War as imperialistic and racist.

Like the nonviolent civil rights movement, the black power movement gave rise to numerous SMO's, leaders, organizers, and tactics. It provided the ideological foundation for the urban rebellions. Leaders associated with the black power philosophy included Malcolm X, Stokely Carmichael, Angela Davis, Huey Newton, H. Rap Brown, Amiri Baraka, Ron Karenga, and many others. SMO's associated with black power included SNCC, CORE, the Black Panther party, the Republic of New Africa, and the Lown-des County Freedom Organization, among many others. Tactics included urban war-fare, political theater, surveillance of police and violent confrontations with agents of social control, numerous cultural innovations, and consciousness-raising. One of the important contributions of the black power movements is that it greatly augmented the infrastructure of the historic black movement.

The overall response to the black power movement was severe oppression by state and local governments. Malcolm X and Martin Luther King, Jr., were removed from the scene, and the exact sources of those assassinations are still unclear. The leadership of the Black Panther party was systematically jailed or murdered. The urban rebellions of the late 1960s were labeled criminal riots and then crushed under the guise of law and order. During these rebellions military tanks rumbled through the African American community, backed by police squad cars where officers rode four deep, openly display-ing automatic weapons. The government spent millions of dollars on repression rather than on social change.

Nevertheless, the legacy of the black power movement includes the development of a powerful oppositional consciousness, the institution of black studies in colleges and universities, the recognition of black culture as a unique entity, the renaming of black people from "Negro" to "black" to "African Americans," an identification of American blacks with African and Third World nations, and the genesis of modern black political organizations which have accomplished the election of black politicians to levels of government impossible 25 years ago. In short, the black power movement diversified and strengthened the infrastructure of the black protest movement and significantly changed how black people view themselves. The black power movement did not overthrow the post-Jim Crow system of white domination. Yet, like the civil rights movement, it sent a powerful signal to domestic and international groups struggling for democracy.

THE MODERN BLACK MOVEMENT AND DOMESTIC DEMOCRACY

The civil rights and black power movements changed the nature of American politics. Social movements have always affected American politics. However, before the modern civil rights movement, the effect of social movements on American politics had been uneven, probably because such movements were relatively isolated in time and space, and focused primarily on single issues. As a consequence, electoral politics, interest group politics, and politics of elite policy makers and elected officials had largely dominated the American political landscape.

By the mid-1960s all this had changed. Indeed, in the 1960s social movements became a formidable political reality. They became the primary vehicles by means of which previously powerless groups organized to pursue power and social change. Thus, ordinary citizens entered into and affected the political process. In this respect, social movements represented the democratic impulse, for they enabled common folk to have input into political decision-making affecting their everyday lives (Flacks 1988). Moreover, by the late 1960s such movements had become numerous and were clustered in time and space. They ranged from small single-issue movements to large complex ones comprised of multiple wings addressing a plethora of issues. The best known of these movements are those that arose among students, women, farm workers, Native Americans, gays and lesbians, environmentalists, the physically impaired, and Chicanos. This highly incomplete list provides a concrete sense of how social movements exploded onto the political scene in the 1960s. Not only did such movements burst forth with regularity, but many of them generated counter-movements, as happened with the abortion and anti-abortion movements. Social movements became so prevalent in America that scholars can now write about a social movement industry (McCarthy and Zald 1977). They have become such an enduring feature of the American political landscape that they are often taken for granted. This was far from true just 25 years ago.

What accounts for this explosion of social movements in the 1960s? To put it differently, we need to know the triggering mechanism behind this important political transformation because therein lies a clue to understanding the prospects for an authentic, robust American democracy. My argument here is that the modern black movement was the central factor giving rise to the proliferation of social movements in the 1960s. The black movement generated the "politics of social movements" that have become so intertwined with the political fabric of America. The black protest movement played this historic role for a variety of reasons: It advocated a universal democracy that was attractive to other powerless groups; it provided a potent oppositional consciousness that could be recast to address the conditions and aspirations of other groups; it developed organizational and tactical blueprints that could be utilized by other groups; and, finally, it served as an actual training ground for many persons who would become key organizers and leaders in other movements.

In its struggle to achieve racial equality, the modern civil rights movement focused its sights on attaining an all-embracing democracy which encompassed all of its citizens regardless of their race, religion, national origin, or class status. Classic democracy was the vision that guided the civil rights movement. In particular, this movement exalted the democratic vision ensconced in the Declaration of Independence and the United States Constitution, and intrinsic in the psychological make-up of the average American. Central to that vision were the values of social justice, human freedom, and human equality. One of Martin Luther King's greatest strengths was the ability to articulate the democratic ideal for all Americans. Thus, he spoke forcefully of how the wells of democracy had been dug deep by the founding fathers and how every American was to fall heir to justice and freedom because of his or her birthright.

But this democratic vision contrasted sharply with all forms of human oppression. The contradiction between blatant racial domination and democracy was especially glaring. The fact that black people were victims of white violence and terrorism, were racially segregated, denied the right to vote, exploited economically, and labeled inferior could not be justified in terms of democratic principles. Yet as long as black people could be excluded from the political process, this contradiction—for the average white person—remained dormant or was even denied. The civil rights movement gave political voice to black people, enabling them to expose the inherent contradiction between racism and democracy. King and the civil rights movement informed America that black people refused to believe that the bank of justice was bankrupt, and that America had to make real the promises of democracy for all its citizens. But King and the civil rights movement did more than expose the ugly nature of racism. By initiating mass social protest they created a source of power for the oppressed, raising them up to warn the forces of oppression that the whirlwinds of revolt would continue to shake the foundations of the nation until the bright day of justice dawned.

This powerful vision of democracy, coupled with a path-breaking protest movement, caught the attention of Americans. A significant number of white Americans joined in the civil rights movement because it rekindled their ardor to make America a real democracy and released them from the charge that the worst enemy of democracy is the silence of the "good people." It would only be a matter of time before many of those whites would come to realize that they, too, were the victims of a democracy that was anemic at best. Even more important, severely oppressed groups in American society took notice of how African Americans—one of the most oppressed, exploited, and stigmatized groups of them all—were challenging their oppressors and raising high the banner of democracy. The farm workers, heavily exploited in the fields, took notice of this brave new development; gays and lesbians, severely stigmatized and scorned by society, sensed the significance of the rising black protest movement for their own situation; inmates in the nation's prisons peered through their bars and asked what relevance the black protest movement had for them; Native Americans, segregated and exploited on the reservations, felt a kinship with the black movement and were challenged to address their wretched condition; physically impaired Americans, tired of being treated as nonpersons, identified with the black cry for human dignity because they realized that their use of wheelchairs, hearing aids, or braille was no reason to stamp a badge of inferiority on them—especially in a society claiming to be democratic. Indeed, all oppressed groups were forced to re-evaluate their situations in the light of the black protest movement. The cry for democracy, backed by an effective protest movement, struck an instant chord in the hearts and minds of oppressed Americans everywhere, because they too had internalized the dream of democracy and they abhorred their own exclusion from it.

By focusing on the origins of the students' and women's movements I will explicate the argument that the black protest movement was the main force that transformed American politics, enabling social movements to become major political actors. However, it is important to bear in mind that similar analyses apply to the wide spectrum of movements that emerged then and continue to emerge today. This is even the case for movements with a conservative agenda. For example, Randall Terry, a leader of the antiabortion movement known as Operation Rescue, claims that the inspiration for its activity came from the American civil rights movement and Martin Luther King, Jr. He clearly explains how the anti-abortion activists have transferred many of the tactics of the civil rights movement into their own movement (Terry 1989:83).

Before the civil rights movement white students had no social movement of their own. Nevertheless, there were white students who held strong democratic values and were interested in promoting democracy. Yet the civil rights movement shocked privileged white students because they had no in-depth understanding of the degree to which democracy was denied to African Americans. They watched in disbelief the brutality and totalitarian tactics black people encountered as they fought racial segregation. The critique of racism and the undemocratic character of American society propounded by leaders like Martin Luther King was absorbed by white students as they developed their own analysis of America's shortcomings. But even more important for these students was that oppressed black people were creatively and courageously acting to overthrow oppression and to establish democracy. The widespread initiation of social protest by black students and the creation of their own independent protest organization— SNCC—were the most decisive factors that pulled white students into social protest and created the conditions out of which a white student movement would develop.

Insofar as protest was concerned, black students became the role models for white students. White students became mesmerized by the black movement because they realized black students were already utilizing and further developing an oppositional consciousness inherited from the historic black movement. That consciousness, expressed through gripping oratory, song, and mass action, identified the enemy of democracy—racism—and specified what needed to be done to correct the problem. Moreover, as white students looked southward they witnessed their black counterparts pioneering protest tactics—such as sit-ins, freedom rides, mass arrests, and the like. They also recognized that black students had taken a very important step when they explicitly decided to create their own independent protest organization. The message was that students themselves had a distinctive and independent contribution to make to the black protest movement and the fight for an authentic democracy. This message was not lost on white students.

Following the model of black students, white students began to initiate social protest against Jim Crow and racism. Many of them initiated such protest in the North and some even went south and joined the civil rights movement, especially the student wing guided by SNCC. As Sale (1973:23) wrote, "The alliance-in-action between southern blacks and young northern whites, founded on a principle that was both morally pure and politically powerful, gave the student movement a strength that it had never before experienced." Those who have studied the period (Heirich 1968; Sale 1973; Carson 1981; Morris 1981; McAdam 1982) have reached what amounts to a consensus: The black civil rights movement, especially its student wing, was the key factor that generated the active phase of the white student movement because it supplied white students with a radical analysis, tactical and organizational blueprints, role models, valuable movement experience, and access to a vibrant movement culture.

What does this conclusion mean in concrete terms? First, the major white student protest organization, Students for a Democratic Society, the one which had the most far-ranging influence over the white student movement, was modelled after SNCC and was often referred to as its northern counterpart. Second, many of the major campaigns—for example, economic and research and action programs, Berkeley free speech movement, etc.—of the white student movement were organized by white students who had received their training directly from the black movement. Third, many of the tactics of the white student movement—sit-ins, mass arrests, marches, teach-ins, etc.—were transferred from the civil rights movement. Fourth, the pace of militancy of the white student movement was influenced by the black movement. Thus, the urban rebellions of the late 1960s and the rise of black power greatly influenced the white student movement to become more radical. Finally, the black movement taught white students that they had to make courageous sacrifices—including the possibility of death—if they were to wage an important struggle for American democracy. In other words, the black movement assisted white students in developing the kind of oppositional consciousness needed to wage a confrontational struggle for democracy. Subsequently, student protest has become an enduring reality of American politics.

The origin and development of the modern women's movement have been significantly shaped by the black movement. Earlier I discussed how the nineteenth-century women's suffrage movement, which finally achieved the franchise for women in 1920, emerged out of the black movement against slavery. In the 1960s a similar process occurred again. After women received the right to vote, their movement entered a dormant phase, recognized only by a few elite women who continued to fight for gender equality (Rupp and Taylor 1987). As a consequence, by the early 1960s, the gender system of human domination remained largely intact. Moreover, during the 1950s, the majority of white women experienced their oppression as a private, taken-for-granted reality. In contrast to women during the suffrage movement, these women possessed neither an oppositional consciousness enabling them to diagnose the nature of their oppression nor a plan of action to destroy it. Rather, in Sara Evans' words (1979:11), "They remained enclosed in the straitjacket of domestic ideology." According to Betty Friedan (1963), women's oppression was the problem with no name. Women were without the kind of consciousness and social organization needed to develop a social movement.

As in the nineteenth century, the civil rights and black power movements opened the door to protest for women in a number of important respects. Scholars of the modern women's movement (Evans 1979; Freeman 1975; Ferree and Hess 1985) agree that the black movement was crucial to the development of both the older professional and younger, more radical wings of the modern women's movement. Generally speaking, the emergence of the modern black movement immediately caught the attention of a number of professional white women who were already concerned about gender inequality and were associated with the Commission on the Status of Women initially established by President Kennedy. These women were acutely aware that black people were protesting against racial oppression and that their struggle contained lessons relevant to their own situation. It was the black struggle in Birmingham, Alabama, in 1963, and the hundreds modeled after it which quickly followed, that proved crucial to the formation of the older branch of the women's movement. In the Birmingham confrontations and the others that followed, black people were beaten and were knocked against walls by jets of water from high-pressure hoses; thousands were arrested, including hundreds of black elementary and high school students. Yet without absorbing the blow of one billy club or spending one night in jail, middle-class white women—indeed all women—benefitted tremendously from the battle waged in the streets of Alabama and the nation.

The 1964 Civil Rights Act, which prohibited all forms of racial discrimination, was the result of the heated protest in Birmingham and elsewhere. As expected, the passage of this bill through the United States Congress was a most difficult task, given the opposition of white segregationist congressmen and their political allies. Howard Smith, an 80-year-old segregationist from Virginia, who was chairman of the powerful House Rules Committee, used his power and political savvy in an impressive effort to defeat the bill. Title VII of the bill, which focused on employment discrimination, initially stated that employers could not discriminate on the basis of race, color, religion, or national origin.

Smith decided that if he amended Title VII by adding the word "sex" he would cause the entire bill to be defeated because he believed a majority of his colleagues would not vote for a bill prohibiting gender discrimination in the work place (Whalen and Whalen 1985:115–17). A small number of congresswomen immediately grasped the significance of the amendment and argued in favor of it. The bill passed with the amendment. Thus a major victory for gender equality had come about because of black protest. It was to have important implications for the modern women's movement.

White males, whether lawmakers or employers, had no intention of honoring the gender-discrimination provision of Title VII. Nevertheless, a group of professional women associated with the Commission on the Status of Women took it seriously. The challenge they faced was to generate the necessary pressure and leverage for its enforcement. To accomplish this task they looked to the civil rights movement for suggestions. They concluded "that sex would be taken more seriously if there were 'some sort of NAACP for women' to put pressure on the government" (Freeman 1975:54). In other words, they saw that a civil rights organization for women was needed in order to reap the gain fortuitously generated by the black movement. Out of this context arose the first major SMO of the modern women's movement—the National Organization for Women (NOW). It was no accident that the moderate wing of the black movement became NOW's organizational and tactical blueprint. These were reform-oriented professional women attracted to the legalistic and mild protest stance of the NAACP.

The younger women who were to develop the radical wing of the women's movement were first attracted to the radical wing of the black protest movement in the South. Like their white male counterparts, these women identified with SNCC, CORE, and SCLC, and with the mass protest championed by leaders like King. Many of them became active in the civil rights movement and some went directly to the battlefronts in the South. As they worked in the southern movement they encountered new role models. Many of the black women associated with the movement were strong, courageous leaders and organizers who put their lives on the line to topple Jim Crow (Evans 1979). The behavior and personalities of these women directly contradicted the domestic ideology internalized by white women. These black women created the possibility of a new womanhood for white women: a womanhood that encouraged protest behavior to achieve democracy at least on the racial front.

The civil rights movement exposed young white women to the black oppositional consciousness that warred against racism and oppression and taught them how to organize social protest. Sara Evans (1979:100) captured the impact that the civil rights movement had on young white women when she pointed out that it provided them with ". . . a language to name and describe oppression; a deep belief in freedom, equality and community—soon to be translated into sisterhood; a willingness to question and challenge any social institution that failed to meet human needs; and the ability to organize."

What we see here, as during the slave period, is that the black movement advocated a broad vision of human emancipation. It was a vision rooted in the belief that total democracy was possible where freedom and equality prevailed. The black movement has been the vehicle that has lifted high the vision of democracy in its purest form. Young white women internalized that vision as they participated in the black movement. They also learned how communities are mobilized and organized for social protest.

Their experiences in the civil rights movement led many of these women to use their new social consciousness to examine women's inequality in the larger society and within the civil rights and student movements. This examination of the "woman's place" caused these women to compare it with the "Negro's place" imposed on black people by white society. In essence, these women had developed a feminist consciousness which enabled them to criticize gender domination and to devise strategies to combat it. As a consequence, they began to organize a radical feminist movement in the United States. This radical wing of the movement was not always unified. Some of the women argued that the primary targets were men, who had created and maintained gender inequality because of the privileges they derived from it. Others argued that gender, race, and class inequality were interconnected and had to be attacked simultaneously.

Nevertheless, what was crucial is that the civil rights and black power movements had played key roles in generating the radical wing of the modern women's movement. As Evans (1979:25) has pointed out, "The sweeping critique of sexual roles that characterized the more radical women's liberation movement of the late sixties first developed from within the ranks, and the revolt, of young southern blacks." These movements provided much of the ideological, tactical, and organizational raw material on which the radical women's movement was able to draw while developing its own strategies (McAdam 1988:185).

Indeed, the black power movement in particular was crucial to the development of the radical wings of the modern women's movement. As argued earlier, the black power movement took an unequivocal stand that African Americans had the right to define themselves and the nature of their struggle for equality and empowerment. The women who developed the radical wing of the women's movement adopted this analysis. It led them to realize that they could not effectively attack gender domination within the black and student movements. Like black power advocates, they decided they needed their own independent movement. Echols has recently demonstrated that the radical women's movement was heavily influenced and shaped by black power. In her words, many of the women who organized the radical branch "took their inspiration from Black Power. Black Power enabled them to argue that it was valid for women to organize around their own oppression and to define the terms of their struggle" (1989:49). Moreover, a similar dynamic occurred throughout the numerous other movements of the 1960s. Thus Adam (1987) explained how organizers of the gay and lesbian movements of the period concluded that they needed to define their own movements for themselves in radical terms as the black nationalists had done.

In short, what has been demonstrated here is the central role that the civil rights and black power movements played in generating and influencing the modern women's movement. We see clearly how the student and women's movements shared this reality in common. But what is the larger meaning of this line of argument?

The larger significance lies in the fact that the modern black movement triggered numerous democratic and even conservative counter-movements in the 1960s and afterward. It was the black movement that transformed American politics, where social movements have become major political actors. As a result, democracy in the United States has gained, because the black movement helped give a political voice to the powerless through the social movement route. Examples abound: The historic black movement has taught the nation that racism and any form of human oppression are fundamentally incompatible with democracy; the student movement taught the nation to question governmental decisions to engage in warfare with foreign nations because of imperialistic motives; the women's movement has shown that a democracy is weak indeed if it maintains a system of domination that claims over half its citizens as victims; the farm workers' movement has called to the attention of the nation the undemocratic practice of exploiting people simply because they lack political and economic power; and neighborhood movements throughout the country have demonstrated that citizens must organize if they are to have a voice. Numerous other victories for democracy could be cited. Whether America is to benefit from these lessons and apply them fully is still unclear. That will be determined to some degree by how effectively the oppressed utilize the vehicle of the social movement. What is clear is that without the historic black movement the nation would be far less democratic overall, for that movement has advanced the challenge of the democratic agenda in its purest form. As a consequence, oppressed people around the world have sensed the relevancy of the black struggle for their own democratic aspirations.

THE BLACK MOVEMENT AND INTERNATIONAL DEMOCRACY

The African American protest movement and its robust vision of democracy have sent an important message to oppressed people around the world. The international significance of the black movement is usually overlooked in America. This is true, in part, because of America's preoccupation with portraying black people as a rather insignificant minority having little power and predisposed to crime and to welfare dependency. Such stereotypes are incompatible with the reality that the actions and visions of African Americans have worldwide significance and that black people in America are in fact important actors on the world stage. Yet, it is hardly surprising that the black protest movement has influenced struggles for liberation everywhere in world, given its focus on justice and democracy for all human beings. The black movement has championed universal human goals and aspirations.

The international influence of the black movement is clearly evident. "We Shall Overcome," the national anthem of the United States civil rights movement, is sung in liberation struggles throughout the world. James Cone (1986:25), one of the major formulators of liberation theology, has pointed out the far-reaching significance of this black freedom song: "The theme song of the Civil Rights Movement, 'We Shall Overcome,' is widely used by oppressed groups in Africa, Asia, and Latin America. I have heard it sung by the masses in many countries on all continents. I will never forget when I first heard it in South Korea." The universal appeal of "We Shall Overcome" stems from the fact that this song came from a people oppressed for centuries by powerful undemocratic forces, yet able to declare with poetic elegance that those barriers to democracy and freedom would be overcome. This message of defiance and ultimate triumph over tyranny has captured the imagination of masses struggling for human emancipation around the globe.

The impact of the African American protest movement has been felt throughout Africa. The case of South Africa is especially instructive. A mutual relationship between black South Africans and black Americans has endured for centuries. Similarities between the systems of white domination in both countries, coupled with the similarities between the two black protest movements, have strengthened this relationship. Patrick Lekota, a national publicity director of the United Democratic Front in South Africa, explains that, "Perhaps, more than anybody else, South Africa has always been very conscious of the AfroAmerican struggle. . . . We in Africa always look across the American continent and understand that the people of color here are really African blood" (interview 1990). He also pointed out that, since many of the leaders of the National African Congress "studied in the United States, they have drawn a lot of inspiration from the struggles that have been waged by African Americans." Moreover, Lekota is very clear about the fact that writings and literature concerning the struggle of African Americans have been and continue to be widely read in black South Africa. Commenting directly on the materials covering the civil rights and black power movements, Lekota reports that in South Africa "it was highly studied material."

Thus, many of the leaders of the National Democratic Front in South Africa, including Reverend Allan Boesak and Bishop Desmond Tutu, have carefully analyzed and debated the leadership tactics of Martin Luther King, Jr., and Malcolm X and the ways in which such leadership applies to their own struggle (Boesak 1978; Cone 1986). They, too, have had to grapple with the questions of nonviolent struggle versus armed struggle and racial integration versus black power. Writing on an experience he had while attending a protest rally in South Africa, Cone speaks of how moved he was when the masses began singing songs from America's black protest movement. He also commented (Cone 1986:162–63) on the similarities between the style and sermon of Reverend Boesak at the rally and that of African American protest leaders: "As I sat there listening to Boesak speak from the depth of this faith, telling the people assembled 'We Shall Overcome' and 'don't get weary, because there is a great camp meeting in the promised land,' I could feel the surge of almighty hope arise in their being. . . . I could not help but think about black people's struggles in the United States, especially during the Civil Rights Movement."

The voices of Malcolm X, Stokely Carmichael, and the black power movement played a direct role in the development of the black consciousness movement in South Africa during the late 1960s. This movement, led by Steve Biko and many others, was especially prevalent among the black youth, and it radicalized the entire black movement in South Africa. Lekota (1990) related that the students in South Africa who developed the black consciousness movement were inspired by Stokely Carmichael and the United States black power movement. According to Lekota, the ideas pushed by black power advocates in the United States, that "black is beautiful" and that black people had to define themselves and lead their own organizations and movements, immediately resonated with young black South Africans—especially in colleges and universities. The impact of the United States black power movement on the black consciousness movement can easily be discerned in the documents of the latter. Thus, Steve Biko, in an article in 1972, explained why that movement rejected racial integration as a strategy and expelled white liberals from the movement. He argued that black liberation had to be achieved by black people. In language almost indistinguishable from Carmichael and Hamilton's statement on black power, Biko argued, "The quintessence of it is the realization by the blacks that, in order to feature well in this game of power politics, they have to use the concept of group power and to build a strong foundation from this. . . . The philosophy of Black Consciousness, therefore, expresses group pride and the determination by the blacks to rise and attain the envisaged self" (quoted in Woods 1978:59).

From the black consciousness movement came numerous SMO's, including the all-black South African Students' Organization (SASO) and Black People's Convention (BPC). The great significance of the black consciousness movement is that it pulled thousands of young people directly into the black liberation struggle, willing to use any means necessary to accomplish freedom and democracy. Moreover, the United States black power movement assisted in the radicalization of the black struggle in South Africa, as it has for numerous struggles within America and elsewhere.

The African American protest movement has influenced the Intifadah movement currently being waged on the West Bank in Israel. In this occupied territory the Palestinians have been struggling for liberation for a long time. To date, Israel has been successful in containing the armed struggle. For guidance in the nonviolent phase of their movement, the Palestinians have begun to apply the lessons of the nonviolent American civil rights movement and Martin Luther King, Jr.

Mubarak Awad, one of the central leaders of the Intifadah movement, explained how the civil rights movement and Martin Luther King have been crucial to their struggle (interview, 1990). According to Awad, because of its successes the United States civil rights movement has become a model for the Intifadah movement. The civil rights movement and Martin Luther King taught black people how to utilize their religion in the fight for liberation. This lesson was an important one for the Palestinians. Awad explains, "What we did—and it has been very helpful for a lot of people who are religious, doesn't matter [whether] Christians or Moslems—is that we taught that through religion you could liberate yourself" (interview, 1990). He went on to say, "What helped us more was the actions of Martin Luther King. The marches. The going to jail to fill the jails." In the Intifadah movement the Palestinians have utilized one of the most important lessons of the civil rights movement: generating costly mass disruption in such a way as to prevent the institutions of the oppressor from functioning as usual. Awad related that they came to understand that Martin Luther King filled the jails to make it highly expensive for the agents of social control to function effectively. Thus a tactic of the Intifadah movement evolved whereby large numbers of Palestinians would fill the jails and cripple the Israeli court system. Awad pointed out that they clogged the court system so that it reached a "zero position where it doesn't work. And we did that. That has been a strong part."

The Intifadah movement continues to study the civil rights movement and Martin Luther King, Jr. Its leaders have acquired films on the black movement and King, and shown them on Jordanian television so that the lessons of that movement can be widely disseminated and applied. Here again, it is clear that the black movement has had influence on another human liberation struggle thousands of miles away.

In summary, all over the world the African American protest movement has influenced struggles for human liberation. In Northern Ireland, thousands of people have marched behind banners declaring that "We Shall Overcome" because we have a civil rights movement. The people of Poland were aware of the need to understand the black movement so they could make their own struggle more effective. Thus, in the early days of Solidarity, Bayard Rustin was invited to Poland for a series of colloquia and speeches because of his work in the civil rights movement and his association with A. Philip Randolph and Martin Luther King, Jr. Rustin revealed how interested the Polish were in the black movement when he stated, "I am struck by the complete attentiveness of the predominantly young audience, which sits patiently, awaiting the translation of my words" (undated report, 15). The influence of the black movement was evident in the 1989 prodemocracy movement in China. One of the leaders of that movement, Shen Tong, who was present during the massacre in Beijing's Tiananmen Square, said, in a speech at the Martin Luther King Center for Social Change in Atlanta, "My first encounter with the concept of nonviolence was in high school when I read about Martin Luther King, Jr., and Mahatma Gandhi" (Tong 1990). Tong clearly revealed the continuing international significance of the black movement:

> We must learn from each other. All our communities must learn peace from each other. And there is much, so much I must learn from you, and from Dr. King. Please teach me. Please help China and the Chinese find that crystal way which will lead to the crystal goal. And together, as one movement for human rights and peace world-wide, we will be able to look at the tyrants and oppressors of history and say to them—in Dr. King's words—"We have matched your

capacity to inflict suffering with our capacity to endure suffering. We have met your physical force with soul force." We are free.

CONCLUSION

In this essay I have traced and analyzed key historic, social, and political contributions that the African American protest movement has made to the black community, the nation, and the world. Throughout history, systems of human domination have been constructed by dominant groups to exploit and oppress the masses. These systems of domination have stood in the path of the human march toward freedom and authentic democracy. Nevertheless, the protest movement has functioned as the historic vehicle through which the oppressed have challenged and at times toppled systems of domination, clearing the path for a momentous leap forward.

The African American protest movement has been such a force. It has had a great deal of success in dismantling slavery and Jim Crow. In the process it has lifted high the banner of democracy and human freedom. In so doing it has helped generate and shape freedom struggles domestically and internationally. There is still a great deal more to be learned from this movement and its broad infrastructure. Many tyrants around the world still sit atop systems of domination. The challenge of the black movement and those who struggle for democracy everywhere is to confront these undemocratic forces head on and topple them with collective blows.

32

THE RISE OF THE CHICANO STUDENT MOVEMENT AND CHICANO POWER

Carlos Muñoz, Jr.

In an effort to provide direction to the efforts of militant Mexican American youth throughout the U.S., the Crusade for Justice hosted a National Chicano Youth Liberation Conference in March 1969. The conference, held at the Crusade headquarters in Denver, Colorado brought together for the first time activists from all over the country who were involved in both campus and community politics. The conference was also significant because it brought together young people of all types—students, nonstudents, militant youth from the street gangs (*vatos locos*), and exconvicts (*pintos*)—to discuss community issues and politics. The majority in attendance, however, were student activists, and most of them were from California. The conference emphasized themes that related to the quest for identity, as popularized by Gonzáles and Valdez, which were eagerly received by students searching for an ideology for the emerging student movement.

Corky Gonzáles and his followers in Denver had developed the image of the Crusade for Justice as "the vanguard" of the rapidly growing Chicano Power Movement. The Crusade, originally a multi-issue, broad-based civil rights organization oriented toward nonviolence, came to symbolize Chicano self-determination and espoused a strong nationalist ideology that militant youth found extremely attractive. Gonzáles articulated this nationalism in a clear and appealing manner:

> Nationalism exists . . . but until now, it hasn't been formed into an image people can see. Until now it has been a dream. It has been my job to create a reality out of the dream, to create an ideology out of the longing. Everybody in the *barrios* is a nationalist. . . . [I]t doesn't matter if he's middle-class, a *vendido*, a sellout, or what his politics may be. He'll come back home, to La Raza, to his heart, if we will build centers of nationalism for him. . . . [N]ationalism is the key to our people liberating themselves. . . . I am a revolutionary . . . because creating life amid death is a revolutionary act. Just as building nationalism in an era of imperialism is a life-giving act. . . . We are an awakening people, an emerging nation, a new breed.

During the week-long conference, Gonzáles and his followers stressed the need for students and youth to play a revolutionary role in the movement. Conference participants were told that previous generations of students, after completing academic programs and becoming professionals, had abdicated their responsibility to their people, to their *familia de La Raza*. This abdication of responsibility was attributed to the fact that Mexican American students had been Americanized by the schools, that they had been conditioned to accept the dominant values of American society, particularly individualism, at the expense of their Mexican identity. The result had been the psychological "colonization" of Mexican American youth.

To liberate themselves from this "colonization," students needed "revolutionary" role models. Street youth and ex-convicts would become the models. Conference speakers proposed that henceforth most crimes committed by Mexican Americans were to be interpreted as "revolutionary acts." The language and dress of the street youth, the *vatos locos,* would be emulated. *Carnalismo* (the brotherhood code of Mexican American youth gangs) would mold the lives of students and become a central concept in the proposed nationalist ideology. From the ranks of this new breed of youth would come the poets, the writers and the artists necessary for the forging of the new Chicano identity. This new identity would base itself on symbols of traditional Mexican culture and would reflect a total rejection of *gabacho* culture—the culture of the white Anglo-Saxon Protestant.

The conference participants developed a series of resolutions outlining the goals of Chicano liberation within the context of the nationalist ideology that Gonzales put forward. The resolutions exhorted students to take up a struggle to unite all Mexican Americans regardless of social class. The basis for unity would be their pride in Mexican ethnicity and culture. It was reasoned that all Mexican Americans, regardless of how indoctrinated they were with the dominant values of U.S. society, ultimately nurtured such a pride. Nationalism, therefore, was to be the common denominator for uniting all Mexican Americans and making possible effective political mobilization.

The resolutions also called for a struggle to win political and economic control of Mexican American communities. Economic practices based on capitalist goals and values were to be rejected in favor of humanistic values thought to be at the core of Mexican and Mexican American culture. Capitalist economic institutions were to be replaced by people's cooperatives. Independent Mexican American political groups were necessary to take the place of the Democratic and Republican party machines, since "the two-party system is the same animal with two heads that feed from the same trough."

The importance of the struggle for community control of the schools received special emphasis. Chicano studies programs were needed to teach Chicanos their history and culture. The resolutions advocated bilingual education to assure the continuity of the Spanish language and Mexican American culture. Mexican cultural values were to be the most "powerful weapon to defeat the gringo dollar value system and encourage the process of love and brotherhood." The resolutions also advocated self-defense and militant protest.

The resolutions as adopted by the conference were put together in a document entitled *El Plan Espiritual de Aztlán* or *The Spiritual Plan of Aztlán*.★ The document was drafted by a committee that included Alurista, one of the better known radical poets from the ranks of the student activists. His poetry, like the work of Luis Valdez, emphasized the Native American aspects of the Mexican American experience. The conference agreed that the conference participants would base all their political work on the premises and program outlined in *El Plan Espiritual*. The participants resolved to disseminate the document at all Mexican American functions on campuses and in Mexican American communities. The following manifesto prefaced the plan:

> In the spirit of a new people that is conscious not only of its proud historical heritage, but also of the brutal "Gringo" invasion of our territories, we, the Chicano inhabitants and civilizers of the northern land of Aztlán, from whence came our forefathers, reclaiming the land of their birth and consecrating the determination of our people of the sun, declare that the call of our blood is our power, our responsibility and our inevitable destiny. . . . Brotherhood unites us, and love for our brothers makes us a people whose time has come and who struggle against the foreigner "Gabacho" who exploits our riches and destroys our culture. . . . We are Bronze People with a Bronze Culture. . . . We are Aztlán.

More than a thousand people had attended the Chicano Youth Conference. It was a week of serious deliberation—and singing and dancing as well. Maria Varela, one of the participants, described it:

> "Conference" is a poor word to describe those five days. . . . It was in reality a fiesta: days of celebrating what sings in the blood of a people who, taught to believe they are ugly, discover the true beauty in their souls during the years of occupation and intimidation. . . . Coca Cola, Doris Day, Breck Shampoo, the Playboy Bunny, the Arrow Shirt man, the Marlboro heroes, are lies. "We are beautiful. . . ." [T]his affirmation grew into a *grito*, a roar, among the people gathered in the auditorium of the Crusade's Center.

★*Aztlán* was the name used by the Aztecs to refer to the place of their origin. Since the Aztecs had migrated to central Mexico from "somewhere in the north," Chicano activists claimed that Aztlán was all the southwestern United States taken from Mexico as a result of the Mexican-American War. This included California, Texas, New Mexico, most of Arizona, large parts of Colorado, Nevada and Utah, and a piece of Wyoming.

The conference was a phenomenal success, going far beyond the expectations of Gonzáles and the conference organizers. For one thing, it made Gonzáles one of the leaders of the Chicano movement. Moreover, the conference promoted solidarity among youth of different social backgrounds and from different parts of the U.S. Puerto Rican youth from Chicago and New York had also attended. Before the conference, very little communication had existed between Mexican American youth in different states, or even between regions of the same state. But it was no surprise that the majority of the participants came from California, because that was where the rapidly developing Chicano student movement first came to maturity.

THE SANTA BARBARA CONFERENCE

Approximately a month after the Denver youth conference, the Chicano Coordinating Council on Higher Education (CCHE) held a conference at the University of California, Santa Barbara. CCHE had been organized as a state network of students, faculty and staff who were interested in creating programs to help Mexican American students attending California's colleges and universities. The goal of the conference was to develop a master plan for the creation of curriculum and the related auxiliary services and structures essential to facilitate Mexican American access to those institutions. The Santa Barbara conference was successful in developing such a plan. The conference had an added significance, however, in that it was the first opportunity for young Chicanos who attended the Denver conference to implement the ideas of *El Plan Espiritual de Aztlán*. Although not one of its original goals, the Santa Barbara conference also became the "founding convention" of the Chicano student movement, which quickly spread across campuses throughout the United States.

At the Santa Barbara conference the student leaders moved to adopt a new name for existing student organizations, a name that would transcend localism and regionalism and align the student movement with the goals of *El Plan Espiritual de Aztlán*. The students envisioned the development of a Mexican American student movement that would play an important role in national as well as community politics. They therefore placed the issue of the name change in a context that would transcend California:

> Since the movement is definitely of national significance and scope, all student organizations should adopt one identical name throughout the state and eventually the nation to characterize the common struggle of *La Raza de Aztlán*. The net gain is a step toward greater national unity which enhances the power in mobilizing local campus organizations.

After intense deliberation on the implications and political significance of a new name, the students voted to drop their current organizational names throughout the state. Thus, the United Mexican American Students, the Mexican American Student Confederation, the Mexican American Youth Association, and the Mexican American Student Association eventually dropped names associated with a particular campus or region and became El Movimiento Estudiantil Chicano de Aztlán (The Chicano Student Movement of Aztlán), based on wide agreement that the new name should reflect the terms *Chicano* and *Aztlán:*

> *Chicano,* in the past a pejorative and class-bound adjective, has now become the root idea of a new culture identity for our people. It also reveals a growing solidarity and the development of pride and confidence.

The adoption of the new name and its acronym, MEChA, signalled a new level of political consciousness among student activists. It was the final stage in the transformation of what had been loosely organized, local student groups into a single structured and unified student movement. A literal translation of the acronym MEChA was "match" or "matchstick." Thus, in the minds of Mexican American student activists the obvious symbol was "fire," with all its connotations of militancy.

In terms of identity and ideology, MEChA symbolized the emergence of a new generation of youth, *La Raza Nueva* or the "new people" or "reborn youth." The adoption of this new name thus encouraged students to see themselves as a part of the new Chicano generation that was committed to militant struggle against U.S. institutions that had historically been responsible for the oppression of Mexican Americans. Adamant rejection of the label "Mexican American" meant rejection of the assimilationist and accommodationist melting pot ideology that had guided earlier generations of activists:

> *Chicanismo* involves a crucial distinction in political consciousness between a Mexican American and a Chicano mentality. The Mexican American is a person who lacks respect for his cultural and ethnic heritage. Unsure of himself, he seeks assimilation as a way out of his "degraded" social status. Consequently, he remains politically ineffective. In contrast, *Chicanismo* reflects self-respect and pride in one's ethnic and cultural background. . . . [T]he Chicano acts with confidence and with a range of alternatives in the political world.

The new student movement wanted to build around the term Chicano the unequivocal rejection of middle-class striving for assimilation:

> Chicanismo simply embodies an ancient truth: that man is never closer to his true self as when he is close to his community. . . . Chicanismo draws its faith and strength from two main sources: from the just struggle of our people and from an objective analysis of our community's strategic needs.

Chicanismo was also seen as an extension of the concept of *La Raza Cósmica*. The term had been coined by the Mexican philosopher José Vasconcellos in his book of the same title. This notion posited that the peoples of mixed indigenous and European bloods throughout the Americas would one day develop into a "superior race." This concept reinforced the idea that Chicanos were *La Raza Nueva*.

The Santa Barbara conference proposed two basic goals for the student movement. In the community, MEChA was to become organically tied to the everyday social and political life of the Mexican American communities, with the aim of developing those communities. On campus, MEChA was to become a permanent, well-organized power bloc for the purpose of redirecting university attention and resources to the needs of Mexican American students and Mexican American communities. In the community, close working relationships with community organizations were to be established, regardless of differences in ideology or orientation. Given the apolitical—and at times negative or conservative—attitudes towards politics within the Mexican American community, MEChA would treat politics in ways that would bring about an understanding of the necessity for political work:

> The student movement is to a large degree a political movement and as such must not elicit from our people the negative responses that we have experienced so often in the past in relation to politics, and often with good reason. . . . We must re-define politics for our people to be a means of liberation. The political sophistication of our Raza must be raised so that they do not fall prey to apologists and vendidos whose whole interest is their personal career or fortune.

A critical element of this political education was the way in which the community viewed the colleges and universities. Chicanos had to understand that these institutions were strategic agencies in any process of community development, and thus it was important to view them as *their* institutions:

> What is needed at this time, more than anything else, is to firm up the rapidly growing identification of the university as a critical agency in the transformation of the Chicano community. Our people must understand not only the strategic importance of the university . . . they must above all perceive the university as being our university.

This position reflected MEChA's understanding that part of its own power on campus would have to derive from community support. If political and educational change were to be won on campus, the community outside the campus would have to be mobilized. The MEChA strategy was to establish itself as both a legitimate community organization and a student group. Legitimacy in the community would in turn depend on a successful effort to form alliances with professionals, workers, and street youth in the surrounding Mexican American communities of each local campus.

MEChA's second broad goal, that of establishing itself as a power base on campus, meant that it would have to undertake an ambitious effort to increase the recruitment of Mexican American students and to teach them the ideology of *Chicanismo*, politicizing them so that they would participate in protest activities on behalf of their people.

> MEChA is a first step to tying the student . . . throughout the Southwest into a vibrant and responsive network of activists that will respond as a unit to oppression and racism and that will work in harmony when initiating and carrying out campaigns of liberation for our people.

The strategy called for students to be organized around social and cultural events that were designed to expose university indoctrination and propaganda based on the Protestant "ethic of profit and competition, of greed and intolerance." MEChA would advocate replacing that ethic with the values associated with the "ancestral communalism" of the ancient Mexican peoples. MEChA would appeal to the sense of obligation to family and community on the part of every student:

> MEChA must bring to the mind of every young Chicano that the liberation of his people from prejudice and oppression is in his hand and this responsibility is greater than personal achievement and more meaningful than degrees, especially if they are earned at the expense of this identity and cultural integrity.

Finally, the MEChA strategy called for the organization to play a substantive role in the creation and implementation of Chicano Studies and support services programs on campus. Chicano Studies programs would be a relevant alternative to established curricula. Most important, the Chicano Studies programs would be the foundation of MEChA's political power base:

> The institutionalization of Chicano programs is the realization of Chicano power on campus. The key to this power is found in the application of the principles of self-determination and self-liberation. These principles are defined and practiced in the areas of control, autonomy, flexibility, and participation. Often imaginary or symbolic authority is confused with the real. Many times token efforts in program institutionalization are substituted for enduring constructive programming. It is the responsibility of Chicanos on campus to insure dominant influence of these programs. The point is not to have a college with a program, but rather a Chicano program at the college.

Allies among sympathetic faculty and administrators were to be cultivated as links to the academic power structure. But an independent and autonomous MEChA would preclude any co-optation. Students would also be the ones to assure that Mexican American faculty and administrators would retain their allegiance to the movement:

> Therefore students must constantly remind the Chicano faculty and adminis-trators where their loyalty and allegiance lies. It is very easy for administrators to begin looking for promotions just as it is very natural for faculty members to seek positions of academic prominence. . . . [I]t is the students who must keep after Chicano and non-Chicano administrators and faculty to see that they do not compromise the position of the student and the community.

MEChA would of course mobilize community support on behalf of those faculty and staff members who, because of their demonstrated commitment to student interests, might jeopardize their own jobs.

Since Chicano Studies programs were at the heart of MEChA's concerns, special measures were advocated—and special concerns were noted. The politics of expediency characteristic of college administrators constituted a particular threat. It was important that Chicano Studies programs not be put in the straightjacket of the usual, academic guidelines. Community input was deemed essential to preclude the complete control of programs by academicians—many of whom accepted a rigid academy-community dichotomy and who therefore would tend toward "business as usual." Adequate Chicano control of the programs could be assured only if people from the community, students and Chicano faculty were all directly involved in the decision-making process of the pro-grams. Dissolving the academy-community dichotomy would thus make possible Chi-cano programs that would become models of "self-determination" and "self-liberation." "Academy" and especially "community" had to be conceptualized in new ways:

> [T]he concept of "community" is all-inclusive. The Chicanos on campus are an organic, integral part of the Chicano community. Among Chicanos on cam-pus there can be no distinctions or separations because of personal occupational differentiations. . . . [T]he Chicano community on campus is an extension of the larger community. The base of the Chicanos on campus is the Chicano community. . . . The primary goals of the various programs must be to serve the interests of the Chicano people.

The Santa Barbara conference lasted three days and involved, over a hundred activists. Most were undergraduates and leaders of campus organizations. But some were graduate students, and several were faculty members or administrators. The proceedings of the conference were subsequently published as *El Plan de Santa Barbara*. The plan was much more detailed and sophisticated than *El Plan Espiritual de Aztlán*. Yet the Santa Barbara document built on the ideological and philosophical foundations laid out in the Denver document. In one important respect, however, it went beyond the Denver document: it specifically focused on the role of the Chicano intellectual and identified the institutions of higher education as strategic targets for political change. The manifesto that prefaced *El Plan de Santa Barbara* was a militant challenge to the university; it announced that the Chicano student movement had officially arrived and intended to play a leading role in the Chicano Power Movement in California and in the United States:

> For all people, as with individuals, the time comes when they must reckon with their history. For the Chicano, the present is a time of renaissance, of *renacimiento*. Our people and our community, *el barrio* and *la colonia*, are expressing a new consciousness and a new resolve. . . . [W]e pledge our will to move against those forces which have denied us freedom of expression and human dignity.

THE DECLINE OF THE STUDENT MOVEMENT

The Santa Barbara conference ended on a high note of solidarity. MEChA did, in fact, play a prominent role in the new politics of protest and confrontation, both on the campus and in the community. The political consciousness of the students rose through the intensification of MEChA's political activity, and much was accomplished. Chicano Studies programs were established at California community colleges located in areas with a substantial Mexican American community, at all the state colleges, and at virtually all of the campuses of the University of California. In some schools they were instituted as regular departments, in others as research centers, and in still other schools as specialized curricula within existing academic units.

Increased Mexican American access to the colleges and universities also became a reality as the student movement pressed for expansion of support services programs. The special focus given to recruitment of Mexican American students was successful as MEChA directly confronted the issue of who should control educational opportunity programs (EOPs). MEChA engaged in power struggles with white liberal and Black administrators, whose overriding emphasis on the recruitment of Black students was perceived as slighting Mexican American. In a few cases these programs were placed in the hands of Mexican American administrators, some of whom were former student activists. But on most campuses the EOPs were divided into two components, one with a Chicano administrator and one with a Black administrator. The results were mixed. On the one hand, Chicano control (or partial control) of the EOPs enabled MEChA to increase the Mexican American student presence on campus. On the other, Chicano influence contributed to bitter and intense conflicts between Mexican Americans and Blacks on several campuses, making viable coalition politics difficult, if not altogether impossible.

Institution-sponsored community programs were another tangible result of the student movement. In some cases, the institutions provided the funds for MEChA to establish community centers that served as a link between students and their communities. Through these centers students provided counseling and tutorial services for youth and adults. Some centers provided a meeting place for community organizations. A few centers also offered bilingual education classes to teach English and academic courses on the same credit basis as college and university extension programs. Many MEChA activists became involved in electoral politics and in community organizations struggling to make changes in the local schools. Alliances were made with other organizations—for example, with the Brown Berets, who were involved in combatting police brutality and drug use in the Mexican American community.

The Brown Berets became the largest nonstudent radical youth organization in the Mexican American community. During their formative period soon after the Los Angeles high school strike of 1968, UMAS and later MEChA activists were important members of the organization. David Sanchez, the founder and prime minister of the Brown Berets, and three other leaders were among the thirteen activists indicted for conspiracy after the student strike. They were students at East Los Angeles City College and California State College, Los Angeles. (Sanchez had been a model high school student leader who had been recruited by the conservative mayor of Los Angeles, Sam Yorty, into his city youth council.) But its leadership and rank and file had become predominantly street youth by 1970. Sanchez and others who had been student activists dropped out of college to become full-time community activists, and they recruited members who were or had been members of gangs. Many recruits came from the ranks of *pintos,* those who had served time in juvenile hall or prison. The Berets thus played a significant role in bringing street youth into the Chicano movement.

The Brown Berets became a paramilitary organization and, because of it, developed an image as the Chicano counterparts of the Black Panther Party. As cultural nationalists, however, they had more in common with US, the militant Black nationalist organization headed by Ron Karenga. They did not share the Marxist/Maoist ideology of the Black Panthers. The Berets adopted as their prime responsibility the defense of the Mexican American community against police harassment and brutality. They were therefore heavily infiltrated by police intelligence agencies and COINTELPRO.

The Berets and MEChA became a significant part of the first major Mexican American demonstration against the war in Vietnam. It took place in Los Angeles on 29 August 1970. The organizing committee for the demonstration was called the Chicano Moratorium, and it was cochaired by Brown Beret Prime Minister David Sanchez and Rosalio Muñoz, former student body president at UCLA and one of the first Mexican Americans to resist the draft. Other draft resisters were Manuel Gómez, a Brown

Beret and student activist at Hayward State College and one of the most eloquent young poets of the Chicano movement; Ernesto Vigil, one of the young leaders of the Crusade for Justice; and Lorenzo Campbell, a student activist at the University of California, Riverside.

The Chicano Moratorium drew over 20,000 people to Laguna Park in East Los Angeles. The rally started in a festive mood, but ended in terror when Los Angeles police and Los Angeles County sheriff's deputies attacked the crowd without provocation. Hundreds were injured and over two hundred were arrested. Those arrested included Corky Gonzáles and his contingent from the Crusade for Justice. Tragically, three Mexican Americans were killed. This police riot provoked the first violent Mexican American outburst in a major U.S. city as thousands of protestors took out revenge by burning businesses and automobiles on Whittier Boulevard, one of the main thoroughfares in East Los Angeles. In response to the police attack, Rosalio Muñoz issued a statement protesting the police violence and making it clear that the Chicano Moratorium committee would continue to protest the war and would not be intimidated by "police totalitarian aggression."

Despite its achievements . . . or perhaps partly because of them . . . student activism had declined dramatically by 1971. New student organizations emerged that were more career-oriented, emphasizing individual advancement. They were also extremely apolitical. Students in engineering and architecture programs formed their own organizations, as did those majoring in health, pre-law, education, and other areas. MEChA had to compete with these new organizations for influence among Chicano students. However, most incoming students lacked the experience of participating in political struggle that would have brought them closer to MEChA's ideological perspective. With protest and confrontation throughout the U.S. on the downswing, mass demonstrations on behalf of Mexican American causes also declined. Most Chicano students no longer perceived MEChA as a viable organization for meeting their academic and social needs.

Meanwhile, the founders of MEChA had graduated. Some had entered graduate or professional schools where they became involved in student organizations independent of MEChA—organizations more attuned to professional career goals. A good example was La Raza Law Students Association, organized by Mexican American student activists in the law schools. Many of those who were graduate students when MEChA was founded and during the height of MEChA's activity had become part-time faculty—mostly in Chicano Studies or similar programs (since few Mexican Americans with doctorates were available for these positions). But priorities shifted as these activists moved from involvement in the politics of confrontation to implementation of programs, and their emphasis often shifted to institutional politics.

Other former student activists became EOP recruiters, counselors, or administrators (often through EOP work-study programs). Consequently they also became part of the university bureaucracy and embroiled in institutional politics. Others had left the campuses and become politically active in community organizations. Still another factor in

MEChA's decline was the fact that many of the activists had neglected their studies because of their political involvement. Many of these students were placed on academic probation and were thus forced to shift their personal priorities from MEChA to academic survival. Attendance at MEChA meetings suffered a noticeable decline.

Within the MEChA groups, students differed on priorities. Some argued that MEChA's priority was campus struggle concerning the issues directly affecting students. Others took the position that MEChA should concentrate its time and energy on community struggles and use its institutional base to generate resources needed in those struggles. These differences eventually widened, becoming more antagonistic, and this debate over strategy only added to the further decline of the student movement.

Efforts were made to revitalize MEChA at a statewide conference held at California State University, Northridge in December 1972. The conference held workshops on the future direction and goals of MEChA, on the concepts of *La Raza* and *Chicanismo,* and on the role of women in the student movement. Several major resolutions were passed. One required MEChA to support La Raza Unida Party. Another stipulated that women would have equal representation in the leadership of MEChA. Others called for MEChA to play a major role in the decision-making process of Chicano Studies and related Chicano programs; to boycott Coors beer in support of striking Mexican American workers; and to continue to support the struggle of the United Farm Workers Union.

The resolution of support for La Raza Unida Party reflected a concern to continue the ideology of *Chicanismo.* But it did generate some controversy because in a very important respect it conflicted with support for the farmworkers' struggle. Chávez and the UFW had consistently worked within the Democratic Party—indeed, the UFW's very existence depended on its ties to the Democratic Party. In return for support of pro-farmworker legislation and other reforms, the UFW endorsed and campaigned for Democratic candidates at the local, state, and national levels.

Ultimately, the conference's farmworker resolution was passed only because of the importance of the union to Mexican American farmworkers. However, the passage of both resolutions reflected contradictions within MEChA and further aggravated divisions within the organization, since some members opted to work actively in support of La Raza Unida while others continued to work actively in support of the farmworkers union (and indirectly for the Democratic Party).

The resolution on the role of women in the leadership of MEChA reflected a rapid acceleration of concern about the issue of sexism. Although women had always played an active role in the student movement (and in a few cases provided the leadership), they had consistently been relegated to secondary roles. As a result, the various stances on sexism became another reason for divisions within MEChA, with many women deciding to spend their energy on the development of their own feminist organizations.

The fact that the MEChA conference found it necessary to pass a resolution calling for more active MEChA involvement in the decision-making process of Chicano programs on campus reflected the ever increasing conflict between students and Mexican

American faculty and administrators. Students had played a key role in the early phases of developing and implementing proposals for Chicano Studies programs on campus. (This was true even before the historic Santa Barbara conference, where the role of students was first "officially" spelled out.) However, once the programs were approved and funded and staff and faculty had secured positions, the role of students became more and more peripheral.

In essence, students had supported the efforts to make the programs an integral part of the institution. However, once programs became part of the institution they came under the general rules and regulations governing all academic programs. In the case of Chicano Studies, this meant that exclusive control of curricula by the faculty was expected to ensure conformance with university policies. Students thus could no longer expect to play an influential role in the further development of Chicano Studies programs unless "understandings" were reached with the program faculty.

Although some programs did make efforts to allow students a direct role in decision making, the usual outcome of institutionalization was the gradual decline of student participation in the governance of the programs. Distrust between faculty, administrators, and students evolved, creating a climate of divisiveness. Students often responded by criticizing the faculty for careerism and opportunism, while faculty members criticized students for not understanding the need to conform to institutional policy to ensure the survival of Chicano Studies programs.

Several other local, regional and statewide meetings and conferences marked efforts to revitalize MEChA and redefine its goals and objectives to be more in tune with the new issues and the changed situation. The general goals of the 1960s had been achieved. Chicano Studies programs had become a reality, and the EOPs and other support services programs had opened the doors to institutions of higher education for thousands of Mexican American youth from low-income families. Although many of these programs were relatively insecure, most new students saw them as part of the status quo and related to them as if they had always been there.

Thus, the issues and objectives outlined in *El Plan de Santa Barbara* could no longer have any meaningful impact on the new wave of students: The plan was not a program for the 1970s and beyond. The easily understood goals of MEChA's founders were not clear to the new MEChA activists, and confusion over goals and ideology began to develop. In response to this uncertainty, the new leaders began to ponder the future direction of the student movement. They attributed the decline of MEChA to the following reasons:

> The lack of vision and adaptability to a new situation made the organization stagnant and nonproductive. This was basically due to the fact that our goals . . . were vague and undefined and that we were trying to build up an organization on false assumptions such as: (1) because we are all Chicanos we would be drawn together and automatically define our goals and directions: (2) that by

simply directing our efforts and energies to the issues facing the Chicano, political consciousness would evolve. These assumptions have been detrimental to the Chicano's advancement for self-determination.

Chicanismo, as defined in *El Plan de Santa Barbara*, had kept the movement generally united during its formative period. But this cultural nationalist ideology, as it was generally understood in 1969, proved unable to accommodate the different levels of political consciousness that characterized the student movement. The ideology of *Chicanismo* had settled the internal confusion over identity. But in spite of this tremendous accomplishment *Chicanismo* could not even begin to answer the substantive questions concerning the ultimate shape of a political ideology and strategy that could take into account the diversity of political orientations within the Mexican American community. There is no question that *Chicanismo* propelled the movements politics against racism. But, as conceptualized in 1969, it did not offer a framework for the concrete analysis of the dominant political and economic institutions of U.S. society and how they affected the different strata of Mexican Americans.

In addition, *Chicanismo* never offered the student movement adequate insight into the nature of the institutions of higher education and their role in society. Breaking some of the barriers to educational opportunity for Mexican Americans, by itself a formidable accomplishment, ultimately proved to be a very limited political goal. Interestingly, some student activists had recognized these limitations soon after the Santa Barbara conference. Those who had become influenced by other left political organizations criticized *Chicanismo* as a reactionary ideology. At a conference that took place at Merritt College in Oakland in July 1969, some of these students put it this way: "What nationalism as an ideology does is deny class society and a class consciousness."

Others, especially those involved in liberal Democratic politics, sought a path toward the acceptance of a liberal capitalism that called for the integration of Chicanos into the existing political economy of society. They argued that Chicano political power was impossible without the development of Chicano capitalist institutions:

> [W]e fail to realize that we . . . lack the power that makes and breaks politicians and turns proposals into laws. We lack monetary power . . . which enables the Anglo-Saxon to buy votes and politicians . . . .We must be able to manipulate politicians through campaign contributions. . . . [W]e shouldn't hesitate to sell our vote to the highest bidder. . . . The solution . . . is for us to become just as capitalistic as the white man. Lets go build Chicano corporations and industrial empires; let's go into business and finance, not being afraid to use the methods that have put the 'man' where he is.

These advocates of Chicano capitalism believed that Mexican American students should major in the natural sciences, business and finance, and engineering. The response to "Chicano capitalism" was a call for a revolutionary Marxism that could provide a critical understanding of how capitalism ultimately functions to the detriment of all working people:

> [W]hite workers are exploited in the factory for their labor in the same manner that Chicanos, blacks, and other minorities are exploited. They suffer from racial discrimination . . . but as a class of people. The ones who benefit from this system are a small percentage of the population . . . who control the means of production. To have . . . Chicanos become big industrialists wouldn't help the Chicano masses any more than the white worker is helped by the white industrialists. What has to be understood is that Capitalism thrives on the exploitation of man by man, and the only way that the oppression of the people will be eradicated is by the destruction of this system and not by its toleration.

The conflict over political ideology intensified, coming to crisis at a statewide MEChA conference held at the University of California, Riverside campus in 1973. Students who urged that MEChA adopt a Marxist ideology criticized cultural nationalism on the following basis:

> Cultural nationalism . . . points to a form of struggle that does not take into account the inter-connectedness of the world and proclaims as a solution the separatism that the capitalist has developed and perpetuated in order to exploit working people further. . . . It promotes the concept of a nation without a material basis and solely on a spiritual basis and tends to identify the enemy on a racial basis, ignoring the origin of racism and that it is simply an oppressive tool of capitalism.

In a heated exchange, the Marxist faction argued that MEChA had ceased to be an effective organization because it had evolved into a bureaucratic and reactionary group. It had lost its will to struggle, as evidenced by the desire of the majority attending the conference to avoid discussions of political ideology. On the second day of the conference the Marxists walked out, along with many of the new, apolitical students who had had an interest in becoming MEChistas.

These new students lacked the experience to understand the political debate. The student movement never recovered from the effects of this split. After the conference, statewide MEChA communication and coordination came to a virtual halt, and MEChA chapters returned to an emphasis on local campus politics.

Most of the students who had adopted a Marxist position at the conference dropped completely out of MEChA. Some formed countergroups, while others became involved with community-based Marxist organizations. One group of Marxists in Los Angeles and Orange counties formed El Comité Estudiantil del Pueblo:

> We have come together ... parting from the conclusion that MEChA has reached its objective limits as an organizational form to wage struggle on the student level. This conclusion was reached through the reflection of our own practice in the Chicano Student Movement.

El Comité was a collective that included Mexican and Puerto Rican students who had links to revolutionary student movements in Mexico and to the Puerto Rican Socialist Party, respectively. The collective operated under the direction of the National Committee to Free Los Tres and CASA (Centro de Acción Social Autónoma). The National Committee to Free Los Tres was formed after the arrest of three activists associated with La Casa del Carnalismo, a community organization whose primary emphasis was to drive dope pushers out of the community. The three activists and the National Committee to Free Los Tres accused the authorities of planting drugs in order to make the bust, with the purpose of subverting the organizing efforts of La Casa del Carnalismo. CASA, the other organization working with El Comité Estudiantil del Pueblo, had been founded by Bert Corona, a labor organizer, former president of MAPA, and long-time political activist, but it had been taken over by the leadership of the radical Los Tres organization:

> We clearly align ourselves with the organizations that put forth the correct political line in theory and foremost in practice, concerning the struggle for self-determination of our people. Both CASA ... and the National Committee to Free Los Tres have shown in practice, their vigilance over the democratic rights of our people through their daily work and open political defiance and resistance to repression in the form of mass demonstrations and mobilizations. ... [B]oth organizations are responsible for taking our struggle to a national level. Also, in developing an independent political line that corresponds to the particular concrete conditions of our people.

Based on its work within these community organizations, El Comité Estudiantil developed a set of political principles that clearly established its Marxist orientation:

(1) Struggle for self-determination as a people against the imperialist system which denies us that right.
(2) University reform.
(3) Creation of Student-Worker Unity.
(4) Anti-imperialist solidarity with student struggles within the United States and throughout the world, particularly with Latin America.

In contrast to MEChA's ideology of cultural nationalism, the ideology of revolutionary nationalism was an attractive alternative to some of the more radical students on campus. The National Committee to Free Los Tres explained the difference between the two outlooks in this way:

> [S]ome Chicano Movement activists obsessively continue to hold on to the view that we must struggle against exploitation, racism, repression and for self determination, guided by the spiritual, cultural and moral values of our Indian ancestors. . . . [They] also hold the view that since the white European Invader is our oppressor, we must reject any ideas . . . that come from white people. . . . But the problems our people face today . . . require concrete solutions. . . . Cultural practices, spiritual beliefs, love . . . Chicanismo . . . do not teach us how to organize a workers strike, how to organize and struggle against police brutality, how to stop the dragnet raids and mass deportations of our people, how to organize a student movement. . . . It does not teach us how to create a society free of exploitation, how as part of the working class we can take power. . . . Our children should not feel proud that they are Mexicanos only because of their color. The strongest national consciousness comes from a knowledge that the masses of our people have made great contributions to the progress and development of organized society, industry and agriculture [and] led . . . great struggles to organize workers against exploitation. . . . Teaching history in this manner . . . creates strong pride in our heritage. But it also recognizes and respects the role of other nationalities as workers and . . . teaches our people true internationalism. It exposes the class nature of U.S. society [and] . . . imperialism as the bloodiest, most brutal exploiter . . . responsible for the underdevelopment of the Third World. . . . [W]e also learn the true nature of racism as having an economic base. . . . [R] evolutionary nationalism entails working class solidarity which knows no borders. A concept especially important to us who exist divided from our people by the border established by the imperialist U.S. powers. True revolutionary nationalism can only be developed in this context. *Un pueblo sin fronteras* [a people without borders].

The revolutionary nationalism defined by the National Committee required the rejection of the Chicano identity defined at the Santa Barbara conference. The concept *sin fronteras,* which for Bert Corona had meant that all workers had to be organized regardless of which side of the border their home was on, now became the basis for a struggle against the politics of Chicano identity. CASA members attempted to persuade other students that Chicano culture did not exist. They argued that the perpetuation of the Chicano identity was harmful because it divided Mexican students in the United States from student movements in Mexico. The National Committee eventually merged with CASA. The Comité Estudiantil del Pueblo ceased to exist as student activists became the dominant constituency and former student activists the leadership of CASA.

Meanwhile, another predominantly Chicano Marxist community organization, the August 29th Movement, had emerged, though its political orientation was very different from CASA's. Comprising mostly former and current Chicano student and youth activists, it had adopted a Marxist-Leninism that emphasized the teachings of Stalin and Mao. ATM attracted left-leaning students who disagreed with CASA's rejection of Chicano identity. Instead, ATM took the position that *Chicanismo* was very much a reality:

> We . . . oppose those forces who say that "there is no Chicano people." . . . These forces . . . claim that Chicanos in the southwest are actually Mexicanos, a part of the country of México. They desire . . . not the right to political independence, but re-annexation to México. To these forces, it must seem that the Chicano people have not yet "earned" their right to be called a people.

ATM credited the student movement of the 1960s with having played the most significant role in the development of the Chicano movement. It acknowledged the decline of MEChA but saw a need to give it direction and to broaden its scope by emphasizing support for worker and campesino struggles. Using Stalin's definition of nation from *Marxism and the National Question,* ATM developed a plan for the establishment of a Chicano nation within those territories of the southwestern United States that had a majority, or a sufficiently large, Chicano population. ATM called on Chicano student activists to join in the struggle to establish a multinational communist party in the United States:

> In every revolutionary movement students have played an important role. We must realize that only one class, the working class, is capable of carrying the revolution to success. But students who believe in the objective of socialism can consciously work for that objective. . . . [S]tudents must take up the disciplined study of the science of the working class, Marxism-Leninism. They must involve themselves with struggles on campus and take leadership roles in those struggles, to educate others as to the fact that our problems derive from the system of imperialism and can only end with the destruction of imperialism. . . . [W]e must remember . . . we were not always students nor will we always be students. There is a class struggle raging and there are only two choices before us, either the side of the imperialists . . . or the side of the proletariat. Let us build a multinational communist party.

CASA and ATM competed with each other in efforts to recruit student activists from MEChA and other organizations. At a few campuses a bitter struggle took place over the control of MEChA or of the Chicano Studies program. But for the most part these organizations failed to have much impact on the majority of Mexican American students. Their intense debates were usually couched in polemical language and alienated the average student, who had no familiarity with Marxist terminology. The result was the reinforcement of anti-Marxist attitudes among most students.

On a statewide basis the dominant forces within MEChA were cultural nationalism and liberal interest-group politics. MEChA continued to decline; few students attended meetings and on some campuses MEChA ceased to function altogether. Nine years after the Santa Barbara conference, MEChA held a statewide constitutional conference at Stanford University to revitalize the student movement and redefine its goals. In a letter to all MEChA leaders in California the conference organizers addressed the significance of the conference in the following terms:

> It is very important that all MEChAs in the state participate in the development of a new constitution. This conference will mark an important stage in the history of the Chicano student movement as it will be the first time since *El Plan de Santa Barbara* . . . that Chicano students will come together to re-define the goals, objectives, and philosophy of *el movimiento estudiantil Chicano.*

By these standards, the Stanford conference was a failure. It did not produce the new document that was to replace *El Plan de Santa Barbara,* nor did it redefine the MEChA's objectives and ideology. MEChA continued to exist on many campuses during the 1970s and was active in varying degrees. On some campuses it ceased to exist entirely, and efforts to revitalize it met with little success.

Outside California, the Chicano student movement developed somewhat differently in both organizational and ideological terms. Few student organizations in other states had changed their names to MEChA. In Texas the Mexican American Youth Organization retained its name and identity, and only one MEChA chapter emerged in that state (at the University of Texas at El Paso in the early 1970s). It was not until 1980 that another MEChA evolved in Texas with the founding of a chapter at the University of Texas at San Antonio. The first statewide MEChA conference in Texas took place in 1982. Eleven student organizations participated and agreed to become members of a statewide MEChA. MAYO, MASA, UMAS, Hispanic Student Alliance, AMAS and even a LULAC chapter, were listed in the MEChA "Member Organizations" list of 1981–82.

In Colorado, only one MEChA chapter emerged and that was at the Metropolitan State campus. At the state's leading college, the University of Colorado at Boulder, UMAS never did change its name to MEChA despite strong support from Corky Gonzales and his Crusade for Justice throughout the state. The same pattern prevailed in Arizona and New Mexico. In the Midwest, UMAS did evolve into MEChA at the University of Notre Dame. But, although the Notre Dame MEChA chapter was active on campus and in the community, the name did not spread to other campuses in the Midwest.

The failure of the MEChA name to take hold outside California was the result of the uneven development of cultural, racial, and political consciousness among Mexican American youth throughout the Southwest and Midwest. For example, the proximity of Texas to the Mexican border has historically resulted in the survival of a distinct Mexican culture and folklore in that state. The identity crisis among youth in Texas has therefore never been as pronounced as in California. In the Midwest, Mexican identity has merged with that of other Latinos, mostly notably Puerto Ricans.

The lack of equal emphasis on the quest for identity outside California did not mean that the Chicano student movement was not significant elsewhere. In terms of the quest for power, the movement was important, especially in Texas, Colorado and New Mexico, where it contributed to the development of La Raza Unida Party and the political mobilization of the Mexican American people.

In spite of internal conflicts, the student movement made significant contributions. It played the principal role in the establishment of programs on campus which produced greater access for Mexican American youth to institutions of higher education—most notably, Chicano Studies and EOF programs. It developed the political consciousness of Mexican American youth. It was always at the center of the development of the broader Chicano Power Movement in California and elsewhere in the United States. From the ranks of the movement have come intellectuals and professionals who are beginning to play a role in leading U.S. political and economic institutions. Some of these intellectuals have participated in organizational efforts to develop new perspectives that challenge the dominant ideology. (The most notable of them have explored and incorporated Marxist, neo-Marxist and feminist concepts into their analysis of the Mexican American experience.) In the absence of a strong student movement, however, most of these intellectuals have assumed roles in institutions that reinforce the dominant values of capitalism. The critiques of "ivory tower intellectualism" that characterized the militant period of the movement are not often heard today, and certainly do not carry the sting they once did.

As with so many other social movements, students were the catalyst in bringing about a polarization between those who were content with the status quo, or who argued for a "gradualist" approach, and those who were committed to quickly bringing about substantive institutional change. The debate continues, because the contradictions still exist. But without a strong student movement, it is not always easy to distinguish between the professionalism and sophistication required to compel social change and the professionalism used to maintain the status quo.

33

The U.S. Central America Peace Movement

Christian Smith

LAUNCHING THE PEACE MOVEMENT

> Their conclusion was always the same . . . that a fight must be put up, in this way or that, and there must be no bowing down. The essential thing was to save the greatest possible number of persons from dying. . . . And to do this there was only one resource: to fight the plague. There was nothing admirable about this attitude; it was merely logical.
>
> Albert Camus, *The Plague*

The U.S. Central America peace movement was not a unified, monolithic entity. Few social movements are. It was, instead, a broad assembly of individual and collective actions and organizations, all of which challenged U.S. Central American policy in some way.

Many of the movement's actions were isolated, relatively uncoordinated deeds of protest and solidarity. Handfuls of demonstrators in small towns held candlelight vigils publicly to mourn El Salvador's war dead. U.S. cities "adopted" and supported individual Nicaraguan cities. Community groups shipped truckloads of clothing and tools to Guatemala's poor. Angry dissidents threw blood on the walls of government buildings. Community leaders wrote searing op-ed articles for local newspapers opposing aid to El Salvador. Ideologically directed consumers bought Nicaraguan-grown coffee in support of the Sandinistas. Activist groups aggressively campaigned and voted against politicians who supported aid to the Guatemalan military. Middle-class citizens undertook hunger strikes and war-tax resistance. Outraged dissenters floated beach balls, painted to resemble explosive mines, in U.S. harbors to protest the mining of Nicaraguan harbors. Suburban homeowners planted in their front yards memorial crosses bearing names of individual peasants killed in Contra attacks. These kinds of grassroots expressions of activism reflected the movement's broad-based diversity and energy.

But what gave the U.S. Central America peace movement its greatest potency and endurance in contesting U.S. policy were its national movement organizations. These organizations mobilized hundreds of thousands of activists across the country, coordinating their energies into targeted strategies of collective action. The most important ones were Sanctuary, Witness for Peace, and the Pledge of Resistance. After only three years of existence, Sanctuary had mobilized more than seventy thousand U.S. citizens to participate in breaking federal immigration laws in order to confront the Reagan administration with the consequences of its low-intensity war in Central America (Golden and McConnell 1986: 3). Witness for Peace activated more than four thousand U.S. citizens to risk their lives by traveling to Nicaraguan war zones to see first-hand the effects of U.S. policy and to return home to struggle to stop it (Taylor n.d.).And in two years, the Pledge of Resistance mobilized eighty thousand U.S. citizens collectively to threaten mass civil disobedience if the U.S. invaded or escalated its war in Central America (Butigan 1991).

This chapter briefly tells the stories of how these organizations formed and what collective actions they produced. It is primarily descriptive. Future chapters will explore why they emerged and what can be learned about social-movement dynamics from their experiences. These chapters will be more analytical in nature. But first, the descriptive histories.

SANCTUARY

Jim Corbett woke up on the morning of May 5, 1981, knowing that he had to do something about the arrested hitchhiker. He did not know, however, that what he was about to do would launch a social movement.

Corbett was a forty-six-year-old semi-disabled Quaker who, with his wife, Pat, raised goats on a ranch outside Tucson, Arizona. The night before, a fellow-Quaker friend of Corbett's, Jim Dudley, had been stopped by the U.S. Border Patrol on his way back from a trip to Mexico, shortly after picking up a Salvadoran hitchhiker. Dudley was on his way to Corbett's house to return a van he had borrowed and to discuss the planned construction of a chapel in a Mexican village. The hitchhiker was arrested. Dudley was interrogated for half an hour and accused of smuggling an illegal alien before being released.

When Dudley finally arrived at Corbett's, he was visibly disturbed. The frightened hitchhiker, he told Jim and Pat, had begged Dudley in the final moments before the abduction to lie about his Salvadoran identity. "Tell them I work for you and we are traveling together," he had pleaded. Dudley now wondered aloud whether he had made a mistake telling the truth. Couldn't he have tricked or eluded the Border Patrol somehow? Jim and Pat thought not. "Once you're stopped, there's not too much you can do"

But as they discussed the incident, their concern for the arrested hitchhiker grew.

They remembered news stories reporting El Salvador's civil war and the assassination of El Salvador's Archbishop Oscar Romero and four North American churchwomen. They recalled that only ten months earlier twenty-seven middle-class Salvadorans had been discovered trying to cross the scorching desert seventy miles west of Tucson. The Salvadorans' paid smugglers—"coyotes"—had gotten lost and abandoned them, and they were forced to drink urine and cologne before the Border Patrol recovered them. Half of the twenty-seven had died of thirst and exposure. The remaining survivors were taken in by several Tucson churches. Frank Shutts, another Quaker also visiting Corbett that night, said that he had heard rumors of entire planeloads of deported Salvadorans being murdered at the San Salvador airport by death squads, as examples to others who might consider fleeing the country.

"There must be some ways to intervene for these people," Corbett said. But none of them knew how. Helplessly, they shrugged their shoulders, noting that the night was getting late and Dudley had to catch a bus to Albuquerque. Frank Shutts drove him to the station. And the Corbetts went to bed. But Jim Corbett did not sleep well. He could not escape the thought of Dudley's arrested hitchhiker being sent home to a death-squad assassination.

In the morning Corbett resolved to follow up on the matter. He called the offices of the U.S. Immigration and Naturalization Service (INS) and the Border Patrol, who told him that they could not give out information on detainees. Corbett then remembered that his name was the same as that of a well-known former Tucson mayor. He called back the Border Patrol office and said in a commanding voice, "This is Jim Corbett here in Tucson, and I need the name of the Salvadoran you picked up late yesterday at the Peck Canyon roadblock. His name, and where he's being held." It worked. The officer looked up and gave him the information.

After a few more phone calls to a local immigration-rights organization, the Manzo Area Council, Corbett learned that the arrested hitchhiker could not be deported without a hearing if an INS G-28 form designating legal council was signed and filed. So, Corbett drove to the Santa Cruz jail, near Nogales, where Nelson, the hitchhiker, was being held. There Corbett met Nelson, who signed the G-28. Corbett also met two other arrested refugees who told him chilling personal stories of abduction and torture in El Salvador. He concluded that their lives would be in danger if they were deported, so he decided to file G-28s for them as well. The jailer said he had no more of the forms, so Corbett drove to the nearby Border Patrol office, where officers delayed him a half hour before giving him G-28s.

Back at the jail, Corbett was told he had to wait before he could see the two other prisoners again. Thirty minutes passed. Corbett grew impatient. He had to leave Nogales soon to get the G-28s filed at the Tucson INS office by five o'clock. He asked again to see the Salvadorans. "Who was it you were waiting for?" the jailer asked. "Oh, you wanted to see those guys? The Border Patrol took them twenty or thirty minutes ago. They're all gone. And there's no way to know where they went."

Corbett was stunned—he had been hoodwinked by agents of his own government. This was not a bureaucratic confusion, he fumed, but a deliberate effort to deprive refugees of their legal rights and deport them as swiftly as possible to what he considered a likely death.

Jim Corbett, it turns out, was the wrong person for the Border Patrol to cross. He was no dolt. With full scholarships, he had completed a philosophy degree at Colgate University in three years and a master's degree in philosophy at Harvard in one year. Corbett was a nonconformist who believed in the Quaker values of honesty and plain speech and who despised abuses of power. A free-thinking and outspoken man, he had lost three separate jobs in one-man-stand protests over the mistreatment of other employees. The Border Patrol stunt was not about to deter him.

The Corbetts borrowed $4,500 against the value of a trailer they owned and bailed four Salvadoran women and a baby out of jail. These refugees, who lived in a small apartment on the Corbett's property, spent hours talking with Jim and Pat about the violence in El Salvador and the terrors of refugee life. Through them, the connection between "the refugee problem" and the U.S.-sponsored war in Central America became increasingly clear. Jim Corbett began to press the system harder to protect Salvadoran refugees from deportation. But the harder he pressed, the more disillusioned and frustrated he became with the INS and the Border Patrol.

On May 30, Corbett and a companion drove to Los Angeles to search in El Centro, a major INS detention center, for the refugees who twenty-five days earlier had been hastily transferred out of the Santa Cruz jail while he waited to see them. When a refugee-rights paralegal had recently traveled to El Centro to process G-28 forms, an INS official took the G-28s out of her hand, tore them up, and threw them in a trash can. Corbett was determined this time to find the refugees he was looking for, especially Nelson Jim, Dudley's arrested hitchhiker.

What he found instead—when a prisoner in the room who knew Nelson interrupted Corbett's conversation with the jail superintendent—was that Nelson had already been deported to El Salvador. Corbett couldn't believe his ears. Nelson's deportation was illegal, since Corbett had filed his G-28 on May 5! The superintendent, Mr. Aguirre had told Corbett upon arrival that he had no record of Nelson. But when the outspoken prisoner insisted otherwise, Aguirre quickly ordered all the prisoners back to their cells and Corbett to leave immediately. Corbett, now angry, refused. Then Aguirre noticed that Corbett's companion had been recording the entire conversation with a tape recorder. Aguirre demanded he hand it over. Corbett replied the guards would have to take it by force, and that they wanted to leave now. Aguirre locked the room's doors and demanded the recorder. Corbett began to lecture Aguirre about refugees' rights. Aguirre stormed out of the room in a rage. After a few minutes, he returned and released them.

The experience was enraging. The U.S. government, Corbett saw, was violating its own law and risking the lives of thousands of Central American refugees. It had to be fought. Corbett began writing a series of "Dear Friend" letters to five hundred Quaker meetings and individual Quakers around the country explaining the plight of the refugees. In them, he criticized INS practices and solicited donations to help pay bond to free jailed Salvadoran refugees while their asylum applications were under review. This was the only legal recourse available for helping illegal aliens. In his first letter, however, Corbett alluded to the possibility of the need to violate immigration laws. "I can see," he wrote, "that if Central American refugees' rights to political asylum are decisively rejected by the U.S. government or if the U.S. legal system insists on ransom that exceeds our ability to pay, *active resistance* will be the only alternative to abandoning the refugees to their fate."

In the nineteenth century, Quakers had helped to organize an underground railroad to help slaves escape the antebellum South. Corbett was now beginning to envision a similar contemporary movement to assist Central American refugees. "The creation of a network of actively concerned, mutually supportive people in the U.S. and Mexico," he wrote, "may be the best preparation for an adequate response [to unjust INS policy]. A network? Quakers will know what I mean."

By June, Corbett and the Manzo Area Council had raised $150,000 to bond refugees out of jail. The Corbetts had twenty Salvadorans living on their property and many refugees living with families from various Tucson churches. But the more money they raised, the more the INS increased the cost of bail for Central Americans—though not for Mexicans. Bail jumped from $250 to $1,000 to $3,000 per alien and more. It was a losing battle.

Another problem was that Central Americans applying for political asylum were being systematically discriminated against by the INS. Granting asylum implicitly acknowledged the existence of gross violations of human and political rights by regimes and forces supported by the U.S. Since this embarrassed the Reagan administration, political asylum for Central Americans was almost always denied. From 1983 to 1986, for example, only 2.6 percent of Salvadorans and 0.9 percent of Guatemalans requesting asylum were approved. This compared to 60.4 percent of Iranians, 51 percent of Romanians, and 37.7 percent of Afghans approved. Thus, bonding Central American refugees out of jail was really only postponing their deportation. Corbett began to despair of the bail-bond strategy. Rather than bonding refugees out of jail for exorbitant sums of money, he reasoned, why not help smuggle the refugees to safety, keeping them out of jail in the first place? Still, for the time, he continued to raise bond money.

June 26 was a turning point. On that day, Corbett took three Salvadorans, who had fled El Salvador under threat of death, to the Tucson INS office to apply for political asylum. He knew their applications would eventually be denied. But the INS had always allowed asylum applicants to go free, under custody of local ministers, while their applications were on appeal—long enough, Corbett still hoped, for the Salvadoran civil war to end. On this day, however, the Tucson INS director, William Johnson, ordered the three applicants arrested and placed bail at $3,000 each. Corbett desperately protested.

This was his only means for working within the system, he argued. If the INS started arresting asylum applicants, Corbett insisted, the churches would have no choice—they would be forced to take their refugee operation underground. According to Corbett, Johnson replied that he was acting under orders from the State Department, that granting asylum to Salvadorans embarrassed the U.S. administration, and that hitherto all applicants would be arrested and sent to El Centro. Corbett and Johnson argued for an hour. At five o'clock Corbett was asked to leave. "We're not just going to abandon these people to their fate," the Quaker warned.

Shortly thereafter, Corbett began putting his intimate knowledge of the desert terrain to use guiding refugees across the border himself and escorting them around INS roadblocks to friends and relatives in Tucson. That such an act broke the law mattered little to Corbett by then. To him, protecting aliens whose lives were in danger was a moral imperative. The Nuremberg trials—which Corbett's lawyer father, Jim recalled, discussed at the family dinner table—had proven that. Corbett next organized a collection of sympathetic students, housewives, professionals, and retirees into a "Tucson refugee support group," which began coordinating a group smuggling operation.[4] The number of refugees aided by their *pro bono* "evasion services" steadily increased. By mid-August, Corbett himself was making one to two trips a day transporting undocumented aliens to Tucson in his pickup truck.

Members of the Manzo Area Council and the newly formed Tucson Ecumenical Council Task Force on Central America (TEC), to which Corbett belonged, however, were more reluctant to break the law. They understood and supported Corbett's work, but chose themselves to continue working to bail Salvadorans out of El Centro. By mid-July they had raised another $175,000 in collateral and freed 115 refugees—every Salvadoran in the detention center.

By late summer, Corbett was beginning to run out of places to leave the refugees. His house was overflowing with Salvadorans, many of whom had serious emotional and drinking problems, and his wife, Pat, had come to the end of her rope. Corbett approached a number of area churches about housing illegal aliens, but each one declined his request. Then, in early autumn, after a TEC meeting, Corbett took aside John Fife, the forty-one-year-old pastor of Tucson's Southside Presbyterian Church, which hosted TEC'S meetings. "John," he said, "we're running out of places to stash people. What about letting the refugees stay in your church?" Fife, it turns out, had already been weighing the possibility of sheltering illegals for weeks. He believed in principle that it was the right thing to do. But he hesitated, concerned for his family's welfare should he be arrested. He told Corbett he would raise the idea at the church's next elders' meeting.

John Fife had a long history of justice activism. Many of his seminary professors were German-emigré scholars who condemned the passivity of the German Protestant churches in the 1930s and '40s. Fife had marched from Selma to Montgomery in 1965, and had been arrested at sit-ins protesting whites-only public facilities and for picketing the suburban lawns of slum landlords. Fife had also done ministry on Indian reservations and in the slums of Canton, Ohio. Still, Fife struggled with Corbett's proposal for several days. No one knew how the government would react to a church willfully committing a felony.

By Southside's next elders' meeting, however, Fife had made up his mind. His faith and ethics gave him no choice but to take in the refugees. To do otherwise, he judged, would be immoral. He explained this to the elders at the meeting, and, after five hours of discussion, they agreed. By a seven-to-zero vote, with two abstentions, the elders decided to shelter illegal aliens in their church building. The next Sunday, Fife announced the decision to the entire church. Within a few weeks, Fife and others from TEC were joining Corbett in transporting the undocumented refugees. Although members of Southside agreed to act as discreetly as possible, it only took a month for the Tucson INS to hear the rumors that city ministers were openly defying immigration laws. Shortly before Thanksgiving, an INS lawyer approached TEC activist Margo Cowan in the city courthouse and told her, "We're not sure what Fife and Corbett are up to. But tell them to quit or we're going to have your asses."

Cowan and Fife called an emergency TEC meeting in Fife's living room. "We can do two things," Fife surmised. "We can continue on and wait for them to indict us. Or we can quit." After a brief discussion, everyone agreed the legal route was grossly inadequate, that they couldn't quit. Fife then observed that there was an alternative to waiting passively for the inevitable arrests. They could go public. "Beat 'em to the punch," Fife said. That way, they could claim the high moral ground and openly explain themselves to the media and their denominations before the INS could brand them just another bunch of "coyotes" and lock them away.

The group, excited now, then had the idea of declaring Southside Presbyterian a sanctuary for refugees. The ancient Hebrews, Fife remembered, declared entire cities sanctuaries of refuge for accused criminals. Christian churches during the Roman Empire and in medieval England had offered themselves as sanctuaries for fugitives of blood revenge. And during the Vietnam War, many churches sheltered conscientious objectors. This idea of sanctuary fit nicely with Corbett's notion of a new underground railroad. The group also realized that public sanctuary could give the refugees a platform to tell their stories about atrocities experienced in Central America—the very stories that had mobilized those in the TEC group to get involved in the first place. Fife agreed to put the idea to his church for approval.

After much soul-searching and self-education, in January 1982 the members of Southside Presbyterian voted 59 to 2, by secret ballot, to endorse the sanctuary idea. The day of the public declaration was set for March 24—the second anniversary of Archbishop Romero's assassination. Tim Nonn, of TEC, sent letters to congregations around the country that worked with refugees asking them to join the sanctuary declaration. Five churches in the San Francisco Bay area and churches in Los Angeles, Washington D.C., and Lawrence, Long Island, agreed also to declare sanctuary. The Episcopal Diocese of Ohio, the Unitarian Universalist Service Committee, the Arlington Street

Church in Boston, and the Social Justice Commission of the Catholic Archdiocese of San Francisco sent endorsements. Noon worked full-time for weeks before the big day, trying to generate media interest and church support.

On the morning of March 24, Fife and others set up a table on the church steps and hung two banners, which read in Spanish, "This is a Sanctuary of God for the Oppressed of Central America" and "Immigration, Don't Profane the Sanctuary of God." By 10:00 A.M. forty news reporters and television crews, including several Europeans and one from Canadian broadcasting, had arrived to cover Southside s public declaration of the movement that was henceforth known as Sanctuary. A church openly breaking federal law was big news.

Corbett began the news conference by telling the reporters that he had been smuggling refugees across the border for months. Manzo Area Council lawyers then explained the injustice of immigration laws. Next, Fife read a letter he had sent the previous day to Attorney General William French Smith and other state and INS officials, which announced the church's violation of the law and declaration of sanctuary. "We believe the current policy and practice of the U.S. Government with regard to Central American refugees is illegal and immoral," it read. "We will not cease to extend the sanctuary of the church to undocumented people from Central America. Obedience to God requires this of us." Finally, a Salvadoran, Alfredo, masked to hide his identity, spoke of the violence in El Salvador which drove him to seek political asylum in the U.S.

That night, three hundred supporters marched in candlelight procession from the Tucson Federal Building to Southside for an ecumenical service observing the welcome of undocumented Salvadoran refugees into the church. Many pastors and rabbis from around the country spoke of the need to endure hardship to defend the poor. The crowd sang stirring renditions of "Through It All" and "We Shall Overcome." Fife closed with a benediction. An undercover Border Patrol agent in attendance later filed this report with his superiors:

> Aside from the old people, most of them looked like the anti-Vietnam war protesters of the early '70s. In other words, political misfits. . . . It seems that this movement is more political than religious, but that the ploy is going to be Border-Patrol "bailing" by that group in order to demonstrate to the public that the U.S. Government, via its jack-booted gestapo Border-Patrol agents, thinks nothing of breaking down the doors of their churches to drag Jesus Christ out to be tortured and murdered. I believe that all political implications should be considered before any further action is taken toward this group.

The INS decided to treat Sanctuary publicly as a trivial novelty that would soon fade into insignificance. No arrests were made. In fact, however, it was later revealed that the INS was deeply worried about Sanctuary and initiated a covert investigation of the movement by paid infiltrators.

In its first year as a sanctuary, Southside Presbyterian harbored sixteen hundred Salvadorans on their way to more permanent homes around the country. And, with national and religious media giving front-page coverage on the movement, word about Sanctuary spread quickly. Steadily, churches scattered across the country began declaring public sanctuary. The movement became truly nationalized, however, when in August 1982 Jim Corbett—feeling overwhelmed by the day to day demands of refugee work in Tucson—asked the Chicago Religious Task Force on Central America (CRTF) to take over the job of coordinating Sanctuaries across the country. The CRTF had been founded, in response to the 1981 murders of four North American churchwomen in El Salvador, to lobby against military aid to that country. Their first year of efforts, however, produced so little fruit that they began to consider shifting their focus to grassroots political education. Corbett's request was enticing. But members of CRTF felt inadequate for the task. But after searching in vain for weeks for a more experienced group, the CRTF—green though they were—finally agreed to become the national headquarters of Sanctuary.

The CRTF aggressively promoted Sanctuary, recruiting churches by phone and publishing and distributing thirty thousand copies of Sanctuary how-to manuals. By early 1983, more than forty-five churches and synagogues had declared public sanctuary and more than six hundred "secondary Sanctuary groups" had offered their endorsements and support. The movement was spreading from New England to southern California. An entire clandestine communication and transportation network—a new underground railroad—was now up and running. Refugee families were being smuggled across the border by the likes of Corbett and driven to Tucson, Los Angeles, and San Antonio. From there a pony express of cars and vans shuttled them across the continent to anxious families waiting to receive them. At first, railroad "conductors"— teachers, truck drivers, businesspeople, farmers—relayed messages through the network with passwords and codes and disguised refugees with wigs and mustaches. But eventually—as the system became routine, no arrests were made, and the coded messages proved more confusing than helpful—the secrecy was abandoned.

The movement's identity soon began to evolve. Sanctuary began as a movement of hospitality that aimed to provide for the humanitarian needs of vulnerable refugees. But Sanctuary quickly become more than that. It grew into a *political* movement that sought to end the human oppression generated by the U.S.-sponsored war in Central America. As more and more churches and synagogues considered declaring sanctuary, they were forced to learn the reasons why so many traumatized and anguished Central Americans were flooding northward. And, by choosing to shelter undocumented refugees, Sanctuaries publicly declared their belief that violence and human rights abuses were epidemic in Central America, that the U.S. was guilty of promoting and financing the violence and atrocities, and that open mass civil disobedience was necessary to confront Washington and demand an end to its bloody war. Thus, heightened grassroots political awareness and the spread of Sanctuary fueled each other.

In 1983, other churches and synagogues made public declarations of sanctuary. Religious groups were by then declaring sanctuary at a rate of more than two a week. In the first six months of 1984, the total number of sanctuaries had more than doubled to 150. And eighteen national religious denominations and commissions had publicly endorsed Sanctuary. Clearly, the Sanctuary movement was not fading into trivial insignificance, as the INS had hoped. Publicly downplaying Sanctuary's importance was not working. So the INS shifted to a more aggressive strategy. In February, 1984, Texas Sanctuary workers Stacey Lynn Merkt and Sister Diane Muhlenkamp were arrested for transporting undocumented refugees. *Dallas Times-Herald* reporter Jack Fischer, who was covering their work, was arrested as well. One month later, TEC Director Phil Conger and Southside volunteer Katherine Flaherty were arrested. In April, Texas Sanctuary worker Jack Elder was arrested. Six months later Merkt and Elder were indicted again on additional charges. Then, in January 1985, the Justice Department announced the indictment of sixteen Arizona Sanctuary workers, including Corbett and Fife, three nuns, two priests, a nurse, a housewife, and a graduate student. The long-awaited, direct confrontation with the government had arrived.

The arrests, however, only served to increase the movement's visibility and produce an outpouring of support from around the country. The National Council of Churches condemned the arrests. Groups of Roman Catholic bishops and religious orders issued statements affirming Sanctuary as biblical and moral. In one week after the Arizona indictments, registration for a TEC-organized national symposium on Sanctuary jumped from three hundred to fifteen hundred participants. The city of Los Angeles and the state of New Mexico declared themselves Sanctuaries. By mid-1985, the number of declared Sanctuaries had climbed to 250. Two years later, the number had grown to four hundred. Despite opposition, the Sanctuary movement was continuing to attract an expanding number of people willing to break federal law to protect aliens and protest U.S. Central America policy.

WITNESS FOR PEACE

On Saturday afternoon, April 9, 1983, thirty dazed North Carolinians stepped off an old yellow school bus in El Porvenir, Nicaragua, and began to wander aimlessly through the smoldering wreckage of the previous night's attack. The sight was devastating. This thriving village and tobacco farm situated on the Honduran border, named "The Future" in Spanish, had been assaulted by U.S.-backed Contra forces. Hours later, the thirty *gringos* stood before the scorched remains—the smoking piles of ashes, mangled tin roofs, burnt crops, scattered mortar shells, and wounded and shellshocked survivors—overwhelmed by the ruin and anguish.

The thirty North Carolinians were traveling on a one-week fact-finding tour, organized by Gail Phares, an ex-Maryknoll nun who had worked with the poor in Nicaragua in the 1960s. In the 1970s, at the urging of the Central Americans she worked with, Phares had returned to the States to work for change in U.S. Central American policy. In 1982 Phares moved to North Carolina, created the Carolina Interfaith Task Force on Central America (CITCA), and began searching for ways to raise awareness about Central America in her new state. When the Contra war surfaced in the media, she decided to lead a group of church people to Nicaragua to see the situation for themselves. Only a few hours after they had arrived in Managua late Friday night, reports of a Contra attack reached Phares and her collection of middle-aged, middle-class religious leaders, pastors, college teachers, and assorted housewives and retirees. At 4:00 A.M. Saturday morning, with little sleep, Phares's group boarded their bus and headed for the village. Ten hours and two stops at other attacked villages later, the exhausted group trudged through the remains of El Porvenir, trying to absorb the horror that lay before them.

"Look over there on that hill," implored a young local militia soldier guarding the village's remains, pointing to a hut a few hundred yards away, across the Honduran border on the horizon. "These are the Contras that attacked us. That is the headquarters of Suicide, their commander. They can see us now."

Jeff Boyer, one of the delegates who years earlier had worked for the Peace Corps in a nearby Honduran village, just on the other side of the mountains, peered through his binoculars and saw contra soldiers wandering about. "Why aren't they shooting now?" he asked.

"Because you are here with us," the youth replied. The wheels began to turn in Boyer's mind. He and others began thinking they should stay the night.

"It's past three o'clock and time to leave," the anxious bus driver insisted. "We need to get out of here and back on the paved road before dark." Phares agreed. But the Nicaraguans did not want the group to leave. They asked them to come see one more house. Inside stood a young mother, shaking. She was in shock. The floors and walls were splattered with blood. A pair of children's shoes lay on the floor in the middle of the room, also stained with blood. The group was told that the woman's mother and three children—an infant and two toddlers—had been wounded in the Contra assault and had been taken away by ambulance that morning. No one knew if they were alive or dead. The trembling mother began to sob. Many in the delegation began to cry. Boyer reached out and held the woman, crying, "What the hell are we doing? We can't just leave these people."

The bus driver was shouting. The bus was getting ready to leave. The hesitant delegation slowly headed back to the bus, saying farewells, embracing the villagers, promising never to forget them. Boyer mumbled in Spanish, "Take care, ma'am," withdrew to the bus, and broke down, weeping bitterly. "Holding that woman was the most empty gesture I have ever made in my life," Boyer later recalled. "To this day, I think we failed those people. We should have stayed." Later, the group learned that the mother's wounded infant died in the hospital.

The bus ride back to Managua was bleak and painful. The delegates burned with rage, helplessness, and guilt. They knew whose tax dollars funded the Contras. They knew it was their own country responsible for devastating El Porvenir, that their own government had shattered that young mother's life. And they knew that the Contras would probably return after dark with more destruction and death. Phares tried to console the group by talking about the need to return home and tell the truth about the Contras. "Somehow," she repeated, "we have to do something to stop our government's war on these people."

Boyer brooded over the young soldier's words: *"Because you are here with us."* Finally, he blurted out, "Look, if the United States is funding this, then let's put fifteen hundred volunteers here to stop this fighting! If all it takes to prevent the killing is a bunch of U.S. citizens in town, then let's do it, let's hold a big vigil in the war zone!" At first, the group laughed off the idea. But the more they thought and talked about the proposal, the more they liked it. The mood in the bus began to shift from guilt and powerlessness to indignation and resolve. Back in Managua, the group spent the rest of the week meeting with Nicaraguan religious, educational, and political leaders, including four Sandinista Commandantes, to learn more about the Nicaraguan situation. In each meeting they posed their idea of a massive U.S. citizens' peace vigil in the war zone and solicited support and advice. Reactions were mixed. But by the end of the week, they had won the approval of evangelical church leaders and the president of Nicaragua, Daniel Ortega.

On the April 15 plane ride home, Phares, Boyer, and Gil Joseph, a University of North Carolina professor, sat together and drafted an outline of their plan. They wanted to organize one thousand people from all fifty states—including celebrities such as Bob Dylan and Bianca Jagger—who were willing to risk their lives by traveling to the war zone and, "standing with the Nicaraguan people," hold a high-visibility peace vigil in clear view of the Contras. The assembly would then return home and spread the word to the media, their religious communities, families, and friends about the government's dirty proxy-war against Nicaragua. They decided to call the event "Action for Peace in Nicaragua." D-Day was set for July 4—two-and-a-half months away. All that remained was to find a national religious organization to sponsor and organize the event.

That, however, proved impossible. Phares, Boyer, and Joseph spent two weeks on the phone and on the road trying to get any number of organizations to sign on to organize the trip. Although many liked the idea, no one would actually take it on. Two months, they said, was not enough time for such an immense and risky project. Boyer and Joseph, in despair, were ready to give up. Phares suggested they sleep on it. A day later they agreed together, "Okay, we'll do it ourselves."

The next six weeks were spent working the telephones in Phare's CITCA office. A small crowd of volunteers, including many members of the first trip, worked around the clock to recruit and train delegates for the July 4 trip. They tapped into the networks of Clergy and Laity Concerned (CALC), the American Friends Service Committee (AFSC), the New York-based InterReligious Task Force on Central America, and local Central America task forces across the country. Gail Phares contacted every religious and political connection she had from her previous work, asking them to join the trip, organize their state, donate money. By July, the volunteers had gathered 153 people from forty states for their "Action for Peace in Nicaragua."[7]

This second delegation arrived in Managua on July 3. They spent the first two days getting acquainted with the Nicaraguan situation, meeting with church, Sandinista, and opposition leaders, visiting social projects and churches, reading local newspapers. Many of them were quite impressed with the social achievements of and popular support for the Sandinista revolution. This, they thought, was not the totalitarian Nicaragua portrayed by the White House and the U.S. news media.

On July 5, the group woke at 4:00 A.M., ate a rice-and-beans breakfast, and began the thirteen-hour bus trip to the refugee town of Jalapa, near the Honduran border. Because of torrential rains and worry about mined roads, the buses arrived three hours later than scheduled. But when they finally did appear, the whole town seemed to come out to greet them. After a merry reception held at the local movie theater, a prayer service concluded the evening's events and the group settled down for a night's sleep in the local high school.

The next morning, the delegates met with a group of Nicaraguans, mostly women, for an emotional, three-and-a-half hour prayer vigil, held on the basketball court behind the high school. The North Americans read passages from the prophet Isaiah and from Thomas Jefferson on the imperative of social justice. The group then presented gifts, including a copy of the U.S. Declaration of Independence, to the Nicaraguans and asked forgiveness for the United States' betrayal of its own revolutionary ideals. Then they prayed. Between each prayer, the North Americans spoke in ritual unison, "For killings and kidnappings funded by us, forgive us and pray for us." Soon, the somber Nicaraguans spontaneously began to answer with quaking voices, "You are forgiven." Back and forth passed the liturgical confessions and pardons until the whole group, overcome by tears, fell silent. Then, the Nicaraguans began to tell, one by one, stories of sons and daughters recently killed, kidnapped, and dismembered by the Contras. At the mention of the name of each killed loved one, the Nicaraguans reverently repeated "Presente," meaning that the persons spirit lived on. With each story of death, the grieved North Americans asked the mothers for their forgiveness. And each suffering mother answered, "You are forgiven."

That afternoon, the North Americans and Jalapans held a peace march, complete with banners, around the city courtyard. They then moved to a field, situated between the Contra positions and the town, held hands in a long line, and sang songs of peace. Delegates planted U.S., Nicaraguan, and United Nations flags in the field. After, some delegates helped plant corn with Nicaraguans. Others met with Nicaraguans throughout the town, ate together, prayed together, exchanged photographs, and pledged to work for peace.

The emotional and spiritual impact of the days' events on the North Americans proved to be extraordinary. The morning prayer vigil was particularly moving. Phyllis

Taylor, a Jewish nurse who became deeply involved in Central America activism, later remembered,

> A profound thing happened to me. When the first mother started telling her story, she began very strong, but started to cry when she got to the day of her son's death. The next mother was the same. By the third mother, they were in tears, I was in tears, we were all in tears, holding each other. The profound thing was that, in comforting each other, the mothers were able to distinguish me from my government. That was a phenomenal breakthrough for me. A strongly self-conscious Jew, I had grown up never having allowed anything German in our house, with a tremendous dislike for Palestinians, without ever even knowing one! Now here I was, this mother not condemning me, but forgiving me, even though her child had died brutally at the hands of my government. It was incredibly moving.

Henri Nouwen, a Dutch theologian and author, said, "I had never been so deeply touched as when those women looked at us and said, 'You are forgiven.' The experience shook up my understanding of faith and left me unable to write anything for months." Similarly, Fran Truitt, a retiring United Church of Christ minister, who went on to become a prime mover in Witness for Peace, later recalled, tearfully.

> After the morning vigil, the oldest of the mothers of these killed came up to me, of all the people. I called for a translator. It was an eternal moment for me. She said, "I have been blessed by God, for I have given the blood of my son for the salvation of our people. I want to share that blessing with you, to share with your people." I fell on my knees, and she kissed me on the forehead. I looked up to the translator and he had tears streaming out of his eyes. The woman's name was Maria Garcia Lopez. But she became the incarnation of Mary for me. I didn't know what all that meant, I just knew it was a very religious moment. It was very sobering, both a blessing and a burden. I was supposed to be retiring. But now I felt chosen. And what do you do with that?

"It was a powerful experience that affected us all very seriously. It made a tremendous impact," recalled Mike Clark, another delegate who later became director of Witness for Peace. "We had seen and experienced something that demanded a response. All of us came back with a solemn mission to carry out."

Before returning to the States, the group met in Managua with the U.S. ambassador to Nicaragua, Anthony Quainton, and told him their story. They showed him pieces of shrapnel from U.S.-manufactured mortar shells they found in bombed villages. Theology professor Jorge Lara Braud charged the U.S. with "legalized murder" and pastor

William Sloan Coffin challenged Quainton to resign in protest. Quainton responded with the official administration's views of the dangers of communism in Central America. This man, the stunned delegates realized, was not talking about the Nicaragua they had come to know in the last few days. Perhaps none of their government's statements on Nicaragua could be trusted. That night, the group held a candlelight vigil outside the U.S. embassy gate, singing "Ain't Gonna Study War No More."

The next morning, forty of the delegates met to begin making plans to establish a permanent North American presence in the war zone. They believed that nothing short of a permanent vigil would have any impact on U.S. policy. Eventually, they chose a task force of nine, which worked all day and through the night. By dawn, they had written a plan they called "Project Witness." Three permanent vigilers would be stationed near border areas where Contras attacked. They and their Nicaraguan co-workers would receive short-term delegations of ten to twenty people. As had been done on the first two trips, the delegates would see the Nicaraguan situation for themselves, go to any village under Contra assault, and report the truth back to the U.S. media and churches. Delegates would be expected to live with Nicaraguans, share the risks of Contra violence, "face death if need be," and become first-hand sources of information on Nicaragua alternative to the U.S. government.

The 153 delegates returned home and began to tell their story in many hundreds of newspaper articles, radio and television interviews, and church pulpits. They received local, regional, and national press coverage, including an article in *Newsweek* and an essay by William Sloan Coffin, "Nicaragua is Not Our Enemy" in the *New York Times*. A three-page draft of the "Project Witness" proposal was circulated widely among church and peace groups. David Sweet, a Santa Cruz Latin American history professor; Jim Wallis, of *Sojourners* magazine; and Henri Nouwen began touring the country calling for peacemaking in Central America and recruiting new delegates. Many from the July trip, who had now become full-time volunteers, worked their own religious denominations and organizations for support. In short order, Clergy and Laity Concerned, the American Friends Service Committee, the Fellowship of Reconciliation, the InterReligious Task Force, the Quakers, the Presbyterian Church U.S.A., the United Methodist Church, the *Catholic Worker* and *Sojourners* magazines, Washington D.C.'s Religious Task Force on Central America, and many other denominations and organizations were lending organizational and financial support for a permanent vigil in Nicaragua.

By August, a National Steering Committee was formed that met on regular telephone conference calls. In October, twenty key leaders met at the Convent of the Good Shepherd in Philadelphia to hammer out a statement of purpose and principles and to hire a coordinator. After struggling through many disagreements (to be discussed in chapter 11), they defined Witness for Peace as "prayerful, biblically-based, non-violent, and politically independent." By mid-November, Witness for Peace had raised more than $38,200 in cash and pledges and had been awarded an additional $13,000 in grants. Around the country, twenty-seven local support groups and seven regional offices worked on publicity, recruitment, and fund-raising. Applications to be long- and short-term delegates began pouring in. According to Phyllis Taylor (1990): "It was wonderful and prophetic and crazy in the beginning. You know, people used their own money and their own travel. We set up trainings in our house. People were asking what our policy was, we didn't have any so we just made them up on the spot. It was that kind of wonderful chaos in beginning."

The first long-term delegates flew to Nicaragua on October 18. Then, the first official short-term delegation was launched with much fanfare on December 2, the third anniversary of the murder of the four U.S. churchwomen in El Salvador. *Sojourners* had hired a top-notch media relations specialist, Dennis Marker, who packaged Witness for Peace for the media as a "shield of love" for the Nicaraguan people, "ordinary people doing a radical thing." The media ate it up. Witness for Peace gained coverage in every major national newspaper. NBC's *Today* show even provided live coverage of the delegation's peace procession in the town of Ocotal.

Short-term delegations began to flow to Nicaragua—from Missouri, South Dakota, New York, Illinois, Maine, all over the country—one after another, at a steady rate of four a month. Delegation after delegation usually encountered the same kind of deeply disturbing experience as had the first two groups—establishing friendships with Nicaraguans, seeing for themselves both the Sandinista revolution and the anguish of the war, weeping with parents whose children and spouses were killed by the Contras, and vowing to return home and struggle to end the killing. Witness for Peace had hit upon a tactic, it seemed, that transformed people, that disturbed and electrified U.S. citizens into fervent political action against their own government. Soon, wave after wave of delegates began returning home on fire with a mission to tell their troubling stories to anyone who would listen and organize to end the U.S.-backed Contra war.

The number of long-term delegates in Nicaragua quickly jumped from three to twenty, increasing capacity to receive a growing number of short-term delegates. Over the course of the decade, a total of four thousand short-term and two hundred long-term delegates traveled to Nicaragua with Witness for Peace, generating the basis of a massive, grassroots domestic opposition to the administration's Central America policy. In time, Witness for Peace was mailing its newsletter to forty thousand readers and its recruitment and fund-raising letters to more than one million contacts a year. Witness for Peace organized more than 1,000 local media and congressional contacts in 380 cities and 49 states. The organization became a regular source of information on Nicaragua for newspapers across the country. And the national office repeatedly helped coordinate major political campaigns to end the Contra war. Anticipating the May 1988 congressional vote on aid to the Contras, for example, Witness for Peace organized an "End Contra Aid!" call-in that generated eleven thousand protest calls to Capitol Hill offices. Thus, the guilt and rage of thirty tired North Carolinians wandering through the smoking wreckage of El Porvenir had been transformed into a well-coordinated challenge to the President's low-intensity war.

THE PLEDGE OF RESISTANCE

On a cold week in early November of 1983, fifty-three Christian peace and justice activists gathered for a retreat at the Kirkridge Retreat Center in northeastern Pennsylvania. These activists, mostly movement leaders and representatives of peace organizations, who called themselves the New Abolitionist Covenant, had been convening each year at Kirkridge for fellowship, Bible study, prayer, and political reflection. But this year, the shadow of an impending crisis loomed large over the assembly. Eight days earlier, almost seven thousand U.S. troops had invaded the Caribbean island of Grenada and deposed its leftist government. Many at the retreat—who were in close communication with alarmed Nicaraguan church leaders—feared that the Grenada invasion was merely a dress rehearsal for the Pentagon's main event: an imminent, full-scale U.S. invasion of Nicaragua.

A sense of urgency and danger weighed heavily on the group as they talked and prayed. Before the retreat's end, a consensus emerged on the need for an organized resistance to such an invasion. Jim Wallis and Jim Rice of *Sojourners* magazine drafted a brief statement called "A Promise of Resistance," which was revised through group discussion and signed by thirty-three of the gathered activists. The statement vowed that, if the U.S. invaded Nicaragua, its signers would gather as many North American Christians as possible to "go immediately to Nicaragua to stand unarmed as a loving barrier in the path of any attempted invasion." It also called upon Christians to "encircle, enter, or occupy congressional offices in a nonviolent prayerful presence with the intention of remaining at those offices until the invasion is ended." *Sojourners* sent copies of the statement to every member of Congress, to the Departments of State and Defense, to the CIA, and to President Reagan. Every retreat participant presented the plan to their own organizations and denominations. And *Sojourners* printed the statement in the December issue, publicizing it to religious activists across the country.

In the first months of 1984 an array of religious organizations endorsed the Kirkridge statement and lent organizational support. With input from these groups, the contingency plan was refined, rewritten, and republished in the August issue of *Sojourners*. Now titled "A Pledge of Resistance," the new plan downplayed the original idea of traveling to Nicaragua to intercept U.S. forces and focused primarily on the occupation of congressional offices. The article described a newly formed implementation plan and communications network—Witness for Peace's seven new regional offices had volunteered to serve as regional communication centers—and published the names, addresses, and phone numbers of regional coordinators.

Meanwhile, in Berkeley, California, a doctoral student in theology and peace activist by the name of Ken Butigan was, by happenstance, given a copy of the *Sojourn-*

ers issue that carried the Kirkridge statement. Nine months earlier, Ken had received a letter from someone in Nicaragua he didn't know. The letter said, in short:

> Listen, we're telling you this: your government is killing our children. We're telling you now so later you cannot say that you didn't know. We're asking you to take steps to stop this killing at a time when we have such hope for our country.

Butigan was deeply affected by the letter. He knew down deep that the letter was right. He and others in his anti-nuclear activist group formed an East Bay chapter of Witness for Peace. Increasingly, however, Butigan felt the need for a U.S.-oriented strategy to complement Witness for Peace's work in Central America. When he read the Kirkridge statement in *Sojourners,* it clicked. "Thirty-three people signed this," he said to himself, "why not three hundred people or three thousand or three million people making this pledge?" Not knowing there were organizers on the East Coast already working on it, Butigan sat down and wrote a pledge document called "A Commitment to Stop the Killing in Central America." He circulated it in the Bay area, explaining his idea to a number of activist groups. But it fell flat. Nobody responded.

A puzzled and discouraged Butigan, however, soon received a call from David Hartsough of the AFSC's San Francisco office, who had heard of the document. They met and debated Butigan's idea for an hour and a half. In the end, Hartsough said, "This is a great idea. We should make it happen across the country!" Hartsough gave Butigan a desk, a phone, AFSC's name, and fifty dollars a week pay. Butigan went to work organizing his version of the Pledge. About this time he discovered *Sojourners'* August revision of the Pledge and rewrote it to say, simply, "If the United States . . . significantly escalates its intervention on Central America, I pledge to join with others . . . in acts of legal protest and civil disobedience as conscience leads me." He then convinced a few people from local Sanctuary, the Committee in Solidarity with the People of El Salvador (CIS-PES), anti-nuclear, feminist, and environmental groups to help collect signatures.

On Tuesday, October 9, 1984, Butigan and his colleagues held the first mass public signing of the Pledge of Resistance. They set up a table and a public address system in front of the San Francisco Federal Building at 11:00 A.M. In the first hour, seven hundred people signed the Pledge. Two hundred of them explained over the microphone to the gathered crowd exactly why they felt compelled to sign on and possibly go to jail. More than half of those explained they did so because of their religious faith. Butigan was thrilled by the response. In the following days the Pledge campaign took off.

Butigan then learned through David Hartsough that *Sojourners* was convening a meeting on October 16 at their Washington, D.C., office. It was to be attended by representatives of eighteen major peace, justice, and anti-interventionist groups to hammer out the organizational details of the emerging Pledge. Butigan got himself invited. At the meeting, different parties advanced disparate visions of how the Pledge should operate. Some argued for an unwritten Pledge with spontaneous protests emerging as conscience led. Others called for a more structured campaign involving coordinated leadership, training seminars, and mass-mail fund-raising. At an opportune time, Butigan passed around a copy of his version of the Pledge, told of his October 9 public signing in San Francisco, and argued for a highly organized but nationally decentralized Pledge. In the end, Butigan's suggestion won out. An "analyst group" was established to monitor and interpret U.S. activities in Central America. An eight-member "signal group" was organized to consult with the analyst group and decide if and when to activate the national network of Pledge protesters. The existing regional Pledge offices were continued and the number expanded from seven to ten. A National Pledge Clearinghouse was set up in the National Council of Churches' Interfaith Task Force on Central America (ITFCA) office in New York. Finally, following Butigan's rewritten version, the decision was made to expand the Pledge to protest not only a U.S. invasion but any major military escalation in Central America, and to offer an optional legal protest to complement the civil-disobedience pledge. With a national organization now in place, Butigan returned home and quickly wrote a hundred-page Pledge of Resistance handbook, called *Basta! No Mandate for War.* Containing detailed information on Central America, the Pledge, nonviolence, and the logistics of protest, it was published by New Society Publishers and distributed nationally.

Meanwhile, Pledge groups were rapidly forming all over the country, collecting signatures, sponsoring nonviolence training seminars, and organizing mailing lists, phone-trees, and affinity groups. Pledge organizers were amazed by the public's positive response. By December, activists had collected 42,352 signatures, half pledging civil disobedience. "In fifteen years of activism," remembered Boston-area Pledge organizer Anne Shumway, "I never saw anything explode the way the Pledge did. It just took off. At public signings, people were just lining up to sign on." Likewise, Janice Hines, the regional coordinator for Texas, Arkansas, and Oklahoma, remarked, "The response was just amazing. The idea caught on so fast and generated so much excitement, we were just trying to keep up with it." Florida, Virginia, North Carolina, and Texas collected 1,000 signatures each. Colorado collected 1,650, Wisconsin 2,000, Massachusetts 2,100, and New Jersey 3,000. Pledge groups at Tufts University and University of California campuses began to organize a national boycott of college classes in the event of a U.S. invasion of Nicaragua. And national organizations—such as the National Lawyers Guild, the League of United Latin America Citizens, the Jewish Peace Fellowship, and Church Women United—continued to endorse the Pledge. To make the message clear, *Sojourners* sent the Department of State copies of the 42,352 signed Pledge forms.

By December, Pledge groups in northern California had collected five thousand signatures. In a few months, that number would grow to nine thousand. Having outgrown the AFSC office, Butigan opened a Pledge office in downtown San Francisco, staffed by two paid organizers and an army of volunteers. They began conducting five nonviolence training sessions a week, which trained fifteen hundred new activists in six months. Pledge activists began holding "peace maneuvers" at the San Francisco Federal Building, role-playing the major demonstration they believed was imminent. And the thousands of Pledge signers were given cards to deliver to their local congressional offices threatening to return to take over and occupy the offices if the U.S. invaded Nicaragua.

By early 1985, the Pledge of Resistance had mobilized the potential to create major social disruption in the event of a U.S. invasion of Nicaragua. The number of local Pledge groups had grown to more than two hundred and the number of Pledge signers had grown to fifty thousand. Activists were trained and communication networks were in place. The Pledge was ready and waiting for the White House to make the wrong move.

In May, the Congress refused to approve $14 million of Contra aid requested by the Reagan administration. In response, one week later, the White House imposed a full trade embargo on Nicaragua. But Pledge leaders were now divided. Should the Pledge react with full force? Or should it "save its ammunition" for a more important political showdown? The national signal group chose to wait. But many local Pledge leaders—including those in Boston and San Francisco—decided to act, despite worries that most of their people might not participate, since the embargo was not really an invasion. Their fears proved groundless, however, as thousands of activists held demonstrations in eighty cities and sixteen states over the next days. In Boston, twenty-six hundred protesters demonstrated and 559 were arrested for occupying the Federal Building. And in San Francisco, three thousand activists engaged in legal protest while six hundred were arrested for committing civil disobedience. In its first major show of force, despite the absence of an official national signal, more than ten thousand Pledge activists demonstrated across the country and more than two thousand were arrested for nonviolent civil disobedience.

As Pledge leaders began to realize that the U.S. might never invade Nicaragua directly with U.S. forces but already was attacking Nicaragua through the Contra armies, Pledge protests began to focus primarily on Contra aid votes in the Congress, arms shipments to Central America, and U.S. military maneuvers in the region. In June, only one month after the first embargo demonstrations, the Congress hastily passed $27 million in aid for the Contras. In response, Pledge activists, this time activated by the national signal group, staged demonstrations again in more than two hundred cities and forty-two states in which more than twelve hundred protesters were arrested for acts of civil disobedience. The Pledge organization, now deeply engaged in political battle, was feeling a surge of confidence and energy. By September, Pledge groups had been organized in more than three hundred U.S. cities and the number of Pledge signers had grown by 40 percent to seventy thousand. In nine months, that number would grow again to its peak of eighty thousand.

Originally, many Pledge organizers, focused on the immediate post-Grenada crisis, expected the Pledge campaign against a U.S. invasion of Nicaragua to last only a few months. Ken Butigan recalls, "When the Pledge first began, I remember bringing a three-month budget to our first meeting. Someone said, 'Hell, we're not really going to be doing this for three months, are we! This will all be over in three months, won't it?' We all hoped so. But we just didn't know." In fact, the Pledge of Resistance spent the next five years mobilizing one campaign of demonstrations after another. All told, the Pledge marshaled forces to fight eight separate congressional Contra aid votes, as well as numerous Salvadoran aid votes, and carried off five major thematic public-awareness campaigns.

In 1986 alone, in response to four successive Contra aid votes in Congress, the Pledge sustained seven months of protest that involved one thousand separate demonstrations and vigils in which some two thousand Pledge protesters were arrested. Tens of thousands of Pledge activists protested in myriad ways. They occupied congressional offices for days; blocked gates of Contra-training military bases: staged funeral processions and mock "die-ins" in city streets and congressional offices; ran "Stop the Lies" advertisements in newspapers and radio stations and distributed sixty thousand "Stop the Lies" tabloids across the country; blocked morning rush-hour traffic with street marches and sit-ins; fasted in protest for weeks on the Capitol steps; rented planes and flew huge "U.S. Out of Nicaraguan Now!" signs over big college football games; trespassed on National Guard bases and blocked airplane runways to obstruct military shipments; staged cross-state marches concluding with rallies at government offices; erected plywood walls in shopping centers painted with the names of hundreds of Nicaraguan civilians killed by Contras; held "Lie of the Week" vigils outside local pro-Contras congressional offices; held a four-day "People's Filibuster" in the Capitol Rotunda; rallied at shopping malls during the Christmas season, unfurling banners and singing politicized versions of Christmas carols; and, with banners and chants, birddogged 160 campaign appearances of forty pro-Contra congressional candidates seeking re-election.

Pledge activism continued strongly into 1987. In response to a major deployment of National Guard troops to Honduras in February, protestors held demonstrations and vigils outside one hundred congressional offices and sent many thousands of letters and postcards to congressional representatives. North Carolina pledge members, for example, sent more than a thousand letters of protest to their newly elected senator, Terry Sandford. The Pledge then took the lead in organizing "April Mobilization" in Washington, D.C., in which one hundred thousand people marched for peace and justice in Central America and South Africa. Afterward, 567 protesters were arrested at a major civil disobedience action at CIA headquarters. Next, the Pledge launched a "Summer of Resistance" that focused on blocking the shipment of arms from the U.S. to Central America. Five hundred protested at the psychological warfare base, in Arlington Heights, Illinois, where sixty-seven were arrested for climbing the base's fences. More than two hundred protested at the Van Nuys Air National Guard base, where thirty-four were arrested for leafletting. In Northern California, three thousand protested at the Concord Naval

Weapons Station, where four hundred were arrested for blocking train tracks leading to the docks. In addition, members of the Baltimore Pledge twice disrupted the Iran-Contra hearings in Washington, unfurling banners and demanding a deeper investigation of the scandal. And a group of Vietnam veterans held a "Nuremberg Action," where they vigiled and leafletted against Contra aid twelve hours a day for three months.

At summer's end the Nuremberg Action group began a forty-day fast and nonviolent blockade of trains and trucks carrying munitions to the Concord Naval Weapons Station. On September 1, Brian Willson, one of the veterans, was run over by an oncoming train while kneeling on the tracks. The train cut off both legs and inflicted severe head injuries. Among the numerous reactions around the country, ten thousand outraged protesters—including Jesse Jackson, Joan Baez, and Daniel Ellsberg—marched on Concord, demanding an end to the war. Afterward several hundred demonstrators tore up one section of train tracks, while others halted all Concord arms shipments by mounting an ongoing, twenty-four-hour human blockade of trains that would last, with the involvement of one thousand protesters, more than two years. They were joined on September 30 by Willson himself, then recently released from the hospital. Altogether, in 1987, twelve hundred Pledge activists were arrested in hundreds of demonstrations.

But by the end of 1987, many Pledge protesters were growing weary of the struggle. Nevertheless, the Pledge continued in its work for two more years. During the fall and winter of 1987–88, 120 Pledge groups and fifty other Central America organizations coordinated a five-month protest campaign, called "Days of Decision," which helped successfully to defeat two new administration requests for Contra aid in February and March of 1988. After the second defeat, the White House deployed thirty-two hundred U.S. troops to Honduras. Fearing an invasion of Nicaragua, the Pledge helped to mobilize tens of thousands to protest in two hundred demonstrations in 150 cities in which nine hundred protesters were arrested. In April, the Pledge orchestrated nonviolent direct action campaigns at thirty military installations supporting the war in Central America, where hundreds were arrested. In October, the Pledge led a coalition of Central America groups in its "Steps to Freedom" campaign, where activists protested in seventy demonstrations across the country. The campaign culminated in a major demonstration at the Pentagon building, where fifteen hundred activists blocked entrances, occupied the heliport, and planted on the lawn five hundred crosses with names of Salvadoran civilians killed in the war. Five hundred protesters committed civil disobedience and 240 were arrested.

In 1989, the Pledge organized nationally coordinated demonstrations and vigils around President Bush's inauguration, the Salvadoran elections, President Cristiani's inauguration in El Salvador, and the Panama invasion. In May, Pledge activists staged a series of surprise, high-visibility actions, where rappellers hung huge "Stop U.S. Aid to the Death Squad Gov't in El Salvador" signs at local and national landmarks, such as Washington, D.C.'s National Press Building, San Francisco's Coit Tower, Philadelphia's Independence Hall, St. Louis's Union Station, Chicago's Daley Plaza, Minneapolis'

Franklin Avenue Bridge, and Boston's Transportation Building. In November and December, Pledge groups responded to renewed U.S.-funded military actions in El Salvador with more than seven hundred protests across the nation in which 2,440 people committed civil disobedience and 1,452 were arrested. And on March 24, 1990, the Pledge helped organize a rally in Washington, D.C., to mark the tenth anniversary of Archbishop Oscar Romero's assassination. Weathering a chilly snowstorm, fifteen thousand people marched and 580—the most of any single Pledge action—were arrested for demonstrating in front of the White House.

CONCLUSION

The Central America peace movement generated in the United States a political mobilization of major significance. Well more than a hundred thousand U.S. citizens had been activated into a fierce, extended struggle against a tremendously popular U.S. President. Year after year they had organized thousands upon thousands of demonstrations, vigils, rallies, and blockades. More than a hundred thousand had engaged in legal protests, many tens of thousands had broken state and federal laws to resist U.S. policy, and more than ten thousand had gone to jail for nonviolent civil disobedience. It was the most protracted, acrimonious political battle and the most enduring and contentious social movement of the decade. The question to which we now turn is: Exactly how and why did such a major movement emerge?

WHAT DID THE MOVEMENT ACHIEVE?

Nothing worth doing is completed in our lifetime; therefore, we must be saved by hope. Nothing true or beautiful or good makes complete sense in any immediate context of history; therefore, we must be saved by faith. Nothing we do, however virtuous, can be accomplished alone; therefore, we are saved by love. No virtuous act is quite as virtuous from the standpoint of our friend or foe as from our standpoint. Therefore, we must be saved by the final form of love which is forgiveness.

Reinhold Niebuhr, *The Irony of American History*

What did the Central America peace movement achieve? In one sense, that is an impossible question. For, without a comparative "control case" of the Reagan Central American policy *unconstrained* by a Central America peace movement, it is impossible to identify with certainty which of history's actual outcomes are attributable to the influence of the movement and which are not. How would events have differed had President Reagan's Central America crusade met little organized opposition? That we can never precisely know.

But lacking ideal comparative conditions does not mean we are totally helpless to venture even a cautious evaluation of the movement's accomplishments. A tentative assessment is better than no assessment at all. Minimally, we can identify what the movement failed to achieve. Beyond that, we can venture a cautious, educated appraisal of the movement's political successes. Finally, we can assess the movement's impact on its participants, and the potential effects of that on future social movements.

FAILURES

The judgment we can make with greatest confidence concerns what the Central America peace movement did *not* achieve: ultimately, the movement was not able to force the Reagan administration to terminate its wars in Central America (see Brett 1994). Despite the movement's fierce opposition, the administration prevailed in sustaining its well-armed counterrevolutionary forces in the field in Honduras and Costa Rica, and so the Contra war in Nicaragua raged on year after year. The Reagan administration also prevailed in maintaining its generous aid package to the embattled regime in El Salvador, sustaining its only lifeline of economic and military viability. Consequently, El Salvador's civil war also ground on for the entire decade. In the end, the Reagan administration essentially had its way. In Nicaragua, the war-weary Nicaraguans cried "uncle," the Sandinistas were ousted from power, the Nicaraguan revolution was terminated, and a U.S.-friendly regime took political control. In El Salvador, an FMLN victory was thwarted, revolutionary social transformations forestalled, and a regime acceptable to the U.S. retained power. Overall, U.S. influence in the region was reasserted and reinforced.

Central America peace activists uniformly recognize their failure in this regard. According to Mike Clark (1992), "We didn't achieve what we wanted to. On the big questions, they won, we lost." Angela Berryman (1990) agreed. "In the end, the Reagan administration got its way. In that sense, our movement was a failure." According to Sam Hope (1992), "Ultimately, Reagan won the battle." Phyllis Taylor (1990) concurred: "That we didn't stop the war was a failure for us." And Dennis Marker (1992) explained, "We could not stop Reagan and Bush from destroying the Nicaraguan revolution. Could not stop tens of thousands from being killed throughout the region. Could not stop the unbelievable amounts of military aid. In those ways, we failed."

A minority of the peace activists also voice another sense of failure: the failure of the movement to fight as entirely effectively as it might have. Cindy Buhl (1993), for example, lamented,

> We really needed to develop more sophisticated, over-arching, long-term, targeted field campaigns for swing-states, to hire crack field staff to go in and organize. We never did. We spent more than one million dollars on Countdown, a short-term campaign. But there was never money for long-term work. And the Central American people paid the price for it. It was the tyranny of the urgent, the fickleness of funders and executive boards who don't understand long-term programs, who'll only fund familiar, short-term campaigns.

Once, they did try the right idea, but implemented it badly and declared the whole thing a mistake. This was the so-called "Southern Strategy." There is still a false folklore that we actually tried to organize South Central states, which is ridiculous. So we are *still* weak in exactly the same states we have always been. And when the next crisis comes up, we'll *still* lose the same goddam votes in exactly those states. That's a failure.

Similarly, some believe the Sanctuary movement failed to capitalize sufficiently on its potential to use the media to challenge the Reagan policy. If so, this may be because, initially, media coverage came easily for Sanctuary, and therefore its leaders were never forced to develop the organizational facility necessary to generate news coverage in later years. According to Jane Guise (1990), "Early on, the media paid lots of attention to the Sanctuary movement, but after the trials, Sanctuary was dropped." Dennis Marker (1992) elaborated:

Sanctuary was golden. It was total integrity, a major movement. But it got much less media attention than it should have because there wasn't anyone doing the press work, interpreting the movement to the media. You had one big splash and an occasional story, but there was no one following up, making the day-to-day contacts, pressing the case. I would have loved to have done it, but I was already over my head. There may have been some media work done, but it mostly seemed they were making it up as they went along. So, Sanctuary's real importance and bigness was not being interpreted to the country. That was a major lost opportunity.

But these were a minority of voices. On the whole, most activists believed that their failure to stop Reagan's wars in Central America was not due to a lack of effort. Most believed they had fought their hardest and best, and had failed anyway.

ACHIEVEMENTS

That the Central America peace movement ultimately failed to force the Reagan administration to terminate its wars in Central America does not mean that the movement cannot also be credited with some successes. To begin, from the perspective of many movement activists, particularly religious activists, the baseline measure of success is faithfulness. Many activists view their actions and their movement as partially successful because they believe that they faithfully acted upon their convictions and principles (Taylor n.d.: 1–2).

For a lot of church people, myself included, success is defined a little differently. Because faith is the reason we get into activism, faithfulness is one of the ways we judge it. Not all the focus is on political goals. Criteria for success can be,

Were you true to your beliefs? Did you adhere to non-violence? Did you help to transform people in the church? Of course, you also want to win. But that's not all. Faith and faithfulness are also what we're about, and they keep us going, pressing on (Rice 1992).

Besides the success, from the activists' perspective, of acting faithfully, the peace movement can also claim one major political accomplishment. Even cautiously judged, it is apparent that the movement made the Reagan administration's Central American policy of low-intensity warfare exceedingly difficult to implement, and therefore helped to limit significantly the severity of its destructiveness. Without the movement's opposition, the administration's policy actions would have been much more overt, intense, and unrelenting, and the human misery and loss of life in Central America would have been greater. Primarily as a result of the massive opposition generated and sustained by the Central America peace movement, with the help of the Vietnam syndrome, the Reagan administration was forced to expend a tremendous amount of political capital to achieve what it *did* accomplish, was prevented from employing as much military force in Central America as it would have liked, and, ultimately, was forced to resort to illegal means to prosecute its war against Nicaragua. In the end, those illegalities threatened to bring down the entire Reagan Presidency. In Sam Hope's (1992) words: "We made a big fight out of something that otherwise would have been a non-issue. We helped escalate the matter to the point that it really became a major bone of contention, and that made a real difference for Central Americans."

The Central America peace movement's primary political leverage consisted in pressuring Congress to cut off or reduce U.S. military aid to Central America. In attempting to procure that aid, the White House's task was made difficult by the Boland Amendment, by congressional hearings on human rights abuses by the Salvadoran regime and the Contras, by congressional oversight and restrictions of CIA covert activities, and by the greatly contested, recurrent Contra aid votes, which the administration often lost. Overall, the Reagan administration was awarded notably less Central American military aid than it requested. And the Central America peace movement was probably the most important force consolidating and sustaining congressional opposition to the Reagan policy. According to Central America Working Group Director and congressional strategist and lobbyist Cindy Buhl (1993), who worked more closely with members of Congress than perhaps anyone else in the movement:

Grassroots activism was critical, not marginal. Without it there never would have been a base of congressional opposition. No one took on Ronald Reagan just for the fun of it. Why should any member of Congress challenge the President at the height of his powers, and put their neck on the line for puny little Central America, unless it were for broad constituent pressure? The Peace movement was active and growing. And members of Congress were acutely aware of that.

Buhl (1993) explains that, in Congress, there were a small committed core of opponents and another of supporters of Reagan's Central American policy. These cores, regardless of what their constituencies said, unwaveringly championed their respective positions because of their firmly held principles and real knowledge about Central America. The rest of the members of Congress were "followers," whose votes—whether they thought the White House Central American policy made sense or not—were decided by the immediate forces of political pressure. This was precisely the Central America peace movement's opportunity:

> When you look at Contra aid votes, over time you see about 180 regular opponents and 180 regular supporters of the policy. Then you have that beautiful, vacillating swing list in between. How did the 180 regular opponents become so constant and loyal? Not because they were educated and committed on this issue. Certainly not because they were Sandinista allies. So, aside from weak party loyalties, why were they always voting against Reagan, no matter how irresolute their personal positions on Central America might have been? Simply because of grassroots pressure. We couldn't have sustained those 180 votes for so many years without the grassroots staying so passionately engaged and constantly growing. Almost all of those 180 regular opponents would say that it was pressure from the grassroots that determined their vote. Even some key swing votes against Contra aid, like Dennis DeConcini in the Senate, credited the movement for exposing them to information that they thought was compelling (Buhl 1993).

According to Gail Phares (1992): "We messed up White House propaganda quite effectively in Congress. We went face-to-face in Washington with our "What We've Seen and Heard" books, with pictures of Contra violence and everything. We continually went to Congress, sat in their offices, and made sure they read our material and saw the reality, so they knew what this vote was about. We did that very effectively."

In addition to pressuring congressional representatives into opposing the President's policy, the Central America peace movement provided congressional allies with useful, supportive information. Mike Clark (1992) has said, "When Congress debated Contra aid, often Witness for Peace was the only source of information. Senators would stand up and say, 'There have been 37 attacks in 18 different places over six months.' They knew those facts because *we* were on the front lines gathering and publicizing them! We were the source of the information that sometimes influenced votes."

Because the peace movement helped create and sustain major congressional resistance to the Reagan Central American policy, and thus partially constrained the administration's ability to intervene in Central America, the extent and intensity of the region's military conflicts were notably diminished. Largely because of movement activism, the Nicaraguan Contras—who, for some years required Oliver North's extra-constitutional intrigues simply to stay alive and together, "body and soul"—had far fewer military resources than they otherwise would have had with which to wage their destructive war. Some evidence also indicates that, because of the physical presence of Witness for Peace delegates in Nicaraguan war zones engaging in protective "interposition," some Contra attacks on Nicaraguan targets were prevented and some Nicaraguan lives were saved (Taylor n.d.: 4–5). Also, largely because of movement activism, the White House was forced to exert continual pressure, which otherwise it would not have, on the regime in El Salvador to curb the army and death squads' gross human rights violations. And it appears that, although Salvadoran army and death-squad atrocities were already rampant, they would have been even worse without the U.S. pressure for improvements. Furthermore, in response to the 1990 murders of the four Salvadoran Jesuits and their housekeepers, protest from the Central America peace movement helped spur Congress into cutting Salvadoran aid in half, which contributed to the negotiated settlement of the civil war: "Just look at how the Salvador policy has gone last year: the Senate voted 75 to 25 to cut military aid in half. That resulted, in part, from our movement's protests. Had there been a 'China-movement' around Tienamen Square, the administration could have never followed its policy of condoning the Chinese government's crackdown. Movements in this country make that kind of a difference" (Butigan 1991).

Finally, although it is impossible to determine, short of a high-ranking Reagan administration official acknowledging the fact, it is not so very unlikely that the peace movement prevented what would have otherwise been a full-scale U.S. invasion of Nicaragua. This possibility is most difficult to judge, and opinions disagree even within the Central America peace movement and among political analysts. It is certainly possible that, even without the movement's widespread grassroots opposition, the Reagan administration would not have launched a U.S. invasion of Nicaragua. But it is also possible that it would have. Other than disruptive domestic protest, it is not clear what might have prevented the President from doing so.

President Reagan unquestionably believed the Sandinistas represented a major threat to U.S. national security interests and plainly stated that he wanted to see the FSLN overthrown. Strategically, he had clearly rejected the diplomatic option of negotiation and compromise. The President approved preludes to and unambiguous acts of war against Nicaragua, including the CIA mining of Nicaraguan harbors. Furthermore, the U.S. armed forces, having repeatedly rehearsed an invasion of Nicaragua in joint military exercises in the region, were fully capable of launching a U.S. invasion to overthrow the FSLN (see Brinkley 1985a, 1985b). Moreover—with factors such as MIG fighter jets allegedly being imported from the Soviet Union, and thousands of U.S. citizens in Nicaragua whose lives could have been claimed, as in Grenada, to have been in danger—the White House was fully capable of creating a "situation" justifying a U.S. invasion. Most importantly, by invading and overthrowing the governments of Grenada and Panama, both Presidents Reagan and Bush demonstrated their complete readiness and willingness to launch full-scale U.S. invasions in the region. Minimally, it would not have been aberrant behavior for President Reagan to have launched a U.S. invasion of Nicaragua. Whether he actually *would* have without a Central America peace movement, however, and whether he actually did not *because* of the Central America peace movement we cannot conclude. The evidence merely suggests this as a real possibility.

Whether or not the peace movement did prevent a full-scale U.S. invasion of Nicaragua, one final political outcome of the movement is certain. The movement helped to force the administration into a position where it had to choose to resort to extraordinary and illegal means to proceed with its policy in Central America. A good part of why the Central America peace movement ultimately failed, especially on Nicaragua, is not because it was unable to use the rules of the political system to accomplish its goals, but because the Reagan administration, when thwarted, chose simply to *disregard* the rules of the political system. Had the White House actually followed the provisions of the U.S. Constitution and other statutes, the movement could have claimed much greater political success, especially with Nicaragua. Instead, the unyielding Reagan administration chose to skirt congressional oversight of covert activities, fabricate human rights improvements in El Salvador, engage in harassment and repression of domestic dissent, unlawfully use tax dollars to fund public diplomacy campaigns, violate established treaties of international law, reject and belittle the rulings of the World Court, and, most astoundingly, secretly divert to the Nicaraguan Contras millions of dollars from the illegal sale of military arms to Iran, a terrorist enemy of the U.S. Having entangled themselves in this snarl of disreputable and illegal activities, with the Iran-contra affair at its pinnacle, members of the administration then attempted a failed cover-up of criminal wrongdoings. In the end, most high-ranking members of the Reagan administration were found to have lied about these improprieties, and twelve players in the administration's Central America intrigues—Caspar Weinberger, Robert McFarlane, Duane Clarridge, Clair George, Elliott Abrams, Alan Fiers, John Poindexter, Carl Channell, Albert Hakim, Richard Miller, Richard Secord, and Oliver North—were convicted of Contra or Iran-Contra-related criminal wrongdoing (Arnson 1993: 297–301). The reputations and authority of President Reagan and many in his administration were damaged and weakened. In this way, the Central America peace movement not only helped to force the Reagan administration to pay a very high price for the success of its Central America policy, but also inadvertently contributed to the ultimate, partial demise of the Reagan Presidency and administration. In the words of Ken Butigan (1991), "The Central America Peace movement forced the creation of Oliver North. Implementing this policy meant going underground, relying on secrecy, skirting the law. And all of this eventually came crashing in on Reagan and his lot."

THE FORMATION OF ACTIVIST IDENTITIES

Perhaps the Central America peace movement's most profound consequences were not seen in the 1980s, but will only become evident in future years and decades. It may be that the movement's most important impact was not accomplishing certain political goals in the 1980s, as important as they may have been, but expanding the base of grassroots activists, especially faith-based activists, who will serve as the core mobilizers of larger, even more consequential peace and justice movements in the future.

Social-movement scholarship has made increasingly clear the critical interconnections between seemingly distinct movements and campaigns. McAdam (1988) has shown that the civil rights movement of the early 1960s was directly responsible for helping to generate the student free-speech, women's liberation, and anti-Vietnam movements of the late 1960s and early '70s. Chatfield (1992) has advanced a view of the U.S. peace movement, not as a single mobilization at one period of time, but as a long tradition comprised of advancing and receding waves. Luker (1984) has posed a comparable view of U.S. anti-abortion campaigns. Rupp and Taylor (1987) have demonstrated the importance of the committed remnant of early twentieth-century suffrage activists in maintaining the women's movement during the doldrum years for its eventual resurgence in the 1960s and '70s. Meyer and Whittier (1994) have revealed that the U.S. women's movement had an important impact on the subsequent U.S. peace movement. And Smith (1991) has shown that the emergence of the liberation theology movement in Latin America was facilitated and conditioned by a host of other prior religious and secular movements and campaigns, which themselves had no intention of generating liberation theology.

Recognizing these interconnections and "spillover effects" (Meyer and Whittier 1994) is vital in assessing the impact of the Central America peace movement. For, not only will that movement likely prove to serve as a sustaining organizational and cultural bridge to important movements in coming years, but, at the individual level, that movement has redirected and transformed the lives of tens of thousands of its participants in ways that will likely promote their involvement in subsequent social movements. As Gail Phares says (1992), "Many of our people will remain active for the rest of their lives. Peace and justice is something you don't just drop. It's a lifelong commitment. We recruited and empowered a lot of people. We taught people how to work with the press, with Congress, with their churches. They know they can make an impact, really do things. That's never going to change."

Theoretically, even limited experience in social movements is significant because it can radicalize participants and familiarize them with the "script" used to play the "social activist" role. When movement activists are seen as engaged in a long-term role-transformation process that gradually deepens their commitment to and participation in political activism, each successive social-movement involvement appears to help activists both become more comfortable with their participation in activism and engage in a broader range of more challenging and disruptive activist tactics. In this way, any significant level of participation may help in the long term to form stronger political-activist identities.

Through the Central America peace movement, a host of North Americans with little prior movement experience were politicized, socialized into the activist subculture, and taught the language and skills of organized, disruptive protest. And for a multitude of other Americans with substantial prior movement experience, participation in the movement reaffirmed their activist identities, refined their organizing and protest skills, and strengthened their political commitments. One Witness for Peace delegate wrote this characteristic comment on her questionnaire: "Anyone who comes on a delegation and sees what U.S. policies are doing here in Nicaragua can't go back without questioning everything we were ever taught by our country. The experience challenged us not just about Nicaragua, but about everything we are as North Americans." According to Mike Clark (1992), "You *thought* you were going to Central America to offer solidarity and moral support, then you discover that your life had been changed. That's what happened. Thousands of people fought Reagan for years because Central America changed their lives. Lots of people experienced struggle and suffering there for the first time."

Central America activist Clark Taylor (1990) disclosed, "I made my first trip to Nicaragua in 1985 and decided to make Central America the issue for the rest of my life. I learned Spanish, have traveled to Central America more than twenty times since, and have become totally immersed in the struggle for Central America."

Phyllis Taylor (1990) recalled, "People's lives were profoundly transformed. When people sleep on a dirt floor in a sleeping bag for the first time; when very wealthy people, surrounded by kids in a refugee camp sit there weeping, just weeping over the realization of what our government's doing, that is change."

The actual numbers involved are impressive. After only three years of existence, Sanctuary had drawn in more than seventy thousand participants (Golden and McConnell 1986: 3). In two years, the Pledge of Resistance mobilized eighty thousand U.S. citizens (Butigan 1991). Witness for Peace provided life-transforming experiences for more than four thousand North Americans, and, even as late as 1990, enjoyed a constituency of forty thousand supporters and newsletter readers. Witness for Peace and the Pledge of Resistance alone taught thousands of people how to use the mass media for political activism, and trained more than eighty thousand people in the philosophy and tactics of nonviolent civil disobedience (Taylor n.d.: 5–6). Thousands were arrested for civil disobedience, very many for the first time in their lives. And the more than one thousand other local, state, and national Central America organizations provided similar experiences and training for their members (Central America Resource Center 1986). All told, counting overlapping involvements, well more than one hundred thousand U.S. citizens appear to have been mobilized into some form of Central America peace activism that gave them exposure to and education in grassroots political protest. From what we know about social-movement mobilization and recruitment, we should expect these now more experienced activists to serve as the core mobilizing base and early joiners of social movements that may emerge in years to come. Cindy Buhl (1993) observed:

> We educated and mobilized an incredible number of people on what would have normally been an obscure foreign policy issue. This was the largest mobilization of Americans around a foreign-policy issue since Vietnam, without even having "our boys" fighting there. The educational effect was amazing. Many church, labor, and left-wing people learned a lot about dealing with Congress policy-making, the media, and about fighting for something worth fighting for. Many religious people have developed a strong, ongoing connection with the poor in Central America. And much of the movement's core has remained intact, unlike the post-Vietnam experience. So there is a core out there, one that can quickly respond again to a new crisis. It will take a long time before we have to start from scratch again.

Dennis Marker (1992) agreed:

> Each new movement involves people from the last movement—Vietnam, anti-nuclear, whatever. Then you also pick up new people. With Central America, we picked up a huge number of religious people. Not everyone joins every succeeding movement. Some may choose to sit out the next issue. But they're still there, a base that's not going to go away. The hope is that you just keep building until it reaches the 100th monkey, when you finally get to where you actually have enough people to make a big difference. Instead of being limited to small changes, you get to where you can actually tip the scales. That's what we're working toward.

Finally, the Central America peace movement also appears to have contributed to the effectiveness of potential social movements in the future by generating two innovative tactics of disruptive political protest. First, Witness for Peace created and implemented the novel idea of an accompanying and interpositioning "shield of love," of sending waves of delegations of ordinary U.S. citizens to hazardous battle zones to try to deter enemy offensives, to document atrocities, and to return to the U.S. as "living media" to challenge and terminate a U.S.-sponsored war. Mike Clark (1992) rightly observes, "Witness for Peace was the first time in American history that large numbers of noncombatant U.S. citizens were put in a war zone to see the war from the other side and, hopefully, through sheer physical presence, to prevent enemy attacks." Second, the Pledge of Resistance formulated and executed the novel idea of proactively organizing the capacity to unleash massive, nationally coordinated civil-disobedient protest *before,* rather than after, a U.S. invasion, in order to deter that invasion from ever happening, rather than trying to reverse the invasion after the fact. Tactical innovations such as these afford challengers important new mechanisms of power with which to struggle against and outmaneuver their adversaries, at least until opponents are able to devise countervailing tactical adaptations (McAdam 1983). Admittedly, the applicability of these particular tactical innovations depends on a particular set of favorable conditions. Nevertheless, the U.S. government throughout the 1980s did seem incapable of adapting an effective tactical response to these innovations. Thus, by expanding the tactical repertoire available to the progressive activist community, the Central America peace movement has enhanced the potential political power of peace and justice movements that may emerge in years to come.

CONCLUSION

The Central America peace movement failed to force the Reagan administration to end its low-intensity wars in Central America. This was partly because the movement was unable to pressure Congress into acting more decisively, especially on El Salvador, and partly because the Reagan administration simply disregarded the law when Congress did act decisively, especially on Nicaragua. Nevertheless, the movement did make the Reagan administration's Central American wars exceedingly difficult to conduct, and, as a result, substantially limited the severity of their destructiveness. As devastating as they were, had the peace movement not challenged the White House, those wars would have been even more devastating. It is possible that the movement even prevented a direct U.S. invasion of Nicaragua. Largely as a result of the movement's resistance to the President's policy, the Reagan administration was forced to pay a very high price for its exploits in Central America. Indeed, the movement helped to create a political context within which the administration felt compelled to make reckless choices and, consequently, began to self-destruct. Finally, the movement innovated new tactics of political protest, and educated and trained tens of thousands of U.S. citizens in the philosophy and methods of grassroots activism and disruptive political rebellion. In so doing, it may very well prove to be a critical wave in the long, historical tradition of grassroots peace and justice activism.

34

The "Four Prisons" and the Movements of Liberation

Asian American Activism from the 1960s to the 1990s

Glenn Omatsu

According to Ali Shariati, an Iranian philosopher, each of us exists within four prisons.[1] First is the prison imposed on us by history and geography; from this confinement, we can escape only by gaining a knowledge of science and technology. Second is the prison of history; our freedom comes when we understand how historical forces operate. The third prison is our society's social and class structure; from this prison, only a revolutionary ideology can provide the way to liberation. The final prison is the self. Each of us is composed of good and evil elements, and we must each choose between them.

The analysis of our four prisons provides a way of understanding the movements that swept across America in the 1960s and molded the consciousness of one generation of Asian Americans. The movements were struggles for liberation from many prisons.

They were struggles that confronted the historical forces of racism, poverty, war, and exploitation. They were struggles that generated new ideologies, based mainly on the teachings and actions of Third World leaders. And they were struggles that redefined human values—the values that shape how people live their daily lives and interact with each other. Above all, they were struggles that transformed the lives of "ordinary" people as they confronted the prisons around them.

For Asian Americans, these struggles profoundly changed our communities. They spawned numerous grassroots organizations. They created an extensive network of student organizations and Asian American Studies classes. They recovered buried cultural traditions as well as produced a new generation of writers, poets, and artists. But most importantly, the struggles deeply affected Asian American consciousness. They redefined racial and ethnic identity, promoted new ways of thinking about communities, and challenged prevailing notions of power and authority.

Yet, in the two decades that have followed, scholars have reinterpreted the movements in narrower ways. I learned about this reinterpretation when I attended a class recently in Asian American Studies at UCLA. The professor described the period from the late 1950s to the early 1970s as a single epoch involving the persistent efforts of racial minorities and their white supporters to secure civil rights. Young Asian Americans, the professor stated, were swept into this campaign and by later anti-war protests to assert their own racial identity. The most important influence on Asian Americans during this period was Dr. Martin Luther King, Jr., who inspired them to demand access to policy-makers and initiate advocacy programs for their own communities. Meanwhile, students and professors fought to legitimize Asian American Studies in college curricula and for representation of Asians in American society. The lecture was cogent, tightly organized, and well-received by the audience of students—many of them new immigrants or the children of new immigrants. There was only one problem: the reinterpretation was wrong on every aspect.

Those who took part in the mass struggles of the 1960s and early 1970s will know that the birth of the Asian American movement coincided not with the initial campaign for civil rights but with the later demand for black liberation; that the leading influence was not Martin Luther King, Jr., but Malcolm X; that the focus of a generation of Asian American activists was not on asserting racial pride but reclaiming a tradition of militant struggle by earlier generations; that the movement was not centered on the aura of racial identity but embraced fundamental questions of oppression and power; that the movement consisted of not only college students but large numbers of community forces, including the elderly, workers, and high school youth; and that the main thrust was not one of seeking legitimacy and representation within American society but the larger goal of liberation.

It may be difficult for a new generation—raised on the Asian American codewords of the 1980s stressing "advocacy," "access," "legitimacy," "empowerment," and "assertiveness"—to understand the urgency of Malcolm X's demand for freedom "by any means necessary," Mao's challenge to "serve the people," the slogans of "power to the people" and "self-determination," the principles of "mass line" organizing and "united front" work, or the conviction that people—not elites—make history. But these ideas galvanized thousands of Asian Americans and reshaped our communities. And it is these concepts that we must grasp to understand the scope and intensity of our movement and what it created.

But are these concepts relevant to Asian Americans today? In our community—where new immigrants and refugees constitute the majority of Asian Americans—can we find a legacy from the struggles of two decades ago? Are the ideas of the movement alive today, or have they atrophied into relics—the curiosities of a bygone era of youthful and excessive idealism?

By asking these questions, we, as Asian Americans, participate in a larger national debate: the reevaluation of the impact of the 1960s on American society today. This debate is occurring all around us: in sharp exchanges over "family values" and the status of women and gays in American society; in clashes in schools over curricular reform and multiculturalism; in differences among policymakers over the urban crisis and approaches to rebuilding Los Angeles and other inner cities after the 1992 uprisings; and continuing reexaminations of U.S. involvement in Indochina more than two decades ago and the relevance of that war to U.S. military intervention in Iraq, Somalia, and Bosnia.

What happened in the 1960s that made such an impact on America? Why do discussions about that decade provoke so much emotion today? And do the movements of the 1960s serve as the same controversial reference point for Asian Americans?

THE UNITED STATES DURING THE 1960s

In recent years, the movements of the 1960s have come under intense attack. One national bestseller, Allan Bloom's *Closing of the American Mind*, criticizes the movements for undermining the bedrock of Western thought.[2] According to Bloom, nothing positive resulted from the mass upheavals of the 1960s. He singles out black studies and affirmative-action programs and calls for eliminating them from universities.

Activists who have continued political work provide contrasting assessments. Their books include Todd Gitlin's *The Sixties: Years of Hope, Days of Rage;* James Miller's *Democracy Is in the Streets: From Port Huron to the Siege of Chicago;* Ronald Fraser's *1968: A Student Generation in Revolt;* Tom Hayden's *Reunion: A Memoir;* Tariq Ali's *Street Fighting Years,* George Katsiaficas' *The Imagination of the New Left: A Global Analysis of 1968* and special issues of various journals, including *Witness, Socialist Review,* and *Radical America.*

However, as Winifred Breines states in an interesting review essay titled "Whose New Left?" most of the retrospects have been written by white male activists from elite backgrounds and reproduce their relationship to these movements.[3] Their accounts tend to divide the period into two phases: the "good" phase of the early 1960s, characterized by participatory democracy; followed by the post-1968 phase, when movement politics "degenerated" into violence and sectarianism.

"Almost all books about the New Left note a turning point or an ending in 1968 when the leadership of the movement turned toward militancy and violence and SDS [Students for a Democratic Society] as an organization was collapsing," Breines observes. The retrospects commonly identify the key weaknesses of the movements as the absence of effective organization, the lack of discipline, and utopian thinking. Breines disagrees with these interpretations:

> The movement was not simply unruly and undisciplined; it was experimenting with antihierarchical organizational forms. . . . There were many centers of action in the movement, many actions, many interpretations, many visions, many experiences. There was no [organizational] unity because each group, region, campus, commune, collective, and demonstration developed differently,

but all shared in a spontaneous opposition to racism and inequality, the war in Vietnam, and the repressiveness of American social norms and culture, including centralization and hierarchy.[4]

Breines believes that the most important contributions of activists were their moral urgency, their emphasis on direct action, their focus on community building, and their commitment to mass democracy.

Similarly, Sheila Collins in *The Rainbow Challenge,* a book focusing on the Jesse Jackson presidential campaign of 1984 and the formation of the National Rainbow Coalition, assesses the movements of the sixties very positively.[5] She contends that the Jackson campaign was built on the grassroots organizing experience of activists who emerged from the struggles for civil rights, women's liberation, peace and social justice, and community building during the sixties. Moreover, activists' participation in these movements shaped their vision of America, which, in turn, became the basis for the platform of the Rainbow Coalition 20 years later.

According to Collins, the movements that occurred in the United States in the sixties were also part of a worldwide trend, a trend Latin American theologians call the era of the "eruption of the poor" into history. In America, the revolt of the "politically submerged" and "economically marginalized" posed a major ideological challenge to ruling elites:

> The civil rights and black power movement exploded several dominant assumptions about the nature of American society, thus challenging the cultural hegemony of the white ruling elite and causing everyone else in the society to redefine their relationship to centers of power, creating a groundswell of support for radical democratic participation in every aspect of institutional life.[6]

Collins contends that the mass movements created a "crisis of legitimation" for ruling circles. This crisis, she believes, was "far more serious than most historians—even those of the left—have credited it with being."

Ronald Fraser also emphasizes the ideological challenge raised by the movements due to their mass, democratic character and their "disrespect for arbitrary and exploitative authority." In *1968: A Student Generation in Revolt,* Fraser explains how these concepts influenced one generation of activists:

> [T]he anti-authoritarianism challenged almost every shibboleth of Western society. Parliamentary democracy, the authority of presidents . . . and [the policies of] governments to further racism, conduct imperialist wars or oppress sectors of the population at home, the rule of capital and the fiats of factory bosses, the dictates of university administrators, the sacredness of the family, sexuality,

bourgeois culture—nothing was in principle sacrosanct. . . . Overall . . . [there was] a lack of deference towards institutions and values that demean[ed] people and a concomitant awareness of people's rights.[7]

THE SAN FRANCISCO STATE STRIKE'S LEGACY

The retrospects about the 1960s produced so far have ignored Asian Americans. Yet, the books cited above—plus the review essay by Winifred Breines—provide us with some interesting points to compare and contrast. For example, 1968 represented a turning point for Asian Americans and other sectors of American society. But while white male leaders saw the year as marking the decline of the movement, 1968 for Asian Americans was a year of birth. It marked the beginning of the San Francisco State strike and all that followed.

The strike, the longest student strike in U.S. history, was the first campus uprising involving Asian Americans as a collective force.[8] Under the Third World Liberation Front—a coalition of African American, Latino, American Indian, and Asian American campus groups—students "seized the time" to demand ethnic studies, open admissions, and a redefinition of the education system. Although their five-month strike was brutally repressed and resulted in only partial victories, students won the nation's first School of Ethnic Studies.

Yet, we cannot measure the legacy of the strike for Asian Americans only in the tangible items it achieved, such as new classes and new faculty; the strike also critically transformed the consciousness of its participants who, in turn, profoundly altered their communities' political landscape. Through their participation, a generation of Asian American student activists reclaimed a heritage of struggle—linking their lives to the tradition of militancy of earlier generations of Filipino farmworkers, Chinese immigrant garment and restaurant workers, and Japanese American concentration camp resisters. Moreover, these Asian American students—and their community supporters—liberated themselves from the prisons surrounding their lives and forged a new vision for their communities, creating numerous grassroots projects and empowering previously ignored and disenfranchised sectors of society. The statement of goals and principles of one campus organization, Philippine-American Collegiate Endeavor (PACE), during the strike captures this new vision:

We seek . . . simply to function as human beings, to control our own lives. Initially, following the myth of the American Dream, we worked to attend predominantly white colleges, but we have learned through direct analysis that it is impossible for our people, so-called minorities, to function as human beings, in a racist society in which white always comes first. . . . So we have decided to fuse ourselves with the masses of Third World people which are the majority of the world's peoples, to create through struggle, a new humanity, a new humanism, a New World Consciousness, and within that context collectively control our own destinies.[9]

The San Francisco State strike is important not only as a beginning point for the Asian American movement, but also because it crystallizes several themes that would characterize Asian American struggles in the following decade. First, the strike occurred at a working-class campus and involved a coalition of Third World students linked to their communities. Second, students rooted their strike in the tradition of resistance by past generations of minority peoples in America. Third, strike leaders drew inspiration—as well as new ideology—from international Third World leaders and revolutions occurring in Asia, Africa, Latin America, and the Middle East. Fourth, the strike in its demands for open admissions, community control of education, ethnic studies, and self-determination confronted basic questions of power and oppression in America. Finally, strike participants raised their demands through a strategy of mass mobilizations and militant, direct action.

In the decade following the strike, several themes would reverberate in the struggles in Asian American communities across the nation. These included housing and anti-eviction campaigns, efforts to defend education rights, union organizing drives, campaigns for jobs and social services, and demands for democratic rights, equality, and justice. Mo Nishida, an organizer in Los Angeles, recalls the broad scope of movement activities in his city:

> Our movement flowered. At one time, we had active student organizations on every campus around Los Angeles, fought for ethnic studies, equal opportunity programs, high potential programs at UCLA, and for students doing community work in "Serve the People" programs. In the community, we had, besides [Asian American] Hard Core, four area youth-oriented groups working against drugs (on the Westside, Eastside, Gardena, and the Virgil district). There were also parents' groups, which worked with parents of the youth and more.[10]

In Asian American communities in Los Angeles, San Francisco, Sacramento, Stockton, San Jose, Seattle, New York, and Honolulu, activists created "serve the people" organizations—mass networks built on the principles of "mass line" organizing. Youth initiated many of these organizations—some from college campuses and others from high schools and the streets—but other members of the community, including small-business people, workers, senior citizens, and new immigrants soon joined.

The *mass* character of community struggles is the least appreciated aspect of our movement today. It is commonly believed that the movement involved only college students. In fact, a range of people, including high-school youth, tenants, small-business people, former prison inmates, former addicts, the elderly, and workers embraced the struggles. But exactly who were these people, and what did their participation mean to the movement?

Historian George Lipsitz has studied similar, largely "anonymous" participants in civil rights campaigns in African American communities. He describes one such man, Ivory Perry of St. Louis:

> Ivory Perry led no important organizations, delivered no important speeches, and received no significant recognition or reward for his social activism. But for more than 30 years he had passed out leaflets, carried the picket signs, and planned the flamboyant confrontations that made the civil rights movements effective in St. Louis and across the nation. His continuous commitment at the local level had goaded others into action, kept alive hopes of eventual victory in the face of short-term defeats, and provided a relatively powerless community with an effective lever for social change. The anonymity of his activism suggests layers of social protest activity missing from most scholarly accounts, while the persistence of his involvement undermines prevailing academic judgments about mass protests as outbursts of immediate anger and spasmodic manifestations of hysteria.[11]

Those active in Asian American communities during the late 1960s and early 1970s know there were many Ivory Perrys. They were the people who demonstrated at eviction sites, packed City Hall hearing rooms, volunteered to staff health fairs, and helped with day-to-day operations of the first community drop-in centers, legal defense offices, and senior citizen projects. They were the women and men who took the concept of "serve the people" and turned it into a material force, transforming the political face of our communities.

THE "CULTURAL REVOLUTION" IN ASIAN AMERICAN COMMUNITIES

But we would be wrong to describe this transformation of our communities as solely "political"—at least as our society narrowly defines the term today. The transformation also involved a cultural vitality that opened new ways of viewing the world. Unlike today—where Asian American communities categorize "culture" and "politics" into different spheres of professional activity—in the late 1960s they did not divide them so rigidly or hierarchically. Writers, artists, and musicians were "cultural workers," usually closely associated with communities, and saw their work as "serving the people." Like other community activists, cultural workers defined the period as a "decisive moment" for Asian Americans—a time for reclaiming the past and changing the future.

The "decisive moment" was also a time for questioning and transforming moral values. Through their political and cultural work, activists challenged systems of rank and privilege, structures of hierarchy and bureaucracy, forms of exploitation and inequality, and notions of selfishness and individualism. Through their activism in mass organizations, they promoted a new moral vision centered on democratic participation, cooperative work styles, and collective decision-making. Pioneer poet Russell C. Leong describes the affinity between this new generation of cultural workers and their communities, focusing on the work of the Asian American Writers' Workshop, located in the basement of the International Hotel in San Francisco Chinatown/Manilatown:

> We were a post-World War II generation mostly in our twenties and thirties; in or out of local schools and colleges. . . . [We] gravitated toward cities—San Francisco, Los Angeles, New York—where movements for ethnic studies and inner city blocks of Asian communities coincided. . . . We read as we wrote—not in isolation—but in the company of our neighbors in Manilatown pool halls, barrio parks, Chinatown basements. . . . Above all, we poets were a tribe of storytellers . . . Storytellers live in communities where they write for family and friends. The relationship between the teller and listener is neighborly, because the teller of stories must also listen.[12]

But as storytellers, cultural workers did more than simply describe events around them. By witnessing and participating in the movement, they helped to shape community consciousness. San Francisco poet Al Robles focuses on this process of vision making:

> While living and working in our little, tiny communities, in the midst of towering highrises, we fought the oppressor, the landlord, the developer, the banks, City Hall. But most of all, we celebrated through our culture; music, dance, song and poetry—not only the best we knew but the best we had. The poets were and always have been an integral part of the community. It was through poetry—through a poetical vision to live out the ritual in dignity as human beings.[13]

The transformation of poets, writers, and artists into cultural workers and vision makers reflected larger changes occurring in every sector of the Asian American community. In education, teachers and students redefined the learning process, discovering new ways of sharing knowledge different from traditional, authoritarian, top-down approaches. In the social-service sector, social workers and other professionals became "community workers" and under the slogan of "serve the people" redefined the traditional counselor/client relationship by stressing interaction, dialogue, and community building. Within community organizations, members experimented with new organizational structures and collective leadership styles, discarding hierarchical and bureaucratic forms where a handful of commanders made all the decisions. Everywhere, activists and ordinary people grappled with change.

Overall, this "cultural revolution" in the Asian American community echoes themes we have encountered earlier: Third World consciousness, participatory democracy, community building, historical rooting, liberation, and transformation. Why were these concepts so important to a generation of activists? What did they mean? And do they still have relevance for Asian American communities today?

Political analyst Raymond Williams and historian Warren Susman have suggested the use of "keywords" to study historical periods, especially times of great social change.[14] Keywords are terms, concepts, and ideas that emerge as themes of a period, reflecting vital concerns and changing values. For Asian Americans in the 1980s and 1990s, the keywords are "advocacy," "access," "legitimacy," "empowerment," and "assertiveness." These keywords tell us much about the shape of our community today, especially the growing role of young professionals and their aspirations in U.S. society. In contrast, the keywords of the late 1960s and early 1970s—"consciousness," "theory," "ideology," "participatory democracy," "community," and "liberation"—point to different concerns and values.

The keywords of two decades ago point to an approach to political work that activists widely shared, especially those working in grassroots struggles in Asian American neighborhoods, such as the Chinatowns, Little Tokyos, Manilatowns, and International Districts around the nation. This political approach focused on the relationship between political consciousness and social change, and can be best summarized in a popular slogan of the period: "Theory becomes a material force when it is grasped by the masses." Asian American activists believed that they could promote political change through direct action and mass education that raised political consciousness in the community, especially among the unorganized—low-income workers, tenants, small-business people, high school youth, etc. Thus, activists saw political consciousness as rising not from study groups, but from involving people in the process of social change—through their confronting the institutions of power around them and creating new visions of community life based on these struggles.

Generally, academics studying the movements of the 1960s—including academics in Asian American Studies—have dismissed the political theory of that time as murky and eclectic, characterized by ultra-leftism, shallow class analysis, and simplistic notions of Marxism and capitalism.[15] To a large extent, the thinking was eclectic; Asian American activists drew from Marx, Lenin, Stalin, and Mao—and also from Frantz Fanon, Malcolm X, Che Guevara, Kim Il-sung, and Amilcar Cabral, as well as Korean Revolutionary Kim San, W. E. B. Du Bois, Frederick Douglass, Paulo Freire, the Black Panther Party, the Young Lords, the women's liberation movement, and many other resistance struggles. But in their obsessive search for theoretical clarity and consistency, these academics miss the bigger picture. What is significant is not the *content* of ideas activists adopted, but what activists *did* with the ideas. What Asian American activists *did* was to use the ideas drawn from many different movements to redefine the Asian American experience.

Central to this redefinition was a slogan that appeared at nearly every Asian American rally during that period: "The people, and the people alone, are the motive force in the making of world history." Originating in the Chinese revolution, Asian American activists adapted the slogan to the tasks of community building, historical rooting, and creating new values. Thus, the slogan came to capture six new ways of thinking about Asian Americans.

- Asian Americans became active participants in the making of history, reversing standard accounts that had treated Asian Americans as marginal objects.
- Activists saw history as created by large numbers of people acting together, not by elites.
- This view of history provided a new way of looking at our communities. Activists believed that ordinary people could make their own history by learning how historical forces operated and by transforming this knowledge into a material force to change their lives.
- This realization defined a political strategy: Political power came from grassroots organizing, from the bottom up.
- This strategy required activists to develop a broad analysis of the Asian American condition—to uncover the interconnections in seemingly separate events, such as the war in Indochina, corporate redevelopment of Asian American communities, and the exploitation of Asian immigrants in garment shops. In their political analyses, activists linked the day-to-day struggles of Asian Americans to larger events and issues. The anti-eviction campaign of tenants in Chinatown and the International District against powerful corporations became one with the resistance movements of peasants in Vietnam, the Philippines, and Latin America—or, as summarized in a popular slogan of the period, there was "one struggle, [but] many fronts."
- This new understanding challenged activists to build mass, democratic organizations, especially within unorganized sectors of the community. Through these new organizations, Asian Americans expanded democracy for all sectors of the community and gained the power to participate in the broader movement for political change taking place throughout the world.

The redefinition of the Asian American experience stands as the most important legacy from this period. As described above, this legacy represents far more than an ethnic awakening. The redefinition began with an analysis of power and domination in American society. It provided a way for understanding the historical forces surrounding us. And most importantly, it presented a strategy and challenge for changing our future. This challenge, I believe, still confronts us today.

THE LATE 1970s: REVERSING DIRECTION

As we continue to delve into the vitality of the movements of the 1960s, one question becomes more and more persistent: Why did these movements, possessing so much vigor and urgency, seem to disintegrate in the late 1970s and early 1980s? Why did a society in motion toward progressive change seem to suddenly reverse direction?

As in the larger left movement, Asian American activists heatedly debate this question.[16] Some mention the strategy of repression—including assassinations—U.S. ruling circles launched in response to the mass rebellions. Others cite the accompanying programs of co-optation that elites designed to channel mass discontent into traditional political arenas. Some focus on the New Right's rise, culminating in the Reagan presidency. Still others emphasize the sectarianism among political forces within the movement, or target the inability of the movement as a whole to base itself more broadly within communities.

Each of these analyses provides a partial answer. But missing in most analyses by Asian American activists is the most critical factor: the devastating corporate offensive of the mid-1970s. We will remember the 1970s as a time of economic crisis and staggering inflation. Eventually, historians may more accurately describe it as the years of "one-sided class war." Transnational corporations based in the United States launched a broad attack on the American people, especially African American communities. Several books provide an excellent analysis of the corporate offensive. One of the best, most accessible accounts is *What's Wrong with the U.S. Economy?*, written in 1982 by the Institute for Labor Education and Research.[17] My analysis draws from that.

Corporate executives based their offensive on two conclusions: First, the economic crisis in the early 1970s—marked by declining corporate profits—occurred because American working people were earning too much; and second, the mass struggles of the previous decades had created "too much democracy" in America. The Trilateral Commission—headed by David Rockefeller and composed of corporate executives and politicians from the United States, Europe, and Japan—posed the problem starkly: Either people would have to accept less, or corporations would have to accept less. An article in *Business Week* identified the solution: "Some people will obviously have to do with less. . . . Yet it will be a hard pill for many Americans to swallow—the idea of doing with less so that big business can have more."

But in order for corporations to "have more," U.S. ruling circles had to deal with the widespread discontent that had erupted throughout America. We sometimes forget today that in the mid-1970s a large number of Americans had grown cynical about U.S. business and political leaders. People routinely called politicians—including President Nixon and Vice President Agnew—crooks, liars, and criminals. Increasingly, they began to blame the largest corporations for their economic problems. One poll showed that half the population believed that "big business is the source of most of what's wrong in this country today." A series of Harris polls found that those expressing "a great deal of confidence" in the heads of corporations had fallen from 55 percent in 1966 to only 15 percent in 1975. By the fall of 1975, public-opinion analysts testifying before a congressional committee reported, according to the *New York Times,* "that public confidence in the government and in the country's economic future is probably lower than it has ever been since they began to measure such things scientifically." These developments stunned many corporate leaders. "How did we let the educational system fail the free-enterprise system?" one executive asked.

U.S. ruling elites realized that restoring faith in free enterprise could only be achieved through an intensive ideological assault on those challenging the system. The ideological campaign was combined with a political offensive, aimed at the broad gains in democratic rights that Americans, especially African Americans, had achieved through the mass struggles of previous decades. According to corporate leaders, there was "too much democracy" in America, which meant too little "governability." In a 1975 Trilateral Commission report, Harvard political scientist Samuel Huntington analyzed the problem caused by "previously passive or unorganized groups in the population [which were] now engaged in concerted efforts to establish their claims to opportunities, positions, rewards, and privileges which they had not considered themselves entitled to before." According to Huntington, this upsurge in "democratic fervor" coincided with "markedly higher levels of self-consciousness on the part of blacks, Indians, Chicanos, white ethnic groups, students, and women, all of whom became mobilized and organized in new ways." Huntington saw these developments as creating a crisis for those in power:

> The essence of the democratic surge of the 1960s was a general challenge to existing systems of authority, public and private. In one form or another, the challenge manifested itself in the family, the university, business, public and private associations, politics, the government bureaucracy, and the military service. People no longer felt the same obligation to obey those whom they had previously considered superior to themselves in age, rank, status, expertise, character, or talents.[18]

The mass pressures, Huntington contended, had "produced problems for the governability of democracy in the 1970s." The government, he concluded, must find a way to exercise more control. And that meant curtailing the rights of "major economic groups."

The ensuing corporate campaign was a "one-sided class war": plant closures in U.S. industries and transfer of production overseas, massive layoffs in remaining industries, shifts of capital investment from one region of the country to other regions and other parts of the globe, and demands by corporations for concessions in wages and benefits from workers in nearly every sector of the economy.

The Reagan presidency culminated and institutionalized this offensive. The Reagan platform called for restoring "traditional" American values, especially faith in the system of free enterprise. Reaganomics promoted economic recovery by getting government "off the backs" of businesspeople, reducing taxation of the rich, and cutting social programs for the poor. Meanwhile, racism and exploitation became respectable under the new mantle of patriotism and economic recovery.

THE WINTER OF CIVIL RIGHTS

The corporate assault ravaged many American neighborhoods, but African American communities absorbed its harshest impact. A study by the Center on Budget and Policy Priorities measures the national impact:

- Between 1970 and 1980, the number of poor African Americans rose by 24 percent from 1.4 million to 1.8 million.
- In the 1980s, the overall African American median income was 57 percent that of whites, a decline of nearly four percentage points from the early 1970s.
- In 1986, females headed 42 percent of all African American families, the majority of which lived below the poverty line.
- In 1978, 8.4 percent of African American families had incomes under $5,000 a year. By 1987, that figure had grown to 13.5 percent. In that year, a third of all African Americans were poor.[19]
- By 1990, nearly half of all African Americans grew up in poverty.[20]

Manning Marable provides a stark assessment of this devastation in *How Capitalism Underdeveloped Black America:*

> What is qualitatively *new* about the current period is that the racist/capitalist state under Reagan has proceeded down a public policy road which could inevitably involve the complete obliteration of the entire Black reserve army of labor and sections of the Black working class. The decision to save capitalism at all costs, to provide adequate capital for restructuring of the private sector, fundamentally conflicts with the survival of millions of people who are now permanently outside the workplace. Reaganomics must, if it intends to succeed, place the onerous burden of unemployment on the shoulders of the poor (Blacks, Latinos and even whites) so securely that middle to upper income Americans will not protest in the vicious suppression of this stratum.[21]

The corporate offensive, combined with widespread government repression, brutally destroyed grassroots groups in the African American community. This war against the poor ripped apart the social fabric of neighborhoods across America, leaving them vulnerable to drugs and gang violence. The inner cities became the home of the "underclass" and a new politics of inner-directed violence and despair.

Historian Vincent Harding, in *The Other American Revolution,* summarizes the 1970s as the "winter" of civil rights, a period in which there was "a dangerous loss of hope among black people, hope in ourselves, hope in the possibility of any real change, hope in any moral, creative force beyond the flatness of our lives."[22]

In summary, the corporate offensive, especially its devastation of the African American community provides the necessary backdrop for understanding why the mass movements of the 1960s seemed to disintegrate. Liberation movements, especially in the African American community, did not disappear, but a major focus of their activity shifted to issues of day-to-day survival.

THE 1980s: AN AMBIGUOUS PERIOD FOR ASIAN AMERICAN EMPOWERMENT

For African Americans and many other people of color, the period from the mid-1970s through the Reagan and Bush presidencies became a winter of civil rights, a time of corporate assault on their livelihoods and an erosion of hard-won rights. But for Asian Americans, the meaning of this period is much more ambiguous. On the one hand, great suffering marked the period: growing poverty for increasing numbers of Asian Americans—especially refugees from Southeast Asia; a rising trend of racist hate crimes directed toward Asian Americans of all ethnicities and income levels; and sharpening class polarization within our communities—with a widening gap between the very rich and the very poor. But advances also characterized the period. With the reform of U.S. immigration laws in 1965, the Asian American population grew dramatically, creating new enclaves—including suburban settlements—and revitalizing more established communities, such as Chinatowns, around the nation. Some recent immigrant business-people, with small capital holdings, found economic opportunities in inner city neighborhoods. Meanwhile, Asian American youth enrolled in record numbers in colleges and universities across the United States. Asian American families moved into suburbs, crashing previously lily-white neighborhoods. And a small but significant group of Asian American politicians, such as Mike Woo and Warren Furutani, scored important electoral victories in the mainstream political arena, taking the concept of political empowerment to a new level of achievement.

During the winter of civil rights, Asian American activists also launched several impressive political campaigns at the grassroots level. Japanese Americans joined together to win redress and reparations. Filipino Americans rallied in solidarity with the "Peoples Power" movement in the Philippines to topple the powerful Marcos dictatorship. Chinese Americans created new political alignments and mobilized community support for the pro-democracy struggle in China. Korean Americans responded to the massacre of civilians by the South Korean dictatorship in Kwangju with massive demonstrations and relief efforts, and established an important network of organizations in America, including Young Koreans United. Samoan Americans rose up against police abuse in Los Angeles; Pacific Islanders demanded removal of nuclear weapons and wastes from their homelands; and Hawaiians fought for the right of self-determination and recovery of their lands. And large numbers of Asian Americans and Pacific Islanders worked actively in the 1984 and 1988 presidential campaigns of Jesse Jackson, helping to build the Rainbow Coalition.

Significantly, these accomplishments occurred in the midst of the Reagan presidency and U.S. polities' turn to the right. How did certain sectors of the Asian American community achieve these gains amidst conservatism?

There is no simple answer. Mainstream analysts and some Asian Americans have stressed the "model minority" concept. According to this analysis, Asian Americans—in contrast to other people of color in America—have survived adversity and advanced because of their emphasis on education and family values, their community cohesion, and other aspects of their cultural heritage. Other scholars have severely criticized this viewpoint, stressing instead structural changes in the global economy and shifts in U.S. government policy since the 1960s. According to their analysis, the reform of U.S. immigration laws and sweeping economic changes in advanced capitalist nations, such as deindustrialization and the development of new technologies, brought an influx of highly educated new Asian immigrants to America. The characteristics of these new immigrants stand in sharp contrast to those of past generations, and provide a broader social and economic base for developing our communities. Still other political thinkers have emphasized the key role played by political expatriates—both right-wing and left-wing—in various communities, but most especially in the Vietnamese, Filipino, and Korean communities. These expatriates brought political resources from their homelands—e.g., political networks, organizing experience, and, in a few cases, access to large amounts of funds—and have used these resources to change the political landscape of ethnic enclaves. Still other analysts have examined the growing economic and political power of nations of the Asia Pacific and its impact on Asians in America. According to these analysts, we can link the advances of Asian Americans during this period to the rising influence of their former homelands and the dawning of what some call "the Pacific Century." Finally, some academics have focused on the significance of small-business activities of new Asian immigrants, arguing that this sector is most responsible for the changing status of Asian Americans in the 1980s. According to their analysis, Asian immigrant entrepreneurs secured an economic niche in inner city neighborhoods because they had access to start-up capital (through rotating credit associations or from family members) and they filled a vacuum created when white businesses fled.[23]

Thus, we have multitiple interpretations for why some sectors of the Asian American community advanced economically and politically during the winter of civil rights. But two critical factors are missing from the analyses that can help us better understand the peculiar shape of our community in the 1980s and its ambiguous character when compared to other communities of color. First is the legacy of grassroots organizing from the Asian American movement, and second is the dramatic rise of young professionals as a significant force in the community.

A stereotype about the movements of the 1960s is that they produced nothing enduring—they flared brightly for an instant and then quickly died. However, evidence from the Asian American movement contradicts this commonly held belief. Through meticulous organizing campaigns, Asian American activists created an extensive network of grassroots formations. Unlike similar groups in African American communities—which government repression targeted and brutally destroyed—a significant number of Asian American groups survived the 1980s. Thus far, no researcher has analyzed the impact of the corporate offensive and government repression on grassroots organizations in different communities of color during the late 1970s. When this research is done, I think it will show that U.S. ruling elites viewed the movement in the African American community as a major threat due to its power and influence over other communities. In contrast, the movement in the Asian American community received much less attention due to its much smaller size and influence. As a result, Asian American grassroots formations during the 1970s escaped decimation and gained the time and space to survive, grow, and adapt to changing politics.

The survival of grassroots organizations is significant because it helped to cushion the impact of the war against the poor in Asian American communities. More important, the grassroots formations provided the foundation for many of the successful empowerment campaigns occurring in the 1980s. For example, Japanese Americans built their national effort to win reparations for their internment during World War II on the experiences of grassroots neighborhood organizations' housing and anti-eviction struggles of the early 1970s. Movement activists learned from their confrontations with systems of power and applied these lessons to the more difficult political fights of the 1980s. Thus, a direct link exists between the mass struggles of activists in the late 1960s and the "empowerment" approach of Asian Americans in the 1980s and 1990s.

But while similarities exist in political organizing of the late 1960s and the 1980s, there is one crucial difference: Who is being empowered? In the late 1960s and 1970s, activists focused on bringing "power to the people"—the most disenfranchised of the community, such as low-income workers, youth, former prisoners and addicts, senior citizens, tenants, and small-business people. In contrast, the "empowerment" of young professionals in Asian American communities marks the decade of the 1980s. The professionals—children of the civil rights' struggles of the 1950s and 1960s—directly benefited from the campaigns for desegregation, especially in the suburbs; the removal of quotas in colleges and professional schools; and the expansion of job opportunities for middle-class people of color in fields such as law, medicine, and education.

During the 1980s, young professionals altered the political terrain in our communities.[24] They created countless new groups in nearly every profession: law, medicine, social work, psychology, education, journalism, business, and arts and culture. They initiated new political advocacy groups, leadership training projects, and various national coalitions and consortiums. They organized political caucuses in the Democratic and Republican parties. And they joined the governing boards of many community agencies. Thus, young professionals—through their sheer numbers, their penchant for self-organization, and their high level of activity—defined the Asian American community of the 1980s, shaping it in ways very different from other communities of color.

The emergence of young professionals as community leaders also aided mass political mobilizations. By combining with grassroots forces from the Asian American movement, young professionals advanced struggles against racism and discrimination. In fact, many of the successful Asian American battles of the past decade resulted from this strategic alignment.

The growing power of young professionals has also brought a diversification of political viewpoints to our communities. While many professionals embrace concerns originally raised by movement activists, a surprisingly large number have moved toward neo-conservatism. The emergence of neo-conservatism in our community is a fascinating phenomenon, one we should analyze and appreciate. Perhaps more than any other phenomenon, it helps to explain the political ambiguity of Asian American empowerment in the decade of the 1980s.

STRANGE AND NEW POLITICAL ANIMALS: ASIAN AMERICAN NEO-CONSERVATIVES

Item: At many universities in recent years, some of the harshest opponents of affirmative action have been Chinese Americans and Korean Americans who define themselves as political conservatives. This, in and of itself, is not new or significant. We have always had Asian American conservatives who have spoken out against affirmative action. But what is new is their affiliation. Many participate actively in Asian American student organizations traditionally associated with campus activism.

Item: In the San Francisco newspaper *Asian Week,* one of the most interesting columnists is Arthur Hu, who writes about anti-Asian quotas in universities, political empowerment, and other issues relating to our communities. He also regularly chastises those he terms "liberals, progressives, Marxists, and activists." In a recent column, he wrote: "The left today has the nerve to blame AIDS, drugs, the dissolution of the family, welfare dependency, gang violence, and educational failure on Ronald Reagan's conservatism." Hu, in turn, criticizes the left for "tearing down religion, family, structure, and authority; promoting drugs, promiscuity, and abdication of personal responsibility."[25]

Item: During the militant, three-year campaign to win tenure for UCLA Professor Don Nakanishi, one of the key student leaders was a Japanese American Republican, Matthew J. Endo. Aside from joining the campus-community steering committee, he also mobilized support from fraternities, something that progressive activists could not do. Matt prides himself on being a Republican and a life member of the National Rifle Association. He aspires to become a CEO in a corporation but worries about the upsurge in racism against Asian Pacific peoples and the failure of both Republicans and Democrats to address this issue.

The Asian American neo-conservatives are a new and interesting political phenomenon. They are new because they are creatures born from the Reagan-Bush era of supply-side economics, class and racial polarization, and the emphasis on elitism and individual advancement. And they are interesting because they also represent a legacy from the civil rights struggles, especially the Asian American movement. The neo-conservatives embody these seemingly contradictory origins.

- They are proud to be Asian American. But they denounce the Asian American movement of the late 1960s and early 1970s as destructive.
- They speak out against racism against Asian Americans. But they believe that only by ending affirmative-action programs and breaking with prevailing civil rights thinking of the past four decades can we end racism.
- They express concern for Asian American community issues. But they contend that the agenda set by the "liberal Asian American establishment" ignores community needs.
- They vehemently oppose quotas blocking admissions of Asian Americans at colleges and universities. But they link anti-Asian quotas to affirmative-action programs for "less qualified" African Americans, Latinos, and American Indians.
- They acknowledge the continuing discrimination against African Americans, Latinos, and American Indians in U.S. society. But they believe that the main barrier blocking advancement for other people of color is "cultural"—that unlike Asians, these groups supposedly come from cultures that do not sufficiently emphasize education, family cohesion, and traditional values.

Where did these neo-conservatives come from? What do they represent? And why is it important for progressive peoples to understand their presence?

Progressives cannot dismiss Asian American neo-conservatives as simple-minded Republicans. Although they hold views similar at times to Patrick Buchanan and William Buckley, they are not clones of white conservatives. Nor are they racists, fellow travellers of the Ku Klux Klan, or ideologues attached to Reagan and Bush. Perhaps the group that they most resemble are the African American neo-conservatives: the Shelby Steeles, Clarence Thomases, and Tony Browns of this period. Like these men, they are professionals and feel little kinship for people of lower classes. Like these men, they oppose prevailing civil rights thinking, emphasizing reliance on government intervention and social programs. And like these men, they have gained from affirmative action, but they now believe that America has somehow become a society where other people of color can advance through their own "qualifications."

Neo-conservative people of color have embraced thinkers such as the late Martin Luther King, Jr., but have appropriated his message to fit their own ideology. In his speeches and writings, King dreamed of the day when racism would be eliminated—when African Americans would be recognized in U.S. society for the "content of our character, not the color of our skin." He called upon all in America to wage militant struggle to achieve this dream. Today, neo-conservatives have subverted his message. They believe that racism in U.S. society has declined in significance, and that people of color can now abandon mass militancy and advance individually by cultivating the content of their character through self-help programs and educational attainment, and retrieving traditional family values. They criticize prevailing "civil rights thinking" as overemphasizing the barriers of racism and relying on "external forces" (*i.e.*, government intervention through social programs) to address the problem.

Asian American neo-conservatives closely resemble their African American counterparts in their criticism of government "entitlement" programs and their defense of traditional culture and family values. But Asian American neo-conservatives are not exactly the same as their African American counterparts. The growth of neo-conservative thinking among Asian Americans during the past 25 years reflects the peculiar conditions in our community, notably the emerging power of young professionals. Thus, to truly understand Asian American neo-conservatives, we need to look at their evolution through the prism of Asian American politics from the late 1960s to the early 1990s.

Twenty-five years ago, Asian American neo-conservatives did not exist. Our community then had only traditional conservatives—those who opposed ethnic studies, the antiwar movement, and other militant grassroots struggles. The traditional conservatives denounced Asian American concerns as "special interest politics" and labeled the assertion of Asian American ethnic identity as "separatist" thinking. For the traditional conservative, a basic contradiction existed in identifying oneself as Asian American and conservative.

Ironically, the liberation struggles of the 1960s—and the accompanying Asian American movement—spawned a new conservative thinker. The movement partially transformed the educational curriculum through ethnic studies, enabling all Asian Americans to assert pride in their ethnic heritage. The movement accelerated the desegregation of suburbs, enabling middle-class Asian Americans to move into all-white neighborhoods. Today, the neo-conservatives are mostly young, middle-class professionals who grew up in white suburbs apart from the poor and people of color. As students, they attended the elite universities. Their only experience with racism is name-calling or "glass ceilings" blocking personal career advancement—and not poverty and violence.

It is due to their professional status and their roots in the Asian American movement that the neo-conservatives exist in uneasy alliance with traditional conservatives in our community. Neo-conservatives are appalled by the violence and rabid anti-communism of reactionary sectors of the Vietnamese community, Chinese from Taiwan tied to the oppressive ruling Kuomintang party, and Korean expatriates attached to the Korean Central Intelligence Agency. They are also uncomfortable with older conservatives, those coming from small-business backgrounds who warily eye the neo-conservatives, considering them as political opportunists.

Neo-conservatives differ from traditional conservatives not only because of their youth and their professional status but most important of all, their political coming of age in the Reagan era. Like their African American counterparts, they are children of the corporate offensive against workers, the massive transfer of resources from the poor to the rich, and the rebirth of so-called "traditional values."

It is their schooling in Reaganomics and their willingness to defend the current structure of power and privilege in America that gives neo-conservative people of color value in today's political landscape. Thus, Manning Marable describes the key role played by African American neo-conservatives:

> The singular service that [they] . . . provide is a new and more accurate under-standing of what exactly constitutes conservatism within the Black experi-ence. . . . Black conservatives are traditionally hostile to Black participation in trade unions, and urge a close cooperation with white business leaders. Hostile to the welfare state, they call for increased "self-help" programs run by Blacks at local and community levels. Conservatives often accept the institutionalized forms of patriarchy, acknowledging a secondary role for Black women within economics, political life and intellectual work. They usually have a pronounced bias towards organizational authoritarianism and theoretical rigidity.[26]

Marable's analysis points to the basic contradiction for African American neo-conservatives. They are unable to address fundamental problems facing their community: racist vio-lence, grinding poverty, and the unwillingness of corporate and government policy-makers to deal with these issues.

Asian American neo-conservatives face similar difficulties when confronted by the stark realities of the post-Reagan period:

- The neo-conservatives acknowledge continuing discrimination in U.S. society but deny the existence of institutional racism and structural inequality. For them, racism lies in the realm of attitudes and "culture" and not institutions of power. Thus, they emphasize individual advancement as the way to overcome racism. They believe that people of color can rise through merit, which they contend can be measured objectively through tests, grades, and educational attainment.
- The neo-conservatives ignore questions of wealth and privilege in American society. In their obsession with "merit," "qualifications," and "objective" criteria,

they lose sight of power and oppression in America. Their focus is on dismantling affirmative-action programs and "government entitlements" from the civil rights era. But poverty and racism existed long before the civil rights movement. They are embedded in the system of inequality that has long characterized U.S. society.

- The neo-conservatives are essentially elitists who fear expansion of democracy at the grassroots level. They speak a language of individual advancement, not mass empowerment. They propose a strategy of alignment with existing centers of power and not the creation of new power bases among the disenfranchised sectors of society. Their message is directed to professionals, much like themselves. They have nothing to offer to immigrant workers in sweatshops, the homeless, Cambodian youth in street gangs, or community college youth.

- As relative newcomers to Asian American issues, the neo-conservatives lack understanding of history, especially how concerns in the community have developed over time. Although they aggressively speak out about issues, they lack experience in organizing around these issues. The neo-conservatives function best in the realm of ideas; they have difficulty dealing with concrete situations.

However, by stimulating discussion over how Asian Americans define community problems, the neo-conservatives bring a vibrancy to community issues by contributing a different viewpoint. Thus, the debate between Asian American neo-conservatives and progressives is positive because it clarifies issues and enables both groups to reach constituencies that each could not otherwise reach.

Unfortunately, this debate is also occurring in a larger and more dangerous context: the campaign by mainstream conservatives to redefine civil rights in America. As part of their strategy, conservatives in the national political arena have targeted our communities. There are high stakes here, and conservatives regard the Asian American neo-conservatives as small players to be sacrificed.

The high stakes are evident in an article by William McGurn entitled "The Silent Minority" appearing in the conservative digest *National Review.*[27] In his essay, he urges Republicans to actively recruit and incorporate Asian Americans into party activities. According to McGurn, a basic affinity exists between Republican values and Asian American values: Many Asian immigrants own small businesses; they oppose communism; they are fiercely pro-defense; they boast strong families; they value freedom; and in their approach to civil rights, they stress opportunities not government "set-asides." McGurn then chastises fellow Republicans for their "crushing indifference" to Asian American issues. He laments how Republicans have lost opportunities by not speaking out on key issues such as the conflict between Korean immigrant merchants and African Americans, the controversy over anti-Asian quotas in universities, and the upsurge in anti-Asian violence.

McGurn sees Republican intervention on these issues strategically—as a way of redefining the race question in American society and shifting the debate on civil rights away from reliance on "an increasingly narrow band of black and liberal interest groups." According to McGurn:

> Precisely because Asian Americans are making it in their adoptive land, they hold the potential not only to add to Republican rolls but to define a bona-fide American language of civil rights. Today we have only one language of civil rights, and it is inextricably linked to government intervention, from racial quotas to set-aside government contracts. It is also an exclusively black-establishment language, where America's myriad other minorities are relegated to second-class citizenship.[28]

McGurn's article presages a period of intense and unprecedented conservative interest in Asian American issues. We can expect conservative commentaries to intensify black-Asian conflicts in inner cities, the controversy over affirmative action, and the internal community debate over designating Asian Americans as a "model minority."

Thus, in the coming period, Asian American communities are likely to become crowded places. Unlike the late 1960s, issues affecting our communities will no longer be the domain of progressive forces only. Increasingly, we will hear viewpoints from Asian American neo-conservatives as well as mainstream conservatives. How well will activists meet this new challenge?

GRASSROOTS ORGANIZING IN THE 1990s: THE CHALLENGE OF EXPANDING DEMOCRACY

> Time would pass, old empires would fall and new ones take their place, the relations of countries and the relations of classes had to change, before I discovered that it is not quality of goods and utility which matter, but movement; not where you are or what you have, but where you have come from, where you are going and the rate at which you are getting there.[29]
>
> C.L.R. James

On the eve of the twenty-first century, the Asian American community is vastly different from that of the late 1960s. The community has grown dramatically. In 1970, there were only 1.5 million Asian Americans, almost entirely concentrated in Hawaii and California. By 1980, there were 3.7 million, and in 1990, 7.9 million—with major Asian communities in New York, Minnesota, Pennsylvania, and Texas. According to census projections, the Asian American population should exceed 10 million by the year 2000, and will reach 20 million by the year 2020.[30]

Moreover, in contrast to the late 1960s, when Chinese and Japanese Americans comprised the majority of Asian Americans, today's community is ethnically diverse—consisting of nearly 30 major ethnic groups, each with a distinct culture. Today's community is also economically different from the 1960s. Compared to other sectors of the U.S. population, there are higher proportions of Asian Americans who are very rich and very poor. This gap between wealth and poverty has created a sharp class polarization in our community, a phenomenon yet to be studied.

But the changes for Asian Americans during the past 25 years have not been simply demographic. The political landscape has also changed due to new immigrants and refugees, the polarization between rich and poor, and the emergence of young professionals as a vital new force. Following the approach of C. L. R. James, we have traced the origins of these changes. We now need to analyze where these changes will take us in the decade ahead.

Ideologically and politically, activists confront a new and interesting paradox in the Asian American community of the 1990s. On the one hand, there is a great upsurge of interest in the community and all things Asian American. Almost daily, we hear about new groups forming across the country. In contrast to 25 years ago, when interest in the community was minimal and when only progressive activists joined Asian American organizations, we now find a situation where many different groups—including conservatives and neo-conservatives, bankers and business executives, and young professionals in all fields—have taken up the banner of Asian American identity.

On the other hand, we have not seen a corresponding growth in consciousness—of what it means to be Asian American as we approach the twenty-first century. Unlike African Americans, most Asian Americans today have yet to articulate the "particularities" of issues affecting our community, whether these be the debate over affirmative action, the controversy regarding multiculturalism, or the very definition of empowerment. We have an ideological vacuum, and activists will compete with neo-conservatives, mainstream conservatives, and others to fill it.

We have a political vacuum as well. In recent years, growing numbers of Asian Americans have become involved in community issues. But almost all have come from middle-class and professional backgrounds. Meanwhile, vast segments of our community are not coming forward. In fact, during the past decade the fundamental weakness for activists has been the lack of grassroots organizing among the disenfranchised sectors of our community: youth outside of colleges and universities, the poor, and new immigrant workers. Twenty-five years ago, the greatest strength of the Asian American movement was the ability of activists to organize the unorganized and to bring new political players into community politics. Activists targeted high-school youth, tenants, small-business people, former prison inmates, gang members, the elderly, and workers. Activists helped them build new grassroots organizations, expanding power and democracy in our communities. Can a new generation of activists do the same?

To respond to this challenge, activists will need both a political strategy and a new ideological vision. Politically, activists must find ways to expand democracy by creating new grassroots formations, activating new political players, and building new coalitions. Ideologically, activists must forge a new moral vision, reclaiming the militancy and moral urgency of past generations and reaffirming the commitment to participatory democracy, community building, and collective styles of leadership.

Where will this political strategy and new consciousness come from? More than 50 years ago, revolutionary leader Mao Zedong asked a similar question:

> Where do correct ideas come from? Do they drop from the skies? No. Are they innate in the mind? No. They come from social practice, and from it alone. . . . In their social practice, people engage in various kinds of struggle and gain rich experience, both from their successes and their failures.[31]

In the current "social practice" of Asian American activists across the nation, several grassroots organizing projects can serve as the basis for a political strategy and new moral vision for the 1990s. I will focus on three projects that are concentrating on the growing numbers of poor and working poor in our community. Through their grassroots efforts, these three groups are demonstrating how collective power can expand democracy, and how, in the process, activists can forge a new moral vision.

The three groups—the Chinese Progressive Association (CPA) Workers Center in Boston, Asian Immigrant Women Advocates (AIWA) in Oakland, and Korean Immigrant Worker Advocates (KIWA) in Los Angeles—address local needs. Although each organization works with different ethnic groups, their history of organizing has remarkable similarities. Each organization is composed of low-income immigrant workers. Each has taken up more than "labor" issues. And each group has fashioned very effective "united front" campaigns involving other sectors of the community. Thus, although each project is relatively small, collectively their accomplishments illustrate the power of grassroots organizing, the creativity and talents of "ordinary" people in taking up difficult issues, and the ability of grassroots forces to alter the political landscape of their community. Significantly, the focus of each group is working people in the Asian American community—a sector that is numerically large and growing larger. However, despite their numbers, workers in the Asian American community during the past decade have become voiceless and silent. Today, in discussions about community issues, no one places garment workers, nurses' aides, waiters, and secretaries at the forefront of the debate to define priorities. And no one thinks about the working class as the cutting edge of the Asian American experience. Yet, if we begin to list the basic questions now confronting Asian Americans—racism and sexism, economic justice and human rights, coalition building, and community empowerment—we would find that it is the working class, of all sectors in our community, that is making the most interesting breakthroughs on these questions. They are doing this through groups such as KIWA, AIWA, and the CPA Workers Center. Why, then, are the voices of workers submerged in our community? Why has the working class become silent?

Three trends have pushed labor issues in our community into the background during the past two decades: the rising power of young professionals in our community; the influx of new immigrants and refugees, and the fascination of social scientists and policy institutes with the phenomenon of immigrant entrepreneurship; and the lack of grass-roots organizing by activists among new immigrant workers.

Thus, although the majority of Asian Americans work for a living, we have relatively little understanding about the central place of work in the lives of Asian Americans, especially in low-income industries such as garment work, restaurant work, clerical and office work, and other service occupations. Moreover, we are ignorant about the role that labor struggles have played in shaping our history.[32] This labor history is part of the legacy that activists must reclaim.

In contrast to the lack of knowledge about Asian American workers, we have a much greater understanding about the role of young professionals, students, and, most of all, small-business people. In fact, immigrant entrepreneurs, especially Korean immigrants, are perhaps the most studied people of our community. However, as sociologist Edna Bonacich notes, the profile of most Asian immigrant entrepreneurs closely resembles that of workers, due to their low earning power, their long work hours, and their lack of job-related benefits. Thus, Bonacich suggests that while the world outlook of Asian immigrant entrepreneurs may be petit bourgeoisie, their life conditions are those of the working class and might better be studied as a "labor" question. Asian immigrant small businesses, she contends, play the role of "cheap labor in American capitalism."[33]

Other researchers have only begun to investigate the extent of poverty among Asian Americans and the meaning of poverty for our community. In California, the rate of poverty for Asian Americans rose from about 10 percent in 1980 to 18 percent in 1990. But more important, researchers found that there are higher numbers of "working poor" (as opposed to "jobless poor") in the Asian American community than for other ethnic groups. Thus, in contrast to other Americans, Asian Americans are poor not because they lack jobs but because the jobs they have pay very low wages. According to researchers Dean Toji and James Johnson, Jr., "Perhaps contrary to common belief, about half of the poor work—including about a quarter of poor adults who work full-time and year-round. Poverty, then, is a labor question."[34]

Activists in groups such as KIWA, AIWA, and the CPA Workers Center are strategically focusing on the "working poor" in the Asian American community. KIWA—which was founded in 1992—is working with low-income Korean immigrants in Los Angeles Koreatown, including garment workers and employees in small businesses. AIWA—founded in 1983—organizes Chinese garment workers, Vietnamese garment and electronics workers, and Korean hotel maids and electronics assemblers. And the CPA Workers Center—which traces its roots to the landmark struggle of Chinese garment workers in Boston in 1985—is composed primarily of Chinese immigrant women. Although their main focus is on workers, each group has also mobilized students and social service providers to support their campaigns. Through these alliances, each group has carried out successful community organizing strategies.

The focus of the three groups on community-based organizing distinguishes them from traditional unions. Miriam Ching Louie of AIWA explains this distinction:

> AIWA's base is simultaneously worker, female, Asian, and immigrant, and the organization has developed by blending together several different organizing techniques. As compared to the traditional union organizing strategy, AIWA's approach focuses on the needs of its constituency. *Popular literacy/conscientization/transformation* [based on the teachings of Paulo Freire] is a learning and teaching method which taps into people's life experiences as part of a broader reality, source of knowledge, and guide to action. *Community-based organizing* takes a holistic view of racial/ethnic people and organizes for social change, not only so that the people can win immediate improvements in their lives, but so that they can also develop their own power in the course of waging the fight.[35]

AIWA's focus on grassroots organizing is illustrated by its "Garment Workers' Justice Campaign," launched in late 1992 to assist Chinese immigrant women who were denied pay by a garment contractor. AIWA organizers shaped the campaign to respond to the peculiar features of the garment industry. The industry in the San Francisco Bay Area is the nation's third largest—following New York and Los Angeles—and employs some 20,000 seamstresses, 85 percent of them Asian immigrant women. The structure of the industry is a pyramid with retailers and manufacturers at the top, contractors in the middle, and immigrant women working at the bottom. Manufacturers make the main share of profits in the industry; they set the price for contractors. Meanwhile, immigrant women work under sweatshop conditions.

In their campaign, AIWA and the workers initially confronted the contractor for the workers' backpay. When they discovered that the contractor owed a number of creditors, they took the unusual step of holding the garment manufacturer, Jessica McClintock, accountable for the unpaid wages. McClintock operates 10 boutiques and sells dresses through department stores. The dresses—which garment workers are paid $5 to make—retail in stores for $175. AIWA and the workers conducted their campaign through a series of high-profile demonstrations at McClintock boutiques, including picket lines and rallies in 10 cities by supporters. AIWA designed these demonstrations not only to put pressure on McClintock and educate others in the community about inequities in the structure of the garment industry, but also to serve as vehicles for empowerment for the immigrant women participating in the campaign. Through this campaign, the women workers learned how to confront institutional power, how to forge alliances with other groups in the community, and how to carry out effective tactics based on their collective power.[36]

Thus, through its activities promoting immigrant women's rights, AIWA is expanding democracy in the community. It is bringing labor issues to the forefront of community discussions. It is creating new grassroots caucuses among previously unorganized sectors of the community, and forming new political alignments with supporters, such as students, young professionals, labor unions, and social service providers. Finally, AIWA is developing a cadre of politically sophisticated immigrant women and promoting a new leadership style based on popular literacy, community building, and collective power.

Similarly, in Boston, the CPA Workers Center is expanding democracy through its grassroots efforts around worker rights. The Center emerged out of the Chinese immigrant women's campaign to deal with the closing of a large garment factory in Boston in 1985.[37] The shutdown displaced 350 workers and severely impacted the local Chinese community due to the community's high concentration of jobs in the garment industry. However, with the assistance of the Chinese Progressive Alliance, the workers formed a labor-community-student coalition and waged an 18-month campaign to win job retraining and job replacement. Lydia Lowe, director of the CPA Workers Center, describes how the victory of Chinese immigrant women led to creation of the Workers Center, which, in turn, has helped other work place campaigns in the Chinese community:

> This core of women activated through the campaign joined with community supporters from the CPA to found a community-based workers' mutual aid and resource center, based at CPA.... Through the Workers Center, immigrant workers share their experience, collectively sum up lessons learned, find out about their rights, and develop mutual support and organizing strategies. Today, the Workers Center involves immigrant workers from each of its successive organizing efforts, and is a unique place in the community where ordinary workers can walk in and participate as activists and decision-makers.[38]

Moreover, forming the Workers Center reshaped politics in the local Chinese community, turning garment workers and other immigrant laborers into active political players. "Previously the silent majority, immigrant workers are gaining increasing respect as a force to be reckoned with in the local Chinese community," states Lowe.

In Los Angeles, the formation of KIWA in March 1992—only a month before the uprisings—has had a similar impact. Through its programs, KIWA is bringing labor issues to the forefront of the Asian American community, educating labor unions about the needs of Asian American workers, and forming coalitions with other grassroots forces in the city to deal with inter-ethnic tensions. KIWA is uniquely positioned to take up these tasks. Out of the multitude of Asian American organizations in Los Angeles, KIWA distinguishes itself as the only organization governed by a board of directors of mainly workers.

KIWA's key role in the labor movement and community politics is evident in the recent controversy involving the Koreana Wilshire Hotel.[39] The controversy began in late 1991 when Koreana Hotel Co. Ltd., a South Korean corporation, bought the

Wilshire Hyatt in Los Angeles. The change in ownership meant that 175 unionized members, predominantly Latino immigrants, were out of jobs. Meanwhile, the new hotel management hired a new work force, paying them an average of $1.50 per hour less than the former unionized work force. The former workers, represented by Hotel Employees and Restaurant Employees (HERE) Local 11, called upon labor unions and groups from the Asian American, African American, and Latino communities to protest Koreana's union-busting efforts. Local 11 defined the dispute as not only a labor issue, but a civil rights issue. With the help of groups such as KIWA and the Asian Pacific American Labor Alliance, Local 11 initiated a letter-writing campaign against Koreana, began a community boycott of the hotel, and organized militant actions outside the hotel, including rallies, marches, and a picket line, as well as civil disobedience at the nearby Korean consulate. In each of these actions, Local 11 worked closely with KIWA and members of the Asian American community. Due to the mass pressure, in late 1992 the Koreana management agreed to negotiate with Local 11 to end the controversy and rehire the union members.

Throughout the campaign, KIWA played a pivotal role by assisting Local 11 build alliances with the Asian American community. In addition, KIWA members promoted labor consciousness in the Korean community by urging the community to boycott the hotel. KIWA members also spoke at Local 11 rallies, mobilized for picket lines, and worked with the union in its efforts to put pressure on the South Korean government. By taking these steps, KIWA prevented the controversy from pitting the Korean community against Latinos and further enflaming inter-ethnic tensions in Los Angeles.

Also, through campaigns such as this one, KIWA is educating Asian immigrants about unions; training workers around the tasks of political leadership; and creating new centers of power in the community by combining the resources of workers, young professionals, and social service providers.

Thus, through grassroots organizing, KIWA—like AIWA and the CPA Workers Center—is expanding democracy in the Asian American community. Moreover, the three groups collectively are reshaping community consciousness. They are sharpening debate and dialogue around issues and redefining such important concepts as empowerment. What is their vision of empowerment, and how does it differ from prevailing definitions?

THE TWENTY-FIRST CENTURY:
BUILDING AN ASIAN AMERICAN MOVEMENT

[A] movement is an idea, a philosophy. . . . Leadership, I feel, is only incidental to the movement. The movement should be the most important thing. The movement must go beyond its leaders. It must be something that is continuous, with goals and ideas that the leadership can then build on.[40]

Philip Vera Cruz

In the late 1960s, Asian American activists sought to forge a new approach to leadership that would not replicate traditional Eurocentric models—*i.e.,* rigid hierarchies with a single executive at the top, invariably a white male, who commanded an endless chain of assistants. In their search for alternatives, activists experimented with various ideas borrowed from other movements, but most of all, activists benefited from the advice and guidance of "elders" within the Asian American community—women and men with years of grassroots organizing experience in the community, the work place, and the progressive political movement. One such "elder" was Filipino immigrant labor leader Philip Vera Cruz, then in his sixties. Vera Cruz represented the *manong* generation—the first wave of Filipinos who came to the United States in the early twentieth century and worked in agricultural fields, canneries, hotels, and restaurants.

Now 88 years old, Vera Cruz continues to educate a new generation of activists. His lifetime of experience in grassroots organizing embodies the historic themes of Asian American activism: devotion to the rights of working people, commitment to democracy and liberation, steadfast solidarity with all who face oppression throughout the world, and the courage to challenge existing institutions of power and to create new institutions as the need arises. These themes have defined his life and shaped his approach to the question of empowerment—an approach that is different from standard definitions in our community today.

Vera Cruz is best known for his role in building the United Farm Workers (UFW), a culmination of his many years of organizing in agricultural fields. In 1965, he was working with the Agricultural Workers Organizing Committee, AFL-CIO, when Filipino farmworkers sat-down in the Coachella vineyards of central California. This sit-down launched the famous grape strike and boycott, eventually leading to the formation of the UFW. Many books and articles have told the story of the UFW and its leader Cesar Chavez. But until recently, no one has focused on the historic role of Filipinos in building this movement. Craig Scharlin and Lilia Villanueva have filled that vacuum with their new publication about Vera Cruz's life.

Following the successful grape boycott, Vera Cruz became a UFW vice president and remained with the union until 1977, when he left due to political differences with the leadership. He was critical of the lack of rank-and-file democracy in the union, and the leadership's embrace of the Marcos dictatorship in the Philippines. Since 1979, Vera Cruz has lived in Bakersfield, California, and has continued to devote his life to unionism and social justice, and to the education of a new generation of Asian American youth.

Vera Cruz's life experiences have shaped a broad view of empowerment. For Vera Cruz, empowerment is grassroots power: the expansion of democracy for the many. Becoming empowered means gaining the capacity to advocate not only for one's own concerns but for the liberation of all oppressed peoples. Becoming empowered means being able to fundamentally change the relationship of power and oppression in society. Thus, Vera Cruz's vision is very different from that of today's young professionals. For them, empowerment is leadership development for an elite. Becoming empowered means gaining the skills to advocate for the community by gaining access to decision-makers. Thus, for young professionals, the key leadership quality to develop is assertiveness. Through assertiveness, leaders gain access to policymakers as well as the power to mobilize their followers. In contrast, Vera Cruz stresses the leadership trait of humility. For him, leaders are "only incidental to the movement"—the movement is "the most important thing." For Vera Cruz, empowerment is a process where people join to develop goals and ideas to create a larger movement—a movement "that the leadership can then build on."

Vera Cruz's understanding of empowerment has evolved from his own social practice. Through his experiences in the UFW and the AFL–CIO, Vera Cruz learned about the empty democracy of bureaucratic unions and the limitations of the charismatic leadership style of Cesar Chavez. Through his years of toil as a farmworker, he recognized the importance of worker solidarity and militancy and the capacity of common people to create alternative institutions of grassroots power. Through his work with Filipino and Mexican immigrants, he saw the necessity of coalition-building and worker unity that crossed ethnic and racial boundaries. He has shared these lessons with several generations of Asian American activists.

But aside from sharing a concept of empowerment, Vera Cruz has also promoted a larger moral vision, placing his lifetime of political struggle in the framework of the movement for liberation. Three keywords distinguish his moral vision: "compassion," "solidarity," and "commitment." Vera Cruz's lifetime of action represents compassion for all victims of oppression, solidarity with all fighting for liberation, and commitment to the ideals of democracy and social justice.

Activists today need to learn from Vera Cruz's compassion, solidarity, commitment, and humility to create a new moral vision for our community. In our grassroots organizing, we need a vision that can redefine empowerment—that can bring questions of power, domination, and liberation to the forefront of our work. We need a vision that can help us respond to the challenge of conservatives and neo-conservatives, and sharpen dialogue with young professionals. We need a new moral vision that can help fill the ideological vacuum in today's community.

Nowhere is this ideological challenge greater than in the current debate over the model minority stereotype. The stereotype has become the dominant image of Asian Americans for mainstream society, and has generated intense debate among all sectors of our community. This debate provides an opportunity for activists to expand political awareness and, in the process, redefine the Asian American experience for the 1990s.

In the current controversy, however, activists criticize the model minority stereotype politically but not ideologically. Activists correctly target how the concept fails to deal with Asian American realities: the growing population of poor and working poor, the large numbers of youth who are not excelling in school, and the hardships and family problems of small-business people who are not "making it" in U.S. society. Activists also correctly point out the political ramifications of the model minority stereotype: the pitting of minority groups against each other, and growing inter-ethnic tensions in U.S. society. In contrast, conservative and neo-conservative proponents of the model minority concept argue from the standpoint of both political realities and a larger moral vision. They highlight Asian American accomplishments: "whiz kids" in elementary schools; growing numbers of Asian Americans in business, politics, and the professions; and the record enrollment of youth in colleges and universities. Conservatives and neo-conservatives attribute these accomplishments to Asian culture and tradition, respect for authority, family cohesion, sacrifice and toil, rugged individualism, and self-reliance—moral values that they root in conservative thinking. Conservatives and neo-conservatives recognize that "facts" gain power from attachment to ideologies. As a result, they appropriate Asian culture and values to promote their arguments.

But is Asian culture inherently conservative—or does it also have a tradition of militancy and liberation? Do sacrifice, toil, and family values comprise a conservative moral vision only—or do these qualities also constitute the core of radical and revolutionary thinking? By asking these questions, activists can push the debate over the model minority concept to a new, ideological level. Moreover, by focusing on ideology, activists can delve into the stereotype's deeper meaning. They can help others understand the stereotype's origins and why it has become the dominant image for Asian Americans today.

Historically, the model minority stereotype first arose in the late 1950s—the creation of sociologists attempting to explain low levels of juvenile delinquency among Chinese and Japanese Americans.[41] The stereotype remained a social-science construct until the 1960s when a few conservative political commentators began to use it to contrast Asian Americans' "respect for law and order" to African Americans' involvement in civil rights marches, rallies, and sit-ins. By the late 1970s, the stereotype moved into the political mainstream, coinciding with the influx of new Asian immigrants into all parts of the United States. But the widespread acceptance of the stereotype was not simply due to the increase in the Asian American population or the new attention focused on our community from mainstream institutions. More importantly, it coincided with the rise of the New Right and the corporate offensive against the poor. As discussed earlier, this offensive economically devastated poor communities and stripped away hard-won political gains. This offensive also included an ideological campaign designed to restore trust in capitalism and values associated with free enterprise. Meanwhile, conservatives and neo-conservatives fought to redefine the language of civil rights by attacking federal government "entitlement" programs while criticizing the African American "liberal establishment."

In this political climate, the model minority stereotype flourished. It symbolized the moral vision of capitalism in the 1980s: a celebration of traditional values, an emphasis on hard work and self-reliance, a respect for authority, and an attack on prevailing civil rights thinking associated with the African American community. Thus, the stereotype took on an ideological importance above and beyond the Asian American community. The hardworking immigrant merchant and the refugee student winning the local spelling bee have become the symbols for the resurrection of capitalist values in the last part of the twentieth century.

Yet, we know a gap exists between symbol and reality. Today, capitalism in America is not about small-business activities; it is about powerful transnational corporations and their intricate links to nation-states and the world capitalist system. Capitalist values no longer revolve around hard work and self-reliance; they deal with wealth and assets, and the capacity of the rich to invest, speculate, and obtain government contracts. And the fruits of capitalism in the last part of the twentieth century are not immigrant entrepreneurship and the revival of urban areas; they are more likely to be low-paying jobs, unemployment, bankruptcies, and homelessness.

However, as corporations, banks, and other institutions abandon the inner city, the immigrant merchant—especially the Korean small business—emerges as the main symbol of capitalism in these neighborhoods. For inner city residents, the Asian immigrant becomes the target for their wrath against corporate devastation of their neighborhoods. Moreover, as this symbol merges with other historical stereotypes of Asians, the result is highly charged imagery, which perhaps underlies the ferocity of anti-Asian violence in this period, such as the destruction of Korean small businesses during the Los Angeles uprisings. The Asian immigrant becomes a symbol of wealth—and also greed; a symbol of hard work—and also materialism; a symbol of intelligence—and also arrogance; a symbol of self-reliance—and also selfishness and lack of community concern. Thus, today the model minority stereotype has become a complex symbol through the confluence of many images imposed on us by social scientists, the New Right, and the urban policies of corporate and political elites.

Pioneer Korean immigrant journalist K. W. Lee—another of our Asian American "elders"—worries about how the melding of symbols, images, and stereotypes is shaping the perception of our community, especially among other people of color. "We are not seen as a compassionate people," states Lee. "Others see us as smart, hard-working, and good at making money—but not as sharing with others. We are not seen as a people who march at the forefront of the struggle for civil rights or the campaign to end poverty."[42] Like Philip Vera Cruz, Lee believes that Asian Americans must retrieve a heritage of compassion and solidarity from our past and use these values to construct a new moral vision for our future. Asian Americans must cast off the images imposed on us by others.

Thus, as we approach the end of the twentieth century, activists are confronted with a task similar to that confronting activists in the late 1960s: the need to redefine the Asian American experience. And as an earlier generation discovered, redefining means more than ethnic awakening. It means confronting the fundamental questions of power and domination in U.S. society. It means expanding democracy and community consciousness. It means liberating ourselves from the prisons still surrounding our lives.

In our efforts to redefine the Asian American experience, activists will have the guidance and help of elders like K. W. Lee and Philip Vera Cruz. And we can also draw from the rich legacy of struggle of other liberation movements.

Thus, in closing this chapter, I want to quote from two great teachers from the 1960s: Malcolm X and Martin Luther King, Jr. Their words and actions galvanized the consciousness of one generation of youth, and their message of compassion continues to speak to a new generation in the 1990s.

Since their assassinations in the mid-1960s, however, mainstream commentators have stereotyped the two men and often pitted one against the other. They portray Malcolm X as the angry black separatist who advocated violence and hatred against white people. Meanwhile, they make Martin Luther King, Jr., the messenger of love and nonviolence. In the minds of most Americans, both men—in the words of historian Manning Marable—are "frozen in time."[43]

But as Marable and other African American historians note, both King and Malcolm evolved, and became very different men in the years before their assassinations. Both men came to see the African American struggle in the United States in a worldwide context, as part of the revolutionary stirrings and mass uprisings happening across the globe. Both men became internationalists, strongly condemning U.S. exploitation of Third World nations and urging solidarity among all oppressed peoples. Finally, both men called for a redefinition of human values; they believed that people in the United States, especially, needed to move away from materialism and embrace a more compassionate worldview.

If we, too, as Asian Americans, are to evolve in our political and ideological understanding, we need to learn from the wisdom of both men. As we work for our own empowerment, we must ask ourselves a series of questions. Will we fight only for ourselves, or will we embrace the concerns of all oppressed peoples? Will we overcome our own oppression and help to create a new society, or will we become a new exploiter group in the present American hierarchy of inequality? Will we define our goal of empowerment solely in terms of individual advancement for a few, or as the collective liberation for all peoples?

> These are revolutionary times. All over the globe men are revolting against old systems of exploitation and oppression, and out of the wombs of a frail world, new systems of justice and equality are being born. The shirtless and barefoot people of the land are rising up as never before. "The people who sat in the darkness have seen a great light." We in the West must support these revolutions. It is a sad fact that, because of comfort, complacency, a morbid fear of communism, and our proneness to adjust to injustice, the Western nations that

initiated so much of the revolutionary spirit of the modern world have now become the arch anti-revolutionaries. . . . Our only hope today lies in our ability to recapture the revolutionary spirit and go out into a sometimes hostile world declaring eternal hostility to poverty, racism, and militarism.[44]

Martin Luther King, Jr.

I believe that there will ultimately be a clash between the oppressed and those who do the oppressing. I believe that there will be a clash between those who want freedom, justice and equality for everyone and those who want to continue the system of exploitation. I believe that there will be that kind of clash, but I don't think it will be based on the color of the skin.[45]

Malcolm X

ENDNOTES

1. Iranian philosopher Ali Shariati's four prisons analysis was shared with me by a member of the Iranian Students Union, Confederation of Iranian Students, San Francisco, 1977.

2. Allan Bloom, *The Closing of the American Mind,* New York: Simon & Schuster, 1987.

3. Winifred Breines, "Whose New Left?" *Journal of American History,* Vol. 75, No. 2, September 1988.

4. Ibid., p. 543.

5. Sheila D. Collins, *The Rainbow Challenge: The Jackson Campaign and the Future of U.S. Politics,* New York: Monthly Review Press, 1986.

6. Ibid., p. 16.

7. Ronald Fraser, 1968: *A Student Generation in Revolt,* New York: Pantheon Books, pp. 354–355.

8. Karen Umemoto, "On Strike! San Francisco State College Strike, 1968–69: The Role of Asian American Students," *Amerasia Journal,* Vol. 15, No. 1, 1989.

9. "Statement of the Philippine-American Collegiate Endeavor (PACE) Philosophy and Goals," mimeograph: quoted in Umemoto, p. 15.

10. Mo Nishida, "A Revolutionary Nationalist Perspective of the San Francisco State Strike," *Amerasia Journal,* Vol. 15, No. 1, 1989, p. 75.

11. George Lipsitz, "Grassroots Activists and Social Change: The Story of Ivory Perry," *CAAS Newsletter,* UCLA Center for Afro-American Studies, 1986. See also, George Lipsitz, *A Life in the Struggle: Ivory Perry and the Culture of Opposition,* Philadelphia: Temple University Press, 1988.

12. Russell C. Leong, "Poetry Within Earshot: Notes of an Asian American Generation, 1968–1978," *Amerasia Journal,* Vol. 15, No. 1, 1989, pp. 166–167.

13. Al Robles, "Hanging on to the Carabao's Tail," *Amerasia Journal,* Vol. 15, No. 1, 1989, p. 205.

14. Warren J. Susman, *Culture as History: The Transformation of American Society in the Twentieth*

Century, New York: Pantheon Books, 1973; and Raymond Williams, *Keywords: A Vocabulary of Culture and Society,* revised edition, New York: Oxford University Press, 1976.

15. John M. Liu and Lucie Cheng, "A Dialogue on Race and Class: Asian American Studies and Marxism," *The Left Academy,* Vol. 3, eds. Bertell Ollman and Edward Vernoff, Westport, CT: Praeger, 1986.

16. See Mary Kao, compiler, "Public Record, 1989: What Have We Learned from the '60s and 70s?" *Amerasia Journal,* Vol. 15, No. 1, 1989, pp. 95–158.

17. Institute for Labor Education and Research, *What's Wrong with the U.S. Economy? A Popular Guide for the Rest of Us,* Boston: South End Press, 1982. See especially chapters 1 and 19.

18. Samuel Huntington, "The United States," *The Crisis of Democracy: Report on the Governability of Democracies to the Trilateral Commission,* ed. Michel Crozier, New York: New York University Press, 1975.

19. Center on Budget and Policy Priorities, *Still Far from the Dream: Recent Developments in Black Income, Employment and Poverty,* Washington, D.C., 1988.

20. Center for the Study of Social Policy, *Kids Count: State Profiles of Child Well-Being,* Washington, D.C., 1992.

21. Manning Marable, *How Capitalism Underdeveloped Black America,* Boston: South End Press, 1983, pp. 252–253.

22. Vincent Harding, *The Other American Revolution,* Los Angeles: UCLA Center for Afro-American Studies, and Atlanta: Institute of the Black World, 1980, p. 224.

23. For analyses of the changing status of Asian Americans, see Lucie Cheng and Edna Bonacich, eds., *Labor Immigration Under Capitalism: Asian Workers in the United States Before World War II,* Berkeley: University of California Press, 1984; Paul Ong, Edna Bonacich, and Lucie Cheng, eds., *Struggles for a Place: The New Asian Immigrants in the Restructuring Political Economy,* Philadelphia: Temple University Press, 1993; and Sucheng Chan, *Asian Americans: An Interpretive History,* Boston: Twayne Publishers, 1991.

24. For an analysis of the growing power of Asian American young professionals, see Yen Espiritu and Paul Ong, "Class Constraints on Racial Solidarity among Asian Americans," *Struggles for a Place,* Philadelphia: Temple University Press, 1993.

25. Arthur Hu, "AIDS and Race," *Asian Week,* December 13, 1991.

26. Marable, *How Capitalism Underdeveloped Black America,* p. 182.

27. William McGurn, "The Silent Minority," *National Review,* June 24, 1991.

28. Ibid,. p. 19.

29. C. L. R. James, *Beyond a Boundary,* New York: Pantheon Books, 1983, pp. 116–117.

30. LEAP Asian Pacific American Public Policy Institute and UCLA Asian American Studies Center, *The State of Asian Pacific America: Policy Issues to the Year 2020,* Los Angeles: LEAP and UCLA Asian American Studies Center, 1993.

31. Mao Zedong, "Where Do Correct Ideas Come From?" *Four Essays on Philosophy,* Beijing: Foreign Languages Press, 1966, p. 134.

32. See "Asian Pacific American Workers: Contemporary Issues in the Labor Movement," eds. Glenn Omatsu and Edna Bonacich, *Amerasia Journal,* Vol. 18, No. 1, 1992.

33. Edna Bonacich, "The Social Costs of Immigrant Entrepreneurship," *Amerasia Journal,* Vol. 14, No. 1, 1988.

34. Dean S. Toji and James H. Johnson, Jr., "Asian and Pacific Islander American Poverty: The Working Poor and the Jobless Poor," *Amerasia Journal,* Vol. 18, No. 1, 1992, p. 85.

35. Miriam Ching Louie, "Immigrant Asian Women in Bay Area Garment Sweatshops: 'After Sewing, Laundry, Cleaning and Cooking, I Have No Breath Left to Sing,'" *Amerasia Journal,* Vol. 18, No. 1, p. 12.

36. Miriam Ching Louie, "Asian and Latina Women Take On the Garment Giants," *Cross-Roads,* March 1993.

37. Peter N. Kiang and Man Chak Ng, "Through Strength and Struggle: Boston's Asian American Student/Community/Labor Solidarity," *Amerasia Journal,* Vol. 15, No. 1, 1989.

38. Lydia Lowe, "Paving the Way: Chinese Immigrant Workers and Community-based Labor Organizing in Boston," *Amerasia Journal,* Vol. 18, No. 1, 1992, p. 41.

39. Namju Cho, "Check Out, Not In: Koreana Wilshire/Hyatt Take-over and the Los Angeles Korean Community," *Amerasia Journal,* Vol. 18, No. 1, 1992.

40. Craig Scharlin and Lilia V. Villanueva, *Philip Vera Cruz: A Personal History of Filipino immigrants and the Farmworkers Movement,* Los Angeles: UCLA Labor Center and UCLA Asian American Studies Center, 1992, p. 104.

41. For an overview of the evolution of the "model minority" stereotype in the social sciences, see Shirley Hune, *Pacific Migration to the United States: Trends and Themes in Historical and Sociological Literature,* New York: Research Institute on Immigration and Ethnic Studies of the Smithsonian Institution, 1977 (reprinted in *Asian American Studies: An Annotated Bibliography and Research Guide,* ed. Hyung-chan Kim, Westport, CT: Greenwood Press, 1989). For comparisons of the "model minority" stereotype in two different decades, see "Success Story of One Minority Group in U.S.," *U.S. News and World Report,* December 26, 1966 (reprinted in *Roots: An Asian American Reader,* ed. Amy Tachiki et al., Los Angeles: UCLA Asian American Studies Center, 1971); and the essay by William McGurn, "The Silent Minority," *National Review,* June 24, 1991.

42. Author's interview with K. W. Lee, Los Angeles, California, October 1991.

43. Manning Marable, "On Malcolm X: His Message & Meaning," Westfield, NJ: Open Magazine Pamphlet Series, 1992.

44. Martin Luther King, Jr., "Beyond Vietnam" speech, Riverside Church, New York, April 1967.

45. Malcolm X, interview on Pierre Breton Show, January 19, 1965, in *Malcolm X Speaks,* ed. George Breitman, New York: Grove Press, 1966, p. 216.

35

Whats "Left" in the Israeli–Palestinian Conflict?

Dick Platkin and Chuck O'Connell

There are many people analyzing the ongoing Israeli-Palestinian conflict who do so with little apparent understanding of the class basis for this conflict and its linkages to imperialism. Their analyses operate within the confines of nationalist interpretations. This approach not only limits their ability to see the conflict's regional context and economic roots, but it also obscures these roots behind self-justifying ethnic and religious claims. What follows is a description and analysis of some movements regarded as "progressive"—the Palestinian Left and the Israeli Peace Movement—but which have replaced class analysis and class conflict with nationalism and religion as analytic and organizational tools.

1. Factionalized Nationalist Movements: Both sides, the Israelis and the Palestinians, have heavily factionalized nationalist movements linked in the past and present to outside imperialist powers. Furthermore, the progressive portions of both nationalist movements are nearly extinguished. What passes for the "Left" among Israelis and Palestinians is largely bourgeois liberalism in the form of advocacy for a two-state solution based on interrelated market economies. Both states would be bourgeois democracies, in which production and investment would remain largely in private hands, not subject to public discussion, debate, or control. The two states would continue to be heavily linked to outside investors and their political and military agents. In neither case would the state be subject to the authority of the workforce.

2. Disintegration of the Palestinian Left: The Palestinian opposition to Israeli occupation of the West Bank and Gaza, in the form of the second Intifada, is, in essence, opposition from the political right. This is despite frequent slogans at support rallies with an anti-imperialist or anti-colonialist ring to them, such as "Free, Free Palestine." These rallies, as well as their agitational material, are careful to exclude any political and economic dimensions of Palestinian freedom, such as political or economic democracy, from their podiums, flyers, newspapers, and Internet sites.

The remnants of the formerly left Palestinian groups such as the Popular Front for the Liberation of Palestine (PFLP), the Democratic Front for the Liberation of Palestine (DFLP), and the Palestine Communist Party (PCP) have no discernible political practices for analyzing or changing class relations within Palestinian society, Israel, or in the region. They are not even focused on finding points of unity between the Palestinian and Israeli working classes, an obvious early step in class struggle, nor with the working classes of other countries in the region, such as Jordan, Lebanon, or Egypt.

Furthermore, within Palestinian society these remnants of the Palestinian left do not appear to engage in class analysis or class struggle, except for ambiguous references on web pages. Other than a militant Palestinian teachers' strike a few years ago, it is difficult to find active class politics in Palestinian society, unless it functions on a clandestine level. At this point, their nationalist outlook is largely separatist and hard to distinguish from the views of the two Islamic movements active in Gaza and the West Bank: Islamic Jihad and Hamas. Their ideologies combine conservative religion, nationalism, and—if recent press reports are correct—an anti-Jewishness which far surpasses any narrow opposition to Zionism or Israeli state policies. Furthermore, these nationalist viewpoints have morphed into racism. The once left organizations now condone (and sometimes initiate) terrorist attacks against Israeli Jewish civilians, regardless of their victims' military role, class position, or political views. Workers, kids, and the elderly are legitimate targets. We also make a comparable analysis of much of the Israeli "Left" below. It, too, is nationalistic, and it has few, if any, links with either Jewish or Palestinian workers. And while the Israeli working class has been historically active through the Histadrut Labor Federation, its activism is strictly focused on wages and benefits, without any criticism of Israeli government policies towards the Palestinians or its cooperation with the United States military, apartheid South Africa, or the Central American contras.

3. Repression in Israel and the Palestinian Authority: The Israeli left and peace movements function within the context of Israeli society, which has veered sharply to the right since the beginning of the second intifada. At this point the Israeli government and much of the Israeli population is profoundly racist, with clear fascist tendencies, but not yet completely fascist. Within Israel's 1948–67 boundaries (i.e., the Green Line) the country still has a bourgeois democracy with more parties, newspapers, debates, and higher electoral turnouts among both Jews and Arabs than in the United States. Furthermore, even though there is intricate discrimination against Israeli Arab Palestinians, they, too, have the trappings of bourgeois democracy, with multiple parties, elections, newspapers, and trade union membership.

Within the West Bank and Gaza, however, there is no doubt about fascism—that is, severe political repression combining physical attacks and prohibitions on political activity—enforced by both the Israeli military and the Palestinian Authority (PA). This fascism, once characterized by death squads and checkpoints, has now escalated into full-scale military invasions. It has been instigated by the Israeli occupation forces, but with no shortage of prior collusion from the Palestinian Authority, with its dozen police agencies, many established by the CIA and Mossad. They are hard at work to keep tight political control, and in early June 2002 CIA Director George Tenet made still another visit to the Palestinian Authority's areas of control. If the PA has not succeeded in implementing the Mossad's and CIA's goals of total political passivity, it is largely a result of incompetence, internal Palestinian political struggles, and the Israeli government's economic sanctions against the Palestinian Authority. Furthermore, many rounds of Israeli military action against the Palestinian Authority have ironically targeted the very police agencies charged with apprehending anti-Israel militants, as well as the civil structures fostered by the European Union.

4. The Israeli Peace Movement: The Israeli Jewish public, for the most part, is highly nationalistic and thus subject to the racism which characterizes all nationalist movements. Their arrogance towards the Palestinians is so widespread that most Israeli liberals are unaware of their own racist assumptions about the conflict. In fact, many of them are still dazed by the Palestinian Authority's rejection of former Israeli Prime Minister Ehud Barak's "most generous offer yet" (for several Bantustans!) that they support the repressive policies of Israeli Prime Minister Ariel Sharon. Their "liberal" racism primarily takes the form of separatism, not yet the ethnic cleansing or "transfer" programs openly advocated by the Israeli right, including some current Cabinet members. This drastic, pregenocidal approach is, however, supported by about 15 percent of Israel's Jewish population. It is also reported by the press to be waiting for the right political events to unfold, such as a regional war beginning with another U.S. attack on Iraq or an India-Pakistan nuclear exchange.

In contrast, most of the Israeli peace movement, which opposes everything from settlements in the occupied territories to torture of Palestinians, wants a two state solution in which Israeli Jews and most Palestinians will lead wholly separate lives. In some cases they even advocate the construction of an impregnable security wall between the two states. These programs, in which ethnic segregation/separation is paramount, is unfortunately, considered "progressive" in most quarters, even though such segregation and separation are defining features of racism. Another source of the Israeli peace movement is the tremendous resentment among many liberal Israelis to three years of mandatory military service in the IDF, an army whose main role now is to defend the two percent of the Israeli population who are settlers in the West Bank and Gaza Strip. In fact, this resentment has given rise to the new "Refusenik" movement. It consists of approximately 1,000 Israeli reservists and active duty soldiers who refuse to serve in the West Bank or in Gaza. It has added a level of critical civil disobedience to the Israeli peace movement which could ultimately make a military difference if it grows.

A more implicitly progressive component is those on each side who are willing to cross ethnic boundaries. There are a number of groups which function at the grass roots level, bringing together Palestinians and Israelis, Muslims and Jews. They are not revolutionary in the sense of advocating a socialized and democratic economy, but they do offer defenses of human rights that reject the inward nationalist outlook of the larger Israeli peace organizations, such as Peace Now.

Here are a few of them:

- *The Israeli Committee Against House Demolitions.* This is an Israeli group working with the Palestinian Land Defense Committee and the Jerusalem Center for Social and Economic Rights to oppose and resist the demolition of Palestinian homes and to rebuild demolished homes. (Since 1967, Israel has demolished over 7,000 Palestinian homes in the West Bank, Gaza, and Arab East Jerusalem. This has rendered at least 30,000 people homeless and traumatized.)
- *Rabbis for Human Rights.* This organization is comprised of Reform, Orthodox, Conservative, and Reconstructionist rabbis and students. It addresses violations of human rights of West Bank Palestinians and Israeli Arabs. It participates in the Israeli Coalition for The Prevention of Home Demolitions and is attempting to find Israeli families who will "adopt" the more than 2,000 Palestinian families who recently have demolition orders on their homes.

Other groups working nonviolently for human rights and Palestinian-Israeli cooperation include:

- *Gush Shalom*—Israeli Peace Bloc
- *Yesh Gvul* ("There Is a Border")—promoting refusal to serve in the Occupied Territories
- *Palestinian Human Rights Monitoring Group*
- *Women in Black*
- *Palestinian Center for Rapprochement between People*
- *International Solidarity Movement*
- *Ta'ayush*

These groups involve Israelis and Palestinians, Muslims and Jews in projects for protection of human rights, rejection of overt racism and ethnocentrism, and "grass roots" activism. For this they are to be commended and supported, including the many groups in the United States, Europe, and elsewhere which are aligned with them.

It should be noted, however, that the struggle waged by these various Israeli and Palestinian groups—courageous as they are—do not apparently address the systemic problems emanating from capitalism (e.g., unemployment, low wage work, lack of democracy) and from imperialism. In this respect they are quite oblivious to the extraordinary military and political involvement of the United States, the EU, and other outside powers in the entire Middle East region to secure the vast oil fields of the Persian Gulf and Caspian Sea areas.

So, on the positive side, these groups for justice show that nonviolent cooperation across nationalist boundaries is possible, but, on the negative side, they pursue policies that only alleviate some of the more severe abuses within the conflict. In other words, their objective, a two state solution, will produce two societies with internal inequality and working class exploitation enforced by local upper classes who are rewarded with a share of the profits by foreign investors and imperialist patrons dedicated to political and economic control of the entire Middle East.

5. Supporting Progressive Elements: With so few class conscious political forces on either the Israeli or Palestinian side, it is important to cultivate what ever contacts we have, especially in the US and Europe, where groups engaged in Arab-Jewish cooperation, political dialogue, and public events are growing. The persistence of such small groups on both sides who have, at least emotionally, discarded exclusive and separatist ideologies is a positive trend through which individuals and groups might develop a critique of nationalism and imperialism, make calls for inter-ethnic unity, and explore the underlying class issues propelling this conflict. If, however, their critiques of Israeli and Palestinian policies are based solely on humanitarian objections, without comprehension of the class basis of the conflict and its place in the imperial designs of larger powers, we will be forced to accept short-term "solutions" to this conflict which only perpetuate it.

This dilemma underscores the need for class conscious scholars and organizations to carefully research and describe the class foundations of both Israeli and Palestinian society, the foreign investment patterns which reinforce it, and the many linkages between this conflict and those in the Persian Gulf and Caspian Sea regions. When this information can be infused into the Israeli-Palestinian conflict, the possibilities for truly progressive political breakthroughs will substantially increase.

36

Thoughts on Urban Unrest

Edna Bonacich

The following is my unexpurgated version of what underlies the recent uprising in Los Angeles. It is based on Marxist theories of race and class, including theories of middleman minorities. I recognize that the language used here is completely unacceptable in the U.S. context, where certain assumptions about the way the system works are not permitted to be challenged. Nevertheless, given the theoretical orientation presented here, the uprising came as no surprise.

1. Urban unrest can be seen as a product of the workings of capitalism, and its concomitant, racism. Capitalism is a system that depends on the private appropriation of socially produced wealth. In other words while everyone contributes to the society's production, only a small class of people are able to expropriate the surplus that is generated, namely, the owners of private property (who take surplus in the form of profit, rent, and interest), and generally credentialed managers and professionals (who take surplus in the form of bloated salaries). At the heart of capitalist society lies a *theft* that has occurred historically and continues on a daily basis.

2. Colonialism was a product of the development of capitalism in Europe, and it added another layer of theft to the general theft of capitalism. This involved stealing the territory of other peoples, stealing the riches of their lands, and stealing their labor and the products of their labor. In some cases, individuals themselves were bodily stolen, in the form of slavery and indentured servitude, and moved to other territories where their stolen labor could be used. Accompanying this colonial theft was racism, *i.e.*, the denigration of the cultures and biological characteristics of the conquered peoples.

3. Despite emancipation from slavery, and formal legal equality, the class system of capitalism remains in place, as does its accompanying racism. Thus, wealth continues to be drained from the poor to the rich, from workers to owners of capital, and from people of color to whites. The earlier thefts established the character of the owning, ruling elite, and although there can be some social mobility both upward and downward, in general its character has not changed much. Having capital (rooted in theft) gives one a tremendous advantage in increasing one's wealth, while working for low wages is a prohibitive barrier to ever crawling out of poverty. The result is that we have an increasingly

polarized population, with the rich controlling billions and billions of dollars in wealth, while others are ground down in poverty.

The rich, it should be emphasized, are not wealthy because they work harder or are more worthy. They are rich because they own property, and often that ownership was based on some form of theft somewhere down the line.

4. The capitalist-racist social order entails the maintenance of racially segregated communities and super-exploited workers. This is clearly seen in Los Angeles with immigrant Latino workers who are maintained as an extra-low wage working class in manufacturing, construction, and services. Their disadvantage is maintained through a host of institutions, including immigration law, housing policy, schooling, welfare, health care, the legal and penal system, etc. Racially skewed unemployment also serves to maintain a relationship between poverty and race.

The globalization of capitalism is exacerbating these trends, by leading to increased international competition, and the decline in labor standards and unionization in the United States. However, although globalization is making things worse, it is only a manifestation of more fundamental ways in which the system works. In other words, the profit system causes gross inequalities, whether profit-making is local or global. The globalization of capital adds to the problem by increasing competition, and pitting workers in different nations against one another.

The globalization of capitalism also stimulates immigration, helping to account for the increasing cultural and racial diversity of Los Angeles. However, the mobility of labor is much more legally restricted than the mobility of capital, creating a legally disabled immigrant workforce who are subject to "super-exploitation."

The police play a special role in relationship to the racially oppressed communities. They serve as a controlling force, protecting the property of the more affluent, generally white, communities from the potential anger and violence of the oppressed. The police serve as a kind of army of occupation, representing the dominant society as opposed to the residents of inner-city neighborhoods.

5. Korean merchants play a particular role in the system of control and exploitation. They perform the function of a "middleman minority," a phenomenon that has been observed in other colonial situations. Rather than having the colonizer or the colonized play the role of shopkeepers and small-scale employers, that role is handed over to a third party, an outsider group. This kind of role was played by Jews in Eastern Europe, by Chinese in Southeast Asia, and by Indians in East Africa.

Having a middleman group play this role is of use to the oppressors. First, the antagonism of the oppressed gets redirected from the primary target, in this case the white corporate establishment, to the middleman group. In other words, the middleman group serves as a scapegoat for the injustices of the system that they did not create. Second, because the middleman group is an outsider group, they can be easily dispensed with. The oppressors have no particular loyalty to them, and so they can be served up as targets for oppressed anger.

Middleman minorities occupy a middle-level position in a system of oppression. To some extent they are beneficiaries of the system. Some of the surplus stolen from the oppressed is appropriated by them, so that the oppressed have a reason to see the middleman as their enemy. On the other hand, most of the surplus is moved on up from the middleman to the white, corporate elites. This second movement is relatively invisible to the oppressed. However, it does mean that the middlemen are also, to a certain extent, oppressed by the white elite, even as they help to oppress those below them in the hierarchy.

6. The uprising in Los Angeles reflects these dynamics:

- The triggering incident of the acquittal in the police trial over the Rodney King beating reflects the festering problem of police relations in racially oppressed neighborhoods. People who experience police victimization on a daily basis were finally in a position to prove beyond a doubt what actually happens to them, only to find that even seeing it with their own eyes could not convince a jury of the atrocities that are committed.
- So-called looting is an expression of the frustration that people experience when they help to create wealth but are not allowed access to it. Theft seems morally justified in a society based upon *legally sanctioned* theft. Of course, the theft committed by "looters" is completely trivial in the context of the large-scale theft committed by billionaire and millionaire property owners.
- The attack on Korean store owners reflects their middleman status in the system. And the fact that the Korean store owners received little protection from these attacks shows how the dominant elite is willing to sacrifice them, when necessary. This was a rude awakening for the Korean community, who learned the hard way that playing the capitalist game by its rules does not protect one from the racist logic of the system.

7. The kinds of solutions being proposed are grossly inadequate to solving the problems of racial and class oppression in Los Angeles (and the United States, in general). The idea that jobs is what is needed arises within the context of accepting the capitalist economic/political system. Providing jobs for workers does not diminish profits for property owners; indeed the theft of surplus from workers will continue, as owners are given incentives to "invest" in the inner city, and thereby extract more profits from these communities.

What is really needed is a system of redistribution of wealth, whereby communities that have been continually robbed of their wealth-making and wealth-controlling capacity have some of the stolen goods returned to them. Thereafter, investment must be turned over to social agents, and not allowed to be kept in the hands of private property owners, whose sole criteria for investment is profit. In other words, instead of creating enterprise zones and Black- and Latino-owned private business, which contribute to corporate profits and help to create a loyal, profiteering sector in the racially oppressed communities, we need to develop economic forms that serve the interests of everyone. This requires breaking with capitalist "business as usual" since the system has proved itself incapable of solving these problems, as class and race inequality have only gotten worse with time.

8. In conclusion, the wealth of this nation cannot be permitted to remain in the hands of a small, largely white elite. It is clear that they are unwilling to give it up, even in the very modest form of increased taxation to cover such basic social expenditures as education and health care. If we cannot even get them to move this far, how can we expect the kind of redistribution that is really needed to solve the massive problems of racial oppression and inequality?

The only solution, it seems to me, is more uprisings. Except that in the future they need to be better organized, with a clearer strategy, and based on well-developed coalitions. They need to be organized with a view toward winning the social struggles that are necessary to produce equality in this nation.

Meanwhile, we can participate in the process of social change by helping to dispel some of the myths that serve to rationalize the current system. The tremendous suffering that occurs at the bottom cannot be denied. It will not disappear through the actions of the "free market" and private investment. We must address directly the social consequences of our system or race and class polarization will only get worse.